Partisan Publics

Princeton Studies in Cultural Sociology

SERIES EDITORS: Paul J. DiMaggio, Michèle Lamont,
Robert J. Wuthnow, Viviana A. Zelizer

A list of titles in this series appears at the back of the book.

Partisan Publics

COMMUNICATION AND CONTENTION
ACROSS BRAZILIAN YOUTH ACTIVIST NETWORKS

Ann Mische

PRINCETON UNIVERSITY PRESS
PRINCETON AND OXFORD

Library of Congress Cataloging-in-Publication Data

Mische, Ann.
Partisan publics : communication and contention across Brazilian youth activist networks /
Ann Mische.
    p.   cm. — (Princeton studies in cultural sociology)
Includes bibliographical references and index.
ISBN-13: 978-0-691-12494-0 (cloth : alk. paper)
1. Youth—Brazil—Political activity. 2. Student movements—Brazil. 3. Political
participation—Brazil. 4. Brazil—Politics and government—1985-2002. I. Title.
HQ799.2.P6M57   2008
322.40835'0981—dc22
2007007148

British Library Cataloging-in-Publication Data is available

This book has been composed in Sabon

Printed on acid-free paper. ∞

press.princeton.edu

Printed in the United States of America

10 9 8 7 6 5 4 3 2 1

To my father, in celebration of life's complexity . . .
and to my son, in appreciation of life's simplicity.

Contents

List of Figures

List of Tables

Abbreviations

Institutional Sectors

R	Religious group
S	General student movement
P	Political party
M	Urban or rural popular movement
D	Antidiscrimination movement (race, gender, ethnicity, sexuality, disability, etc.)
N	Civic/ethical movement or nongovernmental organization
O	Socialist youth organization
L	Labor union or professional organization
C	Course-based student movement
Q	Research organization
B	Business organization

Youth/Student Organizations

AIESEC	International Association of Students in Economic and Accounting Sciences
AP	Popular Action (1960s student movement faction, originally linked to Catholic youth movement)
APML	Marxist Leninist Popular Action (splinter group from AP)
CA	Academic Center (department-based student association)
CA XI	CA Eleventh of August (CA of the Law Faculty, University of São Paulo)
CACS	CA of Social Sciences, PUC—SP
CCA	Council of Academic Centers
CEFEJ	Center for the Formation and Study of Youth
CONEB	National Council of Base Organizations (grassroots deliberative council of UNE, composed of CAs)

CONEG	National Council of General Organizations (higher-level deliberative council of UNE, composed of DCEs and state student unions)
CONUN	National Coordination of Black University Scholars
CONUNE	Congress of UNE
DA	Academic Directorate (another name for CA, instituted during military regime)
DCE	Central Student Directorate (universitywide student association)
DENEM	National Executive Directorate of Medical Students
ECA-Jr	Junior Enterprise of the USP Communication Faculty
EJ	Junior Enterprise
ENECOS	National Executive of Students in Social Communication
ENED	National Executive of Law Students
ENEFAR	National Executive of Pharmaceutical Students
ENECS	National Executive of Social Science Students
ENECON	National Executive of Economics Students
FENEAD	National Federation of Administration Students
FEAB	Federation of Agronomy Students of Brazil
FEJESP	Federation of Junior Enterprises of São Paulo
FENEA	National Federation of Architecture Students
Forum	National Forum of Course Executives
GL	*Grêmio Livre* (independent high school student association)
JAC	Young Catholic Agriculturalists
JEC	Young Catholic Students (secondary students)
JIC	Independent Catholic Youth
JOC	Young Catholic Workers
JUC	Young Catholic University Students
MUDE	Movement for a democratic UNE
NVA	*Não Vou Me Adaptar* (I Won't Adapt: center–left PT thesis at 1997 Congress of UNE)
PeT	*Prazer em Transformar* (Pleasure in Transforming: center–right PT thesis at 1997 Congress of UNE)
PJ	Catholic Youth Pastoral
PJ-Brasil	Youth Pastoral of Brazil (encompasses all of the general and specialized branches)
PJ-Geral	General Youth Pastoral (nonspecialized youth pastoral)
PJE	Student Youth Pastoral
PJMP	Youth Pastoral of the Popular Milieu
PJR	Rural Youth Pastoral
PU	University Pastoral

SECUNE   Secretariat of Communication of UNE
SENUN   National Seminar of Black University Scholars
UC   University Council
UBES   National Union of Secondary Students
UEE   State Student Union
UJS   Union of Socialist Youth
UMES   Municipal Union of Secondary Students
UNE   National Student Union
UPF   *Um Passo a Frente* (One Step in Front: PCdoB thesis at
          1997 Congress of UNE)
____-NC   National coordination
____-RC   Regional coordination

POLITICAL PARTIES/PARTY FACTIONS

ARENA   Alliance for National Renovation (party of the
          military regime)
MDB   Movement for Brazilian Democracy (opposition political
          party during dictatorship)
MR-8   Revolutionary Movement of the 8th of March
PCB   Brazilian Communist Party
PCdoB   Communist Party of Brazil
PDS   Democratic Social Party
PDT   Democratic Labor Party
PFL   Party of the Liberal Front
PMDB   Party of the Brazilian Democratic Movement
PP   Progressive Party
PPB   Brazilian Progressive Party
PPR   Reformist Progressive party
PPS   Popular Socialist Party
PRC   Revolutionary Communist Party
PSB   Brazilian Socialist Party
PSDB   Party of Brazilian Social Democracy
PSTU   Unified Socialist Workers' Party
PT   Workers' Party
PTB   Brazilian Labor party
____-YC   Youth commission/coordination/collective (of a
          specific party)
____-DM   Municipal directorate (of a specific party)

INTERNAL PT TENDENCIES

AE	*Articulação da Esquerda*
AR	*Articulação*
CS	*Convergência Socialista*
DR	*Democracia Radical*
DS	*Democracia e Socialismo*
NE	*Nova Esquerda*
OT	*O Trabalho*
UL	*Unidade na Luta*

UNIVERSITIES

FATEC	Faculty of Technology of São Paulo
FEA-USP	Faculty of Economics and Administration (University of São Paulo)
PUC-SP	Pontifícia Universidade Católica (Catholic University) of São Paulo
UNICAMP	University of Campinas
USP	University of São Paulo

OTHER ORGANIZATIONS AND MOVEMENTS

ABI	Brazilian Press Association
ABJD	Brazilian Association of Democratic Jurists
BANC	Bankworkers' Union
CCC	Command for Hunting Communists
CEB	Ecclesial Base Community (Catholic Base Community)
CEBRAP	Brazilian Center for Analysis and Planning
CEIMAN	Center for Indigenous Studies
CELAM	Latin American Bishops Conference
CEPECS	Center for Social Science Research
CGT	General Workers' Central
CIMI	Indigenous Missionary Council (linked to Catholic Church)
CNBB	National Conference of Brazilian Bishops
CPI	Parliamentary Commission of Inquiry
CPO	Workers' Pastoral Commission
CPT	Pastoral Land Commission

CUT	Unified Workers' Central (controlled by PT)
IBASE	Brazilian Institute for Social and Economic Analysis
ILAM	Latin American Institute
MEB	Movement for Grassroots Education
MEP	Movement for Ethics in Politics
MI	Indigenous Movement
MNU	Unified Black Movement
MOB	Movement Option for Brazil
MST	Landless Worker's Movement
OAB	Order of Brazilian Lawyers (Brazilian Bar Association)
PNBE	National Thought of Business Bases
PO	Workers' Pastoral
PPC	Popular Participation in the Constitution
SBPC	Brazilian Society for Progress in Science
UNEGRO	Union of Blacks for Equality

Acknowledgments

THIS BOOK has been two decades in the making, if you count my initial journalistic sojourn in Brazil during the late 1980s. Many conversations have contributed to its development and entered into this book in both visible and invisible ways. An initial warm thanks goes to Peter Bird Martin, director of the Institute of Current World Affairs, who saw a spark of promise in my philosophical musings on Brazilian youth and sent me— a twenty-two-year-old recent college graduate—to São Paulo from 1987 to 1990 to follow my nose as an observer, writer, and sometimes participant in the local political scene. This experience set the whole project in motion, although it took me in many unexpected directions.

During my many trips to Brazil, I depended on a network of friends and *companheiros* who became a second family to me. A very loving thanks goes to Ana Maria de Oliveira Campos, who has helped me in countless practical, intellectual, and emotional ways along every stage of this adventure. I would also like to thank Toni, Alcilene, Moises, Lucirene, Elisa, Cidinha, Duda, Pedro, Vanilda Neide, Adriano, Arlete, Fernando, Cristina, Sonia, Zé, and other close friends who supported me and taught me much, dating back to my first stay in Brazil (not to mention the children, quickly becoming adults, especially Marina, Mariana, Luanda, and Pedro).

When I returned to Brazil for my dissertation research in the mid-1990s, I acquired a new network of practical and intellectual support. First of all, I would like to thank the young activists who so generously shared their time, stories, reflections, documents, and projects with me. They are too many to mention here by name, but their stories fill this book. I deeply appreciate their insight, patience, and good humor, and apologize for any misrepresentations that might have filtered into this account. (I hope we get a chance to talk about these!) Salvador Sandoval and Sonia de Avelar provided warm hospitality, advice, and intellectual support during my dissertation research in São Paulo. My research assistant, Andresa Cazarine, spent many hours poring over documents and systematizing data. Sara Nelson and Nathalie Lebon shared the stress and excitement of fieldwork. Leonardo Avritzer (my New School colleague) and his wife Ana provided hospitality and intellectual exchange during research trips to Belo Horizonte, giving me useful background on the early student movement as well as on Brazilian academics. I am also grateful for a series of extremely probing discussions of Brazilian youth politics with Helena Abramo, Gisela Mendonça, Miguel Rangel, and Antonio Martins.

As I returned to the United States to write this book, many people provided support and guidance. A huge thanks goes to Charles Tilly, my steadfastly supportive advisor, who helped to focus and clarify my stubbornly ambitious framing of the problem. ("You never take the easy way, do you?" he once asked me in a moment of exasperation.) Harrison White has been a continuing source of inspiration and support, encouraging me to dig under surfaces and trust my instinct for finding lively phenomena. Ira Katznelson provided sage and probing commentary on the dissertation, as did Jose Casanova, who helped to contextualize it in relation to previous moments in Brazilian history.

As I explored the structural side of my analysis, I depended on the mathematical rigor, theoretical imagination, and unmatched hospitality of Philippa Pattison, in a collaboration that extended beyond the dissertation into several trips to Melbourne, Australia. This led to an equally productive collaboration with Melbourne colleague Garry Robins, who helped to extend my understanding of the structural dynamics of these phenomena. Ron Breiger, John Mohr, and Kathleen Carley also provided insight and encouragement as I experimented with the application of formal network analysis techniques to my complex data.

As the book evolved in unexpected ways, I benefited from many conversations with colleagues. I am particularly grateful for copious comments on the whole manuscript from Gianpaolo Baiocchi, Marisa von Bülow, Nina Eliasoph, Mustafa Emirbayer, Robert Fishman, Mimi Keck, and several anonymous reviewers. In addition, Erik Calderoni, Charles Kirschbaum, Paul Lichterman, Eduardo Marquez, David Smilde, Sid Tarrow, and Robin Wagner-Pacifici read chapter drafts at various stages and engaged deeply with the theory and the case material. Many others offered commentary on the articles and prospectuses that led up to the book, including Julia Adams, Angela Alonso, Andy Andrews, Elizabeth Armstrong, Javier Auyero, Nina Bandelj, Peter Bearman, Debbie Becher, Mary Blair-Loy, Carlos Costa-Ribeiro, Mario Diani, Marshall Ganz, Ivan Ermakov, Maria da Gloria Gohn, Jeff Goodwin, Jack Hammond, Jason Kaufman, Michele Lamont, Roy Liklider, Doug McAdam, David Meyer, Kelly Moore, Francesca Polletta, Ziggy Rivkin-Fish, Mimi Sheller, Kim Voss, and Chris Winship. Claudia Dalhrius, Nicole Haia, Sun-Chul Kim, and John Krinsky served as constructive critics on chapters as part of the Columbia University Workshop on Contentious Politics.

I owe a special debt to several Rutgers colleagues who supported me through the frantic rush to complete the manuscript. Paul McLean and Vilna Bashi read and critiqued "hot off the press" first drafts of raw new chapters as part of a crucial book-writing support group. John Levi

Martin also read early draft after early draft and provided provocative commentary that helped me to sharpen my writing and my ideas. Karen Cerulo and Eviatar Zerubavel provided invaluable feedback and publishing advice as I prepared the manuscript for submission. Ellen Idler, Randy Smith and Tom Rudel also gave supportive commentary as I entered the final stretch. In addition, several Rutgers graduate students, including Diane Bates, Crystal Bedley, Sandra Batista, Tom DeGloma, Steph Karpinski, Vanina Leschinzer, and King-to Yeung, collaborated with various stages of data analysis and gave valuable comments on chapter drafts.

I also want to thank my Princeton editor, Tim Sullivan, for his encouragement, advice, constructive criticism, and most of all, his patience, especially as final revisions on the manuscript were repeatedly delayed by the challenges of new motherhood. Likewise, I'm grateful to my excellent copyeditor, Jack Rummel, who smoothed the rough edges in the final stretch.

The spirit of my family echoes through this work. My parents, Pat and Jerry Mische, taught me to be a global citizen and to embrace the complex adventure of life. If my father had lived to see this book completed, he would have recognized many of his own lifelong concerns with networking and coalition building. I thank my two sisters Monica and Nicole, along with my five nieces and two nephews, who sacrificed family time as I traveled to Brazil and holed up in my study. And most of all, I thank my partner David Gibson, who read multiple drafts of the entire manuscript and patiently listened to so many of the arguments in this book worked out over long walks and talks. His intellectual and emotional support has been critical to the project. This book was finished as we awaited the arrival of our son, Jeremy Daniel. These two labors of love and commitment will now make their own ways in the world.

Exploring Brazilian Youth Activism

"*PARTIDARISMO NÃO!*" With these chants against partisanship, a student rally ended in confusion and heated argument. The rally had been organized in July 1988 to pressure for the democratization of the schools, a theme that succeeded in pulling nearly a thousand teenagers out of night classes in ten schools of the Vila Prudente, a working-class neighborhood in the poorer Eastern Zone of São Paulo. The evening rally took place in a dusty parking lot outside a transit hub, with activists speaking from microphones atop a truck equipped with amplifiers. I was attending the rally with two young friends, Teresa and Miguel, who were both activists in the Workers' Party (PT) as well as in the Education Movement of the Eastern Zone. They were among those leading a movement to organize *grêmios livres*—autonomous high school student organizations—which had recently been relegalized after decades of prohibition by the former military regime.

The confusion at this rally was not about the *grêmios* themselves, but about the political groups in defense of them. Most of the students, new at such political happenings, were taken aback by what seemed to be a swarm of representatives from organized political groups pushing their way into the rally. Neighborhood militants of the PT were passing out pamphlets proclaiming, "The PT supports the struggle of the students." Local organizers of CUT, the labor central linked to the PT, had unfurled their banners in the crowd. Representatives of the Communist Party of Brazil (PCdoB) were clamoring to speak from the podium. And when the student organizer leading the rally thanked the PT for use of the sound truck, a large number of students joined in shouting against *partidarismo* (partisanship), although I later found out that the leader of the chants was a militant of the PMDB (Party of Brazilian Democratic Movement).

For weeks prior to the rally, I had accompanied Teresa and Miguel on a flurry of visits to schools in the region to help students organize *grêmios*, often in the face of opposition by school administrators. I also went with them to meetings with teachers, parents, church leaders, party organizers, and other community activists engaged in the broader Education Move-

ment of the Eastern Zone, formed to address precarious educational conditions in the urban periphery. In conversations after the rally, the young
PT activists lamented what they saw as the "depoliticization" of the high
school movement, which they attributed to Brazil's twenty years of authoritarian rule. They argued that partisan bickering along with skepticism toward political parties was stripping the movement of "true dialogue" about educational conditions in Brazil.

However, at the same time as they hoped that the student movement
would become more political, they agreed with almost everyone else that
the movement needed to stay "apartisan," despite their own intense partisan commitments. The confusion at the rally stemmed from several different ways in which the term *apartisan* was being used. Most high school
students, along with Brazilians more generally, equated apartisan with
"apolitical." This was based on the idea that politics is for the politicians,
associated with ambition, corruption, and dirty power politics, as well as
with electoral opportunism and broken promises. This understanding led
to the assertion that politics did not belong in schools, churches, or workplaces, a view eagerly promoted by the military regime and still widespread among many school administrators. In this view, *grêmios* should
stick to organizing dances and sports competitions and keep away from
more combative debate about society or the functioning of the school.

The second use of "apartisan" was as a mask for partisan manipulation. Building on public distrust of politicians, partisan actors wielded
the term as a call to arms against their partisan rivals. The PMDB activist
who led the chants against partisanship was clearly hoping to discredit
the PT, and thereby bring less politicized students under the wing of the
more moderate centrist party. Likewise, the PT leaders themselves tried
to prevent activists from their main competitor, the PCdoB, from speaking on the podium, arguing that the PCdoB was "just" out to recruit
leaders into their more vanguard style of organizing, opportunistically
taking advantage of the PT's hard work raising consciousness in the
schools. Unfortunately, by excluding PCdoB students in the name of
apartisanship, they reinforced the impression that they themselves were
trying to maintain a monopoly for the PT. No one, least of all adolescents
just starting out in political militancy, wants to feel like a pawn of someone else's opportunism.

The third use of the term *apartisan* was a more careful attempt to distinguish "politicization"—conceived as autonomous political conscious-
ness-raising—from partisan manipulation. This is what Teresa, Miguel,
and other young PT leaders meant when they said the movement should
be both "political" and "apartisan," although it was trickier than it
seemed. Most *petistas* (PT activists) openly admitted their partisan affiliation, insisting that there is a legitimate role for political parties in pro-

moting institutional change and actively combating the idea the partisan politics is ugly. But they also insisted—at least in principle—that the student movement had to stay autonomous from the party. They promoted *grêmios livres* as autonomous student forums for strong and open debate, with the right to discuss social issues beginning with the schools and moving out into other areas of political questioning. However, this ideal of autonomy was much harder to pull off in practice. It involved a difficult balancing act in which student activists had to provisionally suppress their avid partisan passions—something they were not always successful in doing. While PT activists tried to distinguish themselves stylistically from what they saw as the vanguardist manipulation of traditional leftist parties, they were locked in partisan battles with these parties for control of local and national student organizations.

I begin with this story because it forms a backdrop for much of this book, posing many of the puzzles I wrestled with over many years of experience with Brazilian youth politics. I first arrived in Brazil in 1987, fresh out of college and the recipient of a journalistic fellowship that allowed me to immerse myself in Brazilian culture and politics and write about it for several years in an exploratory fashion.[1] I was in São Paulo from late 1987 through mid-1990, an exciting period in Brazilian history. The country was moving to civilian rule after twenty years of dictatorship and wrestling with the challenges of writing a new constitution, reconstituting civic and political institutions, and staging its first direct presidential elections in thirty years.

While I had grown up among activists in the United States, mostly in the Catholic peace and justice tradition as well as the international NGO community, I found Brazilian opposition politics in the postauthoritarian period to be something of a mind-blower. Drawing on credentials from my family history (as well as some supportive local contacts), I immersed myself in the complex and contentious activist community of the Eastern Zone of São Paulo. Straddling the roles of journalist and participant, I lived with PT activists and accompanied them in wide variety of church-based, community, student, and labor activities in the region. I followed attempts to revive the high school student movement, helped to start a youth group at a Catholic base community, worked with children in a church at the side of a *favela* (shantytown slum), and helped to organize a program for adolescent children of activists at a labor union school. I was endlessly fascinated with a social movement community that was simultaneously more ideological and more grittily grass roots than anything I had experienced.

What astonished me during this period was that most people I knew were not just involved in one movement, but in five or six. The Eastern Zone of São Paulo, along with other periphery neighborhoods, was a dense network of intersecting movement activity. In the same day, I could accompany activists like Miguel and Teresa from an early morning pamphlet distribution outside a school to a mid-morning health movement assembly at a local clinic to an early afternoon popular culture workshop of the Catholic youth pastoral to a late afternoon meeting of a neighborhood PT "nucleus." We might end the day at an evening rally at an urban land occupation site, stopping at corner bars for snacks, beer, and camaraderie with other activists along the way.

I also went to many local, regional, and municipal meetings of the PT (and some of its factions) as militants vigorously debated the positions and policies of the new party. Founded by an alliance of labor leaders, church-based community activists, and leftist intellectuals, the PT was born in 1980 as Brazil returned to a multiparty system. It billed itself as an internally democratic socialist party, grounded in Brazilian reality rather than on foreign models. The party was organized through a network of local "nuclei" that engaged neighborhood activists in political discussion as well as in the mobilizing tasks of campaigns. Despite the conflicts described above, partisan engagement seemed to serve a bridging function for these activists. Parties like the PT were a source of inspiration and integration, knitting people together across the particularities of neighborhoods, movements, age groups, and community loyalties.

This is not to say that there were not tensions, disputes, and frequent complaints of "depoliticization," as described in the story above. These were part and parcel of these activists' daily lives, which were often exhausting, stressful, and personally costly in terms of finances and family life. At the same time, there was a sense of exhilaration in the late 1980s, as activists were simultaneously building the party, the popular movements, and civic institutions like student organizations, labor unions, health councils, church groups, and community associations. This grassroots enthusiasm carried over into the election campaigns that occurred every few years: for state governments and the national legislature in 1982, the constitutional assembly in 1986, municipal governments in 1985 and 1988, and finally for president in 1989. This intense electoral schedule was sometimes at the expense of the popular movements, as activists were sucked out of local communities into campaign activities (and when the PT won legislative or executive seats, into government bureaucracy). Election activity rose to a fever pitch in the 1989 presidential campaign for the PT's candidate, Luis Inácio (Lula) da Silva, who came within few percentage points of winning the presidency.

And then, following Lula's narrow defeat in 1989 by Fernando Collor de Melo, some of the air seemed to go out of the activist community. Perhaps, as many claimed, they were exhausted by so many years of intense, full-time, self-sacrificing activism. Perhaps there was a generational effect, as young activists got older and decided it was finally time to get their own lives in order. Or perhaps, with the installation of a directly elected president, a new period had begun in Brazilian politics, as the country moved from democratic "transition"—dominated by regime/ challenger polarities—to "consolidation," with elite and opposition groups sorting out more complex institutional roles. In any case, between the time I left Brazil in 1990 to begin my graduate studies and returned in 1994 for two years of systematic research, there was a marked change in activist mood and rhythm. "It's not like '89," I was told mournfully by activist friends from the Eastern Zone. They lamented the "crisis" of the popular movements and described the reshuffled internal politics of the PT, which was increasingly polarized between factions advocating more institutionalized paths to "democratic socialism" and those demanding a return to the PT's more radical challenges to capitalism and neoliberal reforms.

SHIFTS IN THE CIVIC-PARTISAN LINK

In the mid-1990s, I changed the focus of my research from grassroots organizing in the urban periphery to student activism of various types, based mostly in the universities. While I maintained contact with some youth organizations linked to popular movements—particularly sectors of the Catholic youth pastoral—I was interested in the expansion and diversification of student activism as Brazilian democracy consolidated. While urban popular movements were in a self-described crisis, the student movement had received an infusion of energy during the exuberant 1992 movement to impeach President Collor de Melo on corruption charges. High school and college students hit the streets in unexpectedly large numbers as part of a broad civic movement for "ethics in politics." Following Collor's impeachment, there was a surge in student organizations across the country. At the same time, Brazil's traditional, partisan student movement faced challenges from innovative new forms of student associations which were self-consciously "apartisan," including groups organized around race and gender, professional identities, and business involvements. Once again, many student activists participated in several kinds of activism at once.

In this more diversified field of student politics, the arguments about partisanship and politicization that I had witnessed in the late 1980s were back, but in a new guise. Most activists—even those from the PT—no longer wore their partisan identities on their chests as a badge of honor. While factional competition still dominated traditional institutional venues like student or party congresses, other more emergent forms of student organizing tiptoed around issues of partisan identity, pushing references to parties underground. There seemed to be a wedge driven between the ideas of being "civic" and being "partisan," which had previously been seen by activists as closely linked. This put partisan activists who had come of age in the late 1980s on the defensive as they moved on to new roles in university activism. In some cases, I witnessed an odd form of civic one-upmanship, as partisan factions competed to seize the moral high ground and present themselves as more "ethical," "democratic" and "nonsectarian" than their rivals. This led to an unexpected (and sometimes deceptive) veneer of cross-partisan collaboration.

An example can be seen in a national student seminar on science and technology that I attended in May 1996. The seminar was organized in the northeastern state of Bahia under the auspices of the National Student Union (UNE). During most of the 1990s, UNE was controlled by students linked to the PCdoB, although other parties participated in UNE's directorate under a system of proportional representation. The seminar was organized by UNE directors linked to the moderate wing of the PT. The goal of the seminar, according to the PT organizers, was to create a space to discuss the future of the university that would be "elaborative," not "deliberative," that is, oriented toward discussing ideas rather than making policy decisions or disputing organizational control. They explicitly wanted to avoid the highly competitive partisan dynamics of most student movement events, which made such discussion very difficult.

At the same time, the PT leaders admitted, they were trying to expand the influence of their particular camp in the student movement. To this end, they neglected to include other political forces—including rival PT factions as well as the PCdoB—in the organization of the seminar. The leaders of UNE from the PCdoB were furious when they learned of the seminar, and promptly sent UNE's president, Renato, as well as local PCdoB leaders to participate at the last minute (much to the chagrin of the PT organizers). In behind-the-scenes conversations, both PT and PCdoB leaders told me that they were expecting a mudslinging partisan showdown, in which each side attempted to publicly discredit the other in the eyes of less militant students.

To my surprise, almost the opposite happened. In backstage meetings, both PCdoB and PT leaders lamented the partisan tactics of the other side, but then resolved to combat this by publicly taking an ethical stance (an approach I call "ethics as a tactic"). When UNE's president, Renato, met with his local PCdoB copartisans, he fielded anguished comments about exclusion and attack by other forces, to which he responded by affirming the difficulty in facing groups that were not as "broad, democratic, inclusive, and unified" as they were. In a follow-up tactical meeting, PCdoB leaders argued that they would be better able to win the sympathies of the student body by combating the "politics of denunciation" carried out by the PT. Activists were directed to avoid factional squabbling and maintain a strong participation "at the level of ideas and projects." This in fact they did—I was impressed by the thoughtful, well-prepared commentary of the PCdoB activists, who neither descended into ideological slogans nor circled around in vague, disorganized reflections, as some PT students tended to do.

The PT activists, for their part, attributed the absence of overt partisan dispute to their own more open-ended, dialogic, grassroots style of leadership. In the final evaluation session, they produced a document with "practical proposals" for the student movement that was supposed to synthesize the discussions of the seminar, but in fact was written almost entirely by one PT leader. The PCdoB leaders, not to be outdone, promptly presented their own document. In a conciliatory gesture, students resolved to circulate both documents nationally as the resolutions of the seminar. In closing, leaders praised the seminar as a democratic, participatory space, "not of disputes, but of action contributing to a permanent space for elaboration."

This conciliatory space, however, was fragile. At a group lunch following the seminar, youth from the two parties initially gravitated to opposite tables. "Let's unify!" clamored the PCdoB leaders jovially, "everyone together!" Clearly reluctant, the PT activists slowly dragged themselves to a newly joined long table, encouraged by a few go-betweeners. However, the single table did not mean unification. With me and another leader in the intervening positions, there was almost no communication between the two ends of the table. Shortly, lunch was served, and the attempt at conciliation became pro forma.

While similar in some ways, this episode also shows a shift from the student rally described earlier. In both cases, partisan factions confronted a student body that was highly suspicious of partisan motives and disputes. Rival partisan factions were wary, if not hostile toward each other, nursing histories of mutual accusation and distrust. Each side congratulated itself on being more virtuous and democratic than the other. While sincere to a degree, these claims also masked competitive, exclusionary, even manipulative tactics on both sides that lurked not far beneath the surface. The main differences from the late 1980s were in the dynamics of partisan expression—or rather nonexpression. The late-1980s activists took every opportunity to proudly affirm their partisan affiliations, even as they wrestled with the near impossible task of keeping social movements "autonomous" from the parties. The mid-1990s activists downplayed their partisan affiliations as much as possible, even as they took advantage of ostensibly "civic," nonsectarian events (like a science and technology seminar) to advance masked partisan interests.

As I watched events such as these evolve over a period of a decade, I wrestled with the problems and possibilities of both approaches. While more openly sectarian and contentious, the earlier orientation often seemed more vigorous and generative, encouraging activist to throw themselves into the elaboration of proposals for reforms as well as into the hard work of building civic institutions, often from the ground up. While apparently more conciliatory and nonsectarian, the later events seemed to lack some of the drive of the earlier period. The suppression of open partisan dispute sometimes led to richer discussions, but also, in some cases, to an odd sense of paralysis. It was often unclear where those discussions were leading, and how they could contribute to social reforms.

Mid-1990s activists were clearly hungry for what they often called "elaboration of projects," especially as socialist ideals became more ambiguous and involvement in democratic institutions became more absorbing and complex. Many activists complained bitterly that the competitive climate of the traditional student movement prevented such elaboration, disintegrating instead into rigid ideological posturing and backstage manipulation. The emerging new forms of student organizing—such as those oriented around racial, professional, or business identities—actively suppressed partisan affiliations in order to create less competitive spaces for dialogue and project formation. While I certainly saw advantages to this approach, it also left me perplexed and concerned. Does becoming more "civic" necessarily entail curtailing partisan challenges? Or, as the 1980s activists argued, is some degree of partisanship necessary for the elaboration of projects for reform in a complex and contentious field—as well as for acquiring the institutional power necessary to implement those reforms? If so, how can activists mediate between the partisan and civic dimensions of their multiple affiliations as they form new types of publics in an emerging democracy? These are the thorny questions from my Brazilian experiences that inform the analysis and arguments ahead.

RESEARCHING NETWORKS IN FLUX

In studying changes in civic-partisan relations in Brazilian youth politics, I faced a number of challenges. I did not simply want to understand the characteristics of organizations, nor of the individuals who belonged to them, but rather to examine the intersection of multiple networks—student, religious, NGO, antidiscrimination, professional, and business, as well as partisan—in a changing field. Moreover, I wanted to study not just the structure of relations, but also the way that individuals and groups made sense of these networks and responded to the opportunities and dilemmas that they posed. This meant that I had to conduct my research on several different levels, ranging from in-depth interviews and participant observation to more formal analysis of affiliations and careers.

The ethnographic component of my work was particularly daunting, since it did not conform to the usual understanding of ethnography, which focuses on intensive immersion in a culturally cohesive setting. How do you study something that is mobile and shifting, composed of sprawling, fluid, and contentious networks with multiply affiliated activists and overlapping institutional sectors? The political context that I encountered in São Paulo was both structured and chaotic, morphing underfoot just as I thought I was starting to understand it. I found that in order to penetrate this multilayered world, I had to be more than a neutral fly on the wall. Rather, I had to embrace my contradictory position in what theorist Georg Simmel describes as "intersecting social circles." As a Simmelian "stranger," I sought to maintain an outsider's fresh perspective as I moved between social settings and engaged, sometimes intensively, with insiders.[2] This was easier said than done, subject to continual improvisation, learning, and revision as I wrestled with a number of interesting tensions.

Trying to Talk to Everyone

Since I was interested in studying activist networks in a multiorganizational field, I did not have the luxury of spending extensive time within a single organizational setting. Rather, I found myself trying almost impossibly to keep up with the schedules and activities of several different sectors at once. This meant that I made some sacrifices of depth in favor of breadth, although I think that those sacrifices were necessary in order to understand Brazilian activism as a field and not just as a collection of isolated groups. I encountered many of the same activists in several types of settings (for example, in student congresses, party caucuses, religious assemblies, popular protests, or civic forums), although most did not participate in quite so many different kinds of events as I scrambled to attend. I came to know some regions of the field better than others, and some groups no doubt felt hurt that I didn't spend more time with them. Nevertheless, my experience of moving from place to place—often dragged by busy activists themselves—did approximate their own experience of traveling across networks, shifting identities and practices as they went.

As I delved into this world, I explicitly sought out participants from a wide range of groups and attempted to understand the accounts of contending factions. While this helped me to understand the range of perspectives in play, it occasionally led to tensions and difficulties. Activists who had welcomed me into their discussions and bar sessions were sometimes alarmed to find me being equally friendly with opposing groups. My patterns of sociability at cross-network events were intently studied; it was disconcerting to find myself in the position of the "observer who is observed." I found that as my own position in these networks became clearer—and as I took care to segment my more sensitive or reflective conversations—most of the factions welcomed my attention (and again, were hurt if they felt slighted). However, they varied in the degree to which they let me into their internal deliberations. While I attended backroom negotiations, strategy sessions, internal showdowns, and painful self-evaluations of some PT factions, I was only able to conduct personal interviews or attend outer-layer public meetings with the more hardcore communist and Trotskyist groups.

Becoming a Node in the Network

As I moved from place to place, talking with different people and trying to understand the play of events, I found myself unexpectedly becoming a node in the network. Activists would often pump me for information and analysis of what was going on in other groups or sectors. The Catholic activists, for example, were very interested to hear about the student movement congress, which only a few of them attended. More problematically, the different partisan factions were eager to know the views of their opponents. I tried never to pass on information that was expressed to me in confidence, or that I thought was sensitive for ongoing negotiations or the reputation of a group. Nevertheless the cross-network flow of information, gossip, and analysis was so fast and furious that it was almost impossible not to become caught up in the exchange. For the most part, the information I shared was redundant and harmless—if they hadn't heard it from me, it was very likely that they would hear it from the next person they ran into. But occasionally, what I assumed was "common domain" information turned out not to be so for some actors, triggering alarm and renegotiations in the surrounding networks.

Letting Them Know I Know

The fact that I often had valuable insider knowledge created some dilemmas, but also opportunities for deepening my exchanges. As I conducted interviews with leaders of the more closed and guarded groups, I realized that they often initially treated me as they would a journalist. They offered prepackaged, highly ideological, and persistently upbeat views of events, largely devoid of genuine analysis and reflection. To get below the surface, I had to signal that I knew more than they thought I knew—for example, by asking a pointed question about internal disputes, or showing my understanding of the contradictions and dilemmas they were facing. I would sometimes see them look at me quizzically, realize that I was more of an insider than they expected, and then drop the interview down to a whole new level of reflective dialogue. After one such interview—which ran far longer than I had initially hoped—one of the more suspicious leaders of the radical Trotskyist PSTU (Unified Socialist Workers' Party) smiled broadly, shook my hand, and declared that it had been a "good interview." This flies in the face of the "ethnographer as sponge" model; in order to get good information from my intelligent and savvy subjects, I had to show that (like them) I was a thoughtful analyst of the unfolding situation.

"Our Friend from the CIA"

The most difficult part of my fieldwork experience was fending off the barrage of jokingly voiced, back-slappingly delivered references to me as "*nossa amiga da CIA.*" Even some activists with whom I had conducted probing interviews and maintained warm, long-term relationships thought it was hilarious to tease me in this way, part of the natural price of being a *gringa* in this anti-imperialist setting. Since I had spent previous time in Brazil and had influential friends to vouch for me, for the most part these jokes were minor irritations, although people always looked curiously to see if I reacted defensively or good-humoredly. However I made one serious misstep in releasing a very long and detailed questionnaire at a national student council attended by three hundred high-level activists from around the country. While I had developed a stock of trust among São Paulo leaders, activists from other states encountered me for the first time in the gossip-heavy fishbowl of the meeting. Students joked about "filling in their own CIA file" and came up to inquire as to whether it was true that one of the radical Trotkyist factions was boycotting my questionnaire. (It was; in contrast, the PCdoB left the questionnaire up to the "conscience of each person" while most PT youth filled it in happily.)

These tensions were alleviated some months later when I published an article on youth networks in *Teoria e Debate*, the theoretical journal of the PT. The article was widely read and gave me instant legitimation among even some of the most suspicious activists. "Do you remember when we thought you were CIA?" one of the aforementioned Trotskyists laughed near the end of my visit. As other political researchers no doubt know, there is no good response to these sorts of suspicions. I found that the only answer that worked somewhat was to grin and say, "You guys are going to be really disappointed when you find out that I'm just a sociologist."

Which Side Am I On?

One of the dilemmas of studying partisanship (and all politics is about partisanship in one way or another) is that one comes to acquire varying degrees of sympathy with the different camps. While I tried to get underneath the stereotypes, and was wary about critical assessments proffered by opposing groups, I came to "like" not only the ideas and proposals, but perhaps more important, the styles of some groups more than others. Because of my family's own history of Catholic activism, I easily engaged in the intimate rituals and reflections of the Catholic youth pastoral and felt more at home in open-ended discussion groups than in hard-hitting ideological slugfests. I'm sure the activists came to sense those sympathies, although I tried to maintain a critical eye for the difficulties and tensions of these more appealing groups. Perceptions of my affinities were bolstered by my history of living and working with grassroots PT activists in the 1980s; for the PT's partisan rivals, the immediate danger was not that I was CIA, but that I was too close to the PT, and might intentionally or unintentionally pass on sensitive information.

I tried to break out of a pattern of spending too much time with those I was stylistically and ideologically comfortable with, trying instead to seek out more "foreign" points of view. I lobbied hard (if unsuccessfully) to be allowed to attend internal meetings of the PCdoB, to the point that I became something of an irritant even to the PCdoB leaders who were trying their best to help me out. (I was, however, allowed to attend the more public meetings of their associated youth organization, the Union of Socialist Youth.) I had a challenging, if ultimately thoughtful and productive encounter with the Coordination of Black University Scholars, who were less concerned that I might be from the CIA than with my position as a white researcher objectifying black subjects. I also spent time on the other end of the spectrum with more conservative business-oriented youth, among whom I had the unexpected experience of feeling myself underdressed and socially ungraced. I tried always to understand the strengths of those I felt skeptical of, and the limitations of those I felt sympathy for, and in this way to challenge my own preconceptions.

"Thinking the Problem of Youth"

In the end, I did not want to completely submerge my own sympathies, since they were the product of my developing understanding and analysis. The context I was studying was highly self-reflexive. Not only activists, but also their assorted local advisors, supporters, and researchers were engaged in a continual dialogue about youth and politics in Brazil. For the most part, this dialogue was carried out under the implicit assumption that political participation of youth is a good thing, that Brazil needed more of it, and that there were ways it could be nurtured, stimulated, triggered, ignited, detonated, deepened, or enriched, depending on one's preferred metaphor of mobilization. Toward the end of my two years of fieldwork, I was increasingly called on to enter the dialogue, joining the ranks of the locals who were "thinking the problem of youth," as one of the PCdoB youth advisors put it. Some groups invited me to give short presentations or contribute to their informal discussions of youth politics (which I was happier to do in a reflective rather than a strategic mode). My article on overlapping youth networks in the PT journal especially seemed to have touched a nerve, perhaps because it pinpointed live tensions activists felt in juggling multiple involvements. The article was widely used as a discussion text in student, religious, partisan, and community youth groups. Activists often wanted to talk to me about ways I had gotten it right, as well as about the ways in which I hadn't quite.

Perhaps the biggest compliment came right before I left, when one of the PCdoB leaders put his arm around my shoulder and said, "Ann, you have to come back to Brazil! You have to become an advisor to youth politics! But you can't just do it for the PT!" In my position as a Simmelian stranger, I had succeeded, at least in some measure, in transcending local cleavages and digging under the skin of these complex and shifting political networks. This book is my attempt to give voice to the contradictions and possibilities of these networks. I hope to continue to contribute to this Brazilian dialogue, as well as to the discussions of others who are struggling to combine civic and partisan commitments in a world that so often asks them to choose between them.

PART ONE

Institutional Intersections

CHAPTER ONE

Communication and Mediation in Contentious Publics

YOUNG ACTIVISTS beginning political involvement in Brazil during the late 1980s entered a field marked by both dynamism and dispute. The country's slow and cautious transition from military to civilian rule was entering its second decade, with a new constitution on the way and a series of local and state elections paving the road for the country's first presidential elections in almost thirty years. Densely overlapping networks of religious, community, labor, and partisan activism had been mounting challenges to various levels of government since the late 1970s, although there were signs that this mobilization was beginning to weaken. Meanwhile, student activism in high schools and universities was bustling again, attempting to combat decades of student apathy and disengagement. Both traditional leftist student organizations and more experimental forms of student organizing were percolating on college campuses, some focusing on cultural, community-oriented, or preprofessional activity.

During this period, a young agronomy student named Barreto[1] traveled across Brazil to rebuild the Federation of Agronomy Students of Brazil (FEAB), one of Brazil's specialized student organizations focused on areas of professional study. Swept into activism during his freshman year at the Federal University of Rio Grande do Sul, Barreto spearheaded an effort to revitalize the agronomy students' movement by reaching outside of the university, creating links to the burgeoning rural land reform movement. Barreto helped to initiate and design a series of "experiential internships" between university students and the church-based rural workers' movement, which was engaged in land occupations across the country. As he traveled, Barreto also worked to attract students to the newly formed Workers' Party (as well as to his own internal party faction), which was beginning to launch candidates at state and national levels. In a whirl of discussions, meetings of agronomy students spun over into meetings of party or faction, which spun over into strategy sessions on how to win control of Brazil's historic National Student Union (UNE)—recently relegalized after decades of military rule—from the rival Communist Party of Brazil. Success in that campaign led Barreto to assume a position as director of UNE, and to narrowly miss election as president of the organization just before the country exploded into massive student and civic demonstrations for the impeachment on corruption charges of President Fernando Collor de Melo in 1992.

In this heady and exhilarating period of institution building, Barreto became skilled at discursive and organizational maneuvering. He learned when to foreground or background his multiple identities—as student, party member, faction leader, rural activist, and agronomist-in-training—as he pursued several types of projects simultaneously across lively and shifting activist networks. These intersecting identities contributed to his ability to build relations across groups, while expanding the cultural and organizational resources he brought to the various collectivities to which he belonged. However, his overlapping identities were also a source of conflict. The consensual, dialogue-oriented style that Barreto acquired during his experience with church-based popular movements clashed with the much more competitive logic of student politics. He participated in partisan and factional battles within student organizations that undermined student movement unity and disrupted efforts at structural reform. And later attempts to establish a youth research NGO dissolved in a morass of intrafactional rivalries. As he sought to advise younger activists in the more diversified and segmented political field of the mid-1990s, he was deeply critical of partisan disputes in the student movement—which he blamed for curtailing renovation and contributing to the movement's marginalization—even as he acknowledged the role he himself had played in the coupling of partisan and student identities during earlier periods. His perspective on the student movement, expounded at length over a series of interviews between 1993 and 1997, was a mixture of wistful optimism and cynicism over lost possibilities.

Activists like Barreto play an important, if sometimes invisible, role in the tumultuous process of transition between authoritarian and democratic regimes. They are located "in between" in almost too many ways to enumerate: between regime forms; between party, faction, and student movement; between the student movement and the rural-popular movement; between the traditional student movement and new forms of preprofessional student organizing; between experienced militants and new recruits; between regions of the country; and between childhood and their professional futures. Barreto served as a mediator on many fronts, although not necessarily in ways that pointed toward conciliation or consensus. At times he used his growing skills in mediation for adversarial purposes: to consolidate factional dominance, score gains for one or more of his organizations, construct oppositional alliances, or negotiate weighted deals between contending groups. At other times, Barreto's mediating skills helped him to build bridges across different kinds of groups, enabling him to contribute to various forms of institutional innovation.

For example, he helped to convince middle-class students and rural workers that they could learn from each other, and also served as an advocate for new forms of preprofessional organizing within the more conventional leftist student movement. In these senses, his position "in between"—serving as what is sometimes called a broker, but which I will refer to using the more general term of "mediator"—helped to provide dynamism and creativity to the field, at the same time as it generated tension and dispute.

Partisan Publics traces both sides of the mediating roles played by activists like Barreto in Brazil's newly democratic civic arena. On the one hand, young activists located at the intersections of an expanding and diversifying field contributed to innovation, institution-building, and new forms of cross-sectoral communication. On the other hand, their interactions led at times to competition, polarization, and institutional paralysis or breakdown. These contrasting tendencies were in turn influenced by the styles of communication activists learned as they traveled through particular organizations or institutional sectors. For example, activists learned different orientations toward communication and problem solving as they participated within the more consensus-based church or community groups than they did in the highly competitive student or partisan organizations. Likewise, some kinds of groups infused young people with primarily collectivist orientations, while others encouraged the pursuit of more personalized projects.

I argue that variation in styles of political communication resulted not simply from relations within groups, but also from the positions of activists at the intersections of multiple types of organizations. Activists like Barreto, who were situated between groups with varied projects, strategies, and communicative styles, had to find ways to negotiate among these, responding to the problems and opportunities that they created. They synthesized these into their own styles of intervention and mediation as they built their careers as activists. At times they succeeded, and at times they failed. The ways in which they succeeded and failed, innovated or retrenched, built bridges and barriers, had important implications for the structure and dynamics of youth activism in postauthoritarian Brazil. Moreover, I argue that the mechanisms of mediation in play in the Brazilian case can shed light on the inner workings of democratic change processes in many other contexts around the world.

Challenges for Postauthoritarian Publics

The experiences of young Brazilian activists like Barreto reflect a more general paradox of newly democratic public arenas: as actors create new forums for public participation and dialogue, they also create spaces for the pursuit of particularistic and contending projects. These emerging "publics" quickly become "partisan publics," as actors jockey for the prominence of their particular projects, organizational forms, and even definitions of the field itself. Yet communication in such emergent publics cannot be based on pure competition. Actors must also learn ways to talk to each other across institutional and partisan divides, forging new styles of public discussion and collaboration that can sustain civic dialogue in a fractious field. These twin challenges—the elaboration of new projects, repertoires, and institutional forms and the mediation of the divisions and conflicts that these inevitably imply—constitute two of the foundational problems of postauthoritarian public arenas. Without the first, citizens will lack the intermediary organizations that buffer relations between individuals and the state. Without the second, the competing forces in society may polarize to an extent that the fragile democracy is torn apart.

But how do people and groups reconstruct the institutional forms and norms of communication that sustain democratic relations after these have been decimated by decades of authoritarian rule? When do they succeed, and when do they fail? How do attempts to respond to these challenges drive relationships in an emerging political field? One approach to this question, coming from studies of democratic transitions as well as of organizations and the professions, has focused on agonistic or competitive relations among actors, such as bargains between elites, struggles over institutional "jurisdiction," or competition over resources or recruits.[2] A second view, coming from the normative literature on civil society, has focused on the opportunities that newly emerging "public spheres" provide for public communication, dialogue, and consensus-formation, as well as for civic participation, cooperation, and trust.[3]

Neither of these perspectives, taken alone, is adequate for understanding the dynamics of democratic reconstruction in postauthoritarian countries. Such societies *both* experience contention over the direction, contours, and logic of the field, *and* develop new forms of public communication and collaboration—which ironically are necessary for the pursuit of particularistic projects. While some theorists have argued that the competitive logic of particularistic or partisan pursuits necessarily distorts communication in the public sphere, the Brazilian case shows that partisanship plays an important, if sometimes contradictory, role in democratic reconstruction. Sometimes partisanship can help to generate civic networks and institutional innovation. For example, Barreto's enthusiastic militancy in the Workers' Party—as well as the cross-sectoral ties he acquired as a party member—helped give energy and direction to his attempts to renovate student organizations and forge relations with external groups. Yet partisanship can also have divisive, disruptive, or paralyzing effects, as Barreto discovered in the factional struggles that beset the student movement during this period.

These contrasting effects have less to do with the instrumental partisan logic itself than with the way that partisan pursuits are mobilized and demobilized within particular settings. Partisan concerns—in both the broad sense of political advocacy and narrow sense of political party activism—do not necessarily have to be eliminated or suppressed to enable civil communication among contentious actors. However, such communication is facilitated when actors can carve out spaces "in between," that is, not dominated by single identities or membership blocks, but rather positioned at the intersections of multiple identities, projects, and forms of political intervention. Such locations in turn give rise to "publics," a term that I use in this book in a somewhat unusual way. I define publics as interstitial spaces in which actors temporarily suspend some aspects of their identities and involvements in order to generate the possibility of provisionally equalized and synchronized relationships.[4] These spaces buffer relations between individuals and collectivities that otherwise may be engaged in particularistic and contending projects. They often draw on ambiguity and ritual to find points of connection that generate productive relationships and new forms of joint action.

To call such publics "equalized" and "synchronized" does not mean that power differentials, cultural conflicts, or contending projects disappear. As many scholars have pointed out, such divisions are an essential and irreducible dimension of political life.[5] Nevertheless, productive communication does take place across such divides, and this communication drives both the construction of civic institutions as well as new kinds of public collaboration and coalition building. Sometimes this happens in small and localized settings, such as in the university forums Barreto helped to organize between agronomy students, party leaders, and rural workers. At other times these publics are societywide, such as Brazil's huge popular movement for direct elections (*Diretas Já*) in 1984, as well as the mobilizations for the impeachment of President Collor in 1992. Both of these movements had broad cross-sectoral support, including the active participation of political parties.

However, these moments of intensified cross-sectoral dialogue or "civic unity" are extremely fragile and fraught with latent conflict. They set the normative contours of the field and often allow for cross-fertilization of projects and repertoires, but also contribute to the emergence of new forms of competition and contention. To understand these processes, we must examine the mechanisms of communication and mediation by which such provisional "publics" are constructed, sustained, disrupted, and dissolved.

MULTIPLE INVOLVEMENTS ACROSS CHANGING NETWORKS

This book examines the changing composition of activist networks over a twenty-year period (1977–97), as composed by the multiple affiliations of those activists in different kinds of movements and organizations.[6] I track the trajectories of young activists through intersecting institutional sectors, including religious, student, partisan, NGO, antidiscrimination, professional, and business involvements. Through a structural analysis of activist careers (in chapter 3), I show how these intersections changed over time, providing different challenges and opportunities to successive cohorts of activists. The activists responded to such challenges by developing particular styles of communication by which they mediated among their multiple involvements. These communicative styles channeled youth politics in different ways, toward competition versus collaboration, or toward ideas versus actions. These styles of communication in turn informed the ways in which they constructed their publics, that is, provisionally equalized forums for ideas and actions at the intersection of multiple networks of participation.

There are two broader questions underlying these analyses, one political and the other more generally sociological. To take the general question first, I am interested in how people respond to the challenges of moving through multiple social worlds. To sociologists, this is often referred to as the phenomenon of "intersecting social circles," described by nineteenth-century social theorist Georg Simmel as a core problem of modern life.[7] This could mean the overlapping networks of family, work, school, neighborhood, religion, and ethnic or national group, in which most of us participate in some way. Or in the case of the Brazilian youth activists, it could mean the way that people are tugged between student, religious, partisan, professional, and other types of social and political involvements. In what ways does the experience of moving between partially overlapping networks contribute to tension and strain, on the one hand, or innovation and autonomy, on the other? How do these intersections influence the choices and actions of individuals, as well as those of the various collectivities they belong to? This question can be heard in every page of this book, explored from a variety of perspectives.

My political question is one component of this broader sociological concern. How do we combine our civic commitments with partisan and particularistic pursuits? As citizens, we are torn between competing involvements. On the one hand, we are concerned with the good of the whole—whether this is defined as the neighborhood, the polity, the nation, or the global community. This "civic" commitment implies some sort of ideal of a common good negotiated in some way with fellow citizens, even if the scope and range of this commitment varies widely across cultures, localities, and historical periods. On the other hand, we also experience commitments to various "parts" of this whole—the product of our participation in multiple social networks. These can represent private concerns about individual or family well-being, but can also refer to larger collectivities—religious, ethnic, or national groups, for example, as well as other community, professional, commercial, or political interests. For example, we may become involved in fighting for the improvement of our neighborhood, in the case of community activists; or for the protection our co-workers, in the case of labor unions; or for the uplift of our racial or ethnic group, in the case of antidiscrimination movements; or for our career-oriented or profit-making concerns, in the case of professional or business associations. These commitments are not necessarily compatible with each other, and sometimes enter into direct contradiction, making it difficult to see how they all add up to a common "civic" good.

Disagreements over the common good often crystallize into larger ideological and tactical alliances that we come to know as political parties. Partisan politics currently has a bad rap among social commentators, as well as among the public as a whole. Partisanship is often seen as a malaise that paralyzes government, inflames public vitriol, and causes deep polarization in the population. It is blamed for fomenting public disillusionment and apathy, leading to the dismissal of institutionalized politics as the domain of scheming, power-hungry politicians pursuing their narrowly defined interests. No matter that it is often partisans themselves who most fervently brandish the partisan label at their opponents. There seems to be a popular consensus that "civic" is better and that life and government would be vastly improved if we could cast off partisan divisions and learn to "all get along."

This book challenges that popular assessment of partisan politics. Partisanship is not only necessary and unavoidable, but it can also, in some circumstances, be a creative, motivating, and institutionally generative source of civic involvement and reform. Using the example of Brazilian youth politics in the postauthoritarian period, I show how "civic" and "partisan" pursuits are not fundamentally opposed. One can fuel the other, causing conflict and strain for sure, but also building bridges between actors and generating innovative new forms of public participation. In the Brazilian case, this was especially evident in the first decade of democratic transition, when the civic and partisan oppositions were rebuilding themselves simultaneously amidst the rapid political changes of the 1980s. Civic and partisan movements were often composed of the same multiply affiliated activists, who combined political party activism with participation in religious, student, labor, and community-based movements.

However, partisanship can also have many of the negative effects described above. During the second decade of Brazil's return to civilian rule, a cultural wedge was driven between the ideas of "civic" and "partisan" involvement, making it much more difficult for activists to productively combine the two. As I watched this shift in successive visits to Brazil, I began to puzzle over why this was. Why was partisan participation among young activists motivating and generative in the early period of the transition, but increasingly enervating and paralyzing as Brazil's democracy consolidated? Why did activists in the 1980s wear their partisan identities publicly as a source of pride, whereas in the 1990s they tended to be pushed underground? And why was the source of innovation in student politics shifting to areas in which partisanship was barely mentioned—such as antidiscrimination, professional, and business activism—despite the partisan affiliation of many activists in these movements?

Sociological analyses of social movements often focus on the external political environment, such as the openness or closure of the regime, the structure of alliances among elites and challengers, and cultural framings in response to an elite-driven media.[8] While certainly playing a role in this case, these factors only give us part of the answer to the questions I have posed. To address these puzzles, I probe deeply inside the intersecting organizational networks that composed the field of youth politics during this period. In the chapters ahead, I examine structural changes in these networks as young activists traveled through multiple institutional sectors. I also take a more intimate cultural look at the processes of communication that constituted and transformed those networks over the twenty years of the study.

If partisan claims within such publics became more precarious and paralyzing in the 1990s, this was because the structure and dynamics of activist networks had changed dramatically since the early years of the transition. The early field was dominated by full-time, heavily invested activists whose careers often spanned multiple institutional sectors—including intense participation in political parties. The later field was more complex, combining older activists from the early period, as well as younger, less heavily invested activists who were trying to link social commitments with their personal and professional development. The tension between cohorts—as well as between competing styles of communication—generated much of the difficulty in combining partisan and civic pursuits in the 1990s. But at the same time, it also spawned innovative, hybrid forms of publics, which combined competition and collaboration in new ways. This book explores both the possibilities and the problems of these emerging publics, as young activists struggled with the challenges posed by their multiple involvements.

PARTISAN-CIVIC OVERLAP IN THE 1980s

Brazil's extended process of democratic transition began in the late 1970s, when the military regime announced a "slow and secure" process of political liberalization and return to democratic institutions.[9] In the early 1980s, the country saw a return to multiparty elections; a surge in student, labor, human rights, and community-based popular movements; and a massive (if unsuccessful) movement for direct elections (*Diretas Já*). In 1985, Brazil returned to civilian rule under President José Sarney and began the process of writing a new constitution, which was elaborated with strong civic involvement and ratified by Congress in 1988. The period also saw several gripping electoral campaigns, including the 1988 Workers' Party (PT) mayoral victories in several state capitals (including São Paulo) and the narrow defeat of its 1989 presidential candidate Luiz Inácio (Lula) da Silva in the country's first direct presidential elections in nearly thirty years. Young people were involved in many of these movements and campaigns, sometimes centered in the schools and universities, while at other times in the churches and youth groups of the poorer communities.

This is not, of course, to say that most Brazilian youth were involved in political activity of some kind. The 1980s were also a time of political and economic crisis, in which the population swung between the hopes engendered by the return to the democracy and the uncertainty and cynicism generated by economic recession, crippling inflation, several failed economic stabilization plans and continued traces of state corruption and authoritarianism. Having been raised in a climate in which the official mantra was "students study, workers work, and the government governs," most Brazilian youth had little experience of open political debate. The student movement itself was significantly marginalized during much of the period, mired in partisan battles and increasingly distant from the majority of the student population. Yet despite widespread cynicism, there was a palpable sense of a social movement sector on the move. If activists often felt that they were fighting an uphill battle, at least they were energized and in good form, innovating new forms of challenge and introducing new actors to the public arena.[10]

These different forms of participation constituted a densely overlapping activist network, particularly in the urban periphery of São Paulo and other cities. Core leaders in one movement were often linked through partisan, religious, or neighborhood ties to leaders in others; paid party activists served as important movement brokers; participants attended meetings and campaigns together and turned up for each others' rallies.

This overlap of different kinds of movement participation had significant benefits for the movements. It contributed to flows of information, re-sources, and organizational forms; led to higher levels of mobilization for rallies and events; helped in leadership training and consolidation; and generated shared framings of movement goals and opportunities.

But at the same time, these overlapping networks generated tensions and conflicts. Long-time leaders in community-based health or housing movements were shouted off the podium when they became city council candidates for the opposition parties. The electoral success of PT and other parties sucked movement leaders off the street and into administra-tive positions. The funding logic of NGOs created ethical and morale problems within the community movements they sought to support. And nascent student groups were vulnerable to accusations of partisanship from opponents as well as potential supporters. Clearly, the intersections of different organizational forms and logics of participation brought ad-vantages and disadvantages for the actors involved.

DIVERSIFICATION AND DECOUPLING IN THE 1990s

During the 1990s, as Brazil moved from democratic "transition" to "con-solidation,"[11] the intense organizational overlap that had characterized the 1980s began to unravel. Politically motivated young people were in-creasingly wary of the earlier "all or nothing" style of full-time activism and began to seek more specialized and personalized forums of participa-tion. With this shift came increasing unease about the relationship be-tween partisanship and other forms of civic participation, along with ac-tive attempts to decouple these.

Yet even as activists in the 1990s innovated with new organizational forms and styles of communication, they also drew on the partisan styles of political interaction that had been forged a decade earlier. During the 1980s, Brazilian youth politics had been dominated by two quite different (and mostly disconnected) forms of activism, one centered among middle-class university students, the other situated in the poorer urban and rural communities (the history of both are described in chapter 4). The student movement, led by Brazil's historic National Student Union (UNE), played an important role in the first resurgence of democratic protest in 1977, serving as a rallying point in the call for human rights and democratic liberties. However, UNE spent much of the 1980s enmeshed in competition among partisan factions, some of which built on the fragmented Marxist vanguard groups that had survived the military repression. In the urban peripheries and rural areas, many young people had begun to participate in the liberation-theology infused Pastoral de Juventude (Youth Pastoral) of the Catholic Church. The youth pastoral differed from the student movement in its more consensual, dialogic style, which helped to develop leadership for the urban and rural popular movements of the 1980s. These church-based groups also fed many of their leaders into intensive partisan activism, mostly within the Workers' Party (PT) but also occasionally into more traditional vanguard socialist organizations.

By the 1990s, these two forms of activism—both highly partisan, despite clear stylistic differences—were no longer the twin poles of youth politics. Rather, the field of youth activism had become increasingly diversified.[12] In the universities, traditional student organizations (such as UNE) encountered mounting criticism from activists focusing on racial, gender, or other kinds of "specialized" identities, some of which were linked to the NGO-style activism that was flourishing in Brazil during this period. At the same time, young people involved in professional and business-oriented student groups began to contest space within the universities, often in ways that were critical of the partisan dynamics of traditional student politics. Student leaders struggled to adjust to this new pluralism in youth politics, even as they built on the partisan styles and repertoires inherited from the past.

In 1992, the student movement received an infusion of civic energy through its participation in the dramatic public mobilizations to impeach President Fernando Collor de Melo (analyzed in chapter 5). In September 1992, following months of broad-based civic mobilizations for "ethics in politics," President Collor was impeached by the Brazilian Congress for his involvement in a multimillion-dollar patronage ring. Young people played a surprisingly strong and colorful role in these demonstrations, becoming known as the *caras pintadas* (painted faces) for the improvised gesture of painting their faces the colors of the Brazilian flag. While clearly overstating their responsibility for the huge turnout, the leaders of UNE seized the opportunity to take the spotlight, claiming that the rallies represented the "return of the students" to national politics. The student protests received widespread popular and media support and turned Lindberg Farias, the charismatic young president of UNE (and leader of one of Brazil's Communist parties), into a "civic hero" with near pop star status.

The impeachment mobilizations were like a shot in the arm for the ailing Brazilian student movement, allowing it to regain a measure of public prominence that it had not held since the opposition to the dictatorship in the 1960s. In the year or two following the impeachment, young people swelled the ranks of student organizations and showed renewed interest in civic participation of different types—including those focused around specialized racial, professional, and business identities. However, this unexpected infusion of people and energy also created dilemmas for the student movement, as it wrestled with its new "civic" identity. In the more diversified context of postimpeachment politics, the tight coupling of partisan and civic pursuits that had characterized the 1980s could no longer be taken for granted. Issues of partisanship became a flash point for contestation and debate, as more students began to question the highly competitive style of traditional student politics.

MODES OF COMMUNICATION IN COMPLEX PUBLICS

To understand these changes in Brazilian youth politics, I examine how activists renegotiated communicative styles as they built new kinds of publics in an increasingly heterogeneous field. During the 1980s, many activists in the high-school student movement and Catholic youth pastoral learned skills in what I call "partisan bridging," by which they built relations in the overlap between partisan and other kinds of involvements. In the 1990s, many of these same activists were entering the universities, bringing skills and styles learned in earlier relational milieus. Some moved on to top-level leadership in their organizations, or expanded their participation to include other institutional sectors. They interacted with newer cohorts of young people, many of whom began activism in the civic glow of the impeachment movement. The interaction between cohorts contributed to the generation of new styles, as older activists intermingled with younger ones and confronted new types of institutional intersections.

I observed these communicative processes as I attended a wide range of activist encounters during the mid-1990s. Despite the turn toward more segmented and personalized forms of activism, many young people attempted to build bridges across divides of party, ideology, and specialized identities. Some activists tried to bring their specialized projects—related to racial, gender, or professional issues—to more general student publics, such as national congresses or seminars. These proposals were buffeted by intense partisan debates about the form and purpose of student organizing, generating entrenched resistance while also provoking changes in strategy and style. Other activists attempted to set up more specialized nonpartisan forums, arguing that genuine exchange and elaboration of ideas could not happen in a competitive, dispute-driven environment. These groups developed communicative styles in which the expression of partisan identities became nearly taboo. This at times freed up space for more reflective discussion, but at other times seemed to drain such settings of the energy and drive that had characterized earlier periods, when activists like Barreto were much more forthright about their partisan identification.

These struggles over partisanship in Brazilian student politics are examples of more general tensions generated by the relational intersections of which politics is composed. All politics involves a mix of the civic and partisan, combining general and specialized, common and particularized concerns. The texture and quality of political interaction is composed by the ways in which actors compose this mix, or better, slide up and down along the multiple axes along which political relations are composed. Activists learn to do this mixing and sliding differently in particular institutional and relational contexts.

We can challenge the dichotomy between partisan and civic forms of interaction by differentiating between the modes of communication that actors move between in social encounters. In the second half of this book (chapters 6 through 9), I develop a typology that distinguishes between two dimensions of communication—the degree of competition versus collaboration, and the focus on ideas versus actions (or alternatively, on elaboration versus deliberation). These dimensions provide us with four ideal types of communicative performance, which I call exploratory dialogue, discursive positioning, reflective problem solving, and tactical maneuver. These modes of communication are loosely associated with the ideas of Habermas, Gramsci, Dewey, and Machiavelli, respectively. All four modes are important for democratic politics, although they each have characteristic strengths and weaknesses. They allow activists to mediate the relational complexities of different kinds of publics, although they can also can limit and constrain what those publics are able to accomplish.

When used skillfully by movement leaders, these modes of communication can contribute to distinct types of social outcomes: open-ended exchange of ideas, counterhegemonic proposals for reform, pragmatic institutional solutions, or distributions of power and resources. However, groups and individuals rarely stayed fixed in a single mode. Expanding on recent studies of group styles and political discourse,[13] I argue that communicative styles consist of the ways in which actors in particular settings combine, segment, and move between these different modes. Moreover, movement between modes is often cued to the ways in which they activate and deactivate various strands of their multiple identities. As they shape different kinds of publics, activists develop skills in some modes over others, as well as characteristic ways of switching between them.

The attempt to build such publics across partisan and institutional divides created enormous challenges for young activists in the 1990s, generating sometimes productive, sometimes volatile "schools of democracy." The bridging efforts of activists were informed by the changing structure of the political field, as well as by styles and skills of communication that they learned while moving through overlapping forms of social involvements. The process by which such bridging efforts succeed and fail—and the implication of these processes for the robustness and vitality of post-authoritarian public arenas—is the central puzzle of this book.

RESEARCHING BRAZILIAN YOUTH ACTIVISM

This book draws on several years of intensive field research in Brazil during the mid-1990s, based primarily in the São Paulo region, although I made forays to other cities for interviews and events.[14] During this period I built on my previous experience and networks from three years in São Paulo during the late 1980s. The principal organizations whose events I attended are listed in table 1.1 (below). These included the centralized student movement (especially UNE), the Catholic youth pastoral, socialist youth organizations, black student organizations, NGOs, preprofessional (course-based) organizations, and business-oriented student associations. Most do not constitute a single "group," but rather a cluster of linked organizational bodies, organized with varying degrees of hierarchy at the national, regional, and local levels. I also accompanied the youth wings of several political parties, with a focus on three: the Workers' Party (PT), the Communist Party of Brazil (PCdoB), and the Brazilian Social Democratic Party (PSDB). I attended hundreds of events of these groups; conducted formal and informal interviews with their leaders; ate, drank, and traveled with the participants; and contributed to their discussions and debates when requested. I generated extensive field notes as well as more focused meeting logs, and recorded interviews with more than seventy activists (individually or collectively) at different organizational levels.

I also collected more than 330 written questionnaires documenting the participation histories of young activists through different institutional sectors (student movement, religious, partisan, community, NGO, labor, preprofessional, business). In addition to trajectory information, the questionnaires contain data on activists' strategies of prioritization among their involvements, their cultural and extracurricular activities, their socialization networks, their personal and social projects for the future, and their evaluations of youth politics in Brazil. Finally, I collected a wide range of organizational documents, including pamphlets, posters, journals, theses, minutes, correspondence, news clippings, and other original materials. Some documents were gathered at the offices of the organizations, some were distributed at meetings I attended, and some were donated by activists from their personal archives.

In each of the primary organizations described above, I made a formal presentation of my research to the leadership and at least some body of participants. In these meetings I outlined my interest in networks of youth

TABLE 1.1
Principal organizations whose events I attended during fieldwork

Sector	Organization
"General" student movement	UNE: National Union of Students CA XI: Law students' association of University of São Paulo
"Specialized" student movement (Course Executives)	Forum of Course Executives (course-based student associations) & national encounters of the following specific associations: FEAB: Agronomy students' association ENECOS: Communication students' association ENED: Law students' association ENEFAR: Pharmaceutical students' association ENECS: Social science students' association FENEAD: Administration students' association ENECON: Economics students' association
Religious groups	PJ: Catholic Youth Pastoral PJMP: Catholic Youth Pastoral of the Popular Milieu
Antidiscrimination	CONUN: National Coordination of Black University Scholars
Business organizations	FEJESP: State Federation of Junior Enterprises of São Paulo AIESEC: International Association of Students in Economic and Accounting Sciences
Political Parties (includes party factions/youth wings)	PT: Workers' Party (and internal PT factions) PSDB: Brazilian Social Democratic Party PCdoB: Communist Party of Brazil UJS: Union of Socialist Youth (youth organization linked to PCdoB)

activism and stressed that I sought to treat all participants as subjects rather than objects, both in terms of their agency in social movements as well as their participation in the process of research. I also promised to give them a "return" on the research in the form of a discussion of the findings as well as reflections on the research throughout. Many young people were extremely generous with their time and thoughts. They sat down to long interviews about their personal histories, explained the intricacies of organizational structures and practices, and clarified the often dizzying swirl of negotiations and debates. They were eager to swap stories and strategies over beers or on the road, pumping me for comparative reflections on politics and youth activism in the United States.[15]

OVERVIEW OF THE BOOK

In thinking through the complexities of the Brazilian case, I have pulled together ideas from different academic subfields that don't necessarily talk to each other. Thus while I am drawing on the literature on social movements, this is not just a book on social movements, and some of my terminology departs from current conventions in the subfield. I am also drawing on ideas from institutional and network analysis, democratic theory, cultural sociology, and pragmatist and interactionist philosophies. I begin the book by laying out my somewhat unusual theoretical synthesis. As I move into the empirical analysis, my strategy is to begin with a macrolevel structural and historical account of the twenty-year period captured in this book, tracking the trajectories of different cohorts of activists through the field, as well as exploring the tensions they faced in combining civic and partisan pursuits. In the second part of the book, I move to a more microlevel account, based on my ethnographic observations of activist encounters during the mid-1990s.

In the chapters that follow, I combine formal structural analysis of patterns of relations with interpretive analysis of the discourse and practices of young people who were building these relations. These formal mathematical techniques are descriptive in nature; they allow me to find pattern in complexity, but do not drive the overall analysis. Equally important are the voices of the youth themselves, as expressed in interviews, documents, and hundreds of meetings and events that I attended during my fieldwork.

In chapter 2, I present the theoretical framework that underlies this book. I discuss how variation in styles and skills of activism are influenced by the experiences of actors within institutional sectors, as well as by their trajectories across multiple sectors. I argue that we need to combine three angles of vision—systemics, pragmatics, and performances—and discuss the roots of these three approaches in the theoretical literature, including the work of Simmel, Mead, Dewey, Schutz, and Goffman. I also introduce a typology of four leadership positions in a multisectoral field—bridging leaders, entrenched leaders, explorers, and focused activists—which I argue correspond to distinct orientations toward creativity and competition. In chapter 3 I provide the systemic sinews of the book through an analysis of the trajectories of successive "microcohorts" of activists through multiple institutional sectors.[16] I identify five periods from 1977 to 1996, distinguished by changing political environments as well as by the emergence of different sets of institutional actors. Drawing on my questionnaire data, I use the algebraic technique of Galois lattice analysis to examine the structure of overlapping affiliations among each entering cohort, considering how these may have contributed to their styles of participation in successive periods.[17]

In chapters 4 and 5, I address the historical processes underlying these structural changes in the field. In chapter 4, I examine the return of the student movement and radical Catholic organizing during the early years of Brazil's democratic transition, as both movements wrestled with the overlay between partisan involvements and other kinds of participation. This gave rise to two different forms of "partisan bridging," focused more strongly on competitive and collaborative modes of communication, respectively. In chapter 5, I examine how partisan bridging among student leaders contributed to mediation and coalition building in the 1992 impeachment mobilizations. I introduce the idea of "Simmelian mediation," showing how multiply affiliated actors built connections between groups in successive stages of the converging movement. I argue that partisan ties—both expressed and suppressed—played an unexpectedly important role in the self-consciously "civic" coalition.

In part 2, I examine how these historical changes influenced microlevel communicative processes during the postimpeachment period. I discuss the performative dimension of communicative styles in chapter 6 and argue that styles develop in response to the relational challenges of particular settings of interaction. I show how actors moved between four modes of skilled communication—exploratory dialogue, discursive positioning, reflective problem solving, and tactical maneuver—in two highly institutionalized settings with roots in the partisan activism of the 1980s: a congress of UNE and an assembly of the Catholic youth pastoral. I examine in chapter 7 differences in style at three São Paulo universities, in which student activists were responding to increasing skepticism and hostility toward partisan activism. I analyze how local relational contingencies constrained and enabled activists' attempts to build "publics" for crosspartisan debate and action, affecting both the style and the quality of political communication.

In chapters 8 and 9, I explore the ways in which stylistic innovation as well as communicative breakdown are influenced by the leadership positions described in chapter 2. In chapter 8, I examine innovative communicative practices and organizational forms among emerging groups of activists who challenged the dominant style of the traditional student movement. I focus on three loci of innovation: the Coordination of Black University Scholars, the Course Executives, and the Junior Enterprises, all of which rejected the highly competitive, partisan style of traditional student politics, although in quite different ways. In chapter 9, I examine the dramatic breakdown of a student public amidst partisan contention over styles of communication at the 1997 Congress of UNE. To explain this breakdown, I argue that we need to look at the characteristic weaknesses of the four modes of communication, which constrained even highly skilled leaders in responding effectively to the emergent crisis.

I end the book with some concluding reflections on the role of partisanship in postauthoritarian publics. At various times and places, partisan passions among Brazilian youth activists contributed considerable creativity and dynamism to the field, as actors hitched a wide variety of institutional projects and repertoires to overarching partisan narratives. At other times, partisan dispute led to crisis, paralysis, or institutional breakdown, as leaders became mired in polarizing struggles that dragged down associated projects and practices. These findings belie claims that the particularistic or "instrumental" logic of political parties is necessarily bad for public arenas, but they do warrant further reflection into the constructive or destructive effects of partisanship in an emerging democracy. In particular, we should examine the ways that skilled political actors switch between different modes of communication, as well as the ways in which these modes are supported by specific relational contexts and institutionalized practices. As the Brazilian case shows, these modes of political communication—and the multiple networks that shape them—play a critical role in the successes and failures of democratic politics.

CHAPTER TWO

Leadership in the Intersections

IN LATE 1995, about thirty leaders of the Brazilian student movement gathered in São Paulo for a weekend-long meeting of the newly elected directorate of the National Student Union (UNE). Most students knew each other from years of activism at universities around the country. Almost all belonged to one of the five or six political parties (or party factions) represented at the meeting, and others brought experience in community-based popular movements, nongovernmental organizations, the Catholic youth pastoral, or cultural activities such as theater, music, and radio. Despite these diverse involvements, they were committed to the common banner of opposition to neoliberalism and the educational policies of the government of President Fernando Henrique Cardoso. At this meeting, they shared the collective task of evaluating the current direction of UNE and drawing up a plan of alliances and interventions for the coming year. However, it was clear to everyone that the real agenda was different. Underlying the drive toward consensus and joint action was the ever-present battle between partisan forces over the platform, agenda, and resources of the organization. This battle was evident in between-the-lines ideological posturing, as well as in continual rounds of backstage negotiations and the culminating drama of the votes.

Around the same time, a similar meeting was held among a different set of university students, involved in leadership of professionally oriented student organizations (known as "Course Executives") related to particular academic disciplines (e.g., medicine, history, law, agronomy, architecture).[1] These students had a similar array of multiple involvements and were equally opposed to neoliberalism and government educational policies. At least half of the young people belonged to political parties, and one person attended both meetings. However, the climate of the meeting was notably different. There was an unstated taboo against mentioning political party affiliations, although participation in other kinds of movements and organizations could be celebrated. Voting was prohibited in order to foster consensus-making, and backstage negotiation was replaced by endless and exhausting large group deliberations. This self-styled Forum of Course Executives (referred to in this book as "the Forum") prided itself on offering an alternative to the partisan climate and centralized structure of UNE. The participants hoped to create a "network-space" for "elaboration and exchange of experiences," which would bring new energy to student politics.

These two meetings represented two important poles in the field of student politics in the mid-1990s. On the one hand, the meeting of UNE represented the traditional, adversarial style of student politics, with a long and celebrated history going back to the 1930s. Many of Brazil's politicians, judges, and other public leaders had wet their political feet in the historic organization, which prided itself on being present at the major moments in twentieth-century Brazilian history. These included the fight against fascism in the 1930s and 1940s, defense of the national oil industry in the 1950s, resistance to the dictatorship in the 1960s, and most recently, the 1992 movement for the impeachment of President Fernando Collor de Melo. After decades of repression and marginalization, UNE felt itself to be back on its feet, resuming its historic role in defining Brazil's education policy and intervening in other civic questions of the day.

On the other hand, the Forum of Course Executives represented a more recent surge of specialized organizing in the universities that challenged (or at times, sidestepped) the centralized, competitive structure of UNE. This included not only the professional student movement, which organized students within particular academic disciplines, but also other cultural, civic, and even business organizations that had begun to dispute space in the universities. For example, the National Coordination of Black University Scholars challenged the neglect of racial issues within the centralized student organizations, while the new movement of Junior Enterprises recruited students to form mini–consulting firms based on business models. These emergent forms of organizing tended to be fiercely critical of the highly partisan, adversarial orientation of the traditional student movement, which they saw as shutting down debate over the wider array of student concerns.

As the meetings above illustrate, what was at stake in these new forms of organization were not only political projects or ideological positions. These groups were also contending over the forms and practices of democratic politics. Two decades after the military regime's "opening" to democracy, and one decade after the return to civilian rule, the norms and procedures of democratic participation were still very much in dispute within the civic microcosm of Brazilian youth politics. Not only specific proposals, but also day-to-day practices of elaboration, deliberation, and intervention varied significantly among these different groups. In their meetings, activists wrestled over their styles of participation even as they debated projects and agendas.

The difference in styles at these two encounters does not simply represent a split between adversarial versus consensual orientations toward democracy, as embodied in two very distinct institutional forms. Rather, the contrast results from the ways in which activists responded to the challenges posed by their multiple affiliations. In the meetings of UNE, the wide array of organizational memberships among participants tended to funnel down into a more restricted focus on party, faction, and student organization. In the meeting of the Forum, in contrast, partisan identities were forced underground, allowing activists to publicly embrace a wider set of identities and experiences. The distinct character of these events was as much a product of the overlay of multiple organizational involvements—and of the ways activists chose to handle these—as it was of any particular institutional form.

Neither style was clearly "better" than the other, and each presented some characteristic weaknesses. While UNE meetings tended toward power struggles and polarization, those of the Forum often risked exhaustion and paralysis. Both often fell short of elaborating the alternative proposals that they so passionately advocated, and they had decidedly mixed success in building alliances and coalitions. But occasionally, both sets of activists succeeded, sometimes in surprising ways, in breaking out of tendencies toward polarization or paralysis in order to solve problems, elaborate projects, and forge relationships in the political field. Why they were able to do so, I argue, is linked to the styles and skills of communication that actors develop in mediating between multiple forms of social involvement.

In this chapter, I present the theoretical framework that underlies this book, introducing concepts and terminology that I use throughout. I begin with a discussion of how styles and skills in social movements are grounded in institutional intersections. I then delve deeper into the theoretical literature, drawing on the ideas of Simmel, Mead, Dewey, Schutz, and Goffman to understand the systemic, pragmatic, and performative dimensions of these styles. Finally, I present four ideal types of skilled movement leadership that readers can take with them into the more detailed analyses that follow.

While I have developed this framework in dialogue with the particular complexities of the Brazilian case, I engage in sociological and philosophical discussions that go beyond this particular historical context. This book is grounded in a relational approach to social action that focuses on the fluid, interactive, contingent (and yet still structured) character of social process, which is more akin to a conversation or dialogue than to a set of isolated actions.[2] I inquire into the social and cultural mechanisms by which multiply embedded actors engage in dialogue with others—within and across groups—as they project themselves and their collectivities into the future. I hope that readers will be able to take elements of this framework with them as they think about contexts that are much different from the richly contradictory world of Brazilian youth activism.

STYLES AND SKILLS OF COMMUNICATION

How people act in social movement encounters makes a difference for what happens in those movements. This may seem like a trivial observation, but for several decades the role of individuals has been downplayed in studies of political mobilization. To avoid the dangers of an overly psychological approach to explanations of collective action ("they've all gone mad!") as well as the reductionism of narrow choice-based accounts, many analysts have focused on structural factors external to the individual: conditions of opportunity and threat, organizational resources, network relations, cultural schemas or "frames."[3] I argue that social movement analysts should revisit the role of individuals in movement processes and outcomes. However, we must examine individuals not as atomized, self-starting, free-moving actors, but rather in the light of what we know about the range of structural factors influencing movements. The starting point for this task is a relational understanding of styles and skills of communication, particularly among movement leaders.[4]

Individuals in social movements do not act alone; almost by definition, they act as part of more or less organized groups. Most belong to multiple groups simultaneously, including not only those that understand themselves to be engaged in protest (or other efforts at social change), but also other kinds of (more or less overlapping) collectivities—families, neighborhoods, friendship groups, schools, workplaces, racial or ethnic groups, subcultures, cities, regions, and nations. Such collectivities are not just categorical designations. They often entail distinguishable cultural practices that identify members, help them build relationships, establish boundaries with outsiders, and give meaning and orientation to actions. We can call such distinguishable sets of practices "styles," which I join sociologist Harrison White in describing in terms of network-based patterns of social interaction that are considered appropriate or "valuable" within a given relational context.[5]

Such styles, White notes, often have their grounding in what we call "institutions." While there are a number of different understandings of institutions currently circulating in the social sciences, I follow cultural and organizational sociologists in understanding institutions as clusters of self-reproducing practices and relationships sustained by particular "logics" of interaction that distinguish them from the environment around them and give them sustainability over time.[6] They may be more or less formalized through official legitimizing measures (such as marriage licenses or organizational statutes), or thorough less official forms of ritual and recognition (such as secret handshakes or dinner-time prayers). Institutions develop legitimizing narratives and accounts that make sense of their pasts and attempt to give form and direction to their futures, assigning value to sets of practices and relations and disciplining the actions of individuals within them. In this way, institutions give birth to recognizable styles of interaction, which in turn contribute to the sustainability of those institutions.

For movement activists, the institutions that ground their styles include a range of formal and informal forms of social organization, which aim in varying ways to intervene in the social world around them. In the Brazilian case, these include heavily institutionalized forms of association, such as organized religions, political parties, or professional associations. But they also include less-established forms of social organization that can be identified as working according to a recognizable cultural logic: for instance, NGOs, community organizations, and popular movements. Institutions are distinguishable by the logics of action that predominate within them. For example, political parties are dominated by the logic of the pursuit and contestation of state power, even though particular parties may pursue that power in different ways. This differs in fundamental ways from the religious pursuit of transcendental union or redemption, although different religious groups may conceive of this in more or less otherworldly terms (and may be more or less sympathetic with particular partisan orientations). Both of these differ from professional associations, which are concerned with training and legitimating the actions of individuals within the world of work.

These distinct logics supply some minimal forms of mutual recognition and communicability between the different kinds of organizations that compose what I refer to in this book as an *institutional sector*. Expanding somewhat on organizational theory, I define a sector as a set of institutionally differentiated sites of social organization and intervention—such as political parties, student organizations, religious groups, NGOs, professional or business associations—that share important aspects of their institutional logic and derive at least part of this logic from intrasectoral orientations and relationships.[7] Within each sector are characteristic repertoires of institutional practices, from rituals for initiation and solidarity building to procedures for debate, decision making, and leadership selection. While particular organizations within a sector may differ in some aspects of their structure and practice, there are usually analogues if not direct isomorphisms among organizations within a sector. For example, most political parties follow comparable procedures for leadership selection, although they may vary on things such as degree of consultation with party bases. Religious services can usually be identified as such due to familiarity with the institutional form associated with the sector, even if particular religions, denominations, or even places of worship have their own distinguishing features.[8]

These differences in institutional logic inform the discursive practices—which I call "styles of communication"—that underlie the formation of projects, relations, and repertoires of action. Both the elaboration of projects and the mediation of relationships are influenced by how people talk to each other. Some kinds of talk facilitate purposeful thinking through of problems and possibilities, helping people solve organizational dilemmas and construct new understandings of their pasts and futures. Other kinds of talk close down such discussion, or wrap it in existing ideological or conventional templates. Likewise, some kinds of talk are better able to reach across divergent experiences and interests, while others are more defensive and competitive, building boundaries rather than bridges.[9]

To some extent, styles of communication are informed by the institutional logics that predominate in a given organizational setting. For example, leaders who began their involvement in the Catholic youth pastoral were legendary for their greater emphasis on consensual decision making and group integration, even once they had moved on to student or party leadership. In contrast, those who began directly in the political parties often seemed to have a more cutthroat and manipulative sense of factional dispute, as well as strong interpersonal competition. This in turn differed from youth in business organizations, who disdained partisan competition but were often quite interested in individual self-promotion within and outside of their student enterprises.

However, styles are often not determined by a single institutional logic, but rather grow out of negotiation between the multiple forms of identity and involvement in play within an organization or event. To understand this, we need to return to the individual: it is people who practice styles, which they learn through their experiences in different kinds of institutional milieus. Since people belong to multiple groups, they come in contact with a range of different institutional practices, both within the groups they belong to and among other people and collectivities they interact with in the course of their daily activities. Sometimes these styles fuse easily, or allow for smooth transitions between interactions. But other times they come into conflict, either between contending actors (who battle over appropriate styles for a given situation), or within individuals themselves, who have to reconcile two or more possible ways of responding to a given situation.

In this book, I am particularly interested in individuals with experiences in more than one kind of institutional milieu, who therefore come into contact with multiple styles of communication. Such actors must develop what Neil Fligstein calls "social skill": the ability to mediate between different conceptions of identity and interest in order to generate consensus in a complex field.[10] Social encounters vary in the degree of skill they require of activists, in part as a function of the heterogeneity of participants and the complexity of styles and projects in play. Settings in which most participants belong to the same group (or set of groups), and can take institutional styles more or less for granted, may require less skill than those in which participants belong to a complex array of partially overlapping organizations.

Institutional milieus (i.e., the routinized relational settings in which participants in a given sector gather and interact) tend to be composed of individuals whose affiliations cluster in recognizable ways. Any given collectivity will have what I call an "affiliation profile," that is, the array of affiliations in other groups that are typically held by their members. For example, in the mid-1990s, almost all Brazilian student movement leaders belonged to political parties or factions, and some also participated in religious, community, or preprofessional organizations. Most Catholic youth activists were extremely involved in community-based popular movements, with some partisan, student, labor, and NGO involvement. In contrast, very few leaders in business student groups had any partisan, religious, or community involvement, although a few were involved in NGO or preprofessional activism.

Communicative styles develop from the ways that actors wrestle with the problems and possibilities posed by particular institutional intersections. While some aspects of style come from the cultural logic of the institutional sector itself (e.g., church groups versus political parties versus business organizations), subtle but important differences arise from the relational challenges that come from the multiple affiliations of members. Attention to affiliation profiles can help us understand intrasectoral differences. For example, student activists of the rival Workers' Party (PT) and Communist Party (PCdoB) tended to have quite different affiliation profiles, with the PT youth embedded in a wider range of popular, church-based, NGO, and labor organizations (in addition to their student participation), while the PCdoB youth stayed more focused on student and socialist organizing. The PT activists' dispersion of affiliations across sectors versus the PCdoB's concentration within sectors differentiated the communicative practices of these partisan activists, as I will show in the chapters ahead. Likewise, activists in the more radical branches of the Catholic youth pastoral tended have a broader span of sectoral involvements than their more moderate Catholic companions, who focused their activism within the church itself.

These multiple involvements were both facilitative and constraining, a source of ideas, resources, and relations as well as a strain on energy and commitment. Activists' skills in mediating among their multiple involvements are an important part of what becomes a recognizable communicative style. In this book, the term *style* refers to the customary repertoire of discursive practices that are considered to be appropriate forms of mediating the complexity of a particular institutional milieu. The term *skill* refers to the ability of individuals to wield those styles in more or less effective ways (i.e., some communicative interactions within a milieu can be more or less skilled than others). I seek to understand the social origins of both styles and skills by looking at activists' past histories of institutional involvement as well as the current configuration of relations in the field.

The Duality of Trajectories and Fields

This book recounts the experiences of young Brazilian activists during a particularly tumultuous and eventful period in their own lives as well as in the history of Brazil. I examine how they saw their lives-in-formation amidst the changing environment around them, as well as how they came together with others to attempt to intervene in that environment. Part of the story is told from the point of view of the youth themselves, variously positioned as they moved through a challenging set of experiences and events. However, part of my task is to understand how these experiences, perspectives, and positions formed something that was only partly visible to the young people themselves, a set of "dynamics" and "structures" that some saw and understood better than others, but to which no single actor had complete access or an unobstructed line of vision. As an analyst, I also cannot claim to have unfettered access; in fact "access" as a metaphor is misleading since it implies a fixed "thing" beyond the barrier of limited information or understanding. The "thing" that I am attempting to describe and explain is a process of change, the nature and direction of which were contested and composed of multiple and shifting viewpoints. Yet this interplay of viewpoints still gives it form; that form shapes relations; and those relations have effects on the character and consequences of actions.

In examining the interplay of multiple relations, this book addresses a classic problem of sociological theory regarding the complexity and intersections of social life. In the modern world, Georg Simmel argues, people move through increasingly differentiated and overlapping social groups, which leads to conflict and strain as well as to increased capacity for autonomy and freedom.[11] The individual can be seen as the intersection of all of the groups he or she belongs to; conversely, groups can be understood as the intersection of all of their members. Ronald Breiger refers to this Simmelian insight as the "duality of persons and groups," and explains how it can be extended to relationships in a larger network: relations among individuals are formed by the groups they jointly belong to, while relations among groups are formed by the members they share.[12] In the literature on social movements, researchers have used the idea of "duality" to examine how overlapping memberships and projects contribute to recruitment and mobilization, as well as to leadership, mediation, and diffusion of information and identities across groups.[13]

In this book, I focus on the temporal dimension of this Simmelian duality. I consider individuals as the intersection of the set of groups through which they pass over time, that is, their trajectory of overlapping affiliations. Conversely, I understand the trajectories of groups (and institutions) as the intersection of those individuals that pass through them over time. The members that they share across different time periods—and the ways that those members act on their multiple identities in fluid social encounters—help to constitute changing relations across multisectoral fields.

By multisectoral fields, I refer to relations between institutional sectors as shaped by the careers of individuals moving through those sectors. The concept of "field" is both structural and cultural; it refers to how actors are positioned in social space by their relations and affiliations, as well as how they endow those relations with meaning through mutual orientation and discursive positioning.[14] The scope of a relevant field can move up or down: for example, it can be intragroup, referring to the field of power relations among leaders within a student group (or factions within a party); it can be intrasectoral, such as the field of alliances or oppositions among student groups; or it can be multisectoral, such as the field of student, religious, professional, NGO, and business organizations involved in the 1992 impeachment coalition. Fields are multiple and overlapping, and actors switch back and forth among them as different sets of relationships are perceived as mattering for the interaction at hand.

This book focuses primarily on multisectoral fields, highlighting their dual relational structure. The pathways of individuals within and across sectors shape the fields they pass through, just as changes in those fields shape individual pathways. While the principle of duality has received growing attention in the literature on social movement and organizational networks, few researchers have addressed the temporal dimension of this Simmelian idea. Several works have examined the simultaneous shaping of activist lives and movement networks, as well as tensions between movement and nonmovement networks and identities.[15] However, this work has only grazed the surface in understanding how actors build careers across multiple networks, which are themselves undergoing change. Recent work on organizational fields has argued that overlapping relations can lead to institutional innovation through "interstitial emergence."[16] But most of this work has neglected the trajectories of multiply affiliated individuals in this process.[17]

There are two principal ways in which the link between careers and fields has been conceived. We can label the first the "individualist" approach, since it sees careers as the result of individual decisions based on interest calculations at successive points in time. The individual surveys the available options, calculates the costs of particular lines of action, weights costs and benefits, and makes a choice—and proceeds ahead into the future. The career itself has no meaning as a distinct entity with shape and form; it is merely an artifact of accumulated (but discrete) individual choices. A contrasting way of conceiving this link is to concentrate on the institutionalized structure of the field itself. The positions taken by an individual are preset as part of formal or informal organizational structure; there are modular pathways that individuals have little or no choice over, as they are swept along a "career path" that takes them from one position to the next. Ironically, in this conception, the individual career is as much an artifact as in the individualist view, although this time it is a product not of discrete choices, but of the prestructuring of the field itself.[18]

Neither approach takes us far enough in understanding the combination of selection and structure, of positions and possibilities, by which people shape their trajectories across multiple forms of social involvement. Careers vary in their degree of institutionalization; some are highly structured while others offer a wider array of options and choices. Moreover, trajectories through multiple sectors always pose some sort of challenge to reflection, interpretation, and synthesis. We need to look beyond narrowly individualist or structuralist approaches in order to gain a deeper cultural understanding of the processes of communication and interpretation through which people shape their trajectories.

FROM SYSTEMICS TO PRAGMATICS

In this book, I combine a bird's eye look at the *systemic* dimension of these overlapping relations with an analysis of the *pragmatics* of relations on the ground. The systemic dimension focuses on the changing structure of intersecting relationships that may only be partly visible to actors, but which nevertheless constrains opportunities and choices. In other words, to understand what actors can see, say, and do, we have to understand where and with whom they are positioned in the larger system of overlapping relations.

In a more dynamic sense, we also need to understand the systemic effects of a large number of people moving through the system. Activists' structural positions shape the kinds of careers that they develop, influencing which involvements they take on and which they drop or avoid. The choices made by successive cohorts of activists, in turn, influence the future structure of intersections in the multisectoral field. In the chapters that follow, I use a variety of formal mapping techniques to show the systemic effects of cohort trajectories on the political field.

However, to understand how actors respond to systemic constraints, we need a more pragmatic perspective on the challenges posed by overlapping relationships. Such challenges are implied by Simmel when he says that the intersecting affiliations of the modern world diminish an individual's dependence on any particular group (or set of groups), thus allowing greater capacity for judgment, choice, and movement.[19] The individual who is positioned at the intersection of multiple groups must find some way to respond to the conflicts and tensions they create, as well as to the opportunities that they provide for interpretation and synthesis. At the same time, groups face challenges due to the fact that they have multiple members, all with their own array of affiliations.

Here I complement Simmel's structuralist insights with those of the pragmatist and phenomenological thinkers Mead, Schutz, and Dewey.[20] Like Simmel, George Herbert Mead was concerned with the intersection of multiple forms and levels of social organization. He noted that people are active in multiple social systems at once and must therefore respond to tensions and opportunities generated by collision or overlay of social worlds. The problems posed by such intersections, he argued, give rise to the "deliberative attitude," that is, the capacity to "get hold of the conditions of future conduct as these are found in the organized responses we have formed, and so construct our pasts in anticipation of that future."[21] Alfred Schutz also addresses the pragmatic relation between past and future in his idea of the "project," discussing how individuals scan their typified knowledge from past experiences while confronting an uncertain, multipronged array of future possibilities.[22]

Such projections inform the elaboration of ideas as well as deliberation over actions; individuals and collectivities project themselves backward and forward in time, in the effort to understand the present and formulate actions for the future. This process is both diagnostic and prognostic, concerned with inferences gleaned from the social world at hand, as well as from available narratives of historically similar situations. It is carried out from a particular position in a field, but nonetheless attempts to test—through imaginative preconstruction, if not through direct experimentation—the degree of maneuverability, innovation, or challenge that is possible in relation to that field. John Dewey captures this projective and experimental component when he says that "experience in its vital form is experimental, an effort to change the given; it is characterized by projection, by reaching forward into the unknown; connection with the future is its salient trait." Human intelligence is based on the capacity to "read future results in present on-goings."[23] This projective capacity permits the kind of "responsive choice" and inventive manipulation of the physical and social worlds that Dewey thinks is essential to democratic participation.

Systemics influences pragmatics in at least two ways. The first form of influence is synchronic: it involves the interplay of affiliations at a particular point in time. The structure of institutional overlap (i.e., the "affiliation profile") of a given milieu has repercussions for communicative practices. Culturally, such intersections inform the narratives and repertoires that circulate within and between groups, providing resources for the elaboration of projects and strategies. Overlapping memberships also provide opportunities for mediation, collaboration, and coalition building between groups. These intersections constitute the relational challenges to which individuals and groups respond, thus shaping styles and skills of communication.

The second form of influence is diachronic: it involves the movement of cohorts through the field over time. Some aspects of activist careers become routinized and predictable; for example, teenagers who begin activism in a church or high school often move into higher level university leadership. However, there is also a high degree of contingency and uncertainty in the system, due in part to the pragmatics described above. In forming their careers, actors respond to problems and possibilities encountered at particular points in time. These problems are generated by changing political conditions as well as by the intersecting trajectories themselves. Responses to these challenges are systemically influenced by the configuration of the field in previous periods—precisely because youth who were active in previous periods are still moving through the system.

In each period, activists bring styles of communication learned in their prior involvements, as well as skills in mediating the tensions posed by their multiple involvements at previous points in time. These skills are mobilized—and at times challenged or undermined—in interactions with successive cohorts of newcomers who are initiated into activism amidst different configurations of the field. This multitiered dynamic reflects what Jeff Haydu calls "reiterated problem solving," implying both the strongly structuring effects of prior institutional pathways as well as situational response to emergent problems.[24]

SKILLED PERFORMANCES IN PUBLIC ENCOUNTERS

At the point of convergence between trajectories and fields is what happens on a different temporal scale—that of the social encounters in which activists come together in varying combinations. In the ethnographic component of this book, I examine the *performative* dimension of actors' attempts to construct different kinds of publics at the intersection of their multiple involvements. As I described in chapter 1, I understand publics as interstitial spaces in which heterogeneous actors provisionally suspend dimensions of their multiple identities, thereby synchronizing relations and making possible productive communication. Activists use the styles and skills of communication that they have acquired through their trajectories as they attempt to build publics in a wide range of formal and informal settings—including rallies, congresses, assemblies, forums, seminars, bar sessions, and parties.

Publics always involve the selective performance of identities, which I define here as clusters of relations linked by their associated histories and projects. These include relations based on organizational affiliations (e.g., membership in political parties or religious organizations), institutional positions (student, agronomist, citizen), and broad cultural associations (e.g., race, gender, or nationality). Such performances involve representations of alignments and boundaries (distinguishing who you are from who you are not) as well as orientations toward possible future actions. Identities are multiple and shifting, as individuals move between social settings and as those settings themselves are transformed over time.[25]

The multiple identities of activists pose a number of challenges in social movement encounters. Which of their identities and projects can be expressed, and which have to be backgrounded or suppressed? What can and cannot be said in different kinds of movement settings, or in response to particular types of audiences? In such encounters, actors construct what Erving Goffman calls conversational frames or "footings," entailing implicit or explicit norms as to what kind of talk is appropriate, and what identities can or cannot be expressed. These footings are fluid, shifting, and manipulable through "keying" practices, in which actors signal— semantically, gesturally, grammatically—which frame or definition of the situation is being invoked in a given instance.[26] As Paul McLean notes, such keying processes have a network dimension, in that what are often being "keyed" are specific relations between actors—for instance, friendship ties, shared memberships, relations of deference, familiarity, or respect.[27] These performances have an instrumental as well as a ritual component; ties must be strategically represented at the same time as they affirm solidarities.

The performative enactment of selective sets of relations is an important leadership skill. Sometimes activists merge or conflate identities, while at other times these are carefully segmented or compartmentalized. When student activists build coalitions with civic groups, they may need to suppress partisan identities, whereas within internal student forums, student and partisan projects can be openly fused. Likewise, religious identity might be collectively foregrounded or backgrounded depending on the relational contingencies of the public under construction. Often, activists switch readily between identities or play on the ambiguity of who they are "speaking as" at any given point in time.[28] In doing so, they are selectively activating and deactivating networks of relations, and so contributing to the definition of the situation—that is, to the communicative footing—that is perceived as relevant to the interaction at hand.

Such performances play a crucial role in shaping publics, which require the strategic suppression of extraneous or disruptive sets of relations and discourses, as well as the ritual enactment of (provisional) solidarity between participants. Actors located at the intersection of multiple groups have unique opportunities for building such publics, which often require them to mediate between diverse identities and interests. This brokerage-style activity depends on what I have described above as "social skill," which Fligstein defines as the ability to induce cooperation among others through a kind of Meadian empathy with the perspectives of these others.[29] Such entrepreneurial actors—skilled in negotiating ambiguity, communicating definitions of the situation, and finding pragmatic solutions that mediate across groups—are essential both to the reproduction and the transformation of social fields. They serve as Meadian problem solvers in collective contexts, as well as articulators of Schutzian projects, thereby shaping the relations and actions of collectivities as well as their own careers as leaders.

MEDIATION AND LEADERSHIP ORIENTATION

The premise of this chapter has been that skilled communication is an important dimension of political interaction, particularly in complex and heterogeneous civic arenas. The chapters ahead will examine where such skills come from and how they are used in particular kinds of social encounters. However, before beginning this analysis, it is useful to consider what kinds of variation in leadership skills we might expect to find.

Political leaders need to mediate the complex relational intersections out of which political life is composed. However, skills in mediation can work in two contrasting directions. They can be directed toward overcoming differences, inducing mutual understanding, and building new forms of collaboration. Or they can aim at cementing competitive positions, increasing bargaining payoffs, and winning allies for power struggles or ideological disputes. Most mediation contains elements of both, depending in part on the angle of vision. Skilled mediation does not necessarily entail a normatively consensual approach, such as that of the Forum of Course Executives described in the opening of this chapter. Mediation is just as necessary to get things done within the highly contentious meetings of UNE, which is driven by a competitive partisan logic.

Note that in the way I am using the term, mediation goes beyond what is commonly referred to as "brokerage" in the scholarly literature. The importance of brokers—that is, "interstitial" actors capable of negotiating between otherwise disconnected groups—has long been noted by anthropologists, economists, and network analysts.[30] Such entrepreneurial figures often control access to information, resources, and clientage that is essential to the consolidation of political and economic power. In return, brokers often gain some sort of personal advantage, which may come in the nonmaterial form of leadership, social status, or other forms of recognition. A recent overhaul of social movement theory by Doug McAdam, Sidney Tarrow, and Charles Tilly points to brokerage as a key "causal mechanism" that contributes to the explanation of widely differing episodes of political contention. They define brokerage as "the linking of two or more previously unconnected social sites by a unit that mediates their relations with one another and/or with yet other sites."[31]

While my use of the term *mediation* obviously overlaps with these conceptions, there are several senses in which my work both specifies and moves beyond the conventional understanding. Most discussions of brokerage—including the McAdam (et al.) definition above—define brokerage as a link between otherwise disconnected actors or groups. Actors in a network who have no ties between them need a third party to serve as a bridge, constituting the classic "open triangle" formation of the brokerage relation. Other analysts have extended this basic formation not only to situations of disconnect between individuals, but also to "structural holes" between clusters of people or members of disconnected social groups.[32]

However, I argue that we need to extend our understanding of mediation to encompass not only situations of complete disconnect, but also varying degrees of structural overlap. In a Simmelian world, with multiple identities and relations in play, the existence of completely disconnected clusters is only a limiting case in relation to more commonly occurring partial forms of intersection and disjunction. In fact, Simmel argues that it is the partial nature of overlapping affiliations that provides maneuverability and choice in the modern world. This is especially relevant in densely knit social movement communities such as in Brazil, in which overlapping affiliations in partisan, labor, religious, community, professional, or other kinds of organizations create internal cleavages as well as bridging opportunities.

With this kind of variation in mind, I offer an alternative definition: mediation consists of communicative practices at the intersection of two or more (partially) disconnected groups, involving the (provisional) conciliation of the identities, projects, or practices associated with those different groups. There is a decidedly cultural and performative component to such mediation; it involves negotiating between multiple possible public representations of who one is acting "as," as well as what one is acting "for." The goal, again, is relation building: attracting new recruits, constructing alliances, coordinating joint activities, elaborating common proposals or plans of actions. This involves the skilled work of activating and deactivating sets of relations, while developing at least some provisional form of conciliation, coordination, or alignment (if not absolute consensus or agreement) between differing or even contending projects. Sometimes such mediation works through clarification, and sometimes through ambiguity; it may require either the conflation or compartmentalization of identities. This provisional conciliation may not always be perceived as completely satisfying by all of the parties, and some may benefit more than others. However it lets action move forward, often on multiple fronts simultaneously.[33]

Skills in mediation help to distinguish successful movement leaders from less successful ones, both in terms of their own careers and in terms of the various organizations to which they belong. However, as I have argued above, these skills are not uniform, but incorporate varying orientations toward competition or collaboration, as well as toward institutional innovation or reproduction.

To some extent, this stylistic variation comes from the particular institutional sectors in which individuals start activism and through which they make their careers. However, other aspects of style come from actors' positions between sectors, rather than just their experiences within them. Cross-sectoral participation often has an oxygenating effect on social movement activity. It allows for the circulation of projects and organizational forms, permitting activists in bridging positions to draw on a wider range of discursive and organizational repertoires in elaborating proposed solutions to the problems they face. Therefore, we would expect leaders with a higher degree of institutional cosmopolitanism to contribute to the potentiality for innovation within an organization or sector.[34]

If the spread of involvements across sectors contributes to institutional creativity, the concentration of multiple involvements within sectors influences tendencies toward competition. Activists who stack up many organizational involvements within a given sector tend to be more concerned with marking institutional boundaries and engaging in juris-dictional struggles than those with lower investment within a sector. Moreover, they also tend to be more energetic in the promotion and de-fense of institutional influence and control in the larger political field. For example, those who are heavily invested in church-based activity will have more of a stake in promoting religious projects and activities, even outside of the church milieu (for example, they may engage in discussions of how to bring Christian values to the political party or the student movement). Likewise, those deeply involved in student or partisan organizations will argue more vociferously for the relative importance of those forms of organizing (for example, they may be more reluctant to suppress partisan identities in ostensibly nonpartisan settings). In contrast, those with low levels of sectoral involvement will have less of a stake in institutional promotion or defense, and thus may be more willing to engage in cross-sectoral collaboration.

We can combine these two dimensions to locate four different activist positions and corresponding leadership orientations. These are summa-rized in figure 2.1 (below). The two axes differentiate activists according to (1) their level of organizational involvements, defined by the number of distinct collectivities they belong to (y-axis); and (2) the degree to which their organizational involvements span multiple sectors (x-axis). The di-agonal line indicates an increasing level of involvement across positions; that is, it is impossible to span more sectors than the number of groups you are involved in. Those who cluster close to the line have low levels of involvements within sectors, since their sectoral involvement is close to their overall organizational participation.

We would expect those who span many sectors, but who are not deeply involved in any of them, to show a high degree of institutional creativity, plus a general orientation toward cross-sectoral collaboration as opposed to competition. These are cultural and organizational *explorers*, who are willing to experiment with institutional forms and forge new cross-sec-toral relationships. On the other hand, we would expect those with deep involvements within a small number of sectors, but little span across sec-tors, to be more concerned with institutional legitimacy and reproduction than the generation of new forms; moreover, these *entrenched leaders* would be more intent on maintaining organizational (and sectoral) boundaries and prone to jurisdictional competition and dispute. Those whom I call *focused activists*—with low levels of involvement focused within one or two sectors—tend to be neither very creative nor especially competitive, since they have less investment in the promotion or defense of their sector in the broader field. On the other hand, *bridging leaders*—with high levels of participation that span multiple sectors—are a particu-larly interesting (and perhaps unstable) category. They can often be rea-

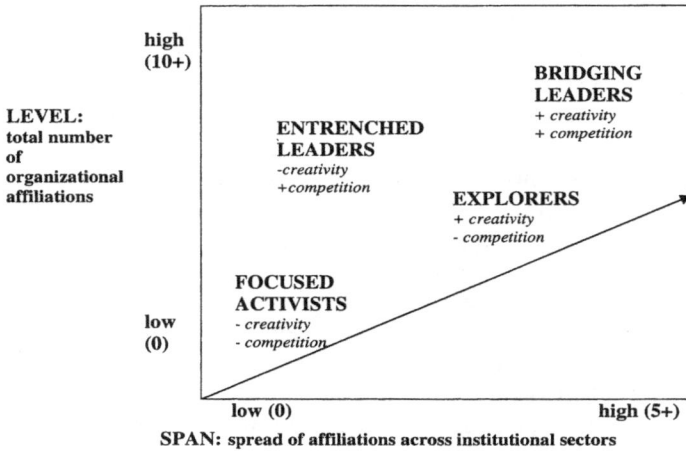

Figure 2.1. Activist positions in a multisectoral field

sonably creative in elaborating ideas and repertoires across sectors, at the same time as they are heavily invested in institutional competition and dispute. They have to defend organizational legitimacy and win space in the field at the same time as they solve problems and build relations across sectoral boundaries.

Figure 2.1 describes a set of ideal types and does not neatly fit all of the possible leadership orientations that I encountered in my research. Nevertheless, the typology is useful in developing comparisons among the leadership skills of differently positioned activists. Here I briefly sketch examples of activists who exemplify each type, keeping in mind that the relative importance of these sets of skills in different regions of the field—as well as the interaction between them—will be explored in the chapters ahead.

Barreto

One example of a *bridging leader* is Barreto, the agronomy student leader described in the opening chapter. His involvements spanned four different institutional sectors: student movement, preprofessional (course-based) student organization, political party, and rural-popular movements. But he had very deep, multilevel involvements in at least two of these sectors. He was deeply involved in the agronomy student movement at local, regional, and national levels, and he also served multiple roles in the Workers' Party (PT) as an internal faction leader and national youth coordinator. He was an institution-building advocate of the emerging course-based student organizations and was quite competitive in wrestling jurisdictional space for this kind of "specialized" activism within the "general" student movement. His competitive spirit also showed as he worked as a committed party- and faction-builder for the PT. At the same time, he demonstrated institutional creativity and skill in cross-sectoral mediation. This could be seen in the new programs he designed linking agronomy students to the rural-workers' movement, as well as in his elaboration of a vision of the course-based movement as a "new" kind of student organizing that could overcome the partisan vices of the old. Barreto's structural position as a bridging leader sheds light on the somewhat odd combination of competitive factionalism and innovative institution building that were the hallmarks of his career.

Ronaldo

A somewhat different example of a bridging leader can be seen in Ronaldo, one of the regional coordinators of a radical branch of the Catholic youth pastoral of São Paulo. Having assumed a variety of leadership roles at local, regional, and national levels since the early 1980s, Ronaldo was deeply invested in Catholic activism. He was also a committed Workers' Party activist who participated in municipal politics and broader electoral campaigns. Over the course of a long career, he flirted with student activism, labor unions, civic and professional movements, and the popular movement on behalf of indigenous rights. He was clearly committed to institution building, as he sought to expand—and eventually, defend—the progressive, liberation-theology-based branch of Catholicism, both within the increasingly conservative church and in the broader society. As a partisan, he was an enthusiastically competitive participant in internal and external disputes. At the same time, he had a strong orientation toward integration and collaboration, a stance encouraged by his Catholic activism. He and companions saw their multiple involvements as strands of a common struggle and self-consciously sought new ways of weaving connections between them.

Antonio

An example of *entrenched leadership* can be seen in the career of Antonio, one of the top youth leaders of the Communist Party of Brazil (PCdoB) within the National Student Union (UNE). Although Antonio's career spanned several sectors—political party, student movement, and socialist youth organization—these sectors were more restricted than those of Barreto. Since one of these involvements, the Union of Socialist Youth, was a semiautonomous offshoot of the PCdoB, this reduced his effective sec-

toral span to only two, with heavy concentration within the student movement and the political party. He had multiple student leadership positions
at university, regional, and national levels (he was the secretary-general
of UNE), and he also played several roles within the PCdoB, serving on
the National Youth Commission as well as the leader of the party caucus
within UNE. While Antonio was a skilled mediator—often serving as his
party's point man in negotiations with the other student factions—these
skills were mostly aimed at cementing PCdoB leadership within UNE as
well as defending the traditional position of UNE as the centralized, unified "voice" of Brazilian students. He was strongly skeptical of the new
approaches to student organizing appearing in the more specialized
course-based organizations, which he saw as a threat to the historical
unification of student politics in Brazil. Strong factional competition
along with jurisdictional defense of existing institutions were features that
informed Antonio's leadership, directing his mediating skills in somewhat
different directions than those of Barreto.

Tomas

A very different approach to student activism could be seen in Tomas, a
leader of the Law Students' Association of the University of São Paulo
(known as the Centro Acadêmico XI de Agosto, or CA XI). Tomas is a
good example of what I call an *explorer*. Structurally, his involvements
spanned a number of different sectors, but he was not heavily invested in
any one of them. His organization, CA XI de Agosto, was the oldest student organization in Brazil, dating back to 1903, which gave its leaders
high status alongside UNE in the general student movement. However,
Tomas was only lightly involved in the general student movement, largely
staying out of disputes at the regional and national level. He expressed
sympathy with both the Brazilian Social Democratic Party (PSDB) and
the PT, but was not officially affiliated with either and avoided internal
factional disputes. He had begun to take part in the emerging course-
based movement of law students at the regional and national level, but
had not taken on any official leadership posts. He also participated in a
"citizenship group" that linked law students with urban and rural popular movements, providing legal aid to slum neighborhoods as well as legal
advocacy for the land reform movement. Because of their perceived neu-
trality, Tomas and his colleagues in CA XI were sometimes called on to
mediate disputes between other factions in the student movement at their
university. Their one point of partisan contention was with their local
rival, a more radical group of law students linked to the Workers' Party,
from whom they had wrested leadership in 1996. In Tomas's exploratory
style we see a much lower level of cross-sectoral competition than either

Antonio or Barreto, while there were also attempts to create new links across sectors.

Marta

Finally, we can see an example of *focused activism* in the career of Marta, a leader in the emerging movement of Junior Enterprises. Junior Enterprises were mini–consulting firms within the universities that were sponsored by faculty and provided services to clients in professional areas. In 1994, Marta joined a Junior Enterprise in the area of communications at the University of São Paulo. The following year, she became a director of the State Federation of Junior Enterprises of São Paulo (FEJESP), which had been founded in 1990. Marta did not belong to a political party and had no involvement in the local student movement; and she participated only marginally in the well-established course-based movement in the area of communications. She focused her energies firmly within the business sector, working to consolidate the movement of Junior Enterprises at the state and national level. Marta did not perceive the Junior Enterprises to be competing with other kinds of student organizations. By and large, she paid little attention to the general student movement, except to critique the high level of partisanship within student organizations. While she certainly saw herself as a movement builder, she used her mediating skills mostly to help coordinate communication among Junior Enterprises and to consolidate the state federation. She did not see that it was her task to suggest new forms or projects for the Junior Enterprises, but rather to cement and diffuse the existing organizational form. Nor did she see a need to create links to other kinds of groups outside of the business sector. In general, Marta's style was characterized by lower degrees of cross-sectoral creativity and competition, in comparison to the other leaders described above.

These four orientations should not be taken as categorically fixed and unchanging, but rather as developing out of the pragmatic challenges that these activists faced as a result of their positions within and between institutional sectors. As we revisit these youth and their organizations in the chapters to come, two points should be kept in view: (1) leadership orientations have a *history*, that is, they are rooted in the trajectories of activists through changing fields of relations; and (2) they are the result of a *synthesis* by activists in response to the challenges and opportunities of their multiple involvements. In chapter 3, I explore these histories through a more systemic analysis of activist trajectories through five periods in Brazil's democratic reconstruction.

CHAPTER THREE

Activist Cohorts and Trajectories, 1977 to 1996

WHEN AND WHERE activists begin their activism makes a difference, both for their subsequent careers and for the dynamics of the field. In the Brazilian activist worlds that I studied, beginning activism often did not mean committing to a single organization or movement. Many activists quickly became sucked into multiple forms of participation, sometimes straddling institutional sectors. Often these intersections expanded as they moved on in their careers. Such cross-sectoral intersections—both in activists' own careers and in the field around them—in turn posed challenges and opportunities to young people active in a given period. In this chapter, I take a bird's eye view of the intertwining of these processes, that is, of how the movement of successive groups of activists through different forms of participation restructured institutional relations over time. I explore the systemic dimension of these changes by mapping the trajectories of five cohorts of activists from 1977 to 1996. I examine how they began activism, their trajectories of institutional involvements, and the interplay of cohorts at different points in time.

Between the democratic "opening" (*abertura*) of the late 1970s and the Cardoso regime of mid-1990s, the structure and experience of Brazilian youth activism changed considerably. These changes, I will show, were at least in part a reflection of the changing structure of institutional intersections. Over the course of the 1980s, religious, student, and popular movement involvement became increasingly coupled with political party activism, interwoven through overlapping memberships and coparticipation in events. While partisan competition generated tension and dispute, it was also an energizing, often creative force that contributed to the building of civic relationships and institutions. However, as Brazil moved into the second decade of democratic reconstruction, the relationship of partisanship to other forms of youth participation became more problematic. The foci of institutional creativity shifted outward, to more specialized cultural, professional, and business organizations that strove for a nonpartisan stance—despite the fact that many participants had partisan sympathies, or even histories of hard-core partisan activism.

How do we explain this shift in partisan dynamics within youth politics over this twenty-year period? Why did partisanship become more disruptive and paralyzing just as Brazil was reaffirming its democratic institutions and settling into a more stable system of electoral succession? Why wouldn't the opposite be true, that actors would forego partisan competition in the early stages of a civic challenge to an authoritarian regime, and then settle into a routinized form of partisan competition as the political field consolidated? It is not at all obvious that the relationship between partisanship and civic reconstruction would work in this way; in fact it runs counter to the usual understanding—drawn mainly from examples of Central and Eastern Europe—of how "autonomous networks of civil society" make way for the reemergence of political society and the restoration of electoral competition.[1]

I propose that we can begin to address this puzzle by focusing not just on external political events, but also on the internal dynamics of the field of youth politics over this twenty-year period. We can shed light on these different experiences of partisanship by tracking the changing shape of the multisectoral field as constituted by the multiple affiliations of activists moving through it. As the political environment was changing, new sets of young people were entering youth politics every few years. Nancy Whittier has described how such "microcohorts" drive movement dynamics, providing fresh energy and ideas while also generating tensions and conflicts over the identity and repertoires of a movement.[2] Here I expand on Whittier's notion by looking at how such microcohorts interact not in a close-knit movement enclave, but in a complex, multisectoral field.

In what follows, I build on the discussion in chapter 2 of what I call the "duality of trajectories and field." I show how activists' trajectories are composed of the intersection of the groups and sectors through which they pass over time. At the same time, I also show how relations between institutional sectors are structured by the multiple affiliations of activists moving though them. I begin with a historical overview, differentiating between five subperiods marked by salient political events as well as by the emergence, consolidation, or decline of particular sets of institutional actors. I give several schematic examples of activist trajectories, including those of Barreto and the other activists introduced in previous chapters. I then switch to the field level, exploring the institutional "entryways" through which successive cohorts of young people began activism. I use an algebraic technique known as Galois lattice analysis to examine the structure of institutional intersections in these five entry periods. I go on to track the changes in each cohort's institutional involvements across the five periods. Finally, I examine what I call "partisan coupling," that is, the degree to which other forms of involvements were combined with political party participation. This allows me to characterize each cohort based on its changing structure of institutional overlap, with a particular focus on the relationship between partisan affiliations and other kinds of activism.

FIVE PERIODS OF DEMOCRATIC RECONSTRUCTION

To understand the interplay between successive cohorts of activists, we need to locate these cohorts within the historical context in which they began activism. To do this, I divided the twenty years of the study (1977–96) into five subperiods, based on significant changes in Brazilian politics. While these periods are of varying lengths, they refer to shifts in what social movement analysts call the "political opportunity structure"—changing relations between powerholders and challengers that affect societal access to the state—as well as in the structure of institutional intersections in Brazil's expanding civic arena.[3]

These five subperiods are mapped in the time line in figure 3.1. We can think of this period in terms of several intersecting waves (or perhaps, "swells") of protest that brought different institutional sectors—as well as sets of leaders—to the fore, while others receded. Following each swell was a period of political jockeying and, importantly, institutional rethinking. In figure 3.1, the events above the time lines represent salient events in the Brazilian political environment, while those below the line represent changes in the field of youth politics.

Here is a brief overview of the highlights of each period (I will revisit these periods in more depth in future chapters):

1. *Abrindo* (opening), 1977–84: This first period of democratic "opening" begin with the return of major street protests in 1977 and ends with the huge (but unsuccessful) campaign for direct elections in 1984. During these years, Brazil saw a softening of the hard-line position of the military government and an increasing restiveness among social movement actors of different kinds. Although President Geisel had announced the beginning of the liberalization process in 1974, public protest did not return to Brazil's streets until 1977, with a sudden surge in student demonstrations, often met with violent police repression. This was followed by the 1979 reconstruction of the semiclandestine National Student Union (UNE), which was finally relegalized in 1984. In addition, there was increasing human rights lobbying by churches, NGOs, and professional associations; a surge of independent trade union mobilization; and the emergence of grassroots popular protests against the high cost of living and scanty social services among the urban poor. While early protests met with varying degrees of state repression, they gained strength as the regime wrestled with internal divisions and continued a slow movement toward civilian rule. Leftist political leaders returned from exile just as opposition parties were relegalized, contributing to the formation in 1980 of the new Workers' Party (PT). The Catholic youth pastoral (PJ) emerged in the liberation-theology-infused Catholic base communities during the late 1970s,

1977 78 79 80 81 82 83 84 85 86 87 88 89 90 91 92 93 94 95 1996

1974: Pres. Geisel announces liberalization process; opposition makes big electoral gains
1977: "April package" restricts opposition, leading to public protests

1978–79: Limited amnesty; return of exiled leaders
1980: POLITICAL PARTY REFORM
1979–85: Deepening economic crisis

1984: Movement for *Diretas Já* (direct elections); huge public demonstrations

1985: Return to (indirect) civilian rule: Pres.-elect Tancredo Neves dies, V.P. Sarney takes office
1986–89: Hyperinflation; failed stabilization plans

1987–88: Constitutional Assembly (with "popular" amendments)

1989: Direct presidential elections; Fernando Collor de Melo defeats Lula
1990–91: Privatizing reforms; economic crisis

1992: Collor corruption scandal; Congressional inquiry and impeachment
1993: V.P. Franco takes office

1994: Fernando Henrique Cardoso defeats Lula
1995–96: Stabilization with recession; privatizing and liberalizing reforms

ABRINDO
("opening"): 77–84
-1977: Widespread student protests; police repression
-1979: UNE reconstituted; re-legalized 1984
-Human rights, labor and popular movement organizing
-Growth of "popular" church; liberation theology (CEBs)
-Catholic youth pastoral grows
-1980: PT formed; opposition parties dispute 1982 elections

RECONSTRUINDO
("reconstructing") 85–88
-1985: High school organizations legalized ("gremios livres")
-1985: Communist parties legalized
-Rebuilding student organizations
-Growth of socialist youth groups
-Partisan clashes in student movement
-Catholic youth pastoral develops specialized branches
-Early course executives (agronomy, communications, medicine)

REPENSANDO
("rethinking") 89–91
-Reevaluation across student, Catholic, and socialist groups
-Ebbing popular movements; growing disillusionment with Collor regime
-Rise of black students, course-based groups, NGOs and business groups

CARA NOVA
("new face") 92–93
-1992: Student/civic mobilizations for Collor's impeachment
-Revitalized student organizations
-1992 Earth Summit
-1993: National Seminar of Black Scholars; formation of National Forum of Course Executives

GLOBALIZANDO
("globalizing") 94–96
-Reorientation to globalizing economy and youth culture
-Partisan student groups on defensive
-Course-based, business groups consolidate national organization
-Catholic, black, and popular movements are struggling

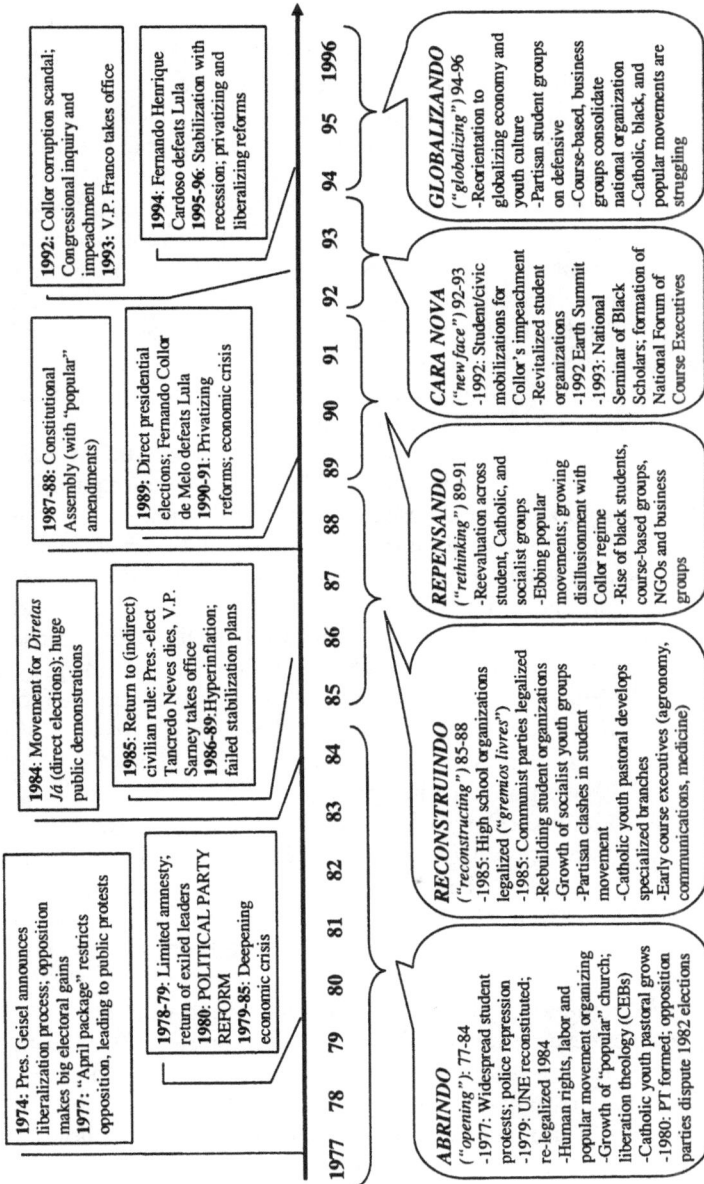

Figure 3.1. Time line of changes in political and youth activist fields

serving as a source of leadership for urban and rural popular movements as well as for opposition parties (particularly the PT). The period culminated with huge mobilizations for direct presidential elections in 1984 (known as *Diretas Já!*), which proved unsuccessful due to backstage elite maneuvering. Despite a return to civilian rule the following year, the country would wait five more years for direct elections.

2. *Reconstruindo* (reconstructing), 1985–88: This period began with the return to civilian rule via indirect elections in 1985 and ended with the approval of a new constitution in 1988. In 1985, President José Sarney took office as part a negotiated pact among elites (after the sudden death of the compromise candidate, Tancredo Neves). During this period, Brazil elected a constitutional assembly and elaborated its new constitution with considerable citizen input, as well as carried out state and municipal elections. In youth politics, the student movement and other youth organizations were busily attempting to "reconstruct" themselves and involve more young people in political participation. The Catholic youth pastoral was developing "specialized" branches in student, rural, and urban popular areas, in an attempt to keep its most active participants from being recruited to the socialist vanguard youth groups that were building a base among high school students. The high school student movement was in ascension, becoming relegalized in 1985 and spearheading an intense campaign for the organization of *grêmios livres* (independent student associations) in public secondary schools. However, exhausted from the factional battles that had recently crystallized into new, party-based alliances, the university student movement was in crisis. The National Student Union (UNE) was polarized in a pitched battle between the dominant PCdoB (the Communist Party of Brazil, legalized in 1985) and their challengers in the PT, which won control of UNE in 1987. A few of the early Course Executives (course-based student associations in specific professional areas of study) were also beginning to reorganize after a period of relative quiescence, particularly in the areas of agronomy, medicine, and communication.

3. *Repensando* (rethinking), 1989–91: The third period was characterized by considerable reevaluation and ferment, as the country moved from its first direct presidential elections in nearly thirty years (in which PT candidate Lula was narrowly defeated by Fernando Collor de Melo) to growing national disillusionment with the policies of President Collor. As the left wrestled with its electoral defeat, the urban popular movements of the 1980s began to ebb and many socialist youth groups entered into post '89 crises of vision and strategy. The Catholic youth pastoral tried to stem the flight of young people from the Catholic Church (often to evangelical churches), while rethinking the role of the more radical "specialized" branches that often challenged the increasingly conservative

church leadership. Meanwhile, the university student movement was regrouping. A switch to proportional representation in UNE's directorship created a new dynamic of collaboration, leading to the organization of several national seminars on the "restructuring of the student movement." At the same time, the Course Executives were beginning to innovate and expand, holding several national meetings with strong participation of PT youth. When PCdoB activists took back the leadership of UNE in 1991 (in alliance with the Social Democratic PSDB), they sought to give the movement a more youthful demeanor, oriented toward culture, sports, and travel. A group of black students began to challenge the lack of attention to racial issues, creating the National Coordination of Black University Scholars (CONUN). And in the business schools, the idea of "Junior Enterprises" (mini–consulting firms within the universities) was imported from France and spurred organization at local and state levels.

4. *Cara Nova* (new face), 1992–93: In 1992, the impeachment movement exploded and the PCdoB leadership of UNE found itself ideally positioned to ride the wave of youth mobilization into national prominence. The "new face" of the movement was represented by the attractive and charismatic young president of UNE, Lindberg Farias, who personified the PCdoB strategy of overcoming the stereotype of the grim, bearded militant. In the year following Collor's impeachment, young people continued to pour into student organizations in high schools and universities, as well as into the youth wings of political parties and NGOs (spurred as well by the 1992 United Nations Conference on Environment and Development [Earth Summit] in Rio de Janeiro). UNE won concessions from the post-Collor government of President Itamar Franco, who granted half-price admission to entertainment with purchase of an UNE identification card, ensuring a flow of resources as well as formal memberships. However, the Course Executives (and the PT) were beginning to articulate themselves in explicit opposition to UNE, creating the Forum of Course Executives and challenging what they saw as the partisan, bureaucratic, and authoritarian leadership of UNE. Other sectors of youth activism were invigorated as well: black students organized a successful national "Seminar of Black University Scholars" in 1993; the radical branch of the Catholic youth pastoral embarked on a reenergized organizing campaign in the urban periphery of São Paulo; and Junior Enterprises began to spread outside of business schools to other universities.

5. *Globalizando* (globalizing), 1994–96: The final period begins with the stabilizing economic reforms introduced by Fernando Henrique Cardoso as finance minister and his subsequent election as president in 1994. The surge of postimpeachment enthusiasm for the traditional student movement began to recede even as activists adapted to an increasingly segmented and globalized political field. UNE found itself once again en-

trenched in partisan battles, facing accusations of corruption and increasing hostility from the media. However the Course Executive movement was exploding across the country, as students from specialized course areas formed national (and sometimes international) organizations. While some still saw themselves in direct opposition to UNE, others began to see themselves as a parallel but autonomous (and nonpartisan) movement. In the meantime, the Junior Enterprises were forming state federations and beginning deliberations toward the formation of a national association. Other internationally oriented business youth groups formed partnerships with NGOs and preached "business citizenship" in a globalizing world. The privatization and liberalization policies of the Cardoso government became a major theme both for these business-oriented groups and for the leftist student groups, which debated how strongly to formulate their opposition to globalization and the "neoliberal plan." Meanwhile, the black student movement struggled, unsuccessfully, to mobilize its second national seminar, while the radical branch of the Catholic youth pastoral sought to sustain the morale of its leaders amidst dwindling local participation.

This highly condensed summary describes transitions between periods in terms of the emergence and struggles of autonomous organizational actors, independently shaping their own position in the field. However, this gives a deceptive picture of the actual dynamics of the field. Many activists had multiple affiliations, creating relationships and interdependencies among organizations and sectors. The passages of young people through the five periods—and the ways that they responded to the challenges of these interdependencies at different points in time—created opportunities and conflicts for the organizations and movements described above. Our challenge, then, is to study activist trajectories across these five periods in such a way as to capture the changing structure of institutional intersections.

MAPPING ACTIVIST CAREERS: SECTORAL INTERSECTIONS

To grasp the meaning of institutional intersections at a personal level, we can look at a few examples of activist trajectories across these five periods. In previous chapters, I introduced Barreto as an example of a *bridging leader*, that is, of a leader who had deep involvements within several different sectors at once, and thus would tend to be stylistically oriented toward both competition and creativity. We can take a more schematic look at Barreto's trajectory by charting sectoral overlap over the course of his career. Barreto's trajectory is described in figure 3.2. (See the key

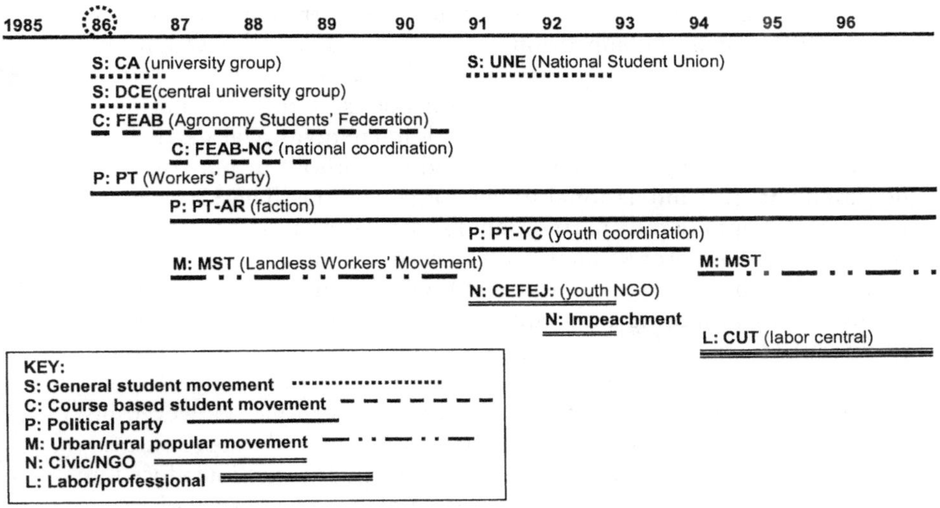

1985	86	87	88	89	90	91	92	93	94	95	96

S: CA (university group)

S: UNE (National Student Union)

S: DCE(central university group)

C: FEAB (Agronomy Students' Federation)

C: FEAB-NC (national coordination)

P: PT (Workers' Party)

P: PT-AR (faction)

P: PT-YC (youth coordination)

M: MST (Landless Workers' Movement)

M: MST

N: CEFEJ: (youth NGO)

N: Impeachment

L: CUT (labor central)

KEY:
S: General student movement
C: Course based student movement
P: Political party
M: Urban/rural popular movement
N: Civic/NGO
L: Labor/professional

Figure 3.2. Barreto's trajectory

for coding of his different sectoral involvements; the year he turned eighteen is circled at the top.)

Barreto began participation at age eighteen during the *Reconstruindo* period (1985–88), and quickly became involved in a multipronged effort in institution building. Within a year of entering the university in 1986, Barreto was engaged not only in general student activism, but also in rebuilding the more specialized preprofessional student movement (through the federation of agronomy students), in expanding a political party (the PT, along with his internal faction), and in assisting popular and labor activism (through the rural worker's movement). He went in and out of these involvements over time, dropping some of his course-based and popular movement involvements as he moved up to higher-level student and party leadership, in UNE and in the PT's youth coordination, respectively. Later in his career, he also took part in an (unsuccessful) attempt to form a youth research NGO as well as in the 1992 impeachment movement. When I talked to him in 1995–96, he was working as a rural advisor to CUT, the labor central associated with the PT, where he was again building links between students and the rural workers' movement.

Despite these wide-ranging involvements, there was no doubt that Barreto was a *partisan* actor. He jumped quickly into partisan and then internal factional politics, as a militant in the young and growing Workers' Party (PT). Note the constancy—and the intensification—of partisan participation over the course of his career. When Barreto began his activism in 1986, partisan competition was in full swing, with elections approaching for the country's constitutional assembly. The energy that Barreto put into building student organizations at the university and national levels was in large measure partisan energy; it was carried out in a climate of intense, at times bitter and tumultuous dispute over the hegemony of local and national student organizations. This spirit of dispute was present not only in traditional student organizations like UNE, but also in the preprofessional course-based organizations such as the agronomy students' association (FEAB), which ironically distinguished themselves by proposing a less confrontational, more dialogic approach to student organizing.

Barreto's trajectory illustrates the cross-sectoral complexity of many activists' trajectories, both simultaneously and over time. However, his was not the only salient set of institutional intersections during those periods. Compare his trajectory to two of his contemporaries introduced in chapter 2: Ronaldo, who began activism four years earlier during the *Abrindo* period (see figure 3.3a), and Antonio, who entered two years later (see figure 3.3b). While both are younger than Barreto, they began their involvements at an earlier age, prior to entry into the university.

Like Barreto, Ronaldo can be described as a *bridging leader*, with deep involvements that spanned many different sectors. He began activism at around age thirteen, participating in his local Catholic base community (CEB), as well as in the leadership of the Catholic youth pastoral in his town in the interior of São Paulo state. In 1986 (not incidentally, a national election year), he suddenly expanded his participation outside of the church, becoming involved in the PT as well as in his high school student movement and the civic movement for popular participation in the Constitution. In 1989, his participation in church-based activism leapt to another level of intensity as he became involved in the construction of one of the specialized (and more militant) branches of the youth pastoral, aimed at youth from poorer urban "popular" neighborhoods (PJMP: the Youth Pastoral of the Popular Milieu). He took part in regional and then national leadership of PJMP over the next few years, remaining in this leadership through the mid-1990s. When I met Ronaldo in 1995, he was regional coordinator of PJMP in the São Paulo region. He also intensified his partisan participation over this period, becoming involved in municipal leadership of the PT in his town. In addition to these intense religious and partisan involvements, he also showed his bridging tendencies by participating sporadically in the student movement, both at the general and specialized level; in the labor movement (when he worked as a leader of the bankworkers' union in his town); in the impeachment movement; and in the movement to

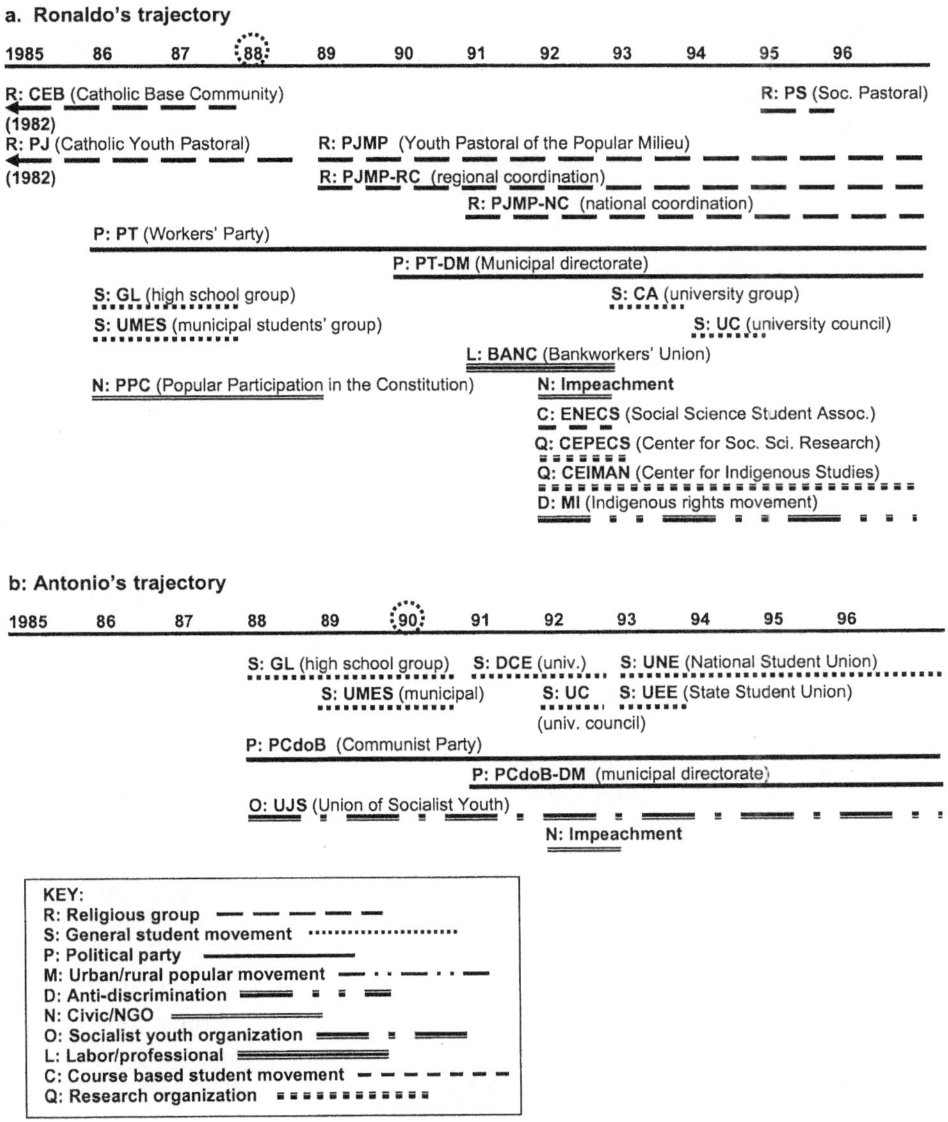

a. Ronaldo's trajectory

| 1985 | 86 | 87 | 88 | 89 | 90 | 91 | 92 | 93 | 94 | 95 | 96 |

R: CEB (Catholic Base Community)
(1982)
R: PJ (Catholic Youth Pastoral)
(1982)

R: PJMP (Youth Pastoral of the Popular Milieu)

R: PJMP-RC (regional coordination)

R: PJMP-NC (national coordination)

R: PS (Soc. Pastoral)

P: PT (Workers' Party)

P: PT-DM (Municipal directorate)

S: GL (high school group)

S: UMES (municipal students' group)

S: CA (university group)

S: UC (university council)

L: BANC (Bankworkers' Union)

N: PPC (Popular Participation in the Constitution)

N: Impeachment

C: ENECS (Social Science Student Assoc.)

Q: CEPECS (Center for Soc. Sci. Research)

Q: CEIMAN (Center for Indigenous Studies)

D: MI (Indigenous rights movement)

b: Antonio's trajectory

| 1985 | 86 | 87 | 88 | 89 | 90 | 91 | 92 | 93 | 94 | 95 | 96 |

S: GL (high school group)

S: DCE (univ.)

S: UNE (National Student Union)

S: UMES (municipal)

S: UC
(univ. council)

S: UEE (State Student Union)

P: PCdoB (Communist Party)

P: PCdoB-DM (municipal directorate)

O: UJS (Union of Socialist Youth)

N: Impeachment

KEY:
R: Religious group ─ ─ ─ ─ ─
S: General student movement ·······················
P: Political party ──────────
M: Urban/rural popular movement ─ · · ─ · · ─
D: Anti-discrimination ▓▓▓ ▪ ▪ ▓▓
N: Civic/NGO ═════════
O: Socialist youth organization ▓▓▓ ▪ ▓▓▓
L: Labor/professional ▓▓▓▓▓▓▓▓
C: Course based student movement ─ ─ ─ ─ ─ ─
Q: Research organization ▪▪▪▪▪▪▪▪▪▪▪▪

Figure 3.3. Early cohort trajectories

defend the rights of indigenous communities, with which he became involved in his research capacity as an anthropology student.

Antonio's career took on a much more streamlined pattern than that of Ronaldo. Antonio represents what I describe in chapter 2 as an *entrenched leader*, concentrating his activism within the political party and student movement. As figure 3.3b shows, he began activism in 1988 (a year of municipal elections), while in high school in the state of Bahia, at around age sixteen. In that year, he participated in the formation of a *grêmio livre* (independent high school student association). He also became involved in one of Brazil's two communist parties, the Communist Party of Brazil (PCdoB), as well as in the Union of Socialist Youth (UJS), the semiautonomous socialist youth organization linked to the PCdoB. While we can't be sure whether he initiated his activism in the *grêmio*, in the party, or in the socialist organization (he says he began "by way of friends"), it is clear that these three forums of participation were tightly linked, remaining steady across his career. He quickly moved his student activism beyond his local high school, becoming involved in the municipal high school student association. On entering the university (and moving to the state of Minas Gerais) in 1991, he became involved in the DCE (Central Student Directorate), as well as the university council; in 1993 he took a jump upward by entering his party's slate both for the State Student Union (of Minas Gerais) as well as the National Student Union (UNE). He served as vice president of UNE for Minas Gerais from 1993 to 1995, and then director of communication from 1995 to 1997, playing an important role as a key negotiator of his party with student leaders of other factions. Unlike Ronaldo, he did not branch out into other kinds of activism over his career but focused on the student-party-socialist intersection. On the other hand, he did participate in the 1992 impeachment movement, in which PCdoB youth leaders played a highly visible role (as I will discuss in chapter 5).

While quite distinct in both form and content, the trajectories of Barreto, Ronaldo, and Antonio share certain characteristics. All three were enthusiastic party-builders, not only affiliating with political parties early in their careers, but also becoming involved in higher-level internal leadership. While Ronaldo and Antonio showed deep and steady involvement in other sectors as well (the Catholic youth pastoral and the student movement, respectively), their partisan identities remained constant. Antonio was more sectorally concentrated than the other two, with less bridging to nonstudent forms of activism, reflecting a stylistic difference between many PT and PCdoB activists (which I will explore in chapters ahead). However all three were marked by the strong partisan ethos among activ-

a: Tomas's trajectory

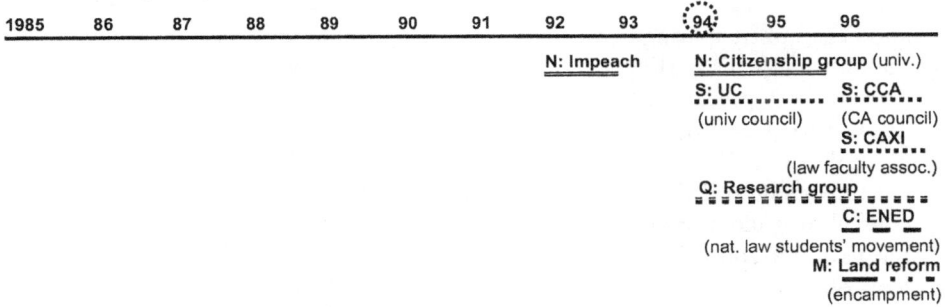

1985	86	87	88	89	90	91	92	93	94	95	96

N: Impeach   N: **Citizenship group** (univ.)

S: **UC** ....   S: **CCA** ...
(univ council)   (CA council)

S: **CAXI**
(law faculty assoc.)

Q: **Research group** ======

C: **ENED**
(nat. law students' movement)

M: **Land reform**
(encampment)

b: Marta's trajectory

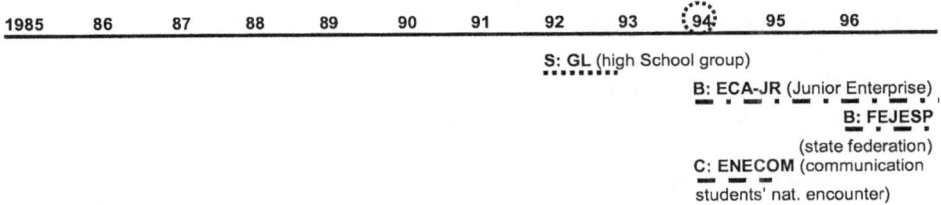

1985	86	87	88	89	90	91	92	93	94	95	96

S: **GL** (high School group)

B: **ECA-JR** (Junior Enterprise)

B: **FEJESP**
(state federation)

C: **ENECOM** (communication
students' nat. encounter)

> **KEY:**
> S: **General student movement**   ·····················
> C: **Course based student movement**   ⎯ ⎯ ⎯ ⎯ ⎯ ⎯
> M: **Urban/rural popular movement**   ⎯ · · ⎯ · · ⎯
> N: **Civic/NGO**   ══════════
> Q: **Research organization**   ============
> B: **Business organization**   ⎯ · ⎯ · ⎯ · ·

Figure 3.4. Later cohort trajectories

ists entering during the 1980s, a pattern they carried with them as they became prominent leaders in the 1990s.

Contrast these trajectories to those of two younger activists who began participation in the early 1990s. Figure 3.4a (below) charts the trajectory of Tomas, whom I describe in chapter 2 as an example of an *explorer.* His involvements spanned a large number of sectors, but he was not (as of 1996) deeply entrenched in any of them. His first experience of participation was as a high school student in the 1992 impeachment movement. This locates him squarely in the *Cara Nova* cohort, entering just as the student movement was going through its dramatic civic renovation. Two years later, when he entered the Law Faculty of the University of São Paulo, he joined a self-titled "Citizenship Group" run by students to provide legal assistance to poor families in the slum areas of São Paulo. He was also elected as a student representative to the Law Faculty council and began participating in a student research group. In his second year in the university, his participation expanded as his slate won control of the law faculty's prestigious student association, the Centro Acadêmico XI de Agosto (CA XI), Brazil's oldest student organization. As secretary-general of CA XI, he was charged with linking the group with the rest of the university and the wider student movement. He participated in the council of student organizations of the University of São Paulo as well as the national council of the law students' movement. Finally, he and a few colleagues were also attempting to get involved with the land reform movement, through legal assistance to land occupations (although perhaps not to the movement's more radical branch). Notably, Tomas was not affiliated with a political party, although he said that he sympathized both with the PT and with the more centrist Party of Brazilian Social Democracy (PSDB).

Finally, figure 3.4b shows a different pattern in the trajectory of Marta, an activist in the movement of Junior Enterprises, whom I have described as an example of a *focused activist*. Marta also began activism as a high school student during the *Cara Nova* period, although unlike Tomas and the others, she did not take part in the 1992 impeachment mobilizations. Two years later, when she entered the Communications Faculty of the University of São Paulo (ECA), she began to participate in a Junior Enterprise, consulting with clients in the area of communication. She also attended the meetings of the National Executive of Communication Students (ENECOS), although she did not play a leadership role and discontinued participation in subsequent years. Instead, she continued to invest in her business-oriented activism. In 1996 she was elected as a director of the State Federation of Junior Enterprises (FEJESP), charged with financial-juridical affairs. Like Tomas, she was not affiliated with a political party, but unlike him, she did not report even sympathizing with any. Her activism was strongly focused within the business sector, avoiding the cross-sectoral bridging of her cohort-mate, Tomas.

Despite these differences, Tomas and Marta were in many ways closer to each other than to the three youth entering during the 1980s. They represent the "civic" and "business" wings, respectively, of the postim-peachment cohorts. They were ambivalent or hostile toward political parties, and found ways to channel their social and political interests in ways that contributed to their personal careers. (This differs markedly from Ronaldo and Antonio, who became social science majors as a means of enhancing their political activism.) While Tomas expressed a stronger sense of political commitment than Marta, both were clearly professionals in the making. They believed that *as professionals*, rather than *as partisans*, young people should play an active role in the social and political life of the country.

General Cohort Comparisons

The trajectories of these five individuals are useful in giving us a sense of the institutional intersections in play across the five periods, as well as pointing toward differences in the experiences of the earlier and later cohorts. But how general are these patterns? To what extent can we generalize from the experiences of these activists to understand the structure of intersections in the larger field? How similar or different were they to others entering at the same time? To explore these questions, we need to examine the patterning of activist trajectories at the aggregate level.

The analysis in this chapter draws on 332 questionnaires that I collected in 1995–96 documenting activists' histories of participation across institutional sectors. There are some limitations to these data: my sample was far from systematic, and the open-ended format sometimes left the responses less clear than I would have liked. Moreover, I do not have information on activists who dropped out of activism in earlier periods, or who moved on to other "nonyouth" forms of participation. While these data thus do not give a completely accurate picture of the political field in the earlier periods, they provide a strong "echo" of those periods, particularly as this echo was carried into mid-1990s politics by long-term activists. By interpreting these data in the light of historical information from those periods, we can gain insight into how early experiences influenced the memories and practices of activists that I observed in my fieldwork.

The largest set of questionnaires (117) was collected at what activists refer to as "general" student movement events, that is, those not divided by specific professional area, but rather tied into the centralized organizational structure of UNE and its affiliates. These included national councils of UNE as well as more local meetings, councils, and seminars. I also collected questionnaires at meetings of the Catholic youth pastoral, professional (course-based) student organizations, partisan youth wings, the National Coordination of Black University Scholars (CONUN), and business student groups, including the State Federation of Junior Enterprises (FEJESP) and a global-minded business student organization (AIESEC— International Association of Students in Economic and Accounting Sciences). A more complete breakdown of where I collected these questionnaires can be found in the Methodological Appendix.

I sorted the reported involvements into 11 institutional sectors, as defined in chapter 2. (A complete list of sector codes along with the details of how I collapsed specific involvements into sectoral categories can be found in the appendix). I divided the respondents into five cohorts based on the period in which they began their activism. Some basic descriptive comparisons between these cohorts are given in the appendix.[4] The mean ages at which each cohort filled out the questionnaires drops quite predictably, since those who started at earlier points in time are likely (though not certain) to be older than those getting involved later. Also predictably, the average age at which respondents started activism rises steadily from 13.35 for Cohort 1 to 19.95 in Cohort 5.[5]

Figure 3.5 (below) shows the mean level of group and sectoral involvements for both the first year of activism and the last year, when the questionnaires were collected. Group involvement refers to the number of distinct activist collectivities (i.e., organizations or movements) the person participated in during a given year, while sectoral involvement refers to the number of institutional sectors that those collectivities span. For the first year, the differences are minimal; youth from all cohorts tended to begin participation with only one to two involvements, with a tendency toward participation in only one (or at most two) sectors during the first year (see figure 3.5a).

By the time I collected the questionnaires, however, many of the activists had diversified their participation considerably. The mean level of group participation during the last year of involvement (i.e., at the time I collected the questionnaires) was 4–5 groups for the first two cohorts, dropping down in each of the next three cohorts to only 3 groups for Cohort 5 (figure 3.5b). Average sectoral involvement was likewise highest for the first two cohorts (around 3), dropping down to about 2.5 for Cohorts 3 and 4, and bottoming at under 2 for the final cohort. Interestingly, many activists had dropped some of their involvements by the time I reached them; for the first four cohorts, the average number of last-year involvements were all lower than the average maximum levels of involvement, that is, the year in which each youth had his or her highest number of distinct forms of participation (figure 3.5c). This indicates that many of the youth reached a point in their careers in which they began to cut back on their level and diversity of activity.

These data suggest that on average, the later cohorts had fewer involvements than the earlier ones, and spanned fewer sectors. This pattern holds when we look not just at simultaneous involvements, but at accumulated sectoral involvements over time (figure 3.5d). For Cohorts 1 and 2, activists participated in an average of 5 sectors during their careers; for Cohorts 3 and 4, sectoral involvement averages between 3 and 4, while for the final cohort, it drops to an average of 2.

Of course, differences in levels of involvement may just be a function of time; that is, the earlier cohorts may have more group and sectoral

a. First year involvement levels (cohort means)

1977-1984	1985-1988	1989-1991	1992-1993	1994-1996
Cohort 1	Cohort 2	Cohort 3	Cohort 4	Cohort 5

b. Last year involvement level (cohort means)

1977-1984	1985-1988	1989-1991	1992-1993	1994-1996
Cohort 1	Cohort 2	Cohort 3	Cohort 4	Cohort 5

c. Maximum involvement levels (cohort means)

1977-1984	1985-1988	1989-1991	1992-1993	1994-1996
Cohort 1	Cohort 2	Cohort 3	Cohort 4	Cohort 5

d. Total number of sectors (across career)

1977-1984	1985-1988	1989-1991	1992-1993	1994-1996
Cohort 1	Cohort 2	Cohort 3	Cohort 4	Cohort 5

■ Groups
▨ Sectors

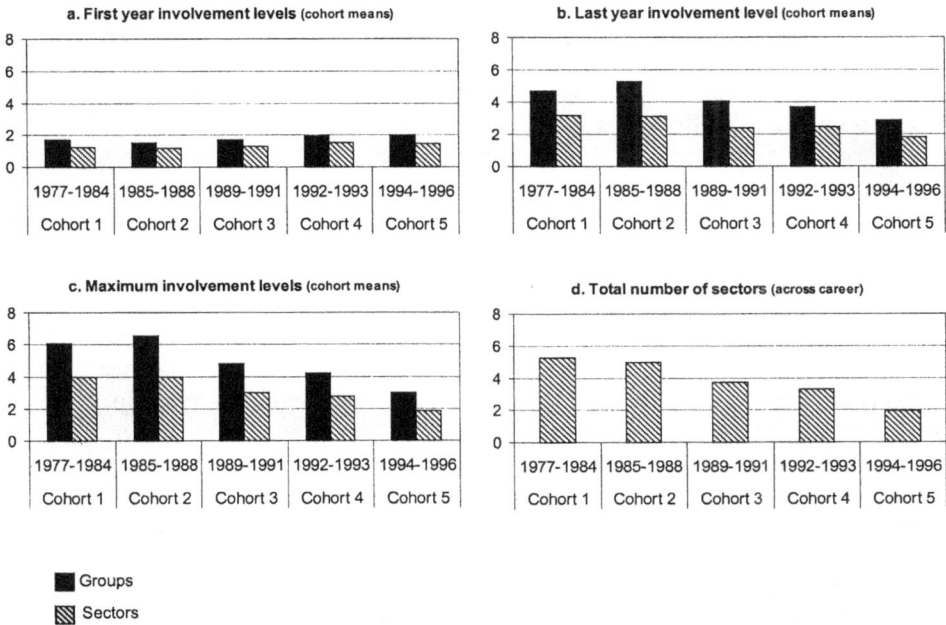

Figure 3.5. Cohort involvement levels (organizations and sectors)

involvements simply because they have had more time to accumulate them. In other words, this many not be a structural difference in tendency between the groups, but rather a temporal difference. Cohorts 3, 4, and 5 might catch up to their predecessors in Cohorts 1 and 2 somewhere down the line. In fact, if we look at the rates of expansion in involvement, rather than the involvement levels themselves, the later cohorts actually expand their sectoral involvement at a faster rate than the earlier ones (although the fastest expansion of *group* involvement comes in Cohorts 2 and 4, both of which entered during periods of intensified youth mobilization).[6]

Whether or not these patterns represent structural differences between cohorts, they have repercussions for the dynamics of the field that I studied in the mid-1990s. During the fifth, *Globalizando* period—in which all of the youth in the study were active—there was a differentiation in levels of group and sectoral involvements between the early and later cohorts. On average, those in the earlier cohorts not only belonged to more groups, but they also spanned more sectors, both simultaneously and over time. This in turn means that they had a heightened experience of intersections between sectors, as a source both of bridging opportunities and of tensions between institutional projects and styles. In contrast, many younger activists had less intense patterns of activism, tending to be involved in fewer organizations and sectors (thus cutting back on the numbers of both entrenched and bridging leaders). This disjunction between the cohorts' experiences of institutional intersections may have contributed to the tension in the field of youth politics at the time I collected the questionnaires.

INSTITUTIONAL GATEWAYS TO PARTICIPATION

While these comparisons show varied levels of participation among the cohorts, we still need to examine how particular institutional intersections left a mark on activists' careers. Young people beginning participation in each of the five periods encountered different political and institutional environments, which changed every few years as Brazil underwent its prolonged process of democratic reconstruction. As Whittier suggests in her study of radical feminist microcohorts, the period in which activists begin participation leaves a mark on the identities and repertoires—that is, on what I call "styles" of participation—that they take with them as the field and their own involvements change.[7]

Figure 3.6 compares the institutional contexts in which youth in the five cohorts began activism. The figure shows the percentage of each cohort that participated in the most active sectors (among respondents) during their initial year of involvement.[8] (Note that since these involvements are overlapping, they don't add up to 100 percent.) While some activists participated in several different organizations during their entry year, more than 65 percent of activists in all five cohorts began in only one sector, and less than 15 percent in any of the cohorts began in three or more.

Note first of all the strong difference in religious involvement. Almost 80 percent of activists in Cohort 1 began their participation in a religious context, most within the Catholic Church. This ranged from assistance in the sacramental life of the church to religious education classes to leadership in the more politicized branches of the youth pastoral. (Simple Catholic affiliation did not count as "involvement" in this analysis—they had to be active participants in the life of the church in some way.) This dropped to 40 percent in Cohorts 2 and 3, and then collapsed to about 10 percent in the last two cohorts. Activists like Ronaldo who began activism in the early years of Brazil's democratic opening—when the Catholic Church was one of the few sources of contestation of the regime—had a much stronger probability of initial influence from a religious context. Note also that almost 20 percent of Cohort 1 began with involvement in urban or rural popular movements, which were strongly supported by the

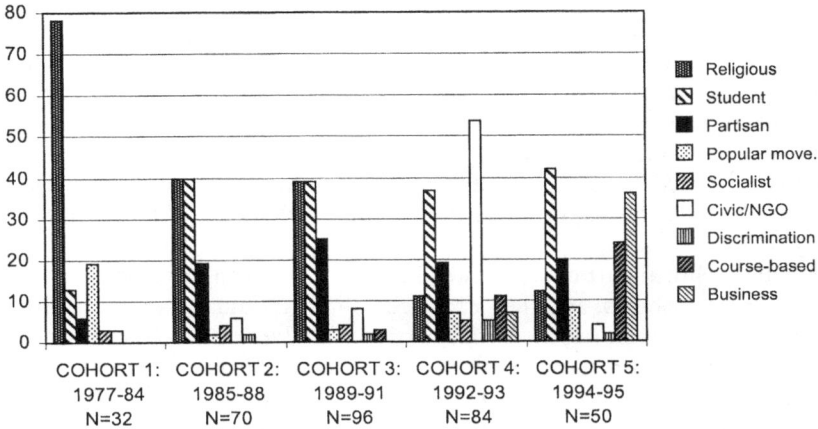

Figure 3.6. Percent of cohorts starting activism in institutional contexts (entry years only)

Catholic Church during this period. This dropped steeply in succeeding cohorts, as the popular movements headed into a period of decline and crisis, although it made a slight recovery as an entryway among a small proportion of those in Cohorts 4 and 5.

The general student movement began to serve as a prominent gateway to activism for Cohort 2, remaining at about 40 percent involvement for all of the remaining cohorts. Included in the category of "general" student movement are high school student groups; university-department-based student groups; universitywide student organizations; governing councils in schools, departments, and universities; and municipal, state, and national student organizations (such as UNE) at both the secondary and university levels. Recall that both Cohort 2 activists described above began activism in general student organizations, Barreto at the university and Antonio at the high-school levels. However, only in the last two cohorts did entrance into activism through the more professional course-based student organizations (such as Barreto's Federation of Agronomy Students) begin to grow; Barreto was an early riser in this respect. Business student participation was also negligible as a starting point until Cohort 4, when Marta entered the scene, and then jumped up to more than 35 percent in Cohort 5. Clearly there was a shift toward more specialized, professionally oriented areas of student participation as a starting point to activism among those entering in the 1990s.

Participation in civic movements and NGOs was a relatively rare starting point for all of the cohorts except for Cohort 4, which entered during the period of the dramatic impeachment mobilizations (participation in the impeachment movement was coded as Civic/NGO). The sudden leap in Civic/NGO entryways to more than 50 percent suggests that, like Tomas, many of the youth entering in 1992–93 had their first experiences of activism in the impeachment mobilizations. Involvement in antidiscrimination movements also increased slightly among those entering in this period. Since the vehicle for antidiscrimination activity often took the form of NGOs, this also reflects the bustling civic/NGO context of the early 1990s.

Finally, political parties as an introduction to activism increased across the first three cohorts, and then dropped somewhat during and after the impeachment mobilizations. Initial partisan involvement rose from only 5 percent in Cohort 1 to a high of 25 percent in Cohort 3, and then dropped down slightly below 20 percent for the last two cohorts. Participation in socialist youth organizations—often linked to parties or party factions, as in the case of Antonio—was a relatively minor entryway to activism among my respondents, with a high of 7 percent in Cohort 2, hovering around 4–5 percent in Cohorts 3 and 4, and then dropping out of sight among those entering in period 5.[9]

EARLY INTERSECTIONS AND THE SHAPE OF THE FIELD

This analysis gives a useful glimpse of the institutional contexts in which activists from successive cohorts began activism. But many activists quickly began to combine multiple kinds of activism, either in their entry years or shortly thereafter. How were early experiences of institutional intersections distributed across cohorts? Here it is interesting to look not only at immediate entry years (in which most activists participated in only one or two forms of activism), but also at the years surrounding their entry as they got their feet wet and began branching out.

One way to do this is through the use of Galois lattices, an elegant algebraic technique for depicting the structure of intersections and inclusions in two mutually associated sets of elements. A more detailed description and references on lattice analysis are included in the appendix. While the lattices look complicated, they are relatively simple to read and understand. For example, figure 3.7 (below) shows the structure of institutional intersections for Cohort 1, during its entry period (*Abrindo*, 1977–84). While there are thirty-two youth in Cohort 1, the unit of analysis here is not individuals, but "youth years," that is, the array of sectoral affiliations a young person participated in during a given year. Altogether, the thirty-two activists of Cohort 1 participated in ninety-two cumulated years of activism during their entry period (1977–84). Their affiliations during this entry period were distributed across eight of the 11 possible sectors.

T1: Abrindo (1977-1984)

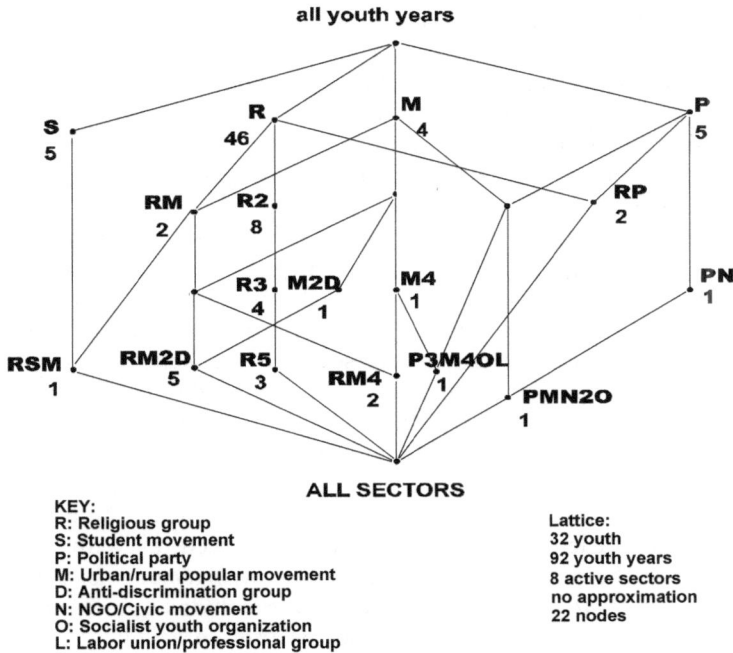

Figure 3.7. Cohort 1: Entry period lattice

The lattice shows ways in which these ninety-two youth years were mapped onto the eight sectors in which the youth participated.

This particular lattice is most easily read from the top down.[10] The clusters of letters corresponding to nodes in the lattice represent distinct combinations of affiliations that appeared in the data. The simplest combinations are at the top; for example, the four top nodes (S, R, M, and P) correspond to participation in just one student organization, religious group, popular movement, or political party, during a given year, with no participation in any other sectors. As you move down the lattice vertically or diagonally, you can see how activists combined those involvements either with others in the same sector or in another sector. The numbers directly following letters indicate multiple involvements *within* sectors. For example, R2 indicates that an activist participated in two kinds of religious activity; this might mean that she took part both in the Catholic youth pastoral and in her church's liturgical direction during that year. M4 might mean that an activist participated in four different kinds of popular movements: e.g., health, transportation, education, and sanitation. And P3 might mean that in addition to his basic political party affiliation, an activist participated in the party's youth commission and in his local directorate. The lattice also shows how activists combined affiliations *across* sectors. For example, RM2D, the second node in from the bottom left of the lattice, indicates a combination of one religious affiliation, two popular movement affiliations, and one antidiscrimination affiliation. Note that the affiliations referred to by a given letter may have been in *different* groups, since I typify groups by institutional sector, not by particular organizations.

The number located below the node indicates how many times that particular combination appeared in the data. The preponderance of early religious participation in this cohort is immediately evident: forty-six youth years, or exactly half of the total, consisted of a single affiliation (R standing for religion). The structure of sectoral intersections can be seen by reading down the lattice from each of the four single sector affiliations. Reading down from Religious affiliation (R), for example, we can see tendencies for keeping multiple affiliation concentrated within the religious sector (reading straight down: R2, R3, R5) as well as the ways that religious participation intersected with other sectors (following the lines down diagonally to the left and right).[11] Note that each sectoral combination is *included* in the ones below it, adding new involvements as you work down the lattice. To see how many youth years included a particular sector, begin at the first appearance of the sector and work downward, summing the numbers associated with all nodes containing that sector. In this case, seventy-three out of ninety-two total youth years (78.5 percent) contained some sort of religious involvement.

This lattice shows an extremely high degree of concentration of affiliations within the religious sector (R). About two thirds of all of the youth years (sixty-six) were completely contained within religious groups, with no overlap with other sectors. However, this cohort did show a notable degree of religious overlap with the popular movements (M), and to a lesser extent, with antidiscrimination movements (D). Political party involvement (P), while beginning to emerge, was not very well integrated with this religious/popular movement clustering, although there was a touch of overlap between parties and NGOs (N). Student movement participation (S) was also just beginning and is relatively marginal from this religious-popular web, although there was one year in which an activist combined participation in religious, student, and popular sectors (RSM).

We have no evidence from this lattice that activists in these overlapping sectors actually knew each other, or even participated in the same exact organizations (in this sense, the lattice is not a "network"). On the other hand, the lattices do indicate the kind of sectoral combinations that were in play when these youth were entering the field. These are certainly not

T2: Reconstruindo (1985-1988)

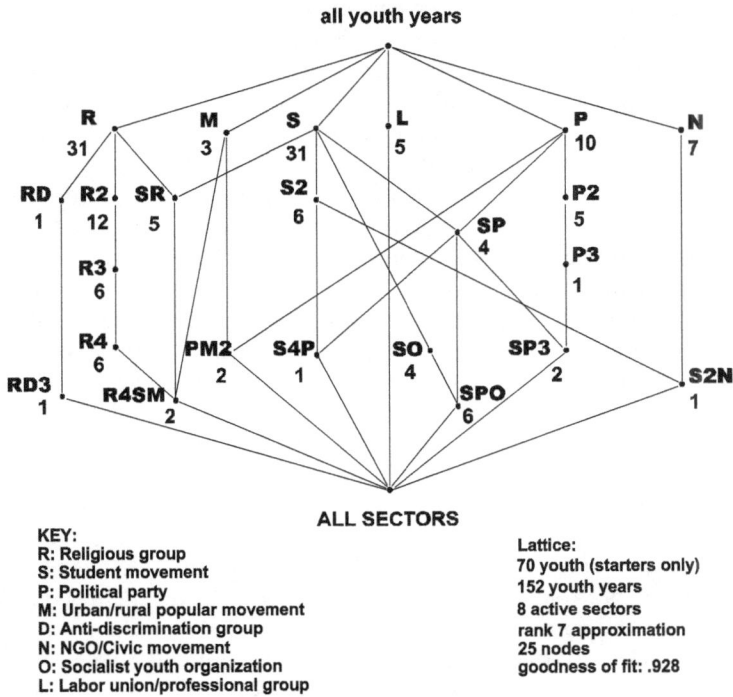

Figure 3.8. Cohort 2: Entry period lattice

the only possible combinations, and there may have been other intersections among those who dropped out or moved into other kinds of non-youth activism (such as labor or party leadership). However, this lattice is consistent with what we know about the *Abrindo* period from other sources: that church-based youth activism was in ascension, that the church was involved with popular movement organizing, and that the student movement and the opposition parties were struggling to get on their feet.

For the second cohort, entering in the *Reconstruindo* period right after the return to civilian rule, the structure of affiliations was beginning to shift. Figure 3.8 (above) shows the distribution of affiliations among respondents beginning their participation from 1985 to 1988.[12] In this lattice, we see that there was still a very high concentration of affiliations within the religious sector, although the religious youth that entered in this period had less involvement with the popular movements (which were beginning to contract at that time). The student movement (S) was growing as an entryway; 45 percent of participation during this cohort's entry period involved some sort of student movement affiliation. While many began participation in a single student organization (S=31), others combined student participation with religious, political party, socialist youth, or even NGO participation. Political party participation (P) was also on the rise, with twenty-nine youth years (19 percent) involving partisan affiliations, even though the intersection of partisan and student involvement was still relatively mild. While labor unions (L) and NGOs (N) were other possible gateways into activism for this cohort, they had little intersection with the other sectors.

The youth of Cohort 3 began activism during the partisan bustle of the 1989 presidential elections as well as the crisis and "rethinking" that followed. Among respondents entering in this *Repensando* period, student and partisan activism were much more intertwined. This increasing overlap among those entering from 1989–91 can be seen in figure 3.9 (below). Religion remained a salient entryway for the respondents in Cohort 3, although religious participation was beginning to have more overlap with student and partisan affiliations (as well as some minor overlap with popular movements and NGOs). But the most notable change was the growth of both student movement and partisan participation overall, as well as the formation of nested clusters of student-partisan overlap (SP, SP2, S2P, S2P3, S2P5, etc.). Course-based student participation (C) made its first appearance in the entries of this cohort, although it was still very limited and largely cut off from other forms of participation.

For activists of Cohort 4, entering in the *Cara Nova* period surrounding the 1992 impeachment mobilizations, the structure of sectoral overlap became a bit more chaotic, losing the neat student-partisan clustering of the previous entry period. The configuration of involvements for those entering in period 4 is depicted in figure 3.10 (below). Echoing the results in figure 3.6, Cohort 4 shows a strong drop in religious entry as well as a leap upward in civic/NGO participation (N), a good part of which was composed by participation in the impeachment mobilizations. While about one-fourth of the youth years (twenty-nine) involved only civic participation, a majority of those who participated in civic mobilizations combined it with other kinds of participation: religious (two), popular movement (three), political party (ten), student movement (sixteen), socialist youth (five) and course-based movement (three). Partisan activism was also widely distributed across the field, although it did not seem to have much penetration among those entering through religious groups during this period. While political parties seem to be their own segmented entryway for a relatively small number of

T3: Repensando (1989-1991)

all youth years

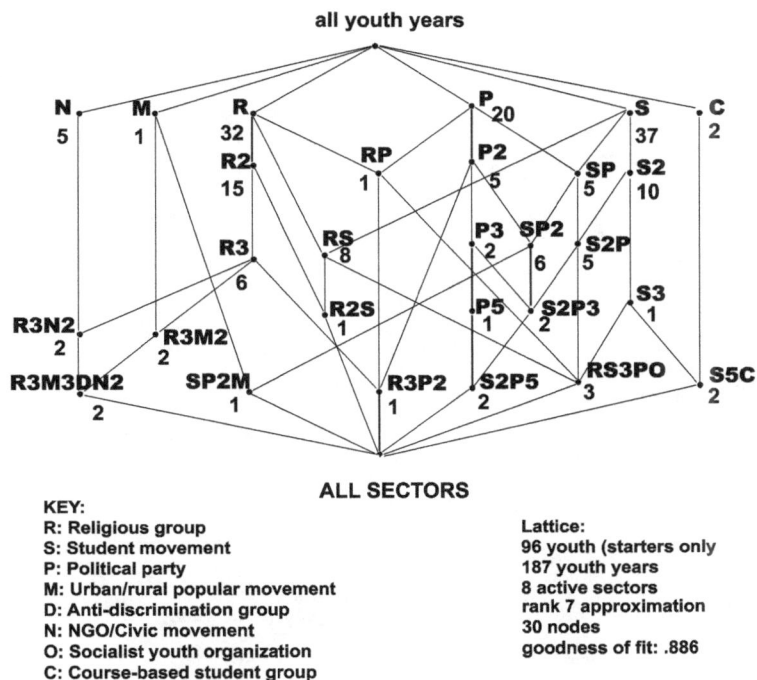

ALL SECTORS

KEY:
R: Religious group
S: Student movement
P: Political party
M: Urban/rural popular movement
D: Anti-discrimination group
N: NGO/Civic movement
O: Socialist youth organization
C: Course-based student group

Lattice:
96 youth (starters only
187 youth years
8 active sectors
rank 7 approximation
30 nodes
goodness of fit: .886

Figure 3.9. Cohort 3: Entry period lattice

youth years (thirteen), there was a stronger probability (twenty out of thirty-five) that partisan affiliation would be combined with other kinds of participation.

Following the tumultuous years surrounding the impeachment mobilizations, the entry field composed by the respondents of Cohort 5, who entered during the final *Globalizando* period, seemed to regain and solidify much of the clear structuring of period 3. This configuration is shown in figure 3.11 (below). For Cohort 5 entrants, the student-party intersection took on a tightly ordered format, incorporating most possible combinations of S and P. Religious, popular movement, and NGO participation dropped way down and were fairly marginal. On the other hand, the course-based student movement (C) saw a big increase among respondents, although it tended to be interwoven with general forms of student movement participation (S). Note, however, the interesting divide among students participating in course-based organizations. While about a third of the involvements of course-based activists were con-

T4: Cara Nova (1992-1993)

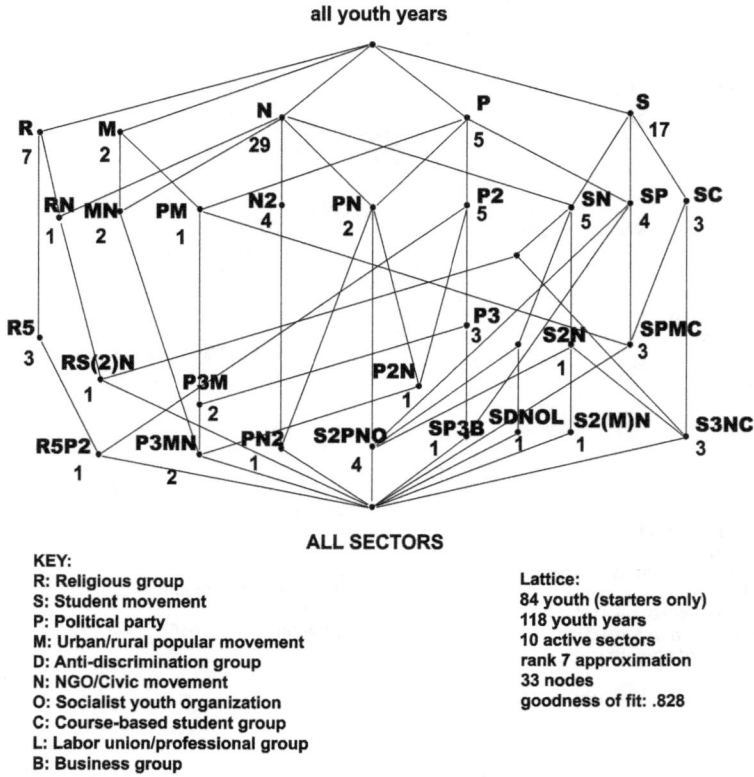

Figure 3.10. Cohort 4: Entry period lattice

KEY:
R: Religious group
S: Student movement
P: Political party
M: Urban/rural popular movement
D: Anti-discrimination group
N: NGO/Civic movement
O: Socialist youth organization
C: Course-based student group
L: Labor union/professional group
B: Business group

Lattice:
84 youth (starters only)
118 youth years
10 active sectors
rank 7 approximation
33 nodes
goodness of fit: .828

nected to political parties (eight out of twenty-two), almost two thirds were not. This points to a split in this entering cohort among the more partisan members of the course-based movement and those who eschewed party participation. The other strong shift in this cohort was the entry of business organizations (B) into the field, although these had very little intersection with partisan or any other form of youth participation.

While these lattices are not complete depictions of the field in the five periods, they are useful in understanding where the five cohorts of young people who were active in the *Globalizando* period were coming from. This, in turn, can give us clues as to what understandings of activism they may have been bringing with them from their early experiences. Activists like Ronaldo, who entered in the first period, brought memories of a field

T5: Globalizando (1994-1996)

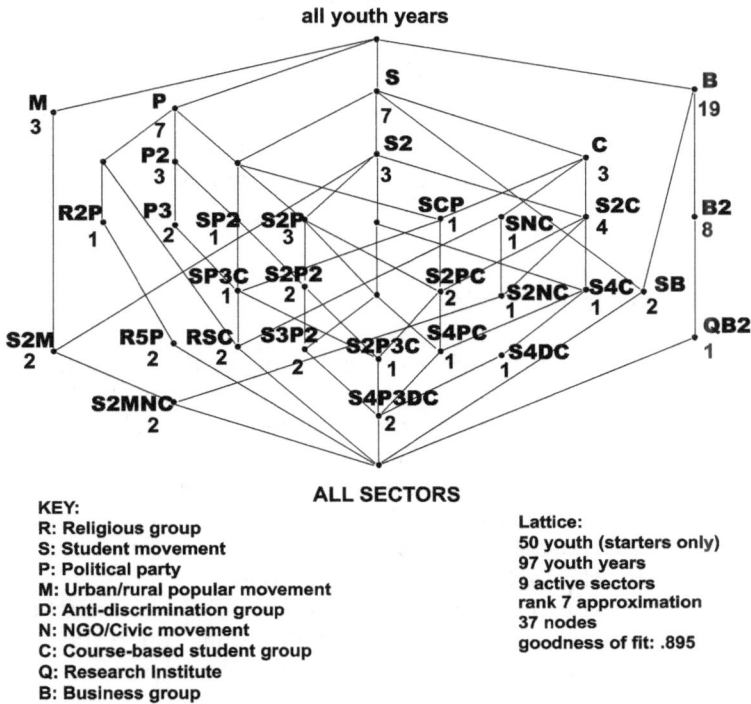

all youth years

KEY:
R: Religious group
S: Student movement
P: Political party
M: Urban/rural popular movement
D: Anti-discrimination group
N: NGO/Civic movement
C: Course-based student group
Q: Research Institute
B: Business group

Lattice:
50 youth (starters only)
97 youth years
9 active sectors
rank 7 approximation
37 nodes
goodness of fit: .895

Figure 3.11. Cohort 5: Entry period lattice

that was dominated by the church, intersected to a moderate degree with popular movements, but was not yet structured by the student-partisan couplings that would play such a strong role in later periods. Both student and partisan participation began to grow as gateways to activism when Barreto and Antonio entered the field in the mid- to late 1980s. These sectors become increasingly interwoven as the opposition parties were caught up in a series of exciting and hard-fought electoral campaigns at the municipal, state, and national levels.

This tight student-partisan relationship was shaken up during the 1992 impeachment mobilizations, as young people like Tomas found an alternative, civic route into activism, which was sometimes connected to student, partisan, and religious participation, but was also to a substantial degree independent of these sectors. Those entering in the *Globalizando* period following the impeachment mobilizations, however, contributed to the construction of a complex field composed of several very different relational dynamics. Many were sucked directly into the strong student-partisan clustering that had reappeared in a significant region of the field, largely dropping the civic intersections of the *Cara Nova* period. Others participated in the growing course-based student movement, often linking this to more general student participation, although a substantial proportion of these activists remained outside of partisan politics. And a new, relatively segmented arena of business youth activism was flourishing, although as in Marta's case, they had little intersection with any other kinds of involvements.

INSTITUTIONAL INVOLVEMENTS OVER TIME

These institutional entries to activism are interesting to the extent that they shape what follows—the trajectories of activists through these changing fields, as well as the styles of communication and problem solving that they developed from wrestling with institutional intersections at different points in time. I will discuss the influence of such intersections on communicative styles in future chapters. Here I will continue the systemic analysis by tracking where the cohorts went next, that is, how their institutional involvements changed over successive periods.

We can examine these patterns by following the waves of activism that emerged over this twenty-year period. I begin by describing cohort trajectories through the religious, popular movement, and political party activism that began to emerge in the late 1970s and early 1980s, during the *Abrindo* period. I then track the cohorts through the student movement and socialist organizing that began to surge in the mid- to late 1980s, during the second and third periods (*Reconstruindo* and *Repensando*). Next I look at the civic/NGO and antidiscrimination activism that was growing in the early 1990s (*Repensando* and *Cara Nova*). Finally, I examine the professional and business student organizing that took off in the last two periods (*Cara Nova* and *Globalizando*).

Religious, Popular Movement, and Partisan Involvement

Figure 3.12 shows a number of quite dramatic patterns in religious, popular movement, and political party participation. First note the strong participation of Cohort 1 in religious participation, beginning at 80 percent in the first period and declining gradually (but remaining high!), arriving at about 60 percent in the final period (figure 3.12a). Cohort 1 clearly contained the most religious of the activists, even if their religious participation dropped over time. This drop may reflect the conservative turn of the Catholic Church in the 1990s, which reduced opportunities for radical

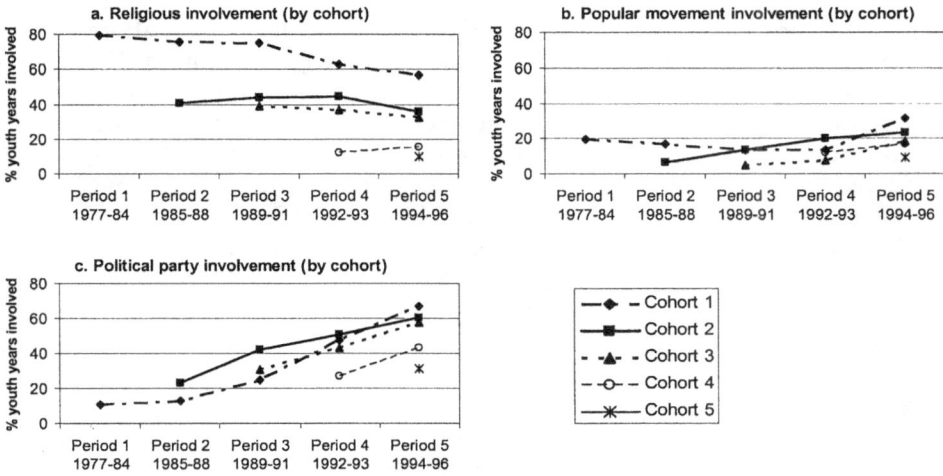

Figure 3.12. Cohort trajectories: Religious, popular, and partisan involvement

lay leadership. Cohorts 2 and 3 also had moderately high level of religious participation, beginning at about 40 percent and again dropping slightly in the final period. Cohorts 4 and 5 were markedly less religious, with participation dropping under 20 percent.

While religious participation did not necessarily go hand in hand with popular movement activism, we do see some evidence that the strongly religious Cohort 1 youth were more heavily invested in popular movements than the other cohorts (figure 3.12b). Their popular movement participation outstripped those of the other cohorts, beginning in the opening period at about 20 percent and reaching more than 30 percent in the final period, after a dip in periods 3 and 4. This shows that the concern with popular, grassroots organizing did not fade for this cohort, even though it lost its salience in the overall field. In fact, some may have returned to popular movement involvement later in their careers, while others began such involvement at higher rates than their younger peers. While the other cohorts also had some moderate involvement in popular movements in the final period, Cohort 5 was less invested than any of the others.

As for political parties, participation remained relatively low until the second period, after Brazil's official return to civilian rule in 1985 (figure 3.12c). The second cohort began with a higher level of partisan involvement than Cohort 1 (above 20 percent), and the participation of all active cohorts jumped up in period 3, which included the dramatic presidential election campaigns of 1989. The partisan involvement of the first three cohorts continued to grow into the 1990s, reaching near or above 60 percent in the final period. In fact, the highly religious youth of Cohort 1 were the most partisan of all in the final period, with 67 percent partisan involvement. One interesting question is whether this high degree of partisan participation was keeping these long-term activists involved in the field, in a sort of inverse relationship to their decreasing religious participation. Note also while Cohorts 4 and 5 started at about the same level of partisanship as Cohort 3, they were markedly less partisan than the earlier cohorts during the final two periods, with participation levels at 43 percent and 31 percent, respectively, at the time I collected the questionnaires.

Student and Socialist Involvement

During the mid- to late 1980s, student activism began to rise, particularly after the 1985 legalization of independent high school organizations. Many high school activists were also involved in partisan battles, some involving socialist youth groups that were often semiattached to political parties. We can see both patterns reflected in the cohort trajectories in figure 3.13 (below). The respondents of Cohort 2 began their student participation at a much higher level than those of Cohort 1 (about 40 percent), and they remained the most highly involved in the student movement, with 64 percent participation in Period 5 (figure 3.13a). Student participation grew for the other cohorts as well, reaching nearly 50 percent or above for all five cohorts in the *Globalizando* period. While socialist organizing was low overall among my respondents (see note 9), Cohort 2 youth reported a higher level of socialist involvement than the other cohorts, hovering at around 20 percent into the final period (figure 3.13b).

Civic and Antidiscrimination Involvement

During the late 1980s and early 1990s, Brazil began to see rapid growth in the NGO sector. In the early 1980s, Brazilian NGOs focused mainly on support for human rights and popular movements, often with links to church-based groups. However, by the turn of the decade the sector had exploded to concentrate on environment, hunger, land reform, gender and racial issues, and indigenous rights.[13] The 1992 United Nations Earth Summit in Rio de Janeiro, held immediately prior to the impeachment movement that same year, reinforced this trend. By the late 1990s, NGO's were increasingly involved in "partnerships" with government and sometimes business organizations, as the Cardoso regime sought to shift provision of some social services to "Third Sector" organizations.

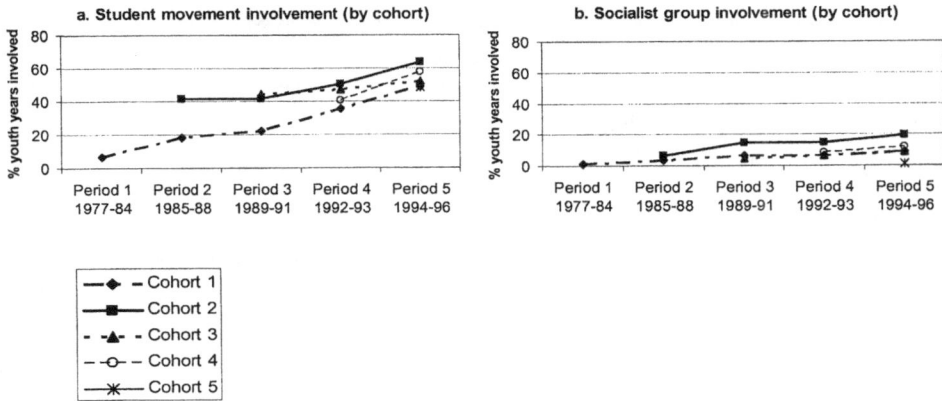

Figure 3.13. Cohort trajectories: Student and socialist involvements

These patterns are reflected in figure 3.14a (below). We can see the sudden jump in civic/NGO participation among all cohorts in period 4, mostly due to participation in the 1992 impeachment movement and (less frequently), the NGO Global Forum at the Earth Summit. Interestingly, the activists with the highest level of civic/NGO involvement in period 4 were Cohorts 2 and 4—that is, those entering the field as well as those who had entered during the highly partisan student activism of the mid-1980s. This civic participation was not necessarily sustained, as levels dropped back down in the final period. This suggests that civic/NGO participation did not leave a strong institutional imprint among these respondents, even in Cohort 4, but rather served as an extension or a gateway for other forms of participation.

One emergent form of early 1990s activism was directed against discrimination toward blacks, women, homosexuals, and indigenous peoples. While this often took the form of NGO participation, I have classified it here into a separate category, since the black student movement was an important component of my ethnographic study. While a low proportion of my respondents overall were involved in antidiscrimination movements, we can still see some interesting cohort differentiation (figure 3.14b). Youth from the two earliest cohorts were more highly involved in antidiscrimination activism than those from the other cohorts, especially in the last two periods, when the movement of black university scholars was picking up steam; both cohorts reached 20 percent in the final period. This suggests that many leaders in the mid-1990s black student movement came from the first two cohorts. Among Cohorts 3 and 4, participation reached 11–12 percent, while only 2 percent of Cohort 5 was involved in antidiscrimination activity of any kind.

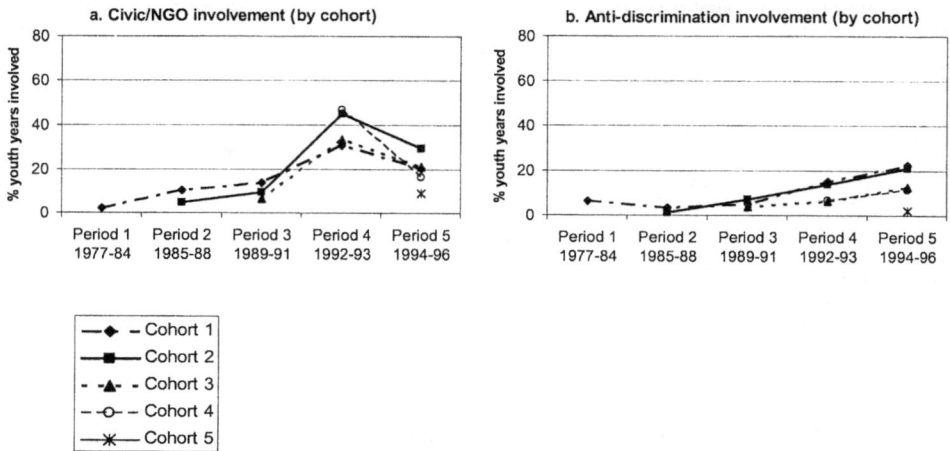

Figure 3.14. Cohort trajectories: Civic and antidiscrimination involvement

Professional and Business Activism

After the civic excitement of the impeachment movement, Brazilian youth politics saw a surge in more specialized forms of activism, often linked to professional or business sectors. Course-based participation began to rise in period 4, with between 20–30 percent involvement of all cohorts in the final period (figure 3.15a). Interestingly, the highest levels of participation in the final period were among Cohorts 1, 4, and 5, all with more than 27 percent involvement. The course-based activism of Cohort 1 activists surged earlier than the others, reaching 20 percent by the fourth period. This suggests that Cohort 1 included pioneers in the course-based student movement, quickly joined by the newcomers in the later cohorts. Finally, there is strong cohort differentiation in business participation, with most business involvement concentrated in the last two cohorts (figure 3.15b). This pattern was strongest in Cohort 5, which had 31 percent involvement in the business sector, followed by Cohort 4 at 16 percent. Very few youth of any of the first three cohorts had any business participation at all over the length of their careers.

This analysis of institutional involvements shows marked changes by cohort and time period. Strong trends include the declining importance of religious participation over time in all cohorts, as well as the rising strength of the student movement and the political parties in the middle periods. This was followed by a decline in the prominence of partisan affiliations in the later two cohorts. Moreover, we see that at least some of the youth in the sectors that were challenging the traditional student

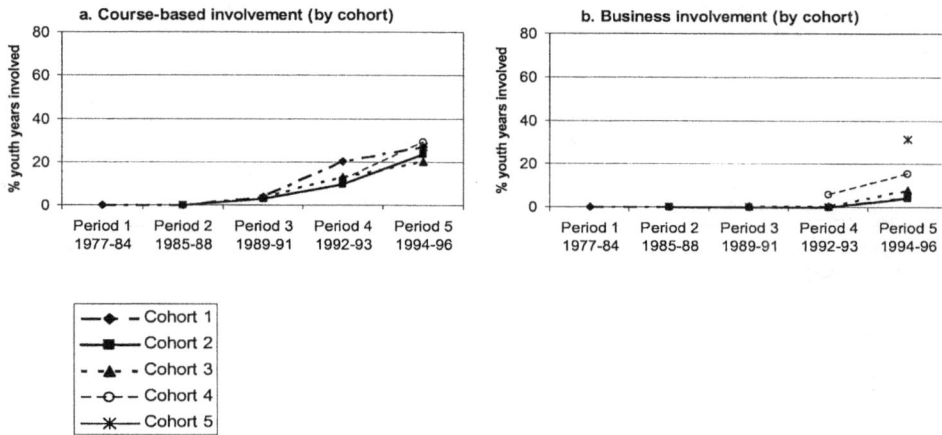

a. Course-based involvement (by cohort)

b. Business involvement (by cohort)

	Cohort 1
	Cohort 2
	Cohort 3
	Cohort 4
	Cohort 5

Figure 3.15. Cohort trajectories: Professional and business involvement

movement in 1990s got their start much earlier—in particular, many early participants in the Course-Executive movement, as well as many black student activists, began participation in periods 1 or 2. On the other hand, some challengers were newcomers: nearly all of the business youth, as well as a strong contingent of the youth in the Course Executives, began activism during or after the 1992 impeachment movement.

PARTISAN COUPLING AND DECOUPLING

The analysis above suggests that at least part of the intramovement tension that I observed during the *Globalizando* period could be attributable to cohort differences. Activists from the earlier periods had different experiences of institutional intersections than those who came later, influencing their styles of communication as well as their subsequent trajectories. I have indicated that one important—and sometimes problematic—component of those intersections is the relationship of partisanship to other forms of activism. So far, I have only looked indirectly at such intersections, which are implicit in the overlapping percentages in the graphs above. To examine these more directly, I analyzed tendencies toward what I call *partisan coupling*, that is, the tendency to combine different forms of activism with political party involvement. To do this, I calculated the conditional probabilities that a particular sectoral affiliation would be combined with partisan participation in a given year.[14]

Figure 3.16 presents tendencies toward partisan coupling in religious and general student movement affiliations, two of the early rising sectors

a. Religious-Partisan coupling
(conditional probabillities)

b. Student-Partisan coupling
(conditional probabillities)

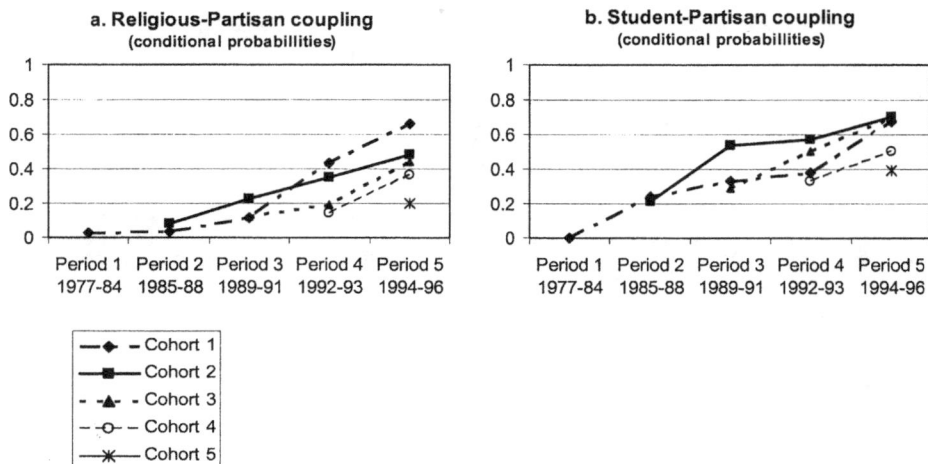

Period 1   Period 2   Period 3   Period 4   Period 5
1977-84   1985-88   1989-91   1992-93   1994-96

—♦— Cohort 1
—■— Cohort 2
- -▲- - Cohort 3
- -○- - Cohort 4
—✳— Cohort 5

Figure 3.16. Partisan coupling in early rising sectors

during the first decade of democratic reconstruction. Figure 3.16a shows the degree to which the youth in each cohort who were religiously active in a given period were also involved in political parties.[15] Note that the highly religious activists of the first two cohorts did not start out with strong partisan involvement, reflecting the trend we saw earlier of single religious involvements in the early years. Participation in political parties only began to rise among religious youth in the third period, most likely surrounding the 1989 presidential elections, and remained at about 20 percent for the last two entering cohorts. Partisanship continued to rise among long-term religious activists in the final two periods; in the final *Globalizando* period, the religious youth of the first cohort were the most partisan of all, with a 0.67 probability of partisan coupling. In the final period, each successive cohort of religious youth had a lower probability of partisan coupling, with the Cohort 5 youth the lowest of all (0.2).

Figure 3.16b shows that there was also cohort variability in partisan coupling among student movement activists. Again, Cohort 1 student activists did not begin with much partisan involvement, but this rose over every successive period and jumped upward in period 5, following the impeachment mobilizations. The vigorous Cohort 2 student activists became partisan at a faster rate, jumping above a 0.5 probability of partisan coupling by their second period of involvement and maintaining partisan dominance into the 1990s. Partisan participation among Cohort 3 student activists also rose steadily, joining the first two cohorts at a nearly 0.7 probability in the final period. In contrast, the two youngest cohorts of student activists had lower partisan involvement in the final periods,

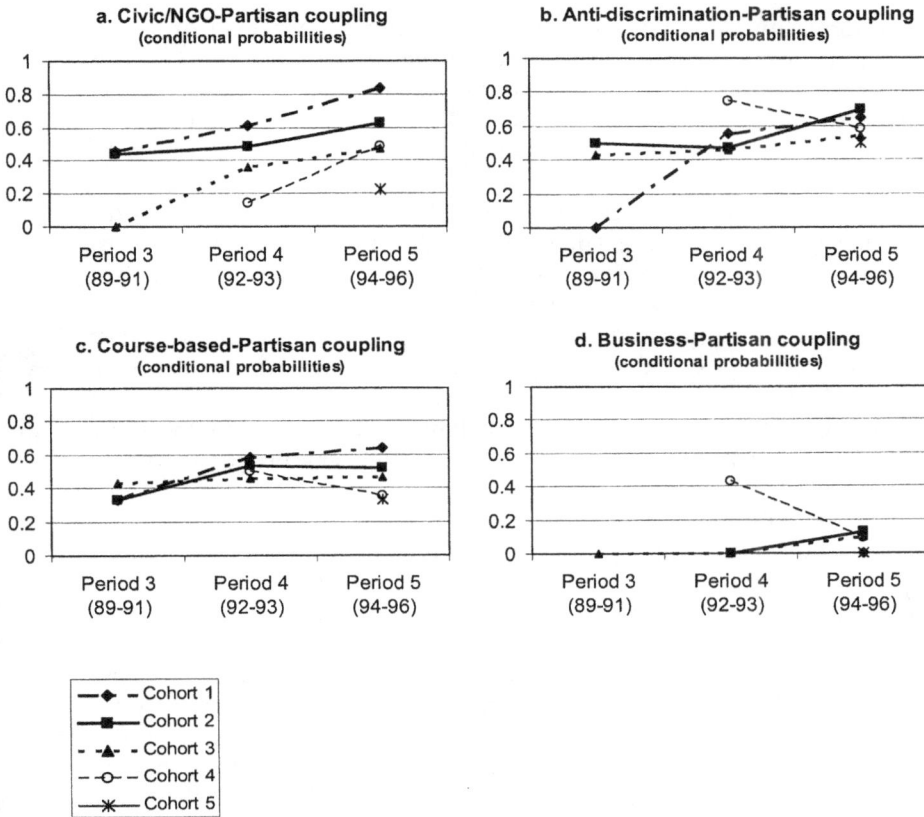

a. Civic/NGO-Partisan coupling
(conditional probabillities)

b. Anti-discrimination-Partisan coupling
(conditional probabillities)

c. Course-based-Partisan coupling
(conditional probabillities)

d. Business-Partisan coupling
(conditional probabillities)

Period 3 (89-91)   Period 4 (92-93)   Period 5 (94-96)

— ◆ — Cohort 1
—■— Cohort 2
- -▲- - Cohort 3
— -o- — Cohort 4
—✳— Cohort 5

Figure 3.17. Partisan coupling in later rising sectors

with that of the final cohort lagging well below the others at 0.4 (although this is still a sizeable proportion).

But what of the new kinds of participation that began to challenge traditional forms of youth activism in the late 1980s into the 1990s? Did young people in civic or NGO activism, antidiscrimination movements, course-based student associations or business groups show similar degrees of partisan coupling as the more traditional student and religious groups? Figure 3.17 (above) tracks levels of partisan coupling among these four sectors. Since participation in these sectors only began to emerge among my respondents in the third (*Repensando*) period, I begin my tracking in period 3.

Not only are these patterns different from religious and student participation, but they are also quite different from each other. They do share one similarity: with a few exceptions, the later cohorts tend to be less partisan than the earlier ones, although the degree and history of this divergence varies. The divergence is particularly marked among participants in civic or NGO activism (figure 3.17a). In period 3, just prior to the impeachment movement, about half of the civic/NGO activists in the first two cohorts combined this with partisan involvement, although none of the incoming Cohort 3 did. During the heat of civic activism in 1992–93, partisan coupling varied markedly by cohort, with a 0.5 to 0.6 probability among the first two cohorts, dropping down to below 0.2 among the new entrants in Cohort 4 (many of whom cut their political teeth in the anti-Collor demonstrations). By the final period, the spread was even more extreme, with civic activists from the first cohort having a 0.8 probability of partisan involvement, while the incoming activists in Cohort 5 had only a 0.2 probability. The probability of combining partisan and civic/NGO activism varied strongly, decreasingly sharply for successive cohorts.

Among antidiscrimination activists (including, but not limited to, the black student movement), the pattern is somewhat different (figure 3.17b). The relatively few Cohort 1 activists involved in antidiscrimination activity in period 3 (5 percent) were not partisan at all. However, as more Cohort 1 and 2 youth became involved in antidiscrimination activity over the next two periods, the probability of partisan involvement soared to nearly 0.7. Partisanship among youth beginning in period 3 held steady at around the 0.5 level, while the few youth beginning antidiscrimination activity during the impeachment period (period 4) had an extremely high level of partisanship (nearly 0.8), quite different that those beginning civic/NGO involvement during the same period. By the *Globalizando* period, the antidiscrimination activists appeared to be more consistently partisan across cohorts than activists from most of the other sectors, bucking the trend toward partisan decoupling visible elsewhere in the field.

Among participants in the professionally oriented course-based student movement, partisan coupling began in Period 3 at around 0.4 probability for all three active cohorts (figure 3.17c). In period 4, all four active cohorts hovered around the same level of partisanship (between 0.4 and 0.6). But then they began to diverge, with Cohort 1 becoming *more* partisan while Cohort 4 became *less* so. Since we have seen above that Cohorts 1 and 4 were the most active in the course-based movement in the final *Globalizando* period, this provides further evidence of a strong split among the professionally oriented youth between more partisan older activists and less partisan recent entries.

Finally, students involved in business activism were quite different than all of the other sectors, with an extremely low probability of partisan coupling. The first three cohorts had very little business activity at all across the five periods, with little or no probability of being combined with political party affiliation (figure 3.17d). Interestingly, however, when the business student movement (such the Junior Enterprises) first started to emerge during the 1990s, a sizable proportion of the Cohort 4 youth (0.43) combined this activism with partisan participation. However, this probability dropped way down as their participation grew (joined by a large number of Cohort 5 youth) in the final period. Strikingly, none of the business youth from the final cohort reported any partisan participation at all. This leads to the interesting question of whether some of the early leaders in the movement of Junior Enterprises may have been more politically inclined—at least to start—than those that followed as the movement consolidated.

Overall, this analysis indicates that while the activists entering in periods 4 and 5 were relatively less likely to be aligned with parties, coupling with partisan affiliation remained very strong in the field overall even in these later periods, with the very notable exception of the stridently apartisan business groups. However, there was strong variability in levels of partisanship across cohorts and sectors. The more long-term religious and student activists eventually reached a very high level of partisan involvement, in which they were joined by the emergent antidiscrimination activists. However partisan coupling with civic and professional activism varied strongly by cohort, with newcomers much less likely to be involved in political parties than their more experienced counterparts. This indicates a split in the later periods between those activists from the early cohorts, who tended to link their student, professional, and civic activism with partisan participation, and those from the later cohorts who showed a much weaker tendency toward such coupling. This split in degrees of partisanship among different cohorts during the postimpeachment period was thus a potential source of tension and debate.

Characterizing the Cohorts

Together, these analyses point toward tensions between what was going on in the cohorts and what was going on in the broader field. They suggest that differences in political orientations and styles of communication may be traced in part to activists' changing experiences of institutional intersections, a point I return to in future chapters. Drawing on these analyses, we can sketch out summary profiles of the five cohorts. While there was certainly individual variation within cohorts, these profiles allow us to get a handle on significant patterns that distinguished young people entering in the five periods.

Cohort 1: God on Earth → God and Party

Activists entering during the *Abrindo* period (1977–84) showed a strong religious affiliation, which, while declining in later years, remained well above the level of any of the successive cohorts. In accord with liberation theology's call to "build the Kingdom of God on earth," they increasingly combined other forms of activism with their religious participation, especially in popular movements, antidiscrimination groups, and NGOs. In later periods they were also among the most partisan, with a strong tendency to link partisan involvement with religious and other forms of activism. Perhaps, as I suggested earlier, they were able to link strong religious narratives to equally strong partisan narratives, contributing to the longevity of their activism. Finally, they seem to include some of the early participants in the course-based movement, which perhaps accounts for the presence in the Course Executives of styles of discussion and consensus-formation that were remarkably like those of the Catholic youth pastoral (I'll return to this point in chapter 8).

Cohort 2: Faction Builders → Civic Bridgers

Activists entering during the *Reconstruindo* period (1985–88) tended to be extremely partisan, but also reached into a wider array of other sectors than any of the other cohorts. As they vigorously rebuilt the high school and university student movements, they also built the role of parties, factions, and other socialist groupings within them. Yet many of them did not stay penned within these two sectors, but rather combined a variety of other involvements with their student and partisan participation. In the impeachment period (period 4), they were the cohort that most vigorously linked their activism to NGO/civic involvement—suggesting that partisan and civic participation were not anathema, but rather, that strong party builders could be quite active in building bridges to other kinds of organizations in an emerging civic arena. However, they were relatively late in joining more specialized, professionally oriented student groups, only mildly catching on in the Course Executives in the final period (perhaps reflecting a tendency to subordinate professional lives to organizational or movement building projects).

Cohort 3: Sustainers → Rethinkers

The activists who began their trajectories in the *Repensando* period (1989–91) seemed in many ways to be a weaker echo of the previous cohort; all of the patterns that were present in Cohort 2 also appeared in Cohort 3, only fainter. Many seemed to jump headfirst into student and party participation, helping to sustain the momentum of the previous cohorts. But by the final period they were branching out tentatively into popular movement, antidiscrimination, and NGO activism, often linking student, partisan, and other forms of participation to one or more of these forms. In addition, slightly more youth from this cohort became involved earlier in the Course Executive movement than their colleagues in Cohort 2. This provides some support for the characterization of their entry period of one of "rethinking": they were continuing the forms they had received but also reaching out tentatively into emerging areas.

Cohort 4: Citizens → Professionals

The cohort beginning in the vicinity of the impeachment mobilizations (the *Cara Nova* period, 1992–93) showed a very strong initial participation in civic/NGO activism (most of which was due to the impeachment itself), although this civic participation dropped off in the final period. They showed strong student participation, but weaker partisan coupling in the 1990s than the previous three cohorts. The tendency toward partisan decoupling was relatively subtle and varied by sector: student and antidiscrimination participation still had a greater than 50 percent chance of being combined with party participation, but this was weaker than the earlier cohorts. On the other hand, this cohort had the highest involvement during the final period in the Course Executives, and some emerging participation in business groups. This suggests a shift from civic to professional identities among those entering during or after the impeachment. Unlike Cohort 1, however, this preprofessional involvement was much less likely to be combined with either religious or partisan participation.

Cohort 5: Specializers versus Party Core

The activists entering during the final *Globalizando* period (1994–96) showed greater tendencies toward segmentation in their institutional couplings. While there was a strong overall tendency toward student participation, student-partisan coupling was lower than for any of the previous four cohorts. There was a strong tendency for a "partisan core" of socialist youth to be linked with student groups and political parties, along with a tendency for antidiscrimination involvement to be coupled with student, preprofessional, partisan, and research activity. But the two newest forms of student participation—the Course Executives and the business groups—tended to be much less connected with the parties, and in fact, business involvement was in a world of its own, with only very slight links to other student, NGO, or research groups. These newcomers were following more specialized paths that either weakened or split from the partisan logic of the field, although at least in the Course Executives, they were interacting with much more partisan youth from the earlier cohorts.

COHORT INTERACTIONS AND COMMUNICATIVE TENSIONS

This dissection of cohort trajectories does more than show us the complexity of the Brazilian political scene. Rather, it provides a systemic grounding for the historical and ethnographic analysis to come. In the chapters ahead, I will turn to the pragmatic and performative challenges posed by changing institutional intersections. Meanwhile, this structural analysis provides a number of clues for the core puzzle of this book: why (and how) the link between partisan and civic engagements seemed to contribute to institution building and cross-sectoral collaboration during the first decade of Brazil's democratic transition, but became more problematic and paralyzing as the country moved into the second decade of democratic consolidation.

The early cohorts had the benefit of starting relatively fresh: everything had to be rebuilt at once, after nearly a decade of enforced quiescence. As I describe in chapter 4, partisan reform came just as exiled leaders were returning and popular movements were surging across the country. Party leaders played mediating roles in the opposition movements, even as partisan narratives—especially among the highly ideological parties of the left—provided overarching, longer-term understandings of the reforms that Brazil was undergoing. By the late 1980s, the opposition region of the Brazilian political field—and in its own heightened way, the field of youth politics—was at once highly integrated and highly competitive, with political parties playing a bridging role in a complex, multisectoral field.

Most of my respondents from the early cohorts were quite young in the 1980s, beginning their involvement in local Catholic youth groups or high school student associations. Their initial involvements were therefore not yet as intense as some of the higher-level student and Catholic leaders I describe historically in chapter 4. However, as these young activists assumed leadership roles, they began reaching out to other sectors, particularly toward the end of the decade in the excitement surrounding the constitutional assembly and the presidential elections. By the 1990s they had higher levels of group involvement, spanning more sectors, than many of those entering in later periods. They were also more partisan than the later entrants, especially beginning in the *Repensando* period as many of them entered the universities. They were building parties—and becoming more partisan over time—at the same time as they built other kinds of institutions in Brazil's emerging civic arena. In fact, as I show ahead, their attempts to wrestle with the tensions between partisanship and other kinds of involvements was itself a source of institutional reflection and regeneration.

Civic-minded young people beginning activism during and after the impeachment had a different understanding of the relationship between partisan and civic participation. They tended to bridge fewer groups and sectors than their more experienced colleagues and had a generally reduced level of political party involvement. While pockets of intense partisan activism remained, these tended to be more closely wedded to the student movement, without the broader link to nonstudent kinds of activism. Moreover, the student movement itself was increasingly split between "general" and "specialized" form of participation, related to professional or course-based areas, as well as to identities based on race or gender. While many activists combined both general and specialized participation, a substantial segment eschewed partisan affiliation. At the same time, a new form of business student activism was emerging that was stridently antipartisan and largely disconnected from other forms of participation. In the final *Globalizando* period, we see a field that was ostensibly more "civic," but less integrated, in which partisan competition had been forced underground.

In this final period, youth from all five cohorts were interacting, although these cohorts were concentrated in different regions of the field. The Catholic youth pastoral, the general student movement, and the black student movement had a higher proportion of respondents from the first three cohorts, while the course-based movement and especially, the business setting showed a higher proportion of youth from Cohorts 4 and 5. Older activists whose experience had led them to stress the partisan side of the partisan-civic balance—but who also had a propensity for cross-sectoral bridging and integration—interacted with those who tended to emphasize the civic dimension, although their experience of activism was more sectoralized.

This disjunction in activist experiences during the period that I was observing—between older activists who were "partisan bridgers" along with younger ones who were "civic but sectoralized"—led to communicative tension in many of the publics I observed. Experienced leaders from the older cohorts were vulnerable to accusations of partisanship that at times paralyzed or disrupted student movement relations and projects. This, in turn, contributed to the strong challenges that UNE and the traditional student organizations were experiencing in the years following their triumphant role in the 1992 impeachment mobilizations.

In the next chapter, I begin to flesh out this systemic account by tracing the historical emergence of two different styles of "partisan bridging," one of which was more collaborative while the other was more adversarial. I examine the relational challenges faced by youth leaders of the early cohorts, who were beginning Catholic and student activism during the first decade of Brazil's democratic reconstruction. The *Catholic-popular-partisan* intersection and the *student-civic-partisan* intersection that emerged in the 1970s and 1980s generated distinct styles of communication, which continued to inform the field of youth politics into the 1990s.

CHAPTER FOUR

Partisan Bridging in Early Student and Catholic Activism

In May 1979, more than five thousand students trekked from the far corners of Brazil to Salvador, Bahia, for the Congress of Reconstruction of the National Student Union (UNE). Ten years after the harsh crackdown by the military regime that sent hundreds of student leaders to prison, exile, or armed resistance, students were attempting to revive and restructure Brazil's historic central student organization. The military regime, in the midst of its slow and cautious *abertura* (opening) to democracy, had declared that the congress was illegal, but not prohibited, in the ambiguous doubletalk typical of the period. The conservative governor of Bahia conceded use of the newly built state convention center for the emotion-packed, two-day meeting. Opposition congressmen, local community leaders, and former student leaders addressed the plenary, with missives read from several leaders still in jail. On the road to Salvador, delegates encountered minor police harassment and slowdowns for searches and name-checking, but most of the state delegations arrived in time for the final deliberation over the mission, structure, and leadership of UNE. Recently formed student factions argued passionately about the future of the organization, amidst backstage maneuvering, leadership negotiations, dramatic plenary sessions, and a few scares of repression. UNE was officially set back on its feet amidst chants of the organization's historic slogan: "A UNE Somos Nos, Nossa Força e Nossa Voz!"[1]

That same year, in the northeast state of Pernambuco, a group of young Catholic activists from nineteen dioceses around the country, along with some of their older advisors, met in the seminary of Olinda for the first interregional encounter of "animators of youth/adults of the popular milieu."[2] Inspired by the radical Catholic Action movement that had been sent underground by the dictatorship in the 1970s, and saddened by the recent collapse of the Young Catholic Workers (JOC) in Recife, the participants in the Olinda meeting sought to develop a line of work that would be "of" and not "for" the *juventude popular* (popular youth), that is, young people from marginalized urban neighborhoods and poor rural areas. The protagonists of this movement would be "impoverished youth who organize within the church of the poor, to construct the Kingdom of

God, a new society, new woman, new man, and new church."[3] They hoped to involve these young people in the nascent popular movements for health, education, sanitation, transportation, and other social needs that the church was beginning to support around the country. One question they faced was whether or not to maintain their autonomy or become an official "pastoral" of the Catholic Church, especially given the stiff resistance they were confronting from the local church hierarchy. Many participants were critical of official attempts to downplay class divisions in the church-sponsored *Pastoral da Juventude* (youth pastoral), arguing that this neglected the distinct experiences and needs of less-privileged youth. While they didn't quite settle this question, the participants left the Olinda meeting energized to articulate the movement at the regional and national levels, seeking to develop a methodology and vision that was specific to poor and working-class young people.

These young student and Catholic activists, like so many others in Brazil at this time, found themselves in a promising, if uncertain, "institutionalizing" moment. Five years into Brazil's "slow and secure" opening to democracy, civic organizations of various stripes were shaking their limbs, testing their feet, and trying to figure out their own visions and the rules of the political game. In some ways, they were starting from scratch: their projects for the future and the organizations through which they hoped to pursue these projects had to be built from the ground up, amidst a very different political conjuncture than Brazil had experienced before the 1964 coup. At the same time, neither set of young people was without models or guidance. Activists from predictatorship periods were present at both gatherings, available for pragmatic consultation even as they handed down the inspirational torch.

The meetings in Salvador and Olinda represent formative moments of what would become two important styles of publics in postauthoritarian youth politics. The students at the Congress of UNE were reviving a tradition of student organizing that reached back to the early 1900s, in which university-based protests often tumbled outside of the universities to engage the civic issues of the day. At once highly factionalized and civic-minded, the student organizations had served as a training ground for generations of Brazil's political leadership, while also serving as a vehicle for semiclandestine leftist organizing. The Catholic youth activists, in turn, were drawing on the rich heritage of Catholic Action, a religious movement with European origins that drew many young Catholics in the 1950s and 1960s to a commitment to social justice and work among the poor, and which played a role in the development of what would become known as "liberation theology" in Latin America.

Yet while activists at both meetings were attempting to build on the tattered threads left from the predictatorship period, they also felt the thrill of embarking on something new, which was in some ways their own and which did not have to follow all of the rules and rituals of previously existing institutions. Both wrestled with internal divisions and contending views of how they should go about building their organizations and programs of action. And they each found themselves at the intersection of several highly charged, emerging networks of political contestation— the civic and leftist opposition to the dictatorship, in the case of UNE, and the community-based (and church-supported) popular movements among the urban and rural poor, in the case of the Catholic youth.

While both sets of youth activists were clearly contributing to Brazil's civic reconstruction, they were also partisan actors—and would become more so over the course of the decade that followed. They were not only fighting for the return of democratic freedoms, but were also engaged in lively and tendentious debates over the substantive direction of Brazilian society. To "participate" not only meant to take part, but to take "a part," or a side, or a position, on the proposed future of the collectivity, whether that referred to the internal workings of one's own organization or its intervention in a wider political field. Partisanship in this broad sense does not necessarily entail membership in formal political parties, although parties can give narrative, associational, and legislative expression to the values and aspirations of such a "part." In 1979, when these two meetings took place, most of these youth did not yet belong to parties (except, in some instances, to clandestine ones), but this would quickly change, as Brazil returned to a multiparty system and opposition parties regained legal status. By the early 1980s, many of the youth at both meetings were enthusiastically involved in party building, even as they were also working hard to build their student, religious, community, professional, and other forms of civic organization. The partisan and civic projects were closely interwoven, providing each other with energy and resources, even if at times they contributed to tension and dispute.

However, out of these two emerging networks came two very different styles of expressing and acting on these partisan associations in the civic arena. Somewhat paradoxically, the student movement, though more competitive and factionalized, was also the more explicitly "civic" of the two, declaring its intention to speak as the unified voice of *all* of the students (and by extension, all of Brazilian society). In contrast, the radical Catholic youth pastoral, while much more consensual, self-reflective, and integrating, was also much more confident in saying that it only represented "a part" of Brazilian youth: the poor, marginalized, and oppressed. The student movement emphasized the "whole"—embodied by the organization UNE (an acronym meaning "unite")—yet was wracked with internal partisan struggle. The youth pastoral emphasized the "part"—as captured in the church's "option for the poor"—yet found in partisanship an integrating link across diverse movements and organizations.

The oft-repeated watchwords for the two groups reflect this difference: the student movement spoke often of "unity," while the church-based popular movements made frequent claims to "autonomy"—words that captured both the normative aspirations and the practical contradictions of the intersection of partisan and civic pursuits. If one set of activists celebrated unity, while the other trumpeted autonomy, it was because those two ideals were highly problematic dimensions of the ways in which they combined multiple kinds of civic and partisan pursuits. These styles were thus as much product of the pragmatics of institutional intersections as they were of a single institutional logic in itself.

In this chapter, I examine the historical origins of these two styles, looking at the pragmatic challenges involved in the coupling of partisan politics with other kinds of social and political involvements. The participation of young people in the *student-civic-partisan* intersection of the student movement as well as in the *religious-popular-partisan* intersection of the Catholic youth pastoral gave rise to different forms of what I call "partisan bridging," that is, the ways in which multiply affiliated activists drew on their partisan projects and relationships as they built other types of institutions and relations in a still fragmentary civic arena.

These two forms of partisan bridging created institutional and stylistic legacies that were still evident when I did my fieldwork in the 1990s. While most of my respondents from the early cohorts were barely wetting their feet during the events described in this chapter, they were nevertheless marked by the tumultuous relations of the 1980s in ways that influenced their later leadership trajectories. In chapter 3, I showed that respondents who started their activism in the first decade of democratic transition, during what I call the *Abrindo* and *Reconstruindo* periods, differed in important ways from those who came afterwards. Those in Cohort 1 (entering activism from 1977 to 1984) tended to be more religious, more involved in popular and antidiscrimination movements, and, eventually, more partisan than the later cohorts. Those in Cohort 2 (entering from 1985 to 1988) were less religious but also highly partisan, with stronger focus on student, civic, and socialist organizing. As these students got older and moved on in activism and leadership, they carried the styles and skills from these early experiences as they entered the university-based movements that I studied in the 1990s. Thus, by examining the pragmatics of these early institutional intersections, we can understand the generativity of partisan coupling in the 1980s as well as how the legacy of these styles may have contributed to the much more troubled partisan relationships in the 1990s.

I begin by giving a historical overview of the relationship between political parties and challenger movements in the early period of Brazil's return to democracy. I then look at the return of the student movement in the late 1970s and early 1980s, examining the ways in which activists in UNE and other student organizations wrestled with the intersection of their student, civic, and partisan identities. I show how their responses to these tensions informed the rebuilding of UNE as an institution, as well as the competitive, often manipulative, and yet unitary and civic-minded style of elaboration and deliberation that would come to dominate student publics into the 1990s. I then turn to the Catholic youth pastoral, showing how radical Catholic activists responded to the relational tensions generated by their location at the intersection of religious, popular, and partisan activism. Their responses to these tensions informed the intensely self-reflective style of grassroots collaboration and combativeness that characterized their own institutionalized publics.[4]

PARTIES AND MOVEMENTS IN THE EARLY TRANSITION

Both styles of partisan bridging—in the student movement and in the Catholic youth pastoral—were critically configured by the convergence of timing that characterized the early years of Brazil's democratic transition. Within the same four year period (1977–80), Brazil saw the reemergence of student, civic, labor, and popular movements, the return from exile of leftist leaders and intellectuals, and the restoration of multiparty electoral competition. The simultaneity of these events contributed to the dense intertwining of partisan with other kinds of civic and social movement participation. To understand these intersections, we need to take a brief historical look at the relationship between the state, political parties, and social movements as Brazil moved from authoritarian to civilian rule.

Brazil's twenty-year period of authoritarian rule began in 1964, when the populist government of President João Goulart was overthrown by a military coup.[5] The self-designated "revolutionary" military regime proposed to restrain what it saw as the excesses of Goulart's populism and suppress dangerous tendencies toward radicalism in land and labor movements. The stated intention of the regime was to return the country quickly to constitutional rule, albeit perhaps under some form of military tutelage. In contrast to many other authoritarian governments, the Brazilian regime did not dismantle Congress, although it abolished the preexisting political parties. In their place, the regime instituted a two-party system—composed of the government party, ARENA (Alliance for National Renovation), and the opposition MDB (Brazilian Democratic Movement)—which it strongly manipulated through legalist maneuvers and intimidation.[6] Over the course of the 1960s, a series of confrontations with opposition actors—including students, trade unions, journalists, and opposition politicians—led to the strengthening of hard-line factions within the military. This trend culminated in the harsh 1968 crackdown on the student movement, which had itself become increasingly radicalized through a wave of mass demonstrations and repeated confrontations with the police. Following the arrest of more than seven hundred students at the Congress of UNE in October 1968, the government released a series of decrees that suspended civil liberties, severely restricted all forms of political organizing, and gave the government unlimited power to decree and enact laws.

The repression of student organizing in 1968–69 marked the onset of the harshest period of the dictatorship. The government's security forces—locked in battle with urban and rural guerrilla forces often led by former student leaders—took on an increasingly prominent role in the infrastructure of state control during the hard-line government of General Emílio Garrastazu Médici. By 1973, these opposition forces had been mostly wiped out, with many of the former student leaders killed, jailed, exiled, or living clandestinely. But beginning in 1974, there were signs of change within the regime, as the incoming president, General Ernesto Geisel, initiated a set of liberalizing reforms. Geisel represented the more moderate wing of the military, which tended to be more sympathetic with the idea that the task of the regime was to return Brazil to a more "stable" democracy. The Geisel government began a dialogue with church leaders, the Bar Association, and other civic organizations about human rights abuses and promised attention to social inequality. In an effort to shore up government legitimacy in the 1974 congressional elections, the government also provided television access to candidates from the official opposition party. To the government's surprise, the MDB nearly doubled its representation in Congress in the 1974 elections. This alarmed hard-liners in the military who were deeply skeptical of Geisel's liberalization policies, while also providing the opposition party with a greater sense of energy and autonomy.

Over the next several years, the push and pull of these various forces resulted in a bumpy and uneven—although in the official mantra, "slow and secure"—loosening of the repressive apparatus and return toward democratic institutions. In 1975–76, a surge of church and civic organizing around human rights issues was accompanied by continued arrests and reports of torture. In April 1977, the government released a set of decrees aimed at limiting the electoral gains of the opposition, contributing to large-scale student demonstrations for the first time in nearly a decade. Following the elections, the government continued liberalizing reforms, with a the abolition of some (but not all) forms of arbitrary state power, the restoration of habeas corpus, the further lifting of censorship, and the revocation of banishment orders for some of Brazil's political exiles. In late 1979, the new president, General João Batista Figueiredo, expanded the amnesty to all except those involved in "blood crimes" against the regime. This led to a flood of returning political leaders, including many prominent figures of Brazil's assorted socialist, communist, and Trotskyist factions. Meanwhile, as I have described in earlier chapters, a wave of labor, human rights, and community-based organizing threatened to take the *abertura* ("opening") beyond what the military could control.

In late 1979, concerned with the growing force of the opposition, the government introduced a reform of the party system that returned the country to multiparty rule for the first time since 1965. The objective of the government was to split the opposition, which was becoming too powerfully concentrated in the increasingly viable MDB. The government party, ARENA, was reconstituted under another name, the PDS (the Democratic Social Party), while the opposition field was opened to an array of new partisan contenders. The MDB indeed split apart, with the bulk of the party minimally renaming itself the PMDB (Party of the Brazilian Democratic Movement). The PMDB remained an umbrella-style party, including conservatives, social democrats, and members of Brazil's two clandestine Communist parties (the Brazilian Communist Party and the Communist Party of Brazil), which were not relegalized until the mid-1980s. The left and right flanks broke off in several directions, including two competitors to the title of "labor" parties, the relatively conservative and clientelistic PTB (Brazilian Labor Party) and the more populist, social democratic PDT (Democratic Labor Party). In addition, an innovative new party, the PT (Workers' Party), emerged out of a rather surprising alliance of the independent labor movement (led by Lula Inácio da Silva), the church-based popular movements, and leftist leaders and intellectuals. The PT advocated a new, specifically Latin American brand of socialist struggle, committed to internal democracy, grassroots social movements, and, increasingly, institutionalized democracy as the path to reform.[7]

While the opposition parties had limited success in the 1982 elections, they began to gain surprising ground over the course of the 1980s, culminating in Lula's nearly successful campaign for the presidency in 1989. While there were a variety of institutional maneuvers that kept the opposition in check, the important point for this analysis is the convergence in timing: a period of intensive party-building at the grassroots level coincided with the emergence of a flourishing network of labor, popular, religious, and civic organizing. Often, as I will show, the same people were involved in both. While partisan participation sometimes caused conflict or sucked people away from grassroots movements,[8] in this early period the effect was arguably synergistic, energizing grassroots militancy with the newly perceived possibility of institutional influence. Partisanship and popular mobilization, at least in the early to mid-1980s, went hand in hand.

Within this tumultuous convergence of civic and political reconstruction, student and Catholic activists were rebuilding their organizations. These two different forms of publics were crucially configured in the late 1970s and early 1980s in ways that would mark relations among youth organizations over the next two decades. In both, partisan participation was a critical component of the militancy of young activists, although they combined partisan and other (student, religious, civic) forms of participation in different ways. This overlap generated bridging opportunities, but also contributed to core, persistent tensions, which reappeared in various guises even as the fields went through significant changes in composition and alignment.

THE RETURN OF THE STUDENTS

Although severely constrained, student organizing had never completely stopped during the dictatorship, continuing in clandestine form even during the years of harshest repression.[9] By 1975, there were visible signs of reorganization at the grassroots levels, marked by the reconstitution of the central student organizations of the University of São Paulo (USP) and Catholic University of São Paulo (PUC-SP). In 1976 the students managed to hold two (still clandestine) student encounters at a national level. These efforts erupted into public form in 1977, with a series of escalating confrontations with university and government authorities. In March 1977, USP students organized protests against funding cuts for teaching and research, while students at PUC-SP and other private faculties protested against tuition increases.

Two months later, following the arrests of eight students and workers at May 1 demonstrations, several thousand students succeeded in gathering in front of the historic USP Law Faculty, located in the city's center, although they were blocked by tear gas and riot police. Similar student protests erupted in other cities, including in Rio de Janeiro, Minas Gerais, and Rio Grande do Sul. Students organized several "National Days of Struggle," which were met with growing police repression. A June attempt to organize a national student meeting in Belo Horizonte resulted in 850 arrests, as police stopped and searched buses entering the city. This meeting was finally held in São Paulo several months later, leading to the violent invasion of Catholic University and the arrest of more than five hundred students, along with faculty and staff. The University of Brasília was occupied repeatedly by police during an extended student strike that lasted nearly three months.

Despite police repression, the 1977 demonstrations helped to publicly relegitimate the student movement, connecting it with broader projects of civic opposition to the dictatorship, while boosting efforts to reorganize within the universities. Student slogans shifted from calls for university reforms to an end to censorship and repression, amnesty for those in prison and exile, and a return to democratic institutions.[10] The student demonstrations were given extensive—and mostly sympathetic—coverage in the recently liberalized press, reflecting a situation in which middle-class civic organizations such as the churches and professional associations were beginning to organize their opposition to human and civil rights abuses of the regime.

Following the 1977 protests, local CAs (Academic Centers, autonomous student associations based in university departments) and DCEs (Central Student Directorates, universitywide student organizations) were reconstructed across the country, although they remained illegal until the mid-1980s. Students in São Paulo managed to reconstitute the State Student Union (UEE), and a national Pro-UNE Commission began planning the Congress of Reconstruction of UNE in Salvador. As repression began to lessen in 1978, students found that they could carry on organizing and fund-raising in relative safety, raising money from, among others, congressional leaders in both opposition and government parties. This effort culminated in the Congress of Reconstruction of UNE held in Salvador in May 1979.

Nascent Factionalism and Political Elaboration

While student activism in the late 1970s helped to resuscitate the civic role of the student movement, students were also reconstructing an internal culture of factional dispute. Throughout the late 1970s and early 1980s, UNE was torn between its external face of civic intervention (requiring unity) and its internal dynamics of partisan struggle (entailing division). Reconciling these two faces would prove highly challenging. Activists attempted to institutionalize ways of handling dissension while maintaining their stance as the unified voice of Brazilian students.

Factional politics in the student movement did not begin in the 1970s, but rather built on remnants of the socialist groupings that splintered in and out of existence in response to the military repression of the 1960s and 1970s. Under the leadership of activists associated with the Young Catholic University Students (JUC), the student movement had undergone a renovation in the years immediately prior to the 1964 coup. In the early 1960s, UNE used innovative methods to spearhead discussions about university reform around the country, including a traveling caravan (UNE-Volante), theater and music performances, and a national strike to democratize the universities. However, the church hierarchy began to resist the increasing radicalization of its activists, leading many Catholic activists to leave JUC and form Popular Action (Ação Popular, AP), an autonomous student organization that originally attempted to fuse humanist and socialist principles.[11] In 1963, after the failure of the national student strike, the leaders of UNE and AP began to encourage student activists to move outside of the university, engaging in the movements of workers and peasants that contributed to the 1964 military coup.

After the coup, many leaders of UNE and AP fled into exile, while others continued to organize in clandestine form. As the student movement skirmished with the police in the mid-1960s, their leaders became increasingly radicalized and dogmatic. In 1966, AP renounced its Christian roots and went through a Maoist reformulation.[12] By the early 1970s, the group had fractured several ways, with one group engaging in urban guerrilla struggles, another joining the PCdoB (one of Brazil's two communist parties, which was in the midst of organizing an ill-fated rural guerrilla movement in Araguaia), and another continuing under a new designation, APML (Ação Popular Marxista-Leninista). At the same time, a myriad of other factions—some coming out of the crisis of the Communist Party in the early 1960s, others multiplying under the spiraling sectarianism of the repressive period—engaged in variations of the armed struggle, until they were effectively crushed by security forces in the mid-1970s.[13]

Despite the splintering and repression of the Brazilian left, the struggles of the 1960s left their marks on youth politics in the late 1970s. The reputed heroism and self-sacrifice of young activists during the fight against the dictatorship took on mythic proportions, eclipsing the tragic dogmatism and narrowly sectarian battles that also characterized the period. When students tentatively took to the streets again in the late 1970s and began rebuilding their organizations, they drew on those heroic memories even as they positioned themselves as the leading edge of a civic movement against the dictatorship. They constructed the unity of the student movement around the historic legacy of the "glorious UNE" and around their position in the broader camp of civic opposition to the dictatorship.

At the same time, the remnants of the 1960s student factions began to reorganize within the universities. These factional groupings (including AP and its various offspring) infused the articulation of student "tendencies" (as they were known) that began to appear the mid-1970s. In the early years, these tendencies were not narrowly instrumental partisan organizations, but rather lively spaces of debate and sociability. Although

TABLE 4.1
Early student movement tendencies and their partisan trajectories

	1970s tendency	*1980s/1990s parties*
Communist parties	*Viração*	PCdoB (UJS)
	Caminhando	PCdoB; PT (PRC, *Nova Esquerda*)
	Unidade	PCB → PPS; PMDB (MR-8)
Marxist humanist	*Refazendo*	PT (*Articulação* and other tendencies)
Trotskyist	*Liberdade e Luta*	PT (*O Trabalho*)
	Novo Rumo	PT (*Convergência Socialista*) → PSTU
	Maioria	PT (*Democracia e Socialismo*)
	Novação (*Organizando, Centelha, Ponteio, Peleia, Resistencia, Travessia, Combate, and others*)	PT (Various left tendencies)

most student tendencies were at least vaguely Marxist, they varied widely in their approach to student organizing. While some adopted a more traditional vanguard approach and debated the finer points of revolutionary strategy, others repudiated ideological dogmatism and tapped into the lively, semianarchistic alternative cultural movements that were active in the universities. The tendencies had vivid names such as *Caminhando* (walking or journeying), *Refazendo* (redoing), *Viração* (turn-around), *Unidade* (unity), *Centelha* (spark), *Resistência* (resistance), *Novo Rumo* (new direction), and *Liberdade e Luta* (freedom and struggle). While the tendencies were fluid, often regionally based, and too numerous to list, the major groupings that played a role in the 1979 congress are described in table 4.1.

These student tendencies formed the initial web of what would become the complex factional composition of the student movement in the 1980s and 1990s. Most student tendencies can be traced forward to the partisan (and intrapartisan) alignments that were on the verge of relegalization at the time of the Congress of Reconstruction in 1979. For example, the students of *Viração* and part of *Caminhando* became the youth of the Communist Party of Brazil (PCdoB), united later in the decade under the banner of the Union of Socialist Youth (UJS), the semiautonomous youth wing of the party. The tendency *Unidade* was linked with a rival Communist Party, the PCB (Brazilian Communist Party) from which the PCdoB split in the early 1960s, and with whom it competed for the mantle of the original Brazilian Communist Party, founded in 1922.[14] Both of Brazil's

Communist parties remained illegal until 1985, although their leaders were often ensconced (and elected to public office) within the mainstream PMDB. Additional clandestine groups also found a home in the PMDB, including the MR-8 (Movimento Revolucionário 8 de Março), a former guerrilla faction that now saw the nationalist bourgeoisie as the pathway to revolution.

Other tendencies gravitated toward the newly formed Workers' Party (PT). Many activists from *Refazendo* became involved in the founding of the PT, principally in its more centrist, moderate branches, sometimes associated with the church and the popular movements. A dissident group in *Caminhando* split with the PCdoB and became associated with a small, Marxist-Leninist faction (the PRC, Revolutionary Communist Party), which took up residence in the PT. By the 1990s, this group had largely dropped its revolutionary intentions and aligned with the "radical democratic" strain of Euro-communism, calling itself *Democracia Radical* (DR). And many smaller Trotskyist tendencies became associated with the proliferation of factions that made up the left flank of the PT, reflecting the dizzying subdivisions of the Fourth International. These included the highly intellectual Mendel-influenced faction *Democracia e Socialismo* (DS) and the more extremist *O Trabalho* (OT). One of the radical Trotskyist tendencies, known as the *Convergência Socialista* (CS), was expelled from the PT in 1991 and formed its own party, the small but strident PSTU (Unified Socialist Workers' Party).

Despite the association of the tendencies with the partisan factions of the 1980s and 1990s, several former student activists that I talked to looked back wistfully on the late 1970s as qualitatively different from the intensely partisan climate that followed. For example, I talked to one former student leader from the University of São Paulo who had links to the church and was working as an aide to a city council member of the PT in 1995. He recalled an effervescent, semianarchistic culturalist movement that advocated freedom of artistic and intellectual expression and opposed the traditional bureaucratic-authoritarian structure of student politics. His local group, called *Delirosque* (a play on "delirium" and "Solidarity," in reference to the Polish labor union), criticized the classical leftist structure of "democratic centralism" as well as what they saw as the attempts at ideological co-optation by organized leftist factions.

Likewise, the sociologist Helena Abramo, a former member of the tendency *Refazendo* who worked as a researcher at an educational NGO during the 1990s, recalled a rich and widespread culture of political elaboration and debate. This process of debate, she said, was "rooted in the schools, in the classrooms." A flurry of manifestos circulated widely through the universities, involving students in discussions about the university, the student movement, the political situation, capitalism, and democracy. According to Abramo, the reconstruction of UNE in 1979—and especially the process of debate leading up to it—served as an important "moment of reflection" for the student movement right at the cusp of the return to democratic institutions. While Abramo and many of her colleagues were disappointed with the direction that UNE took in the 1980s, they took that late 1970s spirit of grassroots dialogue and critique with them into their subsequent political and professional pursuits.

From Elaboration to Deliberation: The Congress of Reconstruction of UNE

The 1979 Congress of Reconstruction in Salvador was important in setting the parameters in structure and style for what would become the highly institutionalized publics of the postdictatorship student movement. At the congress, participants faced the challenge of moving from elaboration to deliberation, that is, from the rich culture of debate within the universities to decisions over organizational program and procedure. To rebuild UNE as an institution, they had to figure out which aspects of their multiple identities could be expressed (or suppressed); how they would manage heterogeneity and dissension; and how they would construct and ritualize their unity despite evident internal differences.

On the surface, the construction of programmatic unity did not seem to be too difficult. The organized student tendencies largely agreed on the main banners of the 1979 congress: more funding for education, a return to democratic liberties, general and unrestricted amnesty, and a repeal of the repressive legislation of the dictatorship. However, the tendencies differed over important questions of program and structure: whether to support the official opposition party, MDB, as opposed to urging the null vote in upcoming elections; whether they should focus their struggles within the university or in the larger political arena; how to elect organizational leadership; and what was the best way to involve the "mass" of students in the movement.

The deliberations at the congress were also shaped by emerging electoral competition. The congress took place amidst anticipation of the 1980 political party reform, with most of the aspiring parties still operating in a semiclandestine state. UNE's public status and proud history of civic intervention made it both a symbolic and a material prize for these parties-in-formation. The different tendencies thus jockeyed for procedures and structures that would give them an electoral advantage within the historic organization.

On the first evening of the congress, following hours of welcoming speeches, the twenty-three hundred delegates (along with several thousand observers) broke into somewhat smaller (although still sizeable!) discussion groups on themes related to Brazilian reality; conditions in the universities; and the statute, principles, program, and structure of UNE. Despite the eagerness for debate, the size and format of the congress made discussion difficult, as two participants noted: "There was no deep discussion of Brazilian reality or even of the university . . . in discussing struggles to be waged, more than 100 proposals emerged—ranging from amnesty and a Constitutional Assembly to the fight against dental cavities."[15] As a result of this chaotic flurry of proposals, the discussion groups were less an exercise in reflective deliberation than in factional positioning: "The statement of the proposals defended by the diverse tendencies ended up serving more to orient accords between the various political groups, in meetings that swept through the night."[16]

The most heavily attended discussion group addressed the electoral process within UNE, with a thousand students reportedly attending (not exactly a number facilitating debate). The format of elections was hotly contested on both ideological and tactical grounds. For example, the tendencies *Viração* and *Unidade* (linked to the two Communist parties) advocated a directorship elected immediately in the congress, arguing that this was necessary to ensure UNE's institutional stability and credibility in the struggle of the "democratic sectors" against the dictatorship. This reflected their own position within the mainstream PMDB and provided opportunities for their favored candidates. Two of the Trotskyist tendencies defended congressional elections with proportional representation, since "only in Congress can all of the positions be deeply debated";[17] more tactically, this was the best way for smaller tendencies to ensure their representation the directorate.

In contrast, the tendency *Refazendo* (which would form the core of the PT), was one of the strongest advocates of direct elections for UNE's directorate in the universities, to be held later in the year. The students argued that they needed to build "a movement of the base," with widespread discussion among students, grounded in university-based struggles for improvement in educational conditions (although also in solidarity with workers' movements around the country). This reflected a stronger emphasis on grassroots organizing than on civic coalitions, a persistent theme among PT students.

In the end, the proposal of *Refazendo* and its allies won out; delegates voted for a provisional directorate, with direct elections for a definitive directorate at the end of the year. This would be the first time in UNE's history that the directorate was elected directly by students in the universities. More than 160,000 students from around the country participated in the October vote, electing a "unity slate" composed of members of most of the major tendencies.

While a spirit of grand debate and ritualized unity thus gilded the return of the organized student movement, the 1979 congress also helped to institutionalize core features of the highly competitive style of student politics. The organized publics of UNE and the student movement in the 1980s and 1990s were composed of large, contentious encounters permeated with semisubmerged factional politics, in which even "small" discussion groups turned into vehicles for political positioning and maneuver. While celebrating their own unity, the congresses culminated in contentious deliberations about organizational structure that determined factional distribution of positions and power.

Partisan Bridging: Reconciling "Civic" and "Partisan"

As the newly elected directorship took control of UNE, leaders wrestled with the intersection of three core identities underlying student activism: that of *students*, attempting to improve education in the universities; of *civic actors*, attempting to expand democracy in the country; and of *partisans*, attempting to gain political space and influence for their political parties. This was not an easy negotiation, and most struggles within the student movement centered on how much weight should be given to one or more of these identities over the others. The fact that so many transformations were happening at the same time—the increase in university-based activism, the surge in civic and popular movements, and the reform of the political party system—intensified this tension, creating opportunities and dilemmas for the renascent student organizations.

The first year of the reconstructed UNE was marked by several public campaigns: tussles with the government over the continuing illegality of UNE, the attempt to retake UNE's historic headquarters in Rio (which had been burned by the dictatorship), and a national student strike for more funding for education. The year also, however, saw increasing strains among the competing tendencies within UNE's leadership. With political party reform, the fluid tendencies of the 1970s were consolidating into polarized partisan camps. While Communist parties remained illegal until 1985, semiclandestine youth groups linked to the PCdoB and other vanguard factions invested intense efforts in recruitment in high schools and universities. Other factions gravitated toward the Workers' Party (PT) and entered into the brand-new party's complex internal factional dance.

In 1980, students voted to reject direct elections and switch to winner-take-all congressional elections. This switch favored factions like the PCdoB that concentrated their efforts within the student movement (and thus could better mobilize activists to attend congresses), rather than those with more dispersed involvements in popular movements outside of the universities (like the PT). A slate controlled by *Viração* (linked to the PCdoB) won the leadership of UNE, leading to a long period of PCdoB control of the directorate, until they were defeated by students from the PT in 1987. In 1991, right before the impeachment movement, the PCdoB took back leadership of UNE, maintaining its dominance in UNE's directorate throughout the 1990s.

The leaders of UNE wrestled with how to maintain the mantle of unity even as the student movement settled into increasingly polarized camps. While the tension between unity and factionalism may seem basic to any centralized, representative organization, in the case of UNE it was heightened by the self-mythologizing, euphoric mode in which it celebrated its own historical unification. The leaders of UNE took great pride in the fact that unlike many European countries—and unlike Brazil's own labor movement—Brazil did not have two or three national student organizations, reflecting different ideological alignments, but only one: a unified central organization that spoke in the name of all Brazilian students. UNE was celebrated not only for its long history of civic intervention, but also for being a "school of democracy," in which of "all" of the competing voices in the national debate (or at least, the left-leaning segments of it) came together to join in a common discussion about the future of the university and the nation.

In principle, the unity of the student movement public required the official suppression of partisan identities: "UNE should not approve or work with the ideas of one or another political current, or of one or another political party . . . but rather carry forward the banners and the struggles of students as a whole," an UNE journal argued in 1983. "Regardless of our political convictions, we students should join forces in defense of UNE and its proposals . . . these proposals express the unity of the Brazilian students, at the side of the democratic and popular sectors of society."[18]

However, the leadership of UNE could not completely elide the question of partisan divisions. As open partisan organizing became more viable, UNE was faced with the question of how to reconcile its "civic," nonpartisan character with what its leaders saw as a very desirable and necessary electoral reform, in which they themselves were highly implicated. In December, 1980, UNE's second postdictatorship president, Aldo Rebelo (who would later become congressman and cabinet minister from the PCdoB), signed a resolution elaborating the organization's relationship to political parties and its support for the partisan reforms. The first two points of the resolution indicate UNE's balancing act in affirming both its organizational nonpartisanship and the possibility of partisan affiliations among its leaders:

1. The directorate reaffirms that, in principle, UNE is an organization that is representative of all Brazilian students, independent of race, color, sex, ideology, or religious belief; *being, therefore, unitary, apartisan, not submitting itself to any Party, and to none of them affiliated.*
2. For this reason, UNE does not delegate to any Director or student the power to represent it within the structure of the Parties. On the other hand, *UNE defends and stimulates the participation of students, including its Directors, in political parties*, as an *individual option,* as a form of contribution to the democratic struggle of the Brazilian people.[19]

Here we see the "civic" (as opposed to partisan) status of UNE swinging on an analytical hinge: UNE *as an organization* was nonpartisan, representing all students. However, UNE's leaders, *as citizens* were permitted and in fact encouraged to participate in parties as part of their democratic duties. This subtle compartmentalization of the identity of the organization from that of its members enabled one form of what I call "partisan bridging," that is, the leveraging of (partially) suppressed partisan identities to build other kinds of relationships in a civic arena. This discursive maneuver allowed UNE to qualify its own actions as civic, rather than partisan, thus enabling its very partisan activists to construct bridges on behalf of UNE with other kinds of civic actors in Brazil. The resolution expresses support for the recent provisional registration of the PT, salutes the convention of the PMDB, and expresses hope that other opposition parties would soon realize their conventions. Finally, the resolution expresses "our commitment on the side of all of the democratic forces in society in the struggle for the freedom of organization for all political parties, including those that today find themselves in clandestinity," a clear reference to the Communist parties to which many directors belonged.

During most of the 1980s, UNE dealt with partisan dispute by reserving it for yearly elections. The winner-take-all structure meant that all members of the directorate belonged to a single party (or at times, partisan alliance), and that opposition tendencies were excluded from organizational control. While such voting procedures lead to extremely contentious elections, they can also lead to relatively more harmonious and productive regimes. During the seven years of PCdoB control of UNE (from 1980 to 1987), students leaders from the PCdoB busily tried to maintain the "civic" face of UNE through a variety of campaigns and projects. They fought for legalization of UNE (approved in 1984), joined with associations of university professors and staff to protest funding cuts for education, opposed tuition hikes in private schools, and supported the broad-based 1984 movement for direct elections. UNE also organized two national seminars, on university reform (in 1985) and the constitutional process (in 1986).

Vanguard Challenges: Entrenchment and Critique

However, at the same time as leaders of UNE were trying to construct bridges with other civic organizations, they were becoming more entrenched and polarized within the student movement. The weakness of the winner-take-all structure is that it eliminates any stake the opposition has in the success of the organization, except during periods of electoral dispute. When the *Viração* tendency (linked to the PCdoB) consolidated its control of UNE in 1980, the other tendencies were largely shut out of leadership. Most of the opposition was caught up in the expansion of the PT, which was taking a hard-line oppositional stance on many of the disputes of the democratic transition. The PT students roundly criticized the directorship of UNE for its decision to support the opposition rather than boycotting Brazil's electoral college in 1984, after the defeat of the movement for direct presidential elections.[20] Likewise, the featured appearance of the minister of education at UNE's 1985 seminar on educational reform was seen as not as an example of civic mediation, but rather of sleeping with the enemy.

At another level, the PCdoB directorship of UNE was also coming under attack for its method and style of leadership. For some activists who valued either anarchist cultural creativity or grassroots reflection and debate, the years following the reconstruction of UNE were bitterly disappointing. For example, Helena Abramo, the former *Refazendo* member cited above, told me that the late 1970s had seen "the gestation of a new idea of the student movement," which emphasized decentralized, grassroots discussion organically linked to alternative forms of cultural expression. This project was defeated, she argued, during the 1980s, with the "ascendance of a new logic" in the student movement. According to Abramo (and the losing group more generally), this was a bureaucratic, centralized, and apparatus-based logic, which stifled grassroots political discussion, impoverished the elaboration of proposals, and alienated a small elite leadership from a rapidly expanding and diversifying student body.

In a highly critical 1985 article, another former *Refazendo* member, Artur Ribeiro Neto, criticized not only the PCdoB leadership, but more generally, the co-optation of the tendencies by organized Marxist political groups (including those that ended up inside the PT). He accused these groups of having an "aristocratic" conception of political leadership, rooted in earlier periods when the universities were the province of a small elite. With the dramatic expansion of access to university education in the 1970s and 1980s, this vanguardist conception was sorely out of touch, portraying the "masses" of students as "political incompetents." Moreover, Ribeiro Neto argued, the seduction of leadership into purist ideological organizations impoverished the quality of thinking within the movement: "It was no longer a matter of thinking about contingent facts . . . even while keeping the revolution in view, but rather, in possessing the truth of the revolution, [seeking] how to reveal it to the students by way of contingent facts; that is, *how* to inscribe the movement of students in the general movement of history."[21]

Ribeiro Neto and others worried that the vanguardist factions' ideological stance as the bearers of revolutionary truth destroyed reflection and creativity at the grass roots. For them, the celebration of UNE's "glorious past" was a self-serving myth used to legitimate the apparatchik strategy of the organized leftist factions. Rather than providing a forum for debate, UNE thus served "to make and legitimize political bargains . . . serving as an institutional structure by which illegal groups can talk to society and, above all, justify their accords with other partisan factions."[22]

The critique by Abramo and Ribeiro Neto reflects the tension between two different political styles emerging among Brazilian social movements during the 1980s. Many of the *petistas* (members of the PT) who were shut out of UNE lamented what they saw as the entrenched, competitive institutionalism of the PCdoB leadership, which they saw as maintaining organizational control at all costs while locked in an outmoded vanguardist mode of communication. Many PT leaders became involved in the urban and rural popular movements, some linked to the Catholic Church, which stressed grassroots reflection and collaboration as the basis for what I will describe in the sections ahead as very different kind of partisan bridging.

According to the PCdoB leadership of UNE, of course, the story was very different. They saw themselves as fighting not only to control the organization, but also to revive UNE as a civic institution with a strong voice in resolving the problems of the day. While they embedded this civic goal within their longer-term revolutionary project, they prided themselves on their pragmatism in building alliances and trying to change institutions from within—a style of partisan bridging born from a long experience of clandestine organizing. They criticized the PT for their narrow sectarianism in avoiding civic coalitions as well as for what became known as *basismo*: a hypervalorization of the grassroots "bases" at the expense of qualified leadership.

At the end of the 1980s, groups involved in both styles of partisan bridging—oriented to alliance-building among civic institutions versus grassroots organizing of popular movements—were undergoing a process of internal reflection and critique, as youth politics entered the *Repensando* period (1989–91). This process echoed the soul-searching going on in the left as a whole, particularly following the 1989 electoral defeat of Lula da Silva, along with the collapse of the former Soviet republics. In the years leading up to the 1992 impeachment, both PCdoB and PT youth would reevaluate their intervention in the student movement and seek changes in movement practices. I will return to these changes in chapter 5. I turn now, however, to the second style of partisan bridging that emerged during the 1980s, within the incubator of the Catholic youth pastoral.

THE REORGANIZATION OF CATHOLIC YOUTH POLITICS

Far from the universities, in the poorer neighborhoods of the urban peripheries, a very different form of youth organizing was also beginning to build momentum during the *Abrindo* period. While the organized student movement trumpeted its unity in the face of intense factional competition, the Catholic youth pastoral was preaching autonomy even as it developed an integrative, collaborative style of communication. As I have argued above, both styles were critically influenced by the location of activists at the intersection of several different institutional sectors: student, civic, and partisan, in the case of the student movement; and religious, popular movement, and partisan, in the case of the youth pastoral. As with the student movement, I first examine the roots of Catholic activism in the precoup period and then show how young activists developed a new style of partisan bridging as they built institutions and relations during the early transition.

Just as the student tendencies of the 1970s built on the remnants of the Marxist factions of the 1960s, the Catholic youth pastoral drew strongly on the legacy of radical Catholic youth organizing in the predictatorship period. The Catholic progressive movement had a long history in Brazil going back to the organization of Catholic Action in the 1930s, associated with an international movement of Catholic laity.[23] Brazil's modernizing bishops originally saw Catholic Action as a way to extend their influence over a rising sector of the country's industrial elite. In Brazil, the church did not follow the approach it took in other Latin American countries by sponsoring a Christian Democratic Party (although there were several attempts in that direction) but instead developed a comprehensive effort to shape the laity as future leaders of the country. This effort was influenced by the philosophical work of Jacques Maritain, whose reflections on liberty, democracy, and human rights would inform later efforts of Catholic clergy and laity to wrestle with the relationship between faith and politics. Nevertheless, there was also a strong conservative strain in the movement; it was militantly anticommunist, focused on elites, and explicitly aimed toward a greater involvement of the church in the emerging power structures of the country

The Catholic Action movement was divided into a several specialized organizations aimed at different sectors of youth. These included JOC (Young Catholic Workers), which was inspired by the Belgian model of Fr. Joseph Cardjin in the 1920s; JUC and JEC, aimed at university and secondary students, respectively; JAC, for agrarian youth; and JIC for independents (these became affectionately referred to "a, e, i, o, u."). The specialized youth branches acquired increasing autonomy from the local hierarchies in the 1950s, particularly under the supportive leadership of Dom Helder Cámera and a small group of progressive bishops at the helm of the National Conference of Brazilian Bishops until 1964.

During the 1950s and 1960s, many branches of Catholic Action went through a radicalization process that went far beyond what most of the hierarchy was willing to support. This process is quite fascinating and too involved to develop here; what is important for this analysis is that it was driven, at least in part, by the multiple affiliations of young Catholic activists. This was especially the case for the Young Catholic University Students (JUC), who wrestled with how to understand the social component of faith even as many participants became involved in the organized student movement, and eventually, in national campaigns for literacy and land reform. Within the universities, many Catholic activists competed and collaborated with more traditional leftist factions, which led them to challenge their own assumptions even as they positioned themselves as a more reflective, humanistic alternative to the Marxist left. The Catholic Action movement encouraged a continual process of self-reflection (known as "revision of life and practice"), as idealized in the "See, Judge, Act" methodology inherited from the international movement. Many JUC activists began to question the distinction between the "spiritual" and the "temporal" that was the bedrock principle of Catholic Action, rethinking their faith in terms of a "historical ideal" that entailed a commitment to social justice and to addressing the problems of poverty and inequality in Brazilian society.

In the years following the 1964 military coup, the church underwent a conservative retrenchment, which included the dismantling of JUC and other branches of Catholic Action in 1966. As Catholic Action disbanded, its members went in a variety of different directions. Some, as we have seen, followed Popular Action as it adopted Marxist-Leninism and set out to organize workers and peasants; others joined factions engaged in the armed struggle against the dictatorship. Still others, particularly the clerical advisors (or "pastoral agents"), began to work in local communities, building what came to be known as *Comunidades Eclesiais de Base* (usually translated as Christian Base Communities, or CEBs).[24] While these small communities of biblical reflection originally focused primarily on evangelization and religious communion, they increasingly became the vehicle of the church's commitment to the poor and to a transformative presence in the world.[25]

After the hardening of the dictatorship in 1968, church leaders began to clash more strongly with the regime, as progressive clergy and laity as well as the remaining Catholic youth activists were targeted for arrest, torture, and even assassination. The moderate archbishop of São Paulo, Dom Paulo Evaristo Arns, became a courageous spokesman against human rights abuses, going head to head with the regime in the case of highly publicized assassinations of students, journalists, and workers. He also became a strong supporter of the CEBs and the progressive church, encouraging the development of the Workers' Pastoral Commission (CPO)—deeply influenced by the Young Catholic Workers' movement (JOC)—and a range of other "pastorals" committed to addressing the problems of the poor urban and rural communities. More conservative clergy were also shocked by attacks on church workers into a more unified criticism of the political and economic policies of the regime. In the early 1970s, most of the hierarchy had at least on the surface adopted the language of the church's "option for the poor" even though many conservatives did not agree with liberation theology's radical fusion of faith and politics, nor with the (implicit or explicit) language of class struggle as the means of establishing the "Kingdom of God on earth."

Amidst this climate of ferment and transformation, church leaders once again began to turn their attention to youth. During the late 1960s and early 1970s, the only visible forms of Catholic youth organizing were evangelical and charismatic youth gatherings—often sponsored by religious orders—that focused on the psychological and affective needs of youth. In the early 1970s, scattered groups of clergy and young people began to talk about organizing a *Pastoral de Juventude* (PJ—youth pastoral) that would be in line with the emerging social commitment of the church. In a series of national encounters from 1973 to 1978, young activists and their clerical advisors called for a new form of youth organization that would be more "organic" (i.e., less vanguardist), closely coordinated with the bishops' General Pastoral Plan, and linked to the needs and realities of youth—all coded critiques of Catholic Action for being elitist, disconnected from the hierarchy, and removed from the conditions and experiences of most Brazilian youth.[26]

Elaborating a Method: See, Judge, and Act

Despite these critiques, the new youth pastoral carried at least two clear legacies from the Catholic Action movement of the 1960s. One was a revival of the reflective methodology of "See, Judge, Act," as "enriched by [both] old and recent experiences."[27] A second was the call for engagement in the "meios específicos" (specific milieus) of young people.[28] As in Catholic Action, this entailed context-based categorizations loosely associated with socioeconomic positions. By the mid-1980s, it included divisions into PU (for university students), PJE (for high school students), PJR (for rural youth) and most important for this book, PJMP, for young people of the "meio popular," that is, of "popular" (i.e., poor and working class) communities.

This proposal of division into "specific" areas fueled one of the early controversies in postdictatorship Catholic youth activism: whether or not to explicitly organize the youth pastoral around social class. This split was partly geographical; many youth leaders and advisors from the Northeast defended a class-based organization, while clerical advisors from the South—particularly Rio Grande de Sul and São Paulo—strongly opposed dividing youth groups along class lines.[29] These debates were heated and emotional, despite the fact that both sides were within the progressive camp of the church, committed to social justice and the "transformation of society" (although this remained vaguely prophetic and undefined).

In a series of meetings in Recife in the late 1970s, young people in the Northeast began to articulate the idea of a "Youth Pastoral of the Popular Milieu" (PJMP) directed specifically at poor and marginalized youth. Inspired by former JOC activists, they argued that poor young people needed a space of their own, separate from middle-class youth. They defended this on theological, sociological, and pedagogical grounds. Jesus's option for the poor and recognition of class contradiction, they argued, presupposes "a direct involvement with the popular strata and a line of vision starting from the poor and their historic project." In addition, the sociological realities of class conflict in Brazil demanded direct confrontation on the part of those working with the marginalized sectors. Finally, they insisted that mixed groups with varying class and educational backgrounds would inevitably result in the silencing of the voices, experiences, and leadership of poorer and less-educated youth.[30]

These debates over the "who" of the Catholic youth pastoral also had repercussions for "how," as PJ debated the methodology with which to work with young people at different levels of involvement. An extraordinary amount of discussion, planning, and textual elaboration went into the pedagogy of PJ, resulting in impressive piles of internal studies, discussion texts, and meeting guides. Everyone seemed to agree that the methodology of PJ should come from Catholic Action's famous triad of See, Judge, Act, as well from the ideas of "revision of life and practice" and "learning in action." However, they were less unified on how this methodology should be carried out.

By the late 1970s, the See, Judge, Act methodology had become closely associated with the "Paulo Freire method," an approach to literacy training as personal and political empowerment (*conscientização*) that deeply influenced the church-based popular movements.[31] Many of the early documents of the youth pastoral built directly on Freire's ideas, particularly on his distinction between "magic," "ingenuous" and "critical" consciousness, in which people are assumed to move from a mythic and fatalistic conception of the world to one that is superficial, "pseudo-scientific" and conformist, and finally to one that is historically aware and oriented toward the "transformation of reality."[32]

Perhaps because of the vanguardist legacy of Catholic Action (which was often accused of "teorismo," i.e., being overly theoretical), the advisors and leaders of PJ were very concerned with how to bring about such "consciousness" in a slow and gradual fashion, linked to the "practice" of the group. Youth pastoral meetings usually took the form of small, intimate discussion groups oriented around socially motivated biblical reflection, often interspersed with song, theater, art, and "group dynamics," that is, exercises for building trust and group integration. There was much discussion about the "natural" rhythm of group development, with most proposals based on stage theories of some type. Some discussion guides jumped right into analysis of class conflict and social injustice in Brazil, while others attempted to gradually develop community spirit and reflection on affective and spiritual issues before turning toward critical reflection on social and political life. Increasingly, advisors were concerned to separate texts and meetings aimed specifically at "initiates" from those aimed at "militants," although the militants themselves didn't always respect this divide.

An example of the more radical stance can be seen in a 1982 booklet elaborated by a team of youth leaders in the archdiocese of São Paulo, called "Pedagogy and Project of a Consequential Youth Pastoral" (note the somewhat tendentious accent on "consequential"). At this meeting, they were assisted by a priest advisor from the northeastern city of Recife, who helped give the resulting text a more radical slant than the local São Paulo hierarchy was probably comfortable with. The booklet suggests five "themes" for group discussions, jumping right into "The society in which we live." The first question is "What are 3 major differences between rich and poor in Brazil?" The booklet proceeds through a schematized discussion of Marxist class theory, as it was circulating through the popular movements of the period, with a historical dissection of class relations in Palestine during Jesus's time. This is followed by a depiction of the pyramid structure of Brazilian society, as shown in figure 4.1.

Figure 4.1. "Situation of Man": PJ—São Paulo (1982)

The analysis accompanying this picture is permeated by a strong critique of capitalism and a highly politicized vision of the "Project of God':

> The social pyramid is rejected by God; nobody should dominate anyone, no one should be on top. Any kind of oppression is against the Gospel. The faith of the people of Israel in one God threw this ideology to the ground. If there is one God, there is no way to justify the differences that exist in society. . . . Before any difference: woman/man, father/son, black/white, worker/boss, ALL ARE EQUAL. Before God, all have the same rights, deserve the same respect, and are called to participate in life. If Yahweh is the only God, the Lord, everyone should be submitted to his project. And his project is UNIVERSAL BROTHERHOOD.[33]

Methodologically, this booklet proposes separate pedagogies for "popular" and middle- or upper-class youth. The text argues that the "See, Judge, Act" method "only has its full meaning if it starts from the reality of the working class." Nevertheless, it does admit that more privileged youth can also use the methodology to perceive class divisions, analyze the sources of exploitation, and eventually come to "betray dominant interests" and serve as "organic intellectuals" of the exploited classes.

In contrast, a pedagogical booklet produced in 1984 by a team of advisors in the southern state of Rio Grande do Sul took a much more cautious approach. The booklet focused on psychological development and group dynamics that only gradually would lead to greater social commitment. It suggests that young people should eventually arrive at "engagement" in some sort of "transformative action" (and even, optionally, a "commitment to the poor"), but only after passing through the "natural" stages of group development. These stages were modeled on the stages of life: prenatal, infancy, adolescence, youth, maturity, and old age. The process of personal and group "maturing" should correspond to a growing sense of independence, human relationship, concern for social justice, capacity for dialogue, emotional equilibrium, deep convictions, and "vital options" in life. The stages of group development envisioned by the booklet are depicted in figure 4.2.

Note that while this picture culminates in a helping relationship with the poor, it does not commit itself to a deeper analysis of the sources of poverty or a broader critique of the Brazilian class system. The team that elaborated the booklet was clearly concerned for social justice and wanted to bring youth to a greater sense of social and political engagement. However, they shied away from the intense politicization and class analysis that characterized the text produced by the more radicalized (and Northeast-influenced) São Paulo team.[34]

Multiple Engagements: Autonomy and Integration

These discussions about pedagogy and social engagement did not happen in a church-enclosed vacuum. Rather, they occurred in response to the relational challenges generated by multiple militancies in the early transition. As Fr. Jorge Boran, national advisor to PJ, wrote in 1986, many different kinds of activism came together within the sheltering space of the church:

> During the military regime *the Church was the principal space of political articulation.* The Church constituted itself as a space of debate, conscientization, and support for claimant movements. When the unions of São Paulo and São Bernardo were closed by the police, parish halls opened their doors for assemblies of strikers, parish houses were used for meetings of the strike command, and parishes turned into centers for collection and distribution of food for [striking] families. Nuclei of the Workers' Party were born and met in the [church-based] communities. The popular movement and the pastoral seemed

Figure 4.2. "Evolutionary stages of a group": PJ—Rio Grande do Sul (1984)

like one and the same. With the political opening, the autonomy and specificity of the pastoral spaces and the intermediate organizations are becoming clearer.[35]

As the youth pastoral was organizing in the late 1970s, the church as a whole was beginning a period of intense material and ideational support for popular movements emerging among poor urban and rural communities. The youth pastoral was only one among many forums that clerical and lay leaders were encouraging for biblically informed critical reflection on society. Small "mothers' clubs," "street groups," "workers' circles," and the Christian base communities (CEBs) themselves were becoming spaces in which residents of poor communities could reflect on the conditions of their lives and, at times, begin to reframe these in terms of human dignity and social injustice. While certainly not all CEBs were as highly politicized as many leaders and advocates (and foreign fans) have suggested, they did provide an unaccustomed, protodemocratic forum in which many poor residents found some sort of voice, even if they did not all go on to become active movement leaders.[36]

Young activists in the budding youth pastoral were some of the most enthusiastic participants in this kind of multiple militancy. Since CEBs and parishes of the poor urban neighborhoods were the nerve center of the new popular challenges to the regime, young Catholic activists became caught up in a wide range of meetings and activities. They energetically took to the street to pass out fliers or collect signatures; went on late-night missions to post (still prohibited) signs and banners; and staged politically informed theater, artistic, and musical presentation to inspire liturgies, assemblies, and protest rallies. They met in parish halls to plot strategy for building (or taking control of) student organizations and joined with other community groups in pressuring for more schools and health, transportation, and sanitation facilities. Following the political party reform of 1980, many of these young people also began to be involved in party building at the grassroots level.

By the mid-1980s, relationships between these diverse forms of activism had become problematic enough to merit significant discussion and textual elaboration. In 1986, a team of advisors led by Fr. Jorge Boran produced a thick booklet entitled "Christian Youth and Political Militancy," in which they wrestled with the difficulties of multiple militancy and proposed a schematic differentiation of five "autonomous spheres" of action for Christian youth, as shown in figure 4.3.

The large sphere on the left was the "space of the pastoral," which ranged from internal religious participation (such as catechism, liturgy, confirmation, and family ministries) to forms of religious participation directed more toward the outside world, such as the Workers' Pastoral (PO), the Pastoral Land Commission (CPT), the Indigenous Missionary Council (CIMI), the general youth pastoral (PJ-Geral) and its various specialized branches (PU, PJE, PJMP, PJR). The other four smaller spheres to the right of the arrows consisted of the "space of the intermediary organisms," including (from top to bottom) the popular movements, the labor movement, the student movement, and the political parties. The "tendencies" (referring to organized socialist groups) are depicted on the right-hand side in contraposition to the space of the church, almost as an invading force directing their action toward the intermediary spaces. "Every sphere has its own ends and specific action, which should be respected by the rest," the booklet admonishes:

ESPAÇO DA PASTORAL

Igreja "adentra"
(ambiente da Igreja)

ESPAÇO DOS ORGANISMOS INTERMEDIÁRIOS

Igreja "adestra"
(lugar da missão)

IGREJA

etc. CIMI CPT
PU
CF PJ Geral PJE
Cateq. PJMP
Liturgia PJR
P.Familiar PO
P.Crisma CEBs

Movimento Popular
Movimento Sindical
Movimento Estudantil
Partidos Políticos

TENDÊNCIAS

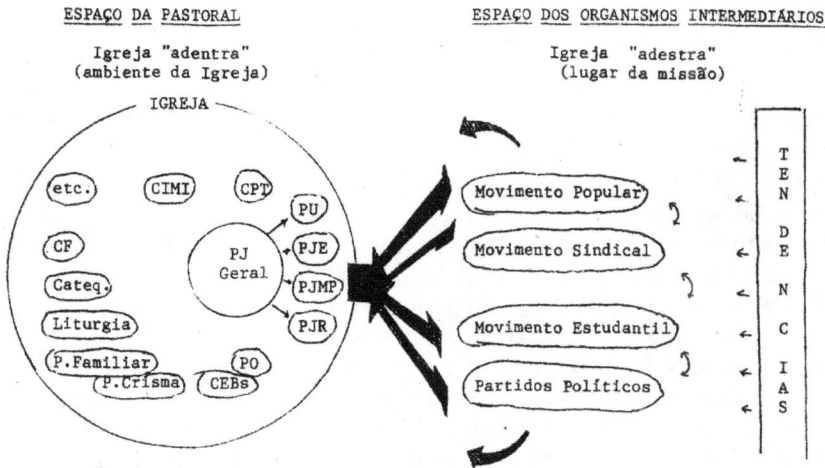

Figure 4.3. The five spheres of Christian militancy

Political militancy should respect the specificity and autonomy of the pastoral, as the pastoral should respect the autonomy and structure of the popular movements, unions, and parties. It would not be good if these were tutored by the Church, if the bishop or priest were to control what the intermediate organizations do or think. . . . On the other hand, its is necessary to avoid the error of absolutizing, of instrumentalizing the pastoral, which could lead to *the mistake of reducing to one and the same* (that is, of everything turning "pastoral"!) the intermediate organism and the pastoral, or reducing the pastoral to the youth wing of the party.[37]

Young Catholics were called to engage in a delicate balancing act: they should "be Church" ("ser Igreja") while engaging in other kinds of social and political involvements, even while not letting either the religious or the nonreligious forms of involvement completely subsume the logic of the other. They should be passionately "integrated" into the differentiated spheres of the community (often several of these at once) at the same time as they restrained themselves on these various fronts, recognizing the different logics in play. The booklet gives the example of a youth group from PJE (Student Youth Pastoral) that won control of a high school student organization, then saw no further need to exist *as PJE*, since "why should we duplicate things?" As a result, the group fell apart; as the booklet admonishes, "they lacked clarity about the specificity and autonomy of each sphere."[38]

Practical Challenges: Commitment and Co-optation

While this enormous effort of reflection and elaboration offered useful distinctions to help Catholic youth analytically separate their various forms of participation, this separation was often much more difficult in practice. With party reform underway, popular and labor movements on the rise, and student organizations in a process of reconstruction, young activists in the early 1980s were sucked almost as they breathed into the dense intersection of religious, popular movement, and partisan activism. The relationship of the church with political parties was especially fraught with challenges, as young activists became caught up in the excitement of electoral politics. In 1982, the new party system received its first test with congressional and state elections. While many in the church and the popular movements were still ambivalent about partisan politics, others threw themselves into the campaign for opposition candidates, particularly for the PT (with some support for other parties well). As Moises Basílio Leal, an early youth pastoral leader from São Paulo (and eventually a committed PT leader) recalls,

> In the election of 1982, a majority of PJ supported the PT, but with different connotations. Some committed to the PT body and soul, while others thought the PT was a necessary evil. I, for example, campaigned in '82, followed the party discussions from a distance, but only began to act in the PT in 1984. Many in PJ prioritized the organization of popular and labor movements, without necessarily linking them to the institutional PT.[39]

However, despite this institutional skepticism, Leal and other leaders of PJ were moving in an increasingly partisan direction—although at that point this was still conceived more in terms of revolutionary project than of institutionalized politics; "It's important to remember that our ideological reference was the revolutionary project on the model of Nicaragua or El Salvador. . . . After all, we were all Christian revolutionaries with Camilo Torres, Cardenal, and other Christians who joined the revolutionary struggle."[40]

This radicalization can be seen in the 1982 booklet, "Pedagogy and Project," described above. This booklet declares boldly that "the God of the Old Testament and the God of Jesus is a PARTISAN GOD." The term partisan here is conceived broadly: "By the life of Jesus, it is clear that God TOOK A PART in the grand conflict that existed in society; He took a part for JUSTICE, the POOR, the EXPLOITED." The text uses the Portuguese phrase "toma partido," which translates best as "took sides," but uses the same word for "party." Clearly there is an attempt to reclaim the very words *partisan* and *party*, cleansing them of connotations of corruption and manipulation, and infusing them with moral righteousness and political commitment.[41]

In the early 1980s, discussions of this sort were still taking place under the official auspices of the church, at least in more progressive centers such as São Paulo, where seminars producing such booklets were supported by the archdiocesan coordination of the youth pastoral. However, by the mid-1980s, the young militants who were articulating the more radical proposal of PJMP began to enter into direct conflict with the local church hierarchy. One event, in particular, shook up internal church relations: two PJMP leaders in Recife left the youth pastoral and revealed that they were members of small militant factions that had been involved in the urban guerrilla warfare of the 1970s. Many other youth in the Northeast broke with the church at the same time. As Moisés Leal notes, this sent shock waves through PJ in the South, leaving the more radical activists vulnerable to the intensifying skepticism of the clergy:

> We, of the PJ of São Paulo, who were organizing PJMP, were confronted by Church hierarchy. The bishops and priest advisors, many of whom already did not agree with PJMP, had reason to suspect that PJMP was an infiltration of leftist political organizations into the Church. The "specific milieus of action" were a negotiated solution for us to continue to organize PJMP in the southern region of the country. It was either this, or leave the Church at that moment. Many left, and went to organize the PT in São Paulo. Those [youth] who had, in fact, a commitment to the Church, rethought the journey and accepted the new formulation.

This "new formulation" was summarized in the organizational chart above (figure 4.3). In this schema, PJMP was subordinated to the "general" youth pastoral (PJ-Geral), becoming one among many of the specific areas of action. The 1986 booklet cited above makes it clear that the specialized branches were a direct response to the concern that Catholic youth groups were becoming a recruiting ground for co-optation by socialist vanguard organizations (the "tendencies"). These included the Union of Socialist Youth (linked to the PCdoB) and a number of other Marxist-Leninist and Trotskyist groups with small cell-like structures that sometimes mirrored the intimate groups of the youth pastoral itself. The advisors worried that many PJ militants seemed attracted to the clear analysis and tight organization (as well as the almost evangelical recruitment methods) of the socialist youth groups, which were gaining a strong foothold in the high school student movement. These advisors complained that "we are preparing leaders and when they are ripe, they are seduced by others and we have to begin everything anew. . . . *We are preparing the bride, for others to marry*."[42]

The flip side of the advisors' concern was the frustration of many youth leaders with the church's hesitation in relation to their broadening political involvement. The activists complained that the church would introduce them to political consciousness, but would then hold them back. As one young activist quoted in the text said rather poetically:

> I was fallen on the ground, and then a priest arrived and helped me to stand up, have faith, walk. They put me on the top of a horse. When I wanted to walk with the horse, they secured the reigns. . . . The Church conscientizes the guy; when he has the capacity to discern, he enters the PT, for example; it's something not anticipated by the priest, the nun, the [pastoral] agent. And they don't participate in this. So necessarily, the guy is going to have contacts that go outside of their control. Then they pull back on the reins.[43]

As young activists began to expand their participation and move outside of the immediate control of the church, they began to see the world from a range of perspectives, and the most active among them began wanting a deeper understanding of what they were looking at. While some, as the advisors feared, were drawn into socialist vanguard groups, many more gravitated to the PT—and from there, to the PT's complex internal factional life. The intense ideological debate within the party provided a set of overarching narratives as well as practical tasks that picked up where the church left off. For many, the socialist humanism of the PT gave them a more elaborated, bridging framework that helped to deepen their social critique while also providing ties to other social movements and political groups. The contentious, if sometimes exhilarating intrapartisan dialogue helped them to locate their participation in the church and the community-based popular movements as part of a larger struggle, which in the short term included intense participation in electoral campaigns. In contrast to the more civic-institutional focus of UNE, this style of partisan bridging was embedded in grassroots community organizing, in which competitive partisan tendencies were tempered by the church's methodological stress on reflective dialogue.

Partisan Bridging and the Reflective Moment

The church's concern to avoid the co-optation of their militants by vanguard socialist groups points to a core stylistic difference between the publics of the Catholic youth pastoral and the student movement. This has to do with the importance assigned to *self-reflection* as a critical component of individual and collective action. The leaders and advisors of the youth pastoral clearly wanted their activists to become involved in community-based popular movements, and the church was becoming reconciled to the fact that this often led into partisan participation. They were quite proud of the bridging and sheltering role that the church had played for opposition movement in the early transition. Yet they were determined to qualify participation in "intermediary organizations" through the reflective orientation that they saw as rooted in faith. Faith was seen not as blind belief or obedience, but rather as the moment of critical reflection beyond ideology, of a transcendence that links human beings to the "suprahistorical" and thus gives them the ability to see "what is lacking" in all idea systems. As the 1986 booklet on Christian militancy declares, "*Christianity is not an ideology, but inspires ideologies.* The construction of the Kingdom, here on earth, passes through ideological mediations. Christianity can be criticized by ideologies, as it is also an instance of criticism of those ideologies."[44]

The purpose of the specialized branches of the youth pastoral (PJMP, PJE, PJR, PU) was to give young activists a space in which they could reflect with like-minded militants on their political practice, "in the light of the Gospels," and thus avoid the overriding of faith by ideology. There is "*an almost total impossibility for a youth to sustain [him]self ideologically* and maintain [his] Christian identity . . . if [he] does not have a space within the pastoral to meet with other militants who are the same level of consciousness and engagement to nourish faith and clarify ideas."[45] Because faith is an essential differentiating moment in the Christian's reflective relationship to theory and practice, the booklet insists, youth groups should at all costs not lose the moment of spirituality, of mysticism or prayer, as some heavily politicized groups of militants were prone to do. Without it, they lose the power of continual criticism, in which the Gospel is "a source of instigation, of provocation." Instead, they turn politics into a totalizing realm that instrumentalizes social relations and strips them of humanity.

The meetings of PJMP, PJE, PJR, and the other more militant branches were charged with providing a space that would combine theological, sociological, spiritual, and human "formation," in which intensely involved young people could combat tendencies toward ideological purism through a continual "revision of life and practice." Most meetings included space for explicit discussion—at times anguished, at other times energizing—of activists' participation in political parties and other kinds of partially overlapping movement sectors. These spaces constituted a form of "public": an interstitial setting, located between the activists' multiple involvements, which was unified and equalized around the idea of religious faith. This public provided a provisional distancing from other kinds of projects and relations, even as it allowed them to be viewed and discussed.

This did not mean that everyone in the church had to share political projects; there was room for political pluralism within the church since what united people was the Gospel, not the political project as such. When acting together outside the church, they should be acting together "as citizens," talking in the name of their "intermediary" organizations and not as the youth pastoral or the church hierarchy. Acting *as citizens*, "they have every right to articulate, to have a more mature intervention in the student, popular, and labor movements, and in the parties."[46] Yet even while acting as citizens, they are still acting *as Christians*. Here they draw on a subtle distinction that fails in English because we have only one word for "as." By acting "enquanto Cristãos"—the strong sense of "as" (or perhaps, "in so far as" they are) Christians—they are representing themselves publicly as religious actors. By acting "como Cristãos"— the weaker form of "as"—they are engaging in secular, civil, lay action, "but inspired by faith."

This distinction is theoretically interesting because it involves a particularly subtle form of identity play: to act *enquanto* (in so far as) means the active foregrounding of an identity, the establishing of the public footing of action. But to act *como* (as) means an active backgrounding; the identity is still there and operative, but not the public grounds for action and relationship. There is an active latency involved—a kind of "private" footing—which may result in the "natural" formation of relationships with others who share a similar latent identity. However, this shared action also involves the (tacit or explicit) agreement to publicly suppress or at least self-consciously restrain the expression of that identity (in this case, religious), while acting on the basis of values implied by that identity.

This subtle distinction is important because it allows for internal heterogeneity or noncomplete overlap in the projects expressed by those who share a common "core" identity, "as Christians." The church is not obliged to "take contradictory positions at times, because of the different options of groups of Christians." On the other hand, the youth are freed from the need to get ecclesial approval for their actions, and thereby "they do not lose . . . the capacity to respond with efficiency and speed to situations that are dynamic and fluid." This in turn, the advisors hoped, would allow Christian youth to retain the "jogo de cintura" (swing of the hips), the improvisational response to emergent situations that Brazilians hold so dear. They worried that many young militants adopted a black-and-white view of the world that kept them from making compromises, negotiating alliances, and seizing opportunities (even if these are partial and therefore "impure"), in short, from engaging in effective politics. Young Catholics should draw on the project and methods that distinguish them "as Christians" even as they learn to pursue politics as "the 'art of the possible.'"

Overall, this 1986 booklet sounds a rather extraordinary call for young Catholic activists both to get their hands dirtied in the political game and to qualify that game with Christian humanist values, a pluralistic ethics and a reflective, generative faith. While this was easier said than done, these guiding ideals formed the basis for the peculiar style of partisan bridging that was rooted in the religious-popular-partisan intersection of the urban peripheries. This style consisted of an integrative approach to multiple involvements that helped to knit together different kinds of grassroots participation. As we have seen, partisan identities were an important component of this style. The bridging narratives supplied by the political parties helped to give discursive consistency to activists' diverse involvements, at the same as the social ties mediated by the parties helped them to feel integrated into a larger historical struggle.

However, because activists were also aware of tensions between the institutional logics of their various involvements, they devoted a good deal of elaborative energy to insisting on the autonomy of these "spheres." While this separation was certainly imperfect—if not impossible—in practice, this discursive emphasis on autonomy schooled activists in a form of reflective self-restraint in negotiating the intersection of their multiple militancies. Partisan bridging for the Catholic youth was not about institutional projection in the civic arena (as it was for the leadership of UNE). Rather, it was about a continual process of collective reflection on the problematics of practice, even as activists pursued several different sets of projects simultaneously as part of the construction of the Kingdom of God on earth.

Partisan Publics and the Play of Identities

The student movement and the Catholic youth pastoral represent two distinct styles of communication that came out of the first decade of Brazil's democratic transition. Both, I have argued, were born at the intersections of multiple institutional sectors, which converged during a critical moment in the early 1980s. In wrestling with the tensions and the opportunities of these intersections, activists from the early cohorts developed skills in building particular kinds of publics.

The students involved in the reconstruction of UNE faced the challenge of rebuilding a *student* organization with a long history of *civic* engagement, even as they were involved in a complex web of renascent *partisan* competition. These three primary identities coexisted uneasily, with considerable internal dissension about how much weight should be given to each. The demands of maintaining a unitary, centralized institution claiming to represent all Brazilian students in the face of evident factionalism required a form of identity play in which activists switched back and forth among those three identities in both strategic and ritualized ways. As we shall see ahead, negotiations between these three identities took center stage in student publics, pushing other, more specialized identities (e.g., professional, religious, race, or gender) to the margins. The resulting style was highly competitive internally yet euphoric in its declarations of unity. Most political elaboration took place inside the factions, while student congresses turned into vehicles for discursive positioning and backstage negotiations. Meanwhile, student leaders engaged in ritualized celebrations of the unified and apartisan UNE, "present in all of the great moments of Brazilian history."

This style of constructing publics trained young activists in a particular set of mediating skills. Internally, activists became skilled in electoral maneuver, bargaining, and coalition building, aimed at control of the centralized organization on behalf of their party or faction. Yearly elections were high stakes and contentious, since UNE was a source of civic status and organizational resources. Once in control of UNE, however, activists could switch from their partisan to their civic hats, downplaying factional identities as they built bridges with other civic organizations and took part in broader publics related to the pressing issues of the day. These publics, however, were precarious, since partisan identities hovered just beneath the surface, threatening to undermine the veneer of apartisan unity projected by student movement leaders.

For activists in the Catholic youth pastoral, the challenge was how to combine their *religious* commitments with participation in the *popular* movements, at the same time as they threw themselves into intense *partisan* activism. The leaders of the youth pastoral saw these as different dimensions of the same struggle, although they struggled with how to integrate these in their daily lives. Recognizing that the institutional logics (and practical demands) of these three forms of activism could overtake and undermine each other, they talked often and forcefully about the autonomy of these different "spheres." But just as the student movement's emphasis on unity marked internal fissures that threatened to divide it, the youth pastoral's frequent reference to autonomy points to a trouble spot—the difficulties in practice of maintaining a separation between these logics in a relational context that was so densely interwoven. In response to the dangers of co-optation and ideological dogmatism, youth leaders and advisors elaborated the idea of faith as the reflective moment, the moment of distance from (or questioning of) all ideologies, which were nevertheless seen as a necessary part of social transformation.

The youth pastoral's emphasis on critical reflection and dialogue gave rise to a very different sort of public, as well as a different set of mediating skills. In their meetings, seminars, and assemblies, the specialized branches of the youth pastoral (especially the more radical PJMP), created publics that drew on the integrative methodology of PJ—linking affective, spiritual, and political growth—even as they elaborated a strong critique of class relations as the basis for social injustice. Radical Catholic activists learned skills in reflective dialogue, consensus-building, and collaborative decision-making, although they had less skill in dealing with internal conflict. They worked enthusiastically within and outside of the church to build an array of social movements, which were often linked through their partisan activism. At the same time, they used church-based publics to discuss the difficulties they faced in combining their multiple militancies. Their style of partisan bridging involved a forthright attempt to use partisan activism to build connections across popular movements, while qualifying their partisan fervor through a religious emphasis on critical reflection and self-restraint.

These two styles of partisan bridging—one highly competitive and institution-oriented, the other more collaborative and embedded in grassroots movement networks—developed in the intersections of the multiple forms of participation that these activists were helping to build in the early transition. Both were highly productive, contributing to the construction of UNE and the Catholic youth pastoral as institutions at the same time as they enabled activists to build relations with other movements and organizations in the expanding field. Young activists from the early cohorts took these styles and skills of communication with them as they moved into other forms of activism in the late 1980s and 1990s. Moreover, aspects of these styles became institutionalized, that is, supported by routinized rules and procedures that sustained these forms of communication over time. I will return to these organizations—and the communicative challenges they faced during the 1990s—in the second part of this book. First, however, I turn to look more closely at one of these forms of partisan bridging in action, as student activists engaged in civic coalition building during the 1992 impeachment movement.

CHAPTER FIVE

Civic Mediation in the 1992 Impeachment Movement

THROUGHOUT THE 1980s and 1990s, Brazilian student activists wrestled with the tension between their student, partisan, and civic identities. For most of the 1980s, the accent was on their partisan affiliations, which, as we have seen, strongly structured the internal debates and battles of student politics. In 1992, civic identities swept into the foreground as the student movement—along with the nation as a whole—converged in a dramatic series of demonstrations for the impeachment on corruption charges of President Fernando Collor de Melo. The impeachment mobilizations allowed the student movement to emerge from the partisan squabbling that had characterized the late 1980s and retake the national spotlight as part of a civic coalition for "Ethics in Politics." In joining this coalition, leftist student leaders were called on to use the skills in "partisan bridging" described in the last chapter. While partisan identities were suppressed, they did not disappear, and even in a state of latency played a critical role in building relations during a moment of national convergence.

President Collor was impeached by the Brazilian Congress in September 1992 for his involvement in a multimillion dollar patronage ring coordinated by his former campaign manager. In a remarkable departure from Brazil's politics as usual, the Movement for Ethics in Politics succeeded in uniting most of Brazil's oppositional and elite actors amidst huge public demonstrations for Collor's impeachment. These demonstrations included colorful and exuberant student rallies, as high school and college students with little previous experience of activism poured into the streets in unexpectedly large numbers. At these carnavalesque protests, young people famously painted their faces yellow and green, the colors of the Brazilian flag, earning them the nickname *caras pintadas*, or "painted faces." Although student leaders were as surprised as anyone at the large turnout, they were quick to claim credit for the mobilizations on behalf of the student organizations and announce the "rebirth" of the student movement in Brazil. The president of UNE (and PCdoB member), Lindberg Farias, was catapulted into public prominence, declaring that the rallies represented the birth of a new "consciousness of citizenship" among youth.

The movement was accompanied by a euphoric celebration of civic identity, capping a decade in which notions of citizenship had been increasingly making their way into public discourse. The term *cidadania* (citizenship) was broad and ambiguous enough to bring together radical student, labor, and popular movement activists—who hailed the term as representing struggles by marginalized groups for political and social rights—with more mainstream professional, NGO, and business actors, some of whom were developing more privatized and institution-oriented understandings of civic responsibility.[1] "Civic" action could encompass general claims to be acting for the "common good" as well as more particularized claims by diverse organizations that considered themselves to be part of "civil society." Often actors would shift back and forth between general and particularized understandings of civic life as they pursued different kinds of social interventions.

During the first decade of the democratic transition, political party activism was also seen as an expression of citizenship as Brazil rebuilt its political institutions. Following the impeachment, however, civic identities increasingly came to be seen in opposition to partisanship and organized politics. The impeachment mobilizations were hailed by the popular media for being "apartisan" and many of the nonactivist youth who showed up in the streets were skeptical if not downright hostile toward partisan politics. Many commentators celebrated the "spontaneity" and "irreverence" of the protests, countering claims that the highly partisan student movement was responsible for the unusually large youth mobilization.

Despite this public skepticism about partisanship, I argue that the partisan affiliations of student leaders did play an important role in the impeachment mobilizations. However, this role had less to do with recruitment and mobilization than with coalition building. The role of partisan identities is subtle and easily missed, often operating behind the scenes in latent or hidden ways. In this chapter, I show how the overlapping memberships of young activists—including partisan affiliations, as well as religious, labor, professional, NGO, and popular movement involvement—enabled forms of mediation that allowed the student movement to emerge from its marginal position and build relations with other civic and political actors in the Movement for Ethics in Politics. At the same time, partisan identities helped to differentiate between the types of mediating roles carried out by student leaders linked to particular parties, bringing some leaders into public prominence while others played supporting or marginal roles.

These forms of mediation provide examples of partisan bridging, that is, the use of partisan identities—often partially or fully suppressed—to build other kinds of relations in a broader civic arena. This often involves complex forms of identity play, as actors foreground and background different dimensions of their multiple affiliations. This type of bridging can be important to the construction of publics, that is, momentarily equalized and synchronized relations among heterogeneous or contending actors, allowing for heightened communication and joint action. The coalition for Ethics in Politics is a great example of such a public, since it combined actors from across the political spectrum, with different partisan associations as well as varying levels of power and resources. Clearly, partisan divisions had to be suppressed in order for the coalition to function, and I expected partisanship to play little or no role in the self-consciously "apartisan" demonstrations. To my surprise, I found that partisan relations worked in a variety of ways to hold the fragile public together. Of course, these same partisan ties also threatened at times to blow it apart—hence the need for skilled leadership and mediation.

In this chapter, I focus on one corner of the impeachment story: the role of the student movement and other types of youth activism as necessary (but not sufficient) contributors to the civic convergence. Leaving aside many of the higher-level negotiations among state, media, and elite actors, I do not try to explain the impeachment per se or tell the whole story of Collor's downfall. I begin by discussing some general theoretical problems posed by what I call "Simmelian mediation," in which relations are constructed across intersecting social circles. I then use Galois lattice analysis to examine the structure of overlapping membership among youth leaders as well as patterns of individual and group participation in events leading up to the impeachment. I flesh out this structural analysis with retrospective interviews with many of the key student leaders involved in the movement. I show that impeachment protests were not as nonpartisan as many of the commentators claimed. Rather, partisan ties among leaders—both suppressed and expressed—constituted the relational sinews of the unexpectedly broad civic coalition.

SIMMELIAN MEDIATION

The role of student organizations in the impeachment movement has evoked considerable disagreement among participants and commentators. Student leaders tried to claim credit for the impeachment rallies by evoking the grand narrative of UNE's "historic role" at the vanguard of Brazilian politics. Other, more skeptical perspectives cite elite interests in removing Collor from power,[2] as well as a media hype that temporarily puffed up UNE's status (and then quickly withdrew its support). Indeed, most commentators give at least partial credit for the youth turnout to a popular television miniseries on *TV-Globo* (called *Anos Rebeldes*, or "Rebellious Years") that romanticized the student opposition to the dictatorship of the 1960s. This miniseries began a week after the opening of the Parliamentary Commission of Inquiry to investigate the corruption charges and finished the week of the first major student demonstrations against Collor. This nostalgia for the 1960s as well as the euphoric media coverage certainly helped to bring many nonactivist young people to the impeachment rallies, on top of widespread frustration with Collor's government.[3]

Both the heroic and skeptical perspectives place a heavy emphasis on UNE's symbolic role in the mobilizations, although this is variously attributed either to the organization's historic legacy or to media manipulation. No doubt, the romanticized history of UNE made it a convenient mobilizing vehicle for elites interested in deposing Collor, just as the student organizations sought to capitalize on the unexpected glow of media attention. However, both perspectives overplay the role of UNE (along with UNE's charismatic president, Lindberg Farias) and downplay the participation of other kinds of organizations and leaders involved in building the Movement for Ethics in Politics. Without the efforts of this broader civic coalition—and its role in instigating and supporting the congressional investigations into Collor's corruption scheme—it is doubtful whether Brazil's elites would have abandoned Collor, even as popular support for his impeachment increased. As Luiz, a young PT activist who also participated in the bankworkers' union, pointed out, many different kinds of organizations contributed to the cross-sectoral mobilization:

> I disagree with UNE, with Lindberg and all, because UNE wasn't the only one responsible. UNE and UBES (the national high school association) never were the only ones responsible for that whole process. A chain of organizations carried it, obviously with support by the media. You have CUT (the labor central) providing space, material, pamphlets, using the labor unions. You have the OAB (the bar association) organizing one sector. The church organized another sector. The problem is that one organization appeared to channel it all.[4]

In the construction of such complex, multisectoral publics, the question of political mediation is critical. How do members of diverse organizations and sectors come into contact with one another, negotiate alliances, and coordinate joint activities? On a cultural level, how do they arrive at broader or narrower representations of their identities and projects, as they attempt to collaborate with very different kinds of actors? Some student leaders who were closest to the articulation of the impeachment movement were aware that links in the organizational chain were often forged through backstage channels, far from the hoopla of more visible events. This process was described to me by Marcelo, president of the prestigious Law Students' Association of the University of São Paulo during the impeachment mobilizations. He recalled these backstage negotiations several years later, from the standpoint of his governmental position as an aide to the state secretary of justice: "It seems pretentious, but it's interesting, in the government today I see this very clearly, how many actions that are visible start with a conversation in a bar. Sometimes you have an idea, the other guy ripens that idea, and in another meeting, he plays that idea and reworks it another manner."

Marcelo's description of these partially hidden discussions highlights the discursive process that Brazilians call "articulation." This is a near ubiquitous term in Brazilian political life that does not quite have an English equivalent. People are continuously going off to "articulate" an idea or project or plan for collaboration with a proposed counterpart, often in a partially hidden corner or hallway or bar (these huddled negotiations have an untranslatable name, *conchavo*, which is also ubiquitous). We can think about this as the "talking of the tie," the spinning of the discursive connections between two or more partially segmented groups or individuals. As Marcelo describes, the "ripening" of ideas jumps between people and contexts, moving into new venues as the seeds of projects are developed into active proposals.

This image of backstage negotiations taking place in a bar or other nonofficial, partially hidden venues meshes well with our conventional understanding of brokerage. Brokerage is generally described as involving links between otherwise disconnected groups that make possible more visible forms of collaboration and alliance. Brokers often gain personal rewards from their capacity to link structurally disconnected actors, to bridge "structural holes," as Ron Burt has argued. In a classic formulation, Peter Marsden defines brokerage as a process "by which intermediary actors facilitate transactions between other actors lacking access to or trust in one another."[5]

However, traditional conceptions of brokerage are problematic on two counts. First, they generally assume complete or near complete disconnection between subgroups, in which a single intermediary controls the link between them.[6] They seldom look at cases in which subgroups overlap. In the case of Brazilian youth activism, overlapping memberships play a critical role in cross-sectoral mediation. Sometimes an entire sector (e.g., the student or labor movement) may share membership in another sector (e.g., political parties or religious groups). In other cases the overlap may be more limited, although equally (or more) powerful, as when smaller professional or church groups bring their political and cultural influence to a broad-based civic or community movement.

Second, traditional accounts of brokerage fail to take into account the social settings in which actors come together. Mediation is not only influenced by shared memberships, but also, perhaps more crucially, by coparticipation in events. Sometimes actors attend events together with all or most of their fellow group members, and sometimes they attend alone, or in small clusters. Moreover, some events have strong cross-sectoral overlap—with many different sectors represented—while others are more limited, restricted to just one or two sectors. Often, participants know each other from several such settings, in which they might hold different positions or leadership roles. In such situations, the question of political representation—who speaks in the name of whom—is tenuous and negotiable, providing leadership opportunities and conflicts that come into play in public encounters.

In analyzing student participation in the impeachment coalition, I focus on what I call "Simmelian mediation": mediation across partially overlapping subgroups in which actors use their multiple identities to build relations and elaborate joint projects. This mediation takes a number of forms. First, it can involve direct attempts to forge alliances between partially disconnected groups, a process that I join the Brazilians in calling *articulation*. Often actors make use of submerged or latent ties as they attempt to build connections across social and discursive distances. Second, such mediation can involve indirect flows of information and ideas across partially overlapping social settings, in ways that contribute to the *amplification* of a movement, even if it does not involve explicit alliance building. For example, a few student activists attending a civic or labor event can bring back news of that event to their student movement colleagues, which may eventually bring more students into civic or labor organizing.

While these first two forms of mediation take place in situations in which subgroups are only partially overlapping, other kinds of mediation are needed when overlap is stronger. When strongly superimposed subgroups create internal cleavages (for example, when student or professional groups are divided along partisan or religious lines), some form of *coordination* is needed to distribute resources and responsibilities across those divisions. In addition, sometimes divisions within extremely heterogeneous settings—for example, in broad civic convergences in which many sectors come together at events—can be overcome by what I call *symbolic bridging*, in which particular actors serve as the symbolic embodiments of larger collectivities. We shall see ahead how Lindberg Farias served in this kind of symbolic role, as the metonymic embodiment of the new civic identity of youth.

These different kinds of mediation all require that actors engage in various types of identity play, as they maneuver among their multiple affiliations. In some cases, they may conflate their identities, playing off of the ambiguity of whom they are "speaking as" (i.e, as a student, a partisan, or a church member), as they target multiple audiences at once. They may also engage in what I call "generality shifting": sliding up and down between the levels of generality at which they are speaking, for example, as they claim to represent their particular student organization, the student sector more generally, or civil society as a whole. At other times, they may compartmentalize their identities, attempting to separate and steer between their multiple affiliations in complex relational settings. They can engage in "identity qualifying," indicating whom they are *speaking as* at any moment, that is, "as UNE" or "as a party member" or "as a citizen."[7]

Such discursive mechanisms highlight the ambiguity and multivocality of the mediator position, that is, the need to speak in multiple voices as settings and audiences shift. Actors participate in many different kinds of events, with and without comembers. There are therefore numerous strands of their relations that they can put into play in any given situation. This creates opportunities for what Padgett and Ansell have called "robust action," that is, multiply targeted (and elusively defined) activity on the part of strategically embedded actors, based on the "fact that single actions can be interpreted coherently from multiple perspectives simultaneously, the fact that single actions can be moves in many games at once, and the fact that public and private motivations cannot be parsed."[8] Such actors may be able to make use of the multivocality of their bridging positions to forge alliances and coordinate action, despite wide differences in projects and positions.

As we shall see ahead, all of these forms of mediation were in play as the student movement engaged with the broader civic coalition. In the early stages of the movement against Collor, the student movement was still partially segmented from the rest of the political field, with only a few student activists attending civic events. These few bridgers were thus able to play important roles in articulating and amplifying the movement. As the impeachment movement converged, more student leaders began to attend events along with an increasingly broad array of actors, including religious, labor, NGO, professional, and business groups. The negotiation of partisan identities in these increasingly "civic" settings posed particular mediating challenges. Such settings required intensive cross-sectoral coordination, but also presented opportunities for symbolic bridging. To understand these processes, we first need to examine how the student movement struggled with its own highly partisan character in the years leading up to the impeachment.

RETHINKING STUDENT POLITICS IN THE COLLOR YEARS

While the impeachment movement seemed to signal a sudden shift in student-civic relations, this shift was preceded by a period of internal evaluation and restructuring that helped to set the stage for UNE's re-emergence into the public spotlight. The changes of the *Repensando* period (1989–91) resulted from the attempts of student leaders to wrestle with the destructive effects of partisan dispute on the movement. As I described in chapter 4, by the mid-1980s there was growing dissatisfaction with the factional entrenchment of the movement, which some thought stripped the movement of the more effervescent, creative, and reflective dialogue that had characterized the late 1970s. At the same time, the late 1980s were a period of intense partisan activity in the Brazilian left, as activists—including students—were caught up in a grueling electoral schedule that brought many opposition candidates into local, state, and national office. As a result, even those activists who were most ambivalent about the partisan dynamic of student politics were sucked into its competitive pressures.

In 1986, partisan tension reached a boiling point as the PT and other opposition forces accused the PCdoB leadership of fraudulent election practices in the attempt to return UNE to nationwide direct elections (abandoned since 1980).[9] Amidst accusations and counteraccusations, the PT resolved not to recognize the new PCdoB leadership of UNE. The PCdoB decided to take office anyway, to avoid dismantling UNE. The PT did not participate in the seminar on the Constitutional Assembly that the PCdoB leaders organized in 1987, further undermining the UNE's attempt to project a civic face. In 1987, factions linked to the PT won control of UNE, which they held until 1991, initiating a series of thoughtful discussions on the "Restructuring of the Student Movement." In 1991, the PCdoB won back control of UNE, maintaining control the following year as the impeachment scandal was heating up.

During this period, three important changes helped to create the conditions for student participation in the civic coalition:

1. *Debating reforms.* First, both the PT and the PCdoB began carrying out parallel conversations on how to reform the student movement. A common refrain during this period was that UNE and other student organizations were facing a "crisis of representativity." UNE was criticized for being locked into outdated ideological discourse and bureaucratic organizational forms, while becoming increasingly distant from the student population. In their internal forums, PT student factions debated proposals for structural reform, including measures to decentralize the organization, return to direct (rather than congressional) elections, and increase

participation of the student base. They also began to focus on course-based organizing as a means of maintaining a closer connection to the professional concerns of students as well as linking students to popular movements (e.g., in health, education, communication, land reform, and other areas). From the PT's perspective, they tragically lost control of UNE just when their projects for reform were coming to fruition. After the 1991 defeat, many PT activists lost interest in UNE, instead devoting their attention to internal factional struggles as well as to their involvement in other kinds of popular movements.

At the same time, the PCdoB was rethinking its intervention in youth politics. Within their associated youth organization, the Union of Socialist Youth (UJS), PCdoB activists wrestled with the collapse of the Soviet Union and the former Soviet republics. They discussed how to adapt to what they called the "new mentality" among youth, oriented toward culture, technology, sports, and travel rather than traditional leftist ideology. While they still clearly advocated socialism (at least within UJS, if not within UNE), they began to shift away from more doctrinal Marxist formulations toward a discourse emphasizing citizenship and "the rights of youth." This shift influenced the PCdoB's choice of candidates for president of UNE, especially the attractive and charismatic young Lindberg Farias in 1992. Lindberg's choice reflected a conscious attempt to bring a "cara nova" (new face) to the student movement, one which they hoped would help UNE (and the PCdoB) break out of the activist ghetto.

2. *Electoral restructuring.* In response to these tensions and debates, student activists proposed structural means of overcoming the partisan polarization within UNE. In 1989, the Congress of UNE voted to switch from a "winner-take-all" system to one of proportional representation. This shift resulted from a spirit of good will between partisan factions that accompanied the 1989 presidential elections, in which the PT, PCdoB, and other leftist parties united to support Lula da Silva in an exhilarating campaign that nearly brought him to the presidency. The spirit of collaboration at the national level filtered down into student politics, enabling alliances that would have been impossible the year before.

As a result of this switch, competing political forces were represented in the directorate in accordance with the proportion of votes they received in UNE's national congress. This intensified the bargaining component of student congresses, leading to flexible and shifting alliances, especially among smaller political forces. It also meant that once elected, the various forces had to work together in the day-to-day operations of the organization. The PCdoB proved particularly adept at working collaboratively in UNE's directorate while it was under PT control, helping to set the stage for retaking control a few years later.

3. *Shifting alliances.* This shift in voting structure generated changing partisan alignments that would prove important for UNE's participation in the civic coalition. The PCdoB students in particular made a number of alliances in order to win back control of UNE. First, the PCdoB allied with the MR-8, a nationalist-revolutionary group inside the mainstream PMDB, known for its strong-arm tactics in the student movement. Second, and more important for the impeachment, the PCdoB allied with the PSDB (Party of Brazilian Social Democracy). Composed of "social democratic" intellectuals, politicians, and technocrats, the PSDB was a relatively new center-left party that split from the PMDB in 1987. While the PSDB would grow in national importance in the next decade—electing a president, Fernando Henrique Cardoso in 1996—it was a very small force in the student movement. The PSDB youth were just wetting their feet in student politics, unsure of their reception by the more radical activists.

As a result of these changes, UNE's leadership in 1992 was composed of activists linked to all of the major political forces. While the PCdoB held majority control of the directorate, the PT's major internal blocs were also represented, along with the MR-8 and PSDB. Many student leaders also had other affiliations that directly or indirectly linked them to labor, religious, NGO, and professional movements. However, despite these external ties, many radical student activists—including some in the PCdoB—were still deeply skeptical of "civic" discourse and action, which they considered too "institutional" (i.e., insufficiently revolutionary). As I will show below, the participation of UNE in the Movement for Ethics in Politics was enabled by the active mediating efforts of the PSDB activists, particularly during the early stages of the movement. This mediation worked in two directions: the PSDB activists used their submerged partisan ties to construct bridges from the radical student movement to the more moderate civic opposition, while also serving as discursive coaches to the more radical leadership of UNE, helping them to tone down their rhetoric and adopt a more effective bridging discourse. Moreover, PCdoB and PT activists positioned at the intersection of student, partisan, and civic groups also helped to articulate, amplify, and coordinate the movement in different ways.

MULTIPLE IDENTITIES: OVERLAPPING MEMBERSHIPS AMONG MOVEMENT LEADERS

The first step in studying the dynamics of mediation in the impeachment movement is to look more closely at the structure of overlapping affiliations. In 1997, I talked to as many youth leaders as I could find who had been involved in organizing the impeachment mobilizations five years

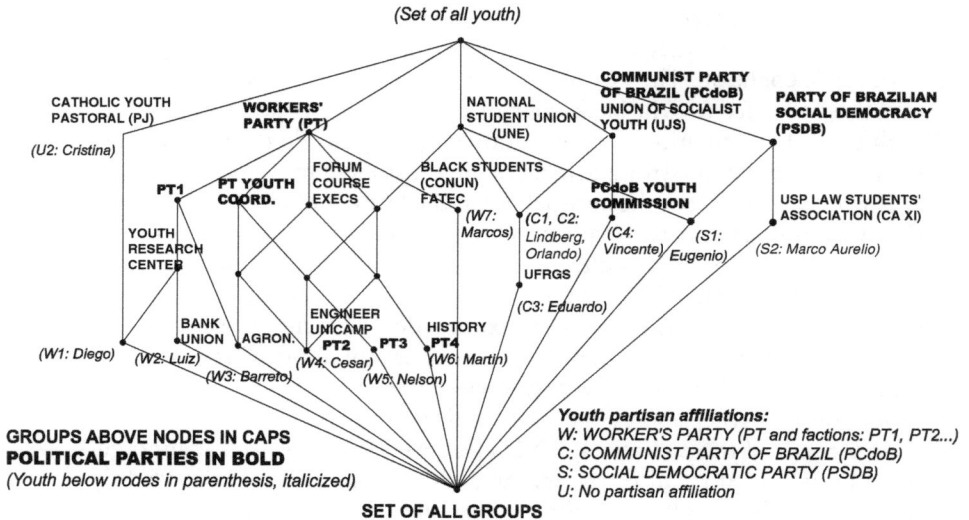

Figure 5.1. Youth leaders by groups lattice

earlier.[10] I collected questionnaires with their affiliation histories as well as their participation in civic, student movement, and other related events in the period leading to the impeachment. Most of the respondents also sat down for longer interviews, which inform the detailed accounts below.

The structure of overlapping memberships among these leaders can be represented using the technique of Galois lattice analysis introduced in chapter 3. Figure 5.1 (above) depicts organizational affiliations among fourteen respondents during the period leading up to the impeachment. As with the previous lattices, this diagram is easier to interpret than it appears at first. Above the nodes (in capital letters) are the names of the organizations that the leaders belonged to at the time of the impeachment; below the nodes (italicized, in parenthesis) are the names of the activists, along with a reference to the political party to which they belonged. (CA or DCE followed by a university refers to a department or universitywide student organization; EC refers to a course-based organization, for example in agronomy, engineering or history; PT-1, 2, 3, 4 refer to internal PT tendencies.) Political parties and internal partisan groupings (factions, youth commissions) are highlighted in bold.

The lattice can be read in two directions, beginning at the top or the bottom. If you read down from any of the organizations, following the lines down vertically and diagonally, you can find all of the leaders who belonged to that organization. For example, reading down from the Workers' Party (PT), we see seven affiliated activists (Diego, Luiz, Barreto, Cesar, Nelson, Martín, and Marcos). If you read up from the leaders, you can find all of the organizations to which they belong. For example, Luiz belonged to the Bankworkers' Union, a Youth Research Center, an internal PT tendency, and the PT. We can also see the points of overlap. Luiz shares membership in the research organization, a PT tendency, and the PT with Diego, but not Diego's comembership with Cristina in the Catholic youth pastoral. The organizations near the top of the lattice have more affiliated activists, while the activists near the bottom belong to more groups.

Three main structural features of this lattice are of interest to this analysis. First, note the strong structuring effects of political party membership. All the activists except one belonged to a political party (and that activist, Cristina of the Catholic youth pastoral, joined the PT shortly after the impeachment). Seven activists belonged to the PT, and six of these also belonged to internal factions of varying degrees of radicalism. Three of these (Barreto, Cesar, and Nelson) also belonged to the PT's youth coordination. Four of the activists—including UNE's president Lindberg Farias—belonged to the PCdoB, and all of these also belonged to the Union of Socialist Youth (UJS). Vincente was also a member of the PCdoB's youth commission. Finally, two of the leaders were associated with the PSDB: Eugênio, a director of UNE; and Marcelo, the president of the student association of the USP Law Faculty (CA XI de Agosto).

Second, UNE served as a bridging context, linking activists from all three parties. UNE's leadership consisted of a national directorate, consisting of thirty to forty leaders from around the country, proportionally distributed among the factions. The day-to-day operations of UNE were run by a smaller executive committee, consisting of eleven high-level leaders, mostly based in São Paulo or Rio. Lindberg, Renato, and Eduardo were all PCdoB leaders in the directorate, with Renato joining Lindberg in the executive. Nelson and Martín represented the PT on the executive, both as members of left Trotskyist factions. Cesar was a lower-ranked member of the directorate, from one of the more moderate PT factions. And Eugênio represented the PSDB on UNE's executive committee.

Third, the lattice shows that that the Workers' Party youth had the most sectorally diversified array of affiliations, beyond the student movement and political parties. Their affiliations included religious, labor, research, antidiscrimination, and course-based associations, in addition to the partisan and student involvements also seen among the PCdoB and PSDB youth. Most were involved in three or more sectors, and can thus be classified as what I called in chapter 2 bridging leaders or explorers, with broad span across sectors, sometimes accompanied by deep involvement in one or two. In contrast, activists from the other parties appear to fall into the categories of entrenched leaders or focused activists, concentrating their involvements more or less deeply within just one or two sectors (in this case, within the student movement and political parties).

What might this mapping of identities allow us to predict about the mediating roles of these leaders in the impeachment movement? From this lattice, we might reasonably expect that the Workers' Party youth would have the best shot at playing an important mediating role in the movement, since so many of its members belonged to other nonstudent organizations (religious, labor, professional, research, etc.) that were part of the Movement for Ethics in Politics. The diversification of affiliations among PT leaders might give them stronger bridging ties to other coalition members, thus leading to prominence in the movement. In contrast, the PCdoB and PSDB youth seemed more focused on student and partisan involvements, and thus might be predicted to be more isolated within the student milieu.

Although this explanation is structurally plausible from the perspective of this lattice, it is clearly wrong historically. Despite the breadth and popularity of the PT (repeatedly indicated in polls as having the highest level of support among university students), and despite the prominence of national PT leaders in the congressional inquiry against President Collor, the PT student leaders were nearly invisible in the euphoric media coverage that accompanied the impeachment mobilizations. They were eclipsed by leaders of the PCdoB, such as UNE president Lindberg Farias, as well as, to a lesser extent, by those of the PSDB. Since reasons for the prominence of these leaders cannot be found simply in the breadth of their memberships, or in the national role of their political parties (minimal for the PCdoB, and small but growing for the PSDB), we need to look beyond static membership to a more temporal analysis of their participation in particular movement settings.

Time Line of Events: From Articulation to Mobilization

To understand the temporal dynamics of mediation, I examine the participation of these fourteen leaders in a series of events leading up to the impeachment, along with the representation at those events of a broad array of civic organizations. Table 5.1 describes a set of twenty-seven events spanning the ten-month period from November 1991, when Brazil saw a surge in cross-sectoral articulation against Collor, through the congressional vote on the impeachment at the end of September 1992.

These events were drawn from organizational documents, newspaper reports, and interviews with participants. At all of the events, the growing critique of the Collor regime was explicitly thematized, although the events had different sectoral characters. (By "sectoral character," I mean the primary self-designation of the event [e.g., as a civic, labor, or student event], although representatives of other sectors may have been present.) Some were self-consciously "civic" (i.e., cross-sectoral forums aimed at

TABLE 5.1
Impeachment related events

#	Name	Place	Sectoral character	Date
T1: Articulation				
1	Movement Option for Brazil (MOB)	São Paulo	Civic/Nonpartisan	11/nov/91
2	Council of Base Orgs.(CONEB)	São Paulo	Student	4-8/dec/91
3	Less Salary and More Taxes	São Paulo	Labor/Business	9/dec/91
4	*Fora Collor* Now	São Paulo	Labor	12/dec/91
5	Vigil Against Recession	São Paulo	Civic/Partisan	12/dec/91
6	National Day of Struggle/CUT	National/SP	Labor	13/mar/92
7	Day of Protest/*Fora Collor*	National/SP	Student	8/april/92
8	International Workers' Day	National/SP	Labor	1/may/92
9	42nd Congress of UNE	Niteroi/Rio	Student	28-31/may/92
T2: Denunciation				
10	Echo of the Oppressed	Rio	NGO/Labor/Partisan	10/jun/92
11	Vigil for Ethics in Politics	Brasília	Civic/Partisan	23/jun/92
12	Rallies against Collor	National/SP	Student/Partisan	3-10/jul/92
13	Campaign rally/Suplicy-PT	São Paulo	Partisan	5/jul/92
14	Annual science conference	São Paulo	Research/Student	12-17/jul/92
15	Launch/Mov.Ethics in Politics (MEP)	São Paulo	Civic/Partisan	13/jul/92
16	Vigil for Land	São Paulo	Popular/Labor	24/jul/92
17	Rallies for Ethics in Politics	National/SP	Civic/Partisan	jul/aug/92
T3: Mobilization				
18	Students' Day March	São Paulo	Student	11/aug/92
19	*Fora Collor* March	Rio	Student/Civic	14/aug/92
20	Battle of the Colors	National/SP	Civic/Nonpartisan	16/aug/92
21	Impeachment rally	São Paulo	Student/Civic	25/aug/92
22	Metalworkers' march	São Paulo	Labor	26/aug/92
23	Congressional demonstrations	Brasília	Civic/Partisan	aug-sept/92
24	Impeachment demonstrations	National/SP	Civic/Partisan	aug-sept/92
25	Rally Against Corruption	São Paulo	Labor/business	11/sept/92
26	Unified Act for Impeachment	São Paulo	Civic/Partisan	18/sept/92
27	Impeachment vote	National/SP	Civic/Partisan	29/sept/92

| 1 | 2,3,4,5 | | | | 6 | 7 | 8 | 9 | 10 | 11 | 12,14, 16 | 18,20,21,23, 25, 27 |
| | | | | | | | | | | | 13, 15 | 17   19   22 24, 26 |

| Nov 91 | D | Jan 92 | F | M | A | M | J | J | A | S |
| | | | | | | * | ** | | *** | **** |

ARTICULATION   DENUNCIATION   MOBILIZATION

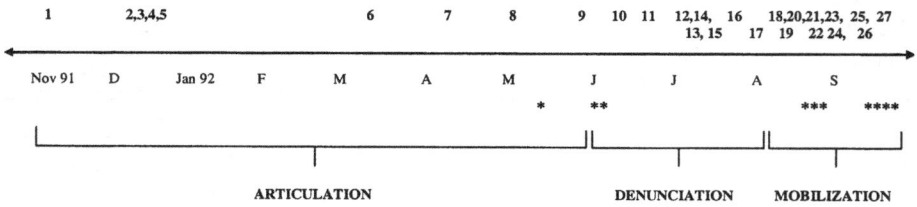

*   First public denunciations of corruption against President Collor, made by his brother, Pedro Collor, May 10, 1992.
**   Installation of a Parliamentary Commission of Inquiry to investigate corruption charges, June 1, 1992.
***   Approval of Parliamentary Commission report confirming corruption by Collor and associates, August 27, 1992.
**** National Congress votes for impeachment, September 29, 1992.

Figure 5.2. Time line of the impeachment movement

dialogue and action related to a jointly defined "public good") while others were more specialized (e.g., a science conference, an environmental rally, a land vigil, a labor demonstration) but served as settings for a general expression of opposition to the Collor regime. (In the case of "civic" events, I have also noted whether they were understood to be "civic/nonpartisan" [no parties were represented] or "civic/partisan" [many parties were represented, although none were formally leading it].) In addition, I have included some events that were internal to the student movement (for example, the national councils and congresses of UNE), which were important sites for elaborating the student movement's anti-Collor stance.

These events can be divided into three different stages, based on major turning points in the movement. These phases, and their corresponding events, are mapped in figure 5.2 (below). The first period, which I call the *Articulation* period, runs from November 1991 through May 1992. It begins with a cluster of forums in late 1991 in which usually segmented actors were coming together to discuss a growing sense of dissatisfaction with the Collor government (that is, they were beginning to "articulate" the discursive linkages that would eventually serve as the basis for the anti-Collor coalition). The second period, which I call the *Denunciation* phase, begins on June 1 with the instauration of a Parliamentary Commission of Inquiry (CPI) to investigate accusations of corruption in the Collor government. The third phase, *Mobilization,* begins on August 11 with the first major student rally that touched off the subsequent huge protest demonstrations across the country. While all three periods were characterized by some degree of articulation, denunciation, and mobilization, I use the names to signal the dominant mode of interaction in each period.

For each event, I compiled information on which organizations from Brazil's broader civic arena were officially represented.[11] I also asked the fourteen leaders which events they attended. From these two types of data—group representation and individual attendance—I composed a somewhat more complex set of lattices for each time period.[12] In what follows, I give a schematized version of those lattices, showing which students leaders and organizations were present at different kinds of events in the three periods leading up the impeachment.

T1: ARTICULATION (NOVEMBER 1991 TO MAY 1992)

Surprised as Brazil was by the outbreak of student demonstrations in August 1992, the protests did not erupt from nowhere onto the political scene. Dissatisfaction with the Collor government had been growing steadily, not only in the popular grumbling and semiresigned complaints common to Brazilian political culture, but also in organized public forums. In the closing months of 1991, six months before the major corruption denunciations against Collor, Brazil saw a surge of organized activities drawing attention to mounting problems in the Collor government and by extension, in the country as a whole.

While these problems had many dimensions, among the most vivid were two failed attempts at economic stabilization. On taking office in 1990, Collor had attempted to vanquish inflation with a "single shot" by freezing savings accounts and implementing a package of monetary reforms (to be accompanied by the privatization of state industries and an opening of the economy to foreign investment). However, by January 1991, inflation was back up to 20 percent per month. A second economic package in early 1991 also failed to control inflation, while leading to industrial recession and growing unemployment, accompanied by painful cuts in social programs. Meanwhile, several minor scandals among Collor appointees and family members were beginning to wear away at the president's populist self-marketing as an anticorruption crusader, through which he had first gained popularity in the late 1980s. Two years after taking office, Collor's originally high popularity had plummeted. At the same time, his congressional base of support was growing irritated with his use of "provisional measures" to impose legislation by decree, leaving him increasingly isolated politically.

Amidst this climate, organized sectors of Brazilian society began to use public forums to call more vociferously for an "alternative" to the current state of affairs. These events, along with the sectors that participated in them, are depicted in the schematized lattice in figure 5.3 (below).[13] The figure classifies the nine events of the *Articulation* period into five main types (in the boxes), based on the self-defined character of the event. The lattice also shows the sectors represented at each (in italics below the events). Below the list of sectors are student groups (in the solid circles)

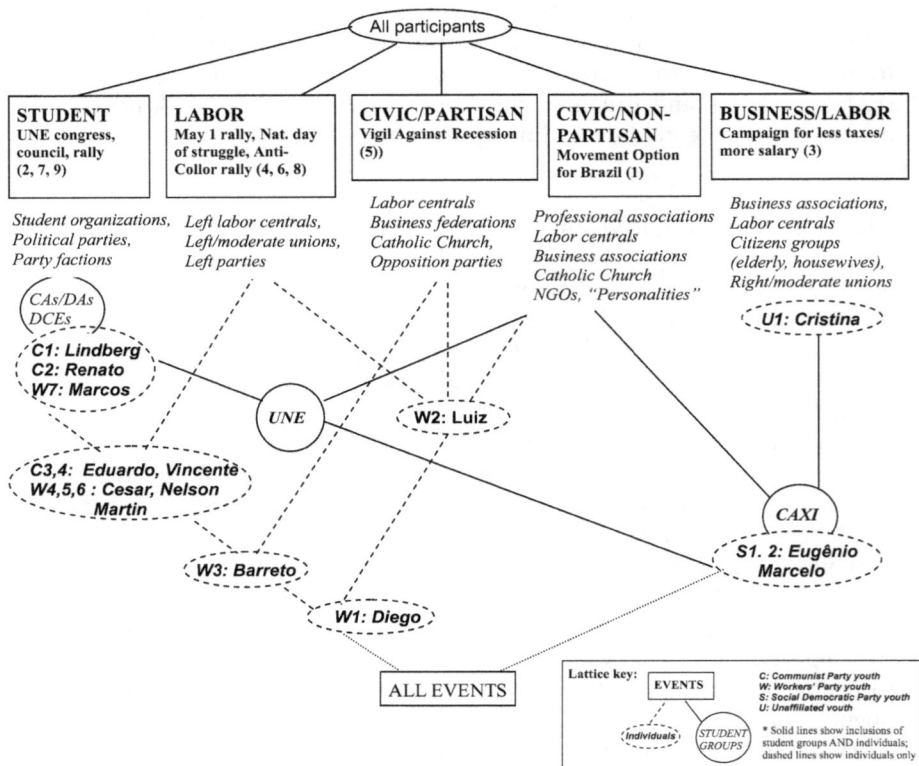

Figure 5.3. T1. *Articulation* lattice (youth and groups at events)

as well as individual leaders (in dotted circles) that were present at each set of events. If you read down from a set of events, you see all of the activists and student groups that participated. If you read up from an activist or group, you see all of the events in which they participated.

This lattice shows a pattern of partial segmentation between student and civic milieus, strongly structured by partisan affiliations. First, note that almost all of the activists attended the student movement events on the left side of the lattice, which included the council and Congress of UNE (events 2 and 9) as well as an April anti-Collor rally (7). A large number of PT and PCdoB activists also attended events organized by the labor movement (although neither of the two PSDB leaders did). However, only a handful of the leaders attended the broader civic events on the center and right side of the lattice. These included three PT members—Barreto, Diego, and Luiz, all from the same centrist tendency of the PT—

as well as the two PSDB leaders and Cristina, the one nonpartisan youth. Note that the PSDB leaders—Eugênio and Marcelo—did not join the PT activists at the civic/partisan Vigil Against Recession (5) in the center of the lattice, organized by Brazil's left-wing labor central (CUT) with participation by church, partisan, professional, and business leaders. The PSDB activists only attended the explicitly nonpartisan events, including the launch of the Movement Option for Brazil (1), as well as an antitax forum organized by business groups and the right-wing labor centrals (3). The Movement Option for Brazil is especially notable in that it was the only broader civic event at which UNE was officially represented, along with the Law Students' Association of the University of São Paulo (CA XI de Agosto). The Movement Option for Brazil was a civic forum involving a loose coalition of intellectuals, politicians, and leaders of professional, labor, religious, and business groups, charged with finding alternative solutions to Brazil's "crisis."

By serving as official representatives of the student movement at civic events which most student leaders did not attend, the PSDB activists were ideally positioned to contribute to the articulation of a student-civic link. As I show below, they helped to build a bridge between the radical student movement and the more moderate civic forum, thus legitimating student representation in the civic movement. But they did this, somewhat ironically, based on their partisan ties to the leaders of the nonpartisan civic forum. Meanwhile, within the forums of the student movement, activists from competing factions were working to create a bridging discourse that would allow them to work together in the coordination of opposition to the Collor regime. To show these mechanisms, in action, I turn to the activists' own accounts of these events. I focus on the two events that were most critical in preparing the interface between the civic and student milieus: the Movement Option for Brazil (MOB) and UNE's National Council of Base Organizations (CONEB).

The Movement Option for Brazil (MOB)

The first student leader among my respondents to participate in the Movement Option for Brazil was Marcelo, director of the Centro Acadêmico XI de Agosto (CA XI, the Law Students' Association of the University of São Paulo). Founded in 1903, CA XI was the oldest student association in Brazil, playing an historic role in the development of Brazilian political leadership.[14] In the second half of 1991, Marcelo and a fellow CA XI director, Roberto, began attending informal meetings of a group that was discussing the need for a civic movement to develop alternatives for Brazil. The meetings were hosted by the Latin American Institute (ILAM), a think tank founded by intellectuals linked to the PSDB. According to Marcelo, they began to participate because of their political party connections to the organizers: Roberto was a leader in the youth wing of the PSDB and Marcelo was a nonaffiliated sympathizer.[15]

Despite this PSDB connection, the nascent movement insisted that it was a nonpartisan forum of intellectuals and prominent individuals (not yet organizations) concerned not with winning elections, but with "the future of Brazil." In addition to intellectuals, key organizers included former government officials and civic-minded business leaders. At that time, Marcelo said,

> Doubts about the morality of the Collor government were beginning to appear more consistently. It was no longer just a partisan thing, since nonpartisan sectors of society were beginning to question [the problems in the Collor government]. There were various people, who, despite being from political parties, were considered as lucid people, consequential, who were not raising moral issues for electoral purposes, but as more fundamental statements about ethics in government.

Note the identity qualifying in play here: participants were attending "as lucid people," not as partisans, despite their partisan affiliation. Nevertheless, this civic norm of nonpartisan intellectuality grew partly out of a partisan tussle between the PSDB and the PT for control of the space (and style) of social critique. Marcelo told me that the idea of the organizers was "to create an ivory tower, a critical intellectual space," in which social criticism would be loosened from the ideological positioning that they associated with the PT. "The idea in the beginning was that you had to disconnect this from the PT. . . . This was a movement of independent intellectuals who questioned the moral and administrative directions of the federal administration. It was something more institutional."

Although organizers took great pains to emphasize the movement's nonpartisan nature, they did invite major party leaders to the launching ceremony, held on November 11 at the Catholic University of São Paulo (PUC). However, these were invited as public figures rather than as formal representatives of their parties; no political parties signed the opening manifesto. The manifesto describes the movement as composed of "organizations of diverse tendencies and persons of different thoughts, looking for democratic alternatives to overcome the crisis." Included among the dignitaries were Lula da Silva, president of the PT, along with former governor André Franco Montoro and Senator Fernando Henrique Cardoso, both of the PSDB. Also present were leaders of Brazil's three competing labor centrals (CUT, CGT, and Força Sindical) as well as the major business federations, the National Conference of Brazilian Bishops

(CNBB), and major professional groups, such as the Bar Association (OAB) and the Brazilian Press Association (ABI).

While more than thirty organizations signed the manifesto, the only student organization among them was CA XI. UNE was not an official signer, although it was represented at the launching ceremony. Marcelo recalls that UNE was invited to the meetings of MOB fairly late in the process: "When we began to feel consistency in the movement . . . we entered in contact with UNE." Representatives of UNE came to a few early planning meetings (including Lindberg Farias, then secretary-general). However, no high-level PCdoB leaders were present at the opening ceremony; instead UNE was represented by Eugênio of the PSDB, who at the time was a low-ranking member of UNE's directorate. He recalled, "I went to the (leadership) table as UNE. I was the only member of UNE at that opening." He attributes this position to skepticism among the more ideological student leaders about this sort of broad civic forum. "It's strange, they resisted participating in these movements. That thing about it being 'institutional.' . . . They don't have time for this. They end up prioritizing other things."[16]

In representing the student movement at the Movement Option for Brazil, the more moderate, institutionally oriented PSDB students were helping to articulate a connection between the partially segmented student and civic milieus. Their partisan affiliations—although suppressed at the event itself—drew them to settings in which very few other student leaders were present. This allowed them to control the student representation, presenting a less confrontational face as they articulated a role for the student movement in the nascent civic forum.

The MOB is a good example of what I have been calling a "public": a heterogeneous space for cross-sectoral discussion, based on the provisional equalization of actors with very different ideological positions and access to power and resources. The narratives of the movement were not limited to a narrowly ethical discourse, but rather included a more substantive set of social issues, ranging from poverty and education to political-institutional reform. However, despite a generally favorable media reception, by early 1992 the MOB began to lose steam, undermined by its own focus on talk rather than action. As Marcelo recalled, "It was always the same people going to the meetings, to discuss the ethereal, nothing concrete." Nevertheless, the MOB laid the basis for the formation several months later of the Movement for Ethics in Politics, which involved many of the same actors. The MOB also set the precedent for the participation of the student movement—and of UNE in particular—in larger civic events, among civic and elite leaders who otherwise might have resisted the more stridently radical student activists.

National Council of Base Organizations (CONEB)

If most student activists stayed away from the Movement Option for Brazil, this did not mean that they were unconcerned with problems in the Collor government. In the first week of December 1991, the student movement held a major student council at the University of São Paulo in which they approved a call for Collor's ouster, although not many people knew about it outside of the student movement and the opposition parties. The Ninth CONEB (National Council of Base Organizations) was regarded as "historic" because it involved about four hundred local grassroots leaders from the universities, instead of the higher-level leaders involved in most of UNE's deliberative councils.

Nearly all of my respondents participated in the CONEB, with the exception of a few of the nonstudent youth. Despite an official focus on science and the environment, the hottest item under discussion (amidst the usual resolutions regarding funding for universities, tuition hikes, and an "intransigent defense of national sovereignty") was which position the student movement should adopt in expressing its opposition to the Collor government. There were three main positions: (1) to call for Collor's immediate ouster (*Fora Collor*) and general elections to replace him (proposed by the more radical, ideological factions of the PT, to which Nelson belonged); (2) to call for Collor's impeachment (considered more moderate and institutionalist, proposed by the MR-8, hidden within the mainstream PMDB); or (3) to call simply for "Opposition to Collor" and "for discussion about solutions to the crisis with the broader society" (which some of the more moderate, dialogue-oriented PT factions defended).

These three positions were hotly debated, often in the context of broader discussions in the political parties and labor movement.[17] For example, the PT youth, after intense internal discussion, decided to support the call for Collor's ouster (*Fora Collor*), breaking with their own national party leadership, which had rejected a similar proposal a few days earlier on the grounds that time was not yet ripe. Nelson told me that his radical Trotskyist tendency had been calling for Collor's ouster from the day that he was elected, calling his victory "a farce." Vincente said that the PCdoB youth supported the *Fora Collor* proposal in line with the party's position within the labor movement. The PSDB activists were divided, with one faction (including Eugênio) encouraged by national party leaders to support the more confrontational proposal, and another faction (including Marcelo and the law students) supporting the more institutionalist call for impeachment. Marcelo's faction emphasized the technical process of the impeachment—parliamentary inquiry, defense, senate approval—"because the defense of the technical process is extremely political." They also hoped to avoid alienating other groups involved in the movement against Collor.

Despite this intensive process of alignment and debate, the students were able to come up with a consensual resolution that incorporated the code words of each of the different factions. According to Eugênio, the imperatives of movement-building ended up winning out over partisan squabbles: "The question emerged, look, maybe we can end up approving *Fora Collor* as a great banner to unify the student movement." The final wording—which Nelson told me proudly was "unanimously approved"—included the impeachment among several possible alternatives, and called on UNE to participate with other organized groups to discuss alternative resolutions to Brazil's political crisis:

> *Fora Collor*. That UNE discuss progressive solutions to the political crisis. Among others, general elections, impeachment, an early plebiscite, etc., mobilizing students for this debate and involving the entire society.

Although this might seem like a lot of fierce debate for a few lines of (rather ambiguous) text, it helped to prepare for the subsequent participation of the student movement in the anti-Collor coalition. The resolution brought together the ideological, dialogic, and institutionalist wings of the student movement around the slogan *Fora Collor*. In the process, it smoothed out many of the kinks in relations among student factions, allowing them to more effectively coordinate their actions (although they continued to debate subtle differences among the slogans). Given the brutal factionalism of post-1979 Brazilian student organizations, this was not as easy as it looked.

The statement also established the principle that UNE should join other organizations in discussing possible forms of opposition to Collor. After the CONEB, top leaders of UNE (including Lindberg Farias) began to participate more consistently alongside PSDB activists in civic forums, especially in the Movement for Ethics in Politics. Although the PCdoB leaders had originally been ambivalent about such "institutional" paths, they were now enabled to walk straight into them, mediated by the PSDB youth and legitimated internally by the "revolutionary" banner of *Fora Collor*.

T2: Denunciation (June 1 to August 10, 1992)

During the first few months of 1992, the critical publics that had begun to form in late 1991 continued, but they struggled to find force and focus. The Movement Option for Brazil began to fade away due to its own lack of concrete proposals, while the student movement tried hard to transform the slogan of *Fora Collor* into a mass mobilization. In April, the student movement tried to organize a nationwide protest against Collor, although this was quite small, with mainly activist participation. The labor movement also organized several anti-Collor rallies, turning up its rhetoric as the slogan of *Fora Collor* began to catch on.

On May 10, these partially segmented milieus gained a common focus as the corruption scandal exploded. The president's brother, Pedro Collor, gave a front-page interview in a major newsmagazine exposing the president's involvement in an elaborate patronage ring run by Collor's close aide (and former campaign manager). The mainstream press jumped on the story, beginning several months of extensive investigative coverage. Meanwhile, congressional representatives of the PT began a campaign to gather material evidence regarding the denunciations, seeking congressional signatures to open a Parliamentary Commission of Inquiry (CPI), the first constitutionally dictated step in impeachment proceedings. Within the student movement, CA XI sponsored several law school debates calling for the congressional inquiry, while the annual Congress of UNE in late May approved a resolution calling for impeachment with general elections. At this congress, Lindberg Farias was elected president and Eugênio, Martín, Nelson, and Renato moved up in rank, representing their political forces in UNE's executive.

I mark the beginning of the second time period on June 1, the day that Congress voted to install the CPI. A schematized lattice for the *Denunciation* period is depicted in figure 5.4. During this period, we see a process of convergence, in which the partially overlapping milieus of the student movement, civic forums, and labor movement began to join in common proimpeachment events.

Figure 5.4 shows a gradual move from partial segmentation among student and civic milieus to increasingly stronger overlap. Some events were still dominated by particular sectors; for example, on the left side of the lattice we see the first round of student rallies in June and July (12) as well as a student ceremony during the national science conference (14). These events had mainly student and partisan participation, although professional and labor groups were also beginning to appear. On the right side, we see the July mayoral campaign rally of the PT coalition (13), and the Vigil for Land Reform (16), organized by the popular movements, labor unions, Catholic Church, and opposition parties. All of these events became platforms for denunciation of Collor. But most participants at these events were also being drawn into the broader cross-sectoral events of the Movement for Ethics in Politics, located in the center of the lattice. These included the launching of the movement (15) at the USP Law Faculty that nearly all of the youth leaders attended.

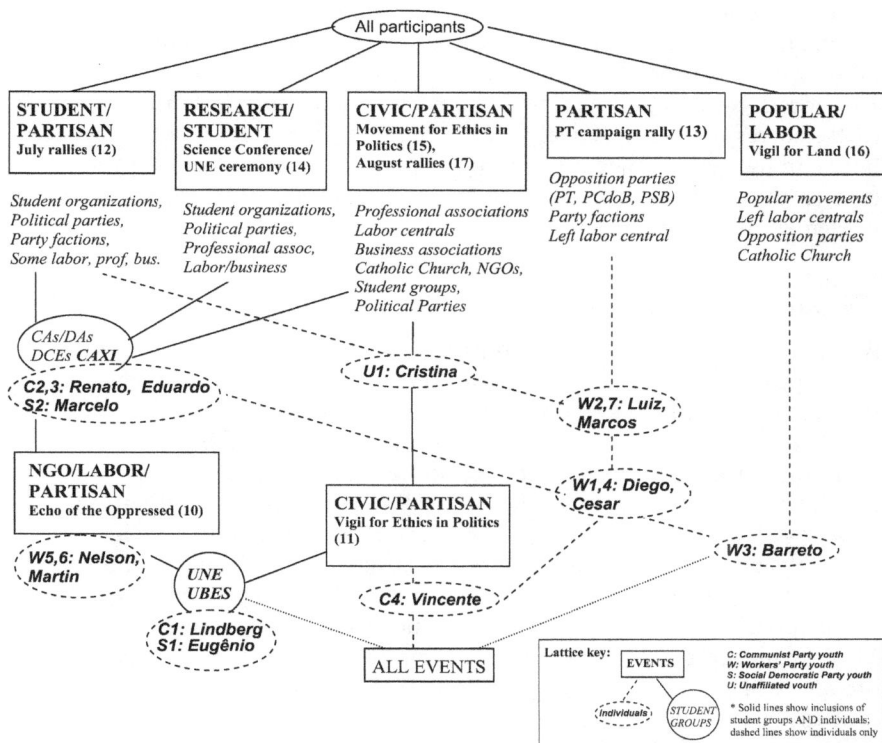

Figure 5.4. T2. *Denunciation* lattice (youth and groups at events)

During this period, there was a shift in the dynamics of mediation. The two social democrats, Eugênio and Marcelo, were still performing an articulatory role, playing on the ambiguity of their student, civic, and (submerged) partisan identities to construct a bridge between the student movement and the growing civic coalition. However, they were increasingly joined in this articulation by the PCdoB leaders, who began attending the broader civic events, thus diluting the exclusivity of the PSDB leaders' previous brokeragelike role. While the PT youth were also attending some prominent civic events, they did not play a central leadership role, in part because many were heavily involved in popular and labor activism as well as in the internal disputes within their own party. However, the multiple affiliations of the PT's bridging leaders did contribute to the amplification of the movement, as more of them began to circulate through these emerging cross-sectoral forums.

In analyzing the roles of these youth leaders, I will explore three sets of events: the "civic forums" of the Movement for Ethics, the *Fora Collor* mobilizations of the student movement, and the more restricted events sponsored by the political parties, unions, and popular movements (these correspond, respectively, to the center, left, and right sides of the lattice in figure 5.4). The positioning of particular youth leaders in relation to these events is important for understanding their roles in the movement's convergence.

The Movement for Ethics in Politics

As the congressional inquiry against Collor got underway, many of the actors previously involved in the Movement Option for Brazil began to reorganize, this time under the rubric of the Movement for Ethics in Politics (MEP). At this point, the focus of the movement shifted from individuals to organizations, including the opposition parties. On June 23, organizers held a "Vigil for Ethics in Politics" (11) in front of the National Congress in Brasília with the participation of professional, religious, labor, business, NGO, and student groups. Signers of the vigil's manifesto included 183 organizations, 10 senators, 65 federal representatives (all from opposition parties), and 35 "personalities."[18] As with MOB, the MEP manifesto did not specifically denounce Collor, but rather issued a broader call for civic participation in defense of institutional ethics and democratic accountability.

Over the next few weeks, radical student activists began to participate more consistently in the Movement for Ethics, although they wet their feet somewhat gradually. Only a handful of student leaders from the PSDB and PCdoB attended the early vigil in Brasília. As figure 5.4 shows, these included Eugênio of the PSDB, who had been relocated by UNE to Brasília, where he was given the job of monitoring the congressional inquiry and other civic demonstrations (aided by his ties with the congressional leadership of the PSDB). However, in contrast to prior civic forums, where he was the sole representative of UNE, Eugênio was upstaged at the vigil by Lindberg, who as the new president of UNE was beginning to move into the spotlight. Also present was Vincente of the Union of Socialist Youth (UJS), signaling the importance that the PCdoB was beginning to give to these civic events.

Many more students showed up several weeks later when the Movement for Ethics was officially launched at a public forum in São Paulo (15), which took place in the historic Hall of Students of the USP Law Faculty. Marcelo hosted the July 13 ceremony in his role as president of CA XI, thus providing a strong bridging context between the civic forum and the student movement. Both UNE and CA XI were on the list of "coordinating organizations" (represented by their respective presidents, Lindberg Farias and Marcelo), along with other prominent civic associations.[19]

In this strong bridging situation, the extensive overlap in organizational memberships allowed for considerable flexibility of informal representation. For example, the youth of the PCdoB could be there either "as UNE" (or whatever student organization they belonged to) "as UJS," or "as PCdoB," leaving it to their discretion which organization(s) they wrote down while signing the attendance list. Marcos told me that he was representing the State Coordination of Black University Students, although he could also have been representing his local student organization or the PT. Likewise Diego was there both "as PJ" (the Catholic youth pastoral) and "as the youth of the PT," while Luiz could have signed in as a bank-worker, as PT, or as the NGO he was involved in starting. In many cases participants left this relationship ambiguous, given that they could run into comembers of their several groups at the event. Their self-identification varied according to which of the constantly shifting *conchavos* (huddled conversations) they were joining on the side while formal speeches were going on at the front.

Although such multiple overlaps may appear to trivialize the possibility of "representation," on the other hand, events like this are rich in opportunities for what I have described as cross-sectoral amplification. While the ceremonial speeches at the front help to anoint formal leadership, in some ways the real action is "on the floor," as members of overlapping subgroups exchange information, set up meetings, compare analyses, and generally assess the scale and scope of an emergent political situation. These leaders could then bring this information back to the various groups they belonged to, thereby helping to bring more people into future civic events.

"Fora Collor" Demonstrations

One important result of the Movement for Ethics ceremony was that young activists began to feel that they were part of a larger, multidimensional movement, no longer limited to the partially segmented student milieu. The leaders of UNE and other student groups worked to expand their civic interface, as student rallies for *Fora Collor* gradually began to incorporate a broader array of organizations and sectors.

In early June, following the Congress of UNE, many student leaders took part in events surrounding the United Nations Conference on Environment and Development (Earth Summit) and the simultaneous Global NGO Forum in Rio de Janeiro. UNE joined labor, community, environmental, and partisan organizations in marches through the center of Rio

(10) denouncing the "farce of the ECO-92" (the Brazilian term for the UN conference), calling the protest the "*Eco dos Oprimidos*" ("Echo of the Oppressed"). The PT activist Martín flippantly described these rallies as "a couple of demonstrations to curse the Americans." However, his more radical copartisan, Nelson adopted a more heroic tone, describing the event as the first "great march" of the impeachment movement. He said that "the axis of the movement was *Fora Collor, Fora Collor* in the mouth of the people."

In early July, UNE attempted to organize another set of student rallies in cities across the country, including Brasília, Rio, São Paulo, Belo Horizonte, Belém, Curitiba, and Recife (12). These were generally small rallies, although they were beginning to call on a broader set of civic organizations. Nelson attributed the small student turnout to the fact that universities were in the midst of winter vacations. Luiz recalled that he was embarrassed by bringing his friends to near-empty rallies: "It was a fiasco, we'd bring people from the schools and the guy would say, look, you brought me here, and there's only us here!"

In mid-July, UNE held its own civic ceremony during the annual science conference of the Brazilian Society for the Progress of Science (14), at the University of São Paulo. The new directorate was sworn in at the event, to which UNE invited an array of dignitaries, including representatives of political parties, labor centrals and professional associations, university rectors, and prominent politicians. Nelson described it as an important public moment for UNE; whereas before the student organization was "weak, worn down," this event helped to give it greater public exposure. In the broader science conference, Renato recalled, there was "a clear consensus against Collor, everyone was against him." Nelson remembered that the president of the conference ended his opening address calling for Collor's ouster; he attributed this strong positioning of the scientific community to the cutting of research funds by the Collor government, which was "a calamity for researchers."

In early August, UNE participated in a series of demonstrations across the country organized by the Movement for Ethics (17). These rallies were marked by considerable contention in self-definition. The left wing unions and political parties joined the student movement in embracing the banners of "*Fora Collor*" and "*Impeachment Já*" ("impeachment now"). However, many professional and business groups were still determined to keep the broad theme of "ethics in politics" separate from calls for Collor's impeachment. They argued that it was still not certain whether they could get the congressional votes to approve the impeachment; therefore they preferred to call for Collor's resignation as an alternative solution to the crisis.

Nevertheless, calls of *Fora Collor* and *Impeachment Já* began to dominate the civic rallies, due to the strong presence at this stage of left-wing militants. This provoked the newspaper *Folha de São Paulo* to complain that "the predominance of militants and sympathizers of the PT, PCdoB, and CUT does not give them the right to appropriate a movement with a clear supra-partisan vocation."[20] In these early, contested civic mobilizations, UNE struggled to be taken seriously by the coordinators of the Movement for Ethics. Barreto recalls that at one MEP demonstration, he had to have "many discussions with Lula" to get the PT leader to announce an upcoming student rally. Likewise, a top leader of UJS said that he had to argue with leaders from the Bar Association and other civic organizations to let student leaders speak at the MEP rally.

Partisan and Popular Movement Events

While leaders linked to the PSDB and the PCdoB were gaining public visibility, those of the PT seemed to disappear from the core leadership of the impeachment movement. In part, this was due to the relative inexperience of the PT leaders who entered the directorship of UNE in 1991–92, as more seasoned leaders abandoned the organization. Because of this, Martín, said, "our intervention was very weak, we never were able to create a political space in which to present our differences from the PCdoB in the student movement." However, there were also deeper stylistic and structural factors. As I described in chapter 4, the activists of the PCdoB and the PT had very different styles of partisan bridging. The PCdoB leaders tended to focus on general student movement events while also promoting UNE's involvement in broader civic forums. In contrast, those of the PT tended to have more dispersed and specialized involvements, often participating in the "specific" (course-based) student movement as well as in grassroots popular, religious, or labor organizing. The PT leaders also tended to be absorbed by the intense internal disputes within their own party.

Nevertheless, PT leaders were involved in a number of more specialized events that contributed to the amplification of the impeachment movement. For example, after Barreto lost the election of UNE in May, he turned his attention to the youth collective of the PT, as well as to other activities linked to labor and popular movements. In late July, Barreto organized two busloads of students from the agronomy student federation (FEAB) to take part in the Vigil for Land (16) in São Bernardo, organized by CUT, the PT, and the land reform movement, with the participation of other church and partisan leaders. Note the importance of Barreto's prior affiliations in the agronomy student movement in constructing opportunities for movement amplification. Like all of the events during this period, the vigil became a forum for the denunciation of Collor's lack of ethics, although there was also more substantive criticism of Collor's neoliberal policies and lack of attention to social programs and agrarian reform.

Moreover, PT youth were also heavily engaged in upcoming municipal elections, which in São Paulo involved a coalition of the PT, PCdoB, and PSB (Brazilian Socialist Party). Luiz of the bankworkers' union and Diego of the Catholic youth pastoral were deeply involved in the youth committee of the campaign; Luiz was fired from his job at the union for spending too much time on partisan activities. On July 5, the PT held a major rally, attended by both PT and PCdoB leaders, to launch its mayoral campaign (13), with *Fora Collor* as one of the central slogans. Luiz recalls that PT youth would go to the impeachment demonstrations "with clipboards in hand, to campaign. To get the names of people, 'look, you want to help Brazil to get better, then give your name and telephone number.' We flirted a lot with that."

In addition to the campaign, the internal dispute within the PT also contributed to the leadership vacuum. At that time, the PT was in the midst of a major realignment, in which the majority tendency, known as the "Articulation" (to which Barreto, Diego, and Luiz belonged) was splitting apart and left-wing factions were increasing their power. This led to uncertain and perilous dynamics at meetings, as factions jockeyed for position and activists weren't sure who was on what side. To some extent, the impeachment rallies helped to smooth such tensions; as Luiz said, "With the impeachment, since the pot was big, with the marches and all, we ended up having a tranquil relationship." The joint excitement of the impeachment and the campaign was a bonanza for youth recruitment, although Luiz noted that they had trouble retaining recruits after the *festa* (party) was over and they tried to turn their attention to other discussions. However, the PT youth didn't lose heart because of this decline; Luiz laughs, "We had the internal struggle to wage, we had a lot of energy to spend!"[21]

In this second period, we have seen how the student and civic milieus moved from a situation of partial segmentation to increasingly stronger overlap, although civic-student relations continued to be tension-ridden, due in part to partisan subcurrents. Marcelo (in São Paulo) and Eugênio (in Brasília) continued to articulate links between the leftist student movement and more mainstream professional, business, and government actors, although the path initially forged by the PSDB students was now being trodden by youth with more diverse affiliations. Meanwhile, the leadership of the PCdoB—especially Lindberg Farias—was moving into the public eye, as UNE gained formal representation at civic activities. In contrast, many PT leaders were caught up in partisan, labor, and popular movement events, contributing to their marginalization from the top leadership of the impeachment movement. However, these involvements did allow them to amplify the movement by bringing other sectors of youth—such as agronomy students, bankworkers, and the Catholic youth pastoral—into anti-Collor events.

T3: Mobilization (August 11 to September 29, 1992)

While the events of the Denunciation period were going on, the CPI was proceeding with its inquiry. The investigation received a huge break in late June with the testimony of the former chauffer of Collor's private secretary, who described deposits made by Collor's aide, P.C. Farias, in the account of the president's wife, mother, ex-wife, and other relatives and employees. Several weeks later, another set of denunciations regarding falsified documents was made by the secretary of a close Collor associate. As evidence began to pour in, the two whistleblowers were celebrated in the press for their "courageous" and "dignified" acts of citizenship.

By early August, the congressional investigations were still underway. Nobody had anticipated the depth and extent of the corruption scheme, which included numerous "phantom" bank accounts and fictional companies. Reports emerged of extravagances by Collor and his family, such as nearly $3 million used to build a "Babylonian garden" within the Collor compound, as well as millions invested in the purchase of an airline and a local television station. His wife Rosane was accused of paying for lingerie and expensive dental treatment with checks from phantom accounts. In all, at least $230 million dollars were involved in transactions traced to the patronage scheme. The CPI concluded its work on August 26, voting 16 to 5 to approve a 369-page report accusing Collor and his associates of passive corruption, prevarication, administrative advocacy, conspiracy, and influence trafficking.

By this time, the massive street demonstrations of the third, *Mobilization* phase were well underway. The schematized lattice for this period is shown in figure 5.5 (below). Note the simplification of the lattice, as the partially overlapping sectors merged into a situation of near complete overlap, as more and more students attended the civic-partisan events.

The period begins with the explosion of student participation in the August 11 "Students' Day" march (18) organized by UNE and UBES. The São Paulo march was followed by rallies in Rio and other major cities, as a sympathetic media flashed pictures of the "caras pintadas" around the country. In the center of the lattice we see all of the major São Paulo rallies held in late August and early September (20, 21, 24, 26),

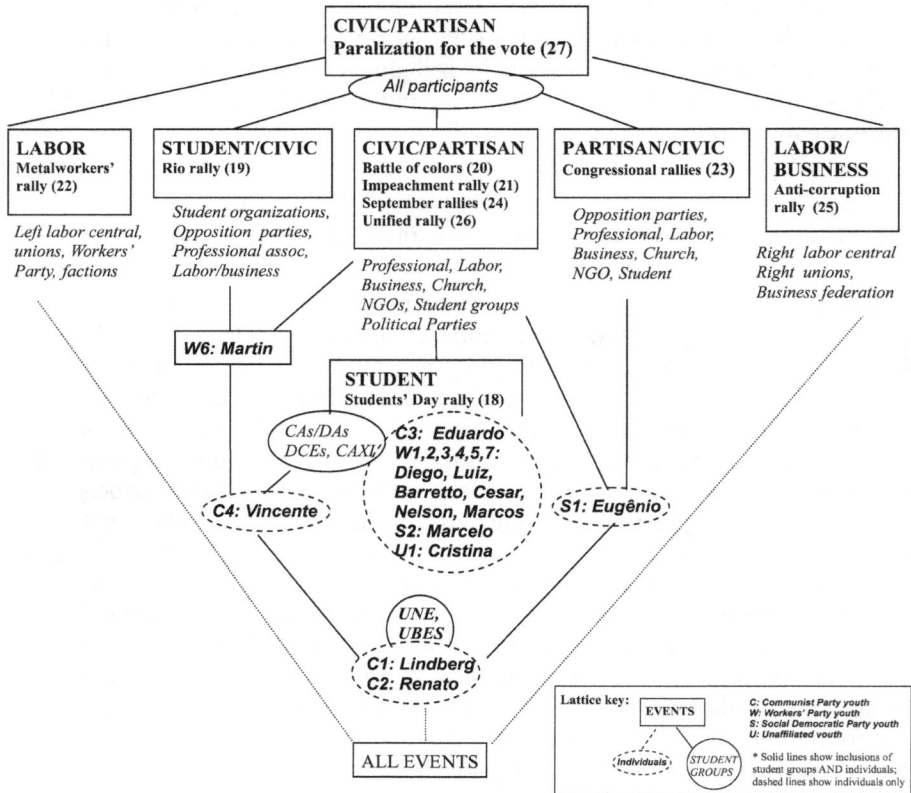

Figure 5.5. T3. *Mobilization* lattice (youth and groups at events)

which nearly all of the youth and the organizations attended, with the exception of the right-wing unions and the business federations.

On either side we see situations with more restricted participation, indicating two regional bases in the movement, in Rio (19), where Martín was located, as well as the national Congress in Brasilia (23), where Eugênio was still temporarily posted by UNE. At the extremities, we see two independent events promoted by rival union groups: a factory sweep by the leftist metalworkers' union to bring workers from the Greater São Paulo industrial region into the anti-Collor demonstrations, and a Rally against Corruption, uniting the right-wing unions and the business federation. Note that all of these actors merge in the rallies that accompanied the congressional vote on the impeachment (27, at the very top of the lattice).

Once again, as the structure of sectoral overlap changed, so did the dynamics of mediation. As the period progressed, there was less need for articulation and amplification, the two most important mechanisms of mediation in the earlier periods. Although Marcelo played an important role at the initial rallies—including brokering relations with state and police actors—he was eclipsed in the later demonstrations, losing his earlier mediating role. His copartisan, Eugênio, continued to play an important backstage role in Brasília, brokering the participation of UNE in congressional hearings and other institutional events. However, the public spotlight shifted dramatically to Lindberg Farias, who by this time was traveling frenetically around the country speaking at rallies and giving high-profile interviews. Lindberg became a symbolic bridger, seeming to embody the spirit and aspirations of Brazilian youth and its citizenry more generally, rather than simply the specific organizations to which he belonged. He was backed up in this position by his copartisans, Renato and Vincente; these fellow communists didn't get the spotlight but did help in the internal coordination of student leadership, contributing to logistical support at the major rallies.

To examine these types of mediation in more detail, I compare four sets of events in this lattice: the first Students' Day march, the more spontaneous street demonstrations that followed it, the backstage articulations in Brasília, and the final sequence of rallies leading toward the impeachment. I try to combine a sense of the collective dramaturgy of these events with an analysis of the cross-sectoral mediations that made them possible.

The Students' Day March

The Students' Day March on August 11 (18) was an important turning point in the impeachment movement for several reasons. First, it marked a change in the relative positions of the student and civic wings of the movement. Whereas previously student leaders had been practically begging for recognition from leaders of the Movement for Ethics, now students (and their organizations) suddenly became the most visible protagonists of the movement. Second, it was the first sign that the movement was extending beyond "organized" sectors of society. What had been a movement of organizations, activists, and intellectuals now suddenly had the beginnings of "mass" participation, in dimensions that surprised everyone, from watching congressmen to student leaders themselves. Third, it marked the emergence of a new set of symbols and repertoires that came to be vividly associated with this cohort of youth, including the colorful gesture of painting their faces (the *caras pintadas*) as well as the march trajectory itself, linking the "new" section of the city (the financial strip of the Avenida Paulista) to the "old" center, traditionally the site of public protests and gatherings.

When student leaders tell the story of this event, they shake their head wonderingly at the turnout, which police estimated at ten to twenty thousand people. "It had been a long time since the student movement had had a demonstration of that size," I was told separately by Barreto, Nelson, Vincente, and Luiz. However, they rejected claims that the march was either spontaneous or media-driven, stressing the important organizing role of UNE and other student groups. The August 11 march had not received advance coverage by the press, unlike the even larger rallies that would follow. It was preceded by planning and coordination among student organizations as well as by intensive pamphleting in the schools.

Plans for the August 11 rally initially emerged out of a collaboration between leaders of UNE and the USP Law Students' Association (CA XI de Agosto). At UNE's Congress in May, students approved a proposal to stage an anti-Collor rally to mark Brazil's traditional *Dia dos Estudantes* (Students' Day), which commemorates the 1827 founding of Brazil's first law course. Marcelo and CA XI (which was named for the "Eleventh of August" date) planned a separate ceremony at the Law Faculty, marking the renewal of a city contract for a legal assistance project. Marcelo recalls that "since the political atmosphere in the country was boiling, that year we resolved to have a bigger demonstration," inviting PT Mayor Luiza Erundina, as well as other dignitaries from professional, business, and community organizations.

Marcelo told the story of how a conversation in a bar between himself, Lindberg Farias, and a few others led to the merging of the two events scheduled for August 11 by CA XI and UNE. The story shows how Marcelo's mediation with state authorities led to the unlikely outcome (given Brazil's history) of police protection for the student protest. It also shows how he helped Lindberg and the other students tone down the confrontational stance of UNE:

> I remember that we were having lunch, with Enrique (a director of UNE), Mário (a director of CA XI), Lindberg, and myself. And Lindberg said to me, "Marcelo, we have to have a big demonstration on this August 11!"
>
> And I said, "Lindberg, we're going to do this thing with [Mayor] Erundina, with others, there will be a ton of people there."
>
> "Then we're going to have a march, we're going to break this thing open, we have to agitate!"
>
> And I said, "Great, then let's do it together."
>
> Three days later, Lindberg calls me. "Marcelo, we're going to bring in 20 buses to the *Largo São Francisco* (site of the Law Faculty, in the

old center), and we're going to close down the Avenida Paulista."

And I said "Lindberg, didn't you read the newspaper?" Fleury [the PMDB governor] had declared that he didn't want any more demonstrations on the Avenida Paulista, after a union rally had caused a tumult, blocking the avenue. So I asked, "Did you let [the authorities] know, Lindberg?"

And he said, "No way, if the police come, we'll let loose on top of them!" At that time the series *Anos Rebeldes* [the TV-Globo program on the student movement] was just starting.

I said, "No, no, Lindberg, that won't work, let me call." So I hung up and called the Secretary of Justice, who was from the Law Faculty. I said, "Secretary, how are you?"

And he said, "Go on, tell me what's up?" I said, "It's the following. In accord with Article 5 of the Federal Constitution, we are *communicating* with the authorities that there is going to be a march on August 11, it's going to leave from the Avenida Paulista, it's going to close the Paulista, and proceed down the Avenida Brigadeiro Luiz Antonio [the major avenue leading to the old center]."

"Marcelo, don't you know that the governor just two days ago made a declaration on television saying that he didn't want any more. . ."

I said, "Look, excuse me, I'm only telling you so as not to have a problem, I'm only complying with the norm." And he said "Wait a minute, I'll call you back."

He hung up, and after 40 minutes he called me back, saying, "I just spoke with the governor, he gives his authorization. He only asks that you meet and converse with the military police to organize it, so as not to have anyone get hurt." I said "That's fine." I called Lindberg, we scheduled the meeting, and organized the thing.

While Marcelo was carrying out these backstage negotiations with state authorities, other students were throwing themselves into the logistical preparation of the rallies. As high-level PCdoB leaders, Renato and Vincente were heavily involved in the coordination of the Students' Day march, distributing tasks among the leaders of the various parties. Vincente told me that they carried out a selective pamphleting operation, "directed toward the schools where we were most organized." Buses were organized to bring students from distant neighborhoods, often from public schools in the poorer periphery that had *grêmios livres* (high school associations) affiliated with UBES (the national high school student association). As a result, this initial rally had a broad demographic mix, not restricted to the middle-class students that would soon dominate the media coverage. In addition, buses came from the University of São Paulo (USP), as well as from the Catholic University (PUC) and other schools.

Most of the footwork of the mobilization was done by high school activists, who were experiencing a rare climate of cross-partisan collaboration. They had just succeeded in reunifying UBES after several years of schism, which alleviated the usual dispute between factions for control of the march. Barreto remembers a climate of "courtship" among the high school activists; "everyone was feeling happy with life." The high school leaders spent ten days prior to the march "visiting schools with *carros de som* ('sound-trucks' equipped with loudspeaking equipment). . . . They believed very strongly in the mobilization of August 11."

Vincente described the climate prior to the march: "We knew during the preparatory activities that it had the possibility of being something big." All the same, he said, "We were surprised. . . . We didn't yet know what the weight of those demonstrations would be. We didn't know whether they would set off a broader process." Renato remembers feeling dejected as he got onto the metro with only a small group of students. But his mood shifted as students from other schools started piling onto the train: "We were completely excited!" The importance of that first rally as a trigger for broader participation could be seen a few days later in a march through the center of Rio, which Vincente said not only was bigger (with fifty thousand people), but already had "another spirit, a greater willingness" on the part of youth.

At the August 11 march, many of the symbols that would become characteristic of the movement were beginning to appear. Newscasts showed a few young people with their faces painted—although mostly with stripes like Indians (not yet with the words *Fora Collor*, which would come to be the movement's trademark).[22] One teenager appeared theatrically dressed as a combination of "Indian, Worker, and Slave," explaining that "this is the situation of all of us here." Banners of student organizations, as well as labor unions and political parties, signaled the strong presence of militants interspersed with unaffiliated youth. The cameras flashed up to show people watching from windows, many cheering and waving, some throwing confetti. As they marched to the city's center, they were accompanied by a cordon of police officers, in a protective rather than repressive role, thanks to Marcelo's mediation. The leaders in the sound truck at the front led the chants of "Fora Collor" and "Estudantes, unidos, derruba os colloridos" ("students, united, will defeat the Collorists") as they proceeded down the Avenue.

Meanwhile, at the Law Faculty, Marcelo was coordinating his own ceremony in the Hall of Students, trying to time the close of speeches with the arrival of the students in the public square outside. When the marchers finally arrived, there were more speeches from student and other leaders, including from Lula (of the PT), who showed up near the end. During the ceremony, Marcelo received a phone call from Governor Fleury (from the

PMDB), saying that he wanted to have lunch. "He wanted to check things out, see the movement."

Marcelo continued his mediating efforts by insisting on pulling Lindberg along with him to lunch with the governor. "He didn't want to go at first, he got all awkward. So I said, 'I'm going, and you're going with me! I'm not going through this alone!'" So Marcelo, Lindberg, and several other student leaders shared lunch with the governor, despite clear political differences between the PCdoB leaders and the more mainstream PMDB. Marcelo justified this exchange by stressing that institutional ties should take precedence over partisan alignments: "I defend what I always defended, the institutional question. . . . I mean, you have to converse with people. You can't close the door, unless you have reasons for this. No, we have to use all the channels of political communication."

The lunch with the governor had the consequence of opening lines of communication between the student organizations and state and media actors, as well as cementing relations between UNE and CA XI. "From that point on, we had a closer conversation with the state government, they praised our organization of the rally." After lunch, Marcelo and Lindberg went together to give an interview at the *Folha de São Paulo*. "After that our conversation with the media began to be a bit more fluid. I had a lot of invitations to go on television, I passed some on to Lindberg, others I went myself. I wrote letters to the newspaper, that kind of thing." Marcelo reports occasionally previewing Lindberg's articles, urging him to tone down his militant language and assume a more civic stance. "Our relationship was very close. There was a strong relationship of partnership between UNE and CA XI during that period."

The Battle of the Colors

While the public and most of the media seemed enchanted with this first strong student demonstration, it was still relatively small compared to the rallies that followed. It took one additional move by Collor to get everyone out into the streets, in an exuberant jumble of organized and spontaneous activities. On Thursday, August 13, Collor made an impassioned speech to taxi-drivers in which he called on "all of Brazil" to go to the streets the following Sunday dressed in green and yellow, the colors of the Brazilian flag, to show their support for the president. In a populist echo of Richard Nixon's preimpeachment discourse, he called on "my people" to show who was the "true majority." The media took up the challenge, speaking of the upcoming "battle of the colors." Newspapers on Saturday carried stories about a counterproposal floated by the opposition to dress in black, to symbolize mourning for Brazil.

On Sunday, August 16, the country erupted in a stream of street protests across the country, as people went out flaunting anything they owned or could improvise in black. Some activities had been planned in the intervening three days, such as a symbolic funeral of Collor and his associates, staged by the São Paulo Artists' Union. The unions and the political parties (PSDB, PT) prepared black ribbons and organized several car processions, setting off from different points in the city. Yet despite these preparations, the striking thing about the August 16 protests (20) is the insistence by almost all of the activists that they were completely spontaneous. For once, student leaders dropped their claims to organizational representation, insisting that they were in the streets that day like everyone else, "como cidadãos" (as citizens). Note the identity qualifying in play: leaders provisionally backgrounded their organizational and partisan identities as they were swept up in the spontaneous demonstrations of the day. Barreto of the PT, for example, said that he didn't have any organizing role; nevertheless, "I was in the streets dressed in black." Another activist spent Saturday in the office of a PT legislator painting a yellow and green banner with a black stripe over. Still, she qualified the Sunday convergence as a "coincidence." "The same idea occurred at the same time, among many different people."

Marcelo of CA XI was among those who declared that the August 16 demonstrations "were absolutely spontaneous." When I pressed him on this, he admitted that there were a few prepared events. "But these were little things. Meanwhile, in the street, everywhere we passed people were beginning to gather. People were dressed in garbage bags, waving flags, that sort of thing . . . whatever they had that was black, they put in the window—a bag, the carpet of a car, a scarf, whatever." He set off with some friends on foot from the Law Faculty, joining a larger group of students: "We made our way all the way to the Avenida Paulista. . . . Then we walked back, those guys didn't want to stop walking. The hour came when I said, 'Okay, let's stop, my feet are hurting.' No, they wanted to walk all the way to the Governor's palace!"

Also in the streets was PCdoB leader Renato, who attended a popular concert that morning at the University of São Paulo. Many students were already dressed in black due to the prior urging of the PT leaders who controlled the central student organization (DCE). The concert turned into an exuberant informal rally for *Fora Collor.* Renato joined a large group of students who took a bus from the concert to the city center, then started off in an impromptu march to the State Assembly. He remembers being swept up and thrilled by the whole thing (which for once he wasn't organizing): "It was tremendous!"

Eugênio of the PSDB watched the battle of the colors from Brasília, where he was helping to articulate UNE's role in the congressional negotiations. He said they had "the biggest car parade in the history of Brazil. Everyone had on black." He went out in his car "like any other person." He noted that some of the movement organizers, including UNE and the Bar Association, originally opposed wearing black, a point that Lindberg had actually made in a national press conference the day before. To Eugênio, this demonstrated that it was not the organized sectors of society that were driving the demonstrations:

> It was like wind, suddenly everyone said, let's go out. There was no commercial at the last minute, "Attention Brazilians," there was nothing like this. And from that point on, no one could hold it back. Collor was the great mobilizer. If he had stayed quiet on that thing with the taxi-drivers. . . . That was the moment.

Eugênio's comments indicate the way in which the battle of the colors differed from many of the other organized events leading up to the impeachment. Although organizations (and their members) were certainly present at the public demonstrations, these groups did not appear to be the driving force behind them. While the parties and unions were still active, they (and the sectoral identities associated with them) fell into the background. The euphoric participation of the day—in which people went out "as citizens" rather than as members of organizations—eclipsed the small-scale preparatory efforts that nevertheless helped to channel part of the flow.

Institutional Articulations

Eugênio's comments also show the degree to which he himself was playing a role in mediating between UNE and elite decision-makers in Congress. Eugênio was sent to Brasília with the task of keeping UNE informed of (and included in) the events of the Movement for Ethics. In doing so, he was also able to make use of his partisan ties with moderate sectors of congressional opposition—including the PSDB and the PMDB—which had more weight and influence in Congress than the PCdoB or the PT. It is very questionable whether congressional leaders would have met as willingly (if at all) with a youth activist of the PCdoB. However, once Eugênio had constructed the bridge, the president of the Congress did not mind shaking hands on national television with Lindberg Farias, in his role not as communist activist, but as the representative of a historic student organization engaged in the defense of democracy.

During the early stages, Eugênio said that he was mostly there alone as the sole articulator of UNE. However, this exclusive, brokeragelike position changed after the first congressional vote on the admissibility of impeachment proceedings (in early September); "Then we began to put more people in Brasília, to be able to work body to body with [congressional] representatives." Eugênio said that he would often do the backstage articulation and Lindberg would come in at the culminating moment of visibility in the press. "Lindberg would enter when it was time to capitalize." He qualified this by saying that there was no competition involved: "We worked well together, there wasn't this thing of trying to profit from it."

During this period, UNE rose to a new level of prestige and recognition in Congress, after legislators began to see the unexpected force (and the broader symbolic appeal) of the student demonstrations. For example, Eugênio took pride in the fact that UNE was able to get privileged access, along with the prestigious Bar Association (OAB) and the Association of Journalists (ABI), to restricted congressional votes, such as the decision on whether to begin impeachment proceedings. "Our great partners were the OAB and the ABI, the whole time," Eugênio reported. UNE succeeded in obtaining credentials for the event "as UNE, as students," through an intense process of negotiation. "The credential came by way of the president of the Congress. . . . So the articulation of UNE was going very well within the institution. That was the moment that we left the ghetto. Our status was the same as the ABI and OAB. It was a historic moment, and very distant today."

Eugênio's mediating role continued after the impeachment, although PCdoB leaders quickly began to move in. He and another PCdoB leader organized a lunch for UNE directors with the new president, Itamar Franco (Collor's former vice president), soon after he took office. Five ministers attended, including the minister of education. "We ate *comida mineira* (food from Minas Gerais, the president's home state), we talked with the president, and in that moment the door of the ministry (of education) did in fact begin to open." In the coming year the PCdoB leadership of UNE would attempt to capitalize on this relationship, negotiating several accords with the government regarding student identification cards, tuition increases, and the restitution of the land from the site of UNE's historic building, which had been burned by the military government in 1964.

Converging toward the Vote

Following the "battle of the colors," the movement began to take on another rhythm. Organized protests began appearing in cities around the country, throwing many student leaders into a dizzying pace of interstate travel. Eugênio recalled, "There were days that I was here [in São Paulo], days I was in Minas Gerais, in Rio de Janeiro, it really exploded. You didn't know where anybody was . . . with Lindberg in Rio, thinking he was in São Paulo, or in São Paulo, imagining that he was in Rio." It became a struggle for the leaders to keep pace with the emerging events; "Things were so dynamic . . . at some moments we were running behind to catch up." However, Eugênio qualifies this by saying that "in the big unified demonstrations, we did have an articulating role, to be able to maximize our force and have a bigger impact."

AUGUST 25

In late August, the student movement and the Movement for Ethics staged one of their largest demonstrations in São Paulo (21), with 200,000 students participating in a student march organized by UNE and UBES in the morning, beginning at the Avenida Paulista, and another 200,000 people participating that evening in a civic rally in the old center (police estimates). The demonstrations continued to be marked by colorful dramaturgy, with symbolic burials of the Collor government, Collor look-alikes, protestors dressed as "phantoms" (a reference to the phantom bank accounts), prison inmates, rats, the dragon of inflation, and many, many painted faces. Luiz went to the march with a chamber pot on his head, a throwback to a character he had developed in community theater in the late 1980s. Luiz was somewhat cynical about the festive motives of most of the participants. He admitted that "there was a sentiment that was one of change. But I think that a significant parcel was there to cut class, for the party, to drink a little, [the street vendors] never sold so much beer!"

In Lindberg's speeches and interviews, he turned this festive element into a virtue, celebrating the mood of "alegria, revolta, e irreverência" (happiness, revolt, and irreverence), which he said signaled the rebirth of a new political spirit among nineties' youth. Lindberg became increasingly skilled in slipping back and forth between his student and civic identities, carefully compartmentalizing his partisan affiliation and ideological beliefs. In one interview he qualified his communist identity by saying that while "I am a socialist by conviction," he was against inclusion of the socialist banner in UNE's program. "*As president of UNE*, I represent the interests of Brazilian students, and have broader positions."[23] His articulate manner and boyish good looks made him a darling of the media, which helped to project him as a metonymic representative of "youth-as-citizen," a larger than life role that transcended his partisan and student movement affiliations. Through this symbolic bridging, unlikely bedfellows across the political spectrum found an attractive symbolic spokesman, enhanced on both ends by the romantic memory of the student movement of 1968 and the modern image of youth in the nineties.

Nevertheless, the rallies were not completely the result of Lindberg's projection by the media. Like the earlier Students' Day march, the August 25 rally was preceded by intense mobilizing and coordinating efforts by student activists, who found a newly receptive audience. Renato remembers that about thirty activists were camped out in the UNE offices in São Paulo, coordinating their efforts across partisan lines: "We would sleep there, we'd leave at six in the morning to go to the schools with the sound-truck, to pass out pamphlets." Nelson said that often they went to schools that didn't yet have student organizations and helped to set up CAs on the spot. Whereas before there had often been resistance to UNE, Eugênio said, "Now we would go to the schools, they would open the door, you didn't need to speak more than half an hour."

The student movement received material support in this mobilization effort from a number of sources. The São Paulo Bankworkers' Union frequently lent them sound trucks and printed posters and pamphlets. Luiz helped to articulate the connection between the union and the student groups, along with several other young union activists. There were also reports that the movement was receiving money, materials, and other support from the state government, funneled through the strong ties of the MR-8 (one of the PCdoB's allies) with the governing PMDB. "Then the money began to roll," Eugênio recalls, "no one asked from where." Renato recalls that they borrowed sound trucks from the mayoral campaign of the PMDB. Because the rallies were taking place close to municipal elections, by the end almost all of the candidates were on board. Even Paulo Maluf, the mayoral candidate of the right-wing PDS (with strong links to the former military regime), flamboyantly painted his face during the August 25 demonstration, videotaping his performance for that evening's nightly campaign broadcast.

Despite official attempts to maintain a "suprapartisan" tone at these demonstration, the partisan dynamic slipped back in through a number of paths. Banners, T-shirts, and other symbols of the parties involved in the movement were evident at the marches and rallies. Barreto asserted that while the PT was poorly represented among movement leaders, "a majority of the youth wore the [star-shaped] buttons of the PT." Partisan currents could also be seen in disputes over the sound trucks, which provided mobile platforms for speeches, chants, and music to animate the crowd. Conflicts erupted over which trucks would lead, who would be allowed to speak or ride on top, and what music to play. Although the lead truck was always the most disputed, there were also trucks coordinated by the universities (e.g., USP, PUC), the bankworkers, UBES, and other groups, each of which had partisan associations. As groups of students arrived, they would fall in behind whichever truck was closest, thus creating a semicaptive audience for the speakers.

However, attempts by partisan representatives to take advantage of the movement did not always go smoothly. At one point a television reporter noted an announcement by the lead truck (which was packed with people) asking candidates not to use the march for their campaigns, since "this is a demonstration of the students, for *Fora Collor* and better educational conditions." The other trucks were then requested to turn off their sound. At other rallies, news reports stressed that many unaffiliated youth booed and hissed at attempts by candidates or partisan representatives to give speeches.

The rallies also provided opportunities for other kinds of organizations to appear as supporters of the impeachment, although it was not always easy for them to gain visibility. Cristina, for example, says that she organized a contingent from the Catholic youth pastoral (PJ) to attend the march "as PJ," complete with banners and flags; they ended up joining other Catholic groups arriving from different parts of the state. Another more problematic example is that of Marcos, of the National Coordination of Black University Scholars (CONUN), who said that he was given the opportunity to speak from the sound truck of University of São Paulo, given his partisan ties to the local PT student leaders. After that experience, however, Marcos and other black student leaders evaluated that it was better for them not to speak at the rallies, given the predominantly white, middle-class character of the demonstrations: "This was not our public, there wasn't receptivity to the black discourse." With so many people trying to talk, he said, "We ran the risk of getting burned," if they attempted to push their own agenda. Unfortunately, this withdrawal reinforced the invisibility of the black movement, as I will discuss in chapter 8.

SEPTEMBER RALLIES

While partisan tension was present at all stages of the movement, we can note a shift from the defensively *nonpartisan* norm of the Movement Option for Brazil (in the first period) to an affirmatively *suprapartisan* self-designation of the later impeachment movement, particularly in the September demonstrations. After the CPI concluded its report and the impeachment proceedings were accepted into Congress, the logic of the moment became more explicitly (and justifiably) partisan, since the goal was now to gain the two-thirds majority in House of Representatives that was needed to send the impeachment proposal on to the Senate.

In early September, there was an intense process of negotiation in São Paulo in the attempt to stage a unified demonstration supporting the impeachment. Early in the month, three separate rallies were planned: by the Movement for Ethics, by the student movement, and by Força Sindical (the right-wing labor central) in conjunction with the business federation. Concerned over this division, Governor Fleury began to articulate the joining of these demonstrations, calling a meeting with the PT mayor of São Paulo, Luiza Erundina, as well as UNE and the Movement for Ethics. They organized a suprapartisan Ato Unitário (Unified Act) on September 18 (26).[24] At this event there were no qualms about inviting politicians to speak; the official participants in the rally (and in the formal lunch at the governor's palace that preceded it) included five state governors, five mayors of capital cities, presidents of political parties, and other political dignitaries, as well as the usual crowd from the Movement for Ethics. Lindberg was present at the lunch and the rally, together with the president of UBES. This demonstration, like the others, was preceded by a student march beginning on the Avenida Paulista. By evening, the military police calculated that 700,000 people were present. The event ended ceremoniously with the singing of Brazil's national anthem, followed by a fireworks display and a giant blazing panel with the word "IMPEACHMENT."

CIVIC SHUTDOWN

The public demonstrations that accompanied the congressional impeachment vote were no less ceremonious, although a bit more chaotic. On September 29, the Movement for Ethics called for a national "civic shutdown" (*paralalização cívica*), in which the population would not go to work and instead go to public squares around the country to follow the vote count. The students, as was by now traditional, gathered on the Avenida Paulista and marched downtown to join the rally organized by the Movement for Ethics. A large screen was set up, showing live television coverage of the vote in Congress. Each vote of "yes" was preceded by heroic litany—e.g. "in the name of the great state of Minas Gerais, for my father and mother, for my children and grandchildren, and for Brazil!"—followed by cheers in Congress and in public squares around the country. When the vote reached 336—the number necessary for approval—onlookers erupted in celebration. The *Folha de São Paulo* described the scene in São Paulo:

> The approval of the process of impeachment against President Collor was commemorated, in São Paulo, as if Brazil had won the World Cup. With hands held and arms raised, the multitude gathered . . . in the center of the city, sang the National Anthem and thrilled to the transmission of the countdown of the last five decisive votes.[25]

After the vote count, many students (and others) headed back up to the Avenida Paulista, where the street festivities organized by UNE and UBES (and animated by popular musicians) continued into the night. The press seemed just as exhilarated as the participants, as they celebrated the *festa cívica* (civic festival) with scenes of people dancing in the streets.

From an organizer's perspective, Eugênio recalls that that final demonstration was as confused as it was exhilarating. "I remember that scene well, it was very disorganized, the singers there, people trying to speak."

He recalls the mayor of São Paulo, Luiza Erundina, sitting on the floor amidst the crush of people. There were some tussles between the labor and student movement, as well as some tension among student leaders over who would represent UNE; in Lindberg's absence, both Eugênio and Renato ended up speaking. On the Avenida Paulista, things weren't much better. Although UNE leaders had spent the previous night setting up the party (in collaboration with the military police), "by that time, the movement was so suffocated by all the various activities that it was a problem, the masses took over the sound truck, confusion set in." By that time, however, it didn't matter; a collective giddiness had set in on the Avenida Paulista and across the country.

MEDIATING PROCESSES IN THE CIVIC CONVERGENCE

This chapter has examined both structural factors and relational contingencies underlying student movement participation in the civic coalition during Brazil's impeachment mobilizations. In the process, I have developed more general ideas about the mechanisms of mediation that contribute to the formation of provisional "publics" in highly contentious fields. I have argued that opportunities for mediation are created by the structure of overlapping affiliations, constituted both by comemberships as well as by copresences at events. In addition to conventional brokerage, *articulators* work to negotiate alliances between partially segmented subgroups, sometimes based on submerged or latent ties. *Amplifiers* help to expand a movement through indirect ties that enable flows of ideas and resources across partially overlapping sectors and milieus. *Coordinators* work to distribute resources and responsibilities across the relational cleavages created by strongly overlapping subgroups. And *symbolic bridgers* enable the convergence of heterogeneous subgroups by serving as multivalent embodiments of larger collectivities.

Over the course of the impeachment movement, the student and civic milieus evolved from partial segmentation in T1, to increasing overlap in T2, to near complete overlap in T3. This shift was facilitated by the cross-sectoral articulation of the PSDB activists, who represented the student movement at early civic nonpartisan events, based on their suppressed partisan ties to the organizers of those events. However, the success of the PSDB leaders' initial mediation made their role increasingly redundant, as more and more student leaders attended civic events. In later stages, their leadership was eclipsed by that of Lindberg Farias, whose role as a symbolic bridger transcended his partisan or organizational location. Supported by enthusiastic media coverage, Lindberg came (for a short time) to embody his entire cohort of civic-minded youth, as symbolized by the *caras pintadas*.

While this articulatory and symbolic work was essential to the student-civic coalition, it was supported by the intensive coordinating efforts of leaders in the more entrenched student-partisan intersection. Students from contending parties succeeded in negotiating a compromise position that fused the demands of radical left activists for Collor's ouster with the call of the moderates for broader social dialogue and institutional procedure. This in turn allowed all of the UNE directors to collaborate in the distribution of tasks and responsibilities as they scrambled to organize the quickly accelerating demonstrations.

Less central activists also used their multiple affiliations to bring more distant groups and sectors into the movement. While PT leaders disappeared from the visible leadership of the movement, their tendency to diversify their affiliations across multiple sectors contributed to the amplification of the movement. I have shown how they brought agronomy students into broader oppositional events; helped to secure infrastructural support from unions; organized contingents from the Catholic youth pastoral; and tried, somewhat unsuccessfully, to represent black students at the rallies. The movement was composed of scores of such mid-level leaders, connected through a web of cross-cutting affiliations, with many less visible opportunities for amplification and support within their own spheres of activity.

This analysis has shown the unexpected importance of partisan relations in building an ostensibly "civic" coalition. In one sense, the civic convergence depended on the suspension of partisanship; the construction of the "public" of the Movement for Ethics in Politics required the provisional suppression of partisan differences, along with other differences in rank, power, or sectoral orientation. This made it possible for leftist college students in the previously marginalized UNE to share the stage with mainstream professional, religious, and business organizations, not to mention with powerful politicians. Most nonactivist youth who hit the streets in such high numbers were quite skeptical of the partisan affiliations of leaders and were eager to shout down politicians that seemed to promote their own electoral agendas.

Nevertheless, if civic passion provided the spirit that pulsed through the streets, partisan identities provided the relational sinews that held the mobilization together. As we have seen, suppressed partisan ties underlay the civic articulations that helped to legitimize student participation in the civic coalition. Explicit partisan commitments fueled the intense investments of time and energy that top student activists put into the coordination of the rallies. And partisan ties provided conduits of information and ideas across popular, labor, religious, and professional movements, thus helping to amplify the movement.

Yet we have also seen that these partisan identities were often tense and uneasy, hovering in the background of the civic ceremony and festival that momentarily unified the nation. Here is the paradox of publics: partisanship both strengthened the civic convergence—providing its hidden joints and connections—but also threatened to tear it apart, draining it of the exhilarating yet fragile spirit of civic unity.

In the second part of this book, I explore these communicative processes in greater depth, focusing on what happened to the field of student politics in the years following the impeachment. I move from a historical and retrospective account of student politics in the democratic transition to an ethnographic analysis of styles of communication in activist settings during the postimpeachment period. I build on the analysis here by examining the communicative mechanisms by which activists maneuvered among their multiple identities, as they built relations and institutions in a changing field.

PART TWO

Contentious Communication

CHAPTER SIX

Modes of Communication
in Institutionalized Publics

IN THE YEAR or two following the 1992 impeachment movement, the student movement continued to bask in the light of its unexpected return to public prominence. UNE showered the universities with colorful documents and posters celebrating the triumphant "return of the students" in the mobilizations to oust President Fernando Collor de Melo. Lindberg Farias, the charismatic president of UNE during the impeachment, had been honored as a *cidadão Paulistano* (citizen of São Paulo) by the city's mayor, cementing his symbolic position as a civic hero (in 1994 he would wage a successful campaign for Congress in Rio de Janeiro on the PCdoB ticket). Student organizations reported a surge of interest in *grêmios livres* and *centros acadêmicos* (CAs)—autonomous student organizations in high schools and university departments, respectively. The mainstream media launched new youth-centered reporting that celebrated youth culture and commented favorably on new forms of student participation.[1]

In academia as well, the focus of scholarship was shifting away from the popular movements—widely regarded to be "in crisis"—to a focus on "citizenship," especially as manifested by the explosion of NGOs in the areas of human rights, antidiscrimination, environment, and hunger.[2] Both analysts and activists pointed to a new "diversification" of youth politics, no longer represented by the full time, hard-core partisan militant of decades past, but rather taking on more specialized forms of civic participation, particularly in cultural and professional arenas. This new pluralism was celebrated as a sign of the strength and robustness of youth politics, in which every young person was potentially a *cara pintada*.[3]

Yet despite this triumphal civic tone, there were also sources of tension and unease. Under the continued leadership of the Communist Party of Brazil (PCdoB), UNE attempted to maintain visibility and momentum, waging a campaign against tuition increases in private schools and universities, as well as participating in civic forums on education, patent law, the environment, and other issues. At the same time, however, the traditional student movement was coming under attack from a variety of directions. Activists linked to the PT mounted a campaign for direct elections in UNE, claiming that this would make the organization more democratic, more responsive to student concerns, and less wedded to partisan disputes. (The leadership of the PCdoB countered that direct elections would actually be *more* partisan and subject to manipulation.) The same year, the National Coordination of Black University Scholars (CONUN) staged a very successful national seminar that was highly critical of the lack of attention to racial issues in the general student movement. Leaders of more professionally oriented ("course-based") student organizations founded the National Forum of Course Executives, counterposed to what they saw as the centralization, bureaucratization, and "partidarization" of UNE. Business-oriented students in São Paulo launched the State Federation of Junior Enterprises (FEJESP), and began to receive positive attention in the press as a possible alternative to the intense partisan climate of student politics. And the mainstream media launched a series of critical reports about the student movement, mapping factional alignments and caricaturing the movement as being composed of "dinosaurs," in other words, fans of Lenin, Stalin, Trotsky, and Che Guevara.

As I waded into these contending milieus, youth politics in the postimpeachment era began to appear less like a pluralistic sphere of civic debate, and more like a loosely veiled battlefield. Struggles over the shape, style, and direction of student politics were being waged by partisan actors in the name of civic nonpartisanship. Student activists in the universities told me that the kiss of death for any would-be slate of leaders would be to admit association with any kind of political party—even those shown by opinion polls to be most popular among the student population. Every move had to be doused in a "civic" or "democratic" light, which meant labeling the opponent as manipulative, authoritarian, instrumental, opportunistic, divisive, monopolistic, or steamrolling—essential components of the local version of what Alexander and Smith call the "counter-democratic code."[4] Rather than seeing political parties as important carriers of the new movement toward democracy (as they arguably were in the 1980s), many students coded parties as almost intrinsically antidemocratic. To win election for the CA of a São Paulo university, one student leader reported that "I had to annul myself as *petista*" (an activist of the PT); her companions demanded that she suppress her PT identity, so that the whole slate would not be "burned."

In this enforced climate of civic nonpartisanship, constructive crosspartisan dialogue was, ironically, elusive and difficult. At the same time as new activist forums were springing up across the country, I heard persistent complaints about the lack of "real discussion" in the student movement, about the impoverishment of political debate, about the distractions and seductions of factional politics, and how this undermined the possibility of dialogue and reform. These criticisms were not limited to the self-designated "apartisan" students, but rather came from all of the partisan camps as well (with blame for this situation often thrown like mud between camps). I found this chorus of complaints somewhat puzzling. If there was such widespread hunger for constructive political debate, what was getting in its way? Why was it so hard for students to create cross-partisan forums for dialogue and joint action, even when they all agreed on the need for such forums?

In the second part of this book, I explore the dynamics of political communication in the uneasy publics of 1990s youth activism. Despite tension and critique, young activists were attempting to create various types of forums for cross-sectoral discussion and action. I stumbled on these contexts sometimes unexpectedly, in open assemblies or backroom discussions, with or without intentional planning or institutional backing. As I watched activists struggle to build such publics—sometimes succeeding, sometimes failing—I began to realize that there were patterned ways that people talked and acted in these settings that contributed to their success and failure. The construction of such publics required mediating skills that were attuned to the relational and institutional complexities of a given setting. These often involved subtle identity play, as well as movement back and forth between collaboration and competition.

In the chapters to come, I examine the performative dimension of such publics—that is, the ways that people maneuver among their multiple identities in ways that nurture or impede productive dialogue and action. By "productive," I mean that such communication gets things done; it sets relations and projects in motion in a relatively intentional manner, even if outcomes are by no means assured. Drawing on ethnographic work in Brazil during the mid-1990s, I look at how young people from different cohorts performed the styles and skills of communication that they acquired throughout their trajectories, putting them to use in different kinds of movement settings. I examine what factors supported or undermined attempts to generate productive communication in such publics, and how these processes contributed to institution-building and relation-formation.

In particular, I examine how activists moved between four different footings or skilled "modes" of communication, distinguished by their relative emphasis on collaboration or competition, as well as on ideas versus actions. I argue that all four modes are important aspects of democratic communication, although people and groups may develop stronger skills in some than in others. By studying how collectivities combine, segment, and switch between these modes, we can locate the communicative practices by which actors construct more or less productive publics in contexts of relational heterogeneity.

In studying such performances, I am interested in four central questions. First, I am interested in how different styles and skills of communication are supported by the *institutional structure* of particular settings. Second, I want to know how individuals adapt these institutionalized styles according to *local relational contingencies*. Third, I want to understand how people *challenge and innovate* on those styles as they build new relations and institutions. And fourth, I am interested in how activists use their skills to build (or break) *alliances and coalitions*, thus contributing to the successes and failures of social movements.

The next four chapters address each of these questions in turn. In this chapter, I compare two highly institutionalized styles of communication that were both forged in the partisan struggles of the 1980s: the competitive style of UNE and the more collaborative style of the Catholic youth pastoral. In chapter 7, I examine the more emergent, contingent, and often defensive negotiation of style in local university settings, amidst the strong antipartisan sentiment of the postimpeachment period. In chapter 8, I examine how the innovative challenger groups of the 1990s—the black university scholars, the Course Executives, and the Junior Enterprises— were both questioning and transforming those earlier styles. Finally, in chapter 9, I examine how weaknesses in communicative skills contributed to a dramatic breakdown in political coalition-building, undermining attempts to reform a student public.

Skilled Modes of Political Communication

In examining communicative styles, I am focusing on the performative aspect of political communication: how people in different relational settings talk to and about each other; how they juggle, merge, or segment their multiple identities; how they manage dissension and ritualize unity; and how they reflect on (and respond to) what they themselves are doing. Recently, students of political culture have begun to focus attention not just on cultural representations (whether understood as symbols, codes, schemas, or narratives) but also on the ways in which these are filtered through what Irving Goffman calls communicative "footings," that is, the shared framing of "what talk is for" in a given setting.[5] Building on Goffman's work, Eliasoph and Lichterman define what they call "group styles" as "recurrent patterns of interaction that arise from a group's shared assumptions about what constitutes good or adequate participation in the group setting."[6]

I build on their definition, but add a stronger relational and pragmatic component. Communicative styles develop out of the social and cultural challenges of local configurations of relations. We can refer to these as "styles" because they are patterned and recognizable to participants as well as to relevant sets of nonparticipants. Moreover, they are to some

degree mobile and transposable. While formed in response to the problems and possibilities of particular institutional settings, they can be carried outside of those settings and put to use elsewhere, to good or ill effect
depending on the receptivity of the new relational context. This mobility
is possible because styles have a habitual element, born of particular institutional configurations. However, their good exercise is also a *skill* that
can be deployed more or less effectively by individuals and adapted to
new settings as they arise.

Styles do not necessarily involve one singular, all-encompassing communicative footing, but rather are composed by the ways in which people switch between different *modes of communication* in particular relational contexts. As activists engage in discussion and relation building,
their communication can move back and forth between a variety of different footings, some of which are more collaborative while others are
more competitive; some are oriented toward elaborating ideas, while
others push toward deliberation over actions. What I am calling a
"style" refers to the patterned ways in which actors in particular institutional contexts emphasize, combine, and move between these different
communicative modes.

To describe these modes, I find it useful to dip into political theory,
drawing on four competing models of political action that are often seen
as being contradictory or incommensurable. I refer to these as *exploratory
dialogue, discursive positioning, reflective problem solving*, and *tactical
maneuver*. At the risk of oversimplification of the work of the theorists
involved, we can see these footings as finding justification in the work of
Habermas, Gramsci, Dewey, and Machiavelli, respectively.[7] These modes
are summarized in table 6.1. While these distilled sketches clearly do not
do justice to the richness of the theorists' writings, they do correspond to
some of the main points of reference that have entered into what we might
call "popular political theory," informing the models of action appro-
priated by different groups of political actors, in Brazil and elsewhere.

While these models are often presented in opposition to each other, I
argue that they correspond to distinct practices of skilled political communication that appear in different contexts and combinations. We can think
of them as ideal types of communication that are discernible in varying
degrees within empirical social settings. Rather than concerning ourselves
with choosing which one is "right" or "best," we should pay attention to
the manner in which groups and individuals move between these modes
in specific settings of interaction.

Before describing each in detail, let me say what I am *not* doing here. I
am not setting these up in normative hierarchy. I am not saying, for example, that a democratic civil society depends on the ideas of Habermas or
Dewey, while partisan politics and other more instrumentally driven

TABLE 6.1
Four modes of skilled political communication

	Collaboration	Competition
Ideas	Exploratory Dialogue	Discursive Positioning
	· *HABERMAS: public sphere* as realm of rational discussion over shared values · communication as mutual learning, search for understanding · debate as persuasion based on shared value claims and collective identities · building a common lifeworld and projects of human emancipation · suspension of instrumental purposes to focus on collective values · *skilled leaders as consensus-builders in dialogue over common good*	· *GRAMSCI: civil society* as terrain of power and struggle between contending classes · communication as ideological dispute in the "field of ideas" · debate as a "war of position"; trenches and breaches · building hegemonies and counter-hegemonies; historical "blocs" · articulation of new "subjects" of political struggles for social reform · *skilled leaders as "organic intellectuals" proposing moral and intellectual reforms*
Actions	Reflective Problem Solving	Tactical Maneuver
	· *DEWEY: democratic community* as locus of attention and improvement · communication as reflective deliberation about shared problems · debate as evaluation of past practices and experimental consideration of future · building democratic relationships and a scientific approach to social problems · intertwining ends and means, value and purpose · *skilled leaders as facilitators of joint learning and problem solving*	· *MACHIAVELLI: the "city"* as an arena of struggle over power, position, and resources · communication as negotiation, bargaining, and discursive maneuver · debate as manipulation of information and rhetoric · building opportunistic relationships and positions of control · distinction between tactic and strategy, ends and means · *skilled leaders as energetic, "virtuous" citizens able to command and control*

forms of action are driven by those of Gramsci or Machiavelli. All of these modes of action are necessary for democratic politics at some time or another. Furthermore, these are not only analytical distinctions, but empirical ones as well. We can observe people switching between these modes as they interact. So there is a performative difference here, a difference in footing—in what communication is understood to be about—within particular social settings. We can also see differences of emphasis. While most political groups involve some combination of these, their leaders may develop greater skills in one than another. Institutionally, groups may develop elaborate methodologies, practices, and self-understandings that sustain some of these modes more than others, thereby accounting for differences in emphases.

We can roughly categorize these modes along two dimensions. The first is their relative emphasis on collaboration as opposed to competition. The theoretical models of Habermas and Dewey put a normative stress on communication as an intrinsically collaborative process, aimed at establishing mutual understanding and joint problem solving, respectively. While both theorists certainly acknowledge the existence of contention and disagreement in society, they maintain a basic optimism about the possibility of overcoming this dissention (at least provisionally) through rational consensus-formation or reflective deliberation. Gramsci and Machiavelli, in contrast, start from the more pessimistic presumption that social life is intrinsically contentious, whether that contention is understood to occur between social classes (or historical "blocs") or between leaders and factions in a fractious city. Again, both certainly admit the possibility of collaboration and alliance, but always with the assumption of an underlying competitive struggle.

The second dimension is the relative emphasis on ideas versus actions. In different ways, Habermas and Gramsci place a greater accent on the elaboration of ideas as opposed to deliberation over actions. Habermas distinguishes the "public sphere" as the realm of rational discussion about shared values, separated from instrumental purposes. Similarly, Gramsci sees civil society as a terrain of cultural struggle, where actors dispute hegemony in the field of ideas (especially when more overt warfare is impossible). While practical action is not inconsequential for these theorists, it does receive a lighter emphasis. In contrast, Dewey and Machiavelli stress the practical and instrumental side of communication. While ideas and discourse are certainly important to both of them, they are seen as being closely intertwined with political purposes and actions. Dewey rejects Habermas's strong distinction between values and purposes, seeing debate as the source of practical problem solving in the democratic community. Likewise, Machiavelli stresses the purposeful dimension of communication, seeing the control of information and rhetoric as tactical tools for gaining and maintaining political power.

These four theorists also present us with different models of skilled leadership. The Habermasian model stresses skill in exploratory dialogue; good leaders are those able to facilitate the free exchange of ideas in order to build a rational consensus among contending ideas of the common good. Deweyian leaders are also seen as being facilitators of joint learning, although they are also charged with reflective problem solving; they help people to evaluate the past and project into the future in order to solve collective problems. For Gramsci, leaders must demonstrate skill in discursive positioning; they serve as "organic intellectuals," proposing moral and intellectual reforms that express the interests and ideals of particular classes or class alliances. Finally, Machiavellian leaders become skilled in tactical maneuver; they must serve as energetic or "virtuous" rulers capable of the relational flexibility necessary for command and control.

Each of these leadership skills is important to the construction of certain kinds of publics, depending on the kinds of relations they bring forward or backward. That is, they can each help to enable productive communication among heterogeneous actors, through the temporary suspension of some aspects of identities and relations. This identity work variously plays up or down the competitive or collaborative dimension of relationships, as well as the focus on ideas as opposed to action. I am not arguing that some of these modes are necessarily "more productive" than others; rather the "products" of such skilled communication vary according to the mode in play. Depending on orientations toward exploratory dialogue, discursive positioning, reflective problem solving, or tactical maneuver, communication in such publics may result in new understandings, cultural reforms, practical solutions or provisional alliances— all important dimensions of political interaction. On the other hand, the *unskilled* or low-quality use of these modes of action may contribute to communicative tension or breakdown: endlessly circling discussions, rigid posturing, narrowly technocratic solutions, or devious manipulation.

I take this argument one step further and argue that movement between modes of communication is in turn tied to the relative salience of different institutional affiliations.[8] The selective identity work by which actors foreground and background some aspects of their identities favors the activation of some modes of communication over others. For example, the salience of partisan identities or other contentious relationships may favor activation of the more competitive modes of discursive positioning and tactical maneuver. Moreover, institutions that understand their identities in collaborative terms—for example, some kinds of religious, cultural, or professional associations—may invoke exploratory dialogue and reflective problem solving. Actors may switch between modes as different identities and relations gain or lose salience within a given interaction.

These modes of communication are not just exogenous categories that I pull from my theorist's hat to apply *ex ante* to social reality. Rather, they were operative models, theoretical references that activists actually talked about, in more or less explicit or coded fashion. Gramscian ideas of hegemony and resistance, for example, had been an important reference for the Brazilian left since the 1980s, particularly amidst a large sector of the PT. In 1988, I attended a course on political formation for social movement activists organized by the center-left factions of the PT; this course used Gramsci to dedogmatize (and bring a cultural awareness to) traditional Marxist ideology. Likewise, church-based popular movements drew heavily on Deweyian ideas of transformative learning from reflection on everyday life, as filtered through the "liberation pedagogy" of Paulo Freire.[9] Habermasian ideas about the public sphere had more recently begun to filter into the debates of the more moderate sectors of the left (billing themselves as either "radical" or "social" democrats), often linked to fashionable 1990s ideas about the "horizontal networks of civil society." And, of course, Machiavelli had long been a favorite reference of traditional Marxist-Leninist organizations, which draw on the language of tactic and strategy in the pursuit of ideologically justified projects of command and control.[10]

While we can suggestively trace the four models to the subregions of the Brazilian left in which these theorists were read and discussed, this gives too cognitive an understanding of how these models work. They were also *modes of action*—involving skilled performances—that supported and were supported by certain relational and institutional configurations. Moreover, even actors who would proudly self-identify as a Gramscian, a Habermasian, a Deweyian, or a Machiavellian switched into the other modes from time to time, perhaps more frequently than they were aware, given the changing configurations of their settings of interaction.

Among the Brazilian youth activists that I studied, I saw all of these leadership skills in action (as well as their less skilled, sometimes harmful variations). However, the four modes of communication do not map neatly onto particular groups and individuals. Instead, they become an important component of specific communicative settings. Different institutional milieus enable some modes over others—as well as ways of switching between them—thereby constituting recognizable institutional styles. Such styles result from the way that people construct their publics, that is, from the relational composition and communicative practices that characterize the institutionalized settings in which people come together. Attentiveness to these modes also helps us understand the different processes by which publics move from elaboration to deliberation, that is, from the generation of ideas and proposals to decision making over the practical steps needed to pursue them.

I turn now to examine two of these institutionalized settings more carefully, showing how the institutional structure and relational composition of these publics favored some modes of communication over others. In the student congresses and councils of UNE, I watched how the more competitive footings of communication, both in relation to ideas and actions, dominated interaction, forcing more collaborative modes onto the sidelines. I contrast this style with the assemblies of the Catholic youth pastoral, in which young people constructed a more collaborative footing for their partisan identities, allowing for a greater degree of exploratory dialogue and pragmatic reflection, although at the cost of partisan diversity.

INSTITUTIONALIZED STYLES: THE LEGACY OF THE 1980s

Many of the criticisms of the organized student movement during the 1990s were directed toward a style of communication developed a decade earlier, during the highly partisan period of the 1980s. As I describe in chapter 4, the highly competitive yet institutionally unified style of the organized student movement was generated out of the (often rocky) attempts by student activists to combine student, civic, and partisan logics of association. Likewise, the more collaborative, yet self-consciously "autonomous" style of the Catholic youth pastoral arose out of the overlay between religious, popular movement, and partisan activism in poor urban and rural communities.

In 1995–96, I attended many events both of the National Student Union (UNE) and of a more radical branch of the Catholic youth pastoral (PJMP). These events ranged in size, purpose, and composition. In the case of UNE, they included huge national congresses with more than five thousand students, smaller national councils with several hundred students, and smaller leadership meetings of UNE's directorate and executive. In the case of PJMP, I attended meetings, seminars, and assemblies organized by the regional coordination of PJMP for the São Paulo area, ranging in size from a handful of activists to about forty to fifty participants.[11] At many of these events, I conducted formal and informal interviews, collected questionnaires, observed and sometimes participated (when invited) in the activities and discussions. I came to know many of the young activists quite well and talked to them frequently during and after the meetings about their interpretations of what was happening and the meaning of these events for participants.

The meetings of UNE and PJMP demonstrate two types of publics that were institutionalized in the 1980s yet still active during the 1990s, although both were facing challenges. UNE, as I said above, was being critiqued by less-partisan students as well as by groups focusing on racial, professional, and business identities. PJMP was struggling with the conservative retrenchment of the Catholic hierarchy, as well as with shrinking participation in the Catholic base communities, as many young people were drawn to evangelical churches. Nevertheless, many of the communicative practices honed in the 1980s were still intact, sustained by activists who had entered the field in earlier periods as well as by the institutional structures themselves.

To explain the persistence of these styles in the very changed context of the 1990s, we must look to the interface between institutional settings and individual trajectories. On the institutional side, the student movement and the Catholic youth pastoral of the 1980s had established routinized settings with rules, procedures, and informal practices that fostered some modes of communication over others, as I will describe in more detail below. On the individual side, many activists who had been schooled in those settings during the 1980s were still active in the 1990s. This trend appears in my questionnaire data; among leaders in both UNE and PJMP, there was a preponderance of youth from the first three cohorts described in chapter 3 (with the UNE leaders concentrated in periods 2 and 3). These leaders became carriers of those contrasting styles into the activist encounters of the 1990s, contributing to their sustainability in a changed political environment.

As I showed in chapter 3, during the 1990s activists from the earlier cohorts tended to have heavier involvements, often spanning more sectors, than more recent entries. Many high-level UNE and PJMP leaders were full-time activists with intensive involvements in more than one sector. However, they differed in the institutional composition of those involvements. To understand the communicative styles in play in each milieu, we need to see what identities activists were juggling, both personally and as a group. In chapter 2, I introduced the idea of a group's "affiliation profile," that is, the array of affiliations in other kinds of groups that are commonly held by members of collectivity. Table 6.2 (below) presents affiliation profiles for UNE's national directorate as well as for the regional coordination of PJMP. The table shows the percent of respondents in the two leadership bodies that were affiliated in each of the eleven sectors analyzed in this book. To get a sense of activist trajectories, I looked at three temporal designations: during the event year (1995), sometime in the past (prior to 1995), and during the activist's start period (see chapter 3).[12]

Table 6.2 shows a number of interesting patterns. First, it shows that among the top leaders of UNE, student and partisan affiliations were without question the most predominant. Nearly all of the directors of UNE participated in both student organizations and political parties, not only during the event year, but also in their previous trajectories. Many of them started in these sectors; others joined later in their activist careers. Moreover, nearly all participated in the 1992 impeachment movement, as reflected in the high level of past civic/NGO participation (although most leaders didn't start in civic/NGO activism, nor did they continue it afterward). The other two most prominent sectors were course-based organizations (in activists' areas of professional study) and socialist youth organizations, such as the Union of Socialist Youth (linked to the PCdoB), as

TABLE 6.2
Affiliation profiles for UNE and PJMP

	Event year	Past	Start period
	a. UNE Directorate (N=21)		
80-100%	S,P	S,N,P	
60-79%			S
40-59%		C,O	P
20-39%	C,O		O,N
10-19%	N,M,Q	M,R,L,Q	C,R,M
1-9%	R		
0%	D,L,B	D,B	D,L,Q,B
	b. PJMP Coordination (N=27)		
80-100%	R	R	R
60-79%			
40-59%	P,M	P	
20-39%	S	N,M	
10-19%	D,L,N	L,S,D	P
1-9%	C,Q	C,Q	S,M,D
0%	O,B	O,B	C,O,L,N,Q,B

Note: sectors are listed in order of descending percentages.
KEY:
R: Religious group
S: General student movement
P: Political party
M: Urban or rural popular movement
D: Anti-discrimination movement
N: Civic/ethical movement or NGO
O: Socialist youth group
L: Labor union or professional organization
C: Course-based student movement
Q: Research organization
B: Business organization

well as a few smaller ones within the PT. Interestingly, these were mostly mutually exclusive; in 1995, only one respondent participated in both Course Executives and socialist youth organizations (in chapter 8, I will discuss how this was a line of demarcation between PT and PCdoB activists). A scattering of students also participated in popular movements, research organizations, and occasionally, labor or religious groups, although participation in these last two had declined over time. None of the UNE respondents reported any participation in antidiscrimination or business groups.

The affiliation profile was quite different among the leadership of PJMP. All of the Catholic respondents obviously had religious participation, many with multiple forms of participation within the religious sector (i.e., in addition to PJMP, they may have participated in Christian base communities, liturgical groups, or other Catholic "pastorals"). This religious participation was relatively steady over their (sometimes long) careers; only three of the twenty-seven leaders did not begin in the church (these began either in political parties or student groups). The next two most prominent forms of participation at the time of questionnaire collection were in political parties and popular movements. Over half of the respondents were affiliated with parties in 1995 and another quarter declared themselves to be sympathizers, mostly with the PT. Likewise, while only a few respondents began activism in popular movements, by 1995, almost half were involved in urban or rural organizing. About a quarter of the activists were involved in the student movement, and a handful took part in antidiscrimination, labor, and NGO activism.[13] Very few participated in professionally oriented activity (in course-based or research groups). Unlike the student movement, none of the Catholic youth were involved in socialist youth organizations, but like UNE, none were involved in business activity.

These analyses suggest that the structural patterns underlying the two forms of partisan bridging described in chapter 4 were still intact. Student and Catholic activists straddled similar sets of sectors as their counterparts in the 1980s—student, partisan, and occasionally, civic participation in the case of the student movement, and religious, partisan, and popular movement activism in the case of the Catholic youth. Most had developed stylized ways in which they maneuvered among their partisan and other kinds of activist identities, as they built relationships and struggled to maintain their institutions.

I summarize the differences between the student and Catholic encounters in table 6.3. In my ethnographic discussion, I look at the institutional purpose and structure of the two settings, as well as their different affiliation profiles. I examine ways in which these affiliation profiles were performatively enacted, that is, the relative salience given to some affiliations over others. I analyze the partisan structure of the settings, comparing the distribution and expression of partisan alignments, as well as the ways in which participants gave expression to specialized identities, that is, those that were understood to have a subsidiary connection to the institutional purpose of the encounter. I also discuss the ways in which they ritually unified their respective publics, despite varying degrees of internal heterogeneity. I show how these elements of the relational composition and performative footings favored certain modes of communication over others, leading to quite distinct and recognizable institutional styles.

THE CONGRESS OF UNE: POSITIONING AND MANEUVER

In mid-1995, student activists around the country began buzzing over the upcoming Congress of UNE. The National Student Union held its national congress every one to two years (in the 1990s it was mostly on a two-year cycle). At these congresses, three thousand to five thousand delegates elected from university departments all around the country converged on some central location to deliberate on the program and structure of UNE, as well as to elect its national leadership. The delegates were chosen at the department level in a variety of ways—sometimes by balloting, at other times by assemblies or by circulating lists of signatures in the classroom. Needless to say, the certification of delegates was a very tricky and contentious business; as a mid-level PCdoB activist named Julio told me somewhat gleefully during the certification process, "We're in a war!" His soon-to-be-elected-president co-partisan, Renato, told me that "the congress is decided here, in the certification."

The reason for this warlike quality was that the congress was high stakes. The directors of UNE not only had a historic, publicly recognized platform (which could be useful for partisan projection as well as for future political careers), but they also had access to the resources and infrastructure of the organization, useful for traveling around the country to promote their own factions or other involvements, along with UNE business.[14] For this reason the leaders of UNE insisted so strongly on the importance of having one, centralized, national organization, rather than have UNE's public voice (and resource flow) diluted by parallel organizations linked to other political forces. Given the number of factions hoping for a slice of the pie, disputes over leadership were intense. Since 1989, the leadership of UNE had been determined through proportional representation among competing slates (often themselves compositions of forces), a change from the winner-takes-all structure that UNE had throughout most of the 1980s. As a result, each faction had an interest in making the strongest showing possible, not only to "win" the congress (only possible through coalitions), but also to gain bargaining power in the battle over space in the directorship, intensely negotiated during and after the congress.

The congresses of UNE consisted of not just one setting, but rather a composite of settings, often overlapping or punctuated during a four-day period. Some of these encounters were highly structured and ritualized

TABLE 6.3
Comparison of student and Catholic publics

	UNE	PJMP
Institutional purpose	Election of leaders, approving platform and plan of action	Evaluation of past year, formulating priorities and projects for next
Affiliation profile	All: student, partisan Many: socialist, course-based Some: antidiscrimination, religious, popular, NGO, research	All: religious Many: partisan, popular movement Some: student, labor, NGO, anti-discrimination, research, course-based
Identity salience	· Marked, unifying student identities ("UNE somos nos!") · Marked partisan/factional identities · Sidelined spaces for professional, religious, anti-discrimination identities · Segmented and cross-cutting socialization	· Marked religious identities · Assumed partisan identity; factional suppression · Featured forums on "intermediate" involvements in student, labor, community, antidiscrimination movements · Focus on recovering "personal" life: affectivity, sexuality
Partisan expression	Competition	Convergence
Specialized identities	Segmentation	Integration
Unifying ritual	Ritualized student chants, music, T-shirts and banners, dance parties	Evocative religious ritual, group games, music, prayer, relaxation, dance parties
Dominant modes	Discursive positioning → Tactical maneuver	Exploratory dialogue → Reflective problem solving
Submerged modes	Reflective problem solving Exploratory dialogue	Discursive positioning Tactical maneuver

while others were fluid and informal. Colorful and rambunctious plenary sessions held in large stadiums alternated with small discussion groups, specialized forums, and backstage strategy meetings. Informal sociability happened everywhere, often segregated within organized political forces but sometimes cutting across them, in buses, lodgings, patios, dining areas, and late-night dance parties.

I attended two of these congresses, held at the University of Brasilia (1995) and at the Federal University of Minas Gerais in Belo Horizonte (1997). While the official purpose of these events was to deliberate program and strategy and elect national leaders, there were also more submerged purposes. The gatherings were spaces for the emergence and consolidation of leadership, for factional realignments, and for ideological and organizational dispute. Because of their mass-based character, the congresses were also grounds for the factional co-optation of recruits, as well as a chance to give UNE public visibility in the media and among the invited dignitaries who attended the opening plenaries.

While the students at the congresses had a wide range of affiliations (from religious and popular movement activism to professional, NGO, or antidiscrimination activity), by far the most prominent identities were student and partisan affiliations. The participants marked their student identities through the historic ritualized chant of "UNE Somos Nos!" ("UNE is us"), often deployed to shore up student unity at moments of high internal or external challenge. By definition, all delegates represented local department-based student organizations (CAs—Academic Centers), and most were also associated with a political party and/or party faction. Many students told me that nonaligned students felt lost and disoriented at the congress; if they weren't associated with a partisan force on arrival, they were much more likely to be so on leaving. Some students did claim independence; the self-designated "League of Independent Students" (LEI) was a visible force at the 1995 congress, although the talk on the ground was that the league wasn't "really" independent, but rather its leaders were promoted opportunistically by assorted parties. In any case, the "independents" constituted a political faction of their own, entering the bargaining process with everyone else.

Partisan relations were clearly characterized by competition, as youth associated with parties and party factions tried to project their force in the dispute for control. Partisan and factional identities were highly salient, marked by colorful T-shirts and banners as well as by constant chants, sloganeering, and drum rolls that resounded through the hallways and plenary sessions. Partisan identifications were lightly masked as "theses," referring to the platforms of contending forces, elaborated prior to the congress and circulated as pamphlets during the proceedings. These theses often had evocative names taken from popular songs or other cultural references; "Those Who Come Full Force Don't Tire," and "Salute to Those with Courage" were two from the reigning PCdoB (and their associated youth group UJS). The opposition theses had provocative names like "UNE for Everyone" (moderate PT), "I Won't Adapt" (left PT), "Indignation" (PDT), "Full Reverse" (PSTU) and "Tomorrow Will Be Another Day" (Independents). These names were stamped on badge-sized stickers with colorful logos; as alliances began to form, students from negotiating camps "flirted" by wearing multiple stickers as a sign of approximation, only to tear them off if the deal went sour.

While student and partisan identities were most salient, other more "specialized" identities also circulated through the congress, although their expression was largely segmented from the main agenda and meeting venues. Socialist youth groups, professional associations, black students, women students, and Catholic youth held their own meetings on the side, sometimes officially sponsored but more often informally staged, without much attention in the plenary debates. While some students were also involved in popular movements, labor activism, NGOs, or research activity, such identities received little or no expression.

The relational and institutional structure of this public—highly marked partisan identities competing for resources, leadership, and recruits, with the segmentation of more specialized or cross-cutting identities into less salient venues—contributed to the dominance of the communicative modes of discursive positioning and tactical maneuver. While there was some evidence of exploratory dialogue and reflective problem solving, these modes played a quite subordinate role. As many people told me, at the Congress of UNE, "Não se discute"; in other words, there was lots and lots of talk, but very little of what either Habermas or Dewey would call discussion, in terms of a genuine attempt to understand the others' point of view or to learn from each other in order to solve joint problems. Rather, the focus of the congress was on partisan competition, expressed through ideological as well as electoral dispute.

Discursive positioning was particularly well developed in the months leading up to the congresses, during which each faction spent months elaborating documents—the omnipresent "theses"—that staked out their position in the discursive field. They circulated those documents within their "camp"—sometimes composed of several allied factions—as they attempted to build internal consensus for the positions that their leaders would argue for on the floor of the congress. The theses developed positions on the "national conjuncture" as well as on issues related to the university system, education policy, the student movement, and the structure of UNE itself. The most contentious issues in national and university politics were usually whether or not to participate in government-sponsored educational forums. The PCdoB and moderates were in favor, the left wing of various stripes vehemently against—evoking counteraccusations of "rigidity" vs. "selling out," as I describe in chapter 9.

In general, the PCdoB took positions that combined general critiques of capitalism and imperialism with pragmatic proposals for building alliances within the current configuration of Brazilian politics. The opposition to the PCdoB was divided ideologically, with a discernible hegemonic battle over the vision and focus of the student movement. On the one hand were groups that criticized the overemphasis of the student movement on broad national questions and its inattention to the educational problems of most concern to students. This position united the moderate and right wing of the PT, the organized Independents, the Social Democrats (PSDB), and the more moderate socialist groups. On the other hand, many students insisted that the historical role of the student movement was to intervene in the major political questions of the day, which at the moment should consist of frontal, proactive opposition to the government of President Fernando Henrique Cardoso (of the PSDB), in the struggle to defeat its neoliberal policies and proposals for constitutional reform. The second position was defended by the left wing of the PT, the radical Trotskyist PSTU, and a number of other small Marxist-Leninist and Trotskyist factions.

The theses elaborated by the various groups became the basis for ideological positioning throughout the congress. This Gramscian positioning happened in the plenary speeches of leaders in support or opposition to specific proposals, as well as in the smaller discussion groups held to generate and debate those proposals. Discussion groups were often used as sounding boards to judge the investment of different groups in ideological positions, as well as their wiggle room for compromise and bargaining. When electoral slates were finally negotiated (usually composites of the original "theses"), a leader would be designated to defend the slate, using the compromise language worked out by the leaders in order to give a veneer of ideological consistency to the newly allied "bloc."

Despite this evident discursive battle, the congress was not all about ideology. As the congress moved from elaboration (writing and debating the "theses") to deliberation (voting on proposals and slates), tactical maneuver dominated the congress. Continuous rounds of backstage negotiations pulsed through the crevices of the event as leaders attempted to stitch together electoral alliances. The system of proportional representation heightened the climate of bargaining, as leaders horse-traded not only on ideological positions, but also on leadership positions in the directorship and access to resources and infrastructure.

These intense huddled negotiations (or *conchavos*) happened in every corner of the congress: in the hallways, in backrooms, on the plenary floor, in the bleachers, at the entrances to the meeting halls, in bars and food stands. Those involved were the *capas pretas* (so-called black cloaks, or top dogs) of the various groups, almost all of them male. You could tell from the structure of the *conchavos* who were the elite and who were the aspirants or second-levels; the former were usually standing square-leggedly in the center of a cluster, while the later were more peripheral and mobile, nosing eagerly around but not getting the same attention or respect. Often I would see people purposively excluded from a cluster, with backs pointedly turned or a selected group pulled away to a more secluded place. Sometimes the *conchavos* were "in-house" (deliberating strategies among leaders of a particular group) and sometimes they were cross-group, as when positions, alliances, and procedures were negotiated with the PCdoB or between leaders of different opposition groups.

The Machiavellian mode was also evident in the dramatic maneuvers carried out in the plenary sessions, especially as the buzz of negotiations was reaching its peak. For example, at a certain point in the 1995 congress, all of the negotiations hinged on one numerical contingency: if all of the opposition forces united, would they have the votes to defeat the PCdoB? Despite deep ideological differences, most of the opposition forces agreed on a basic critique of what they saw as the out-of-touch, bureaucratized, and authoritarian regime of the PCdoB. But would it be worth all of the trade-offs to unite? The costs might include not only ideological concessions, but also possible loss of position in the directorship that they might be able to get independently or in alliance with the PCdoB.

I was seated among the PT delegation when a high-level leader came zooming over from the negotiations at the front, summoning the second-tier activists into an urgent huddle. The top opposition leaders had all agreed to test their strength by zeroing in on a relatively minor question—democratizing UNE's newspaper—and turning it into a showdown with the PCdoB. The drums started rolling and chants of "oposição, unificada!" ("unified opposition!") resounded across the bleachers, as leaders from each of the opposition groups gave impassioned speeches about democratization of the means of communication. A vote was called, first conducted the usual way by waving delegate badges in the air. When the PCdoB tried to declare victory, the opposition demanded a formal vote count (an operation lasting several hours, a significant delay in the proceedings). The vote count showed that the congress was nearly evenly divided, with the PCdoB ahead by a mere hundred votes. The closeness of the votes intensified negotiations, since it signaled that the PCdoB could be defeated if the opposition peeled away a few votes. The opposition frantically tried to stitch together a precarious alliance, which would be threatened if any of the forces decided to go it alone. This in fact is what happened: the internally fractious PT found itself under heavy pressure from party leadership to unite, which it could only do by throwing off its right and left flanks (the independents and the hard-line Trotskyists, respectively). This in turn propelled everyone else into deciding to "mark position" (i.e., assert their own ideological position, rather than make compromises to form alliances), ensuring the victory of the PCdoB. While I was completely taken aback by these sudden developments, most of the leaders assured me that these were typical congressional maneuvers, and that everyone there knew that they were playing a numbers game.

While discursive posturing and tactical maneuver clearly dominated the major settings of the congress, I also found evidence of the more collaborative modes, often in informal or less visible venues. I found pockets of reflective problem solving mostly after the congress, in the postmortem within particular camps. The Deweyian mode was especially evident among the losers, who held long and intense evaluation sessions to figure out what they had done wrong and what they should try to change in the future. While these might shade into tactical maneuver, the tone was different. There was more genuinely a sense of a collectivity trying to learn from mistakes and reflect on what they were about, in relation to both ends and means. They were trying to come up with pragmatic ideas about how they might improve their future interventions in the student movement—and therefore, they hoped, in the wider society.

For example, after the PCdoB and its allies won the 1995 congress, the various subgroups of the PT went home to debrief and rethink their practices. The more moderate groups of the PT ("UNE for Everyone") reflected on their distance from students and resolved that in order to gain support they needed to concentrate on the "everyday experience" of youth, conducting seminars and workshops around the country that touched on issues of education, sexuality, culture, employment, and technology. They also proposed to innovate methodologically by working with theater, music, and video, speaking the "new language" of young people. The reflections of the more radical PT groups ("I Won't Adapt") led them to a different, more Gramscian conclusion, that it was time to radicalize the opposition to the PCdoB by opposing what they saw as the Communist leadership's accommodationist and authoritarian policies. These deliberations over practice had repercussions for the future practices of the two groups, as I will describe in chapter 9.

While these forms of reflective deliberation mostly took place in segregated intrapartisan settings, the Deweyian mode could also occasionally be seen in cross-partisan settings. As the new proportionally elected directorship of UNE took office, the leaders had to carry out the day-to-day operations of the organization—which meant solving problems of coordination, communication, and logistical planning. In subsequent meetings of the Directorate and Executive of UNE that I attended, the meetings would (albeit occasionally) switch out of discursive positioning into this problem-solving mode, in which the directors of various tendencies collaborated in getting things done.

Sometimes cross-partisan episodes of pragmatic reflection happened informally, often in bars and restaurants. For example, in 1996 I had lunch with two PCdoB leaders—including Renato, who had been elected president of UNE at the 1995 congress, as well as two PT leaders, one of whom had been one of the candidates opposing Renato. Renato quizzed the PT leaders on their ideas for an upcoming Latin American Seminar on Education that UNE was organizing, asking for suggestions on how to make the congress "more interactive." They agreed to sit down to go over the program and schedule together to consider methodology and speakers. Renato told me that sometimes such relaxed conversations were "more productive" than formal planning meetings, which tended to disintegrate into confrontations between partisan forces. (In another private conversation, however, Renato confessed to me that he thought he was "very Machiavellian," in response to my complementing him on his ability to dialogue well with other political groups.)

Exploratory dialogue was harder to find in this intensely competitive climate, but still present around the edges. I found inklings of the Habermasian mode not so much in the organized discussion groups, which were mostly taken over by Gramscian positioning, but rather in the informal, backstage discussions that were occurring in spaces of socialization all over the congress. Often these conversations took place between members of a shared camp, but sometimes they happened across camps, especially in situations in which lower-level activists and new recruits got into more free-flowing, less studied debates that explored the ins and outs of various contentious issues. While activists in such settings were not charged with reaching a formal consensus, this was where persuasion, listening, and weighing of different sides could more easily take place.

Within their own intraparty context, the PCdoB called such settings of informal debate the *ativo* (from the word Portuguese word for "active"), referring to a kind of vibrant shared lifeworld among militants in which ideas were debated in a more relaxed, less monitored way, and where problems and tensions emerged that the leadership had to pay attention to. The PT also tried to generate exploratory dialogue in many of its events, often through the technique of going around the room to share experiences and perspectives—again trying to understand the other and construct a joint lifeworld that might make it easier to attain a working consensus.

The movement between these different modes of communication—as supported by institutionalized settings—amounts what I am calling a "style" of political communication. Note that this style is not just about the *student* identity, but also about how actors negotiated the expression or suppression of other aspects of their identities. In this case, the salience of partisan identities—in a heterogeneous, centralized, and competitive public that sidelined less contentious identities—contributed to the dominance of discursive positioning and tactical maneuver. Leaders who achieved high-level positions in this institutional milieu had more settings in which to hone skills in competitive discourse and maneuver than in collaborative dialogue or problem solving. Nevertheless, despite widespread frustration at the lack of "real discussion" (in a more exploratory or reflective sense), the publics of UNE did get things done. UNE's combination of high ritual with partisan contingency contributed to the debate of ideas, formation of alliances, and maintenance of the institutional structure of the student movement as a precariously unified "voice of the students."

THE ASSEMBLY OF PJMP: DIALOGUE AND REFLECTION

Almost diametrically opposed to the highly competitive climate of the Congress of UNE were the assemblies and coordination meetings of the Catholic youth pastoral. In chapter 4, I argued that the youth pastoral helped to generate a different form of partisan bridging than the student movement, in which political party participation (particularly in the PT) was a means of integrating diverse activist involvements, although these were carefully subordinated to a reflective, suprapartisan faith. Here I examine the performative dimension of this style, as expressed in the highly institutionalized publics of the youth pastoral. Like the congresses of UNE, these settings had been shaped within the heyday of partisan activism in the 1980s. However, unlike the student movement, the youth pastoral managed to construct its publics in ways that enabled the more collaborative modes of communication in relation to both ideas and action, although more competitive modes could also occasionally be found.

During my fieldwork, I attended meetings of both the "general" youth pastoral (known as PJ-Geral) and PJMP, the more militant branch of the youth pastoral focusing on poor and marginalized youth in the "popular milieu." Since I was interested in multiple militancies, I spent more time with PJMP activists, who tended to be more intensely involved in other, nonreligious forms of participation. Here I focus on the PJMP Regional Assembly held in November 1995 at a retreat center in the southern zone of São Paulo, although I also draw on observations from other PJMP encounters.

At this Regional Assembly, about thirty leaders from São Paulo and surrounding cities gathered for a weekend meeting to evaluate the experiences of the past year and lay out projects and priorities for the next. As this was a three-day holiday weekend, the activists decided to gather a day earlier than usual, reserving Friday as a day "just for us," to engage in the kind of personal reflection on experience that the progressive church has historically called "revision of life and practice." As at the Congress of UNE, interspersed with these deliberations were copious amounts of high-spirited ritual and sociability, although they took a somewhat different tone: songs, prayers, group games and relaxation techniques, teasing, practical jokes, sexual innuendo, and of course, the obligatory late-night dance party.

As at the Congress of UNE, the relational composition and institutionalized practices of these settings contributed to the predominance of some modes of communication over others. While participants had a wide range of affiliations, religion was clearly the most salient identity. The religious character of the assembly was ritually marked by prayer, music, scriptural reflection, and religious artifacts like crosses (often handmade and artistically expressive of local political themes). The youth also scheduled time for what they called "moments of spirituality" in which the group was plunged into intense emotional and spiritual reflection. In one such moment, a leader played a rap song written by young people describing urban violence and the need for faith and consciousness. After sharing painful personal reflections on the song, participants were asked to get up one by one or in pairs to look in a mirror placed in the center of the room, next to a sheet twisted in the shape of a cross. I found myself in tears at the end of this experience, along with most of the others, until the mood was revived with a lively samba beat.

Alongside this strong religious focus, participants also expressed many of their nonreligious identities. PJMP meetings were just as partisan as the student congresses—the difference was that nearly everyone belonged to the same party. Partisan relations were characterized by convergence, rather than competition; it could be assumed that everyone was either affiliated with or a sympathizer of the PT. While I was assured that PJMP did sometimes have participants from other parties, none were present among the leaders at this assembly. Their partisan identities were not suppressed; rather they were the air they breathed. Discussion groups focused on the relation between the church, the popular movements, and the party, and no one had to inquire what "O Partido" referred to. Many were committed, longtime party activists; some older participants and advisors laid claim to being founding members of the PT. However, factional differences were suppressed. There was almost no mention of the fierce factional battles within the PT, although several activists told me personally that they were associated with one or another PT faction.

A recurrent source of tension and reflection for these activists was the question of how to combine their religious involvement with participation in what they called "intermediate organizations"—the array of community, student, labor, NGO, antidiscrimination, and other forms of activism in which they often had multiple involvements. In contrast to the Congress of UNE, these "specialized" identities were not segmented from the main work of the assembly. Rather, participants dedicated several blocks of time to discussing how to integrate these "intermediate" involvements into their religious activism (and vice versa). In one plenary, three leaders described the tensions and difficulties involved in their participation in the housing movement, literacy education, and the internal politics of the PT. The activists then divided into subgroups focusing on partisan politics, popular movements, education/student movement, community movements, and popular culture (including Afro-Brazilian and indigenous culture).[15]

Some activists had a hard time choosing which group to participate in, since they had several different involvements, usually weighing heavily on their time and energy. A frequent refrain was the need to "prioritize" and "integrate" their various involvements in order to live a coherent, well-balanced life. In addition, there were calls to recover the "personal" and "affective" aspect of their identities, including paying more attention to sexuality and family relations. Sometimes they got so caught up in all of their political involvements, they worried, that "we forget to be young."

In the group on partisan politics, I found a heated discussion about the conflicts generated by partisan involvements. The discussion turned personal: one of the participants, a founding PJMP leader (and committed *petista*), had recently been asked to leave the PT after taking a job with a right-wing candidate (which he said was necessary to support his young family). In addition to ethical concerns, his fellow group members were worried about what this might mean in terms of group camaraderie, especially in electoral periods, when they often went out together to do leafleting, postering, and other campaign activities. But they rejected their friend's proposal to change the name of the discussion group from "partisan politics" to simply "politics," declaring that the relation of the church to the political parties deserved attention all its own. The discussion deepened to analyze two sorts of influence that the PJMP might have on partisan politics. First, they could influence the style of action of militants in the party, by bringing "Christian" values—tolerance, dialogue, ethics, ecumenism, consensus, respect for the human being—to partisan politics. And second, they could help bring new people to ("the") political party by stimulating discussion in community-based movements about the importance of party politics.

This combination of partisan convergence with the integration of more specialized identities made possible a much more collaborative tone than at student movement events. The fact that the assembly took place within a camp helped to enable the exploratory and reflective modes of communication. During the first day of personal reflection, the activists used a number of techniques for exploratory dialogue, focusing on a search for self- and interpersonal understanding. Prior to embarking on evaluations or proposals, the young people engaged what we might call Habermasian "identity work," exploring elements of their shared lifeworld. In writing, in small group, and in larger assemblies they answered the questions "Who am I?" "What are my dreams, desires, and ideals?" "Why did I come to this meeting, and what do I hope to get from it?" They talked about their confusion, ambivalences, fears, but also about their struggles (*lutas*) and their hopes for the "transformation of reality."

One group of women became so involved in talking about their lives that they never got around to the assigned task of writing things down; they began "traveling on our problems" and thought it was better to "let things flow," especially since they all admitted how difficult it was to talk about themselves during their day-to-day lives. Ronaldo, the PJMP activist described in chapter 3 (who was secretary-general of the regional coordination), said that part of the reason he was there was to "see my friends," although one of the other youth present worried that PJMP would turn into "a pastoral of friends of PJMP." Referring to the historic methodology of "See, Judge, Act," he pointed out a typical shortcoming of publics based on exploratory exchange: "there's a lot of see, judge, see, judge. What about action?"

The second day started out with similar open-ended dialogue, although this time at a group level. In small groups as well as in the plenary, the activists attempted to come to a consensus about the core values and mission of the group, which saw itself as expressing hopes and struggles of mostly of poor and working-class young people from the urban peripheries. No decisions were made in these sessions; discussion about PJMP wove into discussion of the "political conjuncture" and was allowed to circle around, until it was usually pulled loosely together by a couple of skilled facilitators.

In later sessions, the group switched quite clearly from an exploratory to a problem-solving mode, moving into Deweyian evaluation and prognosis. They again broke into groups, charged with evaluating what was going wrong and right in their concrete day-to-day practices in their local churches and communities. They spent a good deal of time describing, in sometimes excruciating detail, the history and recent experiences of PJMP in each of the neighborhoods or cities where groups were based. They also engaged in reflective—and sometimes anguished—discussion about the "advances" and the "difficulties" they were facing in various places. This was a period of contraction, not growth, in Catholic base communities (CEBs) throughout Brazil, as Pope John Paul II was clamping down on radical versions of liberation theology and installing a more conservative hierarchy. The young people talked about their lack of resources, money, and spaces to meet; frequent lack of support from church communities; the exhaustion of trying to do so much (and of having so many meetings!); and the frustration and disillusionment when idealism seemed to lead to no concrete victories. They also criticized the lack of adequate attention to spirituality in the groups, which contributed to the loss of participants to the charismatic and evangelical churches that were surging in the poorer neighborhoods. At the same time, they sought comfort from the creativity and energy of some local PJMP groups, which were drawing on theater and culture to engage new young people, as well as contributing to popular movements in their communities.

On the third day, they divided into subregional groups, during which each brainstormed a set of proposals about the structure and priorities of PJMP (including issues of finances, methodology, clerical advising, and future encounters). These proposals were written up in a colored marker on big sheets of newsprint, and two of the leaders led the group through a quite skilled and efficient process of synthesis and elimination, which in only a few cases came to a vote. One controversial question was whether "improving finances" and "building nuclei" should be considered priorities; one activist argued vehemently that these were means and not ends, and they were in danger of organizing for organizing's sake, not for the sake of the larger project. They also voted, in nonsecret, noncompetitive elections, on the leaders charged with coordinating those projects. They seemed to be adverse to open leadership disputes; when there was some backstage discontent with the job one of the current leaders was doing, the proposal was to expand the position by adding names rather than to vote that person down. This part of the meeting was brisk and practiced, certainly a skilled example of what Dewey might call democratic deliberation.

Amidst this highly collaborative and reflective environment, there were still traces of more competitive orientations. The PJMP activists considered themselves to be engaged in a hegemonic struggle with more conservative wings of the Catholic youth pastoral, which objected to the class-centered discourse and practice of the more radical youth. PJMP leaders made a big point of positioning themselves as a pastoral "of poor youth," not "for poor youth," rejecting the paternalism in the latter approach. They reacted angrily on the first day when a visiting priest advisor from the general PJ questioned the value of a pastoral specifically dedicated to impoverished youth. To add insult to injury, the priest said that most of the youth at the meeting were from the "middle class" and therefore not "of the popular milieu" at all. This evoked indignant discussion later during lunch. While most of the leaders present did not live in *favelas* (shantytown slums) and had houses and families, they insisted that the majority lived in poorer neighborhoods of the periphery, went to ill-equipped public schools, worked at low-paying jobs, had very little spending money, and suffered with public transportation and lack of social services. They thereby objected to their disqualification as "subjects" of class transformation.

After the visiting priest had gone, the two young clerical advisors of PJMP (both seminarians) took the floor to engage in a very Gramscian discussion of the "conjuncture" in Brazil and in the church, criticizing the conservative turn of Brazil's Catholic leadership. They described "two churches": one official and conservative and the other popular and progressive (allied with the "elite" and the "people," respectively). Over the years, PJMP had produced piles of texts elaborating its position in relation to the increasingly restrictive church discourse. However, unlike the self-assertive, discourse-prone student activists, the leaders chastised themselves for being "over-intellectualized" and assuming a "posture of superiority" in relation to "less politicized" youth, reminding each other to be "more in the milieu" and not lose touch with the bases.

Tactical maneuver was harder to find, since nakedly instrumental impulses were rarely overtly expressed. However, occasionally, a mildly Machiavellian mode surfaced, as in a discussion of voting procedures in the National Commission of the Youth Pastoral of Brazil (PJ-Brasil). This overarching umbrella commission encompassed both the general youth pastoral (PJ-Geral) and the (usually more politicized) specialized branches: PJMP, PJE, PJR (see chapter 4). As secretary-general, Ronaldo gleefully reported on a new voting structure in which PJMP and the other specialized branches had "parity" with PJ-Geral, giving them equal weight in internal votes, disproportionate to their actual size. This meant they could bring issues to the table and help to pass projects and policies that might not have gotten through when voting was dominated by the more sizeable (but more conservative) PJ-Geral. They hoped that this new voting power would give a more progressive turn to PJ-Brasil, as long as they were not vetoed by the conservative bishops. The intricate calculations involved in the dispute of power within the church show that the "numbers game" (and accompanying manipulations) was not completely foreign to Catholic youth, even though they professed to bring a more ethical stance to political communication.

While the practices of the Catholic youth involved all four modes of political communication, the ways in which activists combined, emphasized, and moved between these modes amounts to a style. This style reflected both the relational composition of their settings of interaction—partisan convergence and participation in intermediate organizations—as well as the institutionalized practices developed in response to the problematic dimensions of those relations. Freed from the challenges of partisan competition—and emphasizing homogeneity in terms of their status as youth "of the popular milieu"—PJMP activists had developed practiced, nonadversarial techniques by which they engaged in exploratory dialogue about their lives and their world, as well as in reflective deliberation about their projects and practices. Because the integration of their multiple militancies was such a problematic dimension of their experiences, they developed forums in which to reflect on those intersections and attempt to gain clarity and direction for their practice. Of course, these forums did not eliminate those tensions—hence their reappearance at encounter after encounter, becoming an institutionalized dimension of the reflective practice of the group.

However, despite this strong collaborative ethic, they were still engaged in larger competitive struggles. They were, after all, highly partisan actors, and unlike many university students, they were not queasy about admitting it. They clearly saw their partisan affiliations as legitimating, not delegitimating, aspects of their identities, although they hoped to make partisan practice "more ethical" than the divisive manipulation they saw around them. They also understood themselves to be engaged in a struggle over hegemony within the increasingly conservative church, and were not above engaging in mild electoral manipulation in order to advance that hegemony.

The Interplay of Styles

The forms of communication I observed at the Congress of UNE and the Assembly of PJMP represent two modal styles in Brazilian youth politics. In the case of UNE, the salience of contending partisan identities and the sidelining of more specialized or cross-cutting affiliations contributed to an extremely competitive style of communication. Strong partisan superimposition along with the institutional demands of electoral dispute contributed to a style dominated by discursive positioning and tactical maneuver, although more collaborative modes could be found around the edges. In PJMP, partisan convergence as well as attempts to integrate religious, partisan, and more specialized forms of participation made possible a more collaborative style. PJMP assemblies included institutionalized forums for discussing these intersections as well as practiced methods for invoking exploratory dialogue and reflective problem solving, although competitive modes also made appearances. Both milieus were highly partisan, although partisan heterogeneity or homogeneity allowed them to *wear* their partisanship in different ways. Both had developed institutional structures and practices that sustained these modes, as well as routinized ways that activists moved between them.

To summarize my broader theoretical claims, I have argued that such styles arise in response to the problems and possibilities of particular relational settings. As movement settings become institutionalized, participants develop patterned ways of expressing or suppressing their multiple affiliations, and these patterns of expression and suppression in turn become the lynchpins of styles. Styles of communication have to do with how participants manage the sometimes contending identities in play in a given setting: for example, by seeking integration or segmentation, or by stressing competition or collaboration. In practice, styles are composed of the ways that actors emphasize, combine, and move between four different modes of political communication: exploratory dialogue, discursive positioning, reflective problem solving, and tactical maneuver. By characterizing these performatively as "modes of action," rather than incommensurable theories of politics in general, we gain a more nuanced understanding of the differences between styles, as well as how these are tied to the composition of particular relational contexts.

In addition, I have argued that productive communication in heterogeneous settings requires the creation of "publics," in which people selectively suspend various components of their identities as they provisionally synchronize and equalize relationships. Such publics involve the interplay between the civic and the partisan, and between general and specialized forms of participation. The two publics that I have described enabled activists to carry out the elaborative and deliberative work of their collectivities—evaluating actions, formulating proposals, debating priorities, and appointing leadership—in very different ways. For UNE, this entailed a ritualized unity "as students" that suspended professional or cultural differences, even as partisan camps engaged in overt contention. For PJMP, this involved using a reflective understanding of religious faith to integrate diverse sectoral involvements, while suspending intrapartisan and interpersonal dispute.

The styles of communication in play at the congresses of UNE and the assemblies of PJMP were highly practiced and institutionalized. Many top leaders had been involved in activism for many years, giving them time to acquire the skills needed to make these publics run in relatively predictable and orderly ways (even if, as in the Congress of UNE, the outcome of negotiations was not always clear ahead of time). These leadership skills had been honed in settings bounded by rules and procedures that facilitated relatively smooth transitions between modes (for example, from Gramscian positioning to Machiavellian maneuver, at the UNE Congress, or from Habermasian dialogue to Deweyan problem solving, in the case of PJMP). These rules—both implicit and explicit—in turn made it difficult for the subordinate modes of communication to break into these public spaces, although they did appear interstitially, in the cracks between the dominant institutional forms.

However, these two modal styles of communication were not the only ones in play in 1990s youth politics. The structure and practices of the traditional student movement were coming under attack precisely because new styles of communication and intervention were being generated in different regions of the field. In the next three chapters, I explore the emergence of these newer modes of communication amidst the tumultuous and contested dynamics of mid-1990s student politics.

CHAPTER SEVEN

Defensive Publics in University Settings

THE CONGRESSES of UNE described in the last chapter were grand, color-ful, and highly ritualized publics, in which the electoral tasks of the stu-dent movement were carried out with much fanfare and public drama. These highly institutionalized publics involved entrenched modes of com-munication that would prove very difficult to change, despite repeated efforts at reform. However, at the grassroots levels in the universities, styles of communication were more tenuous and negotiable. Political communication was shaped by local configurations of relations among student factions, university administrations, and the changing student population. Student activists confronted increasing skepticism of parti-sanship among fellow students, even as they wrestled with the legacies of earlier partisan activism in their local milieus. These local contingencies led to variation in the style and quality of political discussion in different university settings.

Following the civic outpouring of the 1992 impeachment movement, interest in student activism momentarily surged, while partisan activism was discredited or pushed underground. Many student activists faced ac-cusations of manipulation, opportunism, and even corruption in associa-tion with their partisan identities. While activists in the 1980s had also struggled with the delegitimating effects of the partisan label, most felt confident enough of the civic role of their budding partisan identities to affirm these publicly as a code for the construction of democracy along with human, political, and social rights. This was becoming much harder for activists in the mid-1990s, who struggled to create forums for debate and action while feeling forced to downplay one of their salient identities.

One way to explain this increasing skepticism toward partisanship would be to focus on broad cultural shifts. The impeachment arguably provoked a discursive realignment that heightened the civic end of the civic-partisan continuum. Reinforced by confirmation of corruption in Brazil's political class, the national celebration of "civicness" that accom-panied the anti-Collor demonstrations threatened to hurl partisanship into the category of opposition to (rather than support for) democratic relations in civil society. This is somewhat puzzling, since as we saw in chapter 5, political parties and party leaders played an important role in exposing the corruption scandal, as well as in building the broad-based coalition for "ethics in politics." But perhaps in doing so, they contributed to the further delegitimation of their own identities as "partisans." At the same time, the impeachment convergence contributed to the entrance of new actors into the civic arena—including middle-class students (the *caras pintadas*) along with professional and business leaders—who arguably had a more privatized understanding of citizenship than the one that emerged in the popular movements of the 1980s.[1] The discursive field that activists confronted after the 1992 infusion of civic energy had been categorically restructured to classify partisanship as a bad thing for student politics, despite the positioning of clearly partisan actors (like Lindberg Farias) at the head of the parade.[2]

This account, while compelling, is problematic on two counts. First, it places too much stress on the structuring force of discourse in itself, as detached from what was happening to relations on the ground. And second, it does not address the specific local forms taken by challenges to traditional student organizations in the 1990s. The outcry against partisanship was a unifying, if ambiguous, symbol for something else; it condensed and filtered a more textured set of struggles over styles of communication and intervention in a complex, multisectoral field.

In early 1995, I began talking to activists and observing events at three prominent São Paulo universities: the Catholic University of São Paulo (PUC-SP), the University of São Paulo (USP), and Mackensie University. The first two had been important strongholds of student organization and resistance to the dictatorship in the 1960s and had played critical roles in the return of student activism during the democratic opening. The third, Mackensie, was a private institution with a traditionally right-wing student population; students from USP and Mackensie had famously battled in the streets of São Paulo during the 1968 student protests.[3] Student activists at all three schools complained about lack of participation and interest, and they carefully backgrounded their partisan associations in the face of fierce skepticism among the student population. They all tried to create what I am calling "publics": interstitial spaces in which people with different identities and relations provisionally suspended some of those differences in order to engage in productive communication.

However, their efforts to create cross-partisan publics met with quite varied results. In each university, activists developed distinct ways of combining student, partisan, and other involvements, as well as ways of talking with students from other parties. While drawing on the modal style of student politics described in chapter 6, these local styles were shaped by the relational contexts of each university milieu, which enabled some kinds of communication and inhibited or constrained others. At PUC, a legacy of partisan identification and rivalry, combined with the positioning of student groups between a hostile student body and administration, impoverished political debate and exhausted student politics. At USP, a tense and mobile structure of alliance and opposition created conditions for richer cross-partisan debate, although in a confrontational rather than exploratory mode. And rather surprisingly, Mackensie activists were developing quite productive forms of cross-partisan collaboration, perhaps due to enforced partisan suppression by the university administration as well as to the cross-cutting structure of partisan ties.

In contrast to the last chapter, which examined highly institutionalized (and relatively stable) student and Catholic publics, here I look at how more mobile and emergent publics are shaped by local relational contingencies. To understand the differences in political communication between the three universities, I examine four components of the local relational context. First, I show how *spatial and institutional factors* at each university facilitated or impeded student organizing. Second, I examine the *history of partisan dispute*, and the way that this informed 1990s activism. Third I examine the local *configuration of alliances*, drawing loosely on the principles of balance theory in social network analysis. And fourth, I examine the *mediating skills* of local activists as they attempted to steer and manage different kinds of attempted publics. I close by highlighting some of the mechanisms at work in these three cases that may be generalized to other relational contexts.

THE CATHOLIC UNIVERSITY OF SÃO PAULO: PARTISAN EXHAUSTION AND PARALYSIS

The Catholic University of São Paulo (PUC-SP) was the first university milieu that I began to explore in depth, beginning in March 1995. I was more familiar with this campus than the others, having taken classes on education there in 1987–88 (with Paulo Freire, among others) as well as participating in seminars on social movements during the mid-1990s. PUC had been the setting of famous showdowns with the regime, including a violent military occupation in 1977, in which more than five hundred students were arrested. In the 1980s, the university had been the site of protests against rising tuition costs, as the administration tried to pass on the effects of inflation to the students. PUC as an institution had shared the commitment of the church to issues of social justice, and through a broad program of scholarships had attracted many lower-income students with involvements in the church-based popular movements (including some of those I knew from the Catholic youth pastoral).

However, by the mid-1990s, rising tuition costs (and, possibly, the conservative turn of the Brazilian church) had contributed to a student body that was, in the words of Carlos, a graduate student who had been active in the 1980s, "less proletarianized." This was especially true of the more privileged daytime students, who were generally supported by their parents and did not have to work. There was little interest on campus, Carlos said, for political discussion that did not immediately involve students or their families. Carlos expressed nostalgia for the "pleasurable texts" of the more militant past and complained that UNE itself had a discourse that was much more liberal and moderated. "They don't have the rebelliousness of 1969, because the public has no rebellion. That is to say, they have a social rebellion, 'in fashion,' but it's no longer a political rebellion."

Despite widespread apathy, organized student groups persisted on campus, although they were struggling and frustrated. I spent several weeks interviewing students in the CAs (Academic Centers) as well as attending meetings and debates.[4] PUC has an ideal spatial layout for student organizing: classes are concentrated into two adjacent buildings, with wide open-air corridors and ramps between levels with views down to the patio, known as the *prainha* (little beach) because of the propensity of students to lounge around in the sun, eating, smoking, and socializing. The offices of the CAs mostly spill out into this patio, with subterranean rooms for meetings and recreation as well as small businesses that provide income to the CAs: Xerox services, luncheonettes, bookstores and boutiques ("It's like a big shopping center," Carlos told me scornfully). In earlier times, this layout had been highly conducive to mobilization, as it enabled cross-cutting backstage planning (in the underground meeting rooms) as well as rapid-fire communication of anything happening down below in the patio. But while hard-core activists could still be found hanging in the patio, activists complained that the only thing that would get students moving would be beer parties; free drafts usually accompanied any attempt to mobilize against things like tuition increases.

The doldrums of political organizing at PUC marked a shift not only from its historical role in opposing the dictatorship, but also from its more recent history. In the late 1980s, some of the local CAs—in particular, the CA of Social Sciences (CACS)—had been sites for anarchistic, countercultural organizing, turning them into what some described as a hub for drug trafficking. However, in the early 1990s, a particularly lively cohort of activists—many of them linked to the PT (Workers' Party)—took control of CACS and other CAs and reinvigorated the local political scene, protesting against tuition increases and other campus problems. These activists were often tied into larger partisan and movement networks outside the university. As one member of this group told me, "Practically everyone you met in the CA was a *companheiro*" (companion) from local PT nuclei, regional directorates, or popular movements. However, by 1995, most of this cohort had graduated or moved on to graduate school; some had also taken on higher-level leadership in the PT or other movements. "We abandoned the CA," several told me. This left the direction of mid-1990s student politics in younger, less-experienced (but still partisan) hands. However, the younger activists, if they wanted to maintain leadership, had to be much less forthright about their partisan affiliations than those of just a few years before.

In 1995, the leaders of the CAs had a range of partisan affiliations, as well as orientations toward partisanship. While none of the CAs would admit any kind of formal (or even informal) association with a political party, the partisan sympathies of leaders were common knowledge. In private conversations, most leaders would admit their personal sympathies, while carefully detaching them from the organizations they led. For example, the directors of the CAs of Social Sciences, Law, and Philosophy tended to be affiliated with the PT. However, they recounted electoral struggles against other slates that they said were "more" *petista* (linked to the PT), and made a point of saying they were not directly linked to the party, nor did they try to implement the party platform in the projects and activities of the CA. Despite these disavowals, when I accompanied a group of these same *petista* activists from a student meeting to a local bar, talk immediately switched from apartisan "student" issues to internal PT politics, activating another dimension of their shared identities.

The *petista* leaders maintained sometimes cordial, sometimes hostile relations with the leaders of other CAs, associated with different parties. The CA of Economics and Administration was controlled by activists affiliated with the PCdoB (Communist Party of Brazil); however, these leaders denied a direct party link and stressed that their slate also had students from the PSDB (Party of Brazilian Social Democracy), PT, and some independents. The CA of Social Work was controlled by youth linked to a small radical Trotskyist party, the PSTU (Unified Socialist Workers Party); the PT students accused these youth of taking a hard-line, nonnegotiatory stance that undermined their dialogue with the university administration (i.e., "they're 'more' partisan than us"). The Psychology and Journalism CAs were militantly apartisan, heralding their independence and opposition in relation to the "partisan" CAs, although one director admitted hovering between sympathies to the PT and the PSDB. Almost all the CAs, except for the one controlled by the PCdoB, had "collegial" directorships, with no official president and rotating responsibilities. Leadership was selected by slates in yearly winner-takes-all elections, without proportional representation.

Despite these ritual repudiations of partisanship, students in most of the slates came together because they shared political affinities and (usually) because they believed some sort of political participation was important (the exceptions would be the slates that were purely festive or athletic, or that campaigned to "get rid of CA"). Some CAs also had outreach programs that expressed broader social commitments. For example, the law students were involved in legal assistance for the Housing Pastoral of the Catholic Church, while the social science students were involved in community education projects and Afro-Brazilian organizing. The question that troubled many activists was how to "politicize" a CA (and by implication, the student body) without "partisanizing" it. One (somewhat unsatisfactory) way out of this bind was to avoid polarizing ideological issues and instead focus on questions "specific to the university student," such as curriculum reform, quality of teaching, libraries, democratization of the universities, and in the case of private universities (like PUC), scholarships and rising tuition costs.

At PUC, however, the long-term struggle against tuition increases had largely taken over internal student activism and debate, choking the capacity of leaders either to discuss local "quality of education" issues or to engage in more challenging (and rewarding) discussion about the political issues of the day. The issue of tuition increases had been tied by previous cohorts to broader questions about the "elitization" of the university. But the constancy and repetition of the demands and largely futile negotiations with the administration made the struggle seem very narrow and self-interested. In the words of a long-time member of the Law CA, it was a "frustrating and inglorious struggle," diverting time and energy to a battle in which there was little chance of a positive return.

The impoverished quality of political discussion at PUC resulted not only from these historical factors, but also from the more immediate configuration of relations in the local activist milieu. The structure of alliance and opposition at PUC is described in figure 7.1 (below). The positive and negative signs reflect the valence of relationships, showing relations of sympathy and antagonism; the dotted lines indicate provisional alliances. In this and the figures ahead, I draw loosely on the principles of balance theory in social network analysis, which argues that actors experience social pressure for balance in relationships—to be friends of one's friend's friends, for example, or enemies of one friend's enemies, or friends of ones enemies' enemies.[5] A triad is "balanced" if the product of the valences is positive; "unbalanced" triads are unstable and pressure toward resolution by a switch in valence. Here I understand these forces not as psychological pressure (i.e, for conformity or approval), but rather as the cross-pressures of local alliances.

In the triadic relationship on the right-hand side of figure 7.1, we see that the antipartisan students and the independent CAs share a positive relation, as a result of their shared antagonism toward the more partisan

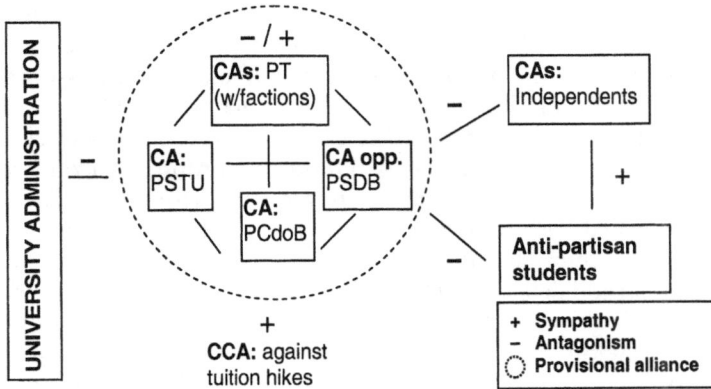

Figure 7.1. Alliance structure at Catholic University of São Paulo (PUC-SP)

CAs (inside the circle). Alternatively, we could interpret this triad as an indication that the independent CAs were playing up their antagonism toward the other CAs (e.g., by labeling them as partisan) in order to maintain a positive relationship with the antipartisan students. In any case, this particular triad is balanced through the shared negativity of the independents CAs and the nonpartisan students toward the allied cluster of the more partisan CAs.

Generally, the CAs linked (indirectly) to the various parties had tense and competitive relations with one another, although they collaborated on a number of internal university activities (hence the − /+ designation within the circle). Most importantly, they came together in their largely unsuccessful attempt to protest tuition hikes by the university administration. The vehicle of this provisional alliance was the CCA (Council of Academic Centers) in which most of the CAs participated, with the exception of the most militantly independent. The CAs were thus locked together on two sides: first, in their losing battle against the administration, and second, in their defensive posture against accusations of partisanship on the part of the independents and the students at large (an accusation with roots in PUC's own history of partisan dispute).

This negative sandwiching between administration and students—along with uneasy partisan competition among the CAs themselves—created an environment in which deeper political debate was difficult, if not impossible. This is not because they didn't try; the CCA repeatedly tried to generate public debate and participation in the form of cross-partisan assemblies to discuss tuition increases and other issues. However, these attempted publics drew only a handful of students, many of whom spent their time bad-mouthing the CAs rather than the university administration. While some of the leaders tried to animate these assemblies with music (a brass band in the patio) and off-color jokes, the discourse was often painfully heavy and long-winded. Younger activists tried to mimic the grand discursive style of the earlier cohort, positioning themselves against the elitization of the university, President Cardoso's "neoliberal project" and the globalizing economy more generally. However, many of these activists lacked the Gramscian skills in discursive positioning of the older students (as described in chapter 6) and ended up sounding stridently ideological and defensive. The student leaders' frustration with this situation was palpable and draining. "I'm so tired of this way of doing politics," one long-time leader (linked to the PT) told me. "I don't have any desire to do anything," said another youth (linked to the PCdoB), who sat slumped in his chair.

This lack of political energy was also evident in the publics formed around the elections for CA leadership at the end of the school year. I attended a series of debates between slates competing for control of the Law CA, in which the incumbent leadership was being challenged from several directions. The opposition included three serious and two "mock" slates, demanding more parties (i.e., festivities) or the legalization of marijuana. "This CA is ridiculous, it doesn't do anything. If it doesn't do anything, why not smoke marijuana?" said one provocative opposition candidate, a prominent PSDB activist, who then proceeded to light up a joint onstage. This tactical maneuver used to contest control of the CA can be construed as narrowly Machiavellian; it entailed the trashing of the current CA leadership by the partisan opposition, while appealing to the self-absorbed, antipartisan sentiment of the larger student body.

I was struck by the almost complete lack of discussion about the social mission of the CA, despite the fact that many of the CA's current leaders were involved in legal aid and citizenship programs among the poor and were sympathizers with the PT. I asked one slate member why they didn't expand the scope of the debate to touch on these broader concerns. She said that there was simply no space for such a discussion, since students didn't want to hear it. Most students were only interested in "integration" (more parties, social events, bars, etc.) and internal matters related to the law program. To talk about "the social role of the law" would have been denounced as demagogy, or worse, as partisanship, the most dangerous word in such elections. Another leader confirmed this analysis, telling me to look around at the students; the cheers from the audience came always in response to talk of parties or social events, the boos in relation to political parties.

As a result of this climate of hypercharged antipartisanship, political discussion at PUC was paralyzed and impoverished. There was little way for students to raise compelling political issues without the discussion degenerating into narrow and frustrating local squabbles (over tuition increases, for instance), on the one hand, or the preaching of an external party platform, on the other. The long and celebrated history of the PUC student movement was more of a burden than a plus, confirming in many students' minds that the more experienced activists were dragging partisan weight along with them, as well as locking them into a historic but losing battle with the administration. The loudest among the younger activists were characterized either by the stridency of their partisan discourse, on the one hand, or by the militancy of their antipartisan stance, on the other. Those seeking a way to express social commitment in a less dogmatic or more politicized fashion were delegitimized from both directions. In this way, the PUC university milieu that might have been expected to have the most dynamic political culture—due both to a history of activism and to spatial and network factors—was in fact stressed, spent, and stripped of meaningful debate.

University of São Paulo:
Partisan Tension and Positioning

At the University of São Paulo (USP), I found a different configuration of relations, and a correspondingly different climate of debate. Like PUC, USP had long been a center for student organizing, particularly during the 1960s when the university's Faculty of Philosophy, Science, and Letters was located in a centralized building in downtown São Paulo. After the 1968 crackdown on student organizing, the military regime restructured the university, building a large new "university city" in the wealthy western suburbs of the city. As a result, the faculties were pried apart into separate complexes separated by long, arid distances (difficult to navigate without a car, as I found out!). This fracturing and dispersion of communication—so different from the dense spatial organization at PUC—proved a considerable impediment to student organizing. The CAs were isolated from each other within dispersed faculties, which formed their own microecologies, making it hard to organize universitywide proposals or campaigns.

As a result, the DCE (Central Student Directorate) of USP was largely segmented from the CAs in the departments, despite its historic status as Brazil's first independent student organization to reorganize after the dictatorship. As at most large universities, the DCE of USP was an autonomous universitywide body, elected from its own set of competing slates, not through delegates chosen by the CAs. Because of the distance between faculties, the DCE leaders formed their own relatively insulated subgroup. The history of the DCE since the mid-1980s was a tangled story of factional lineages and rivalries, most of which were internal to an internal PT tendency, known as the Articulation (the majority faction in the larger party). After many conversations with different sides, I never quite managed to get the story straight. In any case, the DCE was fiercely and historically opposed to the PCdoB leadership of UNE and a proponent of direct elections and winner-takes-all directorates for UNE's national leadership. Within the PT, the DCE leaders adamantly resisted any alliance or collaboration with the PCdoB (including PT participation in UNE's proportionally elected directorate).

I did not spend as much time at USP as I did at PUC, in part because of the logistical difficulties of getting to and around the distant, dispersed campus using public transportation and my own two feet. However, I did attend several debates at USP and interviewed student leaders from the DCE and several CAs. As at PUC, partisanship was a charged and difficult issue, although possibly not of the brittle consistency that it was at PUC. For example, I interviewed eight or nine students from the CA of the Faculty of Economics and Administration (FEA-USP)—all relatively recent entrants into activism—who insisted that they were "completely apartisan" and didn't even know each others' partisan sympathies. However, they admitted that it was customary to talk about the CAs in terms of partisan identification. As one student said, "It's really funny, here at USP, it's very common to identify the CA by the party. They say, 'Oh, Law is of the PT now, Social Science is of the PSTU, UNE is of the PCdoB' and so on." His companion reminded him that their own CA also had a partisan reputation: "in spite of not being so, we are identified as PSDB." This evoked a flurry of conversation, as they tried to reconstruct their history of nonpartisanship; "here in FEA, we have two traditions: one is being apartisan, and the other is being against the DCE."

Along with many other CAs at USP, these students accused the DCE of corruption, streamrolling, and electoral manipulation. The opposition to the DCE included not only self-designated "independents," but also CAs linked to other PT factions, the Trotskyist PSTU, the social democratic PSDB, and the communist PCdoB. In addition, the economics students joined most of the other CAs in their opposition to UNE, or at least, to the directorship of UNE controlled by the PCdoB (and further, they said, to any directorship of UNE unless the organization were to be completely reformed).

Overall, I found that there was a strong three-way tension in the USP political field, which is depicted in figure 7.2 (below). There were three blocks of generally antagonistic relations: between the DCE (and the CAs it considered in its camp), the CAs in the opposition to the DCE, and the

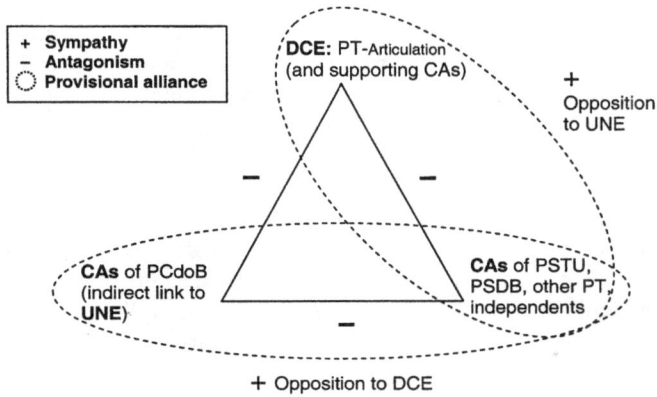

Figure 7.2. Alliance structure at the University of São Paulo (USP)

CAs linked to the PCdoB (and thus indirectly to UNE). In balance theory terms, this created a tense and unbalanced alliance structure that should pressure toward resolution in some way (e.g., as one's enemies' enemies are declared to be friends). This unbalanced triad had a number of possibilities of resolution, through the shifting structure of alliances. The oppositional CAs often joined with the PCdoB in local battles against the DCE, forming provisional alliances surrounding the university's internal electoral disputes. Alternatively, the oppositional CAs sometimes flipped alliances and joined with the DCE (and its allies) in opposing the PCdoB and by extension, UNE, particularly in the period leading up to UNE's national congresses.

Interestingly, I found this fluid triadic structure of factional alliance and opposition—in which the two-against-one groupings could move back and forth—to be more conducive to productive political discussion then the self-enforced partisan suppression of PUC. In May 1995, I attended a debate at the Faculty of Economics and Administration about education policy and the student movement. The organizers invited students from CAs all around the city (including PUC, Mackensie, several private universities, and all of the various faculties of USP). Before the meeting, the leaders told me that they hoped to articulate an independent slate to oppose the PCdoB at the upcoming Congress of UNE. However, they would first try to "feel the climate," since they had invited "everyone" (a code, in this case, for all the different political forces). This cross-partisan forum thus qualifies as a public, in which the participants would try to provisionally set aside their differences in order to construct a common footing for discussion and action.

The intention of the organizers was to use the meeting to "articulate the opposition," that is to begin an exploratory dialogue among the diverse groups opposed to PCdoB in order to move toward a tactical alliance to wrest control of UNE from the PCdoB. In relation to the four modes of communication described in chapter 6, they were hoping to initiate the meeting in a Habermasian footing of open-ended exchange, in order to eventually (perhaps in a later meeting) switch into more Machiavellian negotiations aimed at institutional control. However, this plan was thwarted when students from the PCdoB turned up in force. This included a particularly thoughtful and articulate group of PCdoB activists from the faculties of philosophy, letters, communications, and chemistry, who strode into the meeting and genially greeted the wary organizers. This group took on the task of defending UNE against the onslaught of accusations from the opposing forces, which included activists from the PT, PSTU, PSDB, and independents. The opposition groups pulled no punches, accusing accused UNE (and its PCdoB leadership) of lack of representativity, ideological distance from the students, partisan manipulation and "instrumentalization," bureaucratization, lack of financial transparency and the monopolization of resources and information.

To my surprise, rather than degenerating into a shouting match, the discussion turned into a frank and thoughtful discussion of the Cardoso government's educational reforms, as well as of the strengths and weakness of UNE. The leaders of the various factions squared off discursively, both in the nuance of their critique of the government policy, and in their positioning on the strengths and weakness of UNE. The footing shifted from Habermasian exchange to Gramscian positioning; there was clearly a dispute over the hegemony of the student movement involved in their careful, if heated, debate over the structure and program of UNE. The opposition adopted the tone of zealous moral reformers, and there was no attempt on the part of the organizers to usher the discussion toward consensus (as there might have been had the PCdoB not appeared). Rather, there was close attention to the subtle positioning of each of the speakers—as well as submerged appeals to the construction of an oppositional "bloc"—in the coded language of student activism. The youth from the PCdoB responded to criticisms of UNE at a very high-minded and civil level, carefully meeting each point with their own reasoned defense. Despite the competitive crackle in the air, the students seemed to get beyond sloganeering to wrestle with the complexities of the issues involved.

At several points the PCdoB activists attempted—somewhat unsuccessfully—to change the footing of the debate from discursive confrontation to reflective problem solving, that is, from the Gramscian to the Deweyian mode. A philosophy student named Paulo was particularly lucid in admitting the weaknesses of the student movement, appealing to the group to "look at the history of UNE" in order to analyze the organization's successes and shortcomings. Paulo also tried to engage the other students in a collective, practical reflection on why UNE was "discredited in the eyes of students," saying that UNE needed to learn to "speak the language of the students." He declared that "while I have my own political force," there should be room within UNE to express diverse points of view, not centralized by parties, in order to "debate our reality." He said he often disagreed with people within his own political force, but this debate only led to greater politicization: "UNE should not become a club of friends, only doing parties, camping trips . . . we have to look to the history of UNE to analyze it objectively."

The opposition groups were inclined to dismiss this more reflective, self-critical, and unifying discourse on the part of the PCdoB leaders as a further example of the party's reputation for Machiavellian manipulation. However, I was not so sure. There were both structural and interactional forces at work in creating the conditions for a more probing discussion than I found at PUC. The uneasy triad structure at USP meant that the PCdoB was in an "enemy today, friend tomorrow" position, a past and future ally in the ongoing struggles of the CAs with the DCE. The instability of this alliance structure made rich elaboration necessary— activists had to continually reposition themselves in relation to one another, and so could not rely on easy slogans and formulas as they switched back and forth. As a result, these contending activists had become schooled in talking to each other, in establishing a provisional footing in which debate was possible, without complete degeneration into manipulation and posturing. Moreover, the official format of the setting itself— an exploratory debate, in which there were no immediate electoral stakes, but a mutual interest in sounding each other out—also enabled listening and response. Finally, I think that this particular set of PCdoB leaders was particularly skilled and thoughtful, perhaps as a result of dealing with the relational challenges of the USP milieu. They formed a tight-knit, self-reflective group of mid-level leaders with whom I came to have frequent contact in the councils and congresses of UNE.

The important point here is that the communicative footing arrived at by the students was not predetermined by the institutional context or by the ideological positions of the youth involved. Rather it was negotiated to some extent on the spot, in response to the problematic dimension of the relations in play. The PCdoB students—who were ritually accused of being the most Machiavellian (and who sometimes acted that way in other contexts)—succeeded in switching the discussion into a relatively sophisticated exercise in discursive positioning, tempered by gestures toward reflective problem solving. This footing was enabled by the unstable and shifting alliance structure, which allowed for a somewhat less antagonistic form of interlocution than might have been possible if polarization had been more entrenched. Both the local configuration of relations and the joint construction of the conversational footing enabled a more dynamic, if still tense and precarious set of relations and debates at USP than I found at Catholic University.

MACKENSIE UNIVERSITY: PARTISAN SUPPRESSION AND COLLABORATION

Unlike PUC or USP, Mackensie University did not have a history of left-wing student activism and was known for its conservative leanings. Located in the center of São Paulo, across the street from the former Faculty of Philosophy of USP, the private university had long been a center for the education of the city's right-wing elite. In the famous 1968 street battle with USP students, Mackensie students were reportedly supported by a notorious right-wing paramilitary group, the CCC (Command for Hunting Communists). The university administration had historically opposed any overt political discussion on campus, particularly when linked to political parties.

Spatially, the campus was more similar to PUC than USP, with the faculties centralized in an enclosed, close-knit campus. The campus had the feeling of a private boarding school, with promenades and patios in between more or less stately brick buildings. While it was not modern and high-tech, it was fairly clean and orderly, and did not give the impression of falling apart at the seams as the buildings at PUC and USP often did. The campus was markedly lacking the tumult of political and cultural notices that were taped to the walls at the other universities. I saw an invitation to an athletic league party, a theater notification, ads for swimming lessons and for a business course on "Total Quality Control," and calls for clothing donations from the "Academic Citizenship Nucleus." However, there were no notices that could be identified as even mildly political. Student organizations were scattered around campus with their offices clearly marked, along with their linked athletic leagues. The most prominent was that of the Engineering Faculty, known as the CA Horacio Lane, the oldest and most traditional student organization on campus. This was discernible from the fact that it was the only organization called a "CA" rather than a "DA" (Academic Directorate) since it predated the military regime.[6]

Despite this restrained environment, I found a quite lively political climate when I began visiting Mackensie in June 1995. Students from the CA/DAs were busily preparing delegates, documents, and alliances for the upcoming Congress of UNE, which was being held in Brasília the following week. When I stopped by the Engineering CA, one of the activists quickly filled me in on the local alignment of forces. The Engineering CA had historical ties to the right wing PDS, the party of the military regime. However, in a sign of shifting alliances, the CA was currently led by a negotiated slate, still headed by the right-wing party, although most of the other directors were closer to the center-left PSDB or to the PT. As at the other campuses, partisan affiliation had to be carefully downplayed in electoral disputes, although in this case the suppression was enforced by the university administration, which refused to recognize any explicitly partisan activity.

These submerged partisan associations did not polarize relations between the CAs/DAs; rather, partisan alignments were quite loose and cross-cutting. Like the Engineering CA, most student organizations claimed to have directors from multiple parties as well as nonaligned students. Several other DAs (Economics, Law) had leadership linked to the PSDB, which was quite active on campus, with rival internal factions. PSDB activists ran the charitable Citizenship Nucleus as well as a nonofficial party nucleus. The Law DA had directors linked both to the PSDB and the PT (as well as a number of constructively engaged opposition groups with *petista* sympathies). The DA of Letters, Pedagogy and Psychology was also multipartisan, although its president, Cristina, was a known PT activist, with links to the course-based movement in psychology and the Catholic youth pastoral. (Cristina is the young woman I quoted in chapter 6 as having had to "annul myself as *petista*" in order to head the slate).[7] There was no visible presence of the PCdoB on campus, nor of the more radical student factions (including the left tendencies of the PT and the hard-line PSTU). All of the activists I talked to considered themselves to be opposition to the PCdoB directorship of UNE.

The Mackensie student organizations had a complicated and ambiguous relationship with the university administration, on which they depended for approval, funding, and infrastructure. Cristina told me that this administration was more responsive than previous ones, although it still tried to block student initiatives by "little threats" to withhold funding or approval for events. Up until two years earlier, she said, the administration had controlled election procedures for the student organizations. A campaign by the DCE won the right for independent elections, but at the cost of the "relation of friendship" with the administration (she said that the student organizations nevertheless tried to maintain an "apparent friendship" while avoiding official control).

This official policy of clientelistic control together with enforced partisan suppression contributed to two contradictory styles of communication among the student organization. On the one hand, the flow of offi-

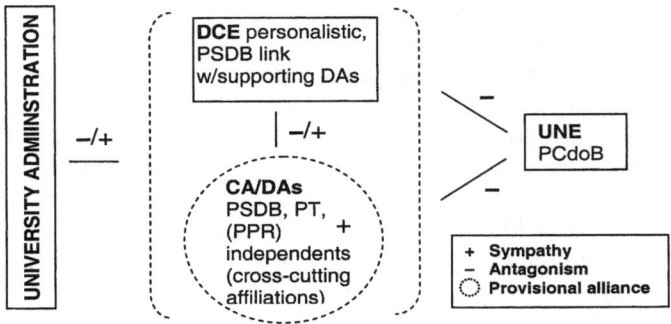

Figure 7.3. Alliance structure at Mackensie University

cial resources helped to sustain a set of leaders in control of the DCE (and some supporting DAs) who were known for their opportunism and self-promotion. While some of these leaders were linked to the PSDB, they were denounced by many of the DA leaders (including their fellow partisans) for using the "machine" of the DCE as a launching pad for personal political careers. The five or six most active CA/DAs were all aligned against the DCE, despite some shared partisan ties with its leadership. On the other hand, the suppression of partisan identities helped to foster collaborative relations among many of the CA/DAs, united by their opposition to the DCE as well as by discussions on other aspects of the student movement.

The alliance structure that I found at Mackensie is summarized in figure 7.3 (above). The most active CAs/DAs were internally linked by their (mostly) hostile relations with the DCE. Note that the provisional alliance among the CA/DAs implies balanced triads; the student groups were allied because they shared opposition to the DCE. Unlike at the other universities, these alignments did not map onto partisan divisions, since most of the student organizations had cross-cutting party affiliations, eliminating a potential source of opposition from the mostly apartisan student body (as at PUC). In addition, there was no third student force outside of this internally polarized relationship, since there was no local CA linked to PCdoB (as at USP). This meant that alliances among the CA/DAs were relatively more stable and conducive to pragmatic collaboration. Yet there was still some relational ambiguity. Despite their strong internal antagonism, the DCE and the CA/DAs were linked by their ambivalent relations with the university administration, as well as by their shared external opposition to the national leadership of UNE. These shared relationships did not overcome local antagonism, but it did mean that the antagonists had an occasional need to work together (i.e., in lobbying the administration or in protesting the policies of UNE).

This local configuration of forces contributed to surprisingly productive forms of cross-partisan dialogue. The CA/DAs that opposed the DCE were talking and collaborating in ways that seemed to transcend partisan divisions. Since most of the CA/DAs could not be mapped neatly onto partisan cleavages—and because activists were officially prohibited from partisan proselytizing in any case—students grew skilled at talking across and beyond those divides. For example, three of the DAs (from Law, Economics, and Letters) collaborated in a letter writing campaign to the federal government to protest policies on tuition increases. While the administration tried to squelch this effort, it provided an important occasion for reflective dialogue and practical collaboration between these student organizations.

In addition to their internal opposition to the DCE, these leaders collaborated in preparations for the councils and congresses of the larger student movement. For example, before a state council of student organizations, Mackensie students from several DAs (and from different parties) met to elaborate their own thesis, working jointly to discuss the position of the delegation, although they didn't vote together on all of the questions. Despite her own PT affiliation, Cristina stressed that their joint positions were "apartisan and independent, not closing ranks with any party," even though they gleaned and synthesized ideas from the proposals of a number of parties. They planned a similar collaboration during the Congress of UNE, meeting *as Mackensie students* (rather than as partisans) to deliberate over the positions of the group (at least to the degree that they were more or less in agreement; if there was real divergence, Cristina said, everyone would be free to vote his or her conscience). Note the identity qualifying involved in construction of this local public; partisan identities were segmented and suppressed, although not completely eliminated from discursive play.

I found another interesting example of a cross-partisan public within the Law Faculty. On my way to try to interview the president of the DA, I stumbled into a meeting of about ten students, sprawled on couches, cushions, and the floor, discussing the upcoming Congress of UNE. They welcomed me in, asked me to sit down, and wanted to know about my project. We then tumbled into a rowdy and probing discussion about UNE and the student movement that lasted over an hour. The meeting had been called to discuss the proposals of Mackensie law students for the Congress of UNE. Their discussion was part of a larger articulation among several groups of law students in São Paulo and other states (from PUC, USP, Mackensie, and other schools). The students were attempting to form a joint law delegation with the purpose of provoking discussion about the purpose and structure of UNE, rather than disputing leadership. The Mackensie law group, which was sending eight delegates to the congress, was elaborating a thesis in which they hoped to agree on principles to guide their intervention during the congress.

While the USP debate described above was front stage ("we invited everyone," the organizers told me), the Mackensie discussion was backstage, held among a dozen delegates in a back room. However, the group was still heterogeneous, containing activists associated not only with different parties (and party factions), but also with groups that had previously competed for control of the Law CA (and who thus had their own backstages). The opposition took the position of being collaborators, although sometimes critical ones, of the current leadership of the DA. The meeting was one of several called to "exchange ideas" and try to arrive at a consensual set of proposals in relation to student politics.

In this sense, the meeting had a Habermasian footing of exploratory exchange—they were energetically trying to see if they could find enough commonality based on their shared experiences as law students (and more broadly, as civic-minded Brazilian citizens) to overcome factional divisions. They did not see themselves as constructing a historical bloc; rather they saw themselves as overcoming a culture of factional divisiveness, partisan manipulation, and personal opportunism, and replacing it with an alternative culture based on reasoned, reflective dialogue about the common good. While I interrupted what was supposed to be the deliberative moment—when they meant to decide what was and wasn't consensual for their intervention in the congress—I got a sense of the vigorous, at times rowdy, but still collegial to and fro that characterized their discussion. It did not have the careful, practiced (if still nuanced and heated) sense of political positioning that characterized the USP debate. Rather, students grappled for the floor, talked over each other, tested out arguments, fielded criticisms, conceded points, and held ground on others—but also listened carefully, learned from each other, and modified their arguments in the attempt to arrive at some position of agreement.

While this spirit of free-floating exchange was somewhat exhilarating, the meeting also had a more purposeful dimension. They were trying to reach some sort of provisional closure on their reformist position in a larger competitive field, that is, to move from Habermasian exchange of ideas to a Gramscian footing of discursive positioning, which would receive full expression at the upcoming congress. The students were militantly apartisan, although they admitted being a mix of sympathizers of the PSDB and the PT. Their scathing critiques of UNE echoed those expressed during the USP debate: ideological and communicative distance

from the students, partisan manipulation, centralization, bureaucratization, corruption, and monopolization of resources.

While the backstage setting of the meeting might seem ripe for Machiavellian scheming, the students tried to prepare a footing of reformist positioning rather than tactical maneuver. The law students had explicitly
agreed not to become involved in the electoral negotiations and factional
bargaining of the congress. They said they were sympathetic with some
of the precongress theses elaborated by the political parties (two of the
students had participated in a meeting in Belo Horizonte to elaborate one
of the PT theses). But they insisted that would they would decide at the
congress whether to ally with different groups on the basis of specific
proposals, "not on partisan questions." They rejected what they saw as
the narrow instrumentalism of the congress, hoping instead to "occupy
space," "make some noise," and take a stand on principles, even though
they were sure that they would lose. (One of the leaders—associated with
the PT—said she personally didn't even intend to vote, although that
stance was not consensual in the group.)

But it is also important to note that this sort of footing—exploratory
dialogue moving toward reformist positioning—was possible because of
who was *not* present. Unlike at the USP debate, there were no representatives of the opposition—in this case, the PCdoB—to turn the meeting
from consensus building to full-blown discursive posturing. The absence
of the PCdoB as an active local political force meant that the center-left
PT/PSDB students could engage in a spirited critique of the structure and
practice of UNE, but without having to engage PCdoB students electorally
or in provisional alliances against the DCE, as at USP. Moreover, the enforced absence in this conservative university of the radical left wings of
the student movement—the PSTU or the left wing of the PT—eliminated
a source of ideological polarization present in other student movement
milieus. As one PCdoB activist told me derisively, "It's easy to have consensus when everyone thinks alike." These students did not all think *exactly* alike, and skilled discursive mediation was still necessary to arrive
at consensual positions. Nevertheless, the absence of either the opposition
or a left flank made the consensus-building conversation easier.

Another (not necessarily contradictory) explanation for Mackensie's
high level of cross-partisan collaboration was the enforced partisan suppression by the administration. The official demand that students suppress partisan identities may have facilitated this kind of discussion, giving students practice in downplaying their partisan sympathies (or in
some cases, active partisan militancies) as they built relations among
themselves. Moreover, Mackensie student organizations did not have a
long history of partisan dispute weighing them down and tainting them
in the eyes of the students, as at PUC; instead, they could start fresh in

their cross-partisan dialogue. And unlike at USP, relations among student organizations were relatively clear and stable, enabling predictable lines of communication and alliance. For these reasons, the climate of political discussion at Mackensie seemed more bridging and productive, without the stagnation and impoverishment of PUC or the tense and shifting balance of forces of USP. The relational composition of the Mackensie milieu allowed activists to negotiate a more exploratory and reflective style of communication, although at the expense of ideological heterogeneity.

Relational and Institutional Constraints on Modes of Communication

In giving the details of these three cases, I am trying to do more than show the complex set of contingencies involved in each. Rather, I want to understand the more general institutional and relational factors that contribute to the style and quality of cross-partisan communication. I close this chapter by highlighting some mechanisms suggested by these cases that can be applied to a wider range of contexts than these three Brazilian universities.

One of the more obvious suggestions of these cases is that the collaborative modes of communication, which I have been calling exploratory dialogue and reflective problem solving, are more possible in homogeneous rather than heterogeneous settings. This is particularly true when this heterogeneity involves antagonistic identities and interests. This is not a new observation; democratic theorists like Jane Mansbridge, Amy Gutmann, Iris Young, and others have noted the difficulties of deliberative communication in situations in which interests and identities conflict (the basis for Mansbridge's distinction between unitary and adversary democracy).[8] The fact that the ideological spectrum among Mackensie activists was much narrower than at the other universities reduced the degree of disagreement that had to be mediated in their local student publics. This may have made local activists more willing or able to downplay partisan identities that were a clear source of contention in other settings. (For example, PSDB and PT activists—close collaborators at Mackensie—were bitter antagonists in national politics, in which the PT was opposition to the government of the PSDB's president Fernando Henrique Cardoso.)

What my work adds to this discussion is the idea that neither identity nor difference is pregiven, but rather has to be constructed in particular settings of interaction. All actors have multiple identities, and all settings involve the provisional activation and deactivation of some of these identities, many of which may be irrelevant to the interaction at hand. What distinguishes publics from more ordinary settings is the emphasis on *deactivation*, particularly of highly charged, situationally relevant identities. Publics involve the active suppression of aspects of identities that participants are aware might prove disruptive to the interaction, in the effort to talk across those potential divides (which nevertheless are never far away, in a kind of active latency that might break into the public at any time). The more disagreement that needs to be suppressed, the more need there is for ritualized displays of unification—hence the ritualized chants of "UNE Somos Nos!" that I have described in earlier chapters at the highly contentious congresses of UNE.

In order to be productive, publics need to actively suppress difference through the construction of provisional homogeneity. In doing so, they arrive at some sort of symbolic equalization of the relations in play. Sometimes this equalization is imagined as extending its reach in space and time, uniting an entire community or social segment. At other times, it is short-lived and fraught with power relations or other divides lurking just beneath the surface. These efforts are constrained both by the institutional location of the public (i.e., within or between recognized institutions) as well as by the degree of ideological disagreement that is at least potentially in play.

In table 7.1, I revisit the four modes of communication introduced in chapter 6, considering the conditions under which each of these modes works best, in the sense of being most productive of new understandings, proposals for reform, practical solutions, or tactical alliances. I also consider the different ways in which these forms of communication construct homogeneity, as well as the focus and reach of their provisional equalization.

I argue that exploratory dialogue works best in settings in which there is low to moderate disagreement, that is, in which actors do not see their core ideals and interest as being fundamentally in conflict. The richest—if more difficult—form of dialogue appears in settings in which there are significant differences in perspective, although there is still a common stock of values and ideals to which participants can appeal. To produce new understandings and enable mutual learning, such publics require a broad array of ideas and experiences. Hence the most productive Habermasian publics (i.e., communicative settings in which exploratory dialogue is the dominant, although not necessarily exclusive, mode) are formed in highly interstitial locations (i.e., self-consciously "between" established institutional settings) in which participants are invited to bring this diversity of experience into public discussion. This debate allows actors to exchange ideas, learn from different points of view, and work toward a provisional consensus over ideas and values. However, participants do not need to bring those ideas to deliberative closure in relation

TABLE 7.1
Relational and institutional constraints on modes of communication

	Collaboration	Competition	Expansive time-space equalization
Ideas	Exploratory Dialogue • works best in low to moderate disagreement, highly interstitial settings • constructs localized homogeneity, connection within the encounter (setting oriented)	Discursive Positioning • works best in high disagreement, partially interstitial settings • constructs segmented homogeneity, structurally equivalent positions (field oriented)	
Actions	Reflective Problem Solving • works best in low disagreement, intrainstitutional settings • constructs long-term homogeneity in an imagined, continuous whole (community oriented)	Tactical Maneuver • works best in moderate to high disagreement, intrainstitutional settings • constructs short-term alliances based on shifting power relations (conjuncture oriented)	Restrictive time-space equalization

to the more concrete, longer-term, and usually more difficult tasks of institution building. The discussions among São Paulo law students (including those at Mackensie) leading up the Congress of UNE are a good example of this. Students from different faculties and partisan factions sought common ground on principles for the student movement and educational policy, but refrained from disputing leadership within UNE or deliberating over the practical steps needed to put those ideas to work in local or national institutions.

In Habermasian publics, participants create *localized homogeneity* by focusing on the immediacy of the encounter. In the time-space bubble of the exchange, everyone is understood—at least on the surface—to be "rational equals" in their capacity to contribute to the debate. Outside the encounter, they might have different levels of authority and prestige, or engage in competition over power and resources. But within the short-term, local space of encounter, these differences are suspended and everyone is considered equally worthy of being heard. I describe this mode as *setting oriented*, in that the equalization may instantly disappear the moment people leave the setting (as when they depart from the coffeehouse or salon in the classic Habermasian examples).

In contrast to this short-term focus, the Deweyian mode of reflective problem solving succeeds by creating a sense of *long-term homogeneity*, which is community oriented, rather than oriented toward the immediate encounter. Actors spend time reflectively evaluating the past and considering the pragmatic implications of imagined future alternatives. Strong Deweyian publics imagine themselves as cohesive wholes, in which everyone is contributing to the collective good. Participants do not have to share all of their affiliations, but they do need to construct a sense of enduring community around at least one dimension of their shared identities, which is seen as extending in space and time. A good example would be the PJMP assemblies described in the last chapter. These assemblies were aimed at evaluating the practices of the Catholic youth pastoral and deciding on programs and priorities for the coming year—that is, they were concerned with sustaining and improving one of the historical institutions to which they all belonged. While they began their assemblies in a free-floating mode of exploratory exchange, they quickly moved to a more practical-minded mode of evaluation and planning, which involved intensive discussion of the past as well as scenario building for the future.

Deweyian publics are most successful when located *within* established institutional milieus, although this does not completely eliminate interstitiality. Reflective problem solving is more difficult when the focus of deliberative attention is institutionally ambiguous or diffuse, as it often is in highly interstitial publics dominated by exploratory dialogue. In the PJMP case, activists had other partially overlapping involvements—in political parties, popular movements, and student, labor, or cultural organizations—that certainly enriched and broadened their discussions. However, these were held in a state of reflective abeyance as they focused on the Catholic identity that they all shared, considering how to integrate these "intermediate involvements" with their religious faith.

When disagreement is strong enough to segment an encounter into opposing subgroups, the two competitive modes of discursive positioning and tactical maneuver come into play. Gramscian publics construct *segmented homogeneity*, in which divisions are strongly drawn between contending subgroups on at least one identity dimension (e.g., race, class, party). Publics dominated by discursive positioning are *field oriented*, directing much of their elaborative work toward the task of marking similarities and differences with other sets of mutually oriented actors. Actors concentrate on the construction of discursive boundaries between opposing camps, playing up difference rather than similarity. At the same time, they also foreground within-camp similarities. This boundary-work generates provisional equalization by means of "structural equivalence" (to use the language of network analysis): everyone is considered equal within a categorical position, defined in relation to surrounding groups.[9] A good example of this kind of Gramscian public is the USP debate described above. While there was a relatively broad spread of potential ideological disagreement (from the moderate independents to the radical left PSTU), the debate ended up in a square-off between the assortment of opposition groups (framed as zealous reformers) and the incumbent PCdoB. The opposition carefully and skillfully tried to suppress differences with each other while highlighting their criticisms of the PCdoB, whose activists responded just as skillfully in defense of their hegemonic position.

As in Deweyian publics, such identities are seen as reaching beyond the immediate setting. Actors envision the "blocs" constructed through this boundary work as having extension in time and place; hence the importance of long-term narratives of continuity and reform. These boundaries can be more or less permeable, depending on the array of affiliations in play. I argue that Gramscian positioning is most productive in partially interstitial settings, in which there is some institutional segmentation (e.g., when members of different groups or factions caucus separately), but still come into contact with those having different affiliations and perspectives. This was true in the USP encounter, which brought together activists from different universities, departments, and partisan factions. This interplay of perspectives is important for nuanced, responsive elaboration, forcing contending groups to wrestle with diverse arguments and thus offer sharper, more developed analysis and prognoses. When elaboration takes place in severely segmented enclaves, with little contact or dialogue between contending positions, ideological purism and rigidity results. I saw this in the more extremist student factions, in which activists had few involvements outside of the party and student movement.

Finally, the Machiavellian mode of tactical maneuver is associated with high disagreement encounters in which contentious subgroups are competing for institutional power. Tactical maneuver works best in intrainstitutional settings, in which the arena of conflict and rules of engagement are relatively clear, even if there is still a fair degree of contingency and uncertainty about outcomes. As in Habermasian publics, those based on tactical maneuver are restricted in time and space; their goal is to generate favorable short-term alliances given the immediate alignment of forces. In this sense, Machiavellian publics are *conjuncture oriented*, responding to shifting opportunities and constraints, rather than forging enduring positions in a field. An example is the Congress of UNE described in the last chapter. Partisan contention was high and the rewards were high stakes, which tended to force cross-cutting identities into the background. The drama of the congress consisted in the working out of complex and shifting partisan alliances, with backstage negotiations supported by discursive positioning and plenary maneuvers. This contention was papered over with the ritualized veneer of unity that helped to hold the centralized institution together in the face of intense partisan dispute.

Lest we think that Machiavellian manipulation runs counter to the whole idea of public communication, I argue that tactical maneuver still provides the footing for a kind of public. Alliance-building always involves a momentary equalization that suppresses difference. This is a relatively thin and fragile construction of homogeneity, through provisional partnerships based on interest and bargaining. Nevertheless, such publics are still productive in the way I mean it here: they produce coalitions, leadership, and institutional control.

One interesting question to consider is the role that relational instability plays in determining the style and quality of publics. Somewhat counterintuitively, in competitive publics, relational uncertainty can heighten the quality of communication. The USP case suggests that the unstable configuration of local alignments contributed to more nuanced discursive positioning than might have been the case otherwise. Since the lines of alliance and opposition at USP were shifting back and forth, activists had to work hard to elaborate boundaries and articulate connections in response to these contingencies. It is possible that this sort of uncertainty actually led to more finely tuned, elaborated, and responsive forms of debate, which might otherwise have degenerated into rigid posturing between the opposing forces. At PUC, in contrast, activists were locked into negative relations on both sides, undermining the discursive connection with opponents and allies needed for rich positional elaboration. As a result, debate was impoverished and activist discourse took on a strident, defensive tone.

Likewise, in competitive deliberative publics such as the Congress of UNE, uncertainty can heighten the quality of communication invested in tactical coalition building. When alignments are unstable, actors are forced to bargain more responsively, working toward an equalization of power relations within the alliance, rather than just steamrolling the opposition or weaker partners. As I described in chapter 6, uncertainty about the alliances needed to win control of UNE led to intensive negotiations and ultimately contributed to a broader distribution of power across contending forces. When student leaders felt that alliances were locked or that they already had the votes to win, they were much less likely to invest in high-quality bargaining efforts.

While it is less clear from these cases, we can speculate about whether the opposite might be true for more collaborative publics. Exploratory dialogue and reflective problem solving might thrive in situations of greater relational stability, such as at Mackensie, in which both internal and external opponents were relatively clear. In such situations, actors are not concerned about the redistribution of power and positions, but rather can settle down to listen and learn from each other. This does not mean that the historical times are necessarily "settled" (a sense of momentous change can certainly contribute to political collaboration), but rather that relational alignments are stable, at least relatively speaking.[10]

I have argued in this chapter that political communication is influenced by the institutional and relational challenges that people face within particular contexts of interaction. The three universities provide examples of how the student-partisan intersection central to Brazilian student politics in general led to quite distinct styles and qualities of cross-partisan communication, given the ways students had learned to communicate amidst local structures of alliance and opposition. While activists at all three universities faced pressure to suppress partisan affiliations, this suppression was debilitating to political discussion at PUC, highly charged at USP, and oddly liberating at Mackensie, given the peculiarities of local configurations of relations.

In the next chapter, I develop these themes further by examining the ways in which challenger groups built on and transformed these communicative styles. The black student movement, course-based organizations, and business-oriented student groups brought these different modes together in new combinations, as they constructed publics that challenged established forms of competition and collaboration. In doing so, they developed new approaches to the role of partisanship within these publics, which sometimes resolved, but at other times exacerbated, the tensions experienced by the local university activists I have described here.

CHAPTER EIGHT

Challenger Publics and Stylistic Innovation

DURING THE MID-1990s, many student activists in Brazil were expressing various degrees of discontent with UNE and the "general" student movement. Even those most committed to UNE as an historic student institution were discussing proposals for institutional reforms (although they often disagreed vehemently over the direction and scope of those reforms). However, the anti-UNE malaise and defensive posture among activists described in the last chapter did not necessarily lead to political paralysis or the impoverishment of political debate. In some cases, this discontent was channeled into attempts to build new types of student participation, engaging different kinds of people, projects, and institutional forms.

In this chapter, I examine several innovative forms of student participation that were emerging in postimpeachment student politics. These include attempts by black university students to put racial issues on the scholarly agenda; the efforts of professionally oriented students to link their course areas to their social commitment; and the emergence of entrepreneurial and civic-oriented participation among business-minded youth. To many left-wing activists, these newer forms of participation (especially the latter two) were worrisome signs of the weakening of the combative stance of the student movement and the encroachment of neoliberal perspectives into student politics. Others enthusiastically welcomed the challenger groups as alternatives to traditional student organizations. These activists argued that students were hungry for some sort of civic participation, but wary of the entrenched partisanship—and fulltime activist commitment—of student politics in the 1980s.

While extremely different in project and style, these three sets of challenger groups shared a number of characteristics. First, they all advocated a shift away from the partisan logic of the 1980s. In the case of the black students and the course-based groups, this required an active effort at partisan suppression, since a sizable proportion of the students belonged to political parties; for the business youth, it involved the explicit repudiation of partisan association of any kind. Second, they all focused on the personal development of activists—whether as researchers, professionals, or business leaders—although they varied in the degree of social commitment that they thought necessary or desirable. And third, they all loosened the expectation that activists should be devoting themselves to full-time, multiple militancy, even though some activists—particularly in the black and course-based movements—still found themselves following this earlier, more intensive model.

My task here is to explain both the similarities among the three challenger groups and their marked stylistic differences. The differences are not just a question of "who" were involved or "what" they were pursuing. Rather, the groups also differed strongly on "how" they went about their projects and activities. I am interested in how they constructed their respective publics, described in previous chapters as bridging contexts in which people with different origins and involvements come together and attempt to create a provisional synchronization in identity and purpose. Stylistically, I have argued that such publics can draw on several possible skilled modes of political communication, described as exploratory dialogue, discursive positioning, reflective problem solving, and tactical maneuver. Styles are composed of the typical practices that publics devise for moving between these different modes. They are supported by the institutional structure of participating organizations as well as by the relational composition of different participatory milieus. During the 1980s, the field was split between two major styles: a more collaborative style, emphasizing dialogue, reflection, and joint problem solving, coming out of the religious-popular-partisan intersection of the Catholic youth pastoral; and a more competitive style, stressing discursive positioning and maneuvering for power, growing out of the student-civic-partisan intersection of organized student politics. While both milieus drew on competitive and collaborative modes at times, they were distinguishable in reputation and practice as favoring one over the other, a distinction recognized among activists from both milieus.

The new forms of youth politics in the 1990s drew selectively on elements of both dominant styles. They combined collaborative and competitive modes in new configurations, variously emphasizing ideas and actions as they built new forums for debate and collaboration. We can account for these styles by looking at the relational composition of these emerging publics as well as at the institutional trajectories of the activists who built and sustained them. As in previous chapters, I argue that different settings of interaction create relational challenges, generating tensions and opportunities. Actors respond to those challenges by drawing on the skills they have developed through their past experiences—which in these cases means their histories of participation in previous and concurrent forms of activism. As people come together in new combinations, new tensions are generated, and new sets of cultural and institutional resources are made available for response. As a result, innovative styles are hybrids of past styles, but generated out of the relational pragmatics of the emergent contexts themselves.

In what follows, I first revisit the typology of activist orientations introduced in chapter 2. I consider how different patterns of intra- and cross-sectoral participation may have contributed to creativity and competition in challenger settings. However, I then argue that these structural patterns cannot in themselves explain the differences in style between the three challengers. Instead, we must also examine the specific institutional resources brought to the table by way of the participants' past and concurrent affiliations. Drawing on ethnographic observations, interviews, and questionnaires, I take a detailed look at the movement of black university scholars, the course-based student movement, and the business-oriented groups. I examine the strengths and the weaknesses of each of the emergent styles, as well as their critical engagement with the dominant forms of the traditional student movement.

THE RELATIONAL SOURCES OF STYLISTIC INNOVATION

As the sociological theorist Harrison White noted in a memorable phrase, "styles mate to change."[1] Innovation, White argues, arises in the overlay between multiple institutional forms and the styles of communication associated with those forms. Because of the way that institutions and styles buttress each other, change in either is difficult, emerging only when there is a historical superimposition of distinct forms and styles. These "turbulent overlays" may result in new hybrid styles, even as they may also generate a counterreaction from one or more of the preexisting styles, which may reassert themselves as separate identities.[2]

While this formulation may appear a bit abstract, it is very useful for understanding the kinds of innovation emerging in Brazilian youth politics during the 1990s. As noted in chapter 3, many activists I encountered in the mid-1990s got their start much earlier, in either the church-based popular movements or the organized student movement. In each of these milieus, the intersection of partisan with other kinds of involvements (religious and popular in the first case, student and civic in the second) gave rise to recognizable styles of communication as well as to institutional structures that mediated and channeled those complex intersections. The period of institutional rethinking that preceded the 1992 impeachment mobilizations resulted from a combination of older activists moving on—to new stages of life, education, and work, as well as activism—along with younger activists moving in. The two dominant styles of the 1980s—themselves the result of previous institutional overlay—began in turn to

Public styles: ACTIONS.......................................IDEAS   Public styles:

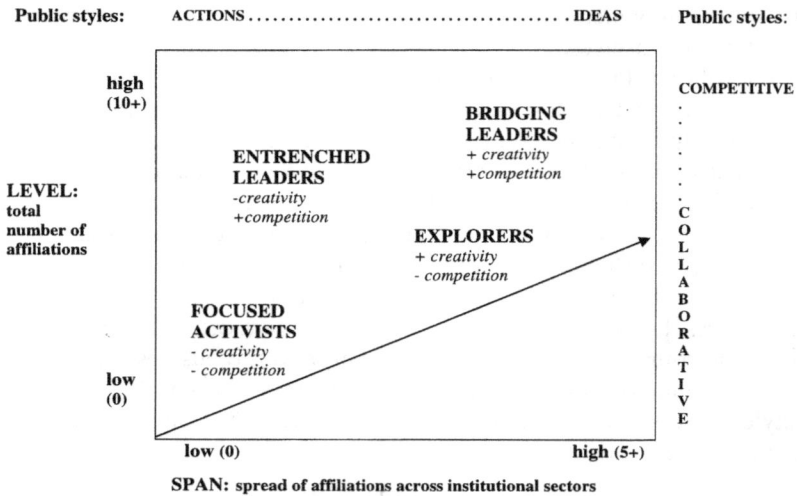

Figure 8.1. Leadership orientations and modes of communication

overlap with others, by means of the successive interactions of cohorts of activists moving through the field.

These changing intersections in the field of student politics contributed to innovative tendencies among some emerging movement leaders. In chapter 2, I introduced a typology of leadership orientations based on the structural positioning of activists within or across sectors. I argued that we can differentiate leadership positions along two dimensions: their number of involvements and the degree to which those involvements span multiple sectors. Those whose institutional affiliations span multiple sectors tend to have a stronger orientation toward cultural and institutional creativity, as opposed to reproduction of existing forms. And those who concentrate multiple affiliations within sectors tend to be more institutionally competitive than those who are only lightly invested in a given sector. Combining these dimensions, I distinguished between four leadership orientations: bridging leaders, entrenched leaders, explorers, and focused activists. Of special interest, I argued, are those I call "bridging leaders," whose high number of involvements *both* span multiple sectors *and* accumulate within sectors, giving them a tendency for creativity and competition. These leadership types are summarized again in figure 8.1 (above).

Here I propose an additional component of this typology, which will link it with my discussion of communicative styles. In publics in which most activists limit involvements to just one or two sectors (i.e, those dominated by entrenched leaders or focused activists), communication may develop a greater focus on actions over ideas. This leads to a focus on institution building—that is, establishing (and at times, defending) the routinized forms of action and organization that sustain institutions over time. This, in turn, leads activists in such settings to emphasize the two *deliberative* modes of communication: reflective problem solving (in more collaborative contexts) or tactical maneuver (where competition is more cutthroat).

In contrast, in publics in which a large number of participants span three or more sectors (either as bridging leaders or as explorers), activists may develop more *elaborative* styles of communication, which emphasize ideas over actions. This happens because such activists have many different foci of attention as well as a more flexible repertoire of discursive resources at their disposal, which makes it harder to focus attention on the nuts and bolts of getting things done. Their more cosmopolitan investments—and the difficulties in coordination and translation that these often pose—challenge them to develop more elaborated "codes" as they travel between sites of participation.[3] While this orientation toward talk can contribute to institution-building (especially to the elaboration of projects underlying institutions), it can also distract actors from practical exigencies. For example, explorers might feel less invested in practical outcomes, reveling in the exchange of ideas for its own sake rather than for instrumental purposes. And while bridging leaders might certainly feel deeply invested in political outcomes, they may see themselves primarily as ideological crusaders as they move across sectors, building counterhegemonies rather than the institutions themselves.

Note that I am not contrasting normative "deliberation" to instrumental "bargaining" in the manner of many democratic theorists.[4] Rather, I am following the usage of Brazilian activists themselves, who consider as "deliberative" any setting that requires collective decision making, whether in a reflective or tactical mode. This includes not just consensus-oriented publics, but also highly adversarial, electorally oriented publics like the congresses of UNE. "Elaborative" settings, in contrast, are for the "exchange" or "debate" of ideas (i.e., either dialogue or positioning) but do not push toward practical or instrumental closure. This revised typology allows us to link the different leadership orientations with the modes of communication described in chapter 6, as summarized in table 8.1. The cells in boldface indicate the strongest skills for each leadership type.

We would expect publics composed mainly of explorers to show a strong tendency toward exploratory dialogue. Such leaders become skilled in the elaborative processes of collective brainstorming, focused on exchanging ideas and establishing mutual understanding within the immediate locus of the interaction setting. However, they are less skilled

TABLE 8.1
Leadership orientations and communicative skills

	Elaboration skills (focus on ideas)	Deliberation skills (focus on actions)	Locus of mediation	Dominant mode
Explorers	**Brainstorming ideas**	Building rational consensus	Setting	Exploratory dialogue
Bridging leaders	**Formulating proposals**	Building ideological camps	Field	Discursive positioning
Focused activists	Reconstructing history	**Resolving collective problems**	Community	Reflective problem solving
Entrenched leaders	Legitimizing power	**Bargaining for control**	Conjuncture	Tactical maneuver

Note: The cells in boldface refer to the generally more strongly developed skills for each leadership type (i.e., a tendency to focus primarily either on elaboration or deliberation, with the other skills in a subordinate or supporting role).

in bringing ideas to closure, relying on consensus-building techniques that often prove to be weak forms of deliberation, especially in the face of heterogeneous identities and interests.[5] Bridging leaders, on the other hand, because of their more competitive orientation, tend to develop skills in discursive positioning. Rather than seeking open-ended dialogue, they try to locate their proposals for moral and political reform within a larger field of competing ideas and power relations. Their goal is to build ideological consensus, but this time within a camp that locates itself in alliance and opposition with others in a contentious field.

We can also note important differences among the two leadership orientations that stress deliberation over elaboration. Publics dominated by focused activists tend to emphasize reflective problem solving within what they understand to be their community of membership. Such activists have less emphasis on cultural elaboration, except for the pragmatic purpose of reconstructing their historical experience in order to evaluate what the collectivity should do in the future. In contrast, publics composed mainly of entrenched leaders tend to understand deliberation as a process of tactical maneuver grounded in the local relational conjuncture, requiring bargaining among competing groups for control of institutional power and resources. They see the process of elaboration primarily as an accessory to the bargaining process, as a means of rhetorically legitimating their institutional position and reinforcing their negotiating power.

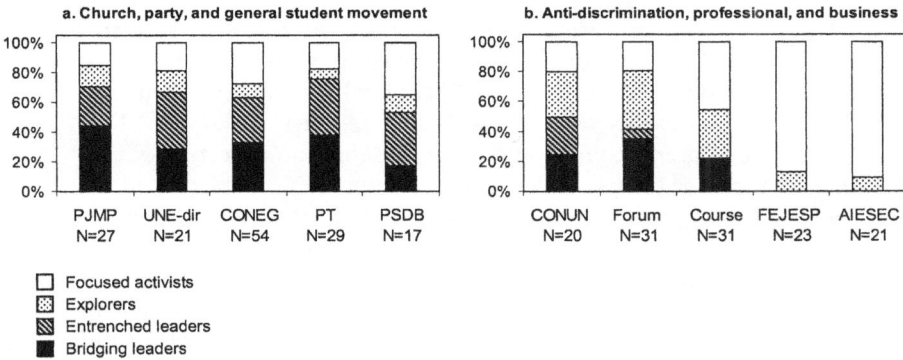

a. Church, party, and general student movement

b. Anti-discrimination, professional, and business

☐ Focused activists
▨ Explorers
▨ Entrenched leaders
■ Bridging leaders

Figure 8.2. Distribution of leadership types within movement settings

To what degree do these leadership orientations map onto the stylistic changes occurring in the three challenger settings? Figure 8.2 (above) shows the distribution of leadership orientations in several activist milieus during the year in which I collected questionnaires (i.e., late 1995 through mid-1996); this means that they do not show the respondents' prior leadership trajectories. The graphs give a rough idea of the distribution of activist positions in the settings in which I carried out my fieldwork, indicating which leadership orientations were potentially in play within the events themselves.[6]

The first graph (8.2a) describes activist positions in what might be called the "old" style settings—those of the Catholic youth pastoral, general student movement, and youth wings of political parties. All of these settings had a marked tendency toward bridging and entrenched leaders, with a smaller proportion of explorers and focused activists. There is some interesting variation among the groups—for example, the radical Catholic leaders in PJMP had more bridging (and fewer entrenched) leaders than some of the other groups, a reflection of the tendency for many Catholic activists to combine religious, partisan, and popular movement involvements. The meetings of the UNE directorate and the CONEG (UNE's national student council) had more entrenched leaders than the Catholic settings, reflecting a concentration of involvements within the student movement and political parties. Among the partisan youth wings, the PT meeting was nearly evenly divided between bridging and entrenched leaders while the PSDB had a somewhat higher proportion of focused activists and explorers (perhaps indicating a somewhat less "hardcore" base among the social democratic youth).[7]

This pattern shifts markedly among the three challenger groups. The second panel (8.2b) shows a dramatic rise in the number of explorers and focused activists, and a corresponding decrease in bridging and entrenched leaders. At the national planning meeting of CONUN (the National Coordination of Black University Scholars), participation was divided more or less evenly among the four categories of leaders. The proportion of explorers jumped up to over one third at a meeting of the National Forum of Course Executives (Forum). Entrenched leaders dropped out entirely among respondents attending the national encounters of specific course-based organizations (Course), while the number of focused activists rose to nearly half.[8] At the two kinds of business student meetings I attended, bridging and entrenched leaders dropped out entirely. Respondents at the meetings of FEJESP (the State Federation of Junior Enterprises of São Paulo) and AIESEC (a civic-minded international association of economics and accounting students) were overwhelming made up of focused activists, with just a handful falling into the category of explorers.[9]

Overall, respondents from challenger groups showed a tendency toward a less intensive style of activism, with fewer involvements per sector, than those in groups that consolidated in the 1980s. This pattern is less marked for the black activists, about half of whom still showed signs of intensive intrasectoral involvement, but becomes more marked for the professional and especially, the business students. In addition, the black and course-based activists shared a tendency for cross-sectoral bridging. A majority of the CONUN activists and three-quarters of the Forum respondents participated in three or more sectors (either as explorers or bridging leaders) at the time of the meetings I observed.

These patterns are suggestive for understanding the orientation toward stylistic innovation in challenger groups. In general, we would expect a decrease in intrasectoral concentration as well as an increase in cross-sectoral bridging to support tendencies toward creativity and collaboration. We find these two patterns reflected in the general rejection of partisan competition among all of the challengers as well as in their organizational innovations (described below), which were often presented in opposition to the entrenched bureaucratic structure of UNE. Activists in all three challenger groups tended to be less entrenched than those in the general student movement, and in the case of the black students and the Course Executives, many had careers spanning several sectors, which would lead us to expect creativity and challenge in the realm of ideas. The business youth mostly stayed within one sector, suggesting a more pragmatic, action-oriented cast to their institution-building efforts.

These trends usefully point toward similarities between the groups, but do not take us far enough in explaining the distinct stylistic innovations emerging in each group. The black students, the Course Executives, and the business student groups were quite different from each other in style and structure, although they were all challenging the traditional student movement. The characteristics of the three types of publics are summarized in table 8.2. I turn now to an in-depth look at the sources and dynamics of stylistic innovation in the three challenger milieus.

BLACK UNIVERSITY SCHOLARS: CHALLENGING RACIAL INVISIBILITY

In the early 1990s, black students from around the country began meeting under the auspices of the annual congresses of UNE. The students discussed the disadvantaged position of black scholars and lack of attention to racial issues within the Brazilian academy. They also turned a critical eye toward the student public that provided the backdrop for their meeting, criticizing the absence of blacks in UNE's national leadership and the invisibility of racial questions in the theses of the student factions. In 1991, they set up a national collective—known as CONUN (National Coordination of Black University Scholars)—which met periodically over the next several years. In 1993, the students staged the first National Seminar of Black University Scholars (SENUN) in the Afro-Brazilian cultural hub of Salvador, Bahia. The highly successful four-day seminar featured prominent black intellectuals and activists as well as practical working groups on the role of racial issues in popular, religious, student, and labor movements. After the first seminar, the national coordination met regularly to plan a second national seminar, which they hoped to hold in 1996.

In their welcoming bulletin, the SENUN organizers described the seminar as "a moment of academic discussion" that proposed to analyze the role of "the university and of Eurocentrism in Brazilian academic production" and "the relation of scientific knowledge with the cultural, political, and religious manifestations of our people."[10] In a discussion text entitled "We, the Blacks," circulated in the year leading up to the first SENUN, the objectives of the seminar were elaborated in more detail. Note the strong focus on elaboration in the description of the conference:

> Among other objectives . . . this should be a permanent event for the presentation of scientific work, exchange of experiences and elaboration of knowledge that contributes to overcoming the invisibility of the black man and woman. . . . It is necessary to overcome the paradigm of *"exotic subservient objects"* in order to have black citizens, with self-esteem, conscious of being black, positively [viewing] their image and that of the other, with the possibility of enjoying the benefits of and transforming Brazilian society.[11]

TABLE 8.2
Characteristics of challenger publics

	CONUN	FORUM	FEJESP
Institutional purpose	Logistical preparation for national seminar of black scholars	Exchange and elaboration of ideas, planning national encounter	Exchange of information and ideas; deliberation over structure and policy
Affiliation profile	All: antidiscrimination Many: partisan, student, religious, NGO, popular Some: labor, research, socialist, course-based	All: student, course-based Many: partisan, popular, antidiscrimination Some: NGO, research, labor, religious	All: business Some: student, NGO/ civic, religion, partisan, research
Identity salience	· Marked racial identities · Selective reference to, student, research, and community involvement · Critique of partisan and NGO experience · Suppressed Christian identities; referencing African religions	· Marked professional identities in specialized fields · Suppressed partisan identities · Selective reference to community, research, and antidiscrimination involvements	· Marked business identities · General references to "professionals-in-training" without mention of specific fields · Suppressed partisan, religious identities
Partisan expression	Subordination	Taboo	Rejection
Specialized identities	Problematization	Linkage	Training
Unifying ritual	Senegalese dance party, African music	Group games, music, collective pizza-making	Coffee hours, cocktail parties, award ceremonies
Dominant modes	Reflective problem solving → Discursive positioning	Exploratory dialogue → Discursive positioning	Reflective problem solving → Exploratory dialogue
Submerged modes	Exploratory dialogue Tactical maneuver	Reflective problem solving Tactical maneuver	Tactical maneuver

In October 1995 I visited the Faculty of Technology of São Paulo (FATEC) to interview Marcos, one of the national coordinators of CONUN. The national coordination was composed of about forty students from different regions of the country who met bimonthly to keep plans for the second national seminar rolling forward. As secretary-general, Marcos was a central node in CONUN's somewhat fragile communication network. From a tiny, sparse office lent by the Academic Center (CA) of FATEC, Marcos manned the telephone, the fax machine, and an ancient computer as he served as a hub for communication and planning among black student leaders across the country. CONUN had no infrastructure of its own, leaving it dependent on borrowed space and resources from the CA and the university as well as support from labor unions and NGOs of the black movement. The office was enlivened by posters from the first SENUN as well as posters celebrating the Afro-Brazilian hero Zumbi. Several African drums and a *berimbau*[12] leaned against the wall in the corner behind the paper-strewn desk.

CONUN was self-consciously *not* an organization, but rather a "working group" or "nucleus" charged with organizing the national seminar. This self-designation was a way of distinguishing itself from the plethora of Brazilian nongovernmental organizations (NGOs) focusing on racial issues. Many of these NGOs were directed toward research, which was also an important component of the mission of CONUN. However, many black activists criticized the encroachment of the NGO logic on the black movement, arguing that it fragmented the movement into lots of separate organizations competing for funding, infrastructure, and attention. This in turn created a territorialist mentality that impeded the sharing of information and ideas. As Marcos told me, "The NGOs are important, they produce important material, but they don't share it. . . . This pulverizes the movement." The decision not to become an NGO was controversial among CONUN leaders, given their precarious resources and infrastructure, which often pushed activist groups toward NGO-oriented funding sources. However, they saw this as a self-protective measure, defending their rights to be students and professionals and not just full-time militants:

> *Marcos*: To the extent that you become a militant . . . of a black movement organization, [the organization] has to act on all of aspects of racial problems. But there are so many [racial problems] in our country, all of the members of N organizations aren't enough. . . . We understood that we have private lives, study, and work . . . it was more important to be acting within the university, in a specific sector . . . because the educational system, I think, is one of the strongest points of the racist society.

This statement points to one similarity between CONUN and the other challenger groups: the focus on personal development together with more specialized social commitments, accompanied by at least a partial retreat from the ideal of full-time militancy. ("To want to be a militant is to want to invest in the hero," Marcos told me, referring to the odd combination of self-sacrifice and self-projection inherent in traditional high-intensity militancy). Yet despite this impulse toward specialization, a large proportion of CONUN leaders did participate in multiple organizations. Table 8.3 (below) describes the affiliation profile of participants at a CONUN meeting I attended in June 1996, that is, the array of affiliations they held in different sectors. Almost all respondents (95 percent) were from the first three cohorts (with 60 percent in the first two), indicating that these were largely long-term activists with previous involvements. This table shows the percentage of respondents who participated in each of the noted sectors, in three temporal designations: during the year of the meeting, sometime in the past, and during each individual's start period (see chapter 3). The table thus has information on entryways and trajectories as well as on concurrent affiliations.

This table points to interesting patterns in activists' trajectories. While nearly all respondents were involved in antidiscrimination movements (D), either currently or in the past, a much smaller percentage actually started in that sector. A large proportion had past experience in the student movement (S) and/or in NGOs (N), although the degree of involvement in both sectors had dropped, showing a tendency toward increased specialization and concentration on black issues. About half got their start (and often continued on) in religious participation (R), and about half had past or current experience in political parties (P) and popular movements (M). This suggests the embeddedness of at least some activists in the religious-popular-partisan intersection of the 1980s. Of partisan affiliations, 80 percent were with the PT, while other affiliations or sympathies were scattered across the PSDB, PCdoB, PDT, PSTU, and other parties. A small but notable proportion were (or had been) involved in labor (L), course-based (C), or research activity (Q), showing signs of a more professionalized activist orientation.

From this profile, we would expect CONUN activists to have brought with them at least some elements of the Catholic style described in chapter 6. This style was grounded in the Deweyian mode of reflective deliberation on shared practice, supported by exploratory dialogue and gesturing toward discursive positioning. However, many also had past or concurrent experience in the student movement, suggesting that they had some skills in the more competitive modes of positioning and maneuver as well. Since the group was almost evenly split between bridging, entrenched, explorer and focused activists, it is hard to predict how, exactly, they would construct their publics, or pull these different stylistic elements together. To understand this, we need to look at the history of CONUN as well as at how activists responded to the pragmatic challenges of straddling multiple sectors.

Marcos and the Emergence of Black Student Organizing

CONUN emerged in the early 1990s in response to the challenges that many black students were experiencing in reconciling the various dimensions of their activist identities. While in some ways these multiple identities supported each other, they also came into conflict. Marcos tells a story about these tensions in recounting how he became involved in the black movement. In late 1990, during his first year as a student at FATEC, he began to get involved in discussions about a government proposal to reform technical education. He became friendly with the directors of the CA, and joined their slate in the next election. He was chosen to be a delegate to the 1991 Congress of UNE, held at the University of Campinas (UNICAMP) in the interior of São Paulo. While attending the congress, he experienced an unexpected clash between commitments and identities:

TABLE 8.3
Affiliation profile: National Coordination of Black University Scholars

	CONUN (n=20)		
	Event year	*Past years*	*Start period*
80-100%	D	D	
60-79%		S,N	
40-59%	P,R	R,P,M	R
20-39%	S,M,L	C	S,P,D
10-19%	N,Q,O	L,Q	M,L,N
1-9%	C	O,B	O
0%	B		C,Q,B

Note: sectors are listed in order of descending percentages.
KEY:
R: Religious group
S: General student movement
P: Political party
M: Urban or rural popular movement
D: Antidiscrimination movement
N: Civic/ethical movement or NGO
O: Socialist youth group
L: Labor union or professional organization
C: Course-based student movement
Q: Research organization
B: Business organization

Marcos: In this period I had minimum consciousness of what would come to be Marcos as a citizen, as a black person in this country. Arriving in the congress of UNE, I had, according to discussion here with the directorate of the CA, I had been chosen to participate in the work group discussing science and technology. In one of the first meals, at the exit of the cafeteria of UNICAMP, I received a pamphlet from the Bahian delegation. . . . It was [titled] "We, the Blacks," and evaluated the social situation of black people in the country. In that pamphlet they convoked a parallel meeting to the plenaries convoked by the directorate of UNE. . . . And it conflicted with the time for the discussion of science and technology that I should have been participating in.

I and another friend who was a delegate from FATEC, we talked, we were torn. I mean, damn. The discussion of science and technology was interesting, but this discussion also interested us. So I went to try to discuss with the rest of the delegation the possibility of changing my discussion theme. The directorate said no, that I had been chosen as a delegate and I had to discuss science and technology. And then I had to prove by A plus B why I thought that the discussion of racial questions was for me more interesting. And after a discussion of almost two hours, with more or less the two of us discussing with at least ten other delegates, we were able to impose . . . it was not even imposition, it was on the basis of good sense that we were able to justify why for us it was more interesting to participate in the discussion about racial questions. And so we went to this discussion.

This "origins" story seemed paradigmatic for Marcos, encapsulating a tension that was one of the core justifications for the national seminar, as well as for his personal militancy in the black movement. Within the student movement, as in society as a whole, issues of race and racism were invisible, seen as low priority and easily trumped by competing commitments, even within the movements and organizations of the left. A key turning point in Marcos's career came when he finally convinced his FATEC colleagues (ambiguously, either "by imposition" or "by good sense") to let him attend the plenary of black students, along with about a hundred "nonwhite" students from thirteen states.

At this 1991 plenary, according to CONUN documents, the students "identified the economistic, Eurocentric axis of the elaboration" produced by the student factions at the UNE Congress. They formed a "national collective" to organize the first SENUN as a means of combating the tendency toward racial invisibility. In São Paulo, Marcos and other leaders organized the first State Encounter of Black University Scholars, followed by encounters in other states. The black students continued to make use of the yearly congresses of UNE to mobilize support for the upcoming SENUN, struggling to get resolutions on racial issues approved by the larger congress. At the 1993 congress, when UNE was still flush from the impeachment mobilizations, CONUN launched a defiant document entitled "Black Youth Don't Have Painted Faces." In this text, they noted the mostly white, middle-class composition of the impeachment demonstrations and once again blasted UNE (and the student movement in general) for lack of attention to racial issues.

Marcos was by this time heavily involved in the state and national coordination. The faculty of FATEC became the headquarters of the São Paulo coordination, as Marcos used his position as director of the CA to hold weekend meetings with black activists from surrounding universities. The location of FATEC near the metro station helped in organization, since most activists were struggling financially and didn't have cars. So did the support of FATEC's director and the CA. Marcos admitted that the infrastructural viability of their project depended on his own position as a mediator. "Our meetings depend to a certain extent on my relationship with them [the CA and the university director]. If there were no Marcos, there would be no meeting. . . . You have to keep negotiating, asking for help, you have to have reputation, a personality so that people trust in your work to be able to concede [space or resources]."

Marcos also served as a bridge to the organized student movement, trying on several occasions to establish relations with the directorate of UNE. These attempts were mostly experienced as tense and unsatisfactory. While black activists were planning the first SENUN, Marcos was promised support by the leadership of UNE, only to have those promises forgotten during the excitement of the impeachment mobilizations. Marcos said that UNE directors failed to show up at several attempted meetings, and when they finally did meet, he was told that UNE could do little to help. He also recounted an incident in which an UNE director from the PCdoB showed up uninvited at a preparatory meeting for the SENUN, apparently alarmed that the black students—many of whom were associated with the PT—were trying to set up a parallel organization to UNE. The black students rejected the charge as ridiculous and took him to task for UNE's neglect of racial issues. Marcos expressed hope that this tense relationship might be changing, especially since in 1995 UNE had elected its first black president, a PCdoB activist named Renato. Many black leaders complained that Renato was primarily a partisan activist with no real involvement in the black movement, despite the fact that he had played up his black identity while campaigning. Nevertheless, Marcos said they were trying to start a dialogue, hoping for institutional support for the second SENUN.

In the scheme described in figure 8.1, Marcos would be an example of a moderately bridging leader, quite conscious—and protective—of his layered role as a mediator. He participated in three sectors: the black movement, the general student movement, and a political party (the PT), although by the time I met him he had significantly cut back on participation in the last two. Unlike other black student leaders, Marcos did not have a history of religious, popular movement, or NGO participation. His entrée to the antidiscrimination sector was through student politics, a particular bridging position that reinforced his skepticism about NGO politicking and led him to focus on UNE as the target of challenge. It also put him in the uncomfortable position of defending student politics to his fellow black activists, such as when he tried to form closer links between CONUN and UNE. This put him at risk of getting "burned" among colleagues who were more hostile critics of UNE and the student movement.

Black Publics: From Pragmatics to Positioning

Over several years of meetings, the student leaders in CONUN developed a particular type of public that combined and rearranged stylistic elements from their prior trajectories. Publics always involve the suppression of some latent (but still lively and potent) set of relations, as well as the construction of provisional homogeneity that allows actors to synchronize ideas and action. In this case, students constructed homogeneity around racial identities, subordinating partisan affiliations and using race to problematize their participation in other sectors. While it may seem obvious that black activists highlight race as a unifying identity, this was not, in fact, inevitable. These activists shared many other dimensions of their identities that were explicitly backgrounded during their encounters as CONUN. Moreover, given Brazil's complex history of miscegenation and lack of state-codified racial categories, the construction of "blackness" was far more tenuous and contested than in the more racially polarized United States, making racially based organizing difficult for black activists.[13]

Like other movements, CONUN leaders wrestled with issues of partisanship in black student politics. In our first interview, Marcos was cagey about his partisan affiliation, admitting that he was involved in a party but not saying which one. In later conversations, he admitted involvement with the PT, although he criticized other black activists for "careerism" within the party and said that he was no longer as involved as he had once been. Apparently this was a source of significant tension, since several prominent black organizations were seen as linked to the PT or the PCdoB, and there were also participants affiliated with the PSDB, PSTU, and other parties. Marcos described long and tumultuous meetings resulting from ideological clashes between activists: "You have black militants linked to diverse parties and from time to time they confuse the ideas of the black movement with the partisan movement." However, he said that they had developed group norms and practices by which they held partisan rivalries in abeyance:

> *Marcos*: I always try to say the following, that the racial question is way above the ideological question, at least for me, since I don't know any party that has this discussion solid, clear, with concrete proposals . . . I have my ideology, but to the extent that I begin to discuss racial questions, I am obliged to have a multipartisan reading, to locate the racial question as the principle axis of my discussion.
>
> *AM*: How successful are you at this, because it can be very complicated.
>
> *Marcos*: No, within our group this was always very clear. We have problems when we have an open event. . . . To the extent that we have been meeting already for four years, some things have already become concrete within the group. People who arrive and who don't fit themselves within the rules of our group, these people tend to leave. Not that our rules are necessarily the correct ones . . .

Marcos described the "rules of our group" as a conscious downplaying of partisan ideology and identity, in order to focus on questions of racial exclusion that were seen as supra-ideological, or at least suprapartisan. Over time, they had worked out a footing that allowed them to do this, even if hotheaded newcomers could occasionally arrive and disrupt that footing. This did not mean that they had relinquished their partisan identities, just that they had learned to subordinate them in order to build a provisionally equalized public focused on something else, that is, the usually backgrounded racial component of their identities as activists and scholars.

This construction of homogeneity around race was clear at the national meeting of CONUN I attended in June 1996. The meeting was held in the offices of a government-linked NGO in Brasilia, with thirty to forty activists from eleven states. My participation was controversial, since the meeting was officially "closed" to outsiders—in part, Marcos told me, because they had so much to do in so little time, and in part because this was a space in which they did not want to be under the eyes of white researchers. While Marcos gained approval for my participation from at least some of his fellow leaders (I was told I could listen, but not talk), not all participants had been forewarned and some were startled by my appearance.[14] In this setting, no one worried that I was from the CIA or a representative of U.S. imperialism (as at some of the traditional student movement events); rather they objected that I was a white researcher objectifying the black experience, just as had happened historically throughout Brazilian academic life. This concern tumbled into view during a discussion of the historical role of blacks in the academy, in a pointed reference to "the example of our friend Ann, who is here studying us."

This open reference to me during the plenary discussion evoked a hush in the audience, along with some nodded heads. I realized with some alarm that there was widespread skepticism about my role there, as reflected in the extremely slow rate of return on my questionnaires. After a couple of reflective conversations with leaders, I was given the right to a short response ("since I was referred to by name"). I described my dialogic stance as a researcher ("treating all of the participants in my research as subjects of their projects and movements") as well as noting that my work was not about black youth per se, but rather about student politics more generally, and if I neglected their movement I would be reinforcing the invisibility that they were trying to overcome. This last point, especially, seemed to strike a chord, and by the close of the three-day meeting nearly all of the more than twenty people who remained to the end had filled out my questionnaire.

Beyond the personal challenge, this incident is interesting for what it reveals about the modes of communication in play at the meeting. The dominant mode was deliberative: they were engaged in reflective problem solving in preparation for the second SENUN. However, there was a hefty dose of discursive positioning as well, not so much in relation to each other, but rather to unify their collective stance *as black researchers* who saw themselves as occupying a privileged position in relation to the scientific understanding of the experiences of the black community. The already delicate balancing act involved in creating a productive public in the face of partisan and other organizational differences depended on being able to unite around a shared identity. My presence disrupted that footing in at least two ways, adding to the complexity that needed to be negotiated. First, as Marcos noted, the purpose of the meeting was the practical one of "getting things done," and having to do bridge work with me was seen as a distraction amidst tight temporal constraints. Second, the discursive positioning that was the justification for the group depended on relegating nonblack researchers to a structurally nonequivalent category, that is, in drawing boundaries between white and black researchers on the grounds that white research turned blacks into exoticized others. My presence meant that they had to be more careful and restrained in their critique of white researchers (although they didn't suppress it entirely). In this context our shared identity as researchers could be perceived as a challenge to the public's foundational positioning, even though eventually it was the tie that allowed us to switch to a friendlier footing.

Throughout the three-day meeting, racial identities were front and center, since they formed the purpose of the group itself. Race was thematized discursively as well as through cultural markings such as posters, music, movement T-shirts, or occasional African-style clothing. A Senegalese dance party ended the hard-working weekend on a ritual note of exuberant celebration. The students' identities as students, as researchers, and sometimes as community activists were also frequently referenced in discussion, although often in the attempt to problematize the lack of attention to racial themes in these more "specialized" domains (seen as specialized in relation to the meta-identity of race). The students occasionally referred to participation in NGOs, although often in a critical light as they discussed how to overcome movement fragmentation. Three prominent black organizations were officially represented: UNEGRO (Union of Blacks for Equality, linked to the PCdoB), the MNU (the Unified Black Movement, an umbrella organization loosely associated with the PT), and the organization of Black Pastoral Agents (linked to the Catholic Church). However, partisan identities were almost never mentioned, except in occasional critiques of the parties' lack of attention to racial issues. The activists' religious participation was also downplayed, except for references to "popular" religiosity of African origins, such as Candomble or Umbanda, in which only three of the participants reported involvement (two of these in addition to the Catholic youth pastoral).

Despite the suppression of religious identities, participants seemed to draw on some (but not all) elements of the Catholic stylistic repertoire, perhaps coming from the prior experience of many in the religious-popular-partisan milieu of the 1980s. The meeting had a Deweyian focus on reflective problem solving, oriented toward practical deliberation within an enduring community. This mode could be seen in the large blocks of time scheduled for the history and evaluation of the black student movement, in which, like the PJMP youth, they self-reflectively pondered the strengths and weaknesses of their own practice. While there was discursive positioning involved in this discussion, it was mostly directed externally—against racism in the academy and the larger society—rather than at each other. Through this process, they generated political proposals for the SENUN as well as practical strategies for national mobilization. They worked as a full group and in small, late-night caucuses to systematize their proposals and turn them into nuts and bolts plans to generate financial and infrastructural support for the seminar. This discussion had a strong collaborative ethos, grounded in a reflective intermingling of the objectives, values, and practical steps involved in the realization of the seminar.

On the other hand, this self-reflective and practical footing was preparatory for a more confrontational stance, which they hoped would characterize the upcoming SENUN. The students saw the SENUN as an elaborative seminar enabling activists to construct a counterhegemony in relation to the dominant Eurocentric orientation of the Brazilian academy. In a very Gramscian formulation, one of the organizers of the first SENUN said that the production of knowledge by and about blacks is "an important and daring project in the dispute of power. Not only in the sphere of knowledge but also in the locations of decision-making, where white scientific production is consolidated by a ethnic-racial project of the state, which implements its racist hegemonic project in Brazilian society."[15]

However, the upcoming seminar was not seen as being completely confrontational; it was also an opportunity for a Habermasian footing of exploratory dialogue (or "exchange of experiences") between black researchers. Plans for the seminar involved a variety of forums and working groups designed to foster free-flowing exchange over issues relevant to the black community. Yet while such exploratory dialogue was planned for the seminar, there was little space for it at the CONUN meeting itself. Unlike at the PJMP meeting described in chapter 6, where participants dedicated time to free-floating discussion of personal experiences, the CONUN meeting had a more consistently focused and purposeful footing. Even during socialization periods, discussion was quite pointed and focused. Participants concentrated on the tasks of evaluating their own practice, generating proposals for the seminar, and resolving the logistical problems involved in staging a national event.

There was also little evidence of tactical maneuver, since internal competition over power and resources was largely suppressed. Any traces of internal competition did not generally take the form of partisan factionalism, as in the student movement, but rather of competitive relations among black NGOs themselves, a problem of organizational entrenchment that the CONUN activists were explicitly trying to avoid. Externally, some traces of tactical maneuver and institutional defensiveness could be seen in CONUN's jockeying with UNE over scheduling and infrastructural support. The CONUN leaders hoped to take advantage of the election of a black president of UNE to secure greater recognition and support, and had made a point to invite Renato to the Brasília meeting. They were angry that UNE did not deem it important enough to send Renato—or any other UNE representative—to the meeting. While Renato later told me he didn't know where the meeting was, the CONUN leaders took his absence as confirmation of the lack of priority given to racial issues within the general student movement.

The main weakness of the black public was in fact its infrastructural fragility, which made it dependent on other organizations—such as UNE, the universities, the government, and the NGOs—to provide the support needed to bring this planning to fruition. By deciding to eschew organizational stability—as a way of avoiding the institutional competition and entrenchment that they saw as plaguing the black community—they did not develop the skills in tactical maneuver, alliance building, and organizational control that are often necessary to sustain institutions over time. When I finished my fieldwork in 1997, the second SENUN had still not been held, as successive schemes for securing infrastructural support fell through.

Nevertheless, the black activists succeeded in generating a quite rich and productive style of communication, which many of them took with them as they moved on in their academic and activist careers. They constructed publics that suppressed partisan and territorial disputes while building homogeneity around a shared racial identity. This allowed them to construct a sense of historical community at the same time as they positioned themselves against the racism of the academy and the larger society. The resulting public was self-reflective, purposeful, and yet still militant in its external positioning. The CONUN public constituted itself as an oasis of dedicated reflective deliberation in an environment in which that sort of deliberation was hard to find.

THE COURSE EXECUTIVES: SOCIALLY COMMITTED PROFESSIONALS

Around the same time that the black student movement began challenging UNE on racial issues, another form of more "specialized" student activism was beginning to surge across Brazil. While UNE represented what was known as the "general" student movement, Brazilian students also historically organized in their professional course areas, staging annual meetings of students of medicine, agronomy, engineering, law, communications and other fields. During the dictatorship, these professional meetings were among the few spaces in which students were allowed to gather, given the regime's perception of them as technocratic rather than political, although they also served as covert sites for reorganizing the student opposition. In the late 1980s and early 1990s, students began to develop more formal organizational structures for these Course Executives (*Executivas de Curso*), some of which engaged in social justice issues and professional reform efforts in their own specialized fields.[16]

While the Course Executives varied in their degree of politicization, most were concerned in some way to link the professional training of students with a broader social commitment. This concern can be seen in the titles of the national encounters held in 1994, shown in table 8.4. A range of explicit political messages were encoded into these titles, which I have listed in roughly declining order of radicalization. Pedagogy, agronomy, and physical education were on the more radical side while engineering was the most politically conservative. Nevertheless, most expressed at least some sort of attempt to get beyond narrow corporatism and examine the role of professionals in the broader Brazilian society.

TABLE 8.4
Titles of National Encounters of Course Executives, 1994

Course	Title of National Encounter
Pedagogy	"Class struggle and education: for a pedagogy in the service of workers"
Agronomy	"Agronomy and youth: in the struggle for true democracy of the land"
Physical education	"Physical education: 15 years—liberation or submission?"
Social science	"The social scientist in a country of contrasts"
Psychology	"Long live difference: identity in diversity"
Medicine	"Brazil: What health do we want?"
Communication	"Communication policy for the country"
Pharmacy	"The pharmacist in multiprofessional teams and for a national medicine policy"
Social work	"Professional formation and student movement in the current conjuncture"
History	"The role of the historian in society"
Forestry	"Forestry and the social question"
Architecture	"Brazilian architecture and national culture in search of an identity"
Philosophy	"Philosophy for the 21st century: perspectives and realities"
Veterinary sciences	"Who are we, academics of veterinary sciences?"
Accounting	"Accounting and the new social order"
Administration	"Administration and social function"
Engineering	"Engineering and quality"

Source: A grid compiled from meetings of Course Executives in a participant's personal archive.

In 1992, a group of course-based activists from several different disciplines founded the National Forum of Course Executives (referred to below as the Forum), in explicit challenge to the traditional model of student politics represented by UNE. The Forum presented the professionally oriented student movement as an alternative not only to the content (as with CONUN) but also, perhaps more importantly, to the logic and methodology of UNE and the general student movement. The student movement was perceived as overly competitive, bureaucratic, authoritarian, and distant from student concerns. In contrast, the Forum presented itself as consensus-oriented, flexible, nonhierarchical, and closely linked to the interests and identities of students. As with CONUN, the Forum organizers insisted that the Forum was not an organization. Rather, it was conceived as a "network-space," as one leader told me, or as most of its documents declared, "a permanent space for exchange of experiences and elaboration" among the course-based organizations.

In November 1995 I participated in a two-day meeting of the National Forum of Course Executives at the University of São Paulo. The Forum was attended by about forty representatives of seventeen different course-based organizations from around the country. Like CONUN, the Forum meeting was called to organize something else, in this case the eighth National Encounter of Course Executives (VIII ENEX), which they hoped to hold the following semester. However, this planning public was much less focused and pragmatic than that of CONUN, harboring a fierce ethic of exploratory exchange tempered by undercurrents of discursive positioning. The planning part of the meeting was subordinated to the goals of elaboration and exchange, particularly since there were many newcomers who needed to be brought up to speed on what the Forum was about.

In marked contrast to the long-term CONUN activists, the Forum participants tended to be more recent entrants. A full 90 percent of respondents came from the last three cohorts, with 65 percent from the last two, meaning that they had begun their activism during or after the 1992 impeachment movement. Two thirds had begun their specialized course-based participation in the past two years (1994–95), although many of these had previous or concurrent involvements in other sectors. Table 8.5 summarizes the affiliation profile of the Forum respondents.

Among the Forum participants, involvement in the "general" and "specialized" student movement was strongly intertwined. Almost all respondents took part in *both* general student organizations (S, ranging from CAs and DCEs to state or national organizations) and the specialized course-based movement (C) in their areas of study. For many, general student movement participation preceded specialized professional student involvement. As in CONUN, nearly half were affiliated with political parties (P), and even more expressed partisan sympathies. Of these, the great majority were associated with the PT, although there were several from the PSTU and smaller socialist parties (but none at all from the PCdoB). A smaller but substantial proportion had other kinds of involvements, especially in popular (M) and antidiscrimination (D) movements, with some NGO (N), research (Q), labor (L), and religious (R) participation. Religious involvement was stronger in the past, suggesting that as in CONUN, some activists may have gotten their starts in church-based groups. None of the participants belonged to socialist youth organizations (O) or business organizations (B).

Given this affiliation profile, we can make some hypotheses about the modes of communication that would prevail in this public. As I showed in figure 8.2, almost three-fourths of the Forum participants were bridging

TABLE 8.5
Affiliation profile: National Forum of Course Executives

| | Forum of Course Execs (n=31) | | |
	Event year	Past	Start period
80-100%	S,C	S	
60-79%		C	S
40-59%	P	P	
20-39%	M,D	M,R	C,P,R
10-19%	N,Q,L,R	N,L	M
1-9%		D,B	N,D,L,Q,B
0%	O,B	O,Q	O

Note: sectors are listed in order of descending percentages.
KEY:
R: Religious group
S: General student movement
P: Political party
M: Urban or rural popular movement
D: Antidiscrimination movement
N: Civic/ethical movement or NGO
O: Socialist youth group
L: Labor union or professional organization
C: Course-based student movement
Q: Research organization
B: Business organization

leaders or explorers, meaning that they participated in three or more sectors at the time of the meeting. We would therefore expect the Forum to have an orientation to ideas over action, stressing the elaboration of ideas and proposals rather than institutional deliberation. However, we would also expect some tension over whether this elaboration should be expressed in a more collaborative or combative mode (i.e, focused on exploratory dialogue or discursive positioning). This tension was clearly evident in the Forum meeting I attended. To analyze the stylistic innovation that characterized the movement of Course Executives—along with its tensions and contradictions—we first need to understand the historical context in which the Forum emerged.

Barreto and Articulation of Course-Based Politics

Despite the nonpartisan stance of the Forum in the mid-1990s, the course-based movement had deep roots in partisan politics. In previous chapters I introduced Barreto, the bridging leader from the agronomy students' movement. Barreto was an early player in the reemergence of the course-based movement, contributing to the growth of the Brazilian Federation of Agronomy Students (FEAB) during the heavily partisan days of the 1980s. But the roots of FEAB and some of the other preprofessional student organizations go back further. The agronomy student movement was the oldest course-based movement in Brazil, dating itself to 1951 (FEAB itself was officially founded in 1972). Agronomy students participated in the land reform movement that helped to trigger the 1964 coup, and like UNE and other student organizations, they were forced underground in 1968 with the hardening of the military repression. However, they were permitted by the military regime to hold yearly "scientific" or "cultural" encounters that played up their technocratic-corporatist side and downplayed other political projects.

When the PCdoB consolidated control over UNE in the early 1980s, the PCdoB activists were initially quite skeptical of the course-based organizations. They saw these as conservative in character, limited by their focus on "specific" issues, in contrast to the more "general" issues of concern to UNE (i.e., those linked to national politics and the government's educational policy). The PCdoB argued that the Course Executives should be organized as specialized branches (or "subsecretaries") of UNE, in order to maintain the centralized structure of the student movement. Nevertheless, several course-based organizations were going through a more autonomous process of politicization and consolidation. In 1986, for example, medical students launched DENEM (the National Executive Directorate of Medical Students), and announced their commitment to the preservation of life and to the unified national health care system. DENEM elaborated a series of highly regarded proposals for evaluation and reform of the medical curriculum, and many young medical students from DENEM went on to participate in the urban health movements in São Paulo, Rio de Janeiro, and other cities.

Likewise, the agronomy students also linked professional orientation with social commitment. In the early 1980s, FEAB began to renew its ties with the land reform movement, participating in debates surrounding President Sarney's national land reform program as well as the constitutional assembly of 1987–88. FEAB helped to organize national encounters on "alternative agriculture," including a large event in 1987—when Barreto was on the national coordination—that included the landless workers movement, the church's Pastoral Land Commission, labor unions, professional associations, political parties, and NGOs linked to environmental and land issues. In addition, FEAB developed an innovative program of "experiential internships" in which college students spent time in land occupations, learning about rural conditions and social movement praxis while offering their professional expertise. Barreto claimed that seventy to eighty students who participated in FEAB during 1987–92 went on to leadership in social movements, including key leaders in the landless workers' movement.

While the intense politicization of the medical and agronomy students was the exception rather than the rule during the 1980s, these movements provided important templates for other professional areas. Most course areas did not have highly structured organizations, but rather consisted of small groups of activists who organized the national encounters from year to year. Many tended to look askance at the highly competitive, vanguardist student tendencies, including those in the PT. They brought stylistic elements that they had learned from their professional milieus (for example, "institutional planning" techniques, on the part of the medical students) as well as from their engagement in grassroots activism, such as the church-based popular movements. For example, Barreto's more consensual, dialogic style, developed through interaction with the church-influenced landless workers' movement, led him to be labeled by fellow student activists as an *igrejeiro*—a "churchy" type, by implication, less revolutionary—even though Barreto insisted on his own irreligiosity: "I didn't believe in that stuff!"

At the 1987 Congress of UNE, FEAB joined with other Course Executives—medicine, dentistry, veterinary, history and others—in launching a thesis entitled "Parameters for a New Intervention in the Student Movement." At that congress, the PT took control of UNE, with one FEAB activist entering the new directorate. At the same time, the PT was going through a process of internal factional restructuring. Barreto helped to build the youth wing of an internal PT group called the "Articulation," a centrist alignment (on the PT spectrum) that was originally seen as an "antitendency" tendency, although it quickly became a political faction in its own right. The Articulation was the dominant tendency of the PT into the 1990s, although it was often attacked by the more militant factions as being authoritarian, bureaucratic, and accommodationist.

We should note the irony here—activists caught up in the thick of factional politics were advocating a new structure for the student movement that would help to undermine factional politics. Barreto was located precisely in this contradictory conjunction of student, partisan, factional, and professional articulation. He describes his mode of operation while traveling around the country as part of the national coordination of FEAB in 1987–88, in which his multiple militancies blended into each other as he pursued several projects simultaneously:

> *Barreto*: We went to a school, we made contact . . . had a meeting with the CA, with the directorate of the CA. . . . There we discussed the problems of the school, saw what contribution we could make, gave some commentary. . . . [Next], we went from classroom to classroom.

In addition to speaking about the [political] conjuncture, the agronomy movement, FEAB, we also touched on their own pressing problems. . . . [If] a school has a movement of alternative agriculture, you go there and talk about alternative agriculture. In another school it was the curriculum, in another it was athletics, in another the debate about youth . . . land reform, the constitution, the student movement. . . . In the first half of our term we were trying to win [control of] UNE, and in the other half we were the principle articulator of UNE. . . . [We called] a meeting with all the students that wanted to come to discuss. Fifty went, forty, at times fifteen, at times a hundred, two hundred, five hundred, depending on the complexity at that school. Second . . . we had a meeting of the PT and the Articulation. At times, when we needed to do the PT, we did the PT, if not, we were initiating the process of [forming] the Articulation. . . . [If] there wasn't organization of the PT there, we organized, had a debate about the PT, what was happening in the PT . . .

AM: As PT?
Barreto: As PT, as PT. . . . So we were always in the schools, and we [also] had a direct participation within UNE. [One of UNE's directors] was from the national coordination of FEAB. So, we did a hell of a process of articulation of UNE . . .
AM: Traveling as FEAB.
Barreto: As FEAB.
AM: But speaking in the name of UNE?
Barreto: No, in the name of FEAB.
AM: Speaking about UNE?
Barreto: Certainly. . . . So, much of the work of UNE that we did, we went there and spoke as FEAB. But we developed and worked on the politics of UNE.

During the three terms that the PT controlled UNE (1987–91), FEAB and the other Course Executives contributed to internal debates about the restructuring of the student movement. However the PT lost control of UNE in 1991, just at the point, the *petistas* claim, that their projects for reform were beginning to ripen. As the PCdoB regained control, many Course Executives resisted attempts by the PCdoB to reinstate the branch model in which they were seen as specialized "subsecretaries" of UNE.[17] At the same time, PT leaders began searching for alternative spaces in which to recoup their forces and, they hoped, eventually mount a campaign to retake UNE. The Course Executives were seen as a fertile field in which to do this, given their ability to challenge UNE on its partisan, bureaucratic structure as well as on its distance from the specific interests of students.

The PCdoB activists, in turn, viewed the growing movement of Course Executives as a double threat. First, it challenged the unified organizational model of UNE, so glorified in the Brazilian left. They feared that the course-based movement might lead to an attempt to form a parallel student organization, thus destroying the historic unity of the Brazilian student movement. Second, the movement threatened the PCdoB's control of student politics, given the dominance of *petistas* among the Course Executive leadership. These concerns intensified during the June 1992 congress, in which FEAB took a radical position against UNE, going so far as to propose an alternative national organization and declaring that the "real" student movement was the course-based movement.

The National Forum of Course Executives was formed in this climate of partisan hostility by seven of the most politicized Course Executives (including FEAB as well as those from medicine, communications, architecture, administration, physical education, and forestry). Barreto was not involved in the founding of the Forum, and was critical of the confrontational tone that the course-based movement took after 1992, when he lost his bid for the presidency of UNE. Nevertheless, after leaving UNE, Barreto helped to organize a 1993 national seminar involving the Course Executives. By most accounts, the closing plenary turned into a rally for the PT-led effort to reform (and retake) UNE, known as MUDE: Movement for a Democratic UNE (the acronym means "change").[18]

From its inception, then, the Forum of Course Executives was straddling partisan and nonpartisan worlds. One the one hand, it rejected the entrenched partisanship of traditional student politics, which it saw as impeding effective communication and the elaboration of projects for reform. On the other hand, the course-based movement was deeply embedded—through the multiple affiliations of many of its members—in this partisan dispute, serving as one of its principal bases. This process was quite generative in terms of institutional and stylistic innovation, although it was also necessarily ridden by ambiguity.

Professional Publics: From Exploration to (Attempted) Closure

For early activists like Barreto, student, partisan, and professional activism were wrapped up in one fast-moving swirl, which was more or less openly acknowledged. But this partisan dance became more difficult in the postimpeachment climate, in which parties as vehicles of democratic participation were under attack, more often perceived as antidemocratic than the reverse. At the 1995 the Forum meeting that I attended, the "new" form of the partisan dance was clearly in play. Leaders struggled to continue the intense conversation between more deeply invested (and often, more partisan) activists that had been going on since the late 1980s, and at the same time open the conversation in meaningful ways to new-comers. In accord with the patterns noted in chapter 3, these newcomers were generally less partisan and had less of a stake in the historical battles of the student movement, even though they were extremely interested in proposals for an alternative form of student politics.

The tone and energy of the 1995 Forum meeting were quite different not only from UNE, but also from the more analogous styles of CONUN and PJMP. Whereas the meetings of UNE were almost frenetic, the meeting of the Forum was studiously relaxed and laid back. The meeting took place in a large, window-laden student lounge in USP's architecture faculty, hosted by the National Federation of Architecture Students (FENEA). The large black puffed cushions in the room were dragged into a ring, contributing to the informal mood (as well as providing space for napping, smoking, eating, and other peripherals). The setting was meant to foster collaborative dialogue, although it also led to a tendency toward dispersion, which was quite different from the highly focused meetings of PJMP and CONUN. Discussions were interspersed with group-building exercises, games, and massage (reminiscent of PJMP) that helped to alleviate tension and revive flagging energy. On Saturday night, leaders tried to foster community by ritually making pizzas together, although this meant that they didn't end up eating until after 11:00 p.m.

The meeting had a number of purposes, somewhat at odds with one another. The leaders insisted that the primary purpose of the Forum was "elaboration," not deliberation, in explicit contrast to the congresses of UNE. They wanted to avoid what they saw as the Machiavellian corruption of this space at all costs. For this reason, they insisted, "the vote does not exist." The meeting was anchored in a Habermasian spirit of exploratory exchange and consensus building, which they contrasted to the partisan logic of the general student movement. At the same time, many activists saw themselves as reformers, wanting to develop proposals for the student movement and the larger society. This required them to move from free-floating exchange of ideas toward discursive closure on joint positions, not a simple task in this relatively heterogeneous group. Finally, the group was also charged with planning a larger national meeting, which meant that they had to come up with practical resolutions on the agenda and logistics of the future event.

The most salient identities at the Forum were those of students and future professionals, although these were often filtered through a social movement prism. In their self-presentations, participants identified themselves as students of agronomy, communications, medicine, nursing, history, law, social science, and other fields. This differed from the events of UNE, in which the tendency was to identify heroically *as students*, but not as a particular kind of student. One theme of the Forum was the need to overcome the distinction between their "specific" and "general" involvements by linking the "micro" world of their profession with "macro" political, economic, and social forces. They frequently made reference to their participation in civic and popular movements related to their professions (e.g., land occupations, legal aid programs, health care reform, alternative radio, democratization of the media, and reform of patent laws, to name a few).

As with CONUN, partisan identities were a delicate component of the Forum, requiring strong normative regulation. Despite the fact that almost three-fourths of the participants had partisan affiliations or sympathies, mention of political parties was almost completely taboo. The closest they came to mentioning parties was to condemn the "logic of dispute" within UNE. I discussed this afterward with one of the leaders, a pedagogy student named Jaime who had been among the early organizers of the Forum. Jaime was a good example of a bridging leader; in addition to course-based leadership, he was also active in local USP student politics, was deeply involved in the PT (and in the Articulation tendency), and had recently been elected as a director of UNE on the PT slate.

Jaime told me that the suppression of partisan identity was part of a deliberate strategy to change the logic of student politics. He argued that this suppression allowed for the kind of political debate and elaboration of alternative proposals that was very difficult within UNE:

> *Jaime*: [The executives] constitute a space that is not as tense, where you don't have to vote on anything, in which you can discuss more calmly and without trying every moment to defeat the other. This makes discussion possible, this makes elaboration possible, which no space of UNE has. It's impossible, right? If you open your mouth in the congress of UNE . . .
>
> *AM*: They're always second-guessing your intentions. . .
>
> *Jaime*: And you have your label. PT, boom, he's PT, he's PT. Fuck what he says, right? And the same thing for the others: he's PCdoB. . . . So, you're labeled, and from there comes prejudice about what you're are going to say, and even if what you say makes sense, they are going to attack because it's the political force, right? So UNE does not make elaboration possible.

The suppression of partisan identity was made simpler by the predominance of PT activists at the Forum, although given intense factional disputes within the PT, it did not eliminate ideological disagreement. However, the footing was very different than at meetings of the radical Catholic youth pastoral (described in chapter 6), which were also dominated by PT activists, but in which partisan identities were openly affirmed. Jaime claimed that even the most ideological activists—such as those linked to the usually hard-hitting and clamorous Trotskyist party, the PSTU—lost their impetus for partisan projection and dispute in the Forum meetings: "They go to a meeting like this, and they are quiet, quiet. They are obliged to stay quiet . . . the PSTU, as PSTU, is isolated because in this space that we have created, they do not have a role."

Nevertheless, Jaime admitted that it was sometimes difficult to carry out this separation of logics, given the fact that so many course-based leaders were also involved in partisan disputes in the general student movement. In affirming my observation that mention of parties was taboo, he noted that the multiple militancy of activists sometimes made things confusing:

> *Jaime*: This thing that you saw, it's true, right? It's taboo to discuss UNE, parties, this is real, right? This is taboo because of the history . . . the PCdoB accuses the Forum historically of wanting to take over UNE, to dispute space with UNE. And . . . in the same way, the people of the Executives put themselves in a defensive posture, of saying, "No, we don't want to take UNE. . . . We are an apartisan space, in contrast to UNE, which is partisan." And . . . this question, people are always . . . even those most linked to political parties stay on the side of this, try to maintain a certain image . . . which is real, in a certain way, it's real, in a certain form. But because we are, many people are linked to the DCE, linked to the CA and dispute directly with UNE, this juxtaposition ends up getting in the way. People are, they don't know what to do . . . should they attack *as CA and DCE*, or maintain more equitable relations *as Executive*. On this point, what you said about superimposition [of networks] is very telling.

The fact that Jaime came back to this point unprompted, and that he seemed to be stumbling uncharacteristically to express himself, signals that it touched a nerve. Many multiply affiliated activists preached non-partisanship in the course-based movement even while waging partisan battles just down the hall, so to speak, in the CA, DCE, or state and national organizations. Jaime himself faced this problem as he moved between his role as a leader of the executives and his new position as a director of UNE. Like Marcos, he acknowledged that bridging two some-times hostile worlds made him vulnerable from both sides, and he had to use all his mediating skill in order to walk this tightrope.[19]

At the Forum meeting, students worked hard to maintain a footing of exploratory dialogue, although this was not always easy. The students scheduled conversational spaces designed to evoke open-ended "ex-change of experiences." They began with prolonged introductions to ex-change notes on different course areas. They maintained this exploratory spirit in an unusually rich and lively discussion of national politics, educational policy, and the university. The discussion circled around and around, deepening like a descending spiral (although it did admittedly tend to stay in the hands of eight to ten leaders, most of them male). There was no moment of coming to conclusions or decisions based on this discussion, which overshot the time limit since, as they said, "the talk is flowing." The pleasure of the exchange was in the discussion of ideas and proposals (and perhaps in the personal satisfaction of being recognized as intelligent and critical), rather than in marking position or competing with other political forces.

However, the students did not always succeed in avoiding their deeply ingrained tendencies toward discursive positioning. As one young woman asked "Could it be that we're really listening? Sometimes we think we're dialoguing but really we're discoursing" (using the Portuguese "*discursando*," which implies monologic speech-making rather than dialogue). The most voluble Forum activists were all PT members associated with different internal factions, well practiced in the PT's internal culture of ideological elaboration and dispute. They subtly staked out mutually recognized positions in a discursive field, regarding the strength of their critiques of neoliberalism, their relative emphasis on curricular reform versus national politics, and their calls for mobilization of the bases. Nevertheless, the meeting had no moment in which participants tried to nail down the Forum's joint position in relation to the student movement, or anything else, for that matter. As Jaime admitted, the Forum *as such* actually elaborated "very little," except for their shared opposition to the partisan logic of UNE. Making the transition from Habermasian open-ended exchange of ideas to Gramscian closure on proposals for reform requires a degree of identity coherence that was difficult for this heterogeneous group to achieve.[20]

While the primary mode of the Forum was elaborative, the students were also charged with the practical task of planning the upcoming national meeting. They hoped to do this through a pragmatic variant of their consensus-building approach, moving from exploratory dialogue to reflective problem solving. However, their efforts snagged on a real disagreement: whether the meeting should feature a rally for land reform in addition to discussions of university reform. Some students (especially the agronomy leaders) insisted that they needed to mobilize rather than just talk, while others argued that time for talk was so scarce that they needed to concentrate on having a productive discussion about issues related to the university. There was clearly submerged discursive positioning in this debate, linked to internal PT factions. As people became increasingly exhausted and stressed, the discussion turned to the process itself. Some newer students suggested that the matter come to a vote. "There is no vote," came the rapid response. One of the longer-term activists gave a short lesson on consensus: "people need to concede. Not to injure their principles, but they have to concede." A deeply involved pedagogy student (one of the few vocal females) acknowledged that "we don't have consensus here. I don't even have consensus with myself." When those opposed to the rally finally faded into silence, only a handful of people remained in the discussion. In such situations, a "consensual" decision becomes a decision of the few who are most persistent.

This incident demonstrates both the strengths and the weaknesses of the attempt to create a Habermasian public. A footing based on exploratory dialogue and consensus building works best either when the setting is relatively homogenous, or, in more heterogeneous settings, when no point of pragmatic or ideological closure is called for. The Forum's careful rules of engagement enabled an unusually rich dialogue on diverse experiences and political views, but broke down when they came up against real ideological and practical dissension on a matter requiring closure. To deal with this, they would have needed to switch into another footing—perhaps a more fully developed style of reflective deliberation—as in the PJMP and CONUN meetings—or failing that, an adversarial clash of proposals. In comparison, I could not imagine either PJMP or CONUN reaching such an impasse—in part, because they had developed more effective institutional supports for reflective problem solving that would culminate, when necessary, in a vote.

Finally, the Machiavellian mode of tactical maneuver was not as absent as the leaders maintained, but rather hovered over the meeting in a state of troubled potentiality. Forum participants were divided on what position to take in relation to UNE: should the Course Executives be completely independent, should they assume a collaborative relationship with UNE, or should they contest leadership of UNE and try to reform its institutional structure? More covertly, as Jaime admitted, many PT activists saw the Course Executives as a base from which to rebuild their partisan force in opposition to the PCdoB. Opponents of this tactic argued that it would "discharacterize" the Executives by engaging them in narrow politicking over leadership, thereby destroying the more dialogic, consensual footing that they had constructed in the Forum.

This issue was becoming more troublesome as the Course Executives expanded and the PCdoB began to rethink its skepticism about the "specialized" movement. Lately, more and more PCdoB activists had been turning up at course-based events. Since the Forum was officially an inclusionary space, there was no legitimate way to turn them away. However, many Forum leaders worried that as PCdoB activists made inroads in the course-based movement, the executives would lose the collaborative footing that was their greatest strength and begin to mirror the partisan disputes of UNE. (More instrumentally, the movement would also lose its potential as an electoral base for the PT). Several PCdoB activists complained bitterly to me that they had been forcibly excluded from Forum meetings, a source of increasing friction within the movement.

As with CONUN, the Forum's rejection of the Machiavellian mode of institutional control contributed to its infrastructural fragility. Since the Forum was self-consciously not an organization, it had no permanent coordinating body to deal with the logistics of institutional maintenance. Tasks such as hosting meetings, writing reports, and communicating about future events were distributed to executives on a rotating basis. Responsibility was dispersed and thus fell on the backs of a few people, sometimes resulting in disasters like one at the meeting I attended, when no food arrived on Sunday at the isolated USP campus until 2:00 p.m., due to the oversleeping of one of the organizers.

Overall, the leaders of the Forum succeeded in building a public that generated a much richer level of exploratory dialogue and exchange of ideas than the publics of UNE. They did this by making parties or partisan dispute practically unmentionable, even though many of the participants were deeply engaged in such disputes. They prided themselves on being an elaborative—not a deliberative—public, eliminating voting altogether as a symbol of the competitive style of deliberation they were rejecting in UNE. They built their provisional homogeneity around this rejection of adversarial logic, which helped to generate lively discussion and debate. However, they risked paralysis or collapse when faced with disagreements on issues requiring pragmatic or ideological closure. Partisan contention stewed backstage, making the Forum a more unstable public than its organizers acknowledged.

Junior Enterprises: Business Idealists in Training

Quite removed from the swirling disputes of the student movement, a very different group of young people were also attempting to build new spaces for specialized participation. Junior Enterprises were mini-consulting firms within the universities in which students developed paid projects for external clients in their area of study, under the supervision of a faculty member. While the enterprises originated in the business-oriented fields of economics and administration, they were quickly spreading to other fields, ranging from engineering, statistics, and agronomy to communications, psychology, and social science. The enterprises were described in the media as an up-and-coming new form of professionally oriented student participation, although they involved a very different profile of activists—in terms of class background as well as organizational affiliations—than the other milieus I was studying. I often heard more traditional student activists refer to the Junior Enterprises as rivals in local student politics, competing for resources and recruits as well as for the ideological "hegemony" of student politics. For the most part, the Junior Enterprises tried to keep themselves out of the fray, preaching a militant nonpartisanship that gazed resolutely inward at the enterprises themselves.

The idea for Junior Enterprises had been imported in the late 1980s from France, where student firms attempted to address the lack of hands-on training in the universities by giving students practical experience in industry. Brazilian students were innovating on the French model in several interesting ways. First, they saw the Junior Enterprises as a form of "university extension" (i.e., university outreach to the community), rather than primarily a contribution to industry. Second, they were consulted mostly by micro- and small businesses, rather than large industries. And third, they focused more strongly than in the French model on the personal growth and autonomy of students. As with many organizations in Brazil during that period, the Junior Enterprises described themselves in the emerging "civic" language, although in this case, the notion of citizenship was less tied to ideas about political and social rights than to personal development and provision of services in a market economy.[21] A text produced by a movement leader on the concept and history of the "Movement of Junior Enterprises" describes them as "not-for-profit civil associations" that "provide services to civil society" by means of consulting projects as well as educational programs that help students make "contact with the professional world."[22]

In October 1994 I visited the Faculty of Economics and Administration of the University of São Paulo (FEA-USP) to talk with Flávio, the incoming president of the Federation of Junior Enterprises of São Paulo (FEJ-ESP). Flávio described the Junior Enterprises to me in similar civic-minded terms, expressing uneasiness with the strong business overtones of their name. "To be honest, I think that the name "enterprise" is a bit displaced. We would like to be always [seen as] a civil association, a group of students that have the opportunity to find a field in which to improve themselves, to put in their knowledge in practice." They were also contributing to society by providing small businesses (for example, the corner bakery, a small manufacturing workshop, a family-owned shop) with quality consulting work at a fraction of the price, guided by a university professor who otherwise could be offering his or her services to large industries for a high fee.

My initial interview with Flávio took place in the bustling offices of Junior-FEA, the Junior Enterprise of USP's Faculty of Economics and Administration. There was a steady flow of people through the reception office while printers and fax machines whizzed in the background. In contrast to the precarious infrastructure of CONUN, the Junior Enterprise had been given three rooms by the faculty administration, and was well equipped with computers, a secretary, and other administrative support. These offices housed not only the Junior Enterprise itself, but also, at the time, the state federation (FEJESP). After the interview Flávio proudly took me to see another project of Junior-FEA: a computerized stock market simulation consisting of eight computers donated by IBM, with a direct line to the stock market and a user-friendly software program that allowed teams in several universities to participate.

Within the Junior Enterprises, students received a modest stipend for their work on consulting projects, similar to an internship or scholarship. In contrast, the student directors of the Junior Enterprises were not paid anything. They were the true activists of the movement, dedicating a tremendous amount of unpaid time and energy to the administrative tasks of making the enterprises work. Often, they gave up opportunities for paid internships in large corporations, which recruited students from top universities as a source of relatively cheap managerial labor, often funneling them into subsequent jobs. Flávio said that the student directors of the enterprises tended to be "idealists," willing to risk less secure career paths because they liked the idea and process of the Junior Enterprises. He said that they often attracted more creative and independent students, who were drawn to the autonomy in carrying out their own projects: "There's a certain satisfaction from the autonomy. You have a very small bureaucracy, you don't need to have big discussions, you have a lot of freedom in carrying out projects . . . there's a personal gain that I think is very interesting, that you have this autonomy, that you can influence society."

In addition, some Junior Enterprises also engaged in unpaid consulting work "of a social cast" (as they called it), providing services to charitable organizations or clients with few resources. Flávio had thrown his heart and soul into two such projects. The first developed an accounting plan for a preschool for low income, mentally disabled children, while the second carried out a socioeconomic mapping of a nearby slum, to assist the local community association in procuring social services (the latter was supervised by Paulo Singer, a well known USP economist associated with the PT). Junior-FEA was able to fund these social projects with the income from their paid projects, which he said were generating about U.S. $100,000 a year. Most other Junior Enterprises were not as well-heeled financially and did not develop probono programs of this type; over the next few years I sensed a movement away from these kinds of social projects.

Table 8.6 presents the affiliation profile of respondents to questionnaires collected at meetings of the FEJESP council, consisting of repre-

TABLE 8.6
Affiliation profile: Federation of Junior Enterprises of São Paulo

	FEJESP (n=23)		
	Event year	Past	Start period
80-100%	B	B	
60-79%			
40-59%		N	B
20-39%		S,R	S,R,N
10-19%	S,N	C,Q	
1-9%	R,P,Q	M,P	P,Q
0%	C,O,M,D,L	O,D,L	C,O,M,D,L

Note: Sectors are listed in order of descending percentages.
KEY:
R: Religious group
S: General student movement
P: Political party
M: Urban or rural popular movement
D: Antidiscrimination movement
N: Civic/ethical movement or NGO
O: Socialist youth group
L: Labor union or professional organization
C: Course-based student movement
Q: Research organization
B: Business organization

sentatives from all of the Junior Enterprises in the state. Like the Forum activists, most participants were relatively recent entrants, with more than 86 percent of questionnaire respondents belonging to the last three cohorts, and 60 percent beginning during or after the 1992 impeachment movement. However, they had fewer overlapping involvements than either the Forum or CONUN activists, with very little experience of activism outside of the university (i.e., in popular, labor, or antidiscrimination movements), with the exception of the civic mobilizations for the impeachment.

At the time of the meetings, 70 percent of the respondents were involved in the business sector (B) alone, with no parallel participation in any other sector. About a third had some past or present participation in the general student movement (S), and about 40 percent had Civic/NGO (N) participation, although most of this was limited to the 1992 impeachment movement. About a fifth of the respondents had some previous experience in religious groups (R), and a handful had participated in course-based activism (C) or research (Q) activity. However, most had abandoned these previous forms of participation by the time I collected the questionnaires, focusing their participation almost exclusively within the business sector. Almost half had started in the business sector, without prior involvement in other sectors. Only one student (Flávio himself) reported any participation in a political party (P).

Since FEJESP was composed primarily of focused activists, with only a handful of explorers bridging lightly into other areas, we would therefore expect FEJESP (and the Junior Enterprises in general) to be oriented toward action over ideas. This was in fact the dominant footing of FEJESP encounters, which had a practical, institution-building style of communication grounded in the collaborative mode of reflective problem solving. However, there were variations on this mode—involving exploratory exchange and tactical maneuver—that had to do with the institutional peculiarities of the business sector. The interplay between modes provoked strong internal debates, as leaders wrestled with the tensions and opportunities of the institution-building process.

Flávio and the Institutionalization of Nonpartisanship

As president of the state federation, Flávio was a passionate advocate of the Junior Enterprises and a committed institution builder. FEJESP had been founded in 1990 with the purpose of providing institutional support for the Junior Enterprises while serving as a forum for integration and exchange. The formation of FEJESP was part of an attempt to provide standards of quality and accountability, as well as to systematize organizational statute and form. FEJESP also dealt with external matters such as publicity and marketing, promotion of protective legislation, and attempts to gain financial sponsorship (and other assistance) from businesses and business associations. In addition, FEJESP organized workshops and educational events aimed at exchanging information and improving the quality of the Junior Enterprises.

Flávio himself was a relatively recent entrant, having begun his participation in Junior-FEA only two years earlier in 1993, when he was a second year economics student at USP. From the beginning he was involved in institutional structuring; his first task was to work on the streamlining of procedures for consulting projects. He then worked at a university-run referral service called "Dial-technology" by which small businesses in need of assistance could call the university—a source of many consulting projects for the Junior Enterprises. After this first year doing internal restructuring and external outreach (two important components of institution building), he became director of projects for Junior-FEA. In addition to coordinating the enterprise's large volume of paid projects, he also dedicated himself to the conceptualization and design of the socially oriented projects, becoming one of their key advocates within FEJESP.

In addition to his intense involvement in the Junior Enterprises, Flávio was one of the few leaders whose involvements spanned multiple sectors. He was the only FEJESP respondent who reported belonging to a political party. On his questionnaire, he said he had been affiliated in the PSDB (Party of Brazilian Social Democracy) since 1992, although "I never came to act effectively." (He made no mention of his party affiliation during the long interview I had with him in 1994). He was also involved in research and cultural activity during some of that time, making him one of the few explorers among the FEJESP activists. This breadth of engagement—as well as his mild experience with partisan positioning—may have contributed to his thoughtfulness and creativity in relation to the ideals and structures of the movement, although he claimed to not have the temperament for partisan dispute.

By the time he was elected president of FEJESP at the end of 1994, Flávio was emerging as one of the important theorists and systematizers of the movement. He enthusiastically reflected on what he saw as the social mission of the Junior Enterprises, as well as their role in Brazil's emerging civil society. At the same time, he was unusually frank and thoughtful about the practical challenges they were facing as they consolidated as an institution. He described three stages in the "structuration" (his word) of FEJESP: (1) constitution, (2) proliferation, and (3) organization of the federation and confederation. He was especially concerned with the two latter stages, and was busily working on questions related to statute reform, the code of ethics, and the possibility of forming a national confederation. The Junior Enterprises had recently held their third national meeting, with three state federations already formed (in São Paulo, Bahia, and Santa Catarina), and several others in formation. He thought that the Junior Enterprises now needed to make a "jump in quality," rather than growing quantitatively (there were now about ninety in São Paulo alone), and he was trying to encourage interdisciplinary projects across faculties.

Not all FEJESP leaders shared Flávio's philosophical bent, nor his concern with the social mission of the Junior Enterprises. Several leaders expressed impatience with so much focus on social and philosophical questions and took a more pragmatic, less discursive approach to building the federation. In contrast, those who came *before* Flávio—the real pioneers of the Junior Enterprises—were even more philosophically oriented. For example, I interviewed Rogério, president of FEJESP in 1992 (during the impeachment), who said that he had noted a change in orientation among the later leaders. Early discussions were "very philosophical and conceptual," as they tried to think about what the enterprises should be. "We were idealists," he told me. Once the structure of the enterprises and the state federation had been settled—so that incoming students received organizations that were "ready-made, prestruc-tured"—the tendency had been to have "more practical and opera-tional" discussions.[23]

Like Flávio, Rogério had an affinity with the PSDB, although he was not affiliated and claimed to choose his candidates "as individuals," not based on their political parties. He admitted that a good number of busi-ness activists did in fact have partisan affinities. Some Junior Enterprises, particularly in the Northeast, had leaders strongly linked to the youth wing of the PSDB, and he thought most leaders at FEA-USP (Flávio's faculty) had sympathies with the PT. Within his own school, the Polytec-nical Faculty of USP (the engineering school), he said, "We had every-thing! It was very eclectic." However, he said that within the Junior Enterprise, they never talked partisan politics. "There were three things we didn't discuss: football, religion, and politics. Because it leads to fights, it's no use."

This suppression of partisanship had been carefully institutionalized in the formal rules and informal practices of the Junior Enterprises. Among other things, these rules required that the Junior Enterprises keep their distance from the CAs and other student organizations, which were often located in the same faculties, right down the hall. As Flávio told me,

> *Flávio*: The Junior Enterprise is, in principle, completely apartisan. The statute itself defines that we have no link with any political party, no link with religion, no link with any interest group . . . we try to stay outside of partisan questions. I don't say political, because everyone is political, but outside of partisan questions within the [faculties], in relation to the CA, for example.

While the Junior Enterprises might occasionally collaborate with the local CA (e.g., producing a newspaper together to save costs), they re-frained from getting involved in any partisan or electoral disputes within the faculty. Flávio told a story of a recent election for the CA in which both slates came to Junior-FEA begging for support, insisting that it would show the "credibility of the enterprise" if they supported one or another candidate. The directors refused, issuing a manifesto saying that "the Junior Enterprise has nothing to do with the CA. Our objectives are others . . . the politics of the CA have to stay inside the CA." The same went for the DCE or UNE; the enterprises stayed out of student politics at the local or national level. However, Junior-FEA did agree to take on UNE as a client, doing an audit of UNE's accounts ("as in any other consulting job, it was in absolute secrecy"). While they charged UNE less because it was a student organization, otherwise they treated UNE as a "normal client."

FEJESP leaders did occasionally wrestle with the limits to this nonpartisan stance. Creating a federation was in itself a political act, as Flávio noted in response to my probing about the 1992 impeachment movement:

> AM: But would you enter into some type of more general political movement? The Movement for Ethics in 1992, for example, for citizenship.
>
> Flávio: Yeah, that was a discussion that emerged right at the time that we were discussing our statute. I remember that there was a very interesting debate, they said, "If we are so radical to the point of being completely apartisan, then we can't take any position within a federation." If you make a federation, certainly you are going to be doing a political action. This is interesting.

He argued that Junior Enterprises should not get involved in any political issues related to educational policy or university administration—they should leave that to the CAs and to UNE. However, they should (and did) get involved in things "that touch the pure interests of the Junior Enterprises." For example, they were currently involved in lobbying the national congress for legislation related to the Junior Enterprises. He also said they might also get involved in debates that had to do with reformulating university internships, or about university outreach, which were directly related to their own interests. "I think that we could be included. Not as the main force behind it, but telling our experiences and carrying the debate forward."

Even in relation to momentous civic events like the 1992 impeachment, the students were restrained, carefully separating their identities "as citizens" from their participation in the enterprises. Rogério told me that the federation had no formal involvement in any discussions or events leading to the impeachment. He personally did not attend any of the rallies, although some participants went to the demonstrations on their own initiative. On the day of the impeachment vote, he was stuck in a traffic jam on the way to a FEJESP seminar on human resources. He heard the vote live on the radio, and remembered the excitement: "Everyone was honking their horns, people were in the windows, shouting, everything stopped! It was very contagious. Because you, as a citizen, are involved in this." He expected the seminar to be cancelled; however FEJESP went ahead with the event. This, for Rogério, was a sign that "the two things were really separate from one another. Those who celebrated [did so] because they were Brazilians, citizens. At this moment, the Junior Enterprises really stayed on the side."

Business Publics: From Pragmatics to Politicking

About a year after my initial conversation with Flávio, I attended several meetings of the directorate and council of FEJESP (1995–96). The council consisted of representatives of all federated Junior Enterprises in the state (about fifty) as well as those "aspiring" for official status. The council met monthly, hosted by faculties in São Paulo or elsewhere in the state. At their peak, Flávio said the council meetings attracted more than one hundred students, although the meetings that I attended had about half that number, ranging in attendance from about forty to fifty people.[24]

The council meetings had a different crowd and climate than the student movement, as well as most of the other activist milieus I was familiar with. Rather than the high-urgency, high-pressure atmosphere of most student movement meetings, the council had a kind of practical conviviality, with students milling around before the meeting, exchanging information, telling jokes, and making contacts. Students had a more polished look, with men dressed in slacks and polo shirts rather than the T-shirt and jeans that prevailed in student politics, reflecting the more privileged socioeconomic background of most participants. The women were also much more "produced," as they say in Brazil, with some wearing skirts, elegant shoes, flowing hair (or chic haircuts), light makeup, and jewelry. The "coffee hour" took on a cocktail party atmosphere, with fancy cookies and savory snacks; occasionally they held more formal cocktail parties to accompany ritual events such as award ceremonies or the installation of a new directorate. These events were intended to be a time for integration and networking, in which students from different faculties and enterprises could cross paths, get to know each other, and "exchange experiences" about their respective enterprises.

Although meetings served as vehicles for exploratory exchange, the council was itself was supposed to be a *deliberative* body, charged with making decisions on FEJESP's organization and policy as well as electing council officers and five executive directors (including the president as well as directors of administration, marketing, quality, and financial/juridical affairs). These directors (and their appointed "teams") ran the federation on a day-to-day basis, although they officially answered to the larger council. The council meetings followed a very orderly procedure, with reports from the directors followed by each item on the agenda, culminating in the noncompetitive, single-candidate election of the new council officers.

In addition to deciding on policy, the council attempted to build community through participants' salient identities as future business leaders and professionals-in-training. In contrast to the Forum of Course Executives, there was remarkably little reference to the particular professional fields of the participants, or to the social role played by those professions in Brazilian society. There were, however, frequent generalizing references to the "professionalism" and the "quality" of the Junior Enterprises, along with the presumption that the firms were preparing students for leadership roles in the private sector. This focus on professionalism, quality, and efficiency—language imported from the business sector rather than their specific fields—was the means by which they attempted to create homogeneity across disciplinary and other differences. This generated a temporally modernizing sense of projected community, without the long historical narratives of the student movement, the Catholic Church, or the black movement. As a result, FEJESP participants spent less time reflectively evaluating the past than, for example, PJMP or CONUN, which were similarly grounded in the Deweyian mode of reflective problem solving.

While FEJESP council meetings tried to maintain a collaborative footing, they did not have the purist emphasis on consensus of the Forum of Course Executives. The meetings tried to create spaces for pragmatic debate while also providing mechanisms for voting in case of disagreement. There were several extremely controversial questions within FEJESP—especially the question of whether Junior Enterprise directors should be paid, as I will describe below. However, these disagreements by and large were not ideological (or not explicitly so), and did not consolidate into settled camps. Most issues seemed to be practical in scope: how to improve the quality and consistency of the Junior Enterprises; how to facilitate communication and participation; how to ensure legal protection and ethical standards; how to build relations with professors and university administrations while maintaining organizational autonomy.

Institutionally, FEJESP tried to avoid the emergence of camps by stipulating that directors and council officers be elected as individuals, not by slate, as was more common in the partisan student movement. Flávio seemed uneasy with this rule, since it could potentially mean that the president and other executive directors could end up disagreeing with each other. He compared this to a government in which "the president has to live with a minister that doesn't share his ideas." So far this had not been a problem, because candidates for the council and directorate had always been consensual. However, Flávio noted that as FEJESP became more consolidated—and organizational leadership began to be seen as more of a prize—they might see intensification of internal electoral dispute, and perhaps with it, some of the forms of tactical maneuver and backstage politicking that they criticized in the general student movement.

While the council served as a lively forum for practical debate, it did not always reach the kind of deliberative closure for which it was officially intended. In fact, large segments of the meetings I attended were not dedicated to deliberation at all, but rather to reports from directors. For example, Flávio gave an update on FEJESP's attempts to improve communication, arguing that the organization should serve as a "data-bank" that collects and redistributes information by means of "net-works." He called on the Junior Enterprises to send in information, experiences, and case studies in order to create a "dynamic of communication" and a "stock of projects" as examples for others. This orientation sounds more elaborative than deliberative, focusing on free-flowing exchange of ideas and information rather than collective decision-making. There seemed to be some tension over this question, based on the perception that real decisions were made behind the scenes in the directorate, rather than in the larger, looser council meeting. One council leader argued that meetings should be held more frequently, with less time spent on reports; this would make them "more deliberative," with "more valid agendas."

Despite this mild tension between the council and directorate, official discussion remained mainly in the collaborative mode, variously emphasizing either reflective problem solving or exploratory dialogue. However, there were also more submerged instrumental concerns tugging the meetings toward tactical maneuver. For example, one young woman from Mackensie University complained bitterly that when she went to visit other Junior Enterprises in order to "collect experiences," she was accused of spying. She declared indignantly that this was contrary to the exploratory, collaborative spirit of the enterprises. But her experience also points to the competitive realities of the market; the enterprises were in fact often competing with each other for projects and clients. They were therefore concerned to protect and promote the reputations of their own enterprises, often at the expense of those of their colleagues.

The fiercest internal debate within FEJESP touched on the interface between the idealism and instrumentalism of the movement. The leaders were deeply divided on whether the directors of the Junior Enterprises should receive some sort of financial compensation for the enormous effort they put into running their organizations. I was amazed at the intensity of this discussion; people from both sides got red in the face as they talked about it. Most of the early idealists of the movement, like Rogério and Flávio, were radically opposed to any sort of payment, saying it would contradict the mission and spirit of the Junior Enterprises and make them much more "political" (i.e., channels for personal promotion) rather than focused on the learning of students. "It's such a beautiful idea, the people who are engaged evolve so much as people and as professionals," Rogério said, that it would be absurd to ask for financial compensation. Flávio added that if money were going to the directors, there would be much more possibility for corruption, which could destroy the reputation (and thus the whole mission) of the enterprises. Yet this idealistic stance also masked subtle class distinctions, which were increasing as the movement expanded. Proponents of compensation argued that that lack of payment restricted leadership to more privileged students—often at higher status public universities—who did not have to work to maintain themselves, thus leading to the elitization of the movement. The compromise position, still under debate, was whether directors should at least receive meal and transportation coupons often given to employees, even if they didn't receive an official salary.

Moreover, as FEJESP consolidated as an organization, the politicking involved in institutional sustenance and control was beginning to grow. At several meetings, students debated whether the state federations should consolidate to form a national confederation. They were under pressure to do so from their French counterparts, who wanted to form an international confederation. This proposal was voted down at their 1996 national encounter in favor of a more open-ended national "Information Network." The coordinator of this network was Marta, the FEJESP director described in chapter 2 as an example of a focused activist. Marta was more consistently pragmatic than Flávio, with little patience for philosophical discussion or more idealistic socially oriented projects. For example, she proposed a prize for "standard projects" to promote quality and consistency rather than for what she called the "mind-blowing" social projects proposed by Flávio and others.

However, when I talked to Marta in 1997 she was feeling a bit disillusioned because FEJESP was turning "very political," "distant from its assistance-giving role in the formation of the enterprises." She thought that too much time and energy were being spent on internal and external politics, including on the ethics and structure of the movement, on clashes with professional associations, on lobbying for legislation, and on the search for financial partnerships. As a result, they were losing the emphasis on reflective problem solving: "There is little space for the Junior Enterprises to discuss their problems." In addition, she and others complained that some directors weren't really committed to the organization, but rather were just in it for narrowly self-interested purposes, to promote their personal careers.

Overall, the business publics constructed by students in the Junior Enterprises depended, like other publics, on the suppression of various kinds of potential divisions. While most students concentrated their participation within the business sector, their occasional overlapping affiliations in partisan, student, religious, or other kinds of groups had to be carefully left at the door. This allowed for a mostly collaborative footing that was grounded—at least in theory—in a Deweyian footing of reflective problem solving, with a strong dose of exploratory exchange. However, both of these collaborative modes required the somewhat more uneasy suppression of other kinds of instrumental projects, related both to organizational control as well as to activists' personal careers. Unlike CONUN and the Forum, FEJESP was quite self-consciously trying to consolidate itself as an organization, in need of public recognition, financial partnerships, and legal support. These concerns tended to drain the group of more reflective, practical discussion about the Junior Enterprises. Moreover, ambitious students were banking their personal careers on the enterprises—often in risky ways—and therefore could sometimes fall into narrowly instrumental maneuvers in relation to each other or to the larger federation. Ironically, the strong organizational component of FEJESP meant that the challenger movement that most strongly rejected the Machiavellian mode of traditional student politics also most ran the risk of moving in that direction.

MEDIATION AND CREATIVITY IN COMPLEX PUBLICS

In all three of the cases examined in this chapter, leaders located at the intersection of multiple institutional sectors played important roles in institutional innovation. While Marcos, Barreto, and Flávio were quite different in their experiences and origins, they shared the challenges of articulating projects and relations across multiple organizational milieus. Marcos and Barreto were both examples of what I am calling bridging leaders, with deep investments across several different sectors: student, partisan, and antidiscrimination, in Marcos's case, and student, partisan, and professional, in the case of Barreto. While Flávio had a fewer number of involvements, his participation also spanned several sectors. This makes him an example of what I am calling an explorer, engaged in business, partisan, and research activity (albeit these last two quite lightly).

While these three were not the only important leaders of their respective organizations, they were all recognized as being key figures in what Brazilians call the "articulation" of the three challenger projects. When leaders are "articulating" a movement (as Brazilian activists say constantly) they are elaborating the projects and strategies of the movements as they talk to people, in the often intense process of building relations and gathering support across partially overlapping milieus. Mediation in this sense takes on a richer, culturally infused character. It is not just about being a node in the flow of information, but rather about marshalling the discursive resources at one's disposal to formulate the ideas and actions of the movement in such a way as to connect to others and catch them up in the promise of the endeavor.

All three leaders were impressive in their articulateness. They were all willing to talk for hours, on multiple occasions, about the histories and purposes of their movements and organizations, as well as to reflect frankly and thoughtfully about the difficulties they were facing. They shared a combination of intensity with restraint, showing care in the way they chose their words (to make sure they "articulated" with the listener) at the same time as they overflowed with the contagious passion of the project. Of the three, Barreto was perhaps the least discursively cautious; perhaps not incidentally, he was also the most forthrightly partisan, belonging to an earlier cohort than the other two. Recall that neither Marcos nor Flávio admitted their partisan affiliations in our first conversations, since they self-consciously decoupled these from their antidiscrimination and business activism, respectively.

The innovative movements they helped to build bore the marks of their—and others'—mediating activity at the intersection of several institutional sectors. CONUN combined repertoires from the student movement—elaborating theses, holding plenaries, proposing resolutions—with the consensual, deliberative style of the church-based popular movements and the research orientation of many NGOs of the black movement. The activists also rejected some of the stylistic elements of each: the partisan contestation of the student movement, the intimate personal reflection of the Catholic youth pastoral, and the organizational territorialism of the NGOs. However, their explicit rejection of a more solid organizational form—as a way of avoiding partisanship and pulverization—meant that they developed less skill in the kind of tactical maneuver often needed to build coalitions, secure resources, and maintain institutional stability over time.

The movement of Course Executives was also influenced by the location of activists like Barreto at the intersection of several institutional sectors. Originally nestled as specialized branches within the student movement, the Course Executives became more autonomous, somewhat paradoxically, as their activists became involved in other sectors. Like CONUN, the Course Executives adopted some aspects of the collaborative style of the church-based popular movement, especially the pedagogic emphasis on small group discussions linking personal and collective reflection. They also drew on methods for institutional planning from professional associations as well as practice in discursive positioning from the political parties. However, they rejected the partisan dispute of the student movement, as well as—at least within the Forum—the more efficient forms of nonadversarial deliberation of the church-based groups. In addition, they tried to avoid the narrow corporatism of many professional groups by linking their specialized concerns with general social issues. As with CONUN, the fierce rejection of tactical maneuver—and with it, any stable organizational or leadership structure—made the Forum quite fragile in relation to resources, infrastructure, and communication.

Finally, the business-oriented youth in the Junior Enterprises also built organizations that were hybrid in conception and structure, although most of the participants did not share the bridging proclivities of leaders like Flávio. The Junior Enterprises were clearly structured on the business model, oriented toward efficient provision of paid consulting services, even if they downplayed the explicit profit motive and tried to frame the benefits to participants in terms of professional training and personal growth. Moreover, explorers like Flávio also incorporated civic language from the nonprofit sector, conceptualizing the Junior Enterprises as civil associations engaged in a form of university outreach to the community. The publics of FEJESP were militantly nonpartisan and strove to maintain a collaborative and practical orientation, although more instrumental calculations were starting to intrude. While a careful process of institution building helped to ensure organizational stability, it also generated tension between the idealism and instrumentalism of the movement.

This chapter has examined the leaders and the publics of three very different—but equally innovative—forms of activism that were challenging the entrenched student movement of the mid-1990s. In all three cases, leaders located at the intersections of multiple sectors drew on some aspects of their prior and concurrent involvements while rejecting others. In this way, they generated hybrid institutional forms that were quite distinct from one another, but similar in their rejection of the partisan contention of traditional student politics. In the next chapter, I will look at how the members of some of these challenger groups came together with more traditional student activists in one of the meta-publics of the student movement: the 1997 Congress of UNE. While many activists in this chapter officially rejected partisanship—at least under the auspices of their antidiscrimination, professional, or business involvements—many were also *student* activists—and often partisan ones as well—concerned with the functioning and control of their national organization. I will examine how some of these multiple identities were activated or deactivated in a very different kind of deliberative public, as activists struggled—and sometimes failed—to build coalitions in the tumultuous dispute for control of UNE.

CHAPTER NINE

Partisan Dramaturgy and the Breakdown of Publics

BY THE LATE 1990s, there was broad consensus in student politics that UNE and the student movement needed to be reformed. Many of the criticisms, as we have seen, were directed at the PCdoB-controlled leadership, often by partisan opponents. However, PCdoB activists were themselves becoming concerned about problems in UNE and developing their own proposals for reform. They also began consciously changing their style, from a tendency toward confrontational tactics and sectarian control to an attempt to present themselves as "broad" and "open," more willing to collaborate across partisan lines. After the congress of 1995 (described in chapter 6), the PCdoB made overtures toward the course-based movement, seemed more receptive to black organizing, and tried to broaden its alliances in electoral coalitions.

The other political forces in the student movement responded to these overtures in different ways. Some of the more moderate groups, including the socialist and social democratic parties and the center-right of the PT, began to enter into more constructive relations with the PCdoB leadership, even as they sought gains for their own forces. Others, including the left wing of the PT and the radical Trotskyist groups, hardened their critique of the PCdoB, seeing the change in style as a cynical manipulation as well as a sign that UNE was losing its historical combativity and becoming co-opted by the "neoliberal" politics of PSDB President Fernando Henrique Cardoso.

Many of these shifts in position and style came to a head in the July 1997 Congress of UNE, held in Belo Horizonte. This congress marked UNE's sixty-year anniversary, a cause for ritual celebration of UNE's historic role in the country's debates and struggles. As usual, the PCdoB leaders expressed the hope that they would be able to construct a "mega-slate" (*chapão*) with all of the contending forces as an expression of student unity. However, this attempt to create a unified public not only fell through; it imploded, leaving all of the political forces except the PCdoB split into pieces, as nearly a third of the registered delegates withdrew from the congress altogether. Badges and banners were burned, T-shirts turned backward, and angry drums resounded through the final plenary as furious delegates walked out in a dramatic display of public repudiation.

Why did this attempted public fail so dramatically? Why, at the very moment in which the PCdoB was admitting many of the problems within UNE and trying to build bridges to other forces, did those bridges break down, both between and within the contending groups? Not only did the congress not end in unity (which no one really expected), but it also failed to lead to the usual mutually recognized electoral distribution of positions among contending forces. Rather, it resulted in the internal division of most of the forces and the rejection of the legitimacy of the congress altogether by a large proportion of the participants.

This chapter examines the breakdown of publics, focusing on the processes of leadership, attempted mediation, and collective dramaturgy involved in the fragmentation and near collapse of the 1997 Congress of UNE. The fractured congress did not, in fact, dissolve, and the next leadership was elected without the departing groups. However, the tumultuous end of the congress left its scars on the contending factions and contributed to a realignment of forces within the student movement. The episode led to the further discrediting of UNE in the mainstream press and intensified critiques of the PCdoB leadership (which nevertheless succeeded in maintaining its control of UNE into the next decade).

We can look at the 1997 congress as the inverse of the convergence of the impeachment movement of 1992, in which all of the opposing forces within the student movement—as well as within the larger civic arena—ended up overcoming their differences in a rare moment of student and national unity. The 1997 CONUNE (as the Congress of UNE was known) was an attempt to realize a very different sort of public, explicitly partisan rather than civic in character, although it was similarly dependent on mediation and ritual. However rather than ending in a ritual convergence, the congress ended in fragmentation, blowing apart attempts at coalition building among contending forces.

Many analysts have explained the success and failures of coalitions by examining shifts in the political environment, particularly in the alignment of state-society relations.[1] Indeed, one factor contributing to tensions at the 1997 congress was the change in the political conjuncture from 1992 to 1997. Whereas the civic convergence of 1992 took place amidst a rare moment of broad, cross-sectoral opposition to the weakened Collor regime, the 1997 congress took place amidst a deepening split in the left over how to respond to the liberalizing reforms of President Fernando Henrique Cardoso, the sociologist turned politician who came into office in 1994 in the first post-Collor elections. Cardoso's social democratic government made symbolic overtures toward civic organizations at the same time as it pursued policies of global economic integration, privatization, and institutional reform. This angered the radical left while moderates struggled over whether to participate in government-sponsored forums on education and other issues, leaving them vulnerable to accusations of accommodation, as I explain more fully below.

However, changes in the external political environment did not determine the convergence or breakdown of these respective publics. The civic convergence against Collor was not at all guaranteed in 1992, but rather depended on a series of contingencies, including an intensive, path-dependent process of cross-sectoral mediation. Likewise, the near breakdown of the CONUNE in 1997 was also not predetermined by the political conjuncture; rather the congress seemed to spin out of the hands of hardworking mediators at the last minute, leaving most of the participants stunned and chagrined.

An alternative line of inquiry is to look not just at the political environment, but at the actors themselves, examining the political projects and relational strategies adopted by participants. The lead-up to the congresses of UNE involved an intense process of preparation and debate, as contending political forces elaborated proposals and formulated tactics for alliance formation. Much of the drama of the congress centered on the building of provisional coalitions to support procedures and resolutions, as well as on the negotiation of electoral alliances to determine the distribution of power in the directorate. As I will show, the resulting field of potential alignments subjected some groups to relational cross-pressures that accentuated internal divisions and heightened the stress in the field. However, once again, the presence of cross-pressures did not determine that the congress would end in fragmentation rather than in a negotiated electoral settlement, although it did increase the demands on the mediating skills of the student leaders.

To understand the mechanisms leading to the breakdown of the student public, we must dig beneath the surface to examine the styles and skills of communication wielded by particular leaders, as well as their contending views of "what the public is about."[2] In past chapters, I have described "styles" as the characteristic ways in which sets of actors emphasize and move between different footings of action, especially the four modes of communication described as exploratory dialogue, discursive positioning, reflective problem solving, and tactical maneuver. Here, I examine how effective leaders were in using these modes of communication to build relations and articulate projects in a complex field.

I argue that the fragmentation of the attempted public at the 1997 CONUNE was due to a clash in style, not just in projects and relations, as well as to the limited skills of leaders in responding to the emergent complexity of the congress. This lack of skill did not result simply from individual weakness or lack of capacity (although there was some of that as well). Rather, it stemmed from the inherent weaknesses and limitations of each of the four modes of communication. I examine how customary modes of political communication constrained even skilled and committed actors from responding to the challenges posed by unexpected situations. Communicative styles impose three main constraints on the construction of publics: (1) they shape discursive practices within groups, making them stronger in some modes of communication than in others; (2) they channel the responses of leaders to emergent situations, limiting their flexibility in response to crisis; and (3) they provide ammunition for denunciation by opponents, who portray such weaknesses as ethically and politically delegitimizing.

In what follows, I first discuss some of the strengths and weaknesses of the four modes of communication. I then describe how these stylistic orientations were distributed among the political forces involved in the 1997 congress. From there, I move to an ethnographic description of the dynamics of the congress. I tell the story as it was unfolding to me and to the participants, giving a sense of both the backstage negotiations and the public dramaturgy of the colorful five-day event. I close with an analytical account of how the styles and skills of communication among leaders contributed to the dramatic breakdown of this attempted public.

Strengths and Weaknesses in Communicative Footings

Skilled actors, in the sense that I have been using that term, are those who are able to marshal the complexity of identity and interest in which they are embedded in order to build relations and projects in a changing field. As Fligstein notes, they can do this in defense of established or hegemonic projects, or as challengers and reformers of the status quo.[3] Situations of greater relational complexity—that is, greater heterogeneity of interest and identity, or complex patterns of network segmentation and overlap—require greater skill in mediation, which can take different forms in response to different relational configurations.

One of my arguments in this book is that skills are not uniform; they differ stylistically, in ways that we can characterize both at the level of operational models (i.e., ethical-political understandings of why and how people act) and in terms of concrete discursive practices. I have described these styles in theoretical terms in chapter 6; here I want to break these down to a more practical level. In table 9.1 (below), I recast the four modes of communication in terms of the specific discursive practices that signal a footing of exploratory dialogue, discursive positioning, reflective problem solving, and tactical maneuver.

The kinds of discursive practices described in table 9.1 can be buttressed by institutions (e.g., regularized ways that meetings are conducted, techniques for reaching consensus, rules for decision making). But they can also

TABLE 9.1
Discursive practices in four modes of communication

	Collaboration	Competition
Ideas	**Exploratory Dialogue (Habermas)** · open-ended discussion, moving toward consensus · tentative, exploratory, or experimental exchanges · attempts to draw the other out, understand what they mean · careful listening and subsequent rethinking of positions Strengths · allows oxygenation of ideas, considering other points of view Weaknesses · tendency toward *idealism*: detached from practical and political consequences	**Discursive Positioning (Gramsci)** · construction of boundaries: similarity and difference · articulation of subject position: *as whom* you are advancing an argument · adversarial self-righteousness; moral-ethical critique of opponents · attempt to build camps and expand the adoption of one's argument Strengths · recognizes incommensurability and power in projects of social reform Weaknesses · tendency toward *purism*: lock-in to rigid, preestablished positions
Actions	**Reflective Problem Solving (Dewey)** · evaluation of strengths and weakness of historical experience · imaginative projection of possible future actions · weighing of group priorities; moral and practical consequences · consideration of values underlying both ends and means Strengths · contributes to institutional learning and collective adaptation to change Weaknesses · tendency toward *appeasement*: avoidance of conflict or dispute	**Tactical Maneuver (Machiavelli)** · control and manipulation of information, symbols, and rhetoric · cost-benefit analysis of tactics and strategies · backstage bargaining over alliances, rules, and resources · front stage displays of prestige and support · tactical adaptation and flexibility, valuing ends over means Strengths · facilitates institutional alliances, projects of command and control Weaknesses · tendency toward *cynicism*: second-guessing and breakdown of trust

to some extent be negotiated on the spot, as actors struggle over appropriate footings for the interaction at hand. As we engage in debate over ideas, are we carrying on an open-ended exchange of ideas in which we are trying to draw the other out, understand the experiences of others, and rethink our own positions (exploratory dialogue)? Or are we involved in an adversarial construction of boundaries, drawing lines of similarity and difference in the attempt to critique opponents and induce others to adopt our arguments (discursive positioning)? While these footings can be fused in practice, they still represent qualitatively different understandings of what conversation is about, and some kinds of settings veer toward one or the other.

Likewise, as we move from the elaboration of ideas to deliberation over actions, we also face choices (and sometimes struggles) over modes of communication. So, for example, deliberation may involve a careful reconstruction of the past, projection into the future, and weighing of priorities in the present, infused with consideration of collective values (reflective problem solving). Or it might entail a narrower calculation of costs and benefits, backstage bargaining over rules and alliances, and front stage control of information and appearances, in which values are subordinated to the goals of success (tactical maneuver). Again, while these footings may shade into each other, there are recognizable qualitative differences that have to do with how we conduct ourselves in conversation.

Table 9.1 also points out some of the strengths and weakness of each of the four modes. Exploratory dialogue is an important component of the elaboration process, as it allows for the oxygenation of ideas, the consideration of a problem from multiple standpoints, and the ability to move beyond one's prior opinions and assumptions. But on its own, the Habermasian mode can also contribute to a tendency toward *idealism*, the belief that differences of power and interest can be reconciled through rational discussion, as well as to a distancing from the practical and political consequences of ideas. In contrast, discursive positioning is based on the recognition that there are often incommensurable differences due to actors' locations in fields of power and resources, and thus complete consensus is impossible. This kind of positioning is essential for elaboration of projects for moral and political reform. However, the Gramscian mode entails the danger of a tendency toward *purism*, of locking interlocutors into rigid, preestablished positions and making it difficult for them to listen to or learn from each other.

The two action-oriented modes also have strengths and weaknesses. Reflective problem solving is an important component of institutional learning and adaptation to change; it allows collectivities to carefully reflect on their practices from the point of view of their values as well as their goals. But because the Deweyan mode has few mechanisms for dealing with conflicts of ideals and interest within the community, it may lead to a tendency toward *appeasement* toward contending interests as a means of avoiding conflict or dispute. Finally, tactical maneuver has the advantage of greater attunement to such conflicts; the Machiavellian mode provides flexibility in forming alliances and pursuing projects of institutional control precisely because it leaves values (provisionally) at the door. But this suspension of values in relation to means leads to a tendency toward *cynicism*, as actors second-guess the motives of their interlocutors, sometimes contributing to a breakdown of trust.

This attention to the limitations as well as the strengths of these modes alerts us to the possibility that groups of activists can be quite skilled in some subset of these practices but can have weaknesses and blind spots in others. What serves them well in building relations and projects in one context may lead to a breakdown in productive communication in others, or leave them ill-equipped to deal with changing or emergent situations. The leaders of these groups—whose mediating skills have been honed in trajectories through particular institutional contexts—may become locked into accustomed ways of responding to problems and challenges. As a result, they may find it hard to see alternative forms of communication that might get them through an impasse.

Moreover, actors may also become morally and politically invested in a given stylistic orientation, so that any departure from it (from those within or outside of their collectivities) is seen as betrayal, hypocrisy, or lack of ethics. In fact, disputes that are, on the surface, about disagreements over projects and relations may more accurately revolve around questions of style, that is, the models of thought and action that actors think are (or should be) in play. The weaknesses that are inherent in a given style become grounds for ethical condemnation, with little acknowledgement of the strengths of the discursive practices involved (i.e., their contribution to productive communication).

In the 1997 Congress of UNE, such conflicts over styles were very much in play. These conflicts emerged as fault lines between and within groups, based in part on differences in leadership position and trajectories, as well as on discursive repertoires within contending groups. The stylistic orientations of the leaders enabled and constrained them in responding to the relational challenges of the congress, especially as it erupted unexpectedly into crisis. My first task is to examine how these stylistic elements informed the repertoires and orientations of the contending forces.

Contending Styles among Partisan Forces

During the 1997 Congress of UNE, the various "political forces" (as they referred to themselves) had recognizably different stylistic orientations. While these styles were routinized and institutionalized in various ways,

	Collaboration	Competition
Ideas	EXPLORATORY DIALOGUE PeT (right PT)	DISCURSIVE POSITIONING Radical Trotskyists: (PSTU, OT) NVA (left PT)
Actions	Socialist/labor: (PDT, PPS, PSB) REFLECTIVE PROBLEM-SOLVING	UPF (PCdoB/UJS) TACTICAL MANEUVER

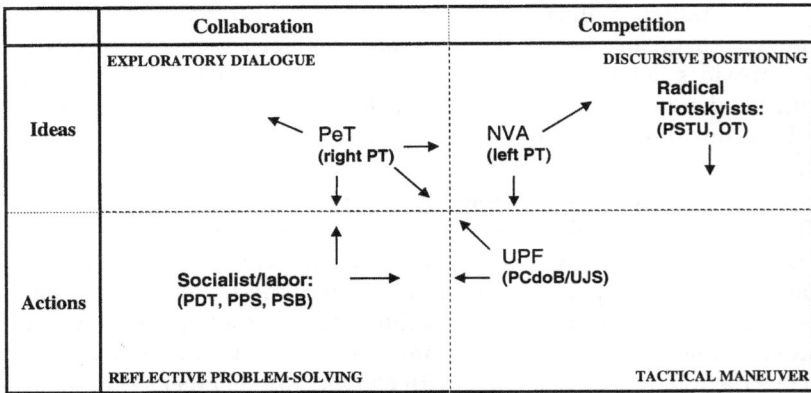

Figure 9.1. Stylistic orientations among partisan forces

they were not static and fixed. Rather, many of the groups were undergoing a process of internal reevaluation of the kinds of discursive practices that they considered to be ethically, politically, and institutionally desirable. These shifts were responses to the changing relational compositions of the different forces as well as to learning processes over the past decade.

Figure 9.1 maps the positions of the major political forces in relation to the four communicative modes. Some of these forces were composed of single political parties, while others were "camps" composed of several parties or internal party factions. In the case of the composite groups, I follow the students' convention by referring to the name of the "thesis" (the text of proposals that each of the forces elaborated ahead of time). These "theses" were the basis for the composition of electoral slates, which sometimes combined several theses, depending on negotiations at the congress. The main locations of the forces in figure 9.1 are based on history and reputation, while the arrows note their internal stylistic complexity, that is, the extent to which their members were engaging, or considering engaging, in modes other than what was considered in the field to be their dominant mode.

Um Passo a Frente (UPF)

The delegates associated with the PCdoB were grouped under the thesis/ slate name of "One Step in Front" taken from a popular rock song. Not all of these delegates had formal PCdoB affiliation; some belonged only to UJS (Union of Socialist Youth), the broader socialist youth group associated with the party, while others were friends and sympathizers swept up in the recruitment effort. Nevertheless, the projects and tactics of the slate were developed by PCdoB leaders, who were determined to maintain their control of the directorate of UNE. The PCdoB had a reputation for manipulative, strong-arm tactics and a tendency for "steamrolling" the other student forces, although as I noted above, they had recently been reevaluating their strategy and making overtures to other groups. The PCdoB leaders gave two different kinds of reasons for this shift. First, they said that they were trying to maintain the ethical high ground in the face of student rejection of partisanship; this required them to seem "broad" and "open," above petty sectarian disputes. Second, they were concerned with the "governability" of UNE, which required working together with the other forces to make UNE as an institution run more effectively. Thus while they had a reputation for skill in tactical maneuver (and indeed, one of their activists had praised Machiavelli to me, as I describe in chapter 6), they were trying to expand their stylistic repertoire toward exploratory dialogue and reflective problem solving, although somewhat warily and within a project of institutional control. However, many of the opposing forces were skeptical of this shift and accused the PCdoB of using "ethics as a tactic," that is, of engaging in cynical manipulation of the civic discourse in relation to their own partisan projects.

The youth of the PT were strongly divided in relation to the party's ongoing internal struggle. At the previous congress in 1995, there had been enormous pressure from the party leadership for a unified PT slate; however, in 1997 the internal struggle was more pronounced and the lines of division were drawn much more solidly. The PT delegates had split into three main camps, consisting of the tendencies of the center-right, the left, and the radical Trotskyists.

Prazer em Transformar (PeT)

The camp on the center-right of the PT gave its thesis the evocative title, "Pleasure in Transforming," by which they tried to differentiate themselves stylistically from the perceived truculence and asceticism of the traditional class-based left. This group consisted of youth from the moderate tendency *Articulation-Unity in Struggle* (which controlled the national leadership of the party) as well as *Radical Democracy* (an intellectually oriented, civic-minded tendency considered to be the right flank of the PT).[4] The camp had a reputation for ideological looseness, that is, being more concerned with grassroots debate and the circulation of ideas as an end in itself than in coming to closure on cohesive ideological projects. They differentiated themselves from the PCdoB by rejecting the communists' strong institutional focus (and accompanying centralization and bureaucracy), focusing instead on grassroots discussion in the universities. But they also differentiated themselves from the left wing of their own party by stressing the need for positive proposals, rather than only mobilization and critique. They were thus the champions of exploratory dialogue, unhitched at least in principle from either ideological dogma or bureaucratic control, although this set them up for accusations of idealism and naiveté. At the same time, they were eager to expand their influence and power within the student movement. Some of their leaders within UNE (most notably, UNE's treasurer, Claudio) had been developing pragmatic and collaborative relations with the PCdoB, arguing that it was important to contribute to UNE as a collectivity even as they schemed tactically about how to increase control (thus combining reflective problem solving and tactical maneuver).

Não Vou Me Adaptar (NVA)

The left wing of the PT also formed a distinct camp, defiantly entitling its thesis "I Won't Adapt." This group was the second largest force of the congress, after the PCdoB-led UPF. It consisted of several PT tendencies, including a center-left faction called *Articulation of the Left*, which had split from the centrist *Articulation* in 1992. The camp also included the intellectually oriented Trotskyist tendency, *Democracy and Socialism*, a Mendel-influenced faction known for defense of environmental and feminist issues and a culturalist approach to Marxism that differed from their more orthodox fellow Trotskyists. Several other smaller leftist tendencies from within and outside of the PT joined them. Stylistically, this group was heavily ideological; it considered itself to be disputing hegemony within the left by defending a more combative, class-based stance, which they saw as under attack even within their own party. As its name signaled, this camp opposed what it saw as the accommodationist tendencies of the PCdoB, the socialists, and the right of the PT. They dedicated their elaborative energy to discursive positioning against Cardoso's "neoliberal plan" as well as against any alliances that would appease the right and dilute the combativity of the student movement. At the same time, they were engaged in tactical maneuvers, in the form of intense negotiations among themselves and with the more radical groups over leadership of their proposed slate and distribution of positions in the directorate of UNE.

Radical Trotskyists

While there were several radical Trotskyist groups visible at the congress, with finely grained ideological distinctions among themselves, they can be considered as a block as they acted in mostly similar ways in relation to projects and alliances and ended up in almost exactly the same place.

The two most important groups were the political party PSTU, which launched a thesis called *Reviravolta* ("Full Reverse"),[5] and the internal PT tendency *O Trabalho* (OT, roughly translated as "Labor" in reference to Marx's capital-labor opposition), whose thesis was entitled *Nem Mais Um Dia Para FHC* ("Not one more day for Fernando Henrique Cardoso"). Like the leftist students of NVA, their dominant mode was discursive positioning, although they usually had a more combative revolutionary discourse that made it seem possible to move from Gramsci's war of position to war of maneuver overnight, if enough energy were put into mobilization. They were accused by many of the other forces (including NVA) of purist tendencies and an ideological disconnect from the practical challenges of revolutionary action in the current political environment. They were often willing to sacrifice electoral victory in order to "mark position" on controversial issues (often noisily, with full drum battery and combative chants). The PSTU, especially, was known for "knocking over tables" in moments of tension (OT took a somewhat more suave, integrating approach, although they could be equally intransigent ideologically). However, they weren't immune from tactical maneuvering and were as concerned as the other forces with securing space in the directorate of UNE, either by going it alone or in alliance with the other leftist forces.

Socialist/Labor

Finally, there were a number of smaller forces that variously defined themselves as socialist or labor parties, which, while differing on some points, can be blocked together in terms of the main projects and relations of the congress. They did not constitute a formal camp, in that they did not launch theses together, but their names were usually uttered in one breath by the other forces when discussing possible configurations of alliances. These included the PDT (Democratic Labor Party), a historic populist-nationalist party; the PPS (Popular Socialist Party), a reformed, "democratic and popular" version of the former Brazilian Communist Party; and the PSB (Brazilian Socialist Party). These parties were divided between three different theses, which differed on institutional points such as whether to support direct elections for UNE and how much to support the government's educational reforms (which they did not reject out of hand, like most of the left forces). One thesis, *Virando a Mesa* ("Turning the Table") was composed of activists from the PDT and PSB; *Construindo o Futuro* ("Constructing the Future") was composed of a dissident group from the PDT; and the self-mocking, high-spirited *Eu Tô Maluco* ("I'm Crazy") was associated with the PPS.

Stylistically, all of the socialist groups can be considered to be primarily grounded in reflective problem solving. They all had strong institutionalist streaks, arguing against partisan divisions in the student movement and calling for more pragmatic engagement with the reforms of the Cardoso government. In addition, they were critical of the strong ideological tenor of student politics, and proposed a less dogmatic internal debate (i.e., involving more exploratory dialogue). They also proposed a broad oppositional front, as opposed to the "classist front" defended by the more leftist students, who accused the socialists of appeasement of neoliberalism. Like the other forces, they also engaged in tactical maneuver as they tried to negotiate alliances that would give them the greatest possible voice in the directorate.

There were a number of other minor forces, including several small revolutionary groups as well as a group of so-called "independents," coming from the Northeastern state of Paraiba, which called itself *Apenas Começamos* ("We're Just Beginning"). A state-based (as opposed to a party-based) grouping was a rarity in this setting; the group entered into negotiations with nearly all of the forces at the conference (although it was closest to PeT). In the chaos at the end of the congress, the group ended up fielding its own slate and winning a slot in the directorate. Almost entirely invisible at the congress was the PSDB (Party of Brazilian Social Democracy), due to the general climate of hostility toward the government of its leader, President Fernando Henrique Cardoso. Unlike at previous congresses, the PSDB youth did not launch their own thesis or appear in any way, although some activists were present.[6]

While I have presented these different forces as more or less unified in style and project, we can take the zoom lens in further to note important internal differences, due in part to the relational composition of the groups. Building on my discussion in chapter 8, I want to briefly link some of these stylistic divisions to the leadership positions and institutional trajectories of participants.

For all of the forces, the high-level leaders tended to be deeply invested in student and partisan organizing. As they assumed national student leadership, they often dropped their previous involvements in other sectors (e.g., in religious, popular, professional, or labor organizing). This positioned them as *entrenched leaders*, with multiple involvements concentrated in one or two sectors. I argued in chapter 8 that entrenched leaders have a tendency toward the Machiavellian mode of tactical maneuver, concerned with seeking and maintaining institutional control. The institutional structure of the congresses of UNE supported (and even demanded) this mode, since leaders had to dedicate a good part of their energies to tactical alliance building, backstage bargaining, and front stage displays of symbolic power in the battle for control of the organization.

Despite this cross-partisan similarity among higher-level leaders, there were clear stylistic differences within and between the different groups. For example, within the camp of *Pleasure in Tranforming* (PeT), there were many middle- and lower-level activists who had multiple involvements that spanned three or more sectors, usually including the student movement, a political party, and some kind of course-based, popular, religious, NGO, or labor activity. However, they varied in how deeply they were invested in these sectors. Many mid-level PeT leaders also had multiple involvements *within* sectors, particularly within the party and student movement, thus qualifying them as bridging leaders, which I have argued would tend to give them an orientation toward discursive positioning. At the same time, they were trying to reach out to less traditional activists, who were often newcomers to student politics. Many lower-level, grassroots activists were less heavily invested than either the mid- or high-level leaders, either as explorers or (less frequently) focused activists. They tended to take a more exploratory and reflective approach, less wedded to ideological boundary-making. In addition, many had prior or concurrent experience in the Catholic youth pastoral, the popular movements, and the Course Executives, also supporting a more reflective, dialogic style. This meant that PeT was split at different levels between youth in all four of the leadership positions. This in turn created the possibility of tension, as many top leaders were oriented toward tactical alliance, some mid-level leaders pulled toward more combative, hegemony-building approaches, and many newcomers pulled toward more dialogic or pragmatic modes of communication.

In contrast, their co-partisans in *I Won't Adapt* (NVA) had a higher concentration of deeply invested, sector-spanning bridging leaders, without the same impetus to provide a "lighter" alternative to traditional militancy (they often referred to PeT disparagingly as "PT-light"). One of the leaders of NVA, Martín (an UNE director during the impeachment, introduced in chapter 5), told me proudly that "our people have more political density." By this he meant that they were more "organically" linked to political forums—including the student movement; political parties; Course Executives; and religious, popular, and labor movements—through multiple militancies and full-time commitments. This contributed to the group's stylistic emphasis on discursive positioning, although as top leaders dropped some involvements and became more entrenched, their orientation to tactical maneuver often intensified as well.

While I have less data on (and experience with) the students in the other forces, my impression is that the association between position and style as laid out in chapter 8 works for these groups as well. The PCdoB youth historically tended to concentrate their energies in the political party and one other sector (in this case, usually the student movement);

this positioned many of them as entrenched leaders concerned with tactical control. However as the student movement diversified, the party began encouraging their activists to expand their involvements, especially in professional and cultural activism, thus contributing to their recent (tentative) shift toward dialogic and reflective approaches. The socialist youth tended to have fewer peripheral involvements, with a higher proportion of focused activists (with the exception of their more entrenched top leaders). Focused activists, I have argued, tend to engage in more collaborative institutional modes, oriented toward reflective problem solving. Finally, the Trotskyists were usually committed participants in popular and labor movements, in addition to their student and partisan involvements (and usually without the more reflective and dialogic influence of the church). This located them firmly as bridging leaders and deepened their tendencies toward discursive positioning.

This distribution of leadership positions helps us to understand the stylistic differences between the political forces. Because of the institutional character of the event—a competitive, deliberative congress aimed at the distribution of institutional control—the Machiavellian mode was very much in evidence among all of the contending forces, as I will show below. But while roundly (and often unfairly) denounced, this tendency toward tactical maneuver was tempered by real differences in—and conflicts over—other aspects of communicative style. These stylistic distinctions were invoked in ethical self-affirmations and condemnations of opposing groups. They enabled some kinds of mediating efforts between groups, but impeded others. And the weaknesses of these styles—the ways that they closed off some possibilities of action—contributed to the tumultuous ending and near breakdown of the congress.

PRECONFERENCE ARTICULATIONS

The short version of the story of the 1997 Congress of UNE is that the PCdoB won again. For the fifth time in a row, and the twelfth time since UNE's reconstruction in 1979, the PCdoB youth won control of the directorate. They did so in a broad, if shallow alliance composed of members of at least five different political parties, including the PT, PDT, PPS, and PSB. The composite slate won by a huge majority, receiving 1,521 of the 1,972 votes cast. Together, the alliance won ten out of eleven positions in the executive, with the PCdoB maintaining majority control. However, despite this veneer of unity, the victory was extremely fragile. The congress ended in disarray, with the internal fragmentation of all of the opposition forces, accusations of authoritarianism and corruption against the

UNE leadership, and the dramatic walkout from the congress of about a third of the credentialed delegates.

This outcome was by no means clear ahead of time. Up until the last evening, the contending forces were busily defending proposals and negotiating alliances, in the usual dance leading up to the final vote. Many opposition leaders were feeling optimistic about their proposed coalitions, sure that they were on the verge of advancing their groups' organizational and ideological interests. What happened to blow this process apart, leaving a divided congress, a disillusioned base, and a weakened directorate?

I attended the 1997 congress during a follow-up research trip to Brazil, having spent two previous years getting to know the groups, leaders, and issues in play in the student movement.[7] I arrived a week before the start of the congress, with precongress articulations busily underway. In São Paulo, the buzz was about a local alliance that the PCdoB had formed with the center-right of the PT, the PPS, and the PSB in the recent election for the State Student Union (UEE). This was a startling break of the moderate *petistas* (PT members) with the left of their own party. The new state directorship included Cristina of Mackensie University (introduced in earlier chapters), along with others I knew from the PT and PCdoB. The big question on the table was whether they would pull off a similar alliance at the national congress the following week. The PT leaders seemed ambivalent about this question. Some seemed optimistic that such an alliance could (and should) be formed, while others worried that their grassroots activists would resist such a move, since the PT had spent the past decade and half denouncing the PCdoB as the incarnation of evil in the student movement.

The anticipation surrounding these negotiations was palpable at a Law School ceremony I attended to swear in the new state directorship. Leaders of the PT and PCdoB bustled around the edge of the auditorium, spinning into the ever-present *conchavos* (small huddled consultations). The current president of UNE, Renato, introduced me to Wilson, the PCdoB's head of slate for the upcoming congress. He then slapped a passing PT activist named Alex on the back, telling me that this was the PT candidate for UNE president. I was surprised; Alex was a relatively young activist from the Northeastern state of Maranhão, who occupied a minor position in the UNE's directorate. He was associated with the civic-oriented PT tendency *Radical Democracy* (part of the *Pleasure in Transforming* camp). In the bar later that evening, Alex confirmed his candidacy as head of slate for PeT, although he noted my surprise: "I wasn't on your map when you left, was I?" While Alex seemed wary of the potential alliance with the PCdoB, he also said that "it's time for us to admit our proximity." On many issues of project and strategy, they were closer to the PCdoB then to their co-partisans on the left of the PT. Many in their camp felt they had betrayed their principles at the 1995 congress, when they were pressured into joining with the left of the party in the name of partisan unity (see chapter 6).

A week later I arrived at the site of the congress, the Federal University of Belo Horizonte, in the interior state of Minas Gerais. The central plaza, known affectionately as "Red Square" (due to a modernist red metal sculpture in the center), was still relatively placid, with a few students unfurling banners and setting up literature tables. I made my way to the congress registration, an all important post where voting credentials, in the form of bright yellow badges hung around delegates' necks, were handed out to approved delegates. This, too, was still relatively calm, although it would soon be mobbed with long lines of arriving students; five thousand delegates and observers were expected from around the country. Registration tables were manned by students with colorful T-shirts and stickers associated with their political forces, charged with maintaining fair play in this critical component of the congressional numbers game. Cristina and her colleagues from São Paulo were there wearing the orange shirts of PeT, sitting next to activists from the PCdoB and other parties that I had met in Rio and Bahia.

I spent most of the afternoon chatting with top leaders from the various forces, who were darting around trying to get a sense of the other groups' opening stances on alliances and proposals. News traveled unevenly, as I found out when I bumped into Celso, a leader of the PDT (Democratic Labor Party) who had just arrived from Rio Grande do Sul. In describing his group's strategy, he told me that "there's no way" they could form an alliance with the PCdoB, since their relationship was very strained; rather their first choice of allies was the center-right of the PT. I mentioned the possibility that *Pleasure in Tranforming* (PeT) might form an alliance with the PCdoB. He looked alarmed and asked "who told you this?" I said I had heard it from some of the leaders, but that it wasn't all a sure thing. He stalked off looking upset. I worried that I might have spilled the beans, although the news hadn't been given to me in confidence, and after the alliance in São Paulo it seemed like an open possibility.

I found my way to the press room above the square, coordinated by Gisela Mendonça, a journalist who had been president of UNE for the PCdoB in 1986 and who now served as communications advisor. Gisela pulled me eagerly into the room, which was equipped with three computers and was bustling with phone calls and organizers. Claudio, one of the top leaders of *Pleasure in Tranforming* (PeT), came in during a planning meeting, talking nonstop on his cell phone (at that time, cell phones were still rare enough to serve as a clear status marker among student leaders). Within PeT, Claudio was one of the chief architects of his camp's new pragmatic and collaborative relationship with the PCdoB, which he carried out from his high-level position as treasurer of UNE. In this practical, institution-building mode, he had a key organizational role at the congress, with lots of last minute details to take care of. While he was there, Celso of the PDT popped his head in and said pointedly to Claudio, "I just talked to your friend" (gesturing to me) "and now I want to talk to you." They went off to huddle in the hallway, with Claudio still glued to his cell phone.

Alex was also buzzing around in his role as head of slate for PeT, which involved the task of negotiating alliances with other forces. He was still cautious about the possibility of an alliance with the PCdoB, concerned that the base of the camp would reject it. In contrast, Maurício, one of the top negotiators of the PCdoB, was more optimistic, although he said that the alliance was still uncertain, given "the internal climate of the PT." Maurício had a reputation for hardball bargaining, although he had also become skilled at working collaboratively with rivals when he served as UNE's vice president under the PT regime of 1989–91. The year before, he had described to me the PCdoB's shift to a "broader, more pluralistic" strategy and criticized the narrow dogmatism of the other forces.

I heard a much more adversarial stance from Francisco, leader of the radical Trotskyist PSTU. He told me that there was no way that the PSTU would enter into a *chapão* (a mega-slate including all of the forces), which was reportedly the proposal of the PCdoB, but was instead trying to form a slate with the other left-leaning forces. He gave me a quick rundown of the main ideological controversies of the conference, which included whether to oppose government subsidies for private universities and what stance to take with regards to Cuba (the PSTU defended a critique of Cuba's recent market-related reforms). The biggest issue for the PSTU was whether UNE should defend a "classist front" or a "broad front of the left" in national politics, including the PDT, PPS, PSB, and other moderate socialist groups. The PSTU was adamantly opposed to the latter, believing that UNE should take a firm position supporting a class-centered critique of Brazilian society and government.

CIVIC CEREMONY AND CHALLENGE

The opening of the congress that evening featured a commemoration of UNE's sixtieth anniversary, with a tribute to the past presidents of UNE. In line with the PCdoB's emphasis on UNE's civic-institutional role, the ceremony highlighted UNE's historic contribution to Brazil's civic and political life. The oldest ex-president at the event was Brazil's minister of justice, Sepulveda Pertences; also present were several congressional representatives and the president of UNE during its dismantling by the dictatorship in 1968. More recent leaders included five ex-presidents from the PCdoB (from 1981 to 1986), along with three PT ex-presidents (from 1987 to 1991). The mayor of the host city, Belo Horizonte, and the rector of the Federal University of Minas Gerais (UFMG) were also present, seated next to Renato, the current UNE president.

The most interesting part of the evening was not the ceremony itself, but rather the dramaturgic interaction between student factions. This dramaturgy reflected stylistic differences between the forces: the PCdoB was determined to maintain a footing of high civic ritual, while the PSTU was equally determined to disrupt it. I arrived early to a near empty auditorium, with a few scattered students beginning to fill in the back of the hall. The calm was soon shattered by drumbeats announcing the arrival of PSTU delegates, who filled the left side of the audience and unfurled their banner along the side wall. As they marked their presence, shouts of "Full Reverse!" (the title of their thesis) reverberated through the room. As delegates from the PCdoB/UJS arrived, chants of "One Step in Front!" (the PCdoB thesis) offered their counterchallenge. These two groups dominated the room, with little or no presence of the PT, which was evident in the lukewarm applause offered to the three *petista* ex-presidents. This was in contrast to the resounding cheers offered by the UJS youth to all ex-presidents of the PCdoB.

To challenge the spirit of civic celebration, the PSTU erupted at several points with chanted denunciations of the mayor of Belo Horizonte (because of the repression of recent strikes), as well as of the justice minister (because of the imprisonment of a leader of the landless workers' movement). The PCdoB was incensed at this challenge to the dignity of their invited guests; they tried to silence the PSTU with the traditional unifying chant "UNE somos nos, nossa força e nossa voz!" ("UNE is us, our force and our voice). I saw Maurício of the PCdoB rush over and gesticulate fiercely in the face of Francisco and other PSTU leaders. Later one of the PT ex-presidents told me that Maurício had threatened to break their drums if they didn't stop. To him, this showed the dark underside of the PCdoB's recent emphasis on civic dialogue; he shook his head and added, "This is the old PCdoB."

The discourses of the ex-presidents also signaled stylistic divisions between the forces. Amidst joint praise for UNE's current directorate and admiration for the history of "the glorious UNE," there was a notable difference in tone. The PCdoB leaders gave exalted, condemnatory speeches against neoliberalism, Fernando Henrique Cardoso, privatization, and the assault on the Brazilian people. In contrast, the PT leaders offered pleas for maturity, ethics, and dialogue as well as exhortations against sectarianism in the student movement (and in the left more generally). Later, one of the PT ex-presidents admitted to me that they hadn't followed their own advice when they were leaders—only now, many years and battles later, could they offer this counsel to the younger cohorts.

Following the ceremony, the three PT ex-presidents were honored guests at a meeting of supporters of the thesis, *Pleasure in Tranforming* (PeT) in the middle of Red Square. They repeated the themes about maturity and dialogue, with one adding that he felt an unprecedented openness in the PCdoB to discuss changes in the structure of the student movement. This meeting had about thirty students, some already wearing the orange T-shirts of the thesis. As national organizer of PeT, Claudio introduced leaders from different states, covered a few logistics, and summarized the major points of contention for the next day's discussion groups. He stressed that their camp was not composed solely of *petistas*, but also of nonaffiliated students who sympathized with their proposals; the focus should be on the proposals rather than the party (this despite the fact that the name of the thesis was clearly designed to highlight the letters "PT"). The question of alliances did not yet come up, although Claudio announced nightly meetings to discuss the progress of negotiations. A headquarters was set up for exchange of information as well as socialization, and names were taken for discussion groups the following day. In what would turn into a chronic (and consequential) problem for this group, no one volunteered for the morning slots, until Claudio said in exasperation at the lack of discipline: "This can't happen!!!" (provoking a few resigned stalwarts to agree to show up early).

OPENING DISCUSSIONS AND THE ARC OF ALLIANCES

On the first full day of the congress, the contending forces continued to feel each other out as backstage negotiations began to heat up. Most of the day was devoted to "discussion groups," in which proposals were initially fielded and debated before being systematized by a committee composed of all of the forces. This year, students reported that the groups were lively and heated, with strong criticisms of UNE and its current leadership. Usually these discussions were dominated by discursive positioning, giving top- and mid-level leaders a chance to be seen and heard as they fired off opening salvos for their factions. The discussion groups were often criticized as not being conducive to thoughtful debate, but rather fostering sloganeering and ideological posturing. The groups were usually too large—and too dominated by the competing leaders—for most grassroots, lower-level delegates to feel like they were part of a reflective, institution-building discussion.

When I returned to Red Square, I ran into Martín, a top leader of *I Won't Adapt* (NVA), engaged in intracamp negotiations with members of his own internal PT tendency (*Democracy and Socialism*), as well as with other left-wing factions. Everyone was in a high state of alertness and unrest, busy with intense and mobile *conchavos* in which the traditional gesture of the hand on the shoulder—accompanied by the urgent statement, "I need to speak to you"—took precedence over all merely sociable conversation. At issue was how to distribute leadership in the slate among the composite forces of NVA (which contained five to six factions from the left of the PT), as well as what kinds of alliances they should form with other forces. While they clearly opposed entering a coalition with the socialists, they were torn on whether to form their own slate, form an alliance with the radical Trotskyists, or expand the "arc of alliance" (as they called it) to include the "right" of the PT and the PCdoB. The Trotskyists would accept both as part of an ideologically based "classist front," while NVA had ethical reservations about the "political practice" (i.e., communicative style) of these two potential allies.

NVA's critique of the PCdoB and PeT is a good example of how opposing forces use perceived weaknesses of communicative styles to ethically and politically discredit opponents. They condemned the PCdoB as cynical, manipulative, and authoritarian, based on its history of Machiavellian tactics in the student movement. They also saw the PCdoB as being too willing to appease the forces of the right, through their pragmatic stress on civic institutionalism and willingness to participate in government-sponsored councils on educational reform (a key point of contention at the congress). While they were not quite as harshly critical of PeT, they were openly scornful of what they saw as their co-partisans' stylistic weakness. NVA thought that PeT was ideologically mushy, overly idealistic, and lacking in combativeness, as a result of the group's antidogmatic embrace of exploratory dialogue. They also condemned PeT for their recent pragmatic "appeasement" of the PCdoB, which they saw as a betrayal of ethical principles for narrow institutional gain.

In contrast, the leaders of PeT saw these same discursive practices as demonstrating the stylistic virtues of their own group: a concern with practical institution building (as opposed to "purist" ideological critique) as well as stronger attention to the personal learning, social integration, and reflective experiences of their members. When I stopped by their headquarters, I found a very different milieu than the intense intracamp negotiations of NVA. The office was filled with orange-shirted students busily engaged with the pragmatics of the event: making phone calls, selling T-shirts, and preparing fliers for that night's festivities. True to the "Pleasure" side of their thesis title, they were planning a late-night party to integrate students from different parts of the country. Top leaders ran in and out between negotiations, greeting me as they passed. Lower-level activists were hanging around, exchanging ideas on politics and their ac-

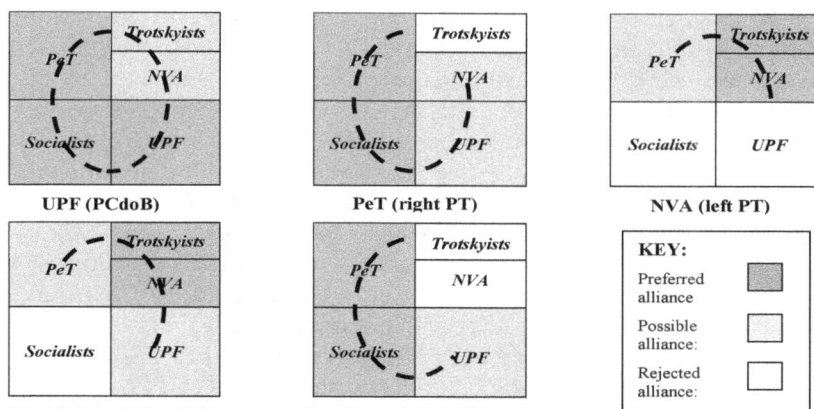

Figure 9.2. Possible "arcs of alliances" among UNE Congress forces

tivist experiences, in an informal footing of exploratory dialogue. A few doors down, music was pouring from a crowded room with pool tables and a stereo system, with delegates dancing, lounging, drinking beer, and otherwise pleasurably engaged.

At the close of the second day of the congress, the dance of alliances between the forces was beginning to come into focus, although it was still fluid and flexible. Each of the force's proposed "arc of alliances" is depicted in figure 9.2, with each force's preferred alliance darkly shaded, and those that it considered possible (but unlikely) in lighter shading.

The PCdoB officially wanted its slate to encompass everyone, although everyone knew that this was impossible, particularly with the left-wing forces. PeT seemed happy to include the socialists, uneasy in relation to the PCdoB, dubious about the left of the PT, and opposed to the radical Trotskyists. The left of the PT (NVA) excluded the socialists and the PCdoB (on ideological and ethical grounds, respectively), was happy to include the radical left, and was conditionally open to the right of the PT. And the Trotskyists were willing to include all of the PT and the PCdoB, but under no terms would they ally with the socialists (the "parties of the right"). The socialists, in turn, rejected an alliance with the ideological left, openly courted the right wing of the PT, and were open but uneasy in relation to the PCdoB.

Given these opening tactical predispositions, there were a number of different ways the forces could have settled into electoral slates, depending on interforce negotiations. However, note the relational cross-pressures placed on PeT by this configuration. All of the forces, in effect, declared themselves willing to include the right of the PT in their coalitions; yet all of their potential allies (except for the PCdoB) had restrictions toward PeT's other potential partners (e.g, NVA rejected the socialists, the socialists rejected NVA and the Trotskyists, and everyone else was uneasy, if not downright hostile, toward the PCdoB). Moreover, any of the alliances could be perceived by PeT as an ideological, organizational, or ethical self-betrayal. If they allied with the left of the PT, they would betray many of their own proposals, which tended to place more stock in institutional change—and less on class confrontation—than their copartisans. If they allied with the socialists, they risked accusations of partisan betrayal for siding with the "parties of the right." And if they allied with the communists, they risked ethical self-betrayal, given their historic condemnation of the style and method of the PCdoB. At this early stage, they were still pleased with being courted; however, these dilemmas intensified over the next few days as the congress developed.

PLENARIES AND POSITIONING

On the third day of the congress, all activities took place in a large sports stadium at some distance from the university. The first event was a political ceremony featuring a lineup of dignitaries from local government, political parties, civic organizations, labor unions, and popular movements, invited to give public credibility to the congress. I stopped by the press room and found a gathering of Brazilian VIPs milling around talking to journalists and slapping each other on the back. The younger folk were marveling at how these national and local leaders leapt at the chance to speak to a congress of students—a sign that UNE did have some weight and glamour in Brazilian society, at least among institutionalized politicians.

Inside the stadium, the forces were slowly positioning themselves, with symbolic attention to their location in the arena. This seating arrangement is mapped in figure 9.3 (below), as it played an important role in the dramaturgy of the congress. The arrangement was for the most part traditional; I had seen nearly the identical seating preferences in the 1995 congress, as well as in other, smaller student councils. However, there were a number of differences this year that signaled the potential realignments in play.

Among the first to enter were the youth of the PSTU (*Full Reverse*), accompanied by chants and drum rolls, occupying the bleachers to the left of the stage. Mingled with them were members of smaller revolutionary groups, which joined the PSTU in most of their dramaturgic gestures but occasionally voted separately.[8] The next section of the bleachers was occupied by the large contingent from the left of the PT (*I Won't Adapt*), followed by the smaller Trotskyist tendency *O Trabalho* (OT). Together,

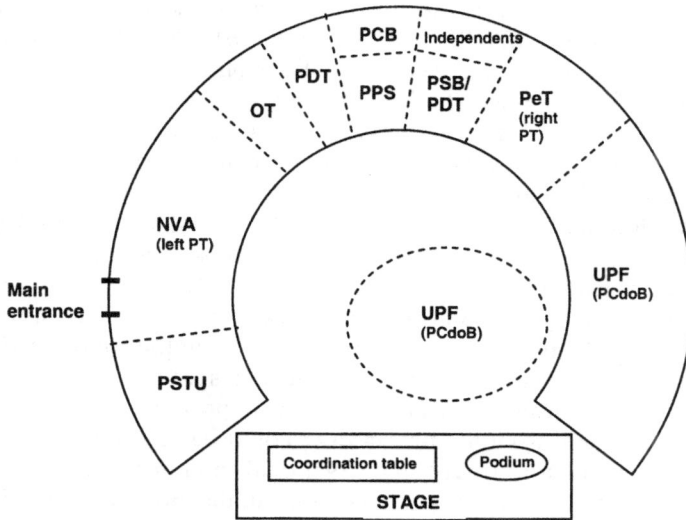

Figure 9.3. The positioning of forces in the major plenary sessions

these forces composed the basis for the potential front of "classist left" that their leaders were working hard to stitch together.

To the right of this block came the socialist parties, starting with a small dissident contingent of the PDT (*Constructing the Future*), led by UNE director Ricardo, who was warring with Celso, the PDT leader I had talked to earlier. The rumor at the congress was that Celso was keeping his own group outside because it was smaller than he had hoped, and he didn't want his force "measured" by the other groups. At the back of the stadium were the remnants of Brazil's other major communist party, the PCB, alongside the more reformist PPS (*I'm Crazy*). Next to them were the PSB/PDT (*Turning the Table*), and the yellow-shirted group of "independents" from Paraiba (*We're Just Beginning*).

The orange-shirted group from right of the PT (*Pleasure in Transforming*) was the last group in the opposition, seated in the center-right bend in the rear of the stadium. I was somewhat surprised by this location, since at the previous congress they had been seated further left, next to their copartisans in the left of the PT. The physical separation of PeT from the rest of the PT, along with the proximity to the PCdoB, signaled the heightened climate of factional dispute within the PT as well as the new spirit of collaboration with the PCdoB, at least among top PeT leaders. However, PeT delegates had a marked tendency (infuriating to the leadership) to disperse around the stadium, perhaps reflecting their discomfort at this unusual location next to the PCdoB. The right side of the bleachers was the territory the PCdoB/UJS (*One Step in Front*). They also occupied the center of the stadium, sprawled on the floor on top of a giant parachute banner. This remained the basic seating plan for the rest of the congress, with some milling at key moments, as I will describe below.

This stadium was the location of the major deliberative plenary sessions, in which the congress voted on proposals in three main areas: the National and International Conjuncture, the University, and the Student Movement. The proposals were gathered through discussion groups, organized by a "systematization committee," and boiled down into consensual versus nonconsensual resolutions. Most resolutions were consensual, requiring simply a blanket mass approval. However, in the controversial areas, contending proposals were hotly defended in speeches by top leaders, accompanied by dramaturgical displays of support and repudiation.

This routine, if still exciting, dramaturgy could be seen on the third evening, in the first major plenary on the National and International Conjuncture. As the PSTU leader Francisco predicted, the most controversial vote was on UNE's position on national alliances. The debate hinged on whether to advocate a broad "democratic and popular" front in opposition to neoliberalism and the Cardoso government, or whether to support a class-based alliance for a "government of the workers," which would "unify students and workers, of the country and city." The "broad front" proposal was supported by the PCdoB, the right of the PT, and the socialist block, while the "classist front" proposal was supported by the left of the PT and the radical Trotskyists.

The initial vote was taken amidst a gripping drumroll of the PSTU. Chants of "Socialist opposition, our front is classist!" and "UNE at the side of the workers!" echoed through the left side of the stadium. In response, the PCdoB whipped its own delegates into derisive counterchants: "Tiny opposition, fits inside a Volkswagen!" As delegates waved their yellow badges in the air for the vote count, the plenary was split down the middle. When UNE President Renato (who was chairing the session) tried to declare victory, the left vociferously demanded a formal vote, chanting "Count, Count!" and "No, no, no, there is manipulation!"

The "broad front" proposal won by a vote of 1,172 to 1,027 (with 2 votes for a third proposal), a very small margin, with a stunningly small total, especially since more than five thousand delegates were thought to be attending the conference. One PCdoB activist told me that many of their less-committed delegates were out sightseeing in Belo Horizonte. PeT was also highly dispersed, as this was not a vote that the right of the PT cared that much about. In contrast, the left was much more disciplined, since it considered this one of the most important votes of the congress. The call for a "classist alliance" was a symbolic marker in the hegemonic struggle to define the left, as well as a unifying banner in the left forces' attempts to form a coalition within the congress.

BACKSTAGE DELIBERATIONS

Outside the stadium, the competing political forces were also engaged in their own segmented deliberations. Sometimes these took the form of small leadership meetings in back rooms, while at other times they consisted of internal plenaries in which delegates could debate and vote on their groups' proposals and alliances. Top-level leaders were constantly shuttling between these internal meetings and their negotiations with leaders of other forces. Some of these segmented plenaries did little more than approve the leadership accords worked out behind the scenes, while others had more lively and contentious internal deliberations.

Such internal disagreement was especially evident in the two PT-linked forces, PeT and NVA. The top leaders had to exercise considerable skill in mediating differences within the camps, rather than just focusing on relations with outside groups. However, the two forces carried out this internal mediation in very different ways. These mediating styles, in turn, channeled and constrained the ability of the leaders to respond to the eventual crisis in the congress.

The left of the PT constructed its internal plenaries in a characteristically Gramscian manner, designed to allow for the discursive positioning of all of the allied forces even as they articulated their commitment to the "camp of the left." One of their early plenaries was held inside the stadium, with students sitting on the floor of the arena in large orderly circle. Leaders hovered and whispered around the sides while speakers tried to project themselves around the ring. The style was declamatory and self-righteous, posturing at fine ideological distinctions among themselves alongside bold critiques of the outside forces. Speakers made resounding calls for a "rescue of the left" from its accommodationist policies in the student movement as well as in national politics.

Interestingly, NVA had very little internal disagreement about the key drama of the congress: the battle of alliances. They were very clear that, for a combination of ideological and ethical concerns, they would not ally with the socialists or the PCdoB, although they were conditionally (if somewhat sneeringly) receptive to PeT ("if they decide that they're of the left"). Their goal was to construct a strong camp of the left to dispute hegemony within UNE, which entailed both democratically expressing, yet operationally suppressing the finer points of their ideological disagreements. However, they suffered strong internal divisions on questions related to institutional control, especially in regard to leadership of the combined slate that they were trying to compose with the PSTU and OT. The next few plenaries were dedicated to heated deliberations over the process by which they would choose the head of slate, with three precandidates nominated from each of the largest internal PT forces. Despite the strong group ethos of discursive positioning, tactical maneuvering for organizational control occupied a large part of the top leaders' mediating energies.

The plenaries of PeT, in contrast, were much more concerned with tensions over alliances than with the leadership of the slate. Since Alex had been designated as head of slate prior to the congress, there was little overt leadership jockeying among the component tendencies of PeT. But there was lively and sometimes anguished discussion regarding the possible alliance with the PCdoB. In contrast to the strongly ideological mode of NVA, there was a much more open-ended, self-reflective, even personalized style of discussion. By the third afternoon, divisions between state delegations as well as between top- and mid-level leaders were beginning to appear. Those in favor of allying with the PCdoB—mostly national and São Paulo leaders—argued that the alliance was important to combat sectarianism and ideological rigidity in the student movement, which they had long regarded as one of the destructive aspects of student politics. Those opposed said it would be a betrayal of their historical critique of the style and method of the PCdoB. Several mid-level leaders said that local relations with the PCdoB were so strained in their states (especially in Brasilia, Minas Gerais, and Bahia) that there was no way that they could explain a national alliance with the PCdoB to their bases in the universities. At the end of this PeT plenary, Claudio and Alex were looking uneasy and stressed as they began to sense the internal disagreement in the group. Claudio closed by saying that these discussions would have to mature over the next few days, as they continued to negotiate with the other forces.

Later that day, I witnessed a conversation between Ivan, a top PeT leader, and several members of NVA, who were sitting outside the dorms where top leaders were bunked. Ivan invited them upstairs to "have a chat" about the possibility of reaching an "accord." NVA activists listened intently, but expressed doubts; they had heard that PeT was close to settling an alliance with the socialists, and wanted to know if this was true. As an experienced negotiator, Ivan did not exactly confirm this, but let them know that there were indeed discussions in progress and it was a possibility. His interlocutors said that this confirmed their suspicion, and their bottom line was no alliance with the socialists. As NVA activists left the room, Ivan and his PeT companions burst into nervous laughter at what they saw as the rigidity of their fellow *petistas'* position.

In the neighboring room, top- and mid-level PeT leaders were lounging on three narrow beds, waiting to begin the first of two leadership meetings that night. The main item of business was Ivan's report on negotiations. He described the "narrowness" of the left of the PT, as well as more promising discussions with PSB, PPS, and PDT, although it wasn't clear yet if the socialist groups would agree to an alliance with the PCdoB. Alex reported that the PCdoB was so eager to have them all join their slate that it had agreed to postpone the question of the division of positions in the directorate, so as to reduce tensions between the forces. As there was nothing to do but wait for negotiations to ripen, they decided to head over to the big dance party in the stadium to mingle with delegates, "show force," and consolidate commitment to the group. I walked to the party with Cristina, who had slapped two PeT stickers on the back pockets of her jeans; "everyone looks anyway, there's no better place to put them."

On the way, we ran into a group of mid-level PCdoB activists from the University of São Paulo with their friend Julio, one of the regional coordinators of UJS. They were drinking *cachaça* (Brazil's traditional sugarcane liquor) in front of one of the food stands. I stopped for a drink, mentioning that the congress still seemed very uncertain. "You think so?" said Julio, smiling and shaking his head. The others grinned knowingly. "The congress is decided. The numbers show it." He confirmed that by their delegate count, the PCdoB already had an "absolute majority." That meant that they would not have to form an alliance with any of the other forces. "But we want to broaden [the slate], we don't want to go out alone," he said, adding that they hoped to settle an accord with PeT and socialist forces. As we walked up the hill toward the dance party, I asked about the recent policy changes of the PCdoB, especially their receptivity toward the historic proposals of the PT. He said that these changes were the result of pragmatic discussions within the party (i.e., their recent turn toward reflective problem solving); "we are very concerned with governability." The proposals were intended to start a broader, more reflective discussion with the other forces about problems within UNE and possibilities for restructuring.

I stopped for a few minutes at the dance party, which featured a live performance of one of Brazil's hottest rock fusion bands. Students were dancing their hearts out, clustered into fluid groups that seemed more permeable than the rigid partisan divisions of the plenaries. Tired and overloaded after an intense day, I decided to head home. On the way out I bumped into Ivan, who was on his way to a midnight meeting of PeT leaders. He invited me to join them, and like a glutton for punishment, I decided to go along. The meeting began with Alex's chilling report that the PCdoB had shown him the numbers: PeT had less than 10 percent of the delegates, meaning that they would not be guaranteed a place on UNE's executive committee if they decided to launch their own slate.[9] There is a moment in the negotiation process when what counts is "simple" mathematics. This meant that PeT must either form an alliance with other forces, or face loss of an executive position, which would be a significant blow in their internal struggle with the left-wing PT tendencies.

PeT leaders remained strongly divided on how to respond to this situation. Many state-level leaders continued to insist that an alliance with the PCdoB would be perceived by their bases as the national leadership "selling out" in exchange for positions in the directorate. On the other side, national leaders—especially those associated with the tendency *Radical Democracy*—passionately defended the need to overcome sectarianism and forge a "broad front" of the parties of the left. Claudio noted real changes in the posture of the PCdoB; as a result, PeT was voting with the PCdoB, and against the left of the PT, on almost all controversial votes. But Claudio was not yet willing to go out on a limb and defend the alliance, trying to sense whether his group could come to a consensus before the end of the congress. The meeting ended at 3:00 am, with a bleary-eyed division of tasks to try to generate greater cohesion and visibility. Inside the stadium, the dance party was still going strong.

Specialized Deliberations: Black Students, Course Executives, and Catholics

Somewhat apart from these intense partisan negotiations, more "specialized" groups were also trying to make use of the space of the congress, often in ways that called the logic of partisanship into question. The black student movement, course-based associations, and Catholic youth all tried to take advantage of the national gathering of students by holding their own meetings, although they had varying success. Not surprisingly, business-oriented groups such as the Junior Enterprises had no presence at all at the congress.

The black student movement had much less visibility than at previous UNE congresses. In 1995, the Coordination of Black University Scholars (CONUN) had organized several plenaries of black students and launched feisty documents and resolutions for the general congress. I was eager to see whether a similar gathering of black students was underway this year. Outside the stadium, the scene was a minifestival of hot-dog vendors, bookstalls, and T-shirt and jewelry stands, often linked to political forces. Walking through the tent of the PSTU, I encountered Jorge, a black student leader (and PSTU activist) whom I had met at a CONUN meeting the previous year (see chapter 8). He told me that CONUN was trying to organize a plenary of black students and showed me a draft statement, which he promised to give me later.

The next afternoon I encountered Jorge again, this time inside the stadium, sitting in the back with a few other black students of various parties, as they waited for the major plenary to begin. He said that they had held a meeting of black students that morning, but it had been very sparsely attended. He gave me a copy of the proposals that they were trying to have included in the official resolutions of the congress, most of which were relatively uncontroversial statements of opposition to racism. But there was also a more challenging proposal to create an official position in UNE's directorate for "racial matters." Jorge said that they were trying to get an executive position, but that the PCdoB was resisting anything higher than the directorate. Jorge and the other students seemed frustrated with the lack of visibility of black students at the congress. This in turn reflected the organizational fragility of the black student movement and the recent difficulties that CONUN activists had been encountering in trying to organize their national seminar.

In contrast to the black students, the course-based movement was given much more official space at the congress, reflecting the PCdoB's shift toward a more conciliatory stance toward the Course Executives. The fourth morning was reserved for separate meetings in each of the course areas. I arrived around noon and stopped by the meetings of FENEA (architecture) and DENEM (medicine). These meetings were not heavily attended; most of the course-based groups I saw ranged from about five to thirty people.

Stylistically, the Course Executives were concerned to ground their discussion in the modes of exploratory dialogue and pragmatic reflection, in a conscious rejection of the discursive positioning and tactical maneuver that dominated the larger congress. While they were not always successful, their meetings were quite different in rhythm and tone than the official UNE "discussion" groups. For example, at the architecture meeting, students went around the circle to "exchange experiences," sharing their personal backgrounds and their thoughts about the congress. The students expressed frustration at what they saw as the poor organization of the congress, as well as the lack of discussion, difficulty in participation, and inattention to student concerns.

In the somewhat larger meeting of medical students, participants were also seated in a circle, discussing the letter sent by the UNE directorate about its relation to the Course Executives. This letter was highly respectful and conciliatory, intended to serve as a gesture of UNE's new good will and disposition to work with the Course Executives. Whether or not the Course Executives were willing to work with UNE was another question; many of the students were clearly uneasy about the new overtures from the PCdoB. One student reminded the group that the purpose of DENEM (the medical student association) was to "act in society, not just in UNE." Another person made the point that the "reapproximation" of UNE and the executives was "our victory, not just their initiative"; they had been trying to develop this relationship for years but had been repudiated by the leadership of UNE (i.e, the PCdoB). Another person wearing the sticker of the PCdoB slate (UPF) tried to maintain a more pragmatic and reflective mode: "Sixty years [the length of UNE's existence] is not six days. UNE is the organization that we have. We have to use what's best in UNE, and criticize what's bad."

Some of the medical students took a more confrontational stance toward UNE. This was particularly the case among the more deeply invested bridging leaders, with multiple militancies in several sectors. One student straddled collaborative and competitive modes by declaring, "We are not just here to beat up on UNE, but we are ALSO here to beat up on UNE." Another person made a Gramscian pitch for the "diversity of the executives" as the basis for "constructing hegemony in UNE." There was also more tactical talk, including a proposal for a new "financial politics" in which the executives could divide the profits from the sale of student IDs (monopolized at the time by UNE, a subject of considerable controversy). The mood seemed to be of cautious receptivity to the gestures of UNE, but with concern to guarantee that the Course Executives would keep their autonomy and not be "steamrolled" by the current structure of the student movement.

I found some evidence of overlap between the Course Executives and the Catholic youth pastoral, although Catholics in general were not very visible at the congress. In the corridor, I encountered an agronomy student with a FEAB T-shirt who was making announcements about a joint meeting of the Course Executives to discuss how they should respond to the new posture of UNE. She introduced me to a fellow FEAB activist who was involved in the Catholic University Pastoral and was trying to organize a meeting of Christian students. I also talked to one activist that I knew from meetings of the São Paulo coordination of PJMP (the radical branch of the Catholic youth pastoral), a somewhat disconcerting crossover from otherwise quite separate worlds.

CONFRONTATION AND CRISIS

On the afternoon of the fourth day, the congress held its second major deliberative plenary, a combined session on the University and on the Student Movement that lasted from 4:00 p.m. to after 11:00 p.m. that night. The evening was filled with controversy and drama, as the most troublesome issues within the student movement came to a head. Over the course of the long evening, the PCdoB won every vote, joined on nearly all of them by PeT. Yet despite this raw numerical dominance, the proceedings were far from cut and dry. The contingencies of the evening triggered fractures between and within the various forces, even as they seemed on the verge of settling alliances.

As the plenary began, the alliances of the congress appeared to be coming into focus. The forces of the left—NVA, PSTU, OT, and associated groups—had nearly negotiated an accord, although they were still working out the details of leadership distribution among the factions. When I entered the stadium these left groups were still involved in their segmented deliberations, mostly taking place in their designated spaces in the arena. The socialist *I'm Crazy* (PPS) group entered with its percussion band and took its place across the stadium from NVA. They started up a lively dance beat, disturbing the deliberations of NVA, whose members angrily tried to shush them by throwing their arms in the air and shouting "eeiiii!!" The PPS youth settled down for a while, but soon thought they had waited long enough and started playing in earnest. When NVA again tried to quiet them, they came forward defiantly with their drums. Challenged, members of NVA began pouring out of the bleachers and running across the floor to force them to be quiet. Finally the leaders calmed down the respective parties, *I'm Crazy* agreed to cool it, and the meeting of NVA resumed.

Meanwhile PeT was engaged in heavy "flirtation" with the socialist groups, as dramatized by delegates from PeT wearing stickers of *I'm Crazy, Turning the Table*, and *We're Just Beginning*. Right before the plenary, leaders reported that a tentative accord had been reached between PeT and the socialist groups. The students of PeT made their grand entrance into the stadium, chanting their name as they danced around in a giant circle in the back half of the arena. They then took up their positions in the bleachers right next to *I'm Crazy*, which started up a joyful dance beat. Soon there was a clearly purposeful intermingling of the four near-allied groups, which succeeded together in composing a significant-looking force.

As the contending forces took their places, the plenary got into full swing. In the first set of votes on the University, there were no dramatic splits, just greater radicalization on the part of the left toward state control of education and opposition to the government's educational reforms. In votes on the Student Movement, the dispute was considerably more polarized. The first major split came over the question of whether UNE's directorate should be elected by congressional or direct elections.[10] This was the one vote in which PeT voted with NVA against the PCdoB, in favor of direct elections. However, some smaller groups from the left and right voted with the PCdoB for congressional elections, which tend to provide more opportunity for smaller parties. By a visual vote (e.g., holding up yellow badges), the congress approved congressional elections, a two-year term for the directorate of UNE, and proportional representation in the directorate, as opposed to a winner-takes all regime.

They then turned to the most controversial vote in the congress, on the creation of regional congresses of UNE. At issue was the PCdoB's proposal to change the election of delegates to UNE's national congress from the current procedure, in which they were elected directly in the university departments, to a "funnel" procedure, in which national delegates would be elected in prior state or regional congresses. The PCdoB claimed that they were adopting a historic proposal of PT for the restructuring and democratization of the student movement, a claim hotly contested by the left of the PT.[11] The left saw the proposal as an attack on the democracy of the student movement and an attempt to "distance UNE even more from the students" through smaller, more manipulable national congresses. The PCdoB argued that smaller national congresses would allow for a higher quality of political discussion and problem solving than was possible in the "great *showmicio*" (combination of show and rally) of the current congress. Note the dispute over style: the left argued that the proposal smacked of Machiavellian manipulation, while the PCdoB declared that it would turn UNE toward Deweyian deliberation.

The importance of the vote could be seen in the fact that each of the factions chose their top leaders to defend their positions. However, no one from PeT spoke in support of this proposal, despite the fact PeT was the only force at the congress to explicitly include the proposal for regional congresses in their precongress thesis. The proposal was not in the UPF thesis, which led to accusations from the left that the PCdoB was staging a last-minute coup.

At the first waving of yellow badges, the plenary seemed to be split right down the middle. As presider, Renato declared that the coordinating commission was unable to arrive at a consensus, and called for another show of badges. Meanwhile drums were rolling, chants were pounding, and the whole plenary was undergoing a shift, as delegates of the PPS, PDT, and PSB moved over to join the left and display a stronger density of votes against the measure. The delegates of UPF were likewise shepherded into a more concentrated position of votes in favor. "True delegates, elected by the base!" resounded from the left side of the stadium from the PSTU all the way over to the PPS, with the two percussion sections of these usually opposing groups exuberantly joining forces. At the second show of badges there was again disagreement, causing the opposition groups to chant "Count, count!" When Renato tried to postpone a count, they again chanted "No, no, no, there's manipulation!" Finally, the commission agreed to count votes by hand, with delegates in favor of the measure occupying the right side of the bleachers, while those opposed

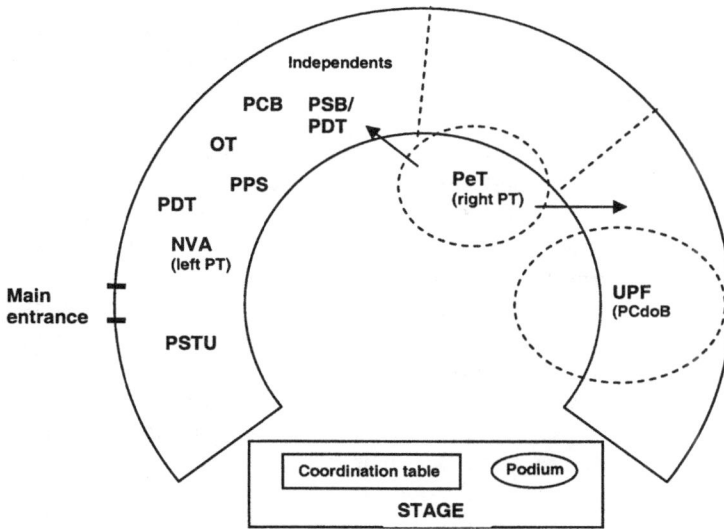

Figure 9.4. Shifts in the plenary: Vote on regional congresses

occupied the left. The PCdoB began to shepherd all of its delegates sitting on the floor into the bleachers; I heard someone from the PT cynically comment, "That's how they herd their sheep."

At this point PeT entered into crisis. The delegates of PeT had actually approved this proposal, "settling an accord" with the PCdoB and confirming support in their internal plenary earlier that day. However at this dramatic moment in the congress, the vote took on other proportions, which superseded the merits of the proposal itself. This was the principal polarizing moment of the congress, the one slight chance that the unified opposition might have to defeat the PCdoB. Even if they lost, it was a dramaturgic chance to deliver a general repudiation of the politics of the PCdoB in the student movement. As such, some of the orange shirts began to move left toward the rest of the opposition.

Expecting them all to move, I was surprised to see the leadership of PeT staying put, engaging in intense discussion among themselves and with the delegates of the base. I went over to see what was going on, and realized the group was divided; part of them, particularly the mid-level leaders from the states that most clashed with the PCdoB (Minas Gerais, Bahia, Brasília) were urging the group to join the rest of the opposition in voting against the measure. At the same time, the top leaders and the São Paulo group were insisting that they had to stay, not just because of the accord with the PCdoB, but because they themselves had approved the proposal! Realizing that they were losing a good part of the base, the leaders tried to move right. But they didn't make it to the bleachers, continuing anguished discussion in orange-shirted clusters on the floor in the rear of the stadium, as depicted in Figure 9.4.

At this point the other forces began to take note of the confusion in PeT. As PeT delegates descended from the bleachers to join the discussion, the left began calling them to join forces: "Come over here, Pleasure in Transforming!" They then upped the pressure by pushing the party loyalty button with the traditional PT chant, "Party, Party, is of the Workers!" Top leaders from the PCdoB came swooping back to see what was going on. I saw Maurício of the PCdoB engaged in a fierce finger-pointing discussion with Diego of PeT, who a short time afterward was repeating the gesture with Alex, who backed away angrily. The argument seemed to be multicentered, with some state-based delegates arguing strongly that the point was to "measure forces," that it didn't matter that they had already approved the proposal. At one point I saw part of the Bahian group split and move right toward UPF, while the group from Brasilia was tugging in the other direction. Cristina and the São Paulo contingent were also armlocked in debate. I heard strongly worded pressures, framed in terms of loyalty and betrayal.

With many delegates nearly in tears, an accord was finally reached among the top PeT leaders, and Alex called the entire group into a huddle. He said that it was obvious that "there is no consensus among us," and that given the clear division in the group and the lack of time to discuss this among themselves, the only thing to do was to liberate everyone to vote his or her conscience. He said they should not feel any "internal division" (i.e., psychological stress) over this choice, but should do what they felt was right at that moment. He also called everyone to a meeting after the plenary was over. At this point the huddle erupted and split into two parts, as half went to join the opposition and half entered the bleachers occupied by UPF.

There was a small tumult during the vote count, when one of the teams that were circling through the two sides of the auditorium suddenly had a discrepancy; the counter representing the UPF appeared to have dropped his count by ten votes. Since he was in opposition territory, this caused a brief uproar in the bleachers, which almost came to blows. When the count was finally in, the PCdoB's proposal for regional congresses had won, although by a very small margin.

With the announcement of the vote count, the UPF erupted in cheers, while the drums rolled ominously among the opposition, to the indignant reprise of "True delegates, elected by the base!" At that point I noticed a kind of sea-motion in the section of NVA. I found Martín standing grimly with his arms folded across his chest while leaders shepherded NVA delegates out of the plenary. "Are you leaving?" I asked Martín in surprise. "From the plenary!" he qualified, saying that he did not know yet if this would be a withdrawal from the congress. Several PCdoB leaders rushed over, trying to convince Martín with angry gestures that this was no way to handle a lost vote. Martín remained impassive. "We're going to leave!" he told them. When the PSTU activists noticed NVA's departure, they began chanting a campaign to convince their neighbor to stay: "Stay to fight!" they repeated, as NVA filed down the narrow stairway and through the tunnel out of the stadium. There was mutual gesturing as NVA tried to convince the PSTU to join them ("Come!"), to no avail. The leaders of the PSTU were especially upset since an important vote was coming up on quotas for women in the directorate, for which they needed the support of NVA.

I followed NVA students outside to the parking lot, where they held an emergency plenary to decide what to do. The vote on regional congresses was denounced by all of the internal forces within NVA as a "coup" on the part of the PCdoB, a fundamentally antidemocratic move with the goal of strengthening the power of the PCdoB. There were also denunciations of the leadership of PeT for entering into an antidemocratic accord "in exchange for positions." They were furious that the PCdoB had not previously discussed the proposal with the opposition, launching it by surprise "on the eve of the congress." There was no consensus yet about what to do; nobody clearly defended withdrawal from the congress, although some leaders suggested that the PCdoB's "fundamental attack" on the structure of the student movement called for a radical response. They finally agreed to set up a commission to try to convince the PCdoB to "reverse the decision," using as leverage their own refusal to participate in future "funnel" congresses, as well as the threat of withdrawal from this congress. They also resolved to negotiate with the other left forces to come up with a joint response to the crisis.

As they were finishing this deliberation, I headed up the hill to the meeting of PeT. On the way I bumped into José, the UNE director from the Trotskyist group *O Trabalho*, who was very upset and eager to tell me his view of the "coup" of the PCdoB, which he said would destroy the "mass-based character" of the congress. He said he wasn't sure yet what his force would do, but that sometime between now and 9:00 a.m. the next morning, they would think of something, even if they had to stay up all night.

Inside the dorm, the meeting of PeT was just beginning. About thirty people crammed into a small room, clearly bunkering in for a long discussion. Claudio asked people to give their frank evaluations of what had just happened. I found out a missing piece of the confusion: shortly prior to the vote, a rumor began to circulate among their own ranks that PeT had "settled an accord" with the PCdoB. This rumor was spread by their neighbors and potential allies from the PPS, PSB, and PDT, who demanded that members of PeT account for what they had heard. This sent many of the mid-level leaders into a panic. Since the question had not been resolved among themselves, this meant that the top leaders must have gone over their heads. As they were bustling among themselves trying to clarify this question, the voting began. Suddenly they were forced into a very definite choice: making a physical move out of the bleachers to join the opposition, or staying put and voting with UPF as agreed. This complex climate of internal confusion, doubt, and accusation erupted into the agonized scene described above.

Among the strongest voices denouncing the defection of the bases was that of Cesar, a leader of the faction *Radical Democracy* (and a director of UNE during the impeachment). He insisted that they could not go back on a decision that had been discussed and approved in their own plenary, arguing that it was "immaturity" to have given such a confused and undisciplined display. A poignant counterattack came from Adriana, a mid-level leader from Minas Gerais, who said that they really didn't have "clarity" regarding the proposal, that in the states they were always in confrontation with the PCdoB, and when it suddenly appeared that this was the one time during the congress that there was the possibility of unifying all of the opposition against the PCdoB, their delegates desperately wanted to be part of it. "Our people long to vote against the PCdoB!" she said. On all other votes they had risked the label of "sell-out" from their fellow *petistas*; this was the one time that they could show party unity as well as opposition to the PCdoB. Besides, she said, there was the warm welcome they received. When the left of the PT began chanting "Come!" and erupting in cheers whenever they won an orange shirt over to their side, slapping them on the back and inviting them to take a seat in their midst, "people felt welcomed, that they were part of something," alleviating the inner tension and feelings of self-betrayal within PeT.

The discussion went on along these lines for hours. Eventually, it began to turn into the "washing of dirty laundry," with Claudio gently but firmly criticizing his companions for lapses in group discipline: for example, for exaggerating the number of delegates, for dispersing in the plenary, for not effectively carrying out the tasks of discussion and dissemination of their proposals. He admitted that the proposal had not been sufficiently discussed among themselves, but he said that this was everyone's fault. He had assumed the lion's share of the work of organizing the congress, having to take care of "a thousand problems," and he hadn't received enough support from the group, contributing to the lack of discussion and organization.

After several hours of this, with people drifting in and out of sleep, they turned to the question of alliances, resolving to settle the question right then, even if it meant continuing until dawn. There was still no consensus about an alliance with the PCdoB, although the numbers were now clear, as were the positions of the other forces. Following the vote on regional congresses, the PPS and part of the PDT and PSB had resolved not to enter into an alliance with the PCdoB. Stung by what they saw as PeT's betrayal, the socialists were disposed to go it alone or to form an accord only among themselves, without PeT.

That meant that PeT had a stark choice; either ally with PCdoB or form their own separate slate. Because of their low numbers, this would effectively mean that they would be out of the executive, perhaps just scraping by in the directorate. Alex (whose position as vice president of UNE was at stake) passionately argued that they couldn't let themselves be isolated, that they had to "come out of sectarianism" and "risk ourselves" in forming a broad alliance against Cardoso; if not they would lose a historic opportunity being constructed in the national congress and the labor movement. Adriana and others argued equally adamantly against the alliance, with some threatening to leave the group if they join with the PCdoB. Claudio gave a somewhat contradictory statement, saying that he had helped to construct the possibility of alliance with the PCdoB, that it was impossible to form an accord with the left of the PT, and yet that he was concerned about the unity of the group, and therefore defended the idea of mounting their own slate.

Finally at nearly 6:30 a.m., with dawn breaking, they woke their dozing *companheiros* for a vote. Before voting, they agreed that they would all adhere to the victorious proposal (all except for the Minas Gerais group, which declared they would on no account support the alliance.) The proposal to form an alliance with the PCdoB was defeated by a very small margin (17 to 14). They closed with a plan to hold a plenary of the group the next day to discuss the decision with the rest of PeT delegates.

As the meeting broke up, Alex, visibly upset, asked to be allowed to "remove my name as head of this slate." He protested that by going alone, they would be no better than the most purist revolutionary sects. As exhausted youth drifted off in small groups, the discussion continued into the hallway, with Alex, backed by Cesar, insisting angrily to Claudio that "I'm out of this!" while Claudio tried to convince him to reconsider; "Let's discuss it!" Cesar, equally upset, told Claudio that "from now on, we're split!" I realized that I was witnessing a dispute between *Radical Democracy* and *Articulation-Unity in Struggle*, the two main internal tendencies within PeT. They were still engaged in this heated huddle when I decided that enough was enough, and took off for a few hours of sleep.

DIVISION, EXIT, AND ACCORD

When I made it back to the stadium around noon, I found a scattering of meetings, as the forces sorted out how to respond to the tumultuous events of the night before. I ran into a loose huddle of the right flank leaders of PeT (including Cesar), who told me that they were "conspiring" to reverse the leadership vote at the group plenary that afternoon. One young woman was deep in conversation with Cesar, saying that she had reconsidered and she now thought the alliance with the PCdoB was the right thing to do. At one point, Claudio walked past with dark sunglasses on, giving barely a greeting, evoking the comment that he and Ivan were "conspiring against." So there was definitely a climate of internal camps drawn.

On the steps leading down to the stadium was a huddle of the leaders of the left, including NVA, the PSTU, and O *Trabalho*. They were still trying to pound out a joint response to the question of the regional congresses. As that meeting broke up I headed to the parking lot where NVA was planning its first plenary of the day. On the way, I ran into some PCdoB leaders who told me that they were just about to "settle our slate." I also crossed paths with Martín, who urged me cheerfully to "come to our plenary!"

When the *I Won't Adapt* (NVA) plenary finally started, Martín began by giving a rundown of the discussions with the various forces. He said that the Trotskyist PSTU and OT wanted to stay in the directorate, but were willing to discuss some sort of opposition, and that PeT was "split," having lost its base after trying to seal an accord with the PCdoB. He suggested that they form a commission to talk with the PCdoB to demand that they "withdraw the proposal." He reiterated his position that this was a fundamental attack on the whole structure of the student movement. The floor was opened to discussion; they were immediately barraged with a rush of people wanting to speak. The first few speakers largely repeated the arguments of the day before; since no decision was imminent, I headed back to see if I could catch the PeT plenary.

I arrived at PeT plenary right at the moment of the vote. The group was gathered under the stairwell, partially cut off from outside observation. Since they had already debated the question of alliances so exhaustively, they did not open up general discussion, but only had defenses of the two proposals, for and against the alliance with the PCdoB. Cesar and another student argued in favor; Claudio and Ivan against. The first show of hands was inconclusive; a second vote was taken, and after some discussion at the front, Claudio declared that the proposal for the alliance had won. I saw Cesar give a quiet handshake to his neighbor. At that moment, however, bedlam broke out as a delegate from Minas Gerais shouted in rage, "With the PCdoB I will not go!!!" As others tried to calm him, he let loose on Alex with angry punches. A fight huddle broke out, and the two were quickly separated. One woman said indignantly, "People, this isn't done, we have to discuss in the plenary and decide in the vote!" In the confusion, the dissident group took off up the stairs. Ivan followed to try to talk to them, while Claudio and Alex tried to pull the meeting back to order. Claudio made a plea to maintain the unity of the group; they had made the decision democratically and would now abide by it. A commission was chosen to discuss their decision with the PCdoB and negotiate any further matters.

Outside, the rumbling of competing sound-trucks was beginning, summoning delegates to the final plenaries of the forces. I stopped briefly by the plenaries of the PSTU and UPF, where their contrasting styles were clearly on display. At the plenary of the PSTU, Francisco was engaged in a long, inflamed discourse on the top of the sound-truck to a grim-faced crowd of copartisans. He denounced the attack on the "mass-based character" of the congress and the accords with groups of the right who were giving "support to the government of FHC (Fernando Henrique Cardoso)." Inside the stadium, the plenary of UPF/UJS was much more exuberant and celebrational, as well as tightly organized and controlled. A mid-level PCdoB leader was on stage trying to arrange students by state delegations, clustered by small friendship groups, each coordinated by a mid-level state leader responsible for morale and camaraderie. Wilson, the PCdoB's candidate for president, was striding around slapping people on the back. Renato stopped by to ask me what I thought of the congress. I gave a noncommittal answer about how complicated the negotiations were, and he laughed. Both he and Wilson were engaged in a steady stream of interviews with the press, along with Alex and Francisco, as other presidential possibilities.

Back out in the parking lot, I ran into a cluster of mid-level NVA leaders lounging restlessly as they waited for their leaders to emerge from a meeting with the PCdoB. As we waited, the activists heatedly debated what should be done. NVA was internally divided; the PT tendency *Articulation of the Left* was arguing in favor of staying in the congress (and thus entering the directorate), while the other NVA forces were leaning toward withdrawal. Edson, the UNE vice president associated with *Articulation of the Left*, appeared looking distressed and pulled a few people off into a huddle. Closer to the stadium, Martín engaged in a huddle with Maurício and other PCdoB leaders. Evidently something was not yet resolved; we waited for another half hour, seated on the asphalt, while the leaders argued off to the side.

The tense meeting finally got underway as the drums from the final grand plenary of the congress were beginning to roll inside the stadium. The PCdoB sent an emissary saying that they were going to begin the final proceedings at 7:00 p.m., with or without NVA. As it was now about 6:30, this evoked a guffaw, as some people muttered "they're going to have to wait." However, for those who wanted NVA slate included in the final vote, this created time pressure that added to the sense of urgency. I was amazed at how inflamed the situation was. Martín reported that the PCdoB had refused to change its proposal. He argued that NVA should therefore withdraw from the congress, reiterating that this was "the most important decision of the PT in UNE in the past ten years!" He argued forcefully that they should not give legitimacy to the authoritarian and antidemocratic attack of the PCdoB on the structure of the student movement. Instead, they should break definitively with the practice of the PCdoB and rebuild the student movement, "starting from the DCEs e CAs," as well as in the Course Executives.

Edson argued against withdrawing in equally passionate terms, saying, "This is the most important intervention I have made in all of my history in the student movement!" While he agreed that this was an attack on the student movement, he argued that they had to stay to fight within UNE in order to have an active role in changing the character and direction of the movement. UNE was the "historic organization of the students" and they could not abandon it or allow it to be divided, especially at this moment when they had the opportunity to create a powerful "front of the classist left." I could tell how close the final vote would be by the almost equally loud applause for each side. As the voting began, I took off toward the stadium, which was now resounding with drums, speeches, chants, and cheers.

Inside the stadium I discovered an astonishing and tumultuous scene of multisided, parallel dramaturgy. Renato was on the stage conducting the remaining official business, which consisted of passing motions of support or repudiation on the part of UNE, accompanied by speeches and cheers on the part of UPF. Meanwhile, there were swirls of movement around the stadium, particularly among the delegations of the PPS and PDT. I realized that the persistent drums of *I'm Crazy* (PPS) were moving across the back of the stadium, as the group crossed the bleachers toward the exit—they were withdrawing! I saw Celso of the PDT standing in the middle of the tumult, arms crossed, surrounded by a few of his lieutenants. "This is a circus!" he told me. I asked if he was going to "settle with the PCdoB," since I had heard a rumor in this direction. He shook his head and clammed up grimly. That's when I noticed that Celso's faction of the PDT was also leaving, having appeared in force for the first time.[12]

Meanwhile, speeches had shifted to defense of the final slates. From the distance I saw Alex at the podium defending the composite slate with the PCdoB. At the last minute, the PCdoB had succeeded in putting together a megaslate that included not only PeT, but also fractures of most of the socialist parties, including Ricardo's group in the PDT, as well as the PPS, PSB, PCB, which had also all split. Celso stood surveying this scene disdainfully until the final moment when he and his lieutenants exited dramatically through the front entrance.

At this point a few people from NVA plenary were beginning to reappear, with drums from outside the stadium signaling the group's approach. I grabbed one of NVA activists who told me that the vote had been 159 to 136 in favor of withdrawal, an extremely close vote, signaling the degree of internal division. As delegates from NVA reentered the stadium, there was a temporary jam-up, since the PPS and PDT were still leaving. Gradually, shouts of "True delegates, elected by the base!" began to take over the stadium. This was answered by a furious rejoinder from the PSTU: "PT, I want to see, unity to defeat PCdoB," and "UNE in struggle, opposition, down with division!" Oblivious and self-righteous, NVA began to mill around the entire left side of the stadium floor, shouting their denunciations of the directorate of UNE.

At one point there was a scuffle at the border between NVA and UPF; several *petistas* came running out carrying a stack of blank yellow badges that they said had fallen out of someone's bag, which NVA presented as evidence of voting fraud on the part of the PCdoB (which could potentially give the badges to nondelegates, such as high school students from UJS, to swell the visual vote). The *petistas* with the badges were lifted on the shoulders of others and paraded around the floor, shouting "PCdoB, is nothing more, than a party sustained by UNE!" Meanwhile delegates of UJS ripped up the remaining blank badges that they could get their hands on. The dramaturgy intensified as members of NVA began to set fire to their own badges, first individually, holding them in the air, and then creating a small bonfire on the floor of the stadium, as media cameras and reporters rushed over to record the scene. The PSTU again responded with a furious repudiation: "Burning badges, leads to nothing, UNE in the fight against the sell-outs!"

Several PCdoB leaders came zooming over with dismayed expressions, resulting in another scuffle as someone punched one of the PCdoB leaders in the face. The antifight apparatus quickly went into action, as mid-level PCdoB leaders set up an arm-link barrier between their delegates and the rest. I saw Julio and the São Paulo UJS crowd shaking their heads disapprovingly, along with higher-level party leaders from the PCdoB who were watching the tumult. Renato issued an appeal for order and respect for the congress, denouncing the burning of badges as "an absurdity!"

that posed a danger to the students in the stadium. Finally, as the dramaturgy exhausted itself, the students from NVA began to file out of the stadium, calling "Come, Come" to the PSTU, OT, and the other forces as they left. The PSTU answered back with "Dividing, for what, this seems like PCdoB!"

As the scene began to calm down, I noticed a subdued group of orange-shirted students in the back bleachers, deserted by their neighbors. I found a very tired Claudio seated in the front row, with a couple of equally exhausted PeT leaders. I asked how he was doing, and he said that he was feeling deeply hurt, "bruised," by what had just happened. He sighed that all his years of experience and dedication could suddenly count for nothing in this sort of public "burning."[13] While I was at the plenary of NVA, I had missed another dramatic sequence, in which dissenters from PeT had entered the stadium with their orange shirts on backwards, painted with messages such as "For ethics in UNE," and "I won't sell myself!" They had processed over to the banner of the thesis and burned it amidst protests, before themselves withdrawing from the plenary. "Do you think we were right?" Claudio asked me mournfully. In contrast, Alex seemed more cheerful and optimistic, since his position as vice president of UNE was assured as a condition of the alliance. He admitted the difficulties to come while expressing confidence that they would be able to "do good work" with the PCdoB and the other forces, eventually helping themselves to grow politically.

POSTCONGRESS EVALUATIONS

The tumultuous events of the 1997 congress left UNE fractured and shaken. On the one hand, the PCdoB succeeded in getting at least part of what it wanted: a broad slate including five to six different parties (to help insure "governability"), as well as an overwhelming victory that gave their composite slate near complete dominance in the directorate. On the other hand, the cost of that victory was the withdrawal from UNE of some of the most vigorous groups on their left flank as well as the internal division and political fragility of most of their allies. In the immediate aftermath, the forces began evaluating what had happened and maneuvering to make the best of it, even as alignments within the student movement were shifting.

The first task facing the leaders was the negotiation of the directorate, always a tense and contested affair. At a meeting in São Paulo a week after the congress, top leaders hashed out the distribution of leadership positions. In addition to the PCdoB-led alliance, three slates had received the requisite 5 percent needed for representation in the directorate, including the PSTU, OT, and the independents from Paraiba, all of which decided to go out alone. The PCdoB leaders declared that the final vote gave its alliance ten of eleven positions in the executive (to be divided among the allied forces), with the last slot going to the PSTU. The other two slates were excluded from the executive (to their dismay) with two positions each in the directorate. Maurício, chief negotiator of the PCdoB, tried to silence protests by whipping out a newspaper editorial attacking the vote on the regional congresses and supporting the opposition's withdrawal. "The bourgeois press is adoring this attempt to divide the student movement," he said, adding that if the left had any sense of political responsibility, it would rush to counter these attacks by reentering the directorate.

The PCdoB had a tactical reason to be tight-fisted: it hoped to reserve a spot in the executive for *Articulation of the Left*. After the congress, the center-left PT tendency—which had opposed withdrawing from UNE in the plenary of NVA—judged that the withdrawal had been a mistake, and that it was essential that they enter the UNE directorate (and hopefully, executive) in order to sustain and project themselves in the student movement. They began negotiations with the PCdoB to enter UNE by the backdoor, via the slate of UPF. This meant a break with Martín's faction, *Democracy and Socialism*, which had defended (and continued to defend) the withdrawal of NVA from the congress.

When I talked to Claudio of PeT after the meeting, he was crowing over this development. "We can only gain from this," he told me cheerfully. Not only did this help to restore the legitimacy of UNE, but, more importantly, from his perspective, it also split the left of the PT. This, he thought, would establish the primacy of his own faction, *Articulation-Unity in Struggle*, among PT youth. It would also give PeT more weight in the leadership of UNE, including the important platform of Alex in the vice presidency.

In contrast, when I had drinks with Martín a few days later, he was livid over the "betrayal" by his fellow NVA members. I met him and Daniel, a fellow student leader from *Democracy and Socialism*, at the office of the faction-run journal, *Em Tempo*, just after they had been raked over the coals by the factional leadership for the decision to withdraw. They told me that they had been criticized for lack of sufficient discussion and "consolidation" of the decision with the other left forces—in other words, for lack of "skill," or what the Brazilians call "*habilidade política*" (political ability). While they admitted that they were now isolated politically, they defended their decision to radicalize in relation to the PCdoB's "antidemocratic coup." They came down hard on *Articulation of the Left* for lack of "ethics," "maturity," and "political responsibility" in not respecting a plenary vote.

In a public response to justify their decision to reenter UNE, Edson and the other leaders of *Articulation of the Left* agreed that the regional congresses were an antidemocratic attack on UNE. However, by withdrawing from the congress, they argued that NVA had lost its big chance to consolidate a "block of the left." They noted that it was not viable to unify the youth of the PT, given PeT's alliance with the PCdoB and the "parties of the right." They also criticized the climate of "sharpened political polarization" that had provoked "the crisis installed in UNE," as shown by the burning of badges and withdrawal not only of NVA, but also of sectors of the PDT, PPS, and PeT, making UNE's new executive "extremely fragile."

This increased fragility and polarization were challenges that UNE and its leaders would have to face in the years to come. The immediate effect of the congress was to blunt nascent internal dialogue over the restructuring of the student movement and to generate further antagonism between the PCdoB and the opposition. The proposal for regional "funnel" congresses was overturned in the next national council of student leaders, as the block of the left reconsolidated. While the PCdoB maintained its grip on the leadership of UNE—now in alliance with the center-right of the PT—it made little headway in convincing other forces that its shift toward more collaborative modes of communication was worthy of mutual investment and trust.

COMMUNICATIVE MECHANISMS IN THE BREAKDOWN OF PUBLICS

How can we account for the tumultuous ending and near breakdown of the 1997 congress? Why did almost every force at the congress end up fractured (with the exception of the PCdoB)? Why weren't they able to do the intra- and interfactional suppression necessary for the construction of an effective public, even a highly partisan one like UNE? While UNE congresses are always contentious, usually the contending forces are able—through a combination of collective dramaturgy, electoral procedures, and backstage negotiation—to arrive at a distribution of proposals and positions that allows them to ritually declare the "unity" of the student movement and to more or less work together over the next year or two. This failed in this case, to the surprise and consternation of most of the participants.

To understand this breakdown, we can look at several different sets of factors. The external political environment (or "political conjuncture," as activists called it) clearly contributed to tensions at the congress, although I argue that this was not the determinant factor in the breakdown. Rather, we need to examine stylistic tensions within and between the forces, as well as the ways in which these styles constrained and limited leadership skills in responding to the emergent crisis.

Conjunctural Factors

While shifts in the larger political field did not directly cause the communicative breakdown, they intensified some of the internal disputes within student forces. In 1997, Brazil was three years into the presidency of Fernando Henrique Cardoso of the PSDB. With varying degrees of radicalism, all of the forces at the congress criticized what they saw as Cardoso's liberalizing reforms, which included privatization of some state industries, opening the country to foreign investment, and attempts to cut the federal bureaucracy, although he also initiated some state sponsored social programs (largely seen as palliative by the left). To win election, Cardoso's PSDB had entered into alliance with some of Brazil's traditional right-wing parties, further alienating the opposition.

Nevertheless, the presence of a self-professedly reformist, social-democratic government provided dilemmas for the traditional left. For example, the Cardoso government created a number of consultative councils, without any binding power, to serve as a channel for civic input into policymaking. These included the "National Education Council," which most national educational organizations (including UNE, as well as labor and professional associations) were invited to join. The left of the student movement denounced these overtures as attempts to co-opt the opposition, and adamantly opposed UNE's participation in the government-sponsored council. In contrast, the more institutionally minded groups, such as the PCdoB and the socialist/labor parties, were inclined to take the foothold offered by the government in order to make whatever institutional improvements were possible. This tension generated some of the mutual accusations of "appeasement" and "rigidity" that opposing camps of the student movement hurled at each other.

This divide was mirrored in other sectors of the opposition, including the labor movement and the national congress. The reformist social-democratic government generated fissures in the left that might not have appeared if they had been united in fighting a more traditional right-wing regime. These fissures put particular pressure on the moderate factions, as we have seen in the case of PeT. The center-right of the PT was caught in the classic dilemma of moderates, chronically on the defensive in relation to their more "combative" left flank even as they sought broader alliances and more institutionalist projects of social intervention. Being dubbed the "right of the left" is never a comfortable position, involving tussles over loyalties and commitments, as well as fear of falling either into purism or appeasement, narrow dogmatism or selling out. The numerical fragility of PeT made it especially vulnerable to relational cross-pressures. While it was a weak force by itself, as a swing faction it was sought by all of the other forces of the congress, which made contradictory demands in terms of alliances and proposals.

Tensions in Styles

Nevertheless, while the larger political conjuncture may have heightened tensions within the left, it certainly did not guarantee that the Congress of UNE would end in disarray, as opposed to in an electoral settlement. To explain this fragmentation, we need to look beneath the public dispute over projects and alliances to examine the deeper contest over style, that is, over the modes of communication by which different actors thought those projects and relations should be built. Conflict over style took place both between and within forces, underlying some of the most painful mutual denunciations in regards to "ethics," "responsibility," and "selling out." In discussing these tensions, I will focus on PeT and NVA, since these forces were the most internally complex, and also the sources of the major divisions in the congress.

The most stylistically divided of the forces at the conferences was PeT. As I noted earlier, there were stylistic tensions between top-, mid-, and lower-level leaders, as well as between the two internal PT tendencies associated with the thesis. Claudio and Ivan's tendency, *Articulation-Unity in Struggle*, had a reputation in the PT for being pragmatic, institutionalist, and bureaucratic (often associated in students' minds with the Deweyian mode), whereas Alex and Cesar's faction, *Radical Democracy*, was more prone to favor broad social dialogue and flexible horizontal networks, rather than traditional hierarchical organizations (qualities often linked to the Habermasian mode). They united in condemning what they saw as the narrow sectarianism and ideological rigidity of the traditional left (i.e., its reliance on Gramscian positioning) as well as the Machiavellian maneuver that they associated with the PCdoB. Nevertheless, while politically and ethically condemning these two competitive modes, they were drawn into them as well. The institutional structure of UNE demanded skill in tactical maneuver to win space in the directorate, especially among the higher-level leaders. Moreover, they still considered themselves to be socialist reformers (although of the loosely "democratic" type). Many mid-level PeT activists were concerned to show that they could be combative and dispute hegemony as well, that they weren't just naïve idealists or pragmatic accommodators to the status quo.

However, their skills in discursive positioning and tactical maneuver were underdeveloped in relation to their counterparts in NVA and PCdoB, and these stylistic weaknesses undermined their ability to respond to the crisis. PeT prided itself as having the most pleasurable, nondogmatic discussion about proposals, with a less hierarchical, more consensus-oriented structure than the PCdoB or other traditional leftist organizations. The precongress elaboration of the thesis involved many such meetings, in which leaders tried to draw new and inexperienced activists into open-ended, exploratory political talk. However, while exploratory dialogue allows for oxygenation of ideas and consideration of other points of view, it can often be difficult to reach closure on political projects. When such closure is required, it tends to be vague, idealistic, and ambiguous, without careful consideration of practical and political consequences (and in many cases, final closure is actually carried out by a small elite group). This can contribute to the dispersion of ideas and people, as well as a lack of commitment to positions. In this case, the base leaders were so uncommitted to their own proposal for regional congresses that they scarcely understood it and abandoned it in a flash when cross-cutting partisan pressures besieged the group. Moreover, the group's nonhierarchical, pleasure-oriented ethic also undermined collective discipline in "marshalling the troops," a key component of the PCdoB's repeated electoral success. As a result of these weaknesses in positioning and maneuver, dispersion was a chronic problem for PeT, perhaps more than for any other force.

Within *I Won't Adapt* (NVA), the stylistic tension was different. All of the left tendencies associated with the thesis considered themselves to be highly ideological and committed to the deep structural transformation of capitalist society. Martín's tendency, *Democracy and Socialism*, tended to be more intellectual, with a higher degree of ideological consistency and self-discipline, while Edson's tendency, *Articulation of the Left*, was somewhat more concerned with institutional control (a difference that would surface in their postcongress split). Nevertheless, the camp as a whole took its discursive positioning extremely seriously, debating proposals thoroughly among the internal forces and only including them if they could achieve clear consensus (and thus commitment) throughout the camp. Moreover, they spent most of the congress repudiating the idea of bringing all of the forces of UNE into one big institutional tent (thus creating a Deweyian community), but rather worked hard to consolidate a clear boundary, between the "classist" left (themselves and the radical Trotskyists) and the "forces of the right" (the socialists and social democrats). As a result of this intense effort in ideological and stylistic boundary work, the base of NVA entered the congress with more commitment (and hence, less ideological or interpersonal dispersion) than PeT.

However, while this strength in discursive positioning clearly benefited the camp on some measures, the weaknesses of this mode also played a role in the congressional crisis. NVA's strongly adversarial positioning helped to generate intracamp cohesion, but it also locked them into rigid and purist evaluations of the other forces. They were clear and unified in evaluating the proposal for regional "funnel" congresses as antidemocratic, dismissing the PCdoB's contention that this would allow for a higher quality of discussion. Instead, they saw the proposal as a cynical attempt by the PCdoB to create smaller forums that would be easier for them to control. While tactical concerns about control may well have entered into the PCdoB's calculus, the leaders of NVA were unable to perceive the genuinely self-reflective discussion that was also going on within the PCdoB. They were not willing to admit or engage the PCdoB's new receptivity to dialogue and problem solving in relation to the structural problems of the student movement. Instead, they decided to radicalize their critique of the antidemocratic tendencies of UNE and force a showdown with the PCdoB.

In these ways, the weaknesses of the dominant styles of PeT and NVA helped to undermine their projects and alliances. While PeT leaders emphasized exploratory dialogue, these conversations were often idealized and open-ended, with a tendency for group dispersion. The pragmatic, institutionalist tendencies of PeT leaders also left them vulnerable to accusations of appeasement and lack of combativity. In contrast, NVA leaders were more cohesive and committed in their discursive positioning, but could also be accused of ideological purism and rigidity.

Leadership Skills

These stylistic tensions, in turn, informed the mediating skills of particular leaders as they attempted to respond to the emergent crisis. Here we have to look not just at strong or weak skills per se, but rather at skills that are stronger in some areas than in others. Claudio, of PeT, and Martín, of NVA, are good examples. Both were located at the points of fracture in their respective forces, and invested considerable mediating efforts in trying to hold their camps together. Both failed in this attempt, and were criticized in this failure for lack of *habilidade política*, that is, political ability, or what I call skill. For both, their customary and well-honed skills in mediation, while effective in other venues, limited their ability to respond to the fast-moving crisis at the congress.

Claudio, as the national leader of PeT, had over the past few years strengthened his skills in reflective problem solving and tactical maneuver, and to a lesser extent, in exploratory dialogue. While serving as UNE's treasurer, he had worked hard to establish a collaborative, pragmatic relationship with the PCdoB. He saw this work in "building UNE from within" not just as a contribution to the community, but also as a tactical maneuver to expand the institutional reach of his own camp, even if it meant distancing from the left of his own party. He also contributed to the group's stylistic shift away from densely ideological discourse, toward a looser, more appealing, less dogmatic style that they hoped would attract the younger cohort of activists in the universities.

However, Claudio's investment in this set of mediating skills meant that his skills in discursive positioning were much less developed. As a result, he was slow to note the lack of ideological closure and commitment among his own delegates. Recall his admission in the postcrisis meeting that the proposal for regional congresses "should have been better discussed" among themselves. He complained that he had been so busy with the logistical organization of the congress (i.e., pragmatic institution building) as well as with negotiating possible alliances (tactical maneuver) that he had no time to dedicate to this discussion. These demands on his time and skills kept him from adequately perceiving—and somehow mediating—the disconnect between the entrenched, tactically inclined leaders at the national level, the more confrontational bridging leaders in the states, and the more dispersed, lightly committed explorers at the base. As a result, he was taken by surprise when his mid-level leaders suddenly decided that their ethical and stylistic opposition to the PCdoB was stronger than their commitment to the groups' own proposals, sweeping much of the base along with them. These mid-level leaders branded Claudio a sell-out and a traitor for appeasing the "right wing" and cynically working with the PCdoB in exchange for power in the directorate.

In contrast, Martín had highly developed skills in discursive positioning, along with a stylistic opposition to what he saw, in moral-ethical terms, as the weaknesses of the other three modes of communication (idealism, appeasement, and cynicism, respectively). As a Gramscian mediator, Martín was highly effective at building consensus within the camp of the left through discursive boundary work that drew ideological and ethical lines between "the classist left" and the other forces. He also saw NVA's withdrawal from UNE as a chance to offer a deep challenge to the PCdoB's "unethical" and "antidemocratic" policies. Given the work they had done to consolidate the camp of the left, he hoped that not only NVA, but also the radical Trotskyists would join in discrediting the leadership of UNE.

However, Martín underestimated the degree to which the other left forces were invested tactically in the dispute for control of UNE as a status- and resource-laden institution, as well as ritually invested in it as the historic, unified voce of the students. As a result, even his allies criticized Martín's ideological rigidity and failure to compromise in response to the surprise proposal of the PCdoB. The camp of the left that he had worked so hard to articulate blew apart, leaving Martín isolated and the other groups fragmented. The other left forces complained bitterly that the withdrawal from UNE should have been "better discussed." They argued that the situation required a switch from purist opposition to tactical flexibility and a concern with the larger unity of the student movement (i.e., a combination of Machiavelli and Dewey), rather than the self-righteous positioning that characterized Martín's style.

These stylistic tensions and lack of skills were also evident in the PCdoB. The PCdoB was experimenting with a new, hybrid repertoire that maintained the party's well-honed skills in tactical maneuver and institutional control while cultivating more pragmatic and dialogic relations with other groups. The lack of trust from other forces shows the inherent weakness of the Machiavellian mode, which tends to engender cynicism about motive and method. While the PCdoB was certainly not as high-minded and community-oriented as it portrayed itself in cultivating the new style, it was also not as accommodationist and cynical as its opponents made it out to be. The party was offering a partial and tentative response to recent calls to strengthen the student movement's historically weak capacity for exploratory dialogue and reflective problem solving, coming in part from the PT-led Course Executives.

On the other hand, the PCdoB also contributed to the breakdown in communication through its own weak skills in cross-partisan articulation. Historically, the PCdoB had developed its ideological positions and tactical planning within its own segmented partisan forums, communicating with the other forces mostly when it came time for bargaining and maneuver. The PCdoB's forays into cross-partisan dialogue and problem solving were still so tentative that its leaders did not adequately discuss their reform proposals with the other forces. The PCdoB appears to have assumed that because regional congresses were a "historic proposal of the PT" (a highly ambiguous claim), its potential PT allies would come on board without commitment-generating discussion and positioning. They were sorely mistaken. When I talked to Renato afterward, he seemed bewildered and exasperated at the accusation that this was a last-minute coup. Clearly, the PCdoB did not exercise the mediating skills that might have allowed the contentious vote to go through without blowing the congress apart.

In all of these cases, limitations in leadership skills—as well as the internal stylistic tension within the camps—contributed to the breakdown in productive communication and the fracturing of subgroups, along with the disruption of UNE as a whole. While the larger political conjuncture generated some of the initial tensions in the field, we get further in understanding the breakdown by looking at communicative processes within the congress. In particular, I have shown how relational cross-pressures, stylistic tension, and limited or inflexible leadership skills contributed to the fragmentation of the student public. This analysis shows the contingency of communicative breakdown; *it could have gone otherwise*, although a nexus of relational factors brought communicative tensions to the breaking point.

This chapter has given a close-up view of the relational tensions, backstage negotiations, and front stage dramaturgy involved in the breakdown of an attempted public. I have focused on how the limitations and weaknesses of communicative styles—as well as of the leadership skills that those styles inform—contributed to the dramatic fracturing of the 1997 Congress of UNE. The fact that the student congress was a highly partisan setting did not make it any less a potential "public," although the modes of communication through which it was composed were undergoing challenge and reorientation. This chapter raises more general questions about the degree to which these different modes of communication can be reconciled with partisan contention and still provide space for productive communication in a democracy. In the concluding chapter, I take this question beyond the intricacies of Brazilian youth politics, into the intersection of contentious politics with democratic communication.

CHAPTER TEN

Conclusion: Parties and Publics

As I WRITE THIS conclusion, the 9/11 Commission has just delivered its final report. In a rather extraordinary accomplishment, the ten-member National Commission on Terrorist Attacks Upon the United States, composed of five Republicans and five Democrats, succeeded in producing a unanimous 567-page report, largely praised as being "balanced" and "nonpartisan."[1] Debates have been circulating about the degree to which individual commissioners flaunted or suppressed partisan leanings during commission hearings, and the final report left a number of gaps in the push to achieve unanimous approval. Responsibility for the 9/11 attacks was assigned to both Bush and Clinton administrations, with scathing critiques of organizational and systemic failures; however, no named individuals were blamed and the commission declined to take a strong position on whether the attacks could have been prevented. Although some 9/11 family members were disappointed, most seemed pleased with the thoroughness of the report and were willing to forego the sharper edges for the moral authority and public legitimacy of a bipartisan statement. As one family member said in an interview with the *New York Times*, "This report lays out a very active plan to make sure something gets done . . . I think this is proof positive that democracy is alive and working."[2]

The 9/11 Commission is an example of one kind of public, in which partisan divisions are provisionally, if precariously, suppressed in the interest of productive communication. For the most part, the commission tried to stay grounded in what I have described in this book as the Deweyian mode of communication: reflective problem solving in relation to the democratic community. This involved the rigorous attempt to evaluate the strengths and weaknesses of historical experience and to imagine future possible actions and their consequences. As commission chair Governor Thomas Kean said in the press conference presenting the report, "We looked back, so we can look forward." While both commissioners and witnesses sometimes lapsed into discursive positioning or tactical maneuver (evoking condemnations of posturing or manipulation), and some points of contention were dropped in the interest of reaching consensual recommendations (leading to accusations of accommodation or appeasement), still, the report was an impressive realization of a high-quality

Deweyian public. The commission made the country's key law-making and law-enforcement bodies look critically and constructively at themselves, providing information and proposals for decisions to come.

This accomplishment was even more impressive for the fact that the report was released in July of an election year, just before the political party conventions, as partisan vitriol was beginning to heat up. Positioning and maneuver filled the media and the halls of Congress as the country geared up for what promised to be one of the most bitterly contentious presidential campaigns in recent history. Commentators noted the increased popularity of partisan sources of news and debate, while sharply partisan documentaries like Michael Moore's *Fahrenheit 9/11* broke box office records. At the same time, politicians and pundits were quick to discredit their opponents by tainting them with time-honored accusations of partisanship—as in the Brazilian case, usually identified with lack of ethics and narrow political manipulation.

These episodes in recent U.S. history raise many of the issues that I have wrestled with in this detailed account of Brazilian youth politics. Democratic politics depends on citizens' ability to express strong and purposeful opinions about the past, present, and future of the polity, and to group together with others to pursue proposals for continuity or change. Citizens also need vehicles by which to access the rules and resources of institutionalized politics. In other words, we need partisans, in the broad sense, and political parties, in a narrower sense. And yet partisanship is persistently flogged (often by partisans themselves) as the enemy of democratic communication.

This tension has historical roots, although as in Brazil, the role of political parties in American civic life has changed over time. "Beware of factions," George Washington famously warned his successors, even as the statesmen and diplomats of the early republic spun into bitter and sometimes violent partisan attacks as they built the country's new party system in the 1790s. During the nineteenth century, political parties played a dynamic role in shaping the ideals and practices of citizenship, although this was often accompanied by cronyism and corruption. In response, the Progressive Era ushered in a more privatized notion of "informed citizenship" largely detached from political parties.[3]

In light of the widely perceived tension between the "partisan" and "civic" dimensions of public life, it is tempting to see these as polar opposites, and demand cynically or idealistically that they be separated. And yet in practice, they are deeply intertwined. Rather than seeing them as categorical opposites, or even as two poles on a continuum, we should look at the different ways in which partisanship and civic life come together. I have argued in this book that we can usefully distinguish between four skilled modes or "footings" underlying democratic communication, which I have called exploratory dialogue, discursive positioning, reflective problem solving, and tactical maneuver. These are loosely associated with the ideas of Habermas, Gramsci, Dewey, and Machiavelli, respectively, although they are not just abstract theoretical models, but rather involve concrete sets of discursive practices. These modes underlie the formation of different kinds of partisan publics, with characteristic strengths and weaknesses. To get past the idea that one or another of these is intrinsically better than the others, we can usefully take a "best practices" approach, looking for examples of the constructive possibilities of each kind of public.

In settings in which there are broad disparities in power and resources, in which views of the world are shaped by different cultural heritages and social locations, and in which contending systems of ideas wrestle for legitimacy and dominance, leaders need skills in drawing boundaries, building relations within them, and elaborating projects of reform that challenge existing orders. In other words, we need provocative and challenging Gramscian publics, with all of their indignation and self-righteousness. Political party conventions—such as those underway in this election year—can be (but are not always) examples of such publics, with their focus on public oratory, programmatic positioning, and unifying ritual. They mediate and suppress differences within a camp as they strive to draw strong and bold contrasts with opponents. They can degenerate into snide bickering or ideological rigidity, or alternatively, dilute their message in pallid and unconvincing pageants of unity. However, when done well, they contribute to the elaboration of critical and compelling narratives that can energize and inspire a partisan camp.

We also need to rescue the much maligned Machiavelli from equation with unethical manipulation and cynical, self-interested calculation—the tar brush that can be used to taint all leaders concerned with institutional control and policymaking in heterogeneous, contentious settings. Since institutional power and resources often facilitate (or impede) the realization of projects of social intervention, leaders must become adept at negotiating the often adversarial world of institutional control. As several PCdoB activists I talked to insisted, tactical maneuver in the interest of a project of command and control is not necessarily based in narrow, self-interested politicking; rather, it can be associated with a larger ideological project or set of societal values. When contests of interests and ideas are too strong (as they often are) for Deweyian problem solving, skill in institutional maneuver and conjunctural alliance making may be necessary for advancing longer-term collective projects. Machiavellian publics require relational flexibility and adaptation to circumstances; leaders must sometimes suspend ideological differences in order to bargain, compromise, and build provisional coalitions. Such mediation is needed not only in the halls of Congress, but also in more local organizational settings in which competing groups struggle over questions of policy and procedure.

While we need the positioning and maneuver associated with political parties, we also need to talk beyond the camps and boundaries that they tend to lock in place. Citizens can and sometimes do talk across those divides, to explore common ground or to propose changes for the larger community. As I have noted, the 9/11 commission is a good example of a self-reflective, pragmatic Deweyian public, made possible by the unifying urgency of a common threat (as well as by the stubborn and watchful pressure of grief-stricken families). While these conditions may seem rare, they may be more possible than we tend to think, particularly in smaller organizations or communities. Deliberative publics grounded in reflective problem solving do not require the absence or elimination of partisan divisions, but they do require their provisional backgrounding or suppression. Skilled leadership can help to keep partisan impulses in check; Chairman Kean's skills as a mediator have often been cited as one reason for the unlikely unanimity of the 9/11 commission. At the same time, partisanship can contribute to the deliberative process. The fact that the ten commissioners were all associated with political parties may have made the final report more probing and honest than it might have been, for example, were it written by nonpartisan technocrats, who may have been more subject to what a recent Senate panel called "groupthink."[4] The checks and pressures of committed, if partisan, public servants on each other, balanced numerically and contained by a skilled mediator, contributed to their ability to push beneath the surface even as they avoided petty accusations.

The 9/11 commission was a public that required closure: an authoritative analysis of what happened in the past and policy recommendations for what should be done in the future. But there is also a need for more open-ended, exploratory publics, which do not necessarily pressure toward final agreement, but which express and probe contending points of view in the attempt to understand and learn from the perspectives of others. I write this with an ear cocked to my favorite talk radio show, hosted by Brian Lehrer on New York public radio, currently commenting on the Democratic convention. Again, Habermasian publics—such as the kind that Lehrer strives to maintain—do not require the absence or elimination of partisanship. Lehrer tries to spark a probing dialogue among citizens and public figures who are often quite partisan, and he himself clearly leans progressive. But he is never happier than when he is gets interviewees or callers willing to suspend partisan positioning and reconsider their prior ideas, in order to think seriously about the community and world. He tries to play different positions against each other, to find common ground as well as to explore blind spots and see what these positions have to teach each other. This sort of exploratory dialogue is important for the oxygenation of ideas and mutual listening that can lead to the elaboration of innovative proposals across partisan divides.

These vignettes from current U.S. politics give examples of the productive possibilities of four kinds of partisan publics. However, such publics are not easy to accomplish. All of the publics that I have sketched here are precarious, subject to intrusion, disruption, or dilution by sudden switches in footing. They depend on careful mediation and leadership in order to maintain the appropriate footing and keep from degenerating into some of the weaknesses I have described in this book: idealism, purism, appeasement, or cynicism. Still, highlighting these different possibilities helps us to see that partisanship and civic dialogue are not diametrically opposed. They can sustain and undergird each other, depending on how citizens mediate and manage the conversational footings on which publics depend.

Note that communication in such publics is not simply dependent on *who* is in them, although skilled leadership can make a difference in their success or failure. These modes of communication are sustained (or undermined) by different kinds of institutional contexts, as well as by the relational composition of local settings. Most leaders have some practice in switching between them, although depending on their history and personality, they may be more skilled in some modes than in others. So, for example, Governor Kean possesses abilities in all four modes of communication, although he seems especially skilled in what we might call the "principled pragmatics" of cross-partisan mediation. As he moves between the Republican convention, the New Jersey state legislature, the 9/11 commission, and an interview on the Brian Lehrer Show, he adopts different types of discursive practices, foregrounding or backgrounding varying dimensions of his multiple identities. As this book has shown, democratic communication—in its possibilities and its pitfalls—lies at the intersection of individuals' leadership skills, their multiple affiliations, and the stylistic orientations of institutionalized settings.

PARTISAN PUBLICS AND DEMOCRATIC RECONSTRUCTION

In a country like Brazil, which was moving from decades of dictatorship into a somewhat shaky return to democratic institutions, partisanship poses a similar set of challenges and conundrums. Political parties are a necessary vehicle for citizen access to and participation in institutionalized politics—or rather, they can be. In reality, they have often been the vehicles for patronage politics, regional feuds, and pacts between elites. In a country with an extremely low level of trust in public officials and politicians in general, the word *political*, let alone *partisan*, has often been turned into an ethical condemnation (an association that the twenty-year dictatorship was all too eager to reinforce). This condemnation shadows the political class as a whole, even those who are trying to reform the political system in terms of access, ethics, and ideas.

This book has been concerned with the relationship between parties and "publics," a term I have used in a restricted sense, to describe heterogeneous forums for cross-sectoral communication that depend on the provisional suppression of some aspects of participants identities and projects. I have been interested in the ways that people with multiple and overlapping involvements find ways to maneuver among their complex identities as they build relations and institutions in an emerging democracy. Partisan affiliations are one component of those multiple identities, but certainly not the only ones in play. The activists I studied moved between partisan, religious, student, popular, professional, NGO, and business activism, concurrently and over time. I found that partisan relations—and attempts to manage these—cut across and influenced the dynamics of almost all of the other sectors, deeply informing the pragmatics of political talk and action within and between groups. Either partisan battles were being fought up front, as in many student movement events; or they were shoved underground, as in some of the preprofessional or business settings; or they formed a kind of overarching bridge, as in many of the church-based popular movements.

This leaves us with a somewhat puzzling phenomenon: parties were everywhere in an emerging civil society—particularly among its most active practitioners—but to be partisan was seen as anticivic. While it may be analytically possible to separate "civil" society from "political" society, as many democratic theorists have advocated, in practice it was often the same people who were involved in both. This raises the question of whether this sort of partisan intersection with other kinds of participation is good or bad for democratic reconstruction, and for democracy more generally. Are partisan pursuits necessarily destructive of attempts to rebuild civic relationships in a postauthoritarian public arena? Do they help or hinder the rebuilding of civic institutions, or the development of new forms of civic dialogue in a complex and contentious field?

If we look to the scholars of democratic politics, the answers are somewhat contradictory. The political scientists who study democratic transitions are emphatic that a strong party system is an essential component of a stable, well-functioning democracy. For example, Scott Mainwaring, in a recent book about party systems in Brazil, argues that parties serve as important agents of public representation. They provide means of access to state power (particularly important in traditionally clientelistic states like Brazil), provide order to legislative life, channel effective leadership, and help to link local or particularized issues to broader public policy agendas. They also can have a mediating, temporizing effect on political contention, since they induce political actors to make compromises and accept losses, thereby channeling social demands in nonpolarizing ways. Mainwaring argues that one of Brazil's problems is that it has traditionally had a very weak party system, incapable of maintaining the loyalties of voters or politicians. This has contributed to an unstable, patronage-base political system, weakened leadership, and the corrosion of public administration and accountability.[5]

So if democratization scholars are bullish on parties, what about the theorists of civil society? Here the attitude toward parties is much more ambivalent. In a recent book on democracy and the public sphere in Latin America, Leonardo Avritzer follows in the Habermasian tradition by making a strong distinction between the instrumental logic of political society—that is, political parties and other means of access to the institutional power of the state—and the discursive or communicative logic of social interaction in the "public space." He celebrates the social movements and neighborhood associations that have appeared in Brazil since the democratic opening as a sign of Brazil's strengthening civil society. But he laments their lack of connection to the state and party system, which, like Mainwaring, he sees as crippled by clientelism and bureaucratization. Avritzer challenges the Habermasian notion that such publics can only be expressive, and not purposeful or deliberative, using the example of participatory budgets in Porto Alegre as an example of how autonomous forms of public deliberation can be institutionalized to monitor and orient state administration.[6]

However, Avrizter elides the point that the "autonomous" social movements and civic associations that he sees as constitutive of new, innovative forms of social organization were permeated through and through with partisan associations. As I have noted in earlier chapters, Brazil returned to a multiparty system in 1980, relatively early in the country's slow transition to civilian rule, just as opposition leaders were returning from exile. This led to a sudden flourishing of small opposition parties, notably the Workers' Party (PT), as well as other labor, socialist, and eventually communist parties. Unlike the traditional parties that Mainwaring critiques, these were by and large parties of ideas, which demanded a higher degree of commitment and active engagement than was customary in Brazilian politics. As a result, the country saw a rush of grassroots party building at the same time as it experienced an explosion of urban and rural popular movements, which had started under the protective umbrella of the Catholic Church in the late 1970s. It was not simply the case that the parties allied with the popular movements, or even that they went to the popular movements to colonize or recruit (although this did happen in some cases). Rather, many leaders in labor and popular movements went to the party; in the case of the PT in particular, they were building the party at the grassroots level. As I have noted, this dense interpenetration of partisan and social movement networks had both positive and negative effects for those movements.

The legacy of this early conjunction of partisan, popular, and civic participation was still being felt in student politics a decade later. Like the popular movements, Brazil's centralized student organizations, such the National Student Union (UNE), as well as local university and high school organizations, returned to legality and strove to rebuild themselves during the highly partisan climate of the 1980s. The student movement experienced intense factional disputes, even as it tried to project a "civic" face. Yet while this period of institutional reconstruction was certainly contentious, it was also extremely energetic and forward moving. Partisan participation served both a bridging and a bonding function in youth politics.[7] Parties helped to give narrative and network cohesion to expanding activist communities, at the same time as these activists built organizations and alliances across institutional sectors.

The 1992 impeachment movement marked a turning point in the relationship between partisan and civic discourse. With the country mesmerized by the civic outpouring of opposition to the Collor government, and further disillusioned by fresh evidence of corruption among Brazil's political leaders, the impeachment deepened the gap between ideas of partisanship and civic virtue. The discourse of citizenship and civic participation became increasingly decoupled from that of partisanship and institutionalized politics (even Lula da Silva, the PT leader, opened up a "Citizenship Institute" that was semiautonomous from the party). This increased wariness about partisanship was somewhat ironic, since as I have shown, partisan mediation played an important role in the convergence of the movement against Collor. The impeachment itself can be seen as a reaffirmation of Brazil's political institutions; the case against Collor was exposed not just by the "apartisan" press, but also by a congressional commission led by partisan opposition leaders.

As Brazil moved into the *Globalizando* period in the mid-1990s, the role of partisanship in civic life became more troubled and complex. The "civic" discourse moved from the popular movements and NGO community into business and professional sectors, reinforced by the Cardoso regime's efforts to shift some social services to "Third Sector" organizations. Some of these actors—as we have seen in the case of the Junior Enterprises—were much less accepting of the strongly politicized understanding of citizenship offered by the popular movements of the 1980s, grounded in notions of social rights, community empowerment and influence on the state. Evelina Dagnino has argued that this led to a displacement of meanings associated with the ideas of "citizenship" and "participation," contributing to a highly privatized, managerial, and entrepreneurial emphasis that "contradict[s] the properly political content of participation as conceived by the democratic project," which sought the "sharing of power between State and civil society."[8]

In this context, it is tempting to see the emergence of the challenger forms of student politics in the 1990s—particularly those linked to cultural, professional, and business identities—as evidence of what Dagnino describes as a clash between the "democratic project" and its privatizing, neoliberal counterpart. Certainly, these emergent movements all placed a greater emphasis on the personal and professional lives of activists than the more collectivist movements of the 1980s. However, labeling these all as "neoliberal" neglects the differences between these challengers, as well as the degree to which conflicts in student politics were not simply over projects, but also over styles of political communication. The traditional student movement was under attack because entrenched partisan competition for institutional control made it difficult to have the exploratory, reflective, and provocative debate that many students craved.

The three challenger groups that I have studied here—black students, course-based organizations, and Junior Enterprises—varied in their orientations toward partisanship, as well as in the ways that they linked personal careers with collective engagement. These differences have their roots in cohort trajectories. The black student coordination was dominated by activists from the early cohorts, contributing to its more confrontational—if "suprapartisan"—stance, highly concerned with mounting a collective challenge to the dominant culture. In contrast, the Junior Enterprises were dominated by newcomers from the later cohorts, contributing to its more privatized, antipartisan orientation, limiting political involvement to narrow protection of interests. Of the three, the Course Executives showed the most stylistic tension, due to the greater degree of commingling of students from earlier and later cohorts. These included experienced partisan leaders who brought more reflective, consensual styles of communication from the church-based popular movements, along with newcomers in the mid-1990s who were more likely to reject partisanship altogether. Students debated how best to link their "specialized" academic pursuits to broader social commitments, and struggled to resist narrow corporatism even as they invested in their professional careers. To avoid what they saw as the pitfalls of the highly competitive student-partisan style, they sometimes resorted to banishing explicitly partisan talk altogether, although partisan pursuits hovered uneasily in the background.

I would argue that these attempts to banish partisan identities were a problem for youth activists in the 1990s, even though they did it in the name of enhancing the quality of democratic communication. While they

TABLE 10.1
Strengths and weaknesses of partisanship

	Positive	Negative
Cultural	· overarching narratives · longer time perspective · joint framings across movements · renovating argument and debate	· encourages posturing and manipulation · discourages listening and learning · drains discussion and debate · party activists tainted as "impure"
Social Structure	· cross-cutting umbrella structure · brokerage and mediation · access to resources and influence	· divisiveness and factionalism · squabbling over resources, allies, recruits · conflicting time frames with other institutional forms
Emotional	· motivation and excitement of a competitive struggle · accepting and explaining loss, disappointment	· in-fighting sucks energy and enthusiasm · disillusionment with opportunism and manipulation

did sometimes succeed in having richer discussions, they risked the paralysis and depoliticization that can come from overreliance on open-ended discussion without pragmatic or ideological closure. This can result in the loss of the more challenging and provocative forms of democratic participation, particularly those committed to expanding social and political inclusion. On the other hand, these young activists had also put their finger on a sore spot for democratic politics: how do you maintain partisan commitments while also engaging in the more exploratory and reflective talk that keeps political communication from degenerating into rigid posturing and manipulation?

STRENGTHS AND WEAKNESSES OF PARTISANSHIP IN CIVIC LIFE

As the experiences of young Brazilian activists have shown us, partisanship has many different dimensions, with both constructive and destructive effects on civic life. In table 10.1, I summarize some of the positive and negative influences of parties on social movements and civic institutions, looking at cultural, social structural, and emotional factors.

At the cultural level, participation in political parties can offer a number of distinct advantages for social movements and civic institutions. As I have noted, the parties that I have studied in this book have mostly been parties of ideas, with ideologically grounded and socially expansive proposals for revolution or reform. They ranged from small revolutionary sects on the left fringe to the more pragmatic and elite-embedded social democrats. Regardless of political orientation, such parties offer overarching narratives of political intervention, broadening activists' understanding of what they are doing and why. These narratives place a movement or organization in a larger time perspective, giving them a sense that they didn't just start yesterday and are not ending tomorrow. Some of these parties arguably offer a view of history that borders on caricature, obscuring more than it reveals. Still, a sense of character and drama, of plot twists and turns, and of extended time horizons can sustain movements and organizations that otherwise might wither when the founding struggle is over. Political parties can provide cultural framings for action that bridge multiple sites of struggle, enabling activists to feel that they are involved in something bigger than the fight for the neighborhood school or busing system or the narrow corporatism of a labor or professional identity. In addition, parties can be sites for the renewal of ideas and projects. For example, the meetings of the Workers' Party that I attended in working class neighborhoods in the late 1980s—ranging from small "nucleus" meetings in people's living rooms to municipal, state, and national encounters—were lively and contentious spaces for the debate of ideas between internal "tendencies," as activists responded to the challenges of their multiple involvements in social movements and local governments.

Political parties can also provide structural support for civic life by bolstering social relations. In settings in which social movements or organizational sectors may be isolated or balkanized, political parties can provide umbrella structures that cut across social networks and institutional sectors. By means of partisan forums and spaces of sociability, people can come in contact with others having very different personal, political, and professional experiences. In the case of the PT, religious activists from the urban periphery could intermingle with students and professionals based on a bond that was not simply one of class or religion, thus expanding the social experience and understanding of otherwise segmented groups. Moreover, partisan ties were often a source of backstage mediation that contributed to civic-coalition building, as I showed in my account of the 1992 impeachment movement. And parties also provided access to material resources and political influence. Elected officials of the PT and other parties contributed much of their official salary and infrastructure to support community organizers and other "professionalized" activists who were involved in building social movements and civic organizations. In many local PT governments, state-controlled spaces were opened for popular debate and deliberation (as in the "participatory budgets" of Porto Alegre and other cities).[9]

Partisanship can also make positive emotional contributions to civic life. The motivation and excitement of a competitive struggle can energize activists in ways that spill over from parties and electoral campaigns into other areas of participation.[10] For example, I showed how Barreto, as a bridging leader, brought his partisan enthusiasm to building the student movement, the movement of agronomists, and the land reform movement, seen as various dimensions of a common struggle. The overtly partisan years of the 1980s were in some ways more emotionally charged and motivating for young Brazilian activists than the more tense and complicated "civic" climate of the 1990s. Partisanship can also help activists to contextualize and accept losses and disappointments, precisely because of the longer temporal structure of partisan narratives, which may serve as what Kim Voss calls "fortifying myths" that help people keep the faith in the wake of defeat.[11]

We need to keep these positive dimensions of partisanship in mind, since partisanship is so often maligned or ignored in studies of civic participation. However, critiques of partisanship also have solid grounding, as I have shown in numerous empirical examples throughout this book. While the discursive positioning involved in partisan debate can energize and inspire, it also encourages rigid posturing or rhetorical manipulation. This in turn can discourage genuine listening and learning among political actors, draining politics of real discussion and debate. Moreover, civic reformers who become involved in electoral contests risk being tainted as opportunists and manipulators. In the late 1980s, I saw a lawyer who had served as a long-term housing activist in São Paulo shouted off the podium at a housing rally when he became a PT candidate for city council. "This isn't politics," people shouted. "This is a movement!" To maintain their apolitical purity, movements may lose opportunities for institutional access and influence. On the other side, politicians may become institutionally entrenched and disconnected from broader projects of social transformation.

Structurally, partisanship can enmesh movements and organizations in divisiveness and factionalism, disrupting attempts to forge provisional unities in order to pursue common projects. Partisan factions in other institutional sectors (or internal tendencies within parties) may become caught up in squabbles over scarce goods such as resources, recruits, and allies, particularly in periods which any or all of these are in short supply. Partisan timetables may be disruptive to the schedules of other sectors, since electoral campaigns are often relentlessly demanding on partisan activists and resources. Campaigning may drain the energy and attention of activists away from other projects and movements, leading to their dilution or collapse. The periodic intensification of partisan posturing that accompanies campaigns may also exacerbate internal competition within other sectors, thus affecting the temporal dynamics of supposedly "nonpartisan" groups.

Finally, partisanship can also have emotional costs on social movements and civic organizations. While partisan competition can sometimes be invigorating, the degeneration of such competition into narrow infighting can suck the energy and enthusiasm from a movement. Partisan disputes can heighten feelings of paralysis and frustration, as well as of indignation and anger that can sometimes turn petty and destructive. In addition, the cynicism that often accompanies tactical maneuver can lead to disillusionment with the opportunism, bargaining, and manipulation that characterizes much of institutionalized politics.

Beyond Competition or Collaboration

This discussion returns us to a thorny question: How can citizens maintain the useful combativeness of partisan positioning while still being able to enter into relations of dialogue and collaboration across partisan divides? To answer this, we need to leave behind idealized, dichotomous views of political communication as being either civic or partisan, consensual or competitive, or as Jane Mansbridge put it in her seminal study of democratic deliberation, divided between "unitary" and "adversary" democracy.[12] We have to focus, rather, on their somewhat troubled but still fertile coexistence.

I have suggested that one way to avoid this dichotomy is to look at the ways in which actors manage the relationship between partisan and other kinds of identities by moving between different modes of communication. I argue that the stylistic orientations that I have called exploratory dialogue, discursive positioning, reflective problem solving, and tactical maneuver—sketched above in relation to U.S. politics—are all essential components of democratic communication, with accompanying strengths and weaknesses. Rather than curtly condemning partisanship and singing the praises of a tamed and declawed "civicness," we should rather pay attention to the more subtle discursive switching that actors engage in as they move between different institutional settings, as well as between contending definitions of what those settings are about.

In distinguishing between the four modes of political communication, I have looked at how forms of talk are differentiated along two axes. The first is the familiar divide in political theory between collaboration and competition, central to the debate between normative and instrumental theories of political interaction. Recent debates in democratic theory sometimes appear as a contest in theoretical worldviews, between those who insist that political life is based on interest, power, and bargaining over preferences, and those who believe that through self-reflective deliberation, citizens can enlarge their understanding and come to a reasoned consensus regarding the common good.[13] This division is grounded in a mutual repudiation of each others' underlying models of social action, sometimes framed as a tension between "how the world is" and "how it should be." We can loosen ourselves from this deadlock by seeing these contending models as modes of communication that people use as the basis for thought and action, with varying degrees of consistency. Yes, certainly, people bargain, maneuver, posture, and jockey competitively for control; but that is not all that they do. Likewise, people do sometimes enter into more reflective, exploratory, and collaborative talk in which they formulate values and proposals for the good of the collectivity. But clearly, this is also not all that they do, and nor should it be, as even normatively oriented theorists such as Walzer, Mansbridge, and Young have argued.[14]

To understand contentious phenomena central to politics—such as social movements and other forms of collective action—we need to break out of these dichotomous models and focus instead on how collectivities fuse collaboration and competition as they move between different modes of political communication. For example, we have seen how organizations that are self-consciously partisan in orientation—such as radical branches of the Catholic youth pastoral—can develop internal relations based on exploratory dialogue and reflective problem solving, even as they militantly position themselves against injustice and oppression in capitalist society. Likewise, organizations that are dominated by internal partisan competition—such as the Brazilian student movement—can work hard (at times) to transcend those divides and develop collaborative relations with other civic organizations.

The second axis is the less familiar, but equally useful distinction between communication oriented toward ideas or actions, or as I also describe it, between talk emphasizing elaboration or deliberation. The literature on deliberative democracy tends to fuse these, intertwining Habermasian open-ended search for mutual understanding with Deweyian reflection on shared problem solving. Yet as we have seen in Brazilian youth politics, these often involve distinguishable sets of discursive practices. Some groups, like the Catholic Youth Pastoral, had institutionalized procedures for moving between exploratory and pragmatic modes of communication, as different moments or stages in the same meetings. Other groups emphasized either elaborative or deliberative modes, neglecting or downplaying the other. For example, the Forum of Course Executives was committed to exploratory dialogue (under the rubric of "elaboration" and "exchange") but fell apart once it needed to reach the closure of practical problem solving. In contrast, the Coordination of Black Scholars maintained a strong footing of reflective problem solving but had less space for exploratory dialogue. The relative strengths and weakness of the groups—what they were able to do together over time— were shaped by these different stylistic orientations.

Studies that focus on the competitive dimension of politics also tend to fuse orientations toward ideas and actions, conflating discursive elaboration with strategic decision making. For example, those working from a rational choice framework usually reduce the cultural component of action to narrowly conceived "norms" and "preferences," stripped of the sophisticated elaboration that often accompanies political processes. And even in the much richer literature of "collective action frames," cultural elaboration often appears overly instrumental and manipulative, as a form of rhetorical maneuver by organizers rather than of narrative positioning in a broader discursive field.[15]

Competitive publics need both elaborative and deliberative modes, although leaders may become more skilled in one or the other. The elaboration of adversarial, self-righteous projects and identities is an essential component of movement building, as is the tactical calculation involved in planning and mobilization. The congresses of UNE involved institutionalized forums that helped to move the proceedings from ideological positioning to the tactical maneuvers involved in electoral dispute. However, some radical left factions stressed ideological positioning at the expense of tactical considerations, while others sacrificed ideological purity to pursue alliances needed for organizational control. These stylistic orientations influenced the fortunes of different factions in the student movement as well as the interventions of the student movement as a whole.

The three challenger groups distinguished themselves from traditional student organizations by developing new ways to fuse collaboration and competition, as well as to link ideas and actions. The Coordination of Black Scholars combined well-honed skills in Deweyian problem solving—gained in part through participants' experience in church-based popular movements—with Gramscian hegemony building in the field of ideas. They constructed homogeneity around racial identities, seeing themselves as subjects of the transformation of Brazilian cultural and scientific production. The Forum of Course Executives combined a fierce ethos of Habermasian dialogue and consensus building with more Machiavellian maneuvering to regain control of Brazil's central student organizations. And the Federation of Junior Enterprises combined a civic-minded form of pragmatic institution building with the more instrumental and personalistic pursuits of ambitious young professionals.

Leadership and Mediation in Partisan Publics

The successes and failures of the types of publics that I have described in
this book depend on the mediating activity of skilled leaders. The litera-
tures on democratic theory and contentious politics both have notable
lacunas when it comes to leadership. Perhaps because of the relative focus
on normative, institutional, or structural conditions, individuals seem to
disappear—except when they are collapsed into individual preference
points in choice-based models of action. I have offered an understanding
of individuals as socially embedded carriers of institutional styles—the
products of where they have come from and where they stand in relation
to overlapping institutional sectors. At the same time, I have sought to
preserve the role of individual interpretation, synthesis, and skill in responding to emergent situations. Before closing, let me summarize my
understanding of leadership and mediation as I have developed it over the
course of the preceding chapters.

In the movements that I studied, leaders play a dual mediating role.
First, they need to mediate between the multiple identities and projects
that are brought into any setting of political action, steering the communication in such a way that some of those identities are "appropriately"
expressed while others are downplayed or suppressed. Second, they must
also negotiate between modes of communication, steering toward more
competitive or collaborative footings, for example, or directing the discussion toward either ideas or actions. While these can be seen as analytically
distinct forms of mediation, they are linked in practice. So, for example,
if leaders in the 9/11 Commission, the Coordination of Black Scholars, or
the Forum of Course Executives wanted to maintain a footing of reflective
problem solving or exploratory dialogue, they would have to carefully
hold in check expressions of partisan identities, sanctioning or redirecting
such expressions should they arise. For black student leaders, the strong
expression of racial identities was a core component of the discursive
positioning of the movement, requiring a quite deliberate suppression of
partisan projects as well as of territorial squabbles among NGOs. And
student leaders with simultaneous involvements in the course-based
movement and in "general" student politics played up and down their
professional and partisan identities, respectively, as they moved between
exploratory dialogue and tactical maneuver.

Leaders gain skills in these types of mediation as they move between
different institutional sectors. I have argued that leadership orientations
are influenced both by the depth of participation within sectors and by
the span of participation across sectors. Activists who have been deeply
involved in several different sectors—those whom I call *bridging lead-*

ers—tend to have a stronger orientation toward ideas rather than actions, as well as a competitive orientation toward movement building; they become Gramscian hegemony builders, and may be quite innovative in combining narratives and frames across their multiple involvements as they articulate projects of reform. In contrast, those who have deep involvements in only one or two sectors tend to be equally competitive, but more focused on institutional legitimation and control. These *entrenched leaders* may become skilled at Machiavellian maneuver and rhetorical manipulation, but they are less apt to present innovative projects of reform.

Likewise, my book suggests that those who are lightly invested within sectors become more skilled in collaborative modes of communication, although they vary in their degree of creativity as well as in the focus on ideas versus actions. *Explorers*, who straddle multiple sectors but are not heavily invested in any of them, can become especially adept and innovative in the play of ideas for their own sake, but are less invested in bringing those ideas to ideological or practical closure. And *focused activists*, who are lightly invested in just one or two sectors, may become pragmatic institution builders without being overly concerned with either the ideational justification for those institutions or their competitive relations with other groups.

This framework highlights the interplay between two different kinds of explanations of communicative styles. One focuses on the institutional content of leaders' affiliations (i.e., on the logic and practices of the particular sectors they have belonged to) while the other focuses on their structural positions in the field (i.e., their depth and breadth of cross-sectoral involvement). Because groups are the intersection of the individuals who are in them, group styles are influenced by the affiliation profile of their members, that is, by the cross-sectoral distribution of where participants have come from, and where they stand in the field. Are activists located in the intersections, or in the enclaves? How deeply invested are they in a given sector or set of sectors? These factors influence the styles of leadership and mediation that come to characterize a collectivity, and therefore shape its interventions in the larger field.

In this book, I have provided evidence of how both institutional and relational factors influence styles and skills of leadership among Brazilian activists. I have drawn on formal structural analysis, leadership interviews, and ethnographic observation to interrogate a rich and complex case. Through these analyses, I have found structural patterns and cultural processes that help us to explain the distinct styles of communication that were in play as youth activists attempted to rebuild democratic institutions. Beyond the Brazilian case, the analysis that I have presented here constitutes a more general framework, which can be applied to the study of political communication in other historical contexts.

Thinking the Problem of Publics

Toward the end of my extended fieldwork in Brazil, I found myself frequently called on to offer commentary and advice on the state of the Brazilian student movement. Sometimes these requests came from particular groups or factions, hoping to strengthen their position in relation to their rivals (such as one late night PT strategy session that took place in my São Paulo apartment, to which we all trooped after the local bar closed). At other times I was asked to provide a more "global" perspective on how Brazilian youth in general could strengthen their political involvement, or on how the student movement could overcome its current "crisis" (variously defined in terms of partisan entrenchment, bureaucratization, stagnation, or distance from the student body). In closing this book, I want to take stock of where my analysis has led me in "thinking the problem of publics," to paraphrase the Brazilian youth advisor quoted in the book's opening.

The publics that I have described in this book are not rarefied zones of abstract and reasoned debate about the common good. They are complex, heterogeneous, and often contentious spaces in which people bring with them too many partially overlapping identities and projects to allow for smooth communication about ideas and action. How do they ever arrive at anything resembling understanding, or get anything jointly accomplished? I have offered the perhaps startling proposition that publics first of all require *suppression*. Not "free expression," not "publicity," not "unrestrained communication," but rather the provisional suspension of potentially distracting, disruptive, or divisive aspects of participants' multiple affiliations. While all communication requires selective attention and the backgrounding of irrelevant aspects of identities, I am talking about something more than the routine deactivation of nonrelevant ties. Publics require the active suppression of situationally potent identities. They are charged places "in between," in which interstitiality heightens the sense of both contingency (something else might happen) and of negotiated restraint.

Theorists of democratic communication implicitly acknowledge such restraint when they refer to "self-limiting civil society," the "economy of moral disagreement," "self-censorship," or the "focusing of debate on the public good."[16] However, these theorists tend to see this kind of suppression primarily in relation to the tension between individual self-interest (or personal moral principles) and the broader public good. The activists that I studied were often negotiating among many different ways of pursuing what they thought of as "the common good," including, in their understanding, their partisan pursuits. When is it important that I bring my identity as a black activist, as an agronomist, as a communist, or as a

Catholic into play? When should I hold these in abeyance as I attempt to build bridges, elaborate projects, and set up institutions? When do these identities contribute to the public under construction, and when do they distract or disrupt? When should I stress the collaborative dimension of my shared identities, and when should I allow competitive relations to come to the fore?

There are no simple answers to these questions, for either the analyst or advisor. But rather than falling back into radical contingency, my book offers a few preliminary suggestions. As I observed debates over Brazilian youth politics, I became increasingly wary of the blanket condemnations of partisanship that seemed to infuse many critiques. These criticisms neglected the more complex identity negotiations that most activists engaged in, of which partisanship was just one—albeit especially problematic—dimension. Student publics that managed this heterogeneity by forcing partisanship underground—such as the Forum of Course Executives—seemed oddly paralyzed, lacking the strong public voice that they claimed to seek. And those that repudiated partisanship altogether—such as the Junior Enterprises—contributed to a thin and depoliticized understanding of citizenship. On the other hand, the entrenched partisan climate of UNE often proved alienating and counterproductive, discouraging dialogue and reflection on how best to reform the "unified" organization of which leaders were so proud.

How then can social movement actors keep their partisan voices in play, without letting these disrupt the complex publics that they are seeking to build? There are two main challenges that movements face in this respect. The first is to strike a balance between interstitiality—their position in between institutional sectors—and institutional focus. Movements should avoid being shut away in narrow or isolated enclaves, and instead allow a diversity of perspectives to enter into the conversation. Activists' multiple affiliations can help them talk across partisan and sectoral divides, especially when they create broad-based settings for exchange of ideas, such as the cross-sectoral encounters that Brazilian activists often dubbed "seminars" or "workshops" or "forums." Such settings encourage exploratory dialogue by not demanding closure; they do not require that participants reach either ideological consensus or practical solutions, but rather just exchange points of view. These kinds of "big tent" encounters—also seen in other settings, such as the World Social Forum of the global justice movement—create a momentary, if somewhat illusory, sense of commonality that suppresses partisan divides and allows for cross-pollination of ideas and experiences.

These kinds of Habermasian publics are often exhilarating and inspiring, but they are not enough. In order to sustain themselves over time, successful movement organizations also need to invest in the pragmatics and maneuvering of institution building. This requires them to solve problems related to day-to-day operations and distribution of power and resources, often in the face of internal dissension. Sometimes such problems can be resolved in the less competitive Deweyian mode, through reflective deliberation that weighs priorities in relation to the good of the whole. To do this, participants need to build a sense of enduring community that suppresses differences in identity and interest. In the case of the Catholic youth pastoral and the black student coordination, strong community narratives grounded in religious and racial identities helped to create a collaborative footing that provisionally overrode factional difference—even though many participants were proudly and openly partisan. However, sometimes those differences are impossible to suppress, requiring more adversarial procedures of bargaining, coalition-building, and voting, as in the congresses of UNE. Movements that completely reject these competitive aspects of institution building are often organizationally fragile and have difficulty sustaining themselves over time, as was the case with the black student coordination and the Forum of Course Executives. Activists need to create institutional procedures that channel the Machiavellian mode without letting its logic become all-consuming, overriding the potential for reflective dialogue.

The second challenge for social movements is to balance constructive self-reflection with more combative proposals for social change. In some ways, the Gramscian mode of discursive positioning, as I have described it here, is the most intrinsically partisan, in that it is concerned with elaborating projects on behalf of a *part* of the larger society, even if actors sometimes frame those projects in more universalistic language. The sense of enduring community that is essential to the more collaborative Deweyian mode is only ever partial; even if a group of people conceives of themselves as members of the "global community" (or as "citizens of the earth," as I was taught to call myself), there will be those that resist this identity and therefore locate themselves in contending positions in the discursive field. While the Catholic youth and black students strove for collaborative, self-reflective internal relations, their discourse turned quite combative when directed against sources of oppression in the larger society. They constructed boundaries based on class and race, respectively, even if the ultimate goal was to create a society in which these divisions ceased to matter. The Gramscian mode entails recognition that efforts at social change often run up against entrenched resistance based on power disparities that are not easily overcome by persuasion or dialogue.

Yet too strong a focus on discursive positioning can have the effect of destroying reflectivity, and with it, the capacity to learn and change. I often watched competing factions in the Brazilian student movement measuring themselves against an imagined *"combatometro"* (or "combat-ometer"), as they jokingly called it, posturing to see who could come off as more combative than the next. This leads to spirals of ideological radicalization, especially when movement leaders are competing for support from a shifting base. It also generates purity regimes that contribute to isolation, detachment, and incomprehension of changing social relations, making it even less likely that the movement will be able to achieve its goals. The capacity to seek out diverse viewpoints and experiences—as well as to look critically at one's own positions and actions—is essential for any collectivity that hopes to intervene responsively in a changing world. In this book I suggest that such openness to change and critical self-reflection are facilitated by activists' multiple affiliations in diverse sectors and organizations. This helps to enliven the play of ideas within publics and generate innovative responses to changing situations. However, such internally diversified Gramscian publics are different from "big tent" forums. Groups that are partially segmented by identity or ideas— such as the black student coordination or partisan factions examined in this book—may have to caucus separately at times in order to achieve coherence and closure in their proposals, something very hard to do in extremely heterogeneous settings.

The Dance of Democracy

Given the importance of all four modes of communication, I'll close with some suggestions for activists. First, I would urge them not to see competition and collaboration as two mutually opposing poles. Too often, actors infuse these modes with moral-political valences that brand opponents as dogmatists and manipulators, on the one hand, or as idealists and appeasers, on the other. In the same vein, I would urge them not to radically separate the elaborative and deliberative dimensions of publics, but rather to find constructive ways to move between ideas and actions. If they want to develop rich and responsive understandings of the changing world, as well as actions that can build bridges and challenge power structures, activists need skills in switching between these different footings.

Political actors should avoid seeing one stylistic orientation as intrinsically better than another. All four modes of communication have characteristic strengths and weaknesses. Groups that are dominated by one particular mode will tend to shipwreck on those weaknesses, limiting the force of their social intervention. They may circle around in the free exchange of ideas until they peter out from lack of concrete proposals. They may retreat into ideological sectarianism, limiting their ability to make alliances or effectively intervene in the political field. They may become enmeshed in devious and cynical manipulations in the attempt to maintain institutional control, losing the trust of potential allies and recruits. Or they may go so far to avoid conflict that they reduce their intervention to technocratic problem solving. This suggests that to be effective, political groups require a plurality of styles and skills, so as to draw on the strengths of these communicative modes and hold the weaknesses in check.

However, stylistic diversity can also lead to conflict, as I showed in the fragmentation of the 1997 Congress of UNE. This is particularly the case when contending styles become coded as "democratic" versus "antidemocratic," or as "combative" versus "accommodationist," serving as partisan labels to promote one's own force and discredit opponents. Stylistic positioning is often a way to stake out a position in a competitive field; hegemonic battles can be waged in relation to styles as well as ideas. Nevertheless, leaders who can suspend these battles and develop skills in moving between footings—as well as between the various identities associated with them—are especially critical to the construction and institutionalization of new kinds of publics, as well as to the success of these publics in articulating joint projects.

These observations about Brazilian youth activism can be extended to other kinds of political contexts. All effective political leadership depends on the mediation of heterogeneous identities and projects. This includes public policymakers at various levels of government as well as local civic leaders, grassroots community organizers, and broad-based challenger coalitions such as the global justice movement. In all of these cases, leaders (and their associated collectivities) are not simply trying to build civic solidarity or social trust, but rather to pursue projects for social intervention in a contested field. That is, they are partisans (in either the broad or narrow sense) as well as citizens. I would urge them not to sacrifice the contentious edge of their intervention in the name of citizenship, or adopt the more privatized, depoliticized understanding of civic participation that I saw among some of the business-oriented youth groups. At the same time, they must not lose the capacity for dialogue and reflection across partisan lines. The skillful movement between modes of communication is part of what Brazilians call the *jogo de cintura*—the swing of the hips— in the dance of democratic politics.

Skill is a difficult thing to explain or predict: you know it when you see it, or sometimes more acutely, when you don't see it. It operates in the charged contingencies of publics, often swinging potential relations in one direction or another. Skilled mediators suppress or highlight aspects of their overlapping identities as they try to carve out provisional spaces of shared thought and action. The more complex and heterogeneous the public, the higher the level of skill required. I have suggested that activists can carry out this mediation in different ways, and that the manner in which they move between modes of communication in turn affects the style and quality of the resulting publics.

This book has provided a framework with which to understand these mediating processes, some of which are undoubtedly quite general, while others are grounded in the particularities of the Brazilian case. I have sought to respect the partisan passions and struggles of young activists while exploring the contradictory effects of partisan involvement on political communication. Partisanship does not necessarily destroy civic dialogue; in fact, it can enrich and extend it. But for this to happen, leaders must be skilled not only in the articulation of joint projects and identities, but also in their provisional suppression. By looking carefully at these processes, here and elsewhere, we can show how the partisan can also be public, engaging the problems and the possibilities of democratic practice.

Methodological Appendix

1. Data Coding in Cohort and Trajectory Analysis

The 332 questionnaires analyzed in chapters 3, 6, and 8 were collected between November 1995 and July 1996 at a wide range of activist events. Figure A.1 presents the distribution of questionnaires by the institutional context in which they were collected (i.e., by the institutional sector primarily responsible for the organization of the event, even though the event may have been attended by young people who also participated in other sectors). I divided the respondents into five cohorts based on the year in which they reported first involvement in one or more of the sectors of interest. See chapter 3 for a description of the periodization for the cohort analysis.

The questionnaire asked activists to list their specific involvements by sector, describing when they started, how long they were involved, and where they took place. The questionnaire prompted them for a wide range of involvements, under the major categories of student movement, political parties, religious groups, popular movements, and civic organizations. In most cases they listed the specific organizations or movement that they participated in, although occasionally they just indicated participation in a general type of organization.

With the assistance of Diane Bates and Steph Karpinski, this information was entered in a large SPSS file with detailed information on the specific involvements of each respondent. This information was then collapsed further to record each respondent's number of involvements within each of eleven sectors in each year since his or her first reported involvement. Occasionally respondents reported involvement since childhood (e.g., in Catholic youth groups). In these cases we set the start date for involvement at the year in which they were ten years of age. Table A.1 reports the types of involvements that were included in each of the eleven categories.

For each "youth year" (i.e., each year in the longer activist trajectory), the array of sectoral involvements was concatenated to form a string depicting the number of involvements within each of the eleven sectoral categories the activist had during that year. For example, if we take the order of the sectors given in table A.1, the string 231001000000 means that the youth had two religious involvements, three student involvements, one political party involvement and one Civic/NGO involvement

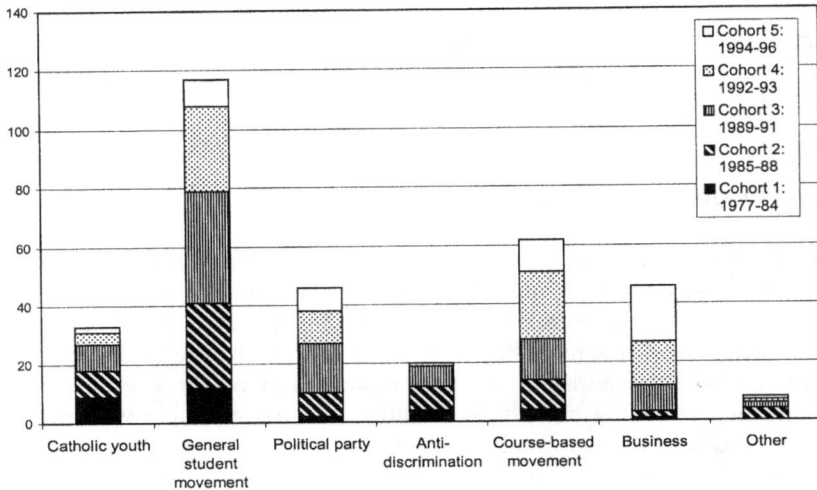

Figure A.1. Cohort distribution by questionnaire context

during that year (this corresponds to the label *R2S3PN* in the lattice analysis in chapter 3). We call the total number of group involvements in a given year the *Level* of involvement for that year, which in this case sums to seven. The number of involvements *within* a sector during a given year (for example, three for student involvement) is the *Depth* for that sector. We call the number of involvements *across* sectors (calculated as the Boolean sum across sectors) the *Span* for that year. For this youth, the span is four, since she belongs to four distinct sectors. Some basic descriptive comparisons between the five cohorts are given in table A.2. These comparisons are discussed in chapter 3.

2. GALOIS LATTICES

In chapters 3 and 5 I use Galois lattice analysis to show patterns of intersections among activists, groups, and events. The initial point of departure for lattice analysis is the work on bipartite graph structures first developed by Breiger (1974) and Wilson (1982). In a seminal formulation, Breiger (1974) uses matrix algebra to describe what he calls the "duality" of the affiliation relationship: individuals are linked by the groups they belong to, and groups are connected by the members they have in common. This duality relationship can be seen as the most basic representation of the interpenetration between two distinct sets of analytic elements (e.g., persons and groups; actors and events; objects and attributes; dis-

TABLE A.1
Classification of sectoral involvements

Code	Sector	Types of involvements included
R	Religious group	Parishes or Catholic Base Communities (liturgy, catechism, ministries, etc) / Catholic youth pastoral (PJ, PJMP, PJE, PU, etc.) / Other Catholic pastorals (land, work, housing, etc.) / Protestant or evangelical churches/youth groups / "Spiritism" or African religions (candomble/umbanda)
S	General student movement	High school organizations (*grêmios livres*) / Municipal/State/National high school student unions (UMES, UPES, UBES, etc.) / University groups in departments (CAs/DAs) / Universitywide student directorates (DCEs) / Student/faculty councils (school/department/faculty levels) / State/National Student Union (UEE, UNE)
P	Political party	PT, PCdoB, PSDB, PSTU, PDT, PSB, PCB, PPS, PV, PPR, PFL, Prona, etc. / Youth councils/coordinations of parties (esp. PT, PCdoB, PSDB) / Local/municipal/regional/state nuclei or directorates / Internal tendencies (in the PT)
M	Urban or rural popular movement	Urban popular movements: education, health, housing, sanitation, transportation, cost of living, etc. / Landless workers' movement (MST); Land occupations/settlements
D	Antidiscrimination movement	Black movement, women's movement, gay and lesbian movement, indigenous people's movement, disabled people's movement
N	NGO/civic/ethical movement	Nongovernmental organizations (environment, human rights, education, anti-hunger, etc.) / Movements for ethics/citizenship; Impeachment movement (1992) / Charitable/social service organizations
O	Socialist youth group	*União de Juventude Socialista* (UJS); *Juventude Revolução* (JR); *Movimento Revolucionário 8 de Março* (MR-8), etc.
L	Labor union/ professional organization	Labor unions: bankworkers, teachers, public servants, metalworkers, postalworkers, journalists, drivers, etc. / Labor centrals: CUT, CGT, Força Sindical / Professional associations (e.g., bar association, agriculturalists, etc.)
C	Course-based student organization	Course executives in the areas of communication, law, agriculture, medicine, pedagogy, physical education, veterinary sciences, economics, pharmacy, history, social sciences, philosophy, letters, geography, administration, social work, statistics, nursing, engineering, etc. / National Forum of Course Executives
Q	Research organization	Research institutes / "Scientific initiation": CNPq, FAPESP, etc.
B	Business organization	Junior Enterprises; State Federation of Junior Enterprises (FEJESP) / International Association of Economics and Accounting students (AIESEC) / Other business associations (PNBE, CIE, FIESP, etc.)

TABLE A.2
Comparison of means across cohorts

	Cohort 1	Cohort 2	Cohort 3	Cohort 4	Cohort 5	All cohorts
Entry years	1977-84	1985-88	1989-91	1992-93	1994-95	
# youth	32	70	96	84	50	332
Age questionnaire	27.35	24.59	22.44	21.31	20.78	22.83
(sd)	(4.38)	(5.0)	(3.3)	(2.96)	(3.13)	(4.2)
Start age	13.35	15.6	16.6	17.88	19.95	16.89
(sd)	(3.59)	(4.92)	(3.34)	(3.07)	(3.23)	(4.07)
First year # involvements						
Groups (level)	1.72	1.57	1.71	1.95	2.02	1.79
(sd)	(1.35)	(0.89)	(1.21)	(1.46)	(1.62)	(1.3)
Sectors (span)	1.25	1.19	1.28	1.54	1.48	1.35
(sd)	(0.67)	(0.46)	(0.64)	(0.88)	(0.81)	(0.72)
Last year # involvements						
Groups (level)	4.72	5.29	4.03	3.69	2.86	4.1
(sd)	(1.96)	(3.18)	(2.14)	(2.27)	(2.01)	(2.5)
Sectors (span)	3.19	3.11	2.41	2.49	1.8	2.56
(sd)	(1.09)	(1.5)	(1.27)	(1.27)	(0.99)	(1.34)
Maximum # involvements						
Groups (level)	6.09	6.53	4.8	4.19	2.98	4.86
(sd)	(2.43)	(3.04)	(2.4)	(2.39)	(2.11)	(2.74)
Sectors (span)	3.94	3.96	2.99	2.74	1.86	3.05
(sd)	(1.52)	(1.45)	(1.34)	(1.27)	(0.97)	(1.49)
Total # sectors (across career)	5.28	5	3.74	3.32	1.94	3.78
(sd)	(2.07)	(1.69)	(1.45)	(1.25)	(1.04)	(1.8)
Involvement rates (lastyear—first year/# years)						
Groups	0.225	0.424	0.354	0.419	0.335	
(sd)	(.247)	(.528)	(.405)	(.567)	(.526)	
Sectors	0.141	0.211	0.195	0.316	0.379	
(sd)	(.108)	(.17)	(.221)	(.457)	(.587)	

course and practice, to name a few recent applications), as determined by each set's association with the other.

Since these early formulations, other researchers have used techniques for discrete structural analysis to develop algebraic representations of such bipartite structures, known as "Galois" or "concept" lattices. Such lattices show the dual orderings between all possible intersection subsets of two distinct (but interdependent) sets of elements. While there have been several attempts to depict this duality in graphical form (including "simplicial complexes" [Doreian 1980; Freeman 1980] and "hyper-graphs" [Seidman 1981]), most of these have resorted to the use of two sets of images—for instance, one showing relationships between actors, the other between organizations. The advantage of Galois lattice analysis is that it makes possible a simultaneous graphical representation of both the "between set" and "within set" relations implied by a two-mode data array (i.e., between actors and groups, between actors and actors, and between groups and groups). In this way, Galois lattices are useful heuristic tools for locating patterns in complex data sets, such as those garnered from cultural, historical, and ethnographic analysis (Mische and Pattison 2000; Mische 1998; Mohr and Duquenne 1997; White and Duquenne 1996; Schweizer 1993, 1996).

The basic lattice procedure applies two algebraic operations—intersection and inclusion—to a two-mode affiliation matrix. First, all possible intersections between the rows of a two-mode matrix are calculated (generating all possible subsets of actors in organizations, or vice versa). The complete set (the vector containing all 1's) is then added to complete the array of subsets, which are then arranged in a special matrix known as a *partial ordering*, showing which subsets are included in larger subsets. This dual ordering constitutes the lattice, which can be graphically depicted in a line diagram in which nodes representing mutually associated subsets of both types of elements are linked to nodes representing the larger subsets in which these are included.

A very clear introduction to Galois lattices is available in Freeman and White (1993); techniques for examining "dual orderings" were discussed by Birkhoff (1940); for recent developments in lattice theory, see Barbut and Monjardet (1970); Wille (1982, 1996a); Lehmann and Wille (1995); Ganter and Wille (1999); and Duquenne (1987, 1991). See also the special 1996 issue of *Social Networks*, edited by Douglas White and Vincent Duquenne, as well as Breiger (2000).

Lattice Approximation

Some of the lattices presented in chapters 3 and 5 are "approximate" lattices, involving clustering techniques that reduce the complexity of the data while maintaining the main structural features of the lattice. In collaboration with Philippa Pattison (Mische and Pattison 2000), I have used two different approximation techniques, both of which are based on Boolean matrix decomposition. Both techniques are designed to find an approximation of a two-mode binary affiliation matrix as a Boolean product of two binary arrays, corresponding to representations in Boolean vector spaces of various ranks. The aim is find a low-rank representation of the original matrix with a low measure of discrepancy.

The approximate lattices in chapter 5 were constructed using the HICLAS algorithm (Hierarchical Class Analysis) described by De Boeck and Rosenberg (1988). HICLAS uses a heuristic approach to matrix decomposition, involving the iterative use of Boolean regression to find the best representation of the original matrix. The lattices in chapter 3 were constructed with the BASA algorithm (Boolean Approximation through Simulated Annealing), which uses a simulated annealing approach to minimize discrepancy directly for a specified rank (see Press et al. 1992). Simulated annealing is well-suited to this form of optimization problem and hence tends to find lower-discrepancy approximations than more heuristic approaches. For further applications of HICLAS and BASA, see Mische and Pattison (2000) and Wilson et al. (2005), respectively.

While approximate lattices may not depict all of the original relationships with the same exactness as a direct lattice, they do provide useful, approximate representations of the original data, which allow for greater interpretability while showing the major relations of inclusion and intersection. These procedures are also useful for handling data that is error-perturbed (which is often the case in empirical research), helping to recuperate a relatively "true correspondence" to the overall structure, even if some of the data are missing or in question.

Notes

PROLOGUE: EXPLORING BRAZILIAN YOUTH ACTIVISM

1. I was in Brazil from 1987 to 1990 as a fellow of the Institute of Current World Affairs, an independent, nonprofit organization that sends young professionals to various parts of the world to immerse themselves in the local culture and write about it in an open-ended, exploratory fashion for a two-year period. Reports take the form of newsletters that combine impressions, reporting, and analysis. In twenty-two newsletters, I wrote about a wide range of topics, including youth and education, the 1988 constitution, municipal and presidential elections, environmental politics, labor-business relations, and other urban and rural social movements of that period.

2. I cannot think of a better model for the ethnographer than Simmel's "stranger" (Simmel 1950). The ethnographer is "in but not of" a social setting, often giving her greater freedom and mobility than participants themselves, able to talk with people on many sides of an issue. She may find participants more willing to share their "confidences"—experiences, reflections and analyses—with her than with their immediate companions, as she catches them outside of the rush of daily activities and negotiations. She might be called on to offer "objective" evaluation and advice, and may end up forging human connections with people. At the same time, as Simmel warned, she is vulnerable to stereotyping and suspicion as a foreign interloper with potentially menacing intentions. See also Simmel (1955) on "overlapping social circles."

CHAPTER 1: COMMUNICATION AND MEDIATION IN CONTENTIOUS PUBLICS

1. All of the names of the youth activists, with one exception, have been changed to protect the privacy of participants in this study. The one exception is Lindberg Farias, who was president of UNE at the time of the 1992 impeachment movement and has since become a congressional representative from Rio de Janeiro.

2. See O'Donnell and Schmitter 1986; Stepan 1989; Skidmore 1989; Przeworksi 1991; Mainwaring et al. 1992; Glenn 2003; Abbott 1988; Mohr and Guerra-Pearson forthcoming; McPherson and Ranger-Moore 1991.

3. See Pateman 1970; Mansbridge 1983; Habermas 1989; Alexander 1990, 1998; Alexander and Smith 1992; Wuthnow 1991, 2002; Cohen and Arato 1992; Calhoun 1992; Seligman 1992; Marcus and Hanson 1993; Emirbayer and Sheller 1999; Schudson 1998; Putnam 1993, 2000; Bohman and Regh 1997; Cohen and Rogers 1998; Avritzer 2002.

4. For a relational understanding of "publics," linking networks, culture, and discursive practices, see White 1995; Mische and White 1998; Mische 2003; Som-

ers 1993; Emirbayer and Sheller 1999; Sheller 2000; Ikegami 2000, 2005; Smilde 2004; 2007.

5. For example, see Young 1990, 2000; Ryan 1990, 1992; Mouffe 1992; Fraser 1992; Gilroy 1993; Honig 1992; Lamont and Fournier 1992; Lamont and Molnar 2002; Marcus and Hanson 1993; Benhabib 1996; Gutmann and Thompson 1996; Alexander 1998; Emirbayer and Sheller 1999; Macedo 1999; Gutmann 2003.

6. In this study, the term *networks* refers mostly to shared memberships in organizations and institutional sectors rather than to personal ties between activists. These shared memberships often resulted in personal ties, which I certainly saw in my fieldwork, although I did not collect data on this aspect of networks. As I explain in chapter 2, the multiple affiliations of activists structured their personal careers as well relations between organizations in the larger political field. For a good discussion of recent research on social movement networks, see Diani and McAdam 2003. For more general introductions to social network analysis, see Wellman and Berkowitz 1988; Emirbayer and Goodwin 1994; Scott 2000; Watts 2004. For other studies focusing on multiple networks, see Gould 1991, 1005; Padgett and Ansell 1993; Padgett 2001; Padgett and McLean 2006.

7. Simmel 1955.

8. For major statements of these positions in the social movement literature, see McAdam 1982; Tarrow 1994; Snow et al. 1986; Snow and Benford 1988, 1992; Gamson 1992, 1995; McAdam et al. 1996.

9. See Stepan 1989 for an excellent collection of essays on this early period of the Brazilian democratic transition; see also Stepan 1988; Skidmore 1988. Other useful collections of essays on this period by Brazilian and non-Brazilian scholars include Krischke 1983; Moisés and Alburquerque 1989; Reis and O'Donnell 1988; and Weffort et al. 1991. For an interesting comparison to the Polish case, see Ekiert and Kubik 2001.

10. For discussions of the role of social movements during the democratic transition, see Singer and Brant 1980; Boschi 1987; Sader 1988; Stepan 1989; Skidmore 1989; Mainwaring 1986, 1989a, 1989b; Keck 1989, 1992; Seidman 1994; Sandoval 1994, 1998; Doimo 1995; Gohn 1995; Escobar and Alvarez 1992; Alvarez, Dagnino, and Escobar 1998; Chalmers et al. 1997; Hochstetler 2000; Avritzer 2002.

11. On Brazil's democratic consolidation, see Reis and O'Donnell 1988; Mainwaring, O'Donnell, and Valenzuela 1992; Kingstone and Powers 2000.

12. On the diversification of youth politics and culture, see Vianna 1988; Lorenzotti 1989; Abramo 1992, 1994; Costa 1993; Bucci 1993; Yudice 1994; Moraes 1995. Most Brazilian commentators on youth culture in the 1980s and 1990s have focused on subcultures, rather than organized youth activism. A notable exception is a recent study by Marcos Mesquita (2003a, b).

13. See especially Eliasoph and Lichterman 2003; other recent studies exploring discursive styles in political interaction include Hart 2001; and Fishman 2004.

14. I carried out dissertation fieldwork in Brazil from 1993 to 1997, beginning with a summer predissertation fellowship from the Janey Program in Latin American Studies in 1993, followed by dissertation fellowships from Fulbright Hays, the SSRC, and AED-NSEP from 1994 to 1996. I returned for a follow-up visit in the summer of 1997.

15. See for the prologue for more probing discussion of the challenges and opportunities of my fieldwork experience.

16. For more about "microcohorts," see Whittier 1995.

17. Galois lattice analysis is an algebraic technique for studying inclusions and intersections in two-mode data (for example, persons by groups, or organizations by projects). For work on Galois lattices, see Freeman and White 1993; Wille 1996a, 1996b; Ganter and Wille 1999; Mohr and Duquenne 1997; Mische and Pattison 2000.

CHAPTER 2: LEADERSHIP IN THE INTERSECTIONS

1. In Portuguese, "course" refers to a discipline or area of professional study, not a specific class. The professional student associations are called "Course Executives" because they plan and coordinate national encounters of students in a professional area as well as serve as a base for policy interventions or movement activity specifically related to that profession. The professionally oriented student movement is also sometimes called the *Movimento Específico* (specific movement, in contrast to the "general" student movement as led by UNE) as well as the *Movimento de Área*, or (professional) area-based movement.

2. For recent examples of this relational and communicative approach to sociological analysis, see Emirbayer 1997; Emirbayer and Goodwin 1994; Emirbayer and Mische 1998; White 1992, 1993, 1995, 2003; Mische and White 1998; Mische 2003; Tilly 1998, 1999, 2002a, 2002b, 2003; Zelizer 1994, forthcoming; Somers 1993, 1994, 1998; McLean 1998, 2007; Steinberg 1998, 1999a, 1999b; Wagner-Pacifici 1987, 1994, 2000; Gibson 2000, 2003, 2005; Polletta 2002a; Smilde 2004, 2005, 2007; Abers and Keck 2003a.

3. Classic statements of what has become known as the "political process" approach to social movement analysis can be found in McAdam 1982; Tarrow 1994; Morris and Mueller 1992; McAdam, McCarthy, and Zald 1996. For a recent rethinking of this approach by three of its founders, see McAdam, Tarrow, and Tilly 2001, as well as Aminzade et al. 2001. On collective action frames, see Snow et al. 1980; Snow and Benford 1988, 1992; Benford 1997; Gamson 1992, 1995.

4. Recently, a number of social movement scholars have issued calls for greater attention to leadership dynamics in movements; for example, see Aminzade, Goldstone, and Perry 2001; Barker et al. 2001.

5. White defines styles as "patterning in profile and sequence of sociocultural processes across some network population." White 2003, 1; see also White 1992, chap. 5. White discusses how the development of styles and institutions are both linked to struggles over values. I develop this point in relation to institutional innovation in chapter 8.

6. For a classic statement of the new institutionalist approach in organizational analysis, see Powell and DiMaggio 1991. On institutional logics, see Friedland and Alford 1991. For a discussion of institutions within cultural sociology, see Swidler 2001; also Mohr forthcoming. Recently, there has been a flurry of discussion between organizational theorists and social movement analysts, often draw-

ing on institutionalist perspectives. See, for example, McAdam and Scott 2002; Scott 1999; Fligstein 2001; Fligstein and McAdam 1995; Rao et al. 2000; Morrill, forthcoming; Armstrong 2002; Clemens and Cook 1999; Clemens 1997. See also Meyer and Scott 1983; Scott and Meyer 1991, 1994; White 1992, 2003; White and White 1965.

7. On societal sectors, see Scott and Meyer 1991.

8. These similarities become even clearer when we reduce the relevant partitioning of the sector to "the Catholic sector" or even "the "Church of the People" (i.e., as one subsector within the Catholic Church). However, in this study, when I refer to sector I am speaking at the more general level of "religious" or "student movement" or "business" sectors.

9. My discussion of "styles of communication" is closely connected to what Lichterman (1996, 1999) calls "styles of community building," referring to the communicative practices by which people "carry" their identities and purposes as they attempt to build relations with each other (see also Lichterman 2005). It also ties into Eliasoph's (1996, 1998) discussion of the types of talk that open or close opportunities for public-spirited conversation. Recently, both have elaborated the idea of styles as based on group settings (Eliasoph and Lichterman 2003); see Hart (2001) for a related discussion of styles of political engagement. I add a focus on how these processes are influenced by the positions of people and settings at the intersections of multiple institutional sectors. See also Wagner-Pacifici (1994, 2000) on hybridization versus contamination of discourse, and the ways that "organic mediators" use hybridization to break down discursive barriers and resolve relational impasses.

10. Fligstein 2001.

11. Simmel 1955.

12. Breiger 1974, 2000.

13. On the importance of overlapping memberships for social movements, see Rosenthal et al. 1985; Fernandez and McAdam 1988; Gould 1991, 1995; Meyer and Whittier 1994; Staggenborg 1998; Diani 1995, 2003; Osa 2001. On the duality of organizations and projects, see Bearman and Everett 1993; Mische and Pattison 2000.

14. There has been a lot of recent attention to organizational and/or institutional fields within the literature on both organizations and social movements (e.g., DiMaggio 1991; Fligstein 2001; Rao et al. 2000; Morrill forthcoming; Lounsbury et al., forthcoming; Klandermans 1992; Curtis and Zurcher 1973). Here I draw on Fligstein's (2001, 108) useful definition of fields as "situations where organized groups or actors gather and frame their actions vis-à-vis one another." If we take "gather" to refer to joint awareness in social space rather than physical copresence, then we can understand fields as flexible analytic categories that denote particular forms of mutual orientation among actors. See Martin (2003) for a cogent discussion of use of the field metaphor in the social sciences, as well as Mohr (forthcoming) on the need to bring an understanding of meaning into spatial metaphors such as fields.

15. For work on the long-term biographical influences on activism, see McAdam 1988; Whittier 1995. On tension between movement and nonmovement identities, see Snow et al. 1980; McAdam and Paulsen 1993.

16. On interstitial emergence, see Morrill, forthcoming; Clemens 1997; Clemens and Cook 1999; Rao et al. 2000; Armstrong 2002.

17. While several recent studies have examined how creativity is facilitated by individuals who bridge multiple network clusters (e.g., Burt 2004; Uzzi and Spiro 2004), most have not linked this analysis to changes in institutional fields. A notable exception that resonates deeply with my study is the work by Padgett and his colleagues on multiple relations in elite networks in Renaissance Florence (Padgett and Ansell 1993; Padgett 2001; Padgett and McLean 2005). For other relevant studies see DiMaggio 1992; Collins 1998; Abers and Keck 2003a.

18. These two approaches to the study of careers have sparked a debate between proponents of techniques for sequence analysis (such as optimal matching techniques; Abbott and Hrycak 1990; Abbott 1995; Abbott and Tsay 2000) and those who take a more stochastic approach to individual transition probabilities (such as event history analysis; Hannon and Tuma 1984). Abbott and Hrycak (1990) have argued that most people see their careers as extended scripts (or "cultural models") due to the highly institutionalized nature of most career paths (see also Abbott 1992). However, these careers are not necessarily static; many studies implementing these techniques have looked at how changing careers intersect with changing institutions; see Stovel et al. 1996; Blair-Loy 1999; Han and Moen 1999; Giuffre 1999; Stark and Vedres 2006.

19. These phenomena also receive attention in Merton's role theory (1968); see especially Coser 1975.

20. On the contributions of the pragmatist and phenomenological thinkers to sociological theory, see Emirbayer 1997; Emirbayer and Mische 1998; Maines et al. 1983; Joas 1985, 1993, 1996; Abbott 2001, chap. 7; Whitford 2002; Gross 2005.

21. Mead 1932, 76. Mead's core idea of "sociality" refers to the capacity of individuals to be both temporally and relationally in multiple systems at once. He argues that the human experience of temporality is based in the social character of "emergence," that is, in interrelated changes occurring throughout the multiple levels of organization within which human beings are embedded. The problematic experience of these intersecting changes leads to reflective evaluation of the past and deliberation over the future. See Emirbayer and Mische 1998.

22. Schutz 1962, 1964, 1967. For a discussion of how Brazilian youth activists elaborate projects for the future across multiple involvements, see Mische 2001.

23. Dewey 1981, 61, 69.

24. Haydu 1998.

25. There is a voluminous literature on identities and identity formation in social movements. My usage of identity is close to the one recently developed by Tilly (2002a; 2005); as well as in the recent volume by McAdam, Tarrow, and Tilly (2001), although I include a stronger focus on the projective dimension of identities. Discussion of the action-oriented and relational aspect of identities can be found in Melucci 1996; see also Melucci 1989, 1995. Other important work includes Taylor and Whittier 1992; Friedman and McAdam 1992; McAdam and Paulsen 1993; Mueller 1994; Polletta 1994, 1998; Bernstein 1997; Snow and McAdam 2000. For a recent article exploring the performative dimension of iden-

tity in movements, see Taylor et al. 2004. For good overviews, see Cerulo 1997; Polletta and Jasper 2001.

26. See Goffman 1959, 1974, 1981. Recently, a number of sociologists have built on Goffman's work to develop a more communicative understanding of culture that focuses on how discourse is constrained by specific settings of interaction. See Eliasoph 1996, 1998; Lichterman 1996; 1999; Eliasoph and Lichterman 2003; McLean 1998; Gibson 2000, 2003, 2005; Perrin 2005, 2006.

27. Paul McLean (1998, 2007) makes this argument in his analysis of patronage letters in Renaissance Florence. He refers to this keying process as "the strategic, selective representation of the agent's network of embeddedness in the course of interaction" (McLean 1998, 53).

28. For discussion of "switching" between networks and associated discursive practices, see White 1995; Mische and White 1998; Mische 2003.

29. Fligstein 2001, 12.

30. On brokerage relations, see Wolf 1956; Geertz 1960; Boissevain 1974; Marsden 1982; Gould and Fernandez 1989; Fernandez and Gould 1994; Burt 1992, 2002, 2004; DiMaggio 1992; Padgett and Ansell 1993; Adams 1996; Diani 2003.

31. McAdam, Tarrow, and Tilly 2001, 26.

32. On structural holes, see Burt 1992, 2002, 2004. For a network typology of mediation between disconnected subgroups, see Gould and Fernandez 1989; Fernandez and Gould 1994. For a seminal statement of the importance of bridging relations in flows of information and ideas, see Grannovetter's 1973 article on "The Strength of Weak Ties."

33. For a description of such multisided (or "robust") action, see Padgett and Ansell 1993, who describe the "multivocality" of the Medici's brokerage activity. In their case, robust action worked through the segmentation of networks; however, in many of the cases I study, such segmentation is not possible, creating different challenges for the multivocality of action.

34. This argument builds on Basil Bernstein's (1975) theory of elaborated and restricted codes and the contrast between cosmopolitanism and provincialism. For studies incorporating Bernsteins's approach into sociological analysis, see Ansell 1997; Swidler 2001. See also White (1992, 1993, 1994, 2003) for a discussion of hybridization in style coming from overlay of institutional systems. Recent discussions of innovation and creativity in the intersections between network clusters or structural formations can be found in Sewell 1992; Collins 1998; Lin 2002; Padgett 2001; Padgett and McLean 2006; Stark 1996; Stark and Bruzt 1998; Burt 2004; Uzzi and Spiro 2005. Abers and Keck (2003a, 2003b) develop related arguments about innovation in their work on water management in Brazil; see also Hochstetler and Keck Forthcoming.

CHAPTER 3: ACTIVIST COHORTS AND TRAJECTORIES, 1977 TO 1996

1. For example, see Arato 1981, 1985; Cohen and Arato 1992; on Brazil, see Stepan 1989. See also Ekiert 1996; Ekiert and Kubik 2001. Ekiert and Kubik describe the transformation of civil and political society in Poland as happening

simultaneously and having some minimal overlap, although they argue that these changes were largely autonomous and disconnected. While some commentators have also noted the weakness of this link in Brazil (e.g., Mainwaring 1999; Avritzer 2002), most have downplayed the important mobilizing—and I would argue, institution-building—role played by the extensive overlap between challenger movements and left-wing opposition parties as Brazil returned to democratic institutions in the 1980s.

2. Whittier 1995.

3. For classic statements regarding political opportunity structures (POS), see McAdam 1982; Kitschelt 1986; Kriesi et al. 1992; Tarrow 1994; McAdam et al. 1996. Tarrow describes several important components of POS: access to the state, shifts in ruling alignments, divisions among elites, elite allies, and the degree of repression or facilitation on the part of state actors.

4. This analysis was conducted with the essential collaboration of my research assistant, Steph Karpinski.

5. These age differences reflect the fact that the questionnaires were collected mainly among university students and in other higher-level leadership venues (i.e., in the political parties and the Catholic youth pastoral), where there were less likely to be very young initiates than in, say, a high school group or a Catholic base community, in which many of the activists in the earlier cohorts got their starts.

6. To measure rates of involvement, Steph Karpinski and I examined the slope of expansion in group and sectoral involvement over time (calculating the difference between the last and first year number of involvements and dividing it by the number of years). The earlier cohorts have a lower rate of sectoral expansion than the later cohorts, which is at least in part a function of the much longer span of years of their trajectories. Interestingly, however, the two cohorts with the highest rates of group (rather than sector) expansion are Cohorts 2 and 4, perhaps reflecting periods of heightened mobilization, for the student movement and political parties in period 2 and for the impeachment mobilization in period 4. After their initial exposure to participation, activists starting during periods 2 and 4 tended to move more quickly into increased activism, given the length of their trajectories, than the other cohorts (suggesting a possible lasting impact from the excitement of their start periods).

7. Whittier 1995. For a broader statement on the role of early formative experiences in shaping political generations, see Mannheim 1952.

8. For readability, I've only included the 9 sectors in which at least 5 percent of one cohort participated in at least one of the five periods. The sectors of labor/professional and research do not meet this threshold, since so few of my respondents began activism in those sectors.

9. The low number of activists reporting entry to activism in socialist youth groups is partly a result of data collection issues. I was not able to collect questionnaires at meetings of the PCdoB or its associated youth group, UJS, where I would have undoubtedly encountered more young people who began their activism in such groups. I did collect questionnaires from PCdoB/UJS activists and members of other socialist groups at general student movement events, and their trajectories are reflected in the data.

10. Lattices can be read from either the top down or the bottom up, given the dual nature of the associations between the two sets of elements (in this case, sectors by youth years). However, this lattice highlights sectors rather than years, and so is best read from the top down.

11. Some nodes do not have labels attached; these refer to combinations that did not actually appear in the data, but were necessary to complete the set of possible intersections among the observed combinations.

12. The lattices for Cohorts 2 through 5 are approximate lattices, constructed using the BASA (Boolean Approximation through Simulated Annealing) program designed by Pip Pattison. Approximation is necessary because of the greater number and complexity of the combinations, given the larger size of the later cohorts. The approximate lattices preserve interpretability while allowing us to see the main structural patterns appearing in the data. Occasional adjustments for approximation are given in parenthesis (preserving the observed combination, even though this is simplified in the approximation). Details on approximation procedures are given in the Appendix.

13. On the growth of NGO sector, see Landim 1991; Scherer-Warren 1993, 1995; Dagnino 1994a, 1994b, 2002, 2005; Doimo 1995; Chalmers et al. 1997; Alvarez et al. 1998; Keck and Sikkink 1998; Teixeira 2003; Hochstetler and Keck Forthcoming.

14. I also calculated the conditional probabilities of all of the other possibilities of institutional coupling. While not presented here, I draw on this broader analysis in the discussion that follows.

15. Here, partisan participation means, at the minimum, formal affiliation in a political party, although it might also include participation in party nuclei, directorates, internal factions, and youth commissions. Those who said they were "sympathizers" with a party, but not officially affiliated, are not included. I believe that this puts these probabilities on the low side, since many partisan milieus included active participants in party activities and debates who were not officially affiliated. For example, the strong overlap of Catholic, popular movement, and partisan activism in the poorer urban regions meant that there was loose transit between religious, popular, and partisan milieus, without necessarily requiring formal affiliation. In addition, law students as a group tended not to be officially affiliated because partisan affiliation would preclude their eligibility for future judicial appointments. Nonetheless, many of these "nonaffiliated" students participated actively in party life.

CHAPTER 4: PARTISAN BRIDGING IN EARLY STUDENT AND CATHOLIC ACTIVISM

1. "UNE is us, our force and our voice!" For a detailed description of the 1979 Congress of Reconstruction, see Romagnoli and Goncalves 1979; also Poerner 1995, 307–11.

2. In Portuguese, this term is *Animadores de Jovens/Adultos do Meio Popular*. This phrase is hard to translate, as it contains words specific to community- and especially church-based organizing in Latin America. An "animator" is a group leader or advisor that animates or "gives life" to meetings. The "meio popular"

refers to marginalized and underprivileged communities, either urban or rural, that have chronic problems with social services such as health, housing, education, and sanitation as well as marginal employment in industry, agriculture, or the informal economy. I will say more about the "popular" component of this below.

3. *Do Meio Popular um Canto Jovem* (Londrina, PR: Secretaria Nacional de PJMP, 1993), 39. Also, *Romaria da PJMP* (Região Nordeste II: Comissão Regional de PJMP Rural e Urbana, 1993), *História da PJ no Brasil* (Porte Alegre, RS: Instituto de Pastoral de Juventude, 1990).

4. This chapter draws on a combination of secondary and primary sources. In addition to published research (cited below), I draw on primary documents of the student movement and the Catholic youth pastoral, as well as on interviews with people who were active in student or Catholic politics in the early years of the transition.

5. On authoritarian Brazil, see: Stepan 1971, 1973, 1988, 1989; Skidmore 1988, 1989; Linz 1978; Linz and Stepan 1978, 1996; Santos 1978; Collier 1979; Lamounier 1989.

6. Many scholars of the Brazilian transition have noted the peculiar role played by the party system under the military regime, in comparison to other authoritarian countries. A Skidmore (1989) notes, the regime left the political infrastructure relatively intact, allowing the opposition to maintain a (mostly muted) presence. This infrastructure was there to build on during the liberalization process, allowing for a much more rapid reconstruction of political society than has happened in other postauthoritarian countries. In addition, as Lamounier (1989) argues, the electoral process provided an important signaling mechanism in state-society relations during the liberalization period, in part *because* of the regime-imposed two-party system, which gave local and state elections a plebiscitary character. See also Lamounier and Meneguello 1986.

7. On the emergence and transformations of the PT, see Keck 1992; Meneguello 1989; Gadotti and Pereira 1989; Bittar 1992; Novaes 1993; Harnecker 1994; Azevedo 1995; Nylen 1997, 2000; Baiocchi 2003a.

8. See, for example, Mainwaring 1989a; Novaes 1993.

9. For a detailed account of the history of the student movement, see Poerner 1995; also Mendes 1981. For accounts of the student movement in the 1960s, see Sanfelice 1986; Martins 1987, 1994; Ventura 1988; Silva 1989; Barcellos 1994; Oliveira 1994; Semeraro 1994; Fávaro 1995.

10. Romagnoli and Gonçalves 1979; Poerner 1995.

11. Many of the activists involved in Popular Action would later become important figures in Brazilian politics and academics. Prominent figures with roots in JUC and AP include Jose Serra (senator, minister and presidential candidate of the PSDB), Hebert José de Souza (Betinho, founder of IBASE and Ação Contra Fome e Pela Vida, a prominent antihunger NGO); Vinicius Caldeira Brandt (CEBRAP social science researcher), Candido Mendes (prominent social scientist); and Aldo Arantes (congressional representative from PCdoB), among others.

12. Lima and Arantes 1984.

13. In tracking the successive divisions and mergers of the Brazilian left, I draw on the book by Antonio Ozai da Silva, *História das Tendências no Brasil* (no

date). The account by Lima and Arantes (1984) of the transformation of AP into the PCdoB was also extremely helpful.

14. The split between Brazil's two communist parties originated in the broader crisis over Stalinism in the late 1950s. In 1958, the Brazilian Communist Party voted to support the changing Soviet line critical of "Stalinist errors," advocating a "unified national front" that would be "national and democratic" rather than explicitly class-based. The previous (now defeated) leadership of the party rejected this "revisionist" line, defending the Stalinist legacy. This dissident group was expelled from the party in 1962, at which point they declared themselves the Communist Party of Brazil (PCdoB), claiming to be the "true" Communist Party founded in 1922 (basing their claim on the fact that the larger party had changed its name in 1961 to the Brazilian Communist Party [PCB]). During the 1960s the PCdoB took a Maoist line in the Sino-Soviet split, which the party eventually abandoned in favor of an idealized Albanian model (finally dropped following the fall of the Soviet regimes in Eastern Europe). Both parties were active in clandestine form during the revival of the student movement in the 1970s, although tendencies linked to the PCdoB eventually gained hegemony during most of the 1980s and 90s. In the 1990s the PCB changed its name to the PPS (Popular Socialist Party), although a small dissident faction calling itself the PCB remained.

15. Romagnoli and Gonçalves 1979, 54.

16. Ibid.

17. Ibid., 61.

18. *Nossa Voz* 12, year 4, no. 4 (December 1983), 1.

19. UNE document, Resolution 12.06.80, italics added.

20. After several months of massive civic mobilizations in 1984 for *Diretas Já* (Direct Elections Now), the proposal for direct elections was defeated in congress and a backstage deal was worked out in which the centrist opposition candidate, Tancredo Neves (from the PMDB) was elected indirectly through an electoral college vote. The PT infuriated the more mainstream opposition by deciding to boycott the electoral college as illegitimate.

21. Ribeiro Neto 1985, 64–65.

22. Ibid., 71.

23. See the accounts of the Catholic left in Souza 1984; Souza Lima 1979; Sigrest 1982; Lima and Arantes 1984; Mainwaring 1986, 1989a, 1989b; Bruneau 1974, 1982; Mendes 1966.

24. For the history and development of the CEBs and the popular church, see Mainwaring 1986, 1989a, 1989b; Levine 1986, 1992; Della Cava 1989; Camargo et al. 1980; Betto 1981; Azevedo 1987, Hewitt 1991; Casanova 1994; Dawson 1999. For recent critical accounts, see Burdick 1993; Nagel 1997.

25. The CEBs were first recognized and approved by the hierarchy in 1965, then received affirmation in 1968 at the pivotal Medellín meeting of the Latin American Bishops Conference (CELAM). The Medellín conference forcefully articulated many of the tenets of what would become known as "liberation theology," including the church's preferential option for the poor, as well as the link between faith and politics and the need for structural reforms to confront political and economic oppression. Discussion of the philosophy underlying liberation theology can be found in Gutiérrez 1973; Boff and Boff 1985; Puleo 1994.

26. *Historia da PJ no Brasil* (Porto Alegre: Instituto de Pastoral de Junventude 1990), 58; *PJ e Movimentos, Caderno de Estudos da Pastoral de Juventude,* 5 (São Paulo: Centro de Capacitação Crista, 1991), 9.

27. *Historia da PJ,* 58.

28. The phrase "meios específicos" is imperfectly translated as the "specific milieus," but also carries connotations of being "in the midst of" as well as working "by means of" specific contexts or environments of social life. According to my Portuguese-English dictionary, the term *meio* can translate, variously as "middle, center, intermediate position, midst; medium, expedient, means, agent, manner, way, course, possibility; ambience, environment, element; sphere; moral or social atmospheres; way of life." This ambiguity is not trivial, as work in the *meios específicos* was supposed to be the "way" or the "path" or the "means" to achieving God's Kingdom, as well as the specific living or working environment of various groupings of youth. This made this a richly evocative and somewhat problematic phrase, the subject of much passion and argument. Debates of being "of" rather than "for" the popular milieu, especially within PJMP, highlight this tension.

29. The more radical posture of the northeastern activists was due to the greater strength of JOC (the Young Catholic Workers) in the region, where it had been protected by sympathetic bishops from the military regime as well as from the 1966 dismantling of Catholic Action by the church hierarchy. See Mainwaring 1986.

30. A careful and spirited exposition of the arguments of the northeastern faction were elaborated by Jairo Umberto Amorim in a 1986 booklet (*Pastoral de Juventude a partir das classes sociais*) that was widely debated in the youth pastoral.

31. The Paulo Freire method taught poor and marginalized people to read through communal reflection on highly charged words from their daily lives (e.g., "land" or "water" or "food"). Through reflection on praxis, according to Freire, people gained critical consciousness, personal and collective empowerment, and the capacity to intervene in social world (thereby becoming "subjects," not "objects," of history). See Freire's *The Pedagogy of the Oppressed* (1968) for the classic statement of his theory and method. In 1963–64, Freire was asked by the Goulart government to redesign the national literacy program. Many young members of Catholic Action participated in this program by means of the Movimento de Educação de Base (MEB). While Freire was exiled after the coup, his work gained international renown and deeply influenced the pastoral agents who were building the popular church in the 1970s. On popular education, see also Brandão 1980; Gadotti and Torres 1994; on Freire's work, see Gadotti 1989.

32. *Roteiros para Grupos Iniciantes* (São Paulo: Centro de Capacitação Cristã), 36 (year unlisted, probably early to mid-1980s).

33. *Pedagogia e Projeto de uma PJ Consequente* (São Paulo: Centro de Capacitação Cristã, 1982), 24.

34. *Grupo de Jovens: Metodologia e Opções.* (Porto Alegre: Instituto de Pastoral de Juventude, 1984). Quotes from 47–49.

35. *Juventude Cristã e militância política* (São Paulo: Centro de Capacitação Cristã, 1987), 46, italics in original.

36. On the limits to the politicization of the CEBs, see Mainwaring 1986, 1989a, 1989b; Doimo 1989, 1995; Burdick 1993; Nagel 1997.

37. Comissão Nacional de Assessores da Pastoral da Juventude, *Os Cristãos e a Militância Política*, rev. ed. (Petropolis: Editora Vizes, 1988), 55–56.

38. Ibid., 56.

39. Moisés Basilio Leal, e-mail interview, October 2003.

40. Ibid.

41. *Pedagogia e Projeto*, 27, caps in original.

42. *Os Cristãos e a Militância Política*, 13, italics in original.

43. Ibid., 13.

44. Ibid., 64.

45. Ibid., 28, italics in the original.

46. Ibid., 75–76; the remaining quotes in this section come from these two pages.

CHAPTER 5: CIVIC MEDIATION IN THE 1992 IMPEACHMENT MOVEMENT

1. Evelina Dagnino (2002, 2004, 2005) has argued that the emergence of the discourse of citizenship in the postauthoritarian period has been marked by a process of "perverse confluence" of two opposing political projects, both of which draw on the language of citizenship, participation, and civil society. The first, nourished in movements for democratization as well as in the popular movements of the 1980s and 1990s, has sought to broaden popular participation and joint action between civil society and the state to respond to problems of exclusion and social inequality. The second project, developed by proponents of the "Third Sector" and linked to dominant business interests, advocates a minimal state and a privatized moral conception of citizen responsibility. On the development of the Third Sector and "business citizenship," see Salamon 1997; Paoli 2002. See also Mische 1996.

2. These analyses attribute the impeachment not to popular mobilization, but rather to Collor's antagonistic relationship with the country's traditional elites, as a result of "neopopulist" politics that brought him to power in 1989. See Colovsky 2002; Skidmore 1999; Avritzer 1999; Rosenn and Downes 1999; Weyland 1993.

3. On the role of the media in Collor's rise and fall, see Bucci 1993; Ribeiro 2000.

4. Unless otherwise noted, all of the quotes from the activists in this chapter are from interviews that I carried out in São Paulo in June and July of 1997.

5. See Burt 1992; Marsden 1982.

6. Even when scholars have acknowledged group identity as playing a key role in mediation, they have focused on *disjoint subgroups*, seldom looking at how mediation works in cases in which subgroups overlap. For example, Gould and Fernandez (1989; see also Fernandez and Gould 1994) distinguish between different types of brokerage roles, as defined by membership in disjoint subgroups (i.e., representatives, gatekeepers, coordinators, liaisons, and itinerant brokers). While

they provide a compelling way to incorporate group identity into structural analysis, their model of brokerage is still based primarily on direct intermediation of two-step ties. They show how affiliations determine types of brokerage, but do not analyze how opportunities for mediation may be structured by sets of affiliations themselves. Moreover, their model imposes the condition that subgroup memberships be nonoverlapping, thereby limiting its application to the Brazilian context.

7. For an expanded discussion of these discursive mechanisms, see Mische 2003.

8. Padgett and Ansell 1993, 1263.

9. What actually happened in the chaotic election is far from clear. The PT says that the PCdoB tried to manipulate the voting process and stack the ballot boxes, while the PCdoB says that the PT tried to disrupt an election that they were clearly going to lose. There were mutual accusations of corruption, burning of ballot boxes, and physical scuffles, often happening in far flung corners of the country. One former activist from that period told me that this experience "discredited a whole generation of student leaders."

10. I was not able to interview all of the leaders of the period, but I did locate a group of important activists who I think are representative of the relational context of that period. To find these activists, I used a targeted snowball technique, looking for youth activists who were recommended by other activists and informants as being highly involved in the impeachment mobilizations, with an attempt to include representatives from all of the different political forces involved in the student movement. While I collected more than twenty questionnaires in all, this analysis is based on the fourteen respondents who were most actively involved at the time of the impeachment.

11. Data on group representation was taken from newspaper accounts and organizational documents, supplemented by activist interviews. Group representation did not mean simply that a member of the group was present, but that there was some formally recognized public presence of the organization at the event, such as cosigning a document and/or having a leader appear on the platform or give a speech *in the name of* that organization.

12. The lattices are known as "multicontext" lattices (Wille 1996b), constructed by stacking two two-mode arrays (in this case, individuals by events and groups by events) and carrying out the lattice operations on the combined matrix. The full multicontext lattices can be seen in my dissertation (Mische 1998). I present a schematized version here so as not to slow down the qualitative narrative.

13. This is based on an approximate lattice constructed using the HICLAS approximation program, which enabled me to find the main clusters of actors and events, even though there may be some minor error in the clusters (for example, Eduardo, Vincente, César, Nelson, and Martín did not all attend all of the student and labor events clustered together, but they attended enough of them together to be considered structurally equivalent). For an explanation of the lattice and HICLAS procedures, see the Methodological Appendix.

14. The CA XI had been an important center for the articulation of the republican movement at the turn of the century as well as successive movements in defense of democracy. Ten presidents of Brazil and fifty-three state governors were former

directors of the CA XI, as well as scores of important jurists. In 1990, the leadership of CA XI had been wrested from the PT by youth linked to the PSDB.

15. Many Brazilian law students refrained from formal affiliation with political parties, even though they were heavily involved in the youth politics of those parties. Some students told me that this was because partisan affiliation could preclude future judicial appointments.

16. Eugênio recalls that because of his link to the PSDB, he ended up representing UNE in an ad hoc manner at a number of similar events that no other UNE leaders attended, including the Campaign for More Salary and Less Taxes: "It was like this in a lot of cases, they wouldn't even let UNE know. Often they would call me, I would go as UNE. I would end up using the credential of UNE in order to expand the range of organizations present at the movement."

17. Parallel debates were going on within the labor movement, which was split among a similar array of partisan factions as the student movement. For an interesting (if partisan) discussion, see Giannotti 1992.

18. Many details of the Movement Ethics were gathered in the dissertation of Carmen Priscila Bocchi (1996). I draw on her account as well as newspapers of the period.

19. The coordinators of the Movement for Ethics in Politics included the OAB (Bar Association), PNBE (National Thought of Business Bases, a civic-minded business group), CUT and CGT (the left and center labor centrals), ABJD (Brazilian Association of Democratic Jurists), IBASE (Brazilian Institute for Social and Economic Analysis); SBPC (Brazilian Society for Progress in Science), the Commission of Justice and Peace (linked to the National Conference of Brazilian Bishops), and the Medical and Engineering Federations.

20. *Folha de São Paulo*, August 12, 1992.

21. In Barreto's analysis, the lack of discussion that followed the impeachment had longer-range, damaging effects on the youth of the PT. New recruits were sucked into the "network of the parties and the tendencies," going directly into the campaign and then into the internal dispute, and thus did not engage the criticisms of (and alternatives for) student politics that were being discussed in the PT prior to the impeachment. This lack of reflection about "the intensive process in which they had participated," led the party to take little advantage of the energy and interest of youth after the impeachment.

22. I received five or six different explanations as to where the painting of faces had come from. Luiz told me it originated in the festive face-painting at a PT campaign rally; in contrast, Eugênio said it started with an upper-middle-class girl from an elite private school. Vincente pointed to two youth with painted paces who appeared in a newspaper picture, one from UJS and the other from the PT, while an activist from the right-wing PDS attributed it to girls from his own party, who pulled out their lipstick and started it off. Renato observed that the gesture of painting faces did not begin with the impeachment, but rather went back earlier to soccer fans. He remembered a World Cup in which Danish fans had appeared with their faces painted; this practice had been picked up by the Brazilians fans,

who felt at home with the carnavalesque gesture. "It was something in the air," Renato said, and thus could be easily picked up by the youth at the rallies.

23. *Folha de São Paulo*, August 32, 1992, italics added.

24. The president of right-wing labor central, Forca Sindical, opted to hold a separate rally, objecting to the location of the unified demonstration in the public square associated with the rallies of the PT. He also bristled when the others rejected the proposal to call for the continuation of Collor's "modernizing reforms." The conservative labor unions held their Rally Against Corruption (and for the reforms) on September 11 (25), with lukewarm business support.

25. *Folha de São Paulo*, September 30, 1992.

Chapter 6 : Modes of Communication in Institutionalized Publics

1. For example, the *Folha de São Paulo* launched a special section called "Folhateen"; the *Estado de São Paulo* launched *Cola*; the *Jornal do Brasil* had "Fanzine" and *O Globo* had "Radical Chic."

2. See, for example, Santos 1979; Lamounier et al. 1981; Weffort 1981; Da Matta 1992; Scherer-Warren 1993, 1995; Benevides 1994; Dagnino 1994a, 1994b, 2002, 2004; Silva 1994; Spink 1994; Telles 1994, 2001; Krischke 1995; Doimo 1995; Viola et al. 1995; Alvarez et al. 1998. For descriptions of the growth of the NGO sector, see Landim 1991; Scherer-Warren 1993, 1995; Keck and Sikkink 1998; Teixeira 2003.

3. *Cara pintada* means "painted face," referring to the seemingly spontaneous practice during the impeachment mobilizations of young people painting their faces the colors of the Brazilian flag. See chapter 5 for more discussion of this phenomenon.

4. Alexander and Smith 1992. See also Alexander 1990, 1992, 1998.

5. Goffman 1959, 1974.

6. Eliasoph and Lichterman 2003, 737. For another relevant discussion of styles linked to institutional innovation, see White 1992, 1994, 2003 (I discuss White's understanding of styles in chapter 2).

7. While the writings of these theorists are too numerous to cover here, the major works that are relevant for this discussion include Habermas 1984, 1987, 1989; Gramsci 1971; Dewey 1987, 1991; Machiavelli 1950.

8. On identity salience in social movements, see McAdam and Paulsen 1993; Stryker 1968, 2000.

9. See Freire 1968. In 1988 I took a class with Freire at the Catholic University of São Paulo, in which he commented that his work was "standing on the back of Dewey."

10. Toward the end of my fieldwork, I began trying out a version of this typology on some of the student leaders, describing these modes as the different "hats" of the student movement. Many were quite intrigued by the typology and could identify themselves as well as their peers (both friends and enemies) as oriented to one mode over another. Interestingly, however, one PCdoB leader strenuously

objected to what he (mis)understood as my pejorative treatment of Machiavelli; "It's all there, in Machiavelli!" he declared, unwilling to see a separation between a focus on tactic and strategy and the pursuit of an ideological project. Perhaps because PCdoB leaders were on the defensive regarding their leadership of UNE, he was also implicitly rejecting the critique of Machiavelli as being unethical or antidemocratic. Clearly some understanding of the civic "virtue" of decisive, tactical action in pursuit of a project of command was part of this activist's self-understanding.

11. The church and its various pastorals had an elaborately developed system of levels of coordination that permeated the parlance of its leaders: "area" (extended neighborhoods) "sector" (more extended urban subregions) "regional" (national subregions—North, Northeast, South, Southeast, West) and "national" (all of Brazil). The group I focused on was the "Regional Coordination" of PJMP, which in practice meant the greater São Paulo area.

12. Note that "Past" and "Start period" are overlapping categories, with the Start period affiliations included in those of the Past. Both designations are useful, since looking at the complete set of past participations indicates the array of cultural and organizational resources that might be in the activists' repertoire, while looking at the Start period lets us see which sectors might have been especially strong influences, serving as the gateway to future participation. It also lets us see what kinds of participation were initiated later in activists' careers, giving an indication of trajectory. See chapter 3 for a discussion of the effects of institutional entries to activism.

13. While the term *popular movement* was sometimes used to refer specifically to urban movements for improvement in community services (e.g., housing, health, education, sanitation, transportation, etc.), the category was somewhat flexible and could also be expanded to encompass other urban and rural movements, including labor movements, antidiscrimination movements (particularly those focusing on gender or racial exclusion, as well as black culture), high school groups (particularly in poorly equipped public schools of the periphery), and NGOs that were often supportive of community-based movements. Using this broader designation, nearly three-quarters (rather than half) of the Catholic youth were involved in some kind of popular movement activism in 1995.

14. After the impeachment, UNE gained the right to issue identification cards to students that ensured half-price admission at movies, concerts, and other cultural events. This ensured a steady source of funding, although it was also a significant bone of contention with the opposition, which accused UNE's leadership of monopolization and corruption.

15. During 1995–96, PJMP activists also organized several encounters in São Paulo that were specifically dedicated to reflecting on the link between their religious faith and the "intermediate organizations." I attended two such meetings, one focusing on popular movements while the other focused on political parties (other meetings addressed the student and labor movements). These encounters featured local leaders from popular movements and the PT. In the meeting on political parties, young people wrestled with the changes in the PT since the party

began winning elections in the 1980s, including issues related to ethics, internal dispute, and the fragmented understanding of socialism in a more "institutionalized" party.

CHAPTER 7: DEFENSIVE PUBLICS IN UNIVERSITY SETTINGS

1. For a discussion of the emergence of a more privatized, entrepreneurial notions of citizenship with the entry of business and "Third Sector" actors, see Dagnino 2004, 2005.

2. For a discussion of how discursive fields structure actions, see Spillman 1995, 2002. See also Alexander 1988, 2003.

3. Romagnoli and Gonçalves 1979; M. Santos 1988.

4. The CAs, or "Academic Centers," were the most basic institutional unit of Brazilian student politics. They took the form of small, autonomous student organizations based in university departments (or in some cases, clusters of departments). The military regime tried to curtail their autonomy by abolishing the CAs and replacing them with DAs ("Aademic Directorates") that were more closely regulated by the university administrations. During the return of student militancy of the late 1970s, most changed their names back to CAs; to not do so was usually a sign of either conservative sympathies or strong university control. The CAs served as spaces for sociability and integration, as well as, at times, for political organizing in both the general and course-based student movement.

5. Balance theory asserts that there is intrinsic pressure for balance in triadic relationships, with balance defined as a positive product of the valence of relations. The original tenets of psychological balance theory were developed by Heider (1946) and later formalized by Harary (1953, 1955) and Cartright and Harary (1956, 1979). The ideas received further evaluation and testing from (among others) Davis (1970), Davis and Leinhardt (1972); Johnsen (1985). For an application to social movement theory, see Kim and Bearman 1997. Here I adapt the principles of balance to alliances without the psychological assumptions of early formulations. When applied to alliance structures, balance theory can help us to locate advantageous or disadvantageous positions in a field of relations, as well as potentially unstable configurations. I extrapolate from this to cultural theory by arguing that certain relational configurations make different kinds of political communication more or less possible.

6. Unlike at most other universities, most student organizations at Mackensie had not changed their names from DA to CA after the end of the dictatorship, a further signal of the conservative leanings of the school. See note 4 in this chapter, above.

7. Cristina was introduced in chapter 5 during the discussion of the 1992 impeachment movement, when she was an activist only in the Catholic youth pastoral. By the mid-1990s she was highly involved in several other kinds of activism, including political party, student movement, and course-based organizations.

8. See Mansbridge 1983, 1986; Gutmann 2003; Gutmann and Thompson 1996; Young 1990, 2000. For good edited collections on deliberative democracy

and democratic theory, see Marcus and Hanson 1993; Benhabib 1996; Bohman and Rehg 1997; Cohen and Rogers 1998; Elster 1998; Macedo 1999.

9. In network analysis, structurally equivalent actors are linked by shared ties to third parties rather than direct relations, allowing attention to network position (or ties between "blocks") rather than simple connectivity. These positions may then become the basis for categorical ties and identity formation. See Lorrain and White 1971; White et al 1976; Breiger et al 1975. For an application to identity formation in social movements, see Gould 1995.

10. On different cultural styles in settled and unsettled times, see Swidler 1986.

CHAPTER 8: CHALLENGER PUBLICS AND STYLISTIC INNOVATION

1. White 1994, 2003.

2. A number of recent scholars have joined White in noting that institutional creativity is often born at the intersections (or in the "interstices") of existing institutions. For example, see Sewell 1992; Clemens 1997; Collins 1998; Lin 2002; Padgett 2001; Padgett and McLean 2006; Armstrong 2002; Burt 2004; Uzzi and Spiro 2005.

3. See Bernstein 1975; Ansell 1997.

4. E.g., Cohen 1997; Gutmann and Thompson 1996.

5. On the difficulties of consensus politics, see Mansbridge 1983; Polletta 2002a.

6. I used a cutoff point of a maximum of two sectoral involvements to differentiate focused and entrenched leaders from bridging leaders and explorers, and a maximum of two involvements in only one of their sectors to differentiate focused activists and explorers from bridging and entrenched leaders. This means that bridging leaders and entrepreneurs belonged *to at least three sectors simultaneously*, although their reported number of sectoral involvements reached as high as eight. Bridging and entrenched leaders had *three or more involvements in at least one of their sectors* (possibly more), *or* two or more involvements in at least two sectors. For this analysis, I counted partisan and socialist youth involvements as one sector, since socialist groups were often equivalent to partisan factions in student politics (e.g., I counted affiliation in the PCdoB/UJS, or in the PT/Juventude Revolução, or in the PMDB/MR-8 as two involvements in the partisan sector rather than involvement in two sectors).

7. Unfortunately, I was not able to distribute questionnaires at meetings of the PCdoB or its associated youth group, UJS, although I did attend local and national UJS meetings. However, many PCdoB activists were among those who filled out questionnaires at meetings of UNE and the CONEG. Among PCdoB activists, I would expect a similar pattern, with a somewhat higher tendency toward entrenched rather than bridging leaders than in the PT due to a tendency to concentrate involvements in the student movement and political party.

8. Each of the Course Executive holds a yearly national encounter, usually in July or August, which can attract up to several thousand students in each professional area from around the country. This is different from the National Forum of Course Executive, in which leaders from many different Course Executives

gathered in different cities to "exchange ideas" and "elaborate projects" cutting across professional areas. In addition to the Forum, I collected questionnaires at the annual encounters of law, communication, economics, and administration students in July–August 1996.

9. While I attended meetings of both FEJESP and AIESEC, and interviewed leaders in both, the analysis of this chapter focuses on the Junior Enterprises, which constituted a broader movement at the time of my study. AIESEC is a very interesting international student-run organization that engages students from economics and administration programs (often in elite business schools such as the Fundação Getúlio Vargas in São Paulo) in considering the social responsibility of business while participating in intensive professionalization, leadership training, and networking activities. Unlike FEJESP, AIESEC activists tend to focus on building ties to large industries rather than small businesses. At the same time, they engage in "social" projects such as education and slum rehabilitation, often by way of business-NGO partnerships. As figure 8.2b shows, activists in the two business-oriented groups show similarities in profile: they were both dominated by focused activists, primarily engaged in the business sector.

10. *1o. SENUN Boletim* 01, September 4, 1993, 1.

11. *Nós, Os Negros* (Subsidio para o 1o SENUN), 1992, emphasis in original.

12. A stringed percussion instrument of African origins used in the dancelike martial art of *capoeira*.

13. On racial identities in Brazil, see Marx 1998; Telles 2004.

14. After I asked to attend meeting, Marcos generously agreed to conduct a consultation on my behalf with his fellow CONUN members. He told me that they didn't have any objection to my participating, as long as I just stayed in the role as listener, without the "right to voice," except for a short presentation of my research (the only time during my fieldwork where I was explicitly given this directive). I later found out that there was considerable resistance to my participation, and that Marcos had thrown considerable friendship weight to back me up. As one participant told me, it also helped that my article on youth politics had recently appeared in the PT journal.

15. "1o SENUN—a Universidade que o povo quer," by Ana Cláudia Lemos Pacheco, *Jornal do MNU*, August–October 1993, 3.

16. Within the universities, the CAs (Academic Centers) in each university department (or "course") served as the "base" for the Course Executives, through which regional and national course-based organizations could communicate with students and recruit them for the national encounters. The CAs were thus in the somewhat ambiguous position of being the base for both the general student movement (i.e., electing delegates for the Congress of UNE) and the specialized or "course-based" movement. In this study I have classified them as part of the "general" student movement, since they were primarily described in that way by student activists.

17. Several of these subsecretariats—notably, those in communication, social work, and eventually administration—changed their names after 1991 to reflect their autonomy. For example SECUNE—the secretariat of communication of UNE—became ENECOS: the National Executive of Students in Social Communication.

18. Alarmed by the clear oppositional slant of the UNE-sponsored seminar, the PCdoB leadership tried to unilaterally cancel the seminar "for lack of ethics." The opposition scrambled to hold the event anyway, and what became known as the "phantom seminar" was attended by three hundred students and ten Course Executives. In an oft-retold incident, the PCdoB sent one of UNE's directors to the meeting, where he declared that "this seminar doesn't exist." He was met with hostility and derision by the gathered students, who were quite sure that they did indeed exist. This incident confirmed to many in the Course Executives that the PCdoB was authoritarian, overly centralized, and hostile to the course-based movement, while confirming to the PCdoB that the course-based movement was a partisan hotbed of the opposition. At least one PT activist I talked to (a former leader of the Communications Executive) lamented that the seminar had turned into a rally for MUDE, arguing that it reduced the reformist impulses of the movement to narrow partisan politicking: "We weren't disputing hegemony in any damn way."

19. This bridging effort backfired several months later when Jaime was publicly denounced by the PCdoB leadership at the CONEG for reputedly proposing a parallel student organization. This was something he told me that he had in fact always *opposed* among the Course Executives, defending instead that the course-based movement build closer ties (if still organizational autonomy) in relation to UNE.

20. The elaboration of proposals was more possible *within* the executives themselves, since they shared long-term disciplinary identities and could focus on reforms within their professional areas. At some of these meetings, course-based activists used a methodology known as "Strategic Institutional Planning" (or sometimes, "Strategic Situational Planning"), featuring focused reflection on problematic areas, diagnosis of complex causation for these problems, and practical suggestions on solutions. In this way, the executives used institutionalized techniques for reflective problem solving to elaborate projects of reform—projects in which the students were quite clear that they were disputing hegemony in society. Interestingly, many of the more traditional leftist student leaders hated this methodology, which they saw as diluting the ideological force of student projects.

21. During the 1990s, the language of citizenship and civic responsibility was increasingly adopted by modernizing sectors of the business community, sometimes in opposition to more entrenched business interests. See Paoli 2002; Dagnino 2004, 2005.

22. Franco de Matos, "Empresa Júnior: o conceito, o funcionamento, a história, as tendencies do movimento," draft manuscript, 1995. This manuscript has since come out as a book (1997).

23. This shift away from more a philosophical approach is interesting in the light of the finding in chapter 3 that early risers in the Junior Enterprises had more partisan involvement than those that followed, perhaps giving them a more elaborative orientation. There was also a tendency for the (few) explorers to come from the earlier cohorts; these cross-sectoral involvements may also have contributed to early expansiveness in ideas.

24. I estimated that 20–30 percent of the participants were women, somewhat lower than at CONUN and the Forum. About 40 percent of both the CONUN and Forum respondents were women, in comparison to only 22 percent of those of FEJESP.

CHAPTER 9: PARTISAN DRAMATURGY AND THE BREAKDOWN OF PUBLICS

1. On coalitions and political opportunities, see Staggenborg 1986; Tarrow 1994; Rochon and Meyer 1997; Meyer 2002. For a recent collection of essays on coalitions that explores issues of brokerage and leadership that I have discussed here, see Bandy and Smith 2004; see also Tarrow 2005.

2. See Eliasoph 1996, 1998.

3. See Fligstein 2001.

4. The tendency *Democracia Radical* was formerly a small Marxist-Leninist party that split from the PCdoB in the 1980s, taking residence in the PT. By the 1990s it had passed through several internal transformations, influenced by developments in Eurocommunism, in which it adopted a progressively more civic and democratic discourse. By the late 1990s the tendency was considered by the more traditional left-wing groups of the PT as the "right wing" of the party, a designation that the activists themselves resisted.

5. The PSTU had, until 1992, been an internal tendency within the PT, called *Convergência Socialista* (Socialist Convergence). It was expelled from the PT in 1992 for using the PT as a "tactical party" rather than a "strategic party," that is, with "instrumentalizing" the PT for it own (revolutionary) purposes rather than working to build the PT for its own sake.

6. Without exception, all of the other parties present considered themselves in opposition to the Cardoso government, approving a consensual resolution stating UNE's official oppositional stance. Most of the other forces were adamantly against allying with the PSDB. Nevertheless, a PSDB activist ended up entering the directorate through the back door, as part of an under-the-table alliance with the PCdoB.

7. My perspective on the congress was shaped by my particular position near the close of several years of research. I had relatively good relations with most top-level student leaders and free transit between public meetings and plenaries of the various forces, although I had more access to the backstage meetings of some groups than of others. In some ways I had a broader view of the congress than many participants, since I could dash between meetings of the competing forces and catch their different perspectives on unfolding events. In other ways, I had a shallower view, in that I heard of many essential intra- or interforce negotiations by second or third-hand report. In that sense, my experience was similar to that of many mid-level leaders, scrambling for reports on fast-moving, high-level negotiations that were for the most part outside their reach (with the difference that I could ask most top leaders directly what was going on, rather than waiting for reports down the hierarchy).

8. These smaller groups included the *Causa Operária, Aliança Revolucionáia Nacional*, and a few others whose names I didn't catch.

9. According to UNE's system of proportional representation, each slate launched at the congress needed to earn 5 percent of the votes to be included in the directorship (composed of about forty students), and 10 percent for a spot in the executive committee (composed of eleven top-level leaders). Exclusion from the executive meant de facto exclusion from day-to-day decision making in the organization.

10. This had been a historical dispute in the student movement since the reconstruction of UNE in 1979, the first and last time that direct elections had been held effectively. An attempt at direct elections ended disastrously with accusations of fraud in 1986 (see chapter 5). The proposal for direct elections was revived as the centerpiece of the PT-led MUDE coalition in 1993, although it was defeated by the PCdoB (see chapter 8). The controversy was whether this method would be more democratic (involving more students in directly electing their leaders) or less (since the elections would be prone to manipulation by forces with more financial resources).

11. The origins and the substance of the proposal for regional congress were highly ambiguous and contested. Both the PCdoB and PeT leaders made a big point of saying that the communists were adopting a historic proposal of the PT, elaborated in the landmark 1991 proposal of the PT for the democratization and structural reform of UNE. This proposal was revived in the thesis of PeT, where it was billed as a means of "amplifying the participation of students in the decision-making spaces of UNE." However, NVA leaders insisted to me that the 1997 proposal was *not* the same as the earlier proposal of the PT. When I checked the original 1991 document, I found that while the PT had indeed proposed regional congresses, the text clearly states that "the delegates for the National Congress of UNE should continue to be elected directly at the base." It is possible that the PCdoB was not aware of this discrepancy; its leaders vigorously insisted that they had indeed adopted the historic proposal of the PT. Oddly, PeT itself seems to have spent very little time discussing the proposal and did not seem to consider it to be especially controversial or worthy of note. Either the leaders of the PCdoB and PeT pulled a sleight of hand—passing off the newer funnel proposal as identical to the older one, in the interest of pushing it through—or else there was genuine confusion within those forces about the two proposals.

12. Celso's faction of the PDT had been in several scuffles over the past few days with Ricardo's faction (*Constructing the Future*). Early on, I encountered Ricardo trying to convince a tearful delegate that she needed to stay in the group, so as not to leave the party to the "bandits." The next day, I found a disconsolate Ricardo sitting in the bleachers; he told me that his group had been attacked in the restaurant by Celso's group, which had stolen and destroyed their theses. While idealistically social democratic in its ideas, the PDT had a reputation as an old-style populist *caudillo* (chieftain or party boss) party, centered on personal loyalty to leaders, and this personal leadership dispute appeared to reflect this pattern.

13. Brazilians use the term *queimação*—"burning"—to refer to the public discrediting or character assassination of a leadership figure.

CHAPTER 10: CONCLUSION: PARTIES AND PUBLICS

1. *The 9/11 Commission Report: Final Report of the National Commission on Terrorist Attacks Upon the United States* (1994).
2. *New York Times*, July 30, 2004.
3. Michael Schudson (1998) makes this argument in his analysis of historical changes in American understandings of citizenship. He argues that currently the

privatized notion of the "informed citizen" coexists with the notion of the "rights-bearing citizen," which may be an alternative (nonpartisan) pathway to collective action, in addition to fostering individual legal action. For another account of the shift from political party–based mobilization to "interest group" politics in the Progressive Era, see Clemens 1997.

4. The term *groupthink* was used in the 2004 Senate Intelligence Committee's *Report on the U.S. Intelligence Community's Prewar Intelligence Assessments on Iraq*. The report drew on the work on Irving Janis (1972), who argued that "groupthink"—which involves uncritical conformity to prevailing viewpoints—is likely to occur in large organizations, committees, and other cohesive subgroups that are sheltered from outside sources of information and argument.

5. Mainwaring 1999.

6. Avrtizer 2002.

7. On bridging and bonding in civic networks, see Putnam 2000.

8. Dagnino 2005, 15. See also Dagnino 2002, 2004.

9. On PT administrations, see Jacobi 1995; Baiocchi 2003a; on participatory budgets, see Abers 2000; Baiocchi 2003b, 2005; on other sorts of deliberative councils in Brazil, see Abers and Keck 2003a, 2003b, forthcoming. On participatory governance more generally, see Wright and Fung 2003.

10. See Collins 2004 on how the "emotional energy" generated by interaction rituals is carried between social encounters.

11. Voss 1996.

12. Mansbridge 1983.

13. This is a broad-stroke caricature; the best work in both "camps" wrestles productively with challenges posed by the other. For example, democratic theorists in the rational choice tradition consider how discussion and argument about the public good do (or don't) lead to better decision making, by expanding information flows, overcoming bounded rationality, and constraining the expression of individual self-interest. See the Elster edited volume (1998) as well as Elster 1997. Likewise, those in the normative tradition wrestle with how consensus-oriented forms of deliberation are constrained by particularistic concerns, such as moral disagreement, cultural identities, and economic and social exclusion. See Gutmann and Thompson 1996, as well as the essays in response to their book (Macedo 1999). On identity and difference in democracy, see also Benhabib 1996; Bohman and Rehg 1997; Young 1990, 2000; Gutmann 2003.

14. For example, see the essays by Walzer, Mansbridge, Young, Simon, and others in Macedo 1999; see also Young 1997.

15. The seminal statements on collective action frames and frame alignment processes can be found in Snow et al. 1986; Snow and Benford 1988, 1992; Gamson 1992. For recent critiques of the framing literature, see Steinberg 1998, 1999a, 1999b; Goodwin and Jasper, 1999; Benford 1997; Polletta 1997, 1999. For a recent study using the framing approach to examine discursive strategies in a complex social movement field, see Ferree et al. 2002.

16. See Cohen and Arato 1992; Gutmann and Thompson 1996; Elster 1997; Cohen 1997.

References

Abbott, Andrew. 1988. *The System of Professions*. Chicago: University of Chicago Press.

———. 1992. "From Causes to Events: Notes on Narrative Positivism." *Sociological Methods and Research* 20:428–55.

———. 1995. "Sequence Analysis: New Methods for Old Ideas." *Annual Review of Sociology* 21:93–113.

———. 2001. *Time Matters: On Theory and Method*. Chicago: University of Chicago Press.

Abbott, Andrew, and Alexandra Hrycak. 1990. "Measuring Resemblance in Sequence Data: An Optimal Matching Analysis of Musicians' Careers." *American Journal of Sociology* 96:144–85.

Abbott, Andrew, and Angela Tsay. 2000. "Sequence Analysis and Optimal Matching Methods in Sociology." *Sociological Methods and Research* 29:3–33.

Abers, Rebecca. 2000. *Inventing Local Democracy: Grassroots Politics in Brazil*. Boulder, CO: Lynne Rienner.

Abers, Rebecca, and Margaret Keck. 2003a. "Networks, Relations, and Practices: Reflections on Watershed Management Organization in Brazil." Paper presented at the XXIV International Congress of the Latin American Studies Association, Dallas, Texas, March 27–29.

———. 2003b. "Mobilizing the State: The Erratic Partner in Brazil's Participatory Water Policy." Paper presented to the American Political Science Association, Philadelphia, PA, August 31–Sept. 3.

———. Forthcoming. "Muddy Waters: The Political Construction of Deliberative Water Basin Governance in Brazil." *International Journal of Urban and Regional Research*.

Abramo, Bia, ed. 1997. *Um Trabalhador da Notícia: Textos de Perseu Abramo*. São Paulo: Fundação Perseu Abramo.

Abramo, Helena Wendel. 1992. "Grupos Juvenis dos Anos 80 em São Paulo: Um Estilo de Atuação Social." Master's thesis, Universidade de São Paulo.

———. 1994. *Cenas Juvenis: Punks e Darks no Espectáculo Urbano*. São Paulo: Editora Página Aberta.

Adams, Julia. 1996. "Principals and Agents, Colonialists and Company Men: The Decay of Colonial Control in the Dutch East Indies." *American Sociological Review* 61:12–28.

Alexander, Jeffrey C. 1988. *Action and Its Environments*. New York: Columbia University Press.

———. 1990. "Bringing Democracy Back In: Universalistic Solidarity and the Civil Sphere." Pp. 157–76 in *Intellectuals and Politics: Social Theory beyond the Academy*, edited by Charles Lemert. Newbury Park, CA: Sage.

Alexander, Jeffrey C. 1992. "Citizen and Enemy as Symbolic Classification: On the Polarizing Discourse of Civil Society." Pp. 289–308 in *Cultivating Differences: Symbolic Boundaries and the Making of Inequality*, edited by Michèle Lamont and Marcel Fournier. Chicago: University of Chicago Press.

———, ed. 1998. *Real Civil Societies: Dilemmas of Institutionalization*. London: Sage.

———. 2003. *The Meanings of Social Life: A Cultural Sociology*. New York: Oxford University Press.

Alexander, Jeffrey, and Phillip Smith. 1992. "The Discourse of American Civil Society: A New Proposal for Cultural Studies." *Theory and Society* 22:151–207.

Alvarez, Sonia E., Evelina Dagnino, and Arturo Escobar. 1998. *Culture of Politics, Politics of Cultures: Revisioning Latin American Social Movements*. Boulder, CO: Westview Press.

Aminzade, Ronald, Jack Goldstone, Doug McAdam, Elizabeth Perry, William H. Sewell Jr., Sidney Tarrow, and Charles Tilly, eds. 2001. *Silence and Voice in the Study of Contentious Politics*. Cambridge: Cambridge University Press.

Aminzade, Ronald, Jack Goldstone, and Elizabeth J. Perry. 2001. "Leadership Dynamics and Dynamics of Contention." Pp. 126–54 in *Silence and Voice in the Study of Contentious Politics*, edited by Ronald Aminzade, Jack Goldstone, Doug McAdam, Elizabeth Perry, William H. Sewell Jr., Sidney Tarrow, and Charles Tilly. 2001. Cambridge: Cambridge University Press.

Amorim, Jairo Humberto. 1986. *Pastoral de Juventude a partir das classes sociais*. São Paulo: Edições Paulinas.

Ansell, Christopher K. 1997. "Symbolic Networks: The Realignment of the French Working Class, 1887–1894." *American Journal of Sociology* 103: 359–90.

Arato, Andrew. 1981. "Civil Society against the State: Poland 1980–81." *Telos* 47:23–47.

———. 1985. "Some Perspectives on Democratization in East Central Europe." *Journal of International Affairs* 38:321–35.

Armstrong, Elizabeth A. 2002. "Crisis, Collective Creativity, and the Generation of New Organizational Forms: The Transformation of Lesbian/Gay Organizations in San Francisco." Pp. 361–95 in *Research in the Sociology of Organization* (vol. 19), edited by Michael Lounsbury and Marc Ventresca. Oxford, UK: Elsevier Science.

Avritzer, Leonardo. 1999. "The Conflict between Civil and Political Society in Post-Authoritarian Brazil: An Analysis of the Impeachment of Fernando Collor de Melo." Pp. 119–40 in *Corruption and Political Reform in Brazil: The Impact of Collor's Impeachment*, edited by Keith S. Rosenn and Richard Downes. Miami: North-South Center Press.

———. 2002. *Democracy and the Public Sphere in Latin America*. Princeton, NJ: Princeton University Press.

Azevedo, Clovis de Bueno. 1995. *A Estrela Partido ao Medo: Ambiguidades do Pensamento Petista*. São Paulo: Entrelinhas.

Azevedo, Marcelo. 1987. *Basic Ecclesial Communities in Brazil*. Washington, DC: Georgetown University Press.

Baiocchi, Gianpaolo. 2003a. *Radicals in Power: The Workers' Party (PT) and Experiments in Urban Democracy in Brazil.* London: Zed Books.

———. 2003b. "Emergent Public Spheres: Talking Politics in Participatory Governance." *American Sociological Review* 68:52–75.

———. 2005. *Militants and Citizens: The Politics of Participatory Democracy in Porto Alegre.* Palo Alto, CA: Stanford University Press.

Bandy, Joe, and Jackie Smith, eds. 2004. *Coalitions across Borders: Negotiating Difference and Unity in Transnational Coalitions against Neoliberalism.* Boulder, CO: Rowman and Littlefield.

Barbut, Marc, and Bernard Monjardet. 1970. *Ordre et Classification.* Paris: Hachette Université.

Barcellos, Jalusa. 1994. *CPC da UNE: Uma Historia de Paixão e Consciência.* Rio de Janeiro: Nova Fronteira.

Barker, Colin, Alan Johnson, and Michael Lavalette. 2001. *Leadership and Social Movements.* Manchester, UK: Manchester University Press.

Bearman, Peter S., and Kevin D. Everett. 1993. "The Structure of Social Protest: 1961–1983." *Social Networks* 15:171–200.

Benevides, Maria Victoria de Mesquita. 1994. "Cidadania e Democracia." *Lua Nova* 33:5–16.

Benford, Robert. 1997. "An Insider's Critique of the Social Movement Framing Perspective." *Sociological Inquiry* 67:409–30.

Benhabib, Seyla, ed. 1996. *Democracy and Difference: Contesting the Boundaries of the Political.* Princeton, NJ: Princeton University Press.

Bernstein, Basil. 1975. *Class, Codes, and Control, III: Towards a Theory of Educational Transmission.* London: Routledge and Kegan Paul.

Bernstein, Mary. 1997. "Celebration and Suppression: The Strategic Uses of Identity by the Lesbian and Gay Movement." *American Journal of Sociology* 103:531–65.

Betto, Frei. 1981. *O Qué É Comunidade Eclesial de Base.* São Paulo: Brasiliense.

Birkhoff, Garret. 1940. *Lattice Theory.* Providence: American Mathematics Society.

Bittar, Jorge, ed. 1992. *O Modo Petista de Governar.* São Paulo: Teoria e Debate.

Blair-Loy, Mary. 1999. "Career Patterns of Executive Women in Finance: An Optimal Matching Analysis." *American Journal of Sociology* 104:1346–97.

Bocchi, Carmen Priscila. 1996. "O Movimento 'Pela Ética na Política' e as Mobilizações Pró-Impeachment: Elementos Para a Análise da Atuação da Sociedade Civil no Brasil Contemporâneo." Master's thesis, University of São Paulo.

Boff, Leonardo, and Clodovis Boff. 1985. *Liberation Theology: From Confrontation to Dialogue.* Maryknoll, NY: Orbis Books.

Bohman, James, and William Rehg, eds. 1997. *Deliberative Democracy: Essays on Reason and Politics.* Cambridge, MA: MIT Press.

Boissevain, Jeremy. 1974. *Friends of Friends: Networks, Manipulators, and Coalitions.* Oxford: Blackwell.

Boschi, Renato Raul. 1987. *A Arte de Associação: Política de Base e Democracia no Brasil.* São Paulo: Vertice.

Brandão, Carlos Rodrigues, ed. 1980. *A Questão Política de Educação Popular.* São Paulo: Brasiliense.

Breiger, Ronald L. 1974. "The Duality of Persons and Groups." *Social Forces* 53:81–90.

———. 2000. "A Tool Kit for Practice Theory." *Poetics* 27: 91–115.

Breiger, Ronald L., Scott A. Boorman and Phipps Arabie. 1975. "An Algorithm for Clustering Relational Data with Applications to Social Network Analysis and Comparison with Multidimensional Scaling." *Journal of Mathematical Psychology* 12:328–83.

Bruneau, Thomas C. 1974. *The Political Transformation of the Brazilian Catholic Church.* Cambridge, UK: Cambridge University Press.

———. 1982: *The Church in Brazil: The Politics of Religion.* Austin: University of Texas Press.

Bucci, Eugênio. 1993. "Guerrilheiros Udenistas." Pp. 111–54 in *O Peixe Morre Pela Boca: Oito Artigos Sobre Cultura e Poder.* São Paulo: Editora Página Aberta.

Burdick, John. 1993. *Looking for God in Brazil: The Progressive Catholic Church in Urban Brazil's Religious Arena.* Berkeley, CA: University of California Press.

Burt, Ronald S. 1992. *Structural Holes: The Social Structure of Competition.* Cambridge, MA: Harvard University Press.

———. 2002. "The Social Capital of Structural Holes." Pp. 148–92 in *The New Economic Sociology,* edited by Mauro F. Guillén, Randall Collins, Paula England, and Marshall Meyer. New York: The Russell Sage Foundation.

———. 2004. "Structural Holes and Good Ideas." *American Journal of Sociology* 110:349–99.

Casanova, José. 1994. *Public Religions in the Modern World.* Chicago: University of Chicago Press.

Calhoun, Craig. 1992. *Habermas and the Public Sphere.* Cambridge, MA: MIT Press.

Camargo, Candido Procoppio Ferreira de, Beatriz Muiz de Souza, and Antônio Flávio de Oliveira Pierucci. 1980. "Comunidades Eclesiais de Base." Pp. 59–81 in *São Paulo: O Povo em Movimento,* edited by Paul Singer and Vinícius Caldeira Brant. São Paulo, Brazil: Editora Brasileira de Ciências.

Cartright, Dorwin, and Frank Harary. 1956. "Structural Balance: A Generalization of Heider's Theory." *Psychological Review* 63:277–92.

———. 1979. "Balance and Clusterability: An Overview." Pp. 25–50 in *Perspectives on Social Network Analysis,* edited by Paul W. Holland and Samuel Leinhardt. New York: Academic Press.

Cerulo, Karen. 1997. "Identity Construction: New Issues, New Directions." *Annual Review of Sociology* 23:385–409.

Chalmers, Douglas, Carlos M. Vilas, Katherine Hite, Scott B. Martin, Kerianne Piester, and Monique Segarra. 1997. *The New Politics of Inequality in Latin America: Rethinking Participation and Representation.* Oxford: Oxford University Press.

Clemens, Elisabeth. 1997. *The People's Lobby: Organizational Innovation and the Rise of Interest Group Politics in the United States, 1890–1925.* Chicago: University of Chicago Press.

Clemens, Elisabeth, and James Cook. 1999. "Politics and Institutionalism: Explaining Durability and Change." *Annual Review of Sociology* 25:441–66.

Cohen, Jean, and Andrew Arato. 1992. *Civil Society and Political Theory*. Cambridge, MA: MIT Press.

Cohen, Joshua. 1997. "Deliberation and Democratic Legitimacy." Pp. 67–91 in *Deliberative Democracy: Essays on Reason and Politics*, edited by James Bohman and William Rehg. Cambridge, MA: MIT Press.

Cohen, Joshua, and Joel Rogers, eds. 1998. *Associations and Democracy (The Real Utopias Project)*. Vol.1. London: Verso Books.

Collier, David, ed. 1979. *The New Authoritarianism in Latin America*. Princeton, NJ: Princeton University Press.

Collins, Randall. 1998. *The Sociology of Philosophies: A Global Theory of Intellectual Change*. Cambridge, MA: Harvard University Press.

———. 2004. *Interaction Ritual Chains*. Princeton, NJ: Princeton University Press.

Colovsky, Salo Vinocur. 2002. "Neoliberalism, Populism, and Presidential Impeachment in Latin America." Master's Thesis, The Fletcher School of Law and Diplomacy, Tufts University.

Comissão Nacional de Assessores da Pastoral da Juventude. 1988. *Os Cristãos e a Militância Política*. Estudos da Pastoral da Juventude, n.1. Petrópolis: Vozes.

Coser, Rose Laub. 1975. "The Complexity of Roles as a Seedbed of Individual Autonomy." Pp. 237–63 in *The Idea of Social Structure: Essays in Honor of Robert Merton*, edited by Lewis Coser. New York: Harcourt Brace Jovanovich.

Costa, Márcia Regina. 1993. *Os Carecas do Subúrbio*. Rio de Janeiro: Vozes.

Curtis, Russel L., and Louise A. Zurcher, Jr. 1973. "Stable Resources of Protest Movement: The Multi-organizational Field." *Social Forces* 52:53–60.

Dagnino, Evelina, ed. 1994a. *Anos 90: Política e Sociedade no Brasil*. São Paulo: Brasiliense.

———. 1994b. "Os Movimentos Sociais e a Emergência de uma Nova Concepção de Cidadania." Pp. 103–55 in *Anos 90: Política e Sociedade no Brasil*, edited by Evelina Dagnino. São Paulo: Brasiliense.

———. 1998. "Culture, Citizenship, and Democracy: Changing Discourses and Practices of the Latin American Left." Pp. 33–63 in *Cultures of Politics, Politics of Cultures: Revisioning Latin American Social Movements*, edited by Sonia E. Alvarez, Evelina Dagnino and Arturo Escobar. Boulder, CO: Westview Press.

———. 2002. *Sociedade Civil e Espaços Públicos no Brasil*. São Paulo: Paz e Terra.

———. 2004. "Sociedade Civil, Participação e Cidadania: De Que Estamos Falando?" Pp. 95–110 in *Políticas de Ciudadanía y Sociedad Civil em Tiempos de Globalización*. Caracas: FACES Universidad Central de Venezuela.

———. 2005. "Citizenship and the Social in Contemporary Brazil." Paper prepared for *After Neo-liberalism? Consequences for Citizenship*. Workshop #2 in the series *Claiming Citizenship in the Americas*, organized by the Canada Research Chair in Citizenship and Governance, Université de Montréal.

Da Matta, Roberto. 1992. "Um Indivíduo Sem Rosto." Pp. 1–32 in *Brasileiro: Cidadão?* edited by Banco Bamirindus do Brasil, S/A. São Paulo: Cultura.

Davis, James A. 1970. "Clustering and Hierarchy in Interpersonal Relations: Testing Two Graph Theoretical Models in 742 Sociomatrices." *American Sociological Review* 35:843–51.

Davis, James A., and Samuel Leinhardt. 1972. "The Structure of Positive Interpersonal Relations in Small Groups." Pp. 218–51 in *Sociological Theories in Progress*, edited by Joseph Berger, Morris Zelditch, and Bo Anderson. New York: Houghton Mifflin.

Dawson, Andrew. 1999. *The Birth and Impact of the Base Ecclesial Community and Liberation Theology Discourse in Brazil*. San Francisco: Catholic Scholars Press.

De Boeck, Paul, and Seymour Rosenberg. 1988. "Hierarchical Classes: Model and Data Analysis." *Psychometrika* 53:361–81.

Della Cava, Ralph. 1989. "The 'People's Church,' the Vatican, and *Abertura*." Pp. 143–67 in *Democratizing Brazil*, edited by Alfred Stepan. New York: Oxford University Press.

Dewey, John. 1981. "The Need for a Recovery of Philosophy." Pp. 58–97 in *The Philosophy of John Dewey*, edited by John J. McDermott. Chicago: University of Chicago Press.

———. 1987 [1916]. *Democracy and Education: An Introduction to the Philosophy of Education*. New York: Free Press.

———. 1991 [1927]. *The Public and Its Problems*. Athens, OH: Ohio University Press.

Diani, Mario. 1995. *Green Networks: A Structural Analysis of the Italian Environmental Movement*. Edinburgh: Edinburgh University Press.

———. 2003. "Leaders or Brokers? Positions and Influence in Social Movement Networks." Pp. 105–22 in *Social Movements and Networks: Relational Approaches to Collective Action*, edited by Mario Diani and Doug McAdam. New York: Oxford University Press.

Diani, Mario, and Doug McAdam, eds. 2003. *Social Movements and Networks: Relational Approaches to Collective Action*. New York: Oxford University Press.

DiMaggio, Paul J. 1991. "Constructing an Organizational Field as a Professional Project: U.S. Art Museums, 1920–1940." Pp. 267–92 in *The New Institutionalism in Organizational Analysis*, edited by Walter W. Powell and Paul J. DiMaggio. Chicago: University of Chicago Press.

———. 1992. "Nadel's Paradox Revisited: Relational and Cultural Aspects of Organizational Structure." Pp. 118–42 in *Networks and Organizations*, edited by Nitin Nohria and Robert G. Eccles. Cambridge, MA: Harvard Business School Press.

Doimo, Ana Maria. 1989. "Social Movements and the Catholic Church in Vitória, Brazil." Pp. 193–223 in *The Progressive Church in Latin America*, edited by Scott Mainwaring and Alexander W. Wilde. Notre Dame, IN: University of Notre Dame Press.

———. 1995. *A Vez e a Voz do Popular: Movimentos Sociais e Participação Política no Brasil pós-70*. Rio de Janeiro: Relume-Dumará/ANPOCS.

Doreian, Patrick. 1980. "On the Evolution of Group and Network Structure." *Social Networks* 2:235–52.

Duquenne, Vincent. 1987. "Contextual Implications between Attributes and Some Representation Principles for Finte Lattices." In *Beitraege zur Begriffsanalyse*, edited by Bernard Ganter, Rudolph Wille, and Karl Erick Wolf. Mannheim: Wissenschaftsverlag.

———. 1991. "On the Core of Finite Lattices." *Discrete Mathematics* 88: 133–47.

Ekiert, Gregortz. 1996. *The State against Society: Political Crises and their Aftermath in East Central Europe*. Princeton, NJ: Princeton University Press.

Ekiert, Grzegorz, and Jan Kubik. 2001. *Popular Protest and Democratic Consolidation in Poland, 1989–1993*. Ann Arbor, MI: University of Michigan Press.

Eliasoph, Nina. 1996. "Making a Fragile Public: A Talk-Centered Study of Citizenship and Power." *Sociological Theory* 14:262–89.

———. 1998. *Avoiding Politics: How Americans Produce Apathy in Everyday Life*. Cambridge, UK: Cambridge University Press.

Eliasoph, Nina, and Paul Lichterman. 2003. "Culture in Interaction." *American Journal of Sociology* 108:735–94.

Elster, Jon. 1997. "The Market and the Forum: Three Varieties of Political Theory." Pp. 3–33 in *Deliberative Democracy: Essays on Reason and Politics*, edited by James Bohman and William Rehg. Cambridge, MA: MIT Press.

———, ed. 1998. *Deliberative Democracy*. Cambridge, UK: Cambridge University Press.

Emirbayer, Mustafa. 1997. "Manifesto for a Relational Sociology." *American Journal of Sociology* 103:281–317.

Emirbayer, Mustafa, and Jeff Goodwin. 1994. "Network Analysis, Culture, and the Problem of Agency." *American Journal of Sociology* 99:1411–54.

Emirbayer, Mustafa, and Ann Mische. 1998. "What Is Agency?" *American Journal of Sociology*, 103:962–1023.

Emirbayer, Mustafa, and Mimi Sheller. 1999. "Publics in History." *Theory and Society* 28:145–97.

Escobar, Arturo, and Sonia E. Alvarez, eds. 1992. *The Making of Social Movements in Latin America: Identity, Strategy, and Democracy*. Boulder, CO: Westview Press.

Fávaro, Maria de Lourdes de A. 1995. *A UNE em Tempos de Autoritarismo*. Rio de Janeiro: Editora UFRJ.

Fernandez, Roberto M., and Roger V. Gould. 1994. "A Dilemma of State Power: Brokerage and Influence in the Mental Health Policy Domain." *American Journal of Sociology* 99:1455–91.

Fernandez, Roberto M., and Doug McAdam. 1988. "Social Networks and Social Movements: Multiorganizational Fields and Recruitment to Freedom Summer." *Sociological Forum* 3:257–382.

Ferree, Myra Marx, William Anthony Gamson, Jürgen Gerhards, and Dieter Rucht. 2002. *Shaping Abortion Discourse: Democracy and the Public Sphere in Germany and the United States*. Cambridge, UK: Cambridge University Press.

Fishman, Robert A. 2004. *Democracy's Voices: Social Ties and the Quality of Public Life in Spain*. Ithaca, NY: Cornell University Press.

Fligstein, Neil. 2001. "Social Skill and the Theory of Fields." *Sociological Theory* 19:105–25.

Fligstein, Neil, and Doug McAdam. 1995. "A Political-Cultural Approach to the Problem of Strategic Action." Unpublished paper, University of California, Berkeley.

Fraser, Nancy. 1992. "Rethinking the Public Sphere: A Contribution to the Critique of Actually Existing Democracy." Pp. 109–42 in *Habermas and the Public Sphere*, edited by Craig Calhoun. Cambridge, MA: MIT Press.

Freeman, Linton C. 1980. "Q-analysis and the Structure of Friendship Networks." *International Journal of Man-Machine Studies* 12:367–78.

Freeman, Linton C., and Douglas R. White. 1993. "Using Galois Lattices to Represent Network Data." *Sociological Methodology* 23:127–45.

Freire, Paulo. 1968. *Pedagogy of the Oppressed*. New York: Seabury Press.

Friedland, Roger, and Robert R. Alford. 1991. "Bringing Society Back In: Symbols, Practices, and Institutional Contradictions." Pp. 232–63 in *The New Institutionalism in Organizational Analysis*, edited by Walter W. Powell and Paul J. DiMaggio. Chicago: University of Chicago Press.

Friedman, Debra, and Doug McAdam. 1992. "Collective Identities and Activism: Networks, Choices, and the Life of a Social Movement." Pp. 156–73 in *Frontiers of Social Movement Theory*, edited by Aldon D. Morris and Carol Mueller. New Haven, CT: Yale University Press.

Gadotti, Moacir. 1989. *Convite á Leitura de Paulo Freire*. São Paulo: Editora Scipione.

Gadotti, Moacir, and Otaviano Pereira, 1989. *Pra Que PT: Origim, Projeto, e Consolidação do Partido dos Trabalhadores*. São Paulo: Editora Cortez.

Gadotti, Moacir, and Carlos A. Torres. 1994. *Educação Popular: Utopia Latino-Americano*. São Paulo: EDUSP.

Gamson, William. 1992. *Talking Politics*. Cambridge, UK: Cambridge University Press.

———. 1995. "Constructing Social Protest." Pp. 85–106 in *Social Movements and Culture*, edited by Hank Johnston and Bert Klandermans. Minneapolis: University of Minnesota Press.

Ganter, B., and R. Wille. 1999. *Formal Concept Analysis: Mathematical Foundations*. Heidelberg: Springer-Verlag.

Geertz, Clifford. 1960. "The Changing Role of the Cultural Broker: The Japanese Kijaji." *Comparative Studies in Society and History* 2:228–49.

Giannotti, Vito. 1992. *Collor, A CUT, e a Pizza*. São Paulo: Editora Página Aberta.

Gibson, David. 2000. "Seizing the Moment: The Problem of Conversational Agency." *Sociological Theory* 18:369–82.

———. 2003. "Participation Shifts: Order and Differentiation in Group Conversation." *Social Forces* 81:1335–81.

———. 2005. "Taking Turns and Talking Ties: Network Structure and Conversational Sequences." *American Journal of Sociology* 110:1561–97.

Gilroy, Paul. 1993. *The Black Atlantic: Modernity and Double Consciousness*. London: Verso.

Giuffre, Katherine. 1999. "Sandpiles of Opportunity: Success in the Art World." *Social Forces* 77:815–32.

Glenn, John K. 2003. "Contentious Politics and Democratization: Comparing the Impact of Social Movements on the Fall of Communism in Eastern Europe." *Political Studies*: 51:1–18.

Goffman, Erving. 1959. *The Presentation of Self in Everyday Life*. New York: Anchor Books.

———. 1974. *Frame Analysis*. New York: Harper and Row.

———. 1981. *Forms of Talk*. Philadelphia: University of Pennsylvania Press

Gohn, Maria de Gloria. 1995. *Historia dos Movimentos Sociais: A Construção da Cidadania dos Brasileiros*. São Paulo: Edições Loyola.

Goodwin, Jeff, and Jim Jasper. 1999. "Caught in a Winding, Snarling Vine: The Structural Bias of Political Process Theory." *Sociological Forum* 14:27–54.

Gould, Roger. 1991. "Multiple Networks and Mobilization in the Paris Commune, 1871." *American Sociological Review* 56:716–29.

———. 1995. *Insurgent Identities: Class, Community, and Insurrection in Paris from 1848 to the Commune*. Chicago: University of Chicago Press.

Gould, Roger V., and Roberto M. Fernandez. 1989. "Structures of Mediation: A Formal Approach to Mediation in Transaction Networks." *Sociological Methodology* 19:89–126.

Gramsci, Antonio. 1971. *Selections from the Prison Notebooks*. Translated by Geoffrey N. Smith and Quintin Hoarse. New York: International Publishers.

Grannovetter, Mark S. 1973. "The Strength of Weak Ties." *American Journal of Sociology* 78: 1360–80.

Gross, Neil. 2005. "Pragmatism, Phenomenology, and Twentieth-century American Sociology." In *Sociology in America: The American Sociological Association Centennial History*, edited by Craig Calhoun. Chicago: University of Chicago Press.

Gutiérrez, Gustavo. 1973. *A Theology of Liberation*. Maryknoll, NY: Orbis Books.

Gutmann, Amy. 2003. *Identity in Democracy*. Princeton, NJ: Princeton University Press.

Gutmann, Amy, and Dennis Thompson. 1996. *Democracy and Disagreement: Why Moral Conflict Cannot be Avoided in Politics, and What Should be Done About It*. Cambridge, MA: Harvard University Press.

Habermas, Jurgen. 1984. *The Theory of Communicative Action*. Vol. 1. *Reason and the Rationalization of Society*. Translated by Thomas McCarthy. Boston: Beacon Press.

———. 1987. *The Theory of Communicative Action*. Vol. 2: *Lifeworld and System: A Critique of Functionalist Reason*. Translated by Thomas McCarthy. Boston: Beason Press.

———. 1989. *The Structural Transformation of the Public Sphere: An Inquiry into a Category of Bourgeois Society*. Translated by Thomas McCarthy. Cambridge, MA: MIT Press.

Han, Shin-Kap, and Phyllis Moen. 1999. "Clocking Out: Temporal Patterning of Retirement." *American Journal of Sociology* 105:191–236.

Hannon, Michael T., and Nancy B. Tuma. 1984. *Social Dynamics: Methods and Models*. New York: Academic Press.

Harary, Frank. 1953. "On the Notion of Balance of a Signed Graph." *Michigan Mathematical Journal* 2:143–46.

———. 1955. "On Local Balance and N-balance in Signed Graphs." *Michigan Mathematical Journal* 3:37–41.

Harnecker, Marta. 1994. *O Sonho Era Possível: A História do Partido dos Trabalhadores Narrada por seus Protagonistas*. São Paulo: Casa América Livre.

Hart, Stephen. 2001. *Cultural Dilemmas of Progressive Politics: Styles of Engagement among Grassroots Activists*. Chicago: University of Chicago Press.

Haydu, Jeff. 1998. "Making Use of the Past: Time Periods and Cases to Compare and as Sequences of Problem Solving." *American Journal of Sociology* 104:339–71.

Heider, Fritz. 1946. "Attitudes and Cognitive Organization." *Journal of Psychology* 21:107–12.

Hewitt, William E. 1991. *Base Christian Communities and Social Change in Brazil*. Lincoln: University of Nebraska Press.

Hochstetler, Kathryn. 2000. "Democratizing Pressures from Below? Social Movements in the New Brazilian Democracy." Pp. 167–82 in *Democratic Brazil: Actors, Institutions, and Processes*, edited by Peter R. Kingstone and Timothy J. Power. Pittsburgh: University of Pittsburgh Press.

Hochstetler, Kathryn, and Margaret Keck. Forthcoming. *Greening Brazil: Environmental Activism in State and Society*. Durham, NC: Duke University Press.

Honig, Bonnie. 1992. "Toward an Agonistic Feminism: Hannah Arendt and the Politics of Identity." Pp. 215–35 in *Feminists Theorize the Political*, edited by Judith Butler and Joan W. Scott. New York and London: Routledge.

Ikegami, Eiko. 2000. "A Sociological Theory of Publics: Identity and Culture as Emergent Properties in Networks." *Social Research* 67:989–1029.

———. 2005. *Bonds of Civility: Aesthetic Publics and the Political Origins of Japanese Publics*. Cambridge, UK: Cambridge University Press.

Jacobi, Pedro. 1995. "Alcances y Límites de los Gobiernos Locales Progresistas en Brasil: Las Alcadías Petistas." *Revista Mexicana de Sociología* 2: 143–62.

Janis, Irving. 1972. *Victims of Groupthink: A Psychological Study of Foreign-Policy Decisions and Fiascoes*. Boston: Houghton Mifflin.

Joas, Hans. 1985. *G. H. Mead: A Contemporary Re-examination of his Thought*. Cambridge, MA: MIT Press.

———. 1993. *Pragmatism and Social Theory*. Chicago: University of Chicago Press.

———. 1996. *The Creativity of Action*. Translated by Jeremy Gaines and Paul Keast. Chicago: University of Chicago Press.

Johnsen, Eugene C. 1985. "Network Macrostructure Models for the Davis-Leinhardt Set of Empirical Sociomatrices." *Social Networks* 7:203–24.

Keck, Margaret. 1989. "The New Unionism in the Brazilian Transition." Pp. 252–96 in *Democratizing Brazil: Problems of Transition and Consolidation*, edited by Alfred Stepan. Oxford: Oxford University Press.

———. 1992. *The Workers' Party and Democratization in Brazil*. New Haven, CT: Yale University Press.

Keck, Margaret, and Katherine Sikkink. 1998. *Activists without Borders: Advocacy Networks in International Politics.* Ithaca, NY: Cornell University Press.

Kim, Hyojoung, and Peter S. Bearman. 1997. "The Structure and Dynamics of Movement Participation." *American Sociological Review* 62:70–93.

Kingstone, Peter R., and Timothy J. Power. 2000. *Democratic Brazil: Actors, Institutions, and Processes.* Pittsburgh, PA: University of Pittsburgh Press.

Kitschelt. Herbert P. 1986. "Political Opportunity Structures and Political Protest: Anti-nuclear Movements in Four Democracies." *British Journal of Political Science* 16:57–85.

Klandermans, Bert. 1992. "The Social Construction of Protest and Multi-Organizational Fields." Pp. 77–103 in *Frontiers of Social Movement Theory*, edited by Aldon D. Morris and Carol Mueller. New Haven, CT: Yale University Press.

Kriesi, Hanspeter, Ruud Koopmans, Jan Willem Duyvendak, and Marco G. Giugni. 1992. "New Social Movements and Political Opportunities in Western Europe." *European Journal of Political Research* 22:219–44.

Krischke, Paulo José, ed. 1983. *Brasil: Do "Milagre" à "Abertura."* São Paulo: Cortez Editora.

———. 1995. "Atores Sociais e Consolidação Democrática na America Latina: Estratégias, Identidades, e Cultura Cívica." Pp. 181–217 in *Meio Ambiente, Desenvolvimento, e Cidadania*, edited by Eduardo Viola et. al. São Paulo: Cortez.

Lamont, Michèle, and Marcel Fournier, eds. 1993. *Cultivating Difference: Symbolic Boundaries and the Making of Inequalities.* Chicago: University of Chicago Press.

Lamont, Michèl, and Virag Molnar. 2002. "The Study of Boundaries in the Social Sciences." *Annual Review of Sociology* 28:167–95.

Lamounier, Bolivar. 1989. "Authoritarian Brazil Revisited: The Impact of Elections on the Abertura." Pp. 43–79 in *Democratizing Brazil: Problems of Transition and Consolidation*, edited by Alfred Stepan. Oxford: Oxford University Press.

Lamounier, Bolivar, and Rachel Meneguello. 1986. *Partidos Políticos e Consolidação Democrática.* São Paulo: Brasiliense.

Lamounier, Bolivar, Francisco C. Weffort, and Maria Vítoria Benevides, eds. 1981. *Direito, Cidadania, e Participação.* São Paulo: T.A. Queiroz.

Landim, Leilah, ed. 1991 *Sem Fim Lucrativos: As Organizaç{{otilde}}es Não-Governmentais no Brasil.* Rio de Janeiro: ISER.

Lehmann, Fritz, and Rudolf Wille. 1995. "A Triadic Approach to Formal Concept Analysis." *International Conference on Conceptual Structures*: 32–43.

Levine, Daniel, ed. 1986. *Religion and Political Conflict in Latin America.* Chapel Hill: University of North Carolina Press.

———. 1992. *Popular Voices in Latin American Catholicism.* Princeton, NJ: Princeton University Press.

Lichterman, Paul. 1996. *The Search for Political Community: American Activists Reinventing Commitment.* Cambridge, UK: University of Cambridge Press.

———. 1999. "Talking Identity in the Public Sphere: Broad Visions and Small Spaces in Sexual Identity Politics." *Theory and Society* 28:101–41.

Lichterman, Paul. 2005. *Elusive Togetherness: How Religious Americans Create Civic Ties*. Princeton, NJ: Princeton University Press.

Lima, Haroldo, and Aldo Arantes. 1984. *História da Ação Popular: da JUC ao PCdoB*. São Paulo: Editora Alfa-Omega.

Lin, Nan. 2002. *Social Capital*. New York: Cambridge University Press.

Linz, Juan J. 1978. *The Breakdown of Democratic Regimes: Crisis, Breakdown, and Reequilibrium*. Baltimore: Johns Hopkins University Press.

Linz, Juan J., and Alfred Stepan, eds. 1978. *The Breakdown of Democratic Regimes: Latin America*. Baltimore: Johns Hopkins University Press.

———, eds. 1996. *Problems of Democratic Transition and Consolidation: Southern Europe, South America, and Post-Communist Europe*. Baltimore: Johns Hopkins University Press.

Lorenzotti, Elizabeth. 1989. "Os Meninos Estão de Volta." *Teoria e Debate* 7:27–29.

Lorraine, Francoise and Harrison C. White. 1971. "Structural Equivalence of Individuals in Social Networks." *Journal of Mathematical Sociology* 1:49–80.

Lounsbury, Michael, Marc J. Ventresca, and Paul M. Hirsch. Forthcoming. "Social Movements, Field Frames, and Industry Emergence: A Cultural-Political Perspective on U.S. Recycling." *Socio-Economic Review*.

Macedo, Stephen, ed. 1999. *Deliberative Politics: Essays on Democracy and Disagreement*. Oxford: Oxford University Press.

Machiavelli, Niccolo. 1950. *The Prince and the Discourses*. Translated by Luigi Ricci. Revised by E. R. P. Vincent. New York: Random House.

Maines, David R, Noreen Sugrue, and Michael A. Katovich. 1983. "The Sociological Import of G. H. Mead's Theory of the Past." *American Sociological Review* 48:161–73.

Mainwaring, Scott. 1986. *The Catholic Church and Politics in Brazil: 1916–1955*. Stanford, CA: Stanford University Press.

———. 1989a. "Grassroots Popular Movements and the Struggle for Democracy: Nova Iguaçu." Pp. 168–204 in *Democratizing Brazil: Problems of Transition and Consolidation*, edited by Alfred Stepan. Oxford: Oxford University Press.

———. 1989b. "Grass-Roots Catholic Groups and Politics in Brazil." Pp. 151–92 in *The Progressive Church in Latin America*, edited by Scott Mainwaring and Alexander W. Wilde. Notre Dame, IN: University of Notre Dame Press.

———. 1999. *Rethinking Party Systems in the Third Wave of Democratization: The Case of Brazil*. Stanford, CA: Stanford University Press.

Mainwaring, Scott, Guillermo O'Donnell, and J. Samuel Valenzuela, eds. 1992. *Issues in Democratic Consolidation: The New South American Democracies in Comparative Perspective*. Notre Dame, IN: University of Notre Dame Press.

Mannheim, Karl. 1952 [1928]. "The Problem of Generations." Pp. 276–322 in *Essays on the Sociology of Knowledge*, translated by. P. Keckemeti. New York: Oxford University Press.

Mansbridge, Jane J. 1983. *Beyond Adversary Democracy*. Chicago: University of Chicago Press.

———. 1986. *Why We Lost the ERA*. Chicago: University of Chicago Press.

Marcus, George E., and Russel L. Hanson, eds. 1993. *Reconsidering the Democratic Public*. University Park: The Pennsylvania State University Press.

Marsden, Peter. 1982. "Brokerage Behavior in Restricted Exchange Networks." Pp. 201–18 in *Social Structure and Network Analysis*, edited by Peter Marsden and Nan Lin. Beverly Hills, CA: Sage.

Martin, John Levi. 2003. "What Is Field Theory?" *American Journal of Sociology* 109:1–49.

Martins Filho, João Roberto. 1987. *Movimento Estudantil e Ditadura Militar: 1964–1968*. Campinas, SP: Papirus.

———. 1994. "Os Estudantes e a Política no Brasil (1962–1992)." *Teoria e Pesquisa* 10. Centro de Educação e Ciências Sociais, Universidade Federal de São Carlos.

Marx, Anthony. 1998. *Making Race and Nation: A Comparison of the United States, South Africa, and Brazil*. Cambridge, UK: Cambridge University Press.

Matos, Franco de. 1997. *A Empresa Júnior no Brasil e no Mundo*. São Paulo: Editora Martin Claret.

McAdam, Doug. 1982. *Political Process and the Development of Black Insurgency, 1930–1970*. Chicago: University of Chicago Press.

———. 1988. *Freedom Summer*. New York: Oxford University Press.

McAdam, Doug, John D. McCarthy, and Mayer N. Zald, eds. 1996. *Comparative Perspectives on Social* Movements: *Political Opportunities, Mobilizing Structures, and Cultural Framings*. Cambridge, UK: Cambridge University Press.

McAdam, Doug, and Ronnelle Paulsen. 1993. "Specifying the Relationship between Social Ties and Activism." *American Journal of Sociology* 99:640–67.

McAdam, Doug, and Richard Scott. 2002. "Organizations and Movements." Paper presented at the Annual Meetings of the American Sociological Association, Chicago, August 2002.

McAdam, Doug, Sidney Tarrow, and Charles Tilly. 2001. *Dynamics of Contention*. Cambridge Studies in Contentious Politics. Cambridge, UK: Cambridge University Press.

McLean, Paul. 1998. "A Frame Analysis of Favor Seeking in the Renaissance: Agency, Networks, and Political Culture." *American Journal of Sociology* 104:51–91.

———. 2007. *The Art of the Network: Strategic Interaction and Patronage in Renaissance Florence*. Durham, NC: Duke University Press.

McPherson, J. Miller, and James R. Ranger-Moore. 1991. "Evolution on a Dancing Landscape: Organizations and Networks in Dynamic Blau Space." *Social Forces* 70:19–42.

Mead, George Herbert. 1932. *The Philosophy of the Present*. Chicago: University of Chicago Press.

Melucci, Alberto. 1989. *Nomads of the Present: Social Movements and Individual Needs in Contemporary Society*. Philadelphia: Temple University Press.

———. 1995. "The Process of Collective Identity." Pp. 41–63 in *Social Movements and Culture*, edited by H. Johnston and B. Klandermans. Minneapolis: University of Minnesota Press.

———. 1996. *Challenging Codes: Collective Action in the Information Age*. Cambridge, UK: Cambridge University Press.

Mendes, Antonio Jr. 1981. *Movimento Estudantil no Brasil*. São Paulo: Brasiliense.

Mendes, Candido. 1966. *Memento dos Vivos: A Esquerda Católica no Brasil*. Rio de Janeiro: Editora Livro.

Meneguello, Rachel. 1989. *PT: A Formação de um Partido, 1979–1982*. São Paulo: Paz e Terra.

Merton, Robert K. 1968. *Social Theory and Social Structure*. New York: The Free Press.

Mesquita, Marcos Ribeiro. 2003a. "Juventude e Movimento Estudantil: Discutindo as Práticas Militantes." *Revista Psicologia Política* 3:89–120.

———. 2003b. "Movimento Estudantil Brasileiro: Práticas Militantes na Ótica dos Novos Movimentos Sociais." *Revista Crítica de Ciências Sociais* 66:117–149.

Meyer, David S. 2002. "Opportunities and Identities: Bridge-building in the Study of Social Movements." Pp. 3–21 in *Social Movements: Identity, Culture, and the State*, edited by David S. Meyer, Nancy Whittier, and Belinda Robnett. New York: Oxford University Press.

Meyer, David S., and Nancy Whittier. 1994. "Social Movement Spillover." *Social Problems* 41:277–98.

Meyer, John W., and W. Richard Scott. 1983. *Organizational Environments: Ritual and Rationality*. Beverly Hills, CA: Sage.

Mische, Ann. 1996. "Projecting Democracy: The Construction of Citizenship across Youth Networks in Brazil." Pp. 131–158 in *Citizenship, Identity, and Social History*, edited by Charles Tilly. Cambridge: Cambridge University Press.

———. 1998. "Projecting Democracy: Contexts and Dynamics of Youth Activism in the Brazilian Impeachment Movement." Ph.D. diss., New School for Social Research.

———. 2001. "Juggling Multiple Futures: Personal and Collective Project-formation among Brazilian Youth Leaders." Pp.137–59 in *Leadership and Social Movements*, edited by Alan Johnson, Colin Barker, and Michael Lavalette, Manchester, UK: Manchester University Press.

———. 2003. "Cross-talk in Movements: Rethinking the Culture-Network Link." Pp.258–80 in *Social Movements and Networks: Relational Approaches to Collective Action*, edited by Mario Diani and Doug McAdam. Oxford and New York: Oxford University Press.

Mische, Ann, and Steph Karpinski. 2003. "Challenging Cohorts: Reconstructing the Institutional Field of Brazilian Youth Activism." Paper presented at the Annual Meetings of the ASA, Atlanta, August 2003.

Mische, Ann, and Philippa Pattison. 2000. "Composing a Civic Arena: Publics, Projects, and Social Settings." *Poetics* 27:163–94.

Mische, Ann, and Harrison White. 1998. "Between Conversation and Situation: Public Switching Dynamics Across Network-Domains." *Social Research* 65:295–324.

Mohr, John. 1998. "Measuring Meaning Structures." *Annual Review of Sociology* 24:345–70.

———. Forthcoming. "Implict Terrains: Meaning, Measurement, and Spatial Metaphors in Organizational Theory." In *Constructing Industries and Markets*, edited by Marc Ventrusca and Joseph Porac. New York: Elsevier.

Mohr, John, and Vincent Duqenne. 1997. "The Duality of Culture and Practice: Poverty Relief in New York City, 1888–1917." *Theory and Society* 26:305–56.

Mohr, John, and Francesca Guerra-Pearson. Forthcoming. "The Duality of Niche and Form: The Differentiation of Institutional Space in New York City, 1888–1917." In *How Institutions Change*, edited by Walter Powell and Dan Jones. Chicago: University of Chicago Press.

Moisés, José Álvarao, and José Augusto Guilhon Albuquerque, eds. 1989. *Dilemas da Consolidação de Democracia*. São Paulo: Paz e Terra.

Moraes, Marco Antonio de. 1995. "Alegria, Alegria, A Onda Jovem da Cidadania: A Construção do Sujeito Social." Master's Thesis, Universidade Federal do Rio de Janeiro.

Morrill, Calvin. Forthcoming. "Institutional Change Through Interstitial Emergence: The Growth of Alternative Dispute Resolution in American Law, 1965–1995." In *How Institutions Change*, edited by Walter W. Powell and Daniel L. Jones. Chicago: University of Chicago Press.

Morris, Aldon D., and Carol Mueller, eds. 1992. *Frontiers of Social Movement Theory*. New Haven, CT: Yale University Press.

Mouffe, Chantal, ed. 1992. *Dimensions of Radical Democracy*. London: Verso.

Mueller, Carol M. 1994. "Conflict Networks and the Origins of Women's Liberation." Pp. 234–63 in *New Social Movements: From Ideology to Identity*, edited by Enrique Laraña, Hank Johnston, and Joseph R. Gusfield. Philadelphia: Temple University Press.

Nagel, Robin. 1997. *Claiming the Virgin: The Broken Promise of Liberation Theology in Brazil*. London: Routledge.

National Commission on Terrorist Attacks upon the United States. 2004. *The 9/11 Commission Report: Final Report of the National Commission on Terrorist Attacks upon the United States*. New York: W. W. Norton.

Novaes, Carlos. 1993. "PT: Dilemmas da Burocratização." *Novos Estudos CEBRAP* 35: 217–37.

Nylen, William. 1997. "Reconstructing the Workers' Party: Lessons from Northeastern Brazil." Pp. 421–46 in *The New Politics of Inequality in Latin America: Rethinking Participation and Representation*, edited by Douglas A. Chalmers, Carlos M. Vilas, Katherine Hite, Scott B. Martin, Kerianne Piester, and Monique Segarra. Oxford: Oxford University Press.

———. 2000. "The Making of a Loyal Opposition: The Workers' Party (PT) and the Consolidation of Democracy in Brazil." Pp. 126–43 in *Democratic Brazil: Actors, Institutions and Processes*, edited by Peter Kingstone and Timothy J. Power. Pittsburgh, PA: University of Pittsburgh Press.

O'Donnell, Guillermo, and Phillipe C. Schmitter, eds. 1986. *Transitions from Authoritarian Rule: Tentative Conclusions about Uncertain Democracies*. Baltimore: Johns Hopkins University Press.

Oliveira, José Alberto Saldanha de. 1994. *A Mitologia Estudantil: Uma Abordagem Sobre o Movimento Estudantil Alagoano*. Maceió: SERGASA.

Osa, Maryjane. 2001. "Mobilizing Structures and Cycles of Protest: Post Stalinist Contention in Poland, 1954–1959." *Mobilization* 6:211–31.

Padgett, John. F. 2001. "Organizational Genesis, Identity, and Control: The Transformation of Banking in Renaissance Florence." Pp. 211–57 in *Networks and Markets*, edited by James E. Rauch and Alessandra Casella. New York: Russell Sage.

Padgett, John F., and Christopher K. Ansell. 1993. "Robust Action and the Rise of the Medici, 1400–1434." *American Journal of Sociology* 98:1259–1319.

Padgett, John F., and Paul D. McLean. 2006. "Organizational Invention and Elite Transformation: The Birth of Partnership Systems in Renaissance Florence." *American Journal of Sociology* 111:1463–1568.

Paoli, Maria Célia. 2002. "Empresas e Responsibilidade Social: Os Enredamentos da Cidadania no Brasil." Pp. 373–418 in *Democratizar a Democracia—Os Caminhos da Democratização Participativa*, edited by Boaventura de Souza Santos. Rio de Janeiro: Paz e Terra.

Pateman, Carole. 1970. *Participation and Democratic Theory*. Cambridge, UK: Cambridge University Press.

Perrin, Andrew J. 2005. "Political Microcultures: Linking Civic Life and Democratic Discourse." *Social Forces* 84:1049–82.

———. 2006. *Citizen Speak: The Democratic Imagination in American Life*. Chicago: University of Chicago Press.

Poerner, Artur José. 1995. *O Poder Jovem: Historia da Participação Política dos Estudantes Brasileiros*. São Paulo: Centro da Memória da Juventude.

Polletta, Francesca. 1994. "Strategy and Identity in 1960s Black Protest." *Research in Social Movements, Conflict and Change* 17:85–114.

———. 1997. "Culture and Its Discontents: Recent Theorizing on Culture and Protest." *Sociological Inquiry* 67:431–50.

———. 1998. " 'It Was Like a Fever . . . ' Narrative and Identity in Social Protest." *Social Problems* 45:137–59.

———. 1999. "Snarks, Quacks, and Quarrels: Culture and Structure in Political Process Theory." *Sociological Forum* 14:67–74.

———. 2002a. *Freedom Is an Endless Meeting: Democracy in American Social Movements*. Chicago: University of Chicago Press.

———. 2002b. "Plotting Protest: Mobilizing Stories in the 1960 Student Sit-In." Pp. 31–51 in *Stories of Social Change: Narrative and Social Movements*, edited by Joseph E. Davis. Albany: State University of New York Press.

Polletta, Francesca, and James Jasper. 2001. "Collective Identity in Social Movements." *Annual Review of Sociology* 27:283–305.

Powell, Walter W., and Paul J. DiMaggio, eds. 1991. *The New Institutionalism in Organizational Analysis*. Chicago: University of Chicago Press.

Press, W., S. Teukolsky, W. Vetterling, and B. Flannery. 1992. *Numerical Recipes: The Art of Scientific Computing*. 2d ed. New York: Cambridge University Press.

Przeworksi, Adam. 1991. *Democracy and the Market*. Cambridge, UK: Cambridge University Press.

Puleo, Mev. 1994. *The Struggle Is One: The Voices and Visions of Liberation*. Albany, NY: State University of New York Press.

Putnam, Robert D. 1993. *Making Democracy Work: Civic Traditions in Modern Italy*. Princeton, NJ: Princeton University Press.

———. 2000. *Bowling Alone: The Collapse and Revival of American Community*. New York: Simon and Shuster.

Rao, Hayagreeva, Calvin Morrill, and Mayer N. Zald. 2000. "Power Plays: How Social Movements and Collective Action Create New Organizational Forms." *Research in Organizational Behaviour* 22:239–82.

Reis, Fábio Wanderly, and Guillermo O'Donnell, eds. 1988. *A Democracia no Brasil: Dilemas e Perspectivas*. São Paulo: Edições Vertices.

Ribeiro, Renato Janine. 2000. *Sociedade Contra O Social: O Alto Custo da Vida Publica no Brasil*. São Paulo: Companhia das Letras.

Ribeiro Neto, Artur. 1985. "UNE: Um Laço Que Não Une Mais." *Desvios* 4:61–71 (special issue, Movimento Estudantil Hoje). São Paulo: Paz e Terra.

Rochon, Thomas R., and David S. Meyer, eds. 1997. *Coalitions and Political Movements: The Lessons of the Nuclear Freeze*. Boulder, CO: Lynne Rienner.

Romagnoli, Luiz Henrique, and Tânia Gonçalves. 1979. "A Volta da UNE: De Ibuína a Salvador." *História Immediata*. Vol. 5. São Paulo: Alfa–Omega.

Rosenn, Keith S., and Richard Downes, eds. 1999. *Corruption and Political Reform in Brazil: The Impact of Collor's Impeachment*. Miami: North-South Center Press.

Rosenthal, Naomi, Meryl Fingrutld, Michele Ethier, Roberta Karant, and David McDonald. 1985. "Social Movements and Network Analysis: A Case Study of Nineteenth-Century Women's Reform in New York State." *American Journal of Sociology* 90:1023–54.

Ryan, Mary P. 1990. *Women in Public: Between Banners and Ballots, 1825–1880*. Baltimore: Johns Hopkins University Press.

———. 1992. "Gender and Public Access: Women's Politics in Nineteenth-Century America." Pp. 259–88 in *Habermas and the Public Sphere*, edited by Craig Calhoun. Cambridge, MA: MIT Press.

Sader, Eder. 1988. *Quando Novos Personagems Entrarem em Cena: Experiências e Lutas dos Trabalhadores da Grande São Paulo, 1970–1980*. São Paulo: Paz e Terra.

Salamon, Lester. 1997. "Estratégias para o Fortalecimento do Terceiro Setor." In *Terceiro Setor: Desenvolvimento Social Sustentado*, edited by Evelyn Berg Ioschpe. Rio de Janeiro: Paz e Terra.

Sandoval, Salvador. 1994. *Social Change and Labor Unrest in Brazil since 1945*. Boulder, CO: Westview Press.

———. 1998. "Social Movements and Democratization: The Case of Brazil and the Latin Countries." Pp. 169–201 in *From Contention to Democracy*, edited by Marco G. Giugni, Doug McAdam, and Charles Tilly. Lanham, MA: Rowman and Littlefield.

Sanfelice, José Luíz. 1986. *Movimento Estudantil: A UNE na Resistência ao Golpe de 64*. São Paulo: Cortez.

Santos, Maria Cecília Loschiavo dos, ed. 1988. *Maria Antônia: Uma Rua na Contramão*. São Paulo: Nobel.

Santos, Milton. 1987. *O Espaço do Cdadão*. São Paulo: Nobel.

Santos, Wanderley Guilherme dos. 1978. *Poder e Política: Crônica do Autoritarismo Brasileiro*. Rio de Janeiro: Forense-Universitária.

———. 1979. *Cidadania e Justiça: A Política Social Na Ordem Brasileira*. Rio de Janeiro: Campus.

Scherer-Warren, Ilse. 1993. *Redes de Movimentos Sociais*. São Paulo: Loyola.

———. 1995. "ONGs na América Latina: Trajetória e Perfil." Pp. 161–80 in *Meio Ambiente, Desenvolvimento, e Cidadania*, edited by Eduardo Viola, Héctor R.

Leis, Ilse Scherer-Warren, Júlia S. Guivant, Paulo Freire Vieira, and Paulo J. Krischke. São Paulo: Cortez.

Schudson, Michael. 1998. *The Good Citizen: A History of American Civic Life.* New York: Free Press.

Schutz, Alfred. 1962. "Choosing among Projects of Action." Pp.67–96 in *Collected Papers.* Vol. 1. *The Problem of Social Reality,* edited by Maurice Natanson. The Hague, Netherlands: Martinus Nijhoff.

———. 1964. "Tiresias, or Our Knowledge of Future Events." Pp. 277–93 in *Collected Papers.* Vol. 2. *Studies in Social Theory,* edited by Arvid Brodersen. The Hague, Netherlands: Martinus Nijhoff.

———. 1967. *The Phenomenology of the Social World.* Translated by George Walsh and Frederick Lehnert. Evanston, IL: Northwestern University Press.

Schweizer, Thomas. 1993. "The Dual Ordering of Actors and Possessions." *Current Anthropology* 34:469–83.

———. 1996. "Actor and Event Orderings across Time: Lattice Representation and Boolean Analysis of the Political Disputes in Chen Village, China." *Social Networks* 18:247–66.

Scott, John P. 2000. *Social Network Analysis: A Handbook.* London: Sage.

Scott, W. Richard. 1999. "A Call for Two-Way Traffic: Improving the Connection between Social Movement and Organizational/Institutional Theory." Paper presented at the conference to honor Mayer B. Zald, University of Michigan, Sept 17–18, 1999.

Scott, W. Richard, and John W. Meyer. 1991. "The Organization of Societal Sectors: Propositions and Early Evidence." Pp. 108–40 in *The New Institutionalism in Organizational Analysis,* edited by Walter W. Powell and Paul J. DiMaggio. Chicago: University of Chicago Press.

———. 1994. *Institutional Environments and Organizations: Structural Complexity and Individualism.* Thousand Oaks, CA: Sage Publications.

Seidman, Gay. 1994. *Manufacturing Militance: Workers' Movements in Brazil and South Africa, 1970–1984.* Berkeley: University of California Press.

Seidman, Steven B. 1981. "Structures Induced by Subsets: A Hypergraph Approach." *Mathematical Social Sciences* 1:381–96.

Seligman, Adam. 1992. *The Idea of Civil Society.* New York: Free Press.

Semeraro, Giovanni. 1994. *A Primavera dos Anos 60: A Geração de Betinho.* São Paulo: Edições Loyola.

Senate Intelligence Committee. 2004. *Report on the U.S. Intelligence Community's Prewar Intelligence Assessments on Iraq.* Washington, DC: Government Printing Office.

Sewell, William H., Jr. 1992. "A Theory of Structure: Duality, Agency, and Transformation." *American Journal of Sociology* 98:1–29.

Sheller, Mimi. 2000. *Democracy after Slavery: Black Publics and Peasant Radicalism in Haiti and Jamaica.* Oxford: Macmillan

Sigrest, José Luiz. 1982. *A JUC no Brasil: Evolução e Impasse de uma Ideologia.* São Paulo: Cortez.

Silva, Antonio Ozai da. n.d. *História das Tendências no Brasil: Origens, Disões e Propostas.* São Paulo: Dag Gráfica e Editorial.

Silva, Jorge da. 1994. *Direitos Civic e Relações Raciais no Brasil*. Rio de Janeiro: Luam.

Silva, Justina Iva de Araújo. 1989. *Estudantes e Política: Estudo de um Movimento (RN 1969–1969)*. São Paulo: Cortez.

Simmel, Georg. 1950. *The Sociology of Georg Simmel*. Translated, edited, and introduced by Kurt H. Wolff. New York: Free Press.

———. 1955. *Conflict and the Web of Group Affiliations*. Translated by Kurt H. Wolff and Reinhard Bendix. New York: Free Press.

Singer, Paul, and Vinícius Caldeira Brant. 1980. *São Paulo: O Povo em Movimento*. São Paulo: Editora Brasileira de Ciências.

Skidmore, Thomas E. 1988. *The Politics of Military Rule in Brazil, 1964–1985*. New York: Oxford University Press.

———. 1989. "Brazil's Slow Road to Democratization." Pp. 5–42 in *Democratizing Brazil: Problems of Transition and Consolidation*, edited by Alfred Stepan. Oxford: Oxford University Press.

———. 1999. "Collor's Downfall in Historical Perspective." Pp. 1–19 in *Corruption and Political Reform in Brazil: The Impact of Collor's Impeachment*, edited by Keith S. Rosenn and Richard Downes. Miami: North-South Center Press.

Smilde, David. 2004. "Popular Publics: Street Protest and Plaza Preachers in Caracas." *International Review of Social History* 49:179–95.

———. 2005. "A Qualitative Comparative Analysis of Conversion to Venezuelan Evangelicalism: How Networks Matter." *American Journal of Sociology* 111:757–96.

———. 2007. *Reason to Believe: Cultural Agency in Latin American Evangelicalism*. Berkeley: University of California Press.

Snow, David, and Robert Benford. 1988. "Ideology, Frame Resonance, and Participant Mobilization." *International Social Movement Research* 1:197–217.

———. 1992. "Master Frames and Cycles of Protest." Pp. 133–55 in *Frontiers in Social Movement Theory*, edited by Aldon Morris and Carol McClurg Mueller. New Haven, CT: Yale University Press.

Snow, David A., and Doug McAdam. 2000. "Identity Work Processes in the Context of Social Movements." In *Self, Identity, and Social Movements*, edited by Sheldon Stryker, Timothy J. Owens, and Robert W. White. Minneapolis: University of Minnesota Press.

Snow, David A., E. Burke Rochford, Jr., Steven K. Worden, and Robert D. Benford. 1986. "Frame Alignment Processes, Micromobilization, and Movement Participation." *American Sociological Review* 51:464–81.

Snow, David A., Louis A. Zurcher, and Sheldon Ekland-Olson. 1980. "Social Networks and Social Movements: A Micro-structural Approach to Differential Recruitment." *American Sociological Review* 45:787–801.

Somers, Margaret. 1993. "Citizenship and the Place of the Public Sphere: Law, Community, and Political Culture in the Transition to Democracy." *American Sociological Review* 58:587–620.

———. 1994. "The Narrative Constitution of Identity: A Relational and Network Approach." *Theory and Society* 23:605–49.

———. 1998. "We're No Angels: Realism, Relationality, and Rational Choice in Social Science." *American Journal of Sociology* 104:772–84.

Souza, Luiz Alberto Gómez da. 1984. *A JUC: Os Estudantes Católicas e a Política*. Petrópolis: Vozes.

Souza Lima, Luiz Gonzaga de. 1979. *Evolução Polítca dos Católicas e da Igreja no Brasil*. Rio de Janeiro: Petrópolis.

Spillman, Lyn. 1995. "Culture, Social Structures, and Discursive Fields." *Current Perspectives in Social Theory* 15:129–54.

———. 2002. "How Are Structures Meaningful? Cultural Sociology and Theories of Social Structure." Pp. 63–83 in *Structure, Culture, and History: Recent Issues In Social Theory*, edited by Sing C. Chew and David J. Knottnerus. Lanham, MD: Rowman and Littlefield.

Spink, Mary Jane Paris, ed. 1994. *A Cidadania em Construção: Uma Reflexão Transdisciplinar*. São Paulo: Cortez.

Staggenborg, Suzanne. 1986. "Coalition Work in the Pro-Choice Movement." *Social Problems* 33:374–89.

———. 1998. "Social Movement Communities and Cycles of Protest: The Emergence and Maintenance of a Local Women's Movement." Working Papers in Social Behavior 98–02, Mc Gill University.

Stark, David. 1996. "Recombinant Property in East European Capitalism." *American Journal of Sociology* 101:993–1027.

Stark, David, and László Bruszt. 1998. *Postsocialist Pathways: Transforming Politics and Property in East Central Europe*. Cambridge, UK: Cambridge University Press.

Stark, David, and Balázs Vedres. 2006. "Social Times of Network Spaces: Network Sequences and Foreign Investment in Hungary." *American Journal of Sociology* 111:1367–1411.

Steinberg, Marc W. 1998. "Tilting the Frame: Considerations on Collective Action Framing from a Discursive Turn." *Theory & Society* 27:845–72.

———. 1999a. "The Talk and Back Talk of Collective Action: A Dialogic Analysis of Repertoires of Discourse among Nineteenth-century English Cotton Spinners." *American Journal of Sociology* 105:736–80.

———. 1999b. *Fighting Words: Working-class Formation, Collective Action, and Discourse in Early Nineteenth-century England*. Ithaca, NY: Cornell University Press.

Stepan, Alfred. 1971. *The Military in Politics: Changing Patterns in Brazil*. Princeton, NJ: Princeton University Press.

———. 1973. *Authoritarian Brazil: Origins, Policies, and Future*. New Haven, CT: Yale University Press.

———. 1988. *Rethinking Military Politics: Brazil and the Southern Cone*. Princeton, NJ: Princeton University Press.

———, ed. 1989. *Democratizing Brazil: Problems of Transition and Consolidation*. Oxford: Oxford University Press.

Stovel, Katherine, Michael Savage, and Peter Bearman. 1996. "Ascription into Achievement: Models of Career Systems at Lloyds Bank, 1890–1970." *American Journal of Sociology* 102:358–99.

Stryker, Sheldon. 1968. "Identity Salience and Role Performance: The Relevance of Symbolic Interaction Theory for Family Research." *Journal of Marriage and the Family* 30:558–64.

———. 2000. "Identity Competition: Key to Differential Social Movement Participation?" Pp. 21–40 in *Self, Identity, and Social Movements*, edited by Sheldon Stryker, Timothy J. Owens, and Robert W. White. Minneapolis: University of Minnesota Press.

Swidler, Ann. 1986. "Culture in Action: Symbols and Strategies." *American Sociological Review* 51:273–86.

———. 2001. *Talk of Love: How Culture Matters*. Chicago: University of Chicago Press.

Tarrow, Sidney. 1994. *Power in Movement: Social Movements, Collective Action, and Politics*. New York: Cambridge University Press.

———. 2005. *The New Transnational Contention*. Cambridge Series in Contentious Politics. Cambridge, UK: Cambridge University Press.

Taylor, Verta, Leila J. Rupp, and Joshua Gamson. 2004. "Performing Protest: Drag Shows as Tactical Repertoire of the Gay and Lesbian Movement." *Research in Social Movements, Conflicts and Change* 25:105–37.

Taylor, Verta, and Nancy Whittier. 1992. "Collective Identity in Social Movement Communities." Pp. 104–29 in *Frontiers of Social Movement Theory*, edited by Aldon D. Morris and Carol Mueller. New Haven, CT: Yale University Press.

Teixeira, Ana Claudia. 2003. *Identidade em Constrção: Organizações Não Governamentais no Processo Brasileiro de Democratização*. São Paulo: Annablume—FAPESP.

Telles, Edward E. 2004. *Race in Another America: The Significance of Skin Color in Brazil*. Princeton, NJ: Princeton University Press.

Telles, Vera da Silva. 1994. "A Sociedade Civil, Direitos, e Espaços Públicos." *Polis* 14: 43–53.

———. 2001. *Pobreza e Cidadania*. São Paulo: Editora 34.

Tilly, Charles. 1998. "Political Identities." Pp. 3–16 in *Challenging Authority: The Historical Study of Contentious Politics*, edited by Michael P. Hanagan, Leslie Page Moch, and Wayne te Brake. Minneapolis: University of Minnesota Press.

———. 1999. *Durable Inequalities*. Berkeley: University of California Press.

———. 2002a. *Stories, Identities, and Political Change*. Lanham, MD: Rowman and Littlefield.

———. 2002b. "Contentious Conversation." Pp. 126–40 in *Stories, Identities, and Political Change*. Lanham, MD: Rowman and Littlefield.

———. 2003. "Social Boundary Mechanisms." Unpublished paper.

———. 2005. *Identities, Boundaries, and Social Ties*. Boulder: Paradigm Press.

Uzzi, Brian, and Jarret Spiro. 2005. "Collaboration and Creativity: The Small World Problem." *American Journal of Sociology* 111: 447–504.

Ventura, Zuenir. 1988. *1968: O Ano Que Não Terminou*. Rio de Janeiro: Nova Fronteira.

Vianna, Hermano. 1988. *O Mundo Funk Carioca*. Rio de Janeiro: Zahar.

Viola, Eduardo, Hector R. Leis, Ilse Scherer-Warren, Julia S. Guivant, Paulo Freire Viera, and Paulo J. Krischke, eds. 1995. *Meio Ambiente, Desenvolvimento, e Cidadania*. São Paulo: Cortez.

Voss, Kim. 1996. "The Collapse of a Social Movement: The Interplay of Mobilizing Structures, Framing and Political Opportunities in the Knights of Labor." Pp. 227–60 in *Comparative Perspectives on Social Movements: Political Opportunities, Mobilizing Structures, and Cultural Framings*, edited by Doug McAdam, John D. McCarthy, and Mayer Zald. Cambridge: Cambridge University Press.

Wagner-Pacifici, Robin. 1987. *The Moro Morality Play: Terrorism as Social Drama*. Chicago: University of Chicago Press.

———. 1994. *Discourse and Destruction: The City of Philadelphia vs. MOVE*. Chicago: University of Chicago Press.

———. 2000. *Theorizing the Standoff: Contingency in Action*. Cambridge, UK: Cambridge University Press

Watts, Duncan. 2004. *Six Degrees of Separation: The Science of a Connected Age*. New York: W. W. Norton.

Weffort, Francisco. 1981. "A Cidadania dos Trabalhadores." Pp. 139–50 in *Direito, Cidadania e Participação*, edited by Bolivar Lamounier et. al. São Paulo: Queiroz.

Weffort, Francisco, Alan Wolfe, Antonio Barros de Castro, Francisco de Oliveira, Carlos Nelson Coutinho, and Guiseppe Vacca. 1991. *A Democracia como Proposta*. Rio de Janeiro: IBASE.

Wellman, Barry, and S. D. Berkowitz, eds. 1988. *Social Structure: A Network Approach*. Cambridge, UK: Cambridge University Press.

Weyland, Kurt. 1993. "The Rise and Fall of President Collor and Its Impact on Brazilian Democracy." *Journal of Inter-American Studies and World Affairs* 35:1–38.

White, Douglas R., and Vincent Duquenne, eds. 1996. "Social Network and Discrete Structure Analysis." Special issue of *Social Networks* 18.

White, Harrison. 1992. *Identity and Control*. Princeton, NJ: Princeton University Press.

———. 1993. *Careers and Creativity: Social Forces in the Arts*. Boulder, CO: Westview Press.

———. 1994. "Values Comes in Styles, Which Mate to Change." Pp. 63–92 in *The Origin of Values*, edited by Michael Hechter, Lynn Nadel, and R. Michod. New York: Aldine de Gruyter.

———. 1995. "Network Switchings and Bayesian Forks: Reconstructing the Social and Behavioral Sciences." *Social Research* 62:1035–63.

———. 2003. "Innovation in Style." Paper presented at The Cultural Turn conference at the University of California, Santa Barbara, March 2003.

White, Harrison C., Scott A. Boorman, and Ronald L. Breiger. 1974. "Social Structure from Multiple Networks. I. Blockmodels of Roles and Positions." *American Journal of Sociology* 81:730–89.

White, Harrison, and Cynthia A. White. 1965. *Canvases and Careers: Institutional Change in the French Painting World*. New York: John Wiley and Sons.

Whitford, Josh. 2002. "Pragmatism and the Untenable Dualism of Ends and Means: Why Rational Choice Theory Does Not Deserve Paradigmatic Privilege." *Theory and Society* 31:3.

Whittier, Nancy. 1995. *Feminist Generations: The Persistence of the Radical Women's Movement.* Philadelphia: Temple University Press.

Wille, Rudolf. 1982: "Restructuring Lattice Theory: An Approach Based on Hierarchies of Concepts." Pp. 445–70 in *Ordered Sets*, edited by Ivan Rival. Dordrecht: D. Reidel.

———. 1996a. "Introduction to Formal Concept Analysis." Technische Hochschule Darmstadt, Fachbereich Mathematik, Preprint-Nr. 1878.

———. 1996b. "Conceptual Structures of Multicontexts." Paper presented at the International Conference on Conceptual Graphs, Sydney, September, 1996.

Wilson, S. J., P. F. Bladin, M. M. Saling, and P. E. Pattison. 2005. "Characterising Psychosocial Outcome Trajectories Following Seizure Surgery." *Epilepsy and Behaviour* 6:570–80.

Wilson, T. P. 1982. "Relational Networks: An Extension of Sociometric Concepts." *Social Networks* 4:105–16.

Wolf, Eric. 1956. "Aspects of Groups Relations in a Complex Society." *American Anthropologist* 58:1065–78.

Wright, Wrik Olin, and Archon Fung. 2003. *Deepening Democracy: Institutional Innovations in Empowered Participatory Governance.* New York: Verso.

Wuthnow, Robert, ed. 1991. *Between States and Markets: The Voluntary Sector in Comparative Perspective.* Princeton, NJ: Princeton University Press.

———. 2002. *Loose Connections: Joining Together in America's Fragmented Communities.* Cambridge, MA: Harvard University Press.

Young, Iris. 1990. *Justice and the Politics of Difference.* Princeton, NJ: Princeton University Press.

———. 1997. "Difference as a Resource for Democratic Communication." Pp. 383–406 in *Deliberative Democracy: Essays on Reason and Politics*, edited by James Bohman and William Rehg. Cambridge, MA: MIT Press.

———. 2000. *Inclusion and Democracy.* Oxford: Oxford University Press.

Yudice, George. 1994. "The Funkification of Rio." Pp. 193–217 in *Microphone Fiends: Youth Music and Youth Culture*, edited by Andrew Ross and Tricia Rose. New York: Routledge.

Zelizer, Viviana A. 1994. *The Social Meaning of Money.* New York: Harper Collins.

———. Forthcoming. "Circuits of Commerce." In *Self, Social Structure, and Beliefs: Explorations in the Sociological Thought of Neil Smelser*, edited by Jeffrey Alexander, Gary T. Marx, and Christine Williams. Berkeley: University of California Press.

Index

420 • Index

elites, 5, 20, 24, 60, 114, 116, 134, 136–
37, 171, 209, 226, 342–43, 348,
371n14, 373n12, 378n2, 385n9
Em Tempo, 329
ENECOS. *See* National Executive of Students in Social Communication
ENEX, VII. *See* Course Executives (National Encounter of)
Enrique, 166
entrenched leaders, 32, 51, 53, 66, 72,
145, 178, 242, 244–46, 250, 298–300,
335, 354, 384nn6 and 7
Erundina, Luiza, 166, 175, 177
Eugênio, 145, 150–51, 153–58, 162, 164–
65, 170–74, 176–77, 380nn16 and 22
Evangelical churches, 60, 192, 208, 363
experiential internships, 17, 263
exploratory dialogue, 29, 33, 187–92, 197,
199, 203, 206–7, 210–11, 215, 224–25,
230–33, 235, 237, 240, 243–44, 248,
250, 258, 262, 267, 269–72, 276, 280,
282–3, 289–92, 294–296, 298–99, 306–
7, 315, 333–34, 336, 340–42, 347, 350–
53, 356. *See also* Habermasian mode
explorers, 32, 51–52, 54, 67, 145, 242–46,
250, 262, 276–77, 284, 286, 299, 335,
354, 384n6, 386n23

factionalism, 9–11, 18, 40–41, 43, 53, 74,
92, 103, 184, 189, 236, 330–31, 339,
347, 349, 358, 374n15, 376n14; in the
black student movement 254–55, 258,
357; in Catholic activism, 127, 197,
205, 209, 357; in the PT, 4–6, 10, 17–
18, 31, 52–53, 63, 128, 141–42, 144–
45, 154, 162, 191, 205 222, 264, 268,
270, 296, 309, 311–13, 320, 323, 331–
33; in student politics, 5–7, 17–18, 21,
41, 105–9, 117, 141, 151, 168, 184,
213, 217, 219, 222–25, 227–28, 230–
31, 234, 236, 247, 258, 345, 355, 357,
384n6; in UNE, 26, 32, 37, 54, 60, 66,
97–99, 109–16, 132, 142, 145, 154–55,
196–204, 287–90, 293–337, 352,
388n12
Faculty of Economics and Administration,
University of São Paulo (FEA-USP), 222,
273–74, 276, 278
Faculty of Technology of São Paulo
(FATEC), 249, 251–53

Farias, Lindberg, 27, 61, 134, 137, 139,
142, 144–46, 150, 153, 155–59, 162–
63, 164–67, 169, 171–73, 176–77, 183,
214, 367n1
FATEC. *See* Faculty of Technology of
São Paulo
FEA-USP. *See* Faculty of Economics and
Administration, University of São Paulo
FEAB. *See* Federation of Agronomy Students of Brazil
Federal University of Rio Grande do Sul
(UFRGS), 17, 144
Federation of Agronomy Students of Brazil
(FEAB), 17, 63–64, 73, 161, 263–66,
316. *See also* agronomy students
FEJESP. *See* Junior Enterprises (State Federation of)
FENEA. *See* National Federation of Architecture Students
fields, alliances in, 43, 140, 222, 244, 289,
358, 383n5; contention in , 8, 19–21,
27, 52, 72, 94–95, 104, 177, 214, 222,
230, 244, 289, 292, 336, 343, 359; creativity in 19, 21, 34, 212, 242, 371n17;
definition of 43, 370n14; diversification
of 6, 18–19, 27–28, 61; of ideas (discursive), 188–89, 199, 214, 244, 270, 352,
357, 383n2; intersections in 8–9, 24, 26,
43–46, 62, 69, 72, 74–82, 91–95, 104,
242 , 354, 368n6; multisectoral, 8–9,
32, 43, 45, 52, 57, 94–95, 214; skilled
mediation in, 20, 29, 41, 48, 177, 289–
90, 354; stylistic orientation toward,
234–35, 244; trajectories through 32,
43–46, 55–57, 62, 82–94, 192, 242
Figueiredo, Joao Batista, 103
Flávio, 273–74, 276–86
Fligstein, Neil, 40, 48, 290, 370nn6, 10
and 14, 372n19, 387n3
focused activists, 32, 51–52, 55, 68, 145,
242, 244–46, 250, 276, 283, 299–300,
354, 384n6, 385n9
footing, 47–48, 130, 185–88, 191–92, 196,
223–26, 230–31, 237, 255–58, 268–69,
271, 276, 281, 283, 289, 290, 292, 304,
307, 339, 342, 352–53, 357–59
Fora Collor, 147, 154–156, 158–62, 168,
170, 175
Força Sindical, 152, 175, 363, 381n24
Forum of Course Executives. *See* Course
Executives (Forum of)

tation of, 285, 293–300, 331–36, 340–
43, 346–47; symbols of, 168, 174, 197,
199 ; tendencies/factions in, 106–8, 111,
144–45, 162, 264–65, 270, 348–49,
375–76n13, 373n14, 380n21, *see also*
factionalism; ties based on, 33, 131,
135–36, 143, 151–152, 171, 175, 177–
78, 215, 228, 348, *see also* partisan
bridging; youth wings of, 30–31, 52, 54,
61, 63, 69, 76, 107, 125, 144–45, 152,
162, 245, 264, 278, 374n15. *See also*
partisanship

Pontifícia Universidade Católica (of São
Paulo) (PUC-SP), 104, 152, 167, 174,
214–23, 225–26, 228–29, 231–32, 237–
38

Popular Action (AP), 106, 375n11,
376n13; Marxist Leninist (APML), 106

popular movements, 363, 382n13; autonomy of, 98, 100, 123–25, 131; church-
based, 5, 18, 84, 98–100, 103, 108,
115–16, 120, 122–24, 126, 128, 132,
178, 191–92, 195, 205, 208, 215, 241,
245, 285, 343–44, 346, 352; civic discourse of, 135, 214, 345, 378n1; connections between, 4, 25–26, 54, 56, 93,
115–16, 126, 128, 131–33, 135, 142,
192, 195, 205, 343–45, 374n15,
382n15; crisis of, 5, 60, 73, 183; education, 1–2, 75, 98, 124, 142, 206, 218,
377n31, 382,13; emergence of, 4, 25,
59, 94, 98, 101, 111, 122–23, 214, 344–
45, 368n10, 378n1; health, 4, 25–26,
75, 98, 124, 142, 263, 268, 382n13;
housing, 26, 206, 218, 349, 382n13; indigenous, 53, 65–66, 84–85, 206; institutional logic of, 39; leadership of, 27, 60,
115, 308, 382n15; participation in, 35,
41, 52–53, 56, 63, 72, 75–84, 92–93,
111, 126, 128, 132, 135, 142, 161, 194–
95, 198–99, 206,208, 216, 235, 241,
245, 250–51, 261–62, 268, 275, 299,
382n13; rural, 17–19, 21, 52–54, 60,
63, 68, 72, 84, 99, 115, 117, 123, 142,
156–57, 161, 194, 251, 262–64, 265,
268, 270, 275, 304, 344, 349, 363,
382n13; sanitation, 75–76, 98, 124,
382n13; stylistic orientation of, 18, 191–
92, 264, 285, 299, 346, 352; transportation, 75, 98, 124, 382n13; urban, 54,
60, 99, 115, 123, 194, 251, 363. *See
also* anti-discrimination movements

popular political theory, 187

Popular Socialist Party (PPS), 107, 294,
297, 300–301, 303, 307, 309, 313, 317–
19, 322–23, 326–27, 330, 363, 376n14

pragmatic communication, 29, 48, 98,
192, 200, 202–3, 228, 235, 244, 246,
254, 261, 270–72, 277, 280–81, 283,
296, 298–99, 302, 306, 313, 315–16,
332, 334–36, 241–42, 347–48, 351–52,
354

pragmatics, 32, 37, 44–46, 55, 94, 100,
186, 241, 251, 272, 343, 356

pragmatist philosophy, 32, 45, 371n20

Prazer em Transformar (PeT – Pleasure in
Transforming), 294–95, 298–99, 301–4,
306–14, 317–24, 326, 328–33, 388

PRC. *See* Revolutionary Communist Party

professional associations, 23, 39, 43, 50,
58, 105, 135, 139–40, 283, 331, 345,
363; institutional logic of, 39; in the
Movement for Ethics in Politics, 146,
150–51, 153, 156–58, 160,162, 164,
166, 178, 214; stylistic orientation of,
190, 285

professional student activism, 8, 17–19,
22, 24, 27, 30, 35–36, 41, 52–53, 56,
60, 63–64, 69,73, 82, 86–87, 90–93, 95,
99, 135, 143, 183–84, 193, 195, 198–
99, 239, 246, 250–51, 259–72, 284,
286, 298, 300, 343, 369n1, 384–85n8;
stylistic orientation of, 264, 386n20. *See
also* Course Executives; course-based
movement

professionals, development of, 18, 24, 68,
92, 142, 239, 248–49, 273, 280, 282,
286, 346, 352, 385n9; identities as, 5, 8,
23, 27, 68–69, 93, 132, 192, 211, 248–
49, 267, 280, 282, 346, 348, 352–53;
projects/interests of, 23, 28, 142; social
role of, 259–260, 263, 285, 346

projects, 37, 47, 185, 285, 292–93,
371n25; civic, 99, 105, 113, 115, 345–
46, 378n1; consulting, 272, 274, 276–
77, 282–83, 385n9; contending, 20–21,
34, 293, 332; Deweyian, 46, 189, 291,
340; elaboration of, 8, 20, 37, 40, 45–
46, 139, 243, 266, 284, 289, 292, 340,
352, 356, 385n8, 386n20; Gramscian,
258, 291, 340, 352, 354, 357; intersection of multiple, 18–19, 21, 34, 41, 43,
47, 50, 72, 129–31, 264, 284, 290, 343,
349, 353–55, 357, 359–60, 371n22;

PRINCETON STUDIES IN CULTURAL SOCIOLOGY

GPSR Authorized Representative: Easy Access System Europe - Mustamäe tee
50, 10621 Tallinn, Estonia, gpsr.requests@easproject.com

www.ingramcontent.com/pod-product-compliance
Lightning Source LLC
Chambersburg PA
CBHW031827270326
41932CB00008B/580